THE TIME OF THE THUNDERER
Mikhail Katkov,
Russian Nationalist Extremism
And the Failure of
The Bismarckian System, 1871–1887

KAREL DURMAN

EAST EUROPEAN MONOGRAPHS, BOULDER
DISTRIBUTED BY COLUMBIA UNIVERSITY PRESS, NEW YORK

1988

EAST EUROPEAN MONOGRAPHS, NO. CCXXXVII

TABLE OF CONTENTS

PART THREE
IN THE MISTS OF ERROR:
THE "KATKOVSHCHINA" OF 1881-1887

ACKNOWLEDGEMENTS

Being a Czech dissident historian, my acknowledgements will necessarily be somewhat unusual. There was no grant, no scholarship. Indeed, the authorities which were imposed upon my country by the Soviet occupation did their utmost to prevent me—as so many others—from scholarly effort. I started working on the theme as a night watchman, with a 69-hour working week. So, firstly, my thanks are due to my former co-workers, colleagues and friends who encouraged me to persist, and to the librarians in Prague who supplied me with the books and journals I needed. (I cannot name those I remember most: it could still complicate their lives.) Secondly, I am deeply indebted to all those who, after I and my family had been forced into emigration, helped us to find a new home in beautiful, generous Sweden and me to become a "full-time" historian again; here, I should like to single out at least Miss Lemne, Vilém Prečan, Józef Lewandowski, Ann and Harald Runblom. Thirdly, I wish to express my appreciation for the services afforded me by the staffs of the Public Records Office in London and the Politisches Archiv des Auswärtigen Amtes in Bonn; my many thanks to Ivor S. Sweigler for practical advice and aid, including hospitality during my research in London; and, above all, my special gratitude to Stephen Fischer-Galati for help in getting my study published. Last but not least, I owe a major debt to my wife, Jarmila. There was not much of a normal family and social life for her: first, the years of material poverty and police harassment; then, the initial trying years in exile. Without her loyalty, courage and sacrifice, this book could not have been written.

ABBREVIATIONS

AA   Auswärtiges Amt. Akten: Russland 82, No. 4. (Katkov)
AP   Accounts and Papers. Parliamentary proceedings.
APP   (Brandenburg, E. et al.) Die auswärtige Politik Preussens 1858-1871
ARTsB   (Pavlovich, P., ed.) Avantiury russkogo tsarizma v Bolgarii
BgB   (Schwertfeger, B., ed.) Zur europäischen Politik, vol. 5. Belgische Gesandtschaftsberichte
DDF-I   Documents diplomatiques français. 1^{ére} série
FO   Public Records Office. The Records of the Foreign Office
GP   (Lepsius, J. et al.) Die grosse Politik der europäischen Kabinette 1871-1914
HvB   (Bussman, W., ed.) Staatssekretär Graf Herbert von Bismarck

IMID   Izvestiia ministerstva inostrannykh del
IS AN   Institut slavianovedeniia Akademii nauk
IsV   Istoricheskii vestnik
IZ   Istoricheskie zapiski
KA   Krasnyi arkhiv

MV   Moskovskiia vedomosti
OBTI   (Nikitin, S. A., ed.) Osvobozhdenie Bolgarii ot turetskogo iga
RA   Russkii arkhiv
RNOBB   (Narochnitskii, A. L., ed.) Rossiia i natsionalno-osvoboditelnaia borba na Balkanakh
RS   Russkaia starina
RV   Russkii vestnik
SEER   Slavonic and East European Review
SR   Slavonic Review

TRHS   Transactions of the Royal Historical Society
VI   Voprosy istorii

INTRODUCTION: THE ERA OF
ARMED PEACE AND
RUSSIAN PUBLIC OPINION

Russian Geography

Moscow, Peter's and Constantine's city
Are the holy capitals of the Russian realm
But where are its outer limits,
Where its borders,
To the north, to the east, to the south,
And where does the sun set?
Destiny will unmask them in future times.

Seven inland seas, and seven great rivers,
From the Nile to the Neva, from the Elbe
                  to China,
From the Volga to the Euphrates,
From the Ganges to the Danube—that is
                the Russian realm.
And never will
It pass, as the Spirit foresaw and
           Daniel predicted.
Tiutchev

No longer meditatingly but almost with cer-
tainty it may be stated that very soon,
—perhaps in the immediate future—Russia
will prove stronger that any nation in
Europe. This will come to pass because all
Great Powers in Europe will be destroyed

for the simple reason that they will be worn out and undermined by the lower-class subjects—their proletarians and paupers.

In Russia, this cannot happen: our demos is content and, as time goes on, it will grow even more content because everything tends towards this condition, as a result of the general mood, or—more correctly—by general consensus. And therefore there will remain on the continent but one colossus—Russia. This will come to pass, perhaps even sooner than people think. The future of Europe belongs to Russia.
Dostoevskii

Who can compare with us? Whom we will not force into submission? Is not the political destiny of the world in our hands whenever we want to decide in one way or another? The truth of my words will be even more manifest if we consider the conditions in other European countries. In contrast to Russia's strength, unity and harmony, we find there nothing but quarrel, division and weakness, by which our greatness—as light by shadow—is still more enhanced . . .

It is known that our present Tsar does not think of any conquest, but I cannot help, I dare not fail to remark as a historian, that the Russian ruler now, without such an intention, without any preparation, quietly seated in his office at Tsarskoe Selo, is nearer to the universal monarchy than Charles V and Napoleon ever were in their dreams.
Pogodin

For long decades until 1871, the pulse of the world had been quickened by big wars, social and national upheavals. These had been times of great expectations, awakening of peoples, achievements in industry, science, arts and letters, but still more, times of fear and insecurity. Military conflicts, often involving great coalitions, ceased to be the business of small professional armies; in their whirlwinds they had caught vast territories and masses of population. Revolutions, too, has been mostly bloody, protracted affairs not limited to one country only; and the following periods of reaction were no less cruel or depressing in their lack of hope. Victors had imposed brutal conditions upon vanquished; many states had disappeared from the map.

Compared with this the years after the Peace of Frankfurt (1871) were perceived by men in the so-called civilized world as an era of tranquility and rest. No European state discontinued its existence and only the decaying Turkish (Ottoman) Empire was afflicted by loss of territories by force of arms. Only there, in the sphere of the perennial Eastern Question, and outside Europe, were accounts settled with guns, peoples subjected to mass cruelties and deprived of independent existence. It seemed as if by the unification of Germany the cycle of general instability was closed and the still emerging tensions and crises were but residues from the past.

As a prominent historian put it,

> Europe had never known such peace and unity since the age of the Antonines. The times of Metternich were nothing in comparison. Then men lived in well-founded apprehension of war and revolution; now they came to believe that peace and security were normal and anything else an accident and an abberation.[1]

Behind this façade, however, arose a reality which was in essential divergence to the hopeful expectations of universal reconciliation and unhindered progress. The factors of unstability remained and accumulated new force. Uneven economic development and cleavages inevitably ensuing from the industrialization process, rising chauvinism, colonial "scramble" and considerable improvements in war machinery—all this made the cherished peace extremely vulnerable and laid a train for a life-and-death struggle as terrible as ever.

In the great European cabinets few wished to play with fire: the old spectres loomed large upon their deliberations and made them resist the temptations. Yet, manifold pressures for change poisoned the atmosphere and serious crises following in short sequence undermined the stabilization effort.

In this development, the possibility of a surprise attack and a "blitz-krieg" was of crucial consequence. Increased mobility due to intense railway construction, military training of a great part of the male population, better organization and planning, enabled to deploy almost instantaneously hundreds of thousands of troops. The Austrian war with the Prusso-Italian coalition in 1866 and the Franco-Prussian war in 1870-1871 demonstrated that the outcome of a fateful conflict could be decided in a matter of weeks and the fragile equilibrium reversed accordingly.

In a memorandum written in 1873, General Obruchev, Russian chief strategist, well expressed the thought of this "Armed Peace era":

> All European Powers share equally the desire for peace, but at the same time all of them continue to develop their armaments. They strengthen cadres and reserves, prepare for their speedy mobilization, build new fortresses and strategic railways. Remaining in peace, all are making preparations for war. Hence, even we have to take steps for the protection of the security of the Empire without delay; the more so as the shift from peace to war is going to happen, so to speak, immediately, in a lightning manner.[2]

No great continental government could ignore this contingency. Scarcely less than in the earlier turbulent times, top decision-making was overshadowed by military considerations, the main work of diplomacy being to procure coalition partners. The military establishments were not slow to take advantage of their enhanced stature. They called for better strategic positions, more secure frontiers, and, most significantly, for preventive wars to render safe the victories achieved, or wars to "restore national honor" after defeats suffered. Increasingly powerful industrial and trade interests seconded them, claiming their place in the sun.

Educated "spokesmen of public opinion" showed equal vehemence and the results of their nationalist sermons were no less disastrous. By appeals for retribution of real or alleged injustices, by claims of racial or cultural superiority, civilizing or liberating missions, by theories of state or national interest, they took on the responsibility for psychological preparation, the mobilization of emotions for war, thus clearing the way for the fatal process described with terrible farsightedness by a minor German poet as the decline "from humanity through nationality to bestiality."[3] In connection with the overwhelming impact chauvinistic propaganda exercised—notably through the daily press—on public opinion, the so-called "democratization of politics" has been correctly marked out among the basic disruptive elements in the Armed Peace era.[4]

From all these aspects, and especially from that concerning the role of extremist nationalism, Russian development was particularly salient.

Regardless of the deeply rooted autocratic tradition, the almost total absence of representative institutions and the inertia of the masses, the St. Petersburg government was exposed to enormous pressures. Western statesmen had to make important concessions and deals with the hawkish groups; they had to open connections with the press, cajole and corrupt it. The space for maneuver at their disposal, however was, as a rule, broader than that available to their Russian counterparts. Tsardom passed through a long-time shattering socio-political crisis and its leadership, moreover, lacked experience and the capabilities necessary for manipulating contradictory interests emerging in the entirely new historical situation after the Crimean War (1853-1856). Effeted, flinching from clear-cut options and scared of revolution, the autocracy adopted, at crucial moments of the Armed Peace era, a defensive position vis-à-vis forces it was unable to harness.

So far, this phenomenon has not been analyzed commensurately to its significance. While Soviet historians have been hindered by dogmas they are unable or unwilling to challenge, the approach of their Western colleagues, in the words of Riasanovsky, "remains in large part vague and even impressionistic."[5]

The prevailing view is still close to that recently expressed by George Kennan:

> It would be idle [he says], in considering the Russia of the 1870s, to speak of such a thing as 'public opinion' in connection with international affairs. The mass of the Russian people had neither knowledge nor means of 'arriving at judgments on questions of foreign policy.' It was the Tsar himself, who had 'in theory, at least, unlimited power to shape Russia's external relations according to his judgments and desires.' Between these two extremes, there was only a body of people, 'probably numbered in the hundreds, scarcely in

the thousands' who 'had in their power to exert, directly or indirectly, some degree of influence upon the reactions of the Tsar
and his responsible ministers. These included persons of elevated
social status at Court (particularly members of the imperial family),
higher officials of the governmental bureaucracy, senior clerical
figures, prominent businessmen, members of the high command of
army and navy, and finally leading editors, publicists and writers.'[6]

Irrespective of all pecularities and limitations, there was definitely a
public opinion in Russia and the great debate on the serfs' emancipation
in 1857-1861 heralded its emergence. In fact, no contemporary statesman
or diplomat familiar with Russian conditions doubted it. Although small
in relative numbers, the politically-minded layers of the populace—nobility,
officialdom, officers, teachers, doctors, artists and scientists, journalists,
students and at least part of the clergy, merchants and artisans—were not
only able to "arrive at their judgments," but voice their views impetuously.
Even the so-called "dark people" had some primitive notion of Russia's
role in the world and her relationship to other nations, and they could
exert their bearing on supreme decisions. This was particularly perceptible
on the crucial Eastern Question.[7]

Consequently, those "probably numbered in the hundreds" had it in
their power to do substantially more than just "exert some degree of influence upon the Tsar and his ministers." To be more precise and closer
to the theme, the extremist nationalist groups wielding prevailing influence on society and strongly represented in the elite[8] could take advantage
of public feeling, create divisions among the policymakers and often at
critical junctures enforce a solution running counter to the will of the
government and sway the Tsar himself.

Russian nationalist extremism, invigorated by the enormous force of
tradition, virtually infected internal development as well as foreign policy.
Moreover, usually identified as "Slavophilism," "Panslavism" or "Old-
Russian current," it incited, in one way or another, chauvinist groups and
public opinion in the key European countries, and largely contributed to
the growth of general instability. The analysis made fifty years ago by
Sumner still passes the historian's scrutiny with honour:

Clearly it was not the organized power or carefully worked-out plan. . . . Yet, the foreign view of it, though exaggerated, had sensed correctly the danger which lay in it. The Panslavs, divided and few in numbers though they were, represented a sounding board of the new, restless Russian nationalism. Through them, with their connections with the Muscovite nobility, the Orthodox Church, the court, the diplomatic service and the army, this nationalism might, if events abroad gave the requisite shock, be capable of eventually diverting or even directing the policy of the Tsar and his immediate advisers.[9]

The key role in rallying public opinion under the extremist banner belonged to the press. And, once again, it was the Russian Empire with its relatively severe censorship and mass illiteracy where at least in the first, "Bismarckian period" of the Armed Peace era the press had been more powerful in this respect than in any other country.

Russian statesmen and foreign observers alike declared newspapers, journals and journalists the only force capable of challenging the autocratic government. Most certainly, nothing can illuminate this thesis and the whole extremist impact on Tsardom's policies better than the case of Mikhail Nikiforovich Katkov. In no other country could a mere publicist standing outside the official power structure exercise such an influence. As a German study put it, "his importance for the development of Russian public opinion as well as his bearing upon the monarch and the highest dignitaries of the Empire can find no analogy in Western Europe and provide a source of exaggeration for friends and foes alike."[10]

Katkov claimed to be the watchdog of the autocracy and this claim was widely recognized. At the same time, both his kinsmen and foreigners considered him with good reason "in principle . . . the most outstanding representative of opposition." He repeated "thousands of times" that "Russian society was sound and only the government was to be blamed"; and "there was hardly a moment when his views would be entirely in accordance with those prevailing in St. Petersburg."[11] His *Moskovskiia vedomosti* (Moscow Gazette) and his office in the dark courtyard of an old University building at Strastnyi Boulevard in Moscow rose into a "state institution" which for a quarter-century became something of an alternative power center.[12]

"And how many ministers, former and future, officers and officials of all titles and shades I have seen during these twenty-five years in the modest study at Strastnyi Boulevard," Prince Meshcherskii recollected.[13] Some joined the ranks of the publicist's "party of order" out of persuasion, some out of sheer opportunism. Others, including the Tsars Alexander II and Alexander III, feared him and sought to appease him by concessions and tokens of sympathy. According to the notorious Pobedonostsev, "there were ministries where not a single important action was undertaken without Katkov's participation."[14]

Although the Moscow editor offered few original ideas, a contemporary compared his spiritual impact with Voltaire's,[15] and a Soviet study on him fittingly declared the *Moskovskiia vedomosti* "the greatest ideological force of absolutism."[16] Katkov's main discovery was precisely that of public opinion as a new, essential element on the political scene; and in the sway of Russian public also lay the main source of his strength.

Inasmuch as he knew "no nation in which democratic instincts were more feeble than in the Russian"—these instincts would merely "in a limited sense permeate the half-aristocratic milieu as an accidental increment and would definitely have no effect whatever on the other classes"[17] —the publicist envisaged only one way in which this element could be used in the state and national interest and not be bewitched by revolutionary destruction: the people should be kept in a permanent state of vigilance, driven by campaigns against both external foes and internal knaves. Pursuing these incessant campaigns with superhuman energy and terrifying inventiveness, he elevated the reactionary instincts of his kin into "sound Russian principles"; and, at the same time, mastered the art of imposing himself as their custodian upon the ruling elite. The force of his pen, the ability to win and destroy, to make people his tools, could hardly be matched.

The "Thunderer from Strastnyi Boulevard" became the pivotal personality in the spectrum of Russian reaction and Russian chauvinism, which the European Powers also had to take into account. Foreign embassies closely watched his editorials and crusades, tried to win his benevolence; the world press named him the "Sage of Moscow." Prince Bismarck, the dominant figure on the international stage in the first twenty years of the Armed Peace era, belonged to those who were most apprehensive about the political and ideological weight he bore.[18]

The fearful expectations in Berlin were well founded indeed. Although there were periods when he strongly advocated understanding with the great Chancellor, no man exerted more direct personal impact on the ultimate failure of the Bismarckian system than the Moscow editor. And what from the German or European angle has been called the Bismarckian era, may from the Russian one be well called the "time of the Thunderer."

PART ONE

THE SETTING OF THE STAGE
(1856-1871)

CHAPTER 1

THE SEARCH FOR IDENTITY

> We have been able to judge all questions sub-
> jected to public consideration exclusively
> from the viewpoint of Russian state interest.
> Our opinions might have been mistaken, but
> we have resolved not to say anything before
> we have convinced ourselves that it com-
> ported with the interest of Russia. The more
> profoundly we have been assured of this, the
> more decisively and perseveringly we have
> considered it our duty to give our opinion.
> Katkov

> God helped me to destroy with several blows
> the revolutionary spectre looming at that
> time over Russia. . . .
> Katkov

"I was born in the same year as Your Majesty. I vividly recall that
time, when in the poor, lonely hamlet, where I lived as a child, the oath
was taken in the churches to Your august father and You, the heir to the
throne . . . . I felt that I was summoned somewhat especially to serve
You," Katkov wrote in a letter to Alexander II. "The circumstances of my
development confined me to the sphere of purely intellectual interest. The
years of my youth flowed by in almost anchor-like solitude. Wholly devoted to the study of speculative matters, I participated neither in practical affairs and interests, and I was alien to all what was around me. It so

happened that the first beginning of my independent public activity co-incided with the accession to the throne of Your Majesty."[1]

In fact, the first thirty-six years in his life, before he could start to "serve somewhat especially" the Tsar, were far from being as uneventful and detached as Katkov depicted them.

Born on 13 November 1818 in Moscow, he joined the tiny educated stratum in the momentuous period of the 1840s. In their heavy-handed manner Nicholas I, his police chief Benckendorff and the Minister of Public Instruction Uvarov silenced dissenting voices. The case of the philosopher Peter Chaadaev (1838-1839), whom the authorities pro-claimed insane for his criticism of Russia and the Russians, loomed like a terrifying omen over all those inclined to serious social debate. Still, this was in the well-known words of Alexander Herzen the time when external constraint stimulated the search for inner liberation.[2]

Political discussions being taboo, the educated youth sought its self-expression mostly in philosophy. Like other bright minds at Moscow University, Katkov found his deliverance in Schellingian and Hegelian teachings and joined the so-called "Westernizer's circle" where Stanke-vich, Belinskii, Granovskii and later Herzen and Bakunin were the leading spirits.[3]

The famous polemics between the Westernizers and the Slavophiles and inside the Westernizers' circle, in which the future luminary of Russian journalism eagerly participated, stimulated him to intellectual perfection; at the same time, though, all the shady sides of his personality surfaced in them.

Delivered to the world in the family of a minor official, lacking money and noble status, Katkov unveiled traits typical of many gifted, low-born, poor men craving to assert themselves. Even towards those who held views not much at variance with his own and who were by no means inferior to him in education and intelligence, he behaved like a "genial boy who has to communicate with well-meaning but limited people." His ungainly appearance (everybody noticed his glassy, yellow-green eyes), choleric nature and bad nerves made things still worse. Nobody questioned his abilities, extensive reading, perfect command of foreign languages; yet nobody cherished a true sympathy for him either. In Belinskii's words, he was held for a "mixture of smugness and egotism," a "remarkable subject for psychological examination," who instead of fighting his complexes became "ever more himself."[4]

With good reason Katkov mentioned, in the quoted letter to the Tsar, his solitude. Groping in the void, he often despaired; and frustrations further nourished the streak of haughtiness, intolerance and, on the other hand, the yearning to be recognized by the mighty ones and climb the social ladder.

Highly significant from this aspect was his intimate life. Much of the estrangement with the Westernizers' circle was due to a "scandal"—in fact, it was hardly more than a platonic relationship—with the wife of Herzen's alter ego, Mrs. Ogareva. Then he lost his head for lovely Miss Delone and both of them intended to get married. He spoiled the romance, however, and shortly afterwards wed the ugly, dull and quite poor Princess Shalikova. "Probably Katkov wished to put his spirit on diet," the poet Tiutchev commented ironically of the match which can be rationally explained only by a burning desire to escape lonliness, mediocrity and belong to people who really mattered.[5]

To elucidate the point it has to be stressed that at the time of emotional failures, moreover, the Nicholas regime destroyed Katkov's budding scholarly aspirations.

The authorities had always eyed the Moscow circles with distaste and suspicion. The enthusiasm for German philosophers was thought untoward the health of the Russian mind, which should imbibe only from the uncontaminated well of the state ideology of "Autocracy-Orthodoxy-Nationality." "As we are a youthful nation, we need not adopt a philosophy which another had evolved in its senile age," one of the vigilants put it.[6] The mighty Metropolitan Philaret was most particular about those who espoused the Shellingian and Hegelian system; Katkov, whom Moscow University employed in 1845, after his postgraduate studies in Germany, as a lecturer in philosophy, logic and psychology, naturally occured on the list of suspects.[7]

Under the impact of the European revolutions of 1848-1849, the official grip tightened still more. Uvarov, hitherto considered by the educated public as the very embodiment of the ultraconservative spirit, was adjudged by the Tsar too irresolute to cope with ideological subversion. The new Minister for Public Instruction, Prince Shirinskii-Shakhmatov, closed down all departments of philosophy at the universities and ordained the sensitive subjects to be removed from the curricula or taken over by theologians. Katkov, not surprisingly, was among the victims. He hoped at least to find a refuge at the chair of pedagogy; a petty personal intrigue, however, prevented even this.[8]

The nervous strain must have been considerable. At the age of thirty-three, Katkov saw his ambitions and talents marred. But, precisely at this moment, fortune offered him the fateful opportunity. One Khlopov, the editor of the University newspaper *Moskovskiia vedomosti,* had been fired for an indecent display of admiration for a foreign danseuse; and Katkov got his job and the official rank connected with it (1851).[9]

Few people would have expected him to succeed. They mostly sized him up as a promising but rather boring scholar;[10] whose interests, moreover, were limited to philosophy, philology and history. The general conditions were signally adverse, too: anything connected with politics would simply be quoted from official sources without comment or the comment would be composed by one of the approved for the task by the authorities.[11] Nonetheless, Katkov resolved to make the best of what he apparently perceived to be his last big chance. He learned to like the new profession, worked with intensity to procure broader knowledge and displayed—in surprisingly contrast to his ineptitude for true friendship—remarkable gifts for winning collaborators and contributors. Soon he commanded esteem and sympathy also for showing courage and imagination in devising ways to circumvent the censorship and disseminate the "new ideas."[12]

When the death of Nicholas I in the midst of the Crimean War disaster (1855) ended the old era, the Moscow editor had already been firmly in the saddle, with good connections to take up new opportunities and become an independent publicist.

In the wake of Alexander II's ascendance he asked for permission to start his own journal. In the application he promised to strive for "liberating the Russian mind from the foreign yoke" and to fight against "disruptive and disturbing agitation." On these grounds he obtained a license to set up a monthly outside the University's control, permitted to report and comment on current affairs—the *Russkii vestnik* (Russian Messenger) with the appendix *Sovremennaia letopis* (Contemporary Chronicle).[13]

Hence, in the infancy of Russian public opinion, Katkov appeared with the means to influence it; and he was going to develop them into a formidable weapon.

* * *

Despite the painfully felt war defeat, the year 1856 brought to Russia an immense feeling of relief and hope. The mood reminded Meshcherskii of a "blue, perfectly clear sky"; and it seemed to him that "sad and scared people had somehow disappeared and had given place to bright, life-loving ones."[14] Dignitaries from the Nicholas era were leaving the scene and those replacing them professed to join the Tsar in an honest endeavour to abandon the system in which, as the future War Minister General Dmitrii Miliutin characterized it, "the defects in the state organism were deliberately veiled by official falsity and hypocrisy."[15] Bonds of mutual confidence appeared to be emerging between the government and the public. While under the deceased autocrat one might only whisper about the most burning problems with intimate friends, now "almost everyone who could write" composed some proposals for improvement and passed them to the authorities.[16]

The Russian press entered into its first era of bloom. Besides Katkov's, dozens of newspapers and journals cropped up, representing every shade in the forming public opinion. The right to comment on political issues was bestowed also to many other periodicals. Censors worked without clear dispositions and, being either sympathetic to the liberal trend or scared to antagonize society, acted in a haphazard manner.[17] The new Tsar, not unlike his father, suspected the intelligentsia of the "most dangerous biases and hidden motives"; still, he repeatedly asserted that "restrictive measures" should be eschewed. In 1858, a special committee was set up with the task to "influence the press, direct it gently, in a paternal and reasonable way, to keep direct contacts with the journalists and sway their views and opinions without resorting to the right of censorship."[18]

Although the "blue sky" was soon covered by the clouds of serious problems, the keywords still sounded: unity, reconciliation and national resurrection through reform. Even Pobedonostsev, the future Torquemada, published in the *Russkii vestnik* articles condemning serfdom and the obsolete judiciary system.[19]

Katkov was conspicious among the advocates of this "positive direction," as he called it. His monthly, wrote a prominent historian of the Imperial era, "became the decisive exponent of political liberalism and the main leader of constitutionalist ideas within society."[20] The editor, on the one hand, from the very first moment enthusiastically welcomed the move of Alexander towards the abolition of serfdom. Warning resisting landowners of a "Pugachev-type" revolt, he canvassed the radical concept of emancipation: not only should the peasant have civil rights but also property rights on the plot he toiled on.[21] On the other hand, he hotly denounced the tendency displayed by the "bureaucratic officials without conscience" to interfere in matters of literature and journalism. Even the "most mistaken and one-sided views," he urged, must be given a forum, because "if they were not openly stated, public opinion would be unable to shake free of them and reject them."[22] When a sympathetic Moscow editor, von Cruze, was dismissed, the editor organized a demonstration and collection of money for his benefit; a deed which was described as the first public protest under the new reign.[23]

Clamouring, mostly under a flimsy pretext of commenting on literary and political events abroad, for an unhindered circulation of ideas as a "guarantee of guarantees," Katkov did not hesitate to conjoin his plea with an acrid criticism of the system erected by Nicholas:

> We 'have seen the cause of all our evils in the superfluous tutelage which has lain heavily upon our life, in the unjustified suspicion towards (independent thought), in the unnecessary desire to adorn and improve it not from within but by means of governmental interference.' This resulted 'in the spirit of despotism on one side, and the spirit of radicalism on the other, both parading behind the mask of an organized "oprichnina," fomenting damage and destruction everywhere instead of conservation.'

As the safest course in removing Russia's perennial ills, he earnestly advised emulation of the "English model." "Up to now," he wrote, "only the English have learned the art of making reforms without revolution, and we shall lose nothing by competing with them on this ground." In England, he admired the firmly established institutions, the rule of law, civil liberties as well as the skill by which the nobility combined organic development with stability. Without a similar basis, he affirmed, "no normal society can exist."[25]

The praise for Katkov and his work in the educated stratum had been overwhelming. The *Russkii vestnik* turned into an "enormous success," and its circulation amounted in 1861 to 6000 copies. The political survey of the monthly, *Sovremennaia letopis,* attracted no less enthusiasm than the literary section, where the best authors—Dostoevskii, Tolstoi, Turgenev, Goncharov—published their masterpieces.[26] No wonder that while the *Sovremennik* (Contemporary), a mouthpiece of left radicalism, commended the journal as "very useful for the preparation of the serious people to the avowal of our attitude,"[27] the reactionaries whom Herzen called the "planters party" identified it with "dangerous influences."[28]

Katkov's critics would emphasize that he had always remained a "borrower of alien ideas" parading behind his skill "an astonishing lack of intellectual originality," a totally eclectic thought.[29] Much in his writing disclosed, indeed, that he was still learning; and he was also too much involved in intense debate to subdue what had been inherent to every quarrel amongst the intelligentsia. Yet no unbiased observer could have refused him a great deal of farsightedness and a bid for constructive dialogue.

Katkov's most direct polemics were aimed against the Slavophile notions of inner reorganization of the country and their evaluation of the past. Although privately referring to them as a "Russian plague,"[30] however, his articles were free from that "murderous sarcasm and mockery"[31] so typical of later campaigns. It seemed that a secure position and the possibility to prove his talents liberated him from his foibles. He tried to soften down discords, maintaining correctly that "Russian society was too weak to afford internecine strife."[32] He was obviously guided by a salutary aspiration to create a broad middle-of-the-road trend which would counterbalance the alarming pressurs coming both from the "planters" and the left radicals. In 1859, he visited Herzen in London, most likely with the intention to agree on a common struggle for the sake of reform.

The meeting with the great exile, though, ended in total estrangement.[33] Soon afterwards the Moscow moderate Westernizer underwent a profound transformation.

The reversal has been customarily proclaimed as "simply an opportunistic switch."[34] This appears to be not a fully satisfactory explanation. "The typical Russian cannot go on doubting for very long," the philosopher

Berdiaev observed. "His inclination is to make a dogma fairly quickly and surrender himself to that dogma wholeheartedly and entirely."[35] Apart from his inordinate ambition Katkov was too much a Russian to remain that English type of compromise seeking liberal he had tried to be. Not unlike the whole Russian intelligentsia, he needed his dogma too. While the left-oriented radicals, whom he commenced to hate intensely, found it in Socialism and Communism, the Moscow editor discovered his programme in enhanced nationalism. And rather than changing sides, he became more and more truly himself.

* * *

Katkov's demeanor mirrored the pattern of general development.

Russian society proved singularly immature in the search for a new identity. The time of hopeful expectations could not last long; the two extremes had to overshadow the moderate forces. On the right, the ultra-conservatives stubbornly defended their vested interests, above all in the crucial strife over the abolition of serfdom. On the left, the young radicals —whom Katkov named the "Nihilists" and who in blind defiance proudly accepted the name[36]—behaved with ostentatious rudeness in condemning all traditional views, values and compromises and finally exhorted the peasants to "snatch at the axe."

Saddled with mental stereotypes, both the elite and the public perceived the threat in the intelligentsia's mood rather than in the ultraconservative obstruction, and their attitudes evolved accordingly.

Leading personalities in the government understood well the implications and took on to stave off the dangerous trend. They advised patience towards young malcontents, wisely pointing out that the repression would only animate their restlessness. "Ignore them," Interior Minister Count Peter Valuev counselled; their writings and deeds were for him only a mild illness which would pass. War Minister Miliutin also declared the left radicalism harmless: "it has come to us from the West and is hence limited to an environment alien to the people."[37] Outside moderate liberal circles, however, such propositions found little sympathy.

Katkov appeared at the helm of the alarmists, producing a diagnosis distinctly adverse from the views he had canvassed earlier. He assessed the Nihilist phenomenon as a "serious social disease," a "frustrated religion" preached by poisonous fanatics:

The religion of negation is directed against the authorities, but it is itself based on the deepest submission to authority. Consequently, its triumph would be followed by a dictatorship of bureaucrats or demagogues, by an oligarchy of the worst kind . . . where the spirit of intolerance and tutelage would prevail even more jealously and captiously than before, where conditions would be even less favorable for freedom of the individual.[38]

After the student demonstrations in 1861, the Moscow editor unreservedly identified Nihilism as the chief element in the "negative direction" and the struggle against it as a supreme service to the national interest.[39] In his campaign—it was in fact the first press campaign in the history of Russian journalism—he asserted that he "belonged to nobody". and still assaulted the reactionaries for their myopic selfishness. "Those conservatives who choose the status quo as their platform no matter how rotten it is, are miserable wretches," he wrote. "They are indifferent to the values of freedom, which creates the spirit of any good conservative."[40] But in fact, he increasingly embraced their stances; and, while denouncing the "spirit of interference and tutelage" of the radical left, he himself was spreading it with no lesser intensity.

"Patriotic" and revolutionary intelligentsia may profoundly differ in their ideas, yet in the pattern of their thinking and behaviour they are identical. By his extreme intolerance, dogmatism and demogogy, Katkov was to become a perfect prototype of this social category.

For the first time, he distinctly demonstrated these qualities in the summer of 1862, when fires broke out in the capital and he meanly connected them with the work of "our foreign refugees", i.e. with Herzen. This disgraceful deed, coupled with the insolent language of his articles, shocked many readers; and not a few in society avoided social contact with him "as if he were contamined by plague."[41] Driven by jealousy towards the great exile and anxious to replace him as the genuine "voice of Russia," however, Katkov knew no restraint. Moreover, of course, there was also an opportunist calculation behind the campaign.[42]

When in January 1863 the Polish uprising broke out, the rising witch-hunt spirit had already been connected with the Muscovite's name ("Katkovshchina"). Meanwhile, he had found his firm place among the proponents of "national interest" in foreign policy, too.

CHAPTER 2

FOREIGN POLICY:
ST. PETERSBURG AND MOSCOW DIMENSIONS

One more century of the present despotism
and all the good qualities of the Russian
people will be destroyed. . . . A long
servitude cannot be accidental, it corresponds
to some element in the national character.
This element can be absorbed and defeated
by other elements, but it can also remain
victorious. If Russia continues the period
of St. Petersburg or returns to the period
of Muscovy, she will have no other vocation
but to throw herself upon Europe, like a
semi-barbarian and semi-corrupted horde,
to devastate the civilized countries and to
perish in the midst of general destruction.

Was it not therefore necessary to call
upon the Russian people by all means to
become conscious of this tragic position?
. . . Instead, the Slavophiles preached submission, . . . the formation of Muscovite
Tsardom; they preached the contempt
of the West which alone could enlighten
the abyss of Russian life; they glorified the
past, which on the contrary it was necessary
to get rid of in favor of a future which
should be common to the East and the West.
Herzen

The programme of Russian foreign policy after the Crimean War was
drafted in memoranda presented by Chancellor Karl Nesselrode to Alexander II in March 1856.

Russia emerged from the conflict with the European coalition weakened and debased, the documents stated, but she was unable to alter this condition swiftly. For the time being, any premature initiative had to be avoided, inasmuch as it would only alarm foreign governments and their public opinions still highly suspicious as to St. Petersburg's intentions. Moreover, Russia was confronted by an 'almost absolute need' to solve her internal problems ; they became her first priority and excluded activities which might disturb the restoration of 'moral and material forces.' The traditional role in international affairs could only be regained after substantial improvement in the domestic situation; and even then, Russia's endeavors ought to be limited to matters in which her direct interests were at stake. She might take part in a war solely in the case of 'unavoidable necessity,' or when its 'evident benefits would be stated beyond any doubt.'[1]

Nesselrode could not retain his office. Society had for long despised him as a "German" who cared for the Holy Alliance instead of Russian interests and the historic objectives in the East. When the Paris Peace (30 March 1856) closed the Crimean chapter by terms considered by the Russians to be highly humiliating,[2] the Tsar dropped him and appointed one of his opponents, Prince Alexander Gorchakov, Minister for Foreign Affairs.

The dossier of the Third Section allegedly contained a description of Gorchakov to the effect that he 'has got the abilities but does not love Russia.' Keeping this in mind, the Prince took over the ministry at the Singers' Bridge (Pevcheskii most) determined to prove the opposite. Alive to the feelings of his kinsmen and being an excessively vain man, he was anxious to placate everybody and win universal admiration by patriotic verbosity. While Nesselrode had had the arrogance to say that he was a servant of the Tsar and Russia did not concern him, Gorchakov always studiously posed as the representative of the 'Tsar and Russia.'[3]

He was the first among Russian statesmen who recognized the power of public opinion and the press in the changed climate. For years he painstakingly cultivated his connections with Katkov and

this alliance helped him at the time of the Polish uprising to reach
the very peak of popularity he so much craved for. He also succeeded in the main prerequisite for political fortune in Tsardom—to
retain the confidence of the autocrat. Alexander II found him a
good choice, compliant to him and adroit in handling foreign statesmen. The Prince was promoted in 1862 to the Vice-Chancellorship
and in 1867 to the Chancellorship of the Empire.

For a while, the fresh wind Gorchakov introduced at the Singers'
Bridge made everybody reasonably happy. In the longer perspective,
though, he could not uphold his patriotic image. Profoundly convinced
that no alternative to the course envisaged in Nesselrode's memoranda
existed, he furnished only a less painful phraseology like the famous
"Russia is not sulking, Russia is recovering."[4] To be sure, he wished
to soothe the injured pride of his compatriots, achieve the revision of the
"humiliating clauses" of the Paris Treaty and re-establish the traditional
influence in the Balkans. Still, however keenly he perceived the importance of success for the government's prestige and his own position,
he was opposed to any risky move: on the Eastern Question, too, the
principle was to be respected that as long as the internal reconstruction
programme remained uncompleted, premature action would be futile
and harmful.[5]

While the Tsar and Gorchakov's colleagues in the government recognized this course as the only possible, the bulk of society felt it too hard
to acquiesce to the patent truths of the economic and military weakness. The reversals suffered by their seemingly invincible army, the Austrian
"treachery" and the conditions imposed in Paris gave rise to a deep trauma.
The Russians were simply not accustomed to see their Tsar and country
in such a humble condition. Above all, there was a painful awareness
of the failure in what had been proclaimed the "holy mission": instead
of a victorious crusade which would wrestle Orthodox and Slavs from
Turkish hands, return the Byzantine double-headed eagle to Constantinople and make the Straits of the Bosphorus and the Dardanelles "the key
to our house," they had to consider gains attained by Peter the Great
and his successors lost or in peril. Inevitably, they were soon to be impatient with the policy of caution. Not even some in the elite, who in
principle shared Gorchakov's prudence, could escape this emotion. (Miliutin,

the pivotal figure of Alexander II's reign, was especially prone to that sort of political schizophrenia.) The notion developed that the formulae offered by the Prince just concealed the absence of any positive programme.[6]

After the Polish episode, the star of Gorchakov was in slow but steady eclipse; and his political and personal liabilities were more and more exposed. It turned out that he was—not unlike Nesselrode—a loner. Although sometimes appreciated as a witty conversationalist and accomplished courtier, he was progressively failing to command the respect due to his high office. The ministers as well as the "great" Ambassadors looked at him with poorly concealed distaste. They ridiculed his vanity which grew with advancing age; because of his love for beautiful phrases, they called him "le Narcissus de l'encrier." Merely in the Chancery of his ministry he had some dedicated friends (Giers, Hamburger, Jomini).

The vulnerability of the Prince and his moderate course was fully revealed only after a decade. The current he tried to impede and which eventually undermined his policies, however, had emerged and gathered strength from the very first post-Crimean days.

* * *

At the outset, there was an initiative of three ladies-in-waiting, Princess Vasilchikova and Countesses Bludova and Protasova, who proposed to establish a Slavic Benevolent Committee to "help our poor co-religionists" in resisting "Latin, Jesuit and political propaganda of the West." The bid sufficed to procure maneuvering space for the notorious Moscow proponents of the "Slav-Orthodox cause"—Ivan Aksakov, Khomiakov, Koshelev, Samarin, Pogodin. Katkov, albeit hostile to the Slavophiles on basic domestic issues, also joined as a curtain-raiser.[7]

Modest in its programme—it envisaged to provide material assistance to Orthodox institutions and schools in Slavic lands and invite young people to study in Russia—and insignificant in the number of participants, the action nonetheless may be earmarked as the first step towards the formation of what we call the "Moscow Panslav-nationalist party."

Dealing with this phenomenon in Russian history, the literature[8] has as a rule described the period prior to the formation of the Slavic Committee as that of purely romatic, humanitarian, "Slavophile" interest in the brotherly peoples abroad, i.e. an interest limited to promoting religious, literary and linguistic ties. Only afterwards, we have been told, did the current appropriate political aims and gradually abandon its authentic basis. Thus, after the "Slavophile," there was a "Panslav" period until the end of the Russo-Turkish war (1877-1878) and then, following the diplomatic setback at the Berlin Congress (1878), came the "nationalist" or "Pan-Russian" period, when the original teachings finally degenerated into a "system of national egotism."

This concept has its indisputable value for periodization purposes, yet ought to be applied with some caution. It particularly pertains to the early, "Slavophile" period of Russian nationalism, which has to be understood in the framework of a régime dwelling heavily on legitimist Holy Alliance principles and strictly prohibitive to any open sermon running counter it. Even in its religious, linguistic and literary confines, Slavophile thought was viewed with utmost suspicion. Nicholas I himself accused its worshippers of concealing "under the guise of compassion for the supposedly oppressed Slavic peoples the idea of rebellion against legitimate authorities in the neighboring, and, in part allied states;" they expect to achieve Slavic unification, he affirmed, "not through God's will but through disorder, which would be ruinous for Russia."[9]

However, just as he failed to escape the abyss of the Eastern Question, Nicholas could neither prevent the educated layer of his subjects from cherishing hopes going far beyond the hated straightjacket of the Holy Alliance. "True Russian feelings," which showed in the enmity to Nesselrode, were also in this "unpolitic" period expressed in ideas later described as "Panslav" or "Pan-Russian."

In 1839, Prince Vasilii Odoevskii published under a pseudonym ('the voiceless one') a fiction 'The Year 4338' strongly reminding us of the famous novel by George Orwell.

In the year 4338, the Prince divined, the world outside America would be divided between Russia and China; with the Chinese, of course, as junior partners learning from their Russian friends. No one would disturb the perfect peace and happiness established in this Russo-Chinese sphere of prosperity, embracing all the Old World. By that time, Western culture would be abandoned and forgotten. As for the former rival Powers which Tsardom had had to fight, they would become bankrupt, and the mightiest one, England, sold to Russia at a public auction. Just 'those unsociable

Americans' would remain as the only ones 'against whom we must maintain troops.'[10]

Odoevskii, though, was not satisfied with this distant prophecy. In his latter writings he asserted that 'the nineteenth century belongs to Russia' and that while 'the West is perishing,' the 'sixth part of the world (is) designed by Providence for a great deed . . . to save not only the body but the soul of Europe as well.'[11]

The historian Mikhail Pogodin, the first recognized Panslav, contemplated in a similar vein. In his letters to the heir apparent, the future Alexander II, he predicted that Russia would decide the destinies of the world, conquer Asia, liberate the Slavs and be transformed into an universal monarchy stretching from the Pacific to the Adriatic Sea, with 'no parallel in history.' As late as 1855, when Sevastopol already lay under prolonged siege, Pogodin still dreamed about the Russian capital at Constantinople and Romanov Grand Dukes sitting on the thrones of Bohemia, Moravia, Hungary, Croatia, Serbia, Bulgaria and Greece.[12]

To exalted artists, the visit of Nicholas in Rome (1845) and the revolutions in 1848-1849 gave inspiration for the boldest auguries. Thus, the painter Ivanov pronounced the Tsar 'entirely equal to Christ in his high authority and belief in God,' and the Russians as the 'great and final people,' elected by Providence to bring humanity 'the wisest rule' and 'eternal peace.'[13] The poet Tiutchev, a diplomat by profession, was more concrete. In a secret notice composed at the time of the Russian intervention in Hungary, he envisaged the end of the 'revolutionary interregnum which had already lasted three centuries' and the opening of a new era, when Russia would swallow Austria, the Tsar return to Byzantium and the two branches of the Christian Church be united by him; there would be an 'Orthodox Emperor at Constantinople, master and protector of Italy and Rome,' as well as an 'Orthodox Pope in Rome, a subject of the (Russian) Emperor.'[14]

The Moscow Slavophiles could not have thought otherwise and be satisfied by mere scientific and cultural exploits. Their very theory of the role of Russia, Slavdom and Orthodoxy in the world had far-reaching political implications; and, as soon as the Crimean War eased the conditions for them, they immediately revealed that Nicholas had not been wrong in assessing their genuine goals. Even Konstantin Aksakov, considered in comparison with his younger brother Ivan a Slavophile unpolluted by politics, circulated in 1854 a memorandum "On the Eastern Question" in quite hardboiled terms: he demanded to discharge the "Christian and fraternal duty" and wage a holy war on behalf of the Slavs, which, at the same time, would attain the most vital "security" objectives—annexation of Constantinople, the Danubian Principalities, Galicia and a "lasting alliance of all Slavs under the supreme patronage of the Russian Tsar."[15]

Indeed, the ground was well prepared when the Muscovites started to set up their Slavic organization. And the fundamentally different internal climate soon allowed them to amplify the plans and dreams with a policy of action.

* * *

Like his father, Alexander mistrusted the Slavophiles no less than the left radicals. "Those gentlemen," he wrote in 1857, "have done much harm in setting in motion this unfortunate trend of undermining the faith of the people in their government."[16] True to his preference for compromise and concession, he nonetheless gave, in February 1858, his blessing to the Moscow Benevolent Slavic Committee.[17]

Several focuses of agitation and activity, more or less connected with the Moscow Committeee and the doctrine of the "historical mission" emerged—at Court, in the Ministry for Foreign Affairs, Ministry of War, among regional military-administrative groups in the eastern and southern provinces and borderlands.

In the terms of everyday personal contact—or, to be more exact, as a direct and permanent annoyance for the Tsar and the government— the Tsarina Maria and her ladies-in-waiting were often most auspicious.

> The German-born wife of Alexander found her source of faith in Tiutchev's and Khomiakov's poetry; she 'believed blindly in the Slavophile teachings and strove to apply them in everyday politics.'[18] So did the daughters of Tiutchev, Anna and Catherine, Countesses Bludova and Protasova in their aggressive, irritating manner.
>
> Anna Tiutcheva, according to her relative, regarded all Russians as barbarians; the only exceptions from that rule which she was prepared to consider were her father and her future husband, Ivan

Aksakov, 'because they were people of pure German culture.' This, of course, would not restrain her from denouncing the Tsar and his ministers as 'unpatriotic.' Her bellicose, barking voice allegedly drove the autocrat off in a panic.[19]

Bludova was most agile among them. Her salon in the Winter Palace, wrote Meshcherskii, served as the gathering point for those who 'shared Russian feelings.' There, 'I remember meeting clever Muscovites, Slavophiles, and professors . . . . Slavs of all kind . . . junior officers as well as generals'; but, he added, he had never seen 'diplomats, Poles and Germans' there.[20] Gorchakov hated the Countess. 'She will not be satisfied until she has the half-moon of St. Sofia (Church at Constantinople) well inserted into her . . . ,' he put it in his familiar cynical manner.[21]

It was in these surroundings that the Grand Duke Alexander, the future Alexander III, grew up. After he became the heir to the throne in 1866 a relatively separate "patriotic" clique formed around him, too. (The Tsarina's and the heir's opposition to the policies of Alexander II can at least to some extent be explained by their feelings of debasement over the existence of a private family' the ruler had with Princess Catherine Dolgorukaia.)

Yet the new nationalism had its true hotbed and center under the Kremlin walls. In Katkov's words, Moscow was "the kernel of the genuine patriotism, the very embodiment of Russia as a historical principle."[22]

With the emergence of public opinion and the political press, the traditional antagonism between St. Petersburg and Moscow took on unparalleled dimensions. Even foreigners, while perceiving the metropole on the Neva as buta grandiose copy of the West, recognized in the old capital "national core," the "quientessence of all that is Russian." An Austrian diplomat observed that St. Petersburg had been a head whereas the Empire's heart had remained in Moscow; and "one has to listen attentively here (in St. Petersburg), because on the Neva the sound of its beating is barely perceptible."[23]

Backed by wealthy businessmen and noble malcontents, the Muscovite ideologues led by Katkov and Aksakov fully developed the notion that their city was the eternal sanctuary in which the Russian state and the national interest had been protected against the alienated city built by Peter.

It would be futile to identify Katkov and the Moscow party entirely with a specific class. Still, behind the rising enmity between the two capitals undoubtedly lay the phenomenon of momentous crisis—the erosion of the social basis of Imperial Russia. Moscow articulated both the protest and ambition voiced by the disintegrating and impoverished landed nobility, old merchant and artisan layers as well as the new "bourgeois" elements, all of them feeling robbed of property, power and privileges by the bureaucracy; whilst St. Petersburg stood precisely for the symbol of that bureaucracy, omnipotent and too jealous, greedy and short-sighted to share its boons with the others.

The Muscovite impact on post-Crimean Russia was to increase as the initial optimistic spirit evaporated and the great reform pushed by the Tsar and liberal group inside officialdom did not produce immediate and visible positive results. During its long rule serfdom had corrupted the muzhik and his owner alike; and they proved signally unfit to accommodate to the new conditions. The Russian village after 1861 shocked everybody as being the place of universal laziness and drunkenness. Frustrated in their hopes, the Muscovites blamed the radical intelligentsia and the bureaucrats on the Neva and sought refuge in extreme nationalism and messianic dreams. They clung to the proposition that national regeneration could be revitalized by a patriotic mobilization, particularly directed towards Russification inside the Empire and the accomplishment of Russia's mission in the Slavic and Orthodox Near East. "Russian national self-consciousness will grow stronger and firmer when realizing its spiritual unity with the Slavic world; then it will no longer feel alone in the war against its internal enemies, the common enemies of Slavdom, the renegades of Russian nationality," Aksakov promised.[24] From these aspects, the Polish uprising bestowed the Moscow doctrine with additional driving force.

The Panslav-nationalist current found sympathy and backing among people of all shades of political opinion, different personal integrity, ambition or group allegiance. Some of them honestly believed in unselfish assistance to the Slavs; some were traditional reactionaries and/or expansionists who used the liberation phraseology as a cover; some were devoid of any true conviction and embraced the creed just in order to obtain posts and promotions; in most cases these motives intertwined, the messianic complex in its peculiar Russian aggressive form being most auspicious. A disillusioned Slavophile described this development in the following words:

> Slavophilism became transformed into some sort of patriotic and Orthodox doctrine, which on the one hand aimed at universal Russification and on the other hand at converting everybody not to the Orthodox Christianity of the people, but quite simply to a police religion. . . . Hence it was able to spread all over the Russian Empire in the early 1860s, and to gain the approval of mammas and generals everywhere, to draw into its fold all the little boys eager to get on in the world. Slavophiles shot up overnight, like mushrooms, together with patriots of a very suspect kind.[25]

Russian society in its entirety underwent the same evolution: unable to solve its problems it looked for substitution in peculiarly conceived national dignity.

CHAPTER 3

FOREIGN POLICY: FIRST STEPS
ON THE NEW PATH
(1858-1862)

> A great age is dawning, one of the greatest in
> world history—a lasting alliance of all Slavs
> under the supreme patronage of the Russian
> Tsar. Moldavia and Wallachia, as regions in-
> habited by people without any individual
> significance, ought naturally to be incorp-
> orated into Russia. It is not likely, either,
> than anyone else will be able to keep posses-
> sion of Constantinople. And since ignoble
> and ungrateful Austria opposes us. . . she
> has released us from obligations and untied
> our hands. There too, Russia will fulfill her
> mission of liberation of the ethnically homo-
> genous and largely Orthodox peoples; she
> will naturally incorporate her former pro-
> vince of Galicia. And the whole Slavic world
> will breathe more easily under the patronage
> of Russia once she finally discharges her
> Christian and fraternal duty.
> Konstantin Aksakov

The programme which the Moscow Slavic Committee formally adopted
in 1858, and which the government approved, was strictly limited to customary cultural and humanitarian aims. At the same time, though, the

Moscow ideologues formulated a genuine creed going far beyond these narrow confines.

All the basic theoretical tenets had already been elaborated by the old Slavophile generation—on the Slavs and particularly Russians as the "chosen people," on Orthodoxy as the only true faith, on the antithesis of Slavdom and the "rotten West." It remained for their inheritors to furnish proper political formulae adequate to the new conditions. The main one was found in the concept of a Slav-Orthodox federation under Russian leadership, which had first been put forward as a objective of Tsardom by its Foreign Minister Adam Czartoryski in 1804 and then can-vassed by Serbian statesman Ilija Garašanin (from the 1840s).

The paramount coherence between Russia's great-power role and her active "Slavic policy" was clearly stated in a treatise on the Eastern Question, written by Prince Vladimir Cherkasskii:

> Russia cannot consolidate herself in her present state. Political, like natural history does not lend eternity to undefined, unfinished forms. All depends now on the solution of the Slavic question. Russia must either extend her primacy to the Adriatic Sea or withdraw beyond the Dnieper. . . . To Europe, which does not desire the independence of the Slavs, the Eastern Question may continue in its present form. . . as an unfinished question involving the dissolution of Turkey. But we Russians have no reason to close our eyes to reality. We must see this notorious question as what it really is— our own Slavic question.[1]

Speaking about the Slavs, Cherkasskii explained that he meant "the whole group of nations which are bound to Russia," i.e. also Magyars, Rumanians, Albanians and Greeks, who "have grown into the compact body of Slavdom and must willy-nilly share its fate." In the "new Slavic Question," which would replace the Eastern Question, the existence of all of them was to "depend exclusively on Russian history."[2]

While Cherkasskii set forth something like "grand strategy," Ivan Aksakov dealt with the same problem in the context of immediate for-eign-policy tasks.

For him, the Slavs were the only "faithful and ardent allies, ready to a man to go to war"; and, at the same time, the "first victims of the final

Western crusade against Russia." Hence, although their liberation ought to result primarily from their own effort, Tsardom should in its supreme interest offer them a helping hand. Even at this stage of the post-war recovery, the architects of official foreign policy should keep in mind that "to liberate the Slavic peoples from psychological and spiritual oppression, to grant them the gift of independent spiritual and, if you please, political existence under the shade of the mighty wing of the Russian eagle—here is Russia's historical calling, her moral right and obligation." Conversely, the Slavs and Orthodox ought to be constantly learnt to understand that their bonds with their protector and saviour must be of obligatory character, that their "own self-styled development and success is unthinkable and impossible" and that they would be asked to act according to Russian higher designs.[3]

In this initial stage, Katkov made only his first tentative steps in commenting on great foreign-policy issues. Nonetheless he already attested that even there his ambition was to be an expounder of the national interest in his own interpretation and that he would eventually challenge the government on this ground. The occasion was given by the Greco-Bulgarian Church dispute.

Contrary to Russian wishful thinking, the Bulgarians perceived the main source of their degradation and the threat to their national existence in Greek cultural and economic supremacy rather than in Turkish rule. The Greek "Phanariots"[4] had jealously protected their overall control of the Eastern Orthodox Church and were unwise enough to impose upon the Bulgarian brethren in faith much higher taxes than did the Turkish state, hinder the development of their schools, the use of their language. Hence, budding Bulgarian nationalism found its first testing ground in the struggle against Phanariot privileges, for a rebirth of a national Church. The conflict, which had already started in the 1820s took increasingly dramatic form after 1856.

The educated Bulgarians explained their standpoint to the Russians:

> However heavy the Turkish yoke, it is far less perilous than the spiritual yoke of the Greeks. The Turks are lazy, indifferent people, now too weak and bent upon the status quo . . . ; they have nothing to do with the Slavs, being only a temporary guests and masters in their house. The Bulgarian can always strike a bargain with them.

> . . . The Phanariots, besides robbing (the Bulgarians) strangle them morally, suffocate their spiritual activity, hamper their development and reject their most sacred dignity, their language and nationality.[5]

The St. Petersburg government, the Holy Synod and the Russian Church would not listen to this reasoning. According to them, the gravest peril in the Balkans lay in Catholic and Protestant propaganda and educational work among the population. Also the documents of the Slavic Committee stressed this danger pointing out that in Bulgaria alone "agents of twelve European societies are actively working" with the intention of using "Jesuit and humanist teachings" to eradicate Russian influence.[6] "I need Church unity," Alexander maintained. The Bulgarians ought to be assuaged by concessions in the matters of language, participation among the hierarchy and a share in the distribution of revenues; however, the Holy Synod rejected as unacceptable their essential claim for an autonomous Church.[7]

Aksakov, Katkov and few others in the Moscow Committee adjudged this approach as shortsighted. "If Russia . . . were to defend the Phanariots against the Slavic stock, then she would destroy the Orthodox inheritance in the East and throw millions of believers into the Roman trap," Aksakov affirmed.[8] The two mouthpieces of the old capital, *Russkii vestnik* and *Russkaia beseda* (Russian Debate), published in 1858 articles by young Bulgarian nationalists Rachinski and Daskalov, violently hostile to the Greeks. Pleading for Russian assistance, the authors attacked the Phanariots as the basest of intriguers, Turkish agents and enemies of the Slavs.[9]

Not unexpectedly, Metropolitan Philaret and the Director General (oberprokuror) of the Holy Synod Tolstoi were enraged: they suspected "foreign intrigue," an attempt to implant hate in the Russian people towards "those who had brought them the Christian faith." But whereas Khomiakov in the name of the *Russkaia beseda* hastened to assure the Synod, Katkov had already reacted in the style of his famous campaigns in the decades to come: in a case where he conceived Russian interest and his own integrity to be at stake, he would never—or almost never—retreat. He refused the proposal volunteered by Minister for Public Instruction Kovalevskii that the *Russkii vestnik* should proclaim the views stated in the incriminated article to be only the author's private opinion. Instead, he launched a counterattack clamouring that the religious

censorship should be applied on questions of dogma only; by their conduct, he charged, the dignitaries had paraded "the principles and spirit
of inquisition" which must be condemned.

Protected by the officials responsible for censorship in Moscow, Bak-
hmetev and von Cruze—incidentally, both members of the Slavic Committee—Katkov held his ground. Unable to influence the debate, the
government had to prohibit its continuation in the press. The Holy Synod
published a special booklet against the *Russkii vestnik*, but the unyielding editor emerged from the strife with flying colours.[10]

* * *

Besides being symptomatic of Katkov's role and attitudes, the Bulgarian Church affair revealed more about the peculiar relationship between
state power, the press and the Moscow party in the post-Crimean period

There were serious frictions concerning Balkan policies from the outset. Aksakov affronted Gorchakov by his attempt to form a "Slavic
Bureau," a sort of shadow "Muscovy" Foreign Ministry; and his weekly
Parus (Sail) was banned after publishing an acrimonious article by Pogodin.[11] Still, the government persisted in its basic approach, preferring
accommodation to confrontation.

The task of supervision over the Moscow Committee was entrusted
to its member Evraf Kovalevskii, the Minister for Public Instruction,
and to his brother Egor, the director of the Asiatic Department of the
Foreign Ministry, also well-known for his sympathy for the Moscow cause.
Through the Asiatic Department, the Committee was to receive governmental subsidies and could keep its own contacts with the diplomatic
mission at Constantinople, consuls in the Balkans and local well-disposed
nationalists.[12]

In the further developments, the arrangement brought about serious
splits and frictions: packed by people close to the Moscow party, the
Asiatic Department was often to assist in actions running counter to the
policies pursued by Gorchakov and his "European-oriented" Chancery.
At this stage, though, tendency to cooperation prevailed. Continuing unrest in the Balkans and particularly the European crisis of 1859 inspired
the Foreign Minister and perhaps even the Tsar to quite considerable
optimism as to the Russian prospects.

Preparing for war with Austria, the Franco-Sardinian alliance sought to secure Tsardom's goodwill. Sardinia gave permission to establish a Russian naval base in the Bay of Villafranca (1858) and on 3 March 1859, a secret Franco-Russian treaty on neutrality and cooperation was concluded. Following negotiations promised still more: Napoleon III talked about a diplomatic common front with the Tsar and his willingness to back the cardinal Russian desiderata, including the establishment of the Balkan federation and the free-city status of Constantinople. This appeared to confirm Gorchakov's calculation that "France remains as a continental and naval power liable to become an ally."[13]

Besides the Russo-French rapprochement, Prince Michael Obrenović, who had recently ascended the Belgrade throne, provided the main source for Russian sanguine expectations.

The Serbian ruler embraced Garašanin's ideas as his own; and, greatly encouraged by the triumphs of the Italian "risorgimento," he resolved to raise his Principality into a South-Slav Piedmont. He elevated Garašanin into the position of his chief lieutenant and together they opened contacts with the Montenegrins and Greeks as well as with the Bulgarian emigres, guerilla leaders in Bosnia-Hercegovina and the "Yugoslav" oriented personalities in the Austrian possessions.

St. Petersburg was very circumspect where the anti-Austrian aspect of the Serbian initiative was concerned. As to the anti-Turkish one, though, it was both positive and hopeful. "Serbia, from the force of circumstances and as a result of her exceptional position," Gorchakov reiterated in his dispatches, "has become the center and the point of support for other Slav areas of Turkey" and "will evolve into a nucleus or basis for the grouping of Christian nations when they resolve to shake off the Turkish dominance."[14]

In June 1860, in a circular to the Powers, the Foreign Minister moved to implement his Eastern policies in a more assertive manner. Pointing to continuous instability in the area, he requested collective pressure on the Porte in order to obtain "real, serious and permanent improvement in her relations with the Christian subjects."[15] He presumably conceived this as the first step to far-reaching events in which Serbia, under the protective umbrella of the Russo-French entente, could go to action.

Moscow, naturally, saw the moment no less propitious and adapted its stance accordingly. While in the first post-war years its main concern had been directed to the Bulgarians and had had a predominately defensive character, now it was transferred, with a pronouncedly offensive penchant, to the western part of the Balkans. Like all the others in the Committee, Katkov was emphatic in the requirement that the Bulgarians must follow the Serbian lead.[16]

The first venture in marshalling the Serbs under the Muscovy banner, performed by Khomiakov, had badly missed the mark. The "Epistle to the Serbs from Moscow," written in 1858, was heavily tainted by Orthodox intolerance and with its anti-Catholic bias it evoked distaste even among people with Russian allegiances. Yet the zealots of the doctrine remained undismayed. That the South Slavs did not like their "Epistle" was only proof of the debilitating impact of "Western decadence"; and they prescribed armed struggle as the best remedy.[17] Aksakov departed for the Balkans to inspect the scene and arrange redress.

The prolonged trip of the Panslav leader brought its most significant result in the deal he made with Matija Ban, Prince Michael's confident and chief propagandist.

Ban, a far-sighted Croat publicist, cherished no illusions about Russian policy: he considered it traditionally selfish and hegemony-seeking and assumed identical motives behind the new interest. Because of this, he also strongly opposed Metropolitan Mihailo, the main Russian stalwart in Serbia, who wanted Orthodoxy to furnish the ideological foundation of the Slav unification: "In Belgrade, we must not raise the banner of Orthodoxy but the banner of the Yugoslav people. With the former we are in Russian hands; with the latter, we remain independent."[18] To Aksakov, too, he made it clear that he would not be a dupe of the "Moscow national party," but for the immediate reasons of expediency he settled with him on building a network of secret organizations which should be supplied by Russian money and eventually trigger a general uprising against the Turks.

Following the Aksakov-Ban understanding, the Moscow Committee set up a special fund and local businessmen were approached for contributions. In autumn 1860, Ban received the first subsidies.[19]

The Panslav-oriented diplomats worked to the same purpose. Among them Alexander Ionin, the agent in Ragusa (Dubrovnik), had a prominent role, being a mediator between Serbia, Montenegro, the Asiatic Department and the Moscow Committee.[20]

Warmed up, the official St. Petersburg more and more outstretched its hand. It not only tolerated the collection of funds for the uprising but also offered Prince Michael 900,000 rubles as an interest-free loan and decided for arms deliveries to Serbia. Taking into consideration political and financial conditions in Russia—these were times of severe stringency, rising tensions in Poland and large-scale military operations in the Caucasus—it may be assumed that Tsardom was tempted to go far beyond the proclaimed course of strictly "moral" assistance to the South Slavs.

Europe was at that time alive with the most fantastic rumors. British diplomatic and intelligence reports claimed that Napoleon III was planning an agreement with Russia on a "great action in the Orient" and that the Winter Palace intended to create two big vassal states in the Balkans —one, comprising the Danubian Principalities and Bulgaria and headed by a relative of Alexander, the Duke of Leuchtenberg, the other led by Michael, extended as far as Salonika and Albania.[21]

No big events, however, took place. The Russo-French talks on a common front in the East stalemated and the Serbian Prince was an astute enough politician to play the game prudently. True, his preparations were vigorous: in September 1861, he introduced universal military service and in the course of intensive negotiations with other Balkan states concluded a potentially highly significant alliance treaty with Otto, the King of Greece. But when the crisis broke out in July 1862 by the Turkish bombardment of Belgrade, he rejected appeals for war, soberly judging the Balkan conditions unripe, his armed forces and their armaments inadequate[22] and the international situation unclear.

Inconclusive French talks and looming Polish troubles also cooled down optimism in St. Petersburg. After the Belgrade incident, the envoy in Berlin, Baron Budberg, was sent to Paris for consultations, the instruction he received, however, suggested peaceful settlement; albeit confirming Russian interest in Serbia as a center of the anti-Turkish forces, the Singers' Bridge pointed out that owing to internal complications, "further sacrifices for foreign policy aims" were out of the question. Budberg agreed with the French that the two Powers should demand the withdrawal of Turkish garrisons (except Belgrade) from Serbian soil,[23] and this was also the compromise solution approved by both the Prince and the Porte.

The reaction of the Moscow party to this outcome was highly illuminative.

Impatient and inspired by Slavophile dreams rather than by detached political calculation, Aksakov scolded Michael for his diffidence, for what he called a "come-il-faut policy"; instead of being an old-type Balkan guerilla leader standing at the helm of his armed people, he contended, the Prince entered on the wrong path of building up an ordinary European state and army.[24]

Katkov, on the contrary, gave the affair a realistic assessment, taking into account Serbian and Russian weakness and the European conditions.

Comparing Piedmont with Serbia, the editor of the *Russkii vestnik* emphasized the substantial disadvantages of the latter: Piedmont had only to settle accounts with Austria and could rely on the powerful and direct assistance of the French ally, while Serbia was surrounded by enemies, the Turks and the Austrians, and her ally was "far away." Belgrade must be circumspect and start its struggle only at the moment when the trump-cards were in Slavic hands. In general, both Russian and South Slav leaders ought to set about rather for a gradual broadening of autonomy and should not forget that Turkey still remained a partner in the European power-balance system.[25]

So, even in foreign policy sphere where he had so far only been learning his part, Katkov reaffirmed his aspiration to be an independent arbiter scrupulously observing and judging events but from the viewpoint of highest state interest.

* * *

The developments in 1858-1862 for the first time indicated what would be the differences between the "St. Petersburg" and the "Moscow" approach, as well as between the two main currents in the framework of the Muscovy doctrine—the more traditionally conceived "Panslav line," best personfied by Ivan Aksakov, and the "national direction" with Katkov as its chief expounder.

Concerning the latter aspect, the nuances were well stated in an analysis by the Austrian Ambassador, Count Wolkenstein:

> Aksakov and his like perceived the Near-Eastern mission as the
> only important task for Russia, 'the basis of her existence . . . the

fulfillment of her destiny.' Katkov and other 'pure' nationalists looked on the Slavic-Orthodox world with entirely unsentimental, utilitarian eyes: 'the Balkan and Bosphorus policies' were for them 'just one postulate,' albeit crucial one, in the broader perspective of Russian ambition.[26]

The lofty keywords were for Katkov hardly more than of propagandist significance. "Panslavism" in his interpretation meant simply "faith in Russia, her interests and her own national policy"; and, national policy was "a law of every civilized state, every self-respecting nation and government," recognizing no moral obligation to the others, whether small or great.[27]

As he had shown in his comments on the Serbian crisis, the editor more than other Muscovites took into account international realities and the internal weakness of Tsardom. For that reason, until the end of the 1860s he mostly backed Gorchakov's cautious line in the Near East; and even later there were periods when he recognized circumspection as inevitable. Despite this, though, a liberal critic correctly described his fundamental position as the "exclusive cult of naked power, a power an sich and für sich."[28]

He preached unadulterated Machiavellism:

> In 'the international context, the voice of moral has no significance . . . . Governments have no other obligation than the benefit (polza), only benefit and nothing else than the benefit of their nation, their own country.' Hence, 'politicians seek to be directed in their deeds exclusively by the interests of their countries and do not accept any consideration of any abstract idea of justice and magnamity.' Benefits cannot be obtained and state interests furthered otherwise than from the position of strength; foreign policy cannot be other than offensive. 'A state among other states is restrained by nothing more than by the simple impossibility of going farther. It is not its duty to ask the question whether its power does not grow too much; this question must be asked by others and solved by them.' Particularly for Russia expansion was a matter of supreme necessity: if she failed to keep pace with her rivals, then 'our state would not only lose its position as a Great Power, but also be driven out of Europe,' relegated to the state of an 'Asiatic khanate.'[29]

No diplomatic achievement could substitute for the true means of a great-power policy. "Diplomatic accomplishment is a secondary matter and nowhere does national interest rely on greater or lesser talent in the presentation of diplomatic arguments," wrote Katkov. When a situation he assessed as favorable would arise, then no negotiations were permissible save those safeguarding Russian spoils. Russia was strong enough for bold moves, he would invariably argue in such moments, and those who disputed this on the grounds of her military and economic deficiencies he would stigmatize as internal enemies, perpetrators of Nihilism in the foreign policy sphere.[30]

From these premises, Katkov also drew the fundamental line of division in Russian policy between those who were ready to follow his interpretation and who were not; or, as he put it, between the "national Russian party" and the "anti-national and anti-Russian" one.[31]

Both currents in the Moscow mainstream would agree with Gorchakov on one substantial point only: that Tsardom ought to avoid permanent obligations of the Holy Alliance type and break with the dynastic tradition of fixed bonds with Berlin and Vienna.

"This idea has tied us hand and foot not only in Western Europe but also in the East," claimed Aksakov. "The closer our alliance with Austria and Prussia, the weaker our influence will be." It should be recognized that a non-alligned, free-hand policy was best suited to the furthering of national purpose. What the other Powers regarded as an isolated position, "is better for Russia than any alliance. The greater freedom she retains, the stronger will be her national position and the more genuinely national the character of her policy."[32]

Owing to its Machiavellian and anti-Western undertone, however, the Muscovy interpretation of free-hand policy was to veer progressively away from Gorchakov's. While the Prince looked for Russia's advancement in diplomatic combinations and agreements in the framework of the "Concert of Europe," the nationalist extremists emphasized "unfavorable neutrality" towards all the big ones and their rivalries as "our best political alliance." Tsardom should take advantage of these rivalries and enter only into temporary understandings beneficial to its purposes. Danilevskii put it flatly in his famous "Russia and Europe":

We must abandon the notion of any kind of support for European interests, any kind of connection with this or that European configuration. Above all, we must achieve complete freedom of maneuvre, the right to a potential alliance with any European state, regardless of what political principles it represents at any given moment, and on the sole condition that this alliance is in our interest.[33]

In Russian continental and Near-Eastern ventures of 1856-1862, future trends and disputes on "national interest policy" were still hardly discernible. Meanwhile, in the Caucasus and Central Asia, where the formidable military and diplomatic offspring of the Moscow party operated in more favorable circumstances, they had already been fully exposed.

CHAPTER 4

THE MILITARY: THE CAUCASUS AND
CENTRAL-ASIAN PATTERN
(1856-1862)

> It is our endeavour to raise the numbers of
> our troops, increase profits, intimidate
> other nations, expand our territories often
> with the help of lies.
> Khomiakov

> The time has come to justify all the sacri-
> fices Russia has made in the last half century.
> Only relatively minor increases in expendi-
> ture and numbers of troops are needed. With
> this, Russia will be rewarded by new sources
> of enrichment and by a first-rate position in
> Asia.
> Bariatinskii

That the Moscow Committee attracted a great group of officers serving
in the Caucasus was no accident. Notwithstanding the defeat in the Crimean War, the army in its entity had not suffered much harm either in
influence or prestige. Their humiliated pride even stimulated the younger
generation in the officer corps in the resolve to prove Russian martial
virtues and their own superiority over the "muzurka-dancers" of the old
era. The conditions in the Caucasus offered perfect ground for this reas-
sertion; and the benevolence of the new ruler assured his "eagles" almost
unhindered outlet.

To be sure, the decisions for the Tsar were far from easy. The financial situation and the Crimean experience, sharpened by memories of his father's last excruciating days, led him to accept the policy advocated by his ministers. On the other hand, the military in the words of General Miliutin reminded him that "thanks to the army, Russia has become a first-class Power, (and) only by maintaining the army can Russia uphold the position she has acquired."[1]

Alexander read this message correctly, not just as a warning against excessive cuts in military expenditures demanded by the desperate Finance Ministry: with the hopes for speedy internal recovery receding, the autocracy had to enlist the loyalty of its subjects in the traditional way, i.e. by the triumphs of arms. The Tsar chose—apparently via facti rather than by forethought—to overcome his dilemma by giving free rein to eager officers in the regions where limited resources and international conditions would allow it.

Hereby, the decades after 1856 ripened into heydays for the militarists in the Caucasus and other Asiatic borderlands. Already under Nicholas, the mighty proconsuls in the East—Perovskii, Muraviev-"Amurskii," Vorontsov—had displayed a marked tendency to "act first and report afterwards."[2] Now their stature grew even more powerful. Exploiting favorable circumstances, they could run a forward policy which was often in sharp contrast to that officially adopted.

This development was initiated in 1856, when Alexander appointed his long-time close friend Alexander Bariatinskii as the Viceroy (namestnik) and Commander-in-Chief in the Caucasus and bestowed him with extensive powers.

The nominee was an outstanding figure in the Russian aristocracy. Strikingly handsome, he had been known as the "first Don Juan" at Court.[3] But he would not be satisfied only with the conquest of female hearts. Life among the happy few furthered in him a keen taste for power and his subsequent service in the Caucasus added to it convenient lofty purpose. Russia's might and glory, inextricably woven into his personal aspirations, had become the value he cherished most. Recklessly courageous in battles with mountaineers, Bariatinskii had already prior to Alexander's ascendance been recognized as one of the best commanders on the spot; and when the new ruler had offered him any position he wished he had not hesitated in his choice.

Surrounded in Tiflis by Oriental pomp, with a personal "court" where native nobles mingled with adjutants from the Russian jeunesse dorée, the Prince felt called by the Providence for the role of an Empire-builder. The Caucasus should be subjugated once and for all to Russian rule to serve as a springboard for great exploits.

Like his lieutenants who joined the Moscow Committee, he wished to see Tsardom "politically dominant over the Slavic world, having a firm influence in the East, and, in consequence, a leading position in Europe."[4] Contrary to the customary outlook, however, the key to this goal lay in his vistas not in the Balkans but in Asia. In this way, he epitomized both the new role of the military in the Eastern borderlands and the "Asiatic" challenge to the traditionally oriented foreign policy.

In the beginning, Bariatinskii's concept appeared to be pure fantasy. Even the conquest of the Caucasus was considered a remote perspective. Guerillas counted tens of thousands of relatively well armed men perfectly adapted to war in mountains and woods; and they controlled areas of about one million inhabitants. The War Ministry, expecting no substantial improvement, was at one with the Finance Ministry that the wisest course would be that of containment, strict economy and troop reductions. So, the Prince had first of all to persuade the Tsar. He affirmed that another great conflict with the English was in the offing; and, because of this, the best possible position had to be obtained to prevent a second Crimean disaster. That, he claimed, could not be achieved unless the Caucasus were pacified and communications with Trans-Caucasia made safe.[5]

Alexander abhorred the notion of another big confrontation. Nonetheless, albeit in his correspondence with the Prince he declined to believe in war and dwelt on the "absolute necessity" of strict economy and even on "restraining our military operations,"[6] the Caucasus command always at the end got what it had asked for.

Events were to prove that Bariatinskii evaluated the conditions more correctly than St. Petersburg's military authorities. After a half-century of bloody and devastating campaigns, and after their hopes for massive outside assistance during the Crimean War failed to materialize, the exhaustion and isolation of guerillas took its heavy toll. Russian forces, more than 200,000 strong, now better equipped and organized,[7] could set out for decisive actions.

The Caucasus command deployed the bulk of its troops in Daghestan and Chechnia against the most formidable enemy, Imam Shamil. After two years of ruthless warfare, in which mountaineer's settlements (auls) and forests were systematically destroyed, it succeeded where all its predecessors had stumbled. In the summer of 1859, the legendary Moslem leader asked for truce.

The image of Shamil still loomed large in St. Petersburg and War Minister Sukhozanet anew seconded to Gorchakov's claim that peace in the Caucasus would give Russia "ten times more weight in the councils of Europe."[8] Also Alexander leaned towards a negotiated settlement: he wished to have at least a portion of Bariatinskii's forces on the western frontier, where—because the approaching war between Austria and the Franco-Sardinian alliance—"we have a greater need of them than ever."[9] But the Prince refused to comply and, as usual, he forced his will upon the capital. On 6 September 1859, the Russians stormed the last retreat of the Imam on the Ghunib mountain and took him prisoner. Only relatively unimportant and isolated regions remained unvanquished.

Discussing the future strategy in the area, the St. Petersburg policymakers once again suggested that large-scale and costly operations should cease; and, once more Bariatinskii prevailed on the Tsar in advocating the very opposite line of "permanent offensive war." "The East is soon going to rise into a stage where big controversial questions are to be solved for good," he repeated, "and if the Caucasus is not entirely subdued . . . then we will not have a single soldier of our glorious army free to cross the border."[10]

Even in its conclusive phase, the conquest was to be performed with the same vigour and brutality which had been employed against the Chechnia stronghold.

As in the past, now, and time to come, the Russian military were never to suffer qualms of conscience in effecting the Muscovite philosophy of national interest. Standing over the body of a native women killed by a soldier's bayonet, Katkov's admirer reasoned:

> They will order us burn and destroy the auls later anyway. Why here, in the midst of such a bloody mess, ask troops to behave towards women like gentlemen; one way or another, to harmonize war and humanitarian ideas is but an empty dream.[11]

* * *

In the meantime, the opening years of the 1860s witnessed the climax of the Caucasus warlord's game. Awarded the title of Field Marshal, Bariatinskii rose into a de-facto ruler of his extending satrapy, with his own Council and Chancery substituting for governmental organs. No wonder that he felt even less compulsion than in the past to accommodate himself to the "weaklings" on the Neva; on the contrary, he set out to impose himself above them.

First General Sukhozanet, the War Minister who had been opposing him, was to go. For some time the Tsar resisted, but the painfully slow concentration of troops during the crisis of 1859—it took five months to move four corps on the Austrian border—gave the Prince the trump card he needed. Miliutin, his subordinate, was named Sukhozanet's deputy and then, in November 1861, the minister.

After this initial step, Bariatinskii unfolded his big design in a proposal to introduce the Prussian system in the relationship between the ruler and the armed forces. The position of the Imperial Chief of Staff ought to be established and a respected military figure appointed to it (i.e. the Prince himself), who would be responsible to the Tsar for supreme politico-military decisions. In another innovation, an Imperial Military Chancery was to be created and his most trusted lieutenant with important connections to the Moscow Committee, General Rostislav Fadeev, to serve as its head. Miliutin would retain the War Ministry, with responsibilities, however, limited to administrative and logistic functions.

Furthermore, Bariatinskii undertook to reassert himself as the man of the new foreign policy concept and undermine Gorchakov's position. Since July 1861 he had been submitting to Alexander memoranda requiring a complete change in the approach to the Polish and Eastern Questions: Russia was to grant to the Polish Kingdom independence and then, freed from this embarrasing burden, adopt a hard line against the Turks and the Austrians and openly take over the leadership in the Slavic world.

However, the climate in the elite of late Imperial Russia was unhealthy for a Napoleon or for any overpowering personality for that matter. The Caucasus warlord, too, overrated his chances. Rather than winning allies, his triumphs and bold challenge to St. Petersburg's routines alerted many at Court, in the army and in the government. A special commission set up by the Tsar to discuss his proposals turned them down. The failure of Count Lambert, his client sent to Warsaw with a mission of appeasement, brought him an additional setback. And when an unsavoury affair with a subordinate's wife compromised him personally, his enemies were turned loose.[12]

In January 1863, the Prince tendered his resignation, a painful gout being probably only a cover story for injured pride. In any case, his spell was broken and, although still towering in the future military-political debates, he was to be invariably on the loser's side. None of his army schemes materialized. The post of the Chief of Staff was established in 1865, but with vaguely specified and generally subordinated functions vis-à-vis the War Minister. Miliutin became his chief opponent and in the long strife on military reform in the end obtained the laurels of victory over the Field Marshal. In the sphere of the Slavic policy, the Polish question was handled in traditional style and on the Eastern Question the extremist initiative was appropriated by others.

Still, in its Asiatic dimensions, the "Bariatinskii heritage" was to evolve into an integral part of the hawkish programme and the area east and south of the Caspian Sea into a huge scene for its execution.

* * *

Whereas in the Caucasus the first half of the 1860's marked the final stage of the Russian conquest, a similar process in Central Asia was only just beginning to set its pace and dimensions.

Until then, there had been a slow advance from the Orenburg and Siberian lines of forts into the Kirghiz steppe (Kazakhstan), protecting the Central-Asian khanates—Bukhara, Kokand, Khiva—and further on, Afghanistan. To reach Samarkand with an expedition sent from Orenburg would take at least six months; and no only the fate of the famous Cossack expedition ordered by the mad Tsar Paul I to go to India, but also more modest yet abortive attempt of Perovskii against Khiva (1839) revealed almost unsurmountable obstacles for big achievements. Thus the plans, or rather fantasies, projecting a drive to India or Afghanistan, elaborated during the Crimean war by Generals Tornau, Duhamel and Chikhachev left the khanates mostly aside.[13] To be sure, the Siberian military were not idle: in 1852, Perovskii occupied the Kokanese fortress of Ak-Mechet on the Syr-Daria and two years later General Hasford founded the fortress of Vernyi (Alma-Ata). But even some time after the Crimean War they were not eager to be involved in large-scale ventures. The initiative for forward policy came from Tiflis, not from Orenburg or Omsk.

In 1856-1857, pushing his concept of a drive into Asia, Bariatinskii requested that ports be constructed as well as a railroad which would connect the Aral Sea and the Syr-Daria.

> The government, the Prince maintained, 'must strive to win Central Asian and Persian trade,' link the seas on the southern borders with Russia and in this way 'open new untaped resources,' create better conditions for transportation of goods and troops. Besides proper communications, the occupation of a Central-Asian outpost should provide the instrument to control of Turkoman tribes, the Persians, the Emir of Bukhara, and the starting point for the advance Herat, Kabul and Kandahar. If this advice were neglected, he warned, then the British would master the Persian Gulf and Afghanistan, buy off Central Asian rulers and enjoy an enormous advantage in the future great war.[14]

Opinions were sharply divided. Grand Duke Konstantin and a group of businessmen headed by V.A. Kokorev backed the Tilflis warlord. Among the military the Sevastopol hero General Khrulev joined them in pleading for vigorous move against the English; and, prompted by the Sepoy uprising in India, he circulated a project which would bring Russian regiments into the very heart of the British colonial empire. On the other hand, the ministries for foreign affairs and war strenuously resisted Eastern adventures. In an analysis "On the possibility of an untoward war in Central Asia," written by Generals Lieven and Neverovskii and defended by both ministers, the claims of an alleged English threat were dismissed as groundless and the Indian expedition unequivocally rejected. The document insisted that Russian policy in the area should not be unlike that pursued in Europe, i.e. that it ought to be "temporizing, not offensive."[15]

Alexander approved the Lieven-Neverovskii memoir and accepted Bariatinskii's reasoning as a guideline "for the future."[16] However, the

Prince and his supporters obtained an important concession: three missions were dispatched to Persia, the west-Chinese province of Sinkiang and to Bukhara and Khiva, to reconnoitre the routes and collect all useful information. "I am convinced that this will have the most weighty consequences in paving the way for our forthcoming activities," Grand Duke Konstantin commented, "and will deny posterity the right to say that we stood with folded arms when unfortunate India struggled to overthrow the hated English yoke."[17]

This was the occasion when the young Nikolai Ignatiev, entrusted to lead the mission to Bukhara and Khiva, emerged as a rising extremist star. Upon his return, seemingly arguing in favor of peace and cooperation with the khanates, the budding soldier-diplomat enlarged in a lengthy memoir Bariatinskii's scheme:

> Intense political and economic contacts with areas separating us from the British possessions would raise influence and prosperity and at the same time ensure better security for our borders. There is also 'the only field left for our commercial activity for the expansion of (markets for) our industry,' and above all 'in the event of a breach with Britain' the only space of land 'where we can fight her with some chance of success and harm Turkey into the bargain. So long as the peace endures, the difficulties brought on Britain in Asia and the extension of our prestige (there), . . . will be the best guarantee for avoiding war with her.'[18]

In the document Ignatiev thus coined the thesis which subsequently towered in the arguments of the military: the bolder we shall be in Central Asia, the more accomodating will the London cabinet be elsewhere, notably in the Near East.

Meanwhile, the offensive current had received a considerable boost by the events in the Far East and their repercussions on the Neva.

The East-Siberian Governor General Nikolai Muraviev and his entourage, in complete disregard of the orders coming from the capital, had seized vast territories on the left bank of the Amur considered so far to be a part of the Chinese Empire. Once the Chinese yielded to Muraviev's intimidations and by the Treaty of Aigun (1858) recognized the river as the new frontier, St. Petersburg performed a volte-face: while earlier it had threatened the unruly East-Siberians with a court-martial for unauthorized actions, now it awarded them and bestowed their chief with the title of "Count Muraviev-Amurskii."

In 1860, Ignatiev was sent on another great Eastern mission, this time as an extraordinary envoy to the Chinese capital. He took advantage of the Third Opium War and the Taiping Rebellion and further enlarged Russian gains: by the Peking Treaty, Tsardom obtained sovereignty over the region between the Ussuri River and the Pacific as well as trade privileges in Mongolia and Chinese Turkestan. The very name of the newly founded Vladivostok ("the ruler of the East") indicated the rising "ambition of Russian imperialism."[19]

Now, the heretofore complacent administrators in Orenburg learned their lessons. Seeing that the wind in the capital was changing and jealous of their rivals at Tomsk and Tiflis, they stepped forward with their own initiative. Instead of the drive to Central Asia across the Caspian Sea, Governor General Katenin and his successor Bezak pleaded for advance for the Kirghiz steppe: first the gap between the Orenburg and Siberian fort lines should be closed and a firm position on the Amu-Daria established; then, with a push from the north and the east, Tashkent and Bukhara should be subdued.

Numerous extraordinary councils and commissions dealing with the Asiatic issues offer a complex picture, with the moderates desperately resisting hawkish charges and the respective military groups fighting each other.[20] The general tendency, though, unmistakably pointed to the extremist supremacy.

The plea for a bold course had been greatly sustained by economic considerations. The American civil war and the resulting scarcity of cotton on European markets made the valleys of the Syr-Daria and Amu-Daria extremely attractive. And the risks that the advance would en-kindle serious complications were minimal. In what Kipling called the "Great Game" of the Anglo-Russian contest in Asia, the English proved much less formidable opponents that has generally been believed. An American scholar correctly remarked that "prior to 1869, the British cabinet registered no great concern over the progress of Russian arms and influence in Central Asia."[21] The same may be said about the In-dian administration headed by Sir John Lawrence.

After Miliutin had entered the St. Petersburg government, the de-cisive shift took place in the Asiatic councils: the hitherto existing unity between the ministries for foreign affairs and war ended and the new colleague denounced Gorchakov's policies east of the Caspian Sea as a "system of total conservatism" unduly timid towards the British response.[22] Moreover, appointed upon his triumph in Peking the director of the Asiatic Department, Ignatiev emerged in the debates as a stout ally of the War Minister.

Just as it was the hallmark in Russia's domestic development, the Polish uprising with its external implications may also be considered the point of departure in the conquest of Central Asia: in the sequel of plans, debates and tentative moves the time had now arrived for big deeds.

CHAPTER 5

THE TASTE OF POWER:
THE POLISH UPRISING AND AFTER
(1863-1866)

These are really grave times—almost imposing the question of "to be or not to
be"; and they are even more critical than
the year 1812.
Nikitenko

The whole Europe except Prussia took the
side of Poland, although only by collective
demarches. This was the moment when
Katkov conquered the feelings of Russian
society, hitherto directed by Alexander
Herzen in a European revolutionary sense,
and converted it as if by magic want into the
now so much inflated national-Russian
direction.
von Schweinitz

If events before 1863 had signalled failure, then the Polish uprising
of 1863-1864 pronounced the fatal verdict on the quest of Russian society
for inner liberation. Perennial anti-Polish hatred surfaced and took hold
of the sophisticated upper layer as it did of the ignorant masses. Almost
all those who had stoutly defended the cause of peasant freedom and the
course of reform joined the hard-boiled reactionaries in refusing the

"historical enemies" even the right of limited self-government. Liberal
bureaucrats from St. Petersburg (the brothers Miliutin) and the Moscow
critics of serfdom (Cherkasskii, Koshelev) were among the chief executors
of brutal repression. The courageous handful who dared to go openly
against the current were hunted down. And while Herzen or Grand Duke
Konstantin were now then men ostracized "as if contaminated by plague"[1]
because of their sympathy for conciliation, Katkov and the military
butchers—personified at their worst by General Muraviev, the "Hangman
of Vilna"—were hailed as heroes and saviors of Russia.

The conservative philosopher Konstantin Leontiev expressed most
succintly the impact of the Polish drama on the way of thinking. In
1864, he recalled,

> I began to love monarchy. I began to love army and the military.
> I began to pity and appreciate the landed nobility. I began to ad-
> mire Muraviev-Vilenskii and the articles of Katkov.[2]

During the two tense years preceding the uprising, the Moscow publicist pursued a circumspect line and followed the lead of the army paper,
Russkii invalid. When, however, the Poles resorted to arms and the St.
Petersburg government occured on the defensive before the angry public,
he quickly overshadowed all the others in his chauvinistic outcry.[3] Having
just obtained a much stronger weapon in the daily *Moskovskiia vedomosti*,[4]
he opened in its leading articles that verbal barrage which brought him the
nickname of the "Thunderer from Strastnyi Boulevard."

Arguing in the *Russkii invalid*, Miliutin and his lieutenants contended
that nothing the Russians could possibly do would induce the Poles to
conciliation.[5] There, undoubtedly, lay the weakpoint of appeasement.
The majority in the government, and, albeit with utmost reticence, Alexander as well, were willing to make concessions and did even grant them.
The Poles, however, wished to sever ties with Tsardom and, above all,
clamoured for a return to the historical frontiers existing before the three
divisions.

Katkov unfolded the reasoning of Muliutin's circle with—at least for
the Russian mind—enormous persuasive strength. The Pole, he charged,

> will not be satisfied with simple independence. He wants domin-
> ance. He will not be satisfied to liberate himself from the foreign

yoke; he wants to destroy his triumphant foe. He will not be satisfied to be a Pole; he wants the Russians to become Poles, or else, move beyond the Urals . . . . And instead of the contemporary powerful Russia, a powerful Poland with Kiev and Smolensk would take its place, from the Baltic to the Black Sea.

'There, on the banks of the Vistula, the first stage of the most important and essential question of any government is now being decided—that of the integrity and security of its own rightful possessions.' Hence, any retreat would bring about the 'end of Russia as a Great Power,' a 'death certificate for the Russian people.' Between Poland and Russia, 'history has always posed the fateful question of life and death. Both states were not simply rivals, but enemies who could not live side by side, enemies to the end. Between them, the question was not which will be in first place, which will become mightier; rather the question was which one of them will exist.'

Because of all this, those in the government pleading for making accomodation with the Poles were implicitly enemies, too—such were the disturbing connotations of the Katkovian sermon. The special status granted in 1815 to the so called Polish Kingdom ought to be destroyed, holding the Poles under "force of arms" recognized a maxim of national policy. "The sword is the symbol of the state" and must be applied without hesitation to induce the hostile nation to acknowledge a "new political life, in common with Russia." "Our troops are entitled to know that they defend the national, Russian cause."[6]

The circulation of the Thunderer's daily increased virtually with every issue and it was avidly read even in the remostest provinces. The awareness that the public found in his editorials the genuine expression of their wishes and feelings, poised the publicist for the more and more reckless attacks. In vain a censor implored that he should observe "utmost caution in the *Moskovskiia vedomosti* (because it is) read by the common people;" he made, according to one of his correspondents, "the whole of Russia witness to the weak and haphazard governmental actions."[7]

Feoktistov, the later press lord, recollected in his memoirs:

It was the first case in Russia where a man without contacts and protectors and only by the sheer force of his burning convictions, gained an unheard of dictatorship over minds. . . . The *Moskovskiia vedomosti* went from hand to hand until it turned into shreds. His name thundered across all Russia.' The peculiar relationship between the authorities and the publicist which was to be symptomatic of the years to come now took its shape: 'the government was afraid of him and at the same time fawned upon him.'[8]

* * *

The abortive interference by France, England and Austria into the Polish imbroglio much helped to enhance the Moscovite's hold over both the public and the elite.

When the first Western protests were registered in St. Petersburg in March, Gorchakov took them light-heartedly as mere maneuvres to allay the spirits aroused in their countries: "neither France nor England would go too far."[9] The Vice-Chancellor earnestly hoped that the moderate policies just inaugurated in Warsaw by the new Viceroy, Grand Duke Konstantin, would bring about appeasement and turn Western attitudes to Tsardom back to normalcy. However, once the three "pro-Polish" Powers simultaneously presented their notes (on 17 April) and the conciliatory moves in the Polish Kingdom produced no effect, the worries in the Neva markedly increased. Gorchakov and his colleagues responsible for the army, navy and finance—Muliutin, Admiral Krabbe and Reutern—sounded the alarm. Suddenly they saw Russia at the verge of another armed conflict with the "Crimean coalition" for which, as all of them stressed, she was manifestly unprepared.[10] "Great excitement and general expectation of war," the British embassy in St. Petersburg reported, also prevailed "in all classes of society." It was assumed—and such was the opinion in Europe too—that Napoleon III was purposely striding towards a showdown.[11]

Contrary to the ministers, Katkov remained undismayed. From the outset of the Western "war of démarches" he had insisted that hesitations on the Neva rather than military repression on the Vistula incited foreign interference; and that once strength and determination was shown, Russia's enemies would be compelled to shrink back.[12] So, he condemned the system introduced in Warsaw by Konstantin and praised the Vilna dictatorship of Muraviev as a model for the provinces where fighting was going on and perhaps for the whole of Tsardom.[13] People as different as Counts Bludov, Panin and Prince Gagarin, poets Tuitchev and Fet, Metropolitan Philaret, moderate liberals Kavelin and Academician Nikitenko shared his view. The last named protested against the "wretched system of concessions" and reiterated that the "only way to avoid war is to show Europe that we don't fear it"; vacillations, he admonished, would deprive the government of the "last shred of prestige" and it "would be hard to imagine the kind of anarchy it would lead to."[14]

Katkov and his alike refused to be intimidated by the Crimean spectre. Firstly, they were perfectly aware that "if threatened from abroad the whole Russian people would take up arms and offer their fortune and their lives for their Emperor, their national destiny and their Church"; and that the "danger of war would be blindly and boldly met."[15] Secondly, they disclaimed the proposition that the three Powers would fight for the sake of Poland.

> Indeed, the possibility of war was largely exaggerated. Lord Palmerston, the architect of the anti-Russian policy in the past, now resorted to démarches merely because intense pro-Polish feeling 'among the middle and lower classes' forced him to it. The London government approved Vienna's caution and dampened Napolean's tendencies to more dramatic steps. 'The cabinet will not back the French proposition which smells of gunpowder dreadfully,' Foreign Secretary Russell admonished the Tuileries, 'Austria and England are pacific.' And on 8 June, in a statement in the House of Lords, he made it obvious for everybody: For my part, I can see no advantage that could arise from armed intervention on behalf of Poland. I can see nothing but confusion and calamity likely to arise from an interruption of the peace of Europe . . . .'[16]

So, when Paris, London and Vienna presented on 17-18 June their "decisive" notes requesting a general amnesty, provisional armistice, return to the constitutional system in the Kingdom and a conference of the signatories of the Vienna Treaty (1815), the Moscow publicist could successfully insist on their explicit repudiation.[17]

Certainly, the foremost role of the Tsar in turning down the Western desiderata cannot be questioned: Alexander disapproved of the policy of moderation[18] and must have found the June diplomatic action the final proof that the conciliatory effort had been barren. Still, the measure of Katkov's participation was astounding.

Although the harangues coming from Strastnyi Boulevard manifestly clashed with his opinion, Gorchakov had taken every precaution so that the wrath of the Thunderer would not hit him. During the critical months he used Tiutchev to keep him in permanent contact with Moscow. He had first given the draft of the reply to the three Powers to the Tsar and Katkov for revision; and only then, on 8 July, did he set it before the Ministerial Council for formal confirmation. Most significantly, too, the final text—the circular of 13 July—was published simultaneously in the official *Journal de St. Pétersbourg* and the *Moskovskiia vedomosti,* purportedly as a token of appreciation "for the services offered to the state" by the editor.[19]

Sequel to the episode was no less telling. As foreseen by Katkov, Russian refusal to give assent to the Western terms was met only by important protests. And the Vice-Chancellor, whatever his doubts might have been, procured "the biggest leaf in his laurel crown." The *Moskovskiia vedomosti* and then the rest of the press proclaimed him the "saviour of Russian dignity." Even illiterate, peasant women, the old vain man might boast, were buying scarfs with his portrait.[20] This, naturally, would not pass unnoticed by many who sought after posts and promotions. Gorchakov's fame provided additional strength for Katkov's position. Strastnyi Boulevard became virtually a place of pilgrimage for supplicants of all sorts, "from high dignitaries to representatives of religious sects"[21] and this stream was never to cease under Katkov's lifetime.

Even people who privately disliked the publicist, deemed it useful to win his favour.

Count Peter Valuev, the powerful Interior Minister and anti-Muscovite par excellence, had been, besides the Vice-Chancellor, the first explorer along this path. Already on 10 April 1863, long before the "dark people" started to look for Gorchakov's pictures, the cool haughty politician approached the publicist:

> I extend to you a request and I offer you a proposal. The request is that you should conclude an agreement with me—a 'pactum'—for the purpose of the future exchange of views and thoughts. I am

prepared within the limits of possibility to give you a confidential
answer to any question which you may pose to me and I hope in
return to have the possibility of turning to you confidentially for
information on your views concerning these questions. . . . Yes
or no?[22]

The authority exercised by the Strastnyi Boulevard, however, was not
limited to those who were swayed by its chauvinistic sermon or who
hoped to further their career through it. Baron Brunnov, the Ambassador
to St. James' Court, belonged to none of these categories. The diplomat,
a prototype of an official of Nicholas' era, cynical and without convictions, detested the Muscovites and their creed as much as they disliked
him for lack of patriotic ardor; in the words of Meshcherskii, he "loved
Russia like any Englishman." But, during the Polish crisis, Brunnov confessed later, he had scanned the *Moskovskiia vedomosti* for directives
instead of reading dispatches from the Singers' Bridge. "I have always
preferred an original to a copy," he explained.[23]

In the meantime, each day had perhaps brought Katkov new proof
of his "dictatorship over minds." He had been showered by collective
letters coming from different social layers and parts of the Russian realm.
His correspondents in St. Petersburg acquainted him with the admiring
words pronounced by the universally respected Grand Duchess Helen,
by Gorchakov, Bludov, Kovalevskii. In the Winter Palace, as they had
intimated, the Moscow daily was read aloud in the Tsar's presence; and
the Tsarina wept over the editorial praising the loyalty of muzhik to the
throne. The publicist had been elected to the most exclusive English
Club, to the Moscow city council (duma), to the learned councils of Moscow and Kiev universities.[24]

Indeed, this was the finest hour of the Thunderer.

* * *

In 1864, the Poles were again trampled into the dust, but Tsardom
was protracted in a feverish state. Amidst executions and deportations
the sinister figure of Katkov and Count Mikhail Muraviev continued to
loom large in the limelight.

The latter, alluding to the fate of his cousin, who had been hanged
for taking part in the Decembrist coup (1825), put his credo bluntly:

"I am one of the hanging Muravievs, not one of the ones who get hang-ed."[25] And in order to stay in charge even in the future when the hanging would be over, he triggered a campaign for the stern Russification of Poland, the Baltic region and the so-called Western provinces.[26]

The activities and plans of the Vilna dictator were perfectly suited to Katkov's political philosophy. The programme, which the Hangman for-warded to Alexander and which the publicist enlarged in his editorials, aimed to destroy the power and property of the Catholic and Lutheran Churches, the Polish "shlakhta" and the German barons; furthermore, it envisaged a thorough purge in the administration, a privileged position for Orthodoxy, the dominant position of Russian in schools and official communications.[27]

The Moscow Panslav-nationalists were all for it. Aksakov praised Muraviev for "striking salutary fear" and the Slavic Committee presented him an icon of St. Michael the Archangel as the "restorer of Orthodoxy in our western borderlands."[28] In St. Petersburg, though, only the notor-ious circles in the Winter Palace and the Miliutin group approved, while the majority of the elite protested and implored the Tsar for return to normalcy. That ministers Valuev, Golovnin, Adlerberg, Zamiatin, the chief of the Third Section Prince Dolgorukov and Governor General of the capital Prince Suvorov denounced the Hangman and his like as "hor-rible monsters from the Apocalypse,"[29] reverberated more than just a disgust over the deeds which again made Russia, in European eyes, a barbarous land. The upper classes, alerted by the "red" agrarian policies in Poland and the Western provinces, where the military and liberal of-ficials incited peasants against landowners, saw the whole social and power structure in peril. Particularly the Baltic Germans who held key positions at Court, in administration, army and diplomacy, must have felt endangered almost as much as the Polish nobles.

Increasingly, the feud assumed the familiar form of a strife between the old and the new capital. Perhaps never before had Moscow's envious hatred for its privileged rival been so open and intense. There, the very word "St. Petersburger" was regarded as an insult, and the blame for every real or imaginary evil put squarely on the shoulders of the "bastion of cosmopolitan bureaucracy." The city on the Neva, the Muscovy Senator Lebedev complained, could impress everybody by its European order and tidiness; it displayed the splendor of the Court, ministries and the Guards; its high officialdom lived in abundance and enriched itself still more by railway speculation; while its luxury only worsened the budget deficit, Moscow remained in "dirt, ignorance and poverty."[30]

Katkov both exploited and incited the resentment. Before the uprising, he had identified Nihilism as the main expression of the "negative direction"; now he pinpointed this stigma on "federalist cosmopolitanism" and "internal separatism" allegedly nurtured on the Neva. Muraviev's programme appeared in his arguments as the only means to forestall the brewing of the great conspiracy aiming to broaden autonomy of the Finnish type to Poland, the Baltic and Western provinces and to the Ukraine, to transform that way the Russian Empire into a feeble body like that of Austria or Turkey.[31]

In the course of the crusade, Katkov developed what may perhaps be assigned as his most essential contribution to the theory of Russian nationalism—the concept of the integrity of the Russian state. This integrity, according to him, rested on the unity and dominance of the Russians. Other nationalities of the Empire—or "tribes" (plemiona) as he called them all—might keep their customs, language and eventually their religion, but at the same time they were to recognize the "leading role" of the Russian language and Russian patriotism as the indisputable attribute of the state's unity. Catholics, Protestants and Jews ought to use Russian in their church services and prayer books, Polish, Finnish or German subjects consider themselves above all Russians. There should be no non-Russian "political nationality":

> The sole integral state and sole language acknowledged by the government, or what is identical to it, the sole political nationality —that is the quintessence of the question, and must be stated beyond any doubt and hesitation.
>
> We do not want coercion or persecution or constraints against ethnic peculiarities, dialects and languages, or still less against the religious conscience of non-Russians; but we do indeed propose that the Russian government can be solely Russian throughout the whole expanse of the possessions of the Russian power, which have been gained by Russian blood. This is not coercion . . . it is a law of both life and of logic. We consider that throughout the whole expanse of the Russian power no other political nationality can be recognized but the Russian one.[32]

On the same grounds, Katkov also evolved his fundamental concept of "permanent high tension of the national spirit."[33] The "spontaneous" petition campaign he initiated at the time of the uprising appeared to him not efficacious enough to silence the cosmopolitan and revolutionary foes. All the "healthy forces" should be marshalled behind the autocracy in an active manner and the enemies hit by all weapons at the state's disposal. So, he not only unreservedly assented to the "red" agrarian policies against the Polish gentry[34] but clamoured for the organization of a broad movement of mass vigilance. Requesting Valuev to "employ every means at hand to protect public security," he proposed to set up civil guards, some sort of people's militia, which would "harness the evil elements. . .wandering here in the midst of our society." Along with quelling diverse dissident elements, these guards should be employed in case of war as the force safeguarding internal safety in the Empire. If the present patriotic upsurge were not utilized and given stable forms and permanent basis, Katkov affirmed, and if it were left for long without purpose, enthusiasm would gradually evaporate, perhaps never to return. This would be to the greatest harm of the state at the moment when "an acute patriotic need" would occur.[35]

The idea was carried out—at least on a semi-official basis—after the assassination of Alexander II and then in the ill-famed movement of the "Black Hundreds." Now, however, except for some "red" bureaucrats (Miliutin brothers) and Katkov's admirers (Bludov), the elite had still been wise enough—or afraid of what it perceived as a "garde civique nationale" of revolutionary type—to resist this madness or nationalism running amuck.[36]

* * *

In the atmosphere still bordering on hysteria, the pattern of Katkov's behaviour was much closer to that of Torquemada than a publicist operating in a modern European state. Living in permanent tension, suffering intense insomnia, he entirely succumbed to the delusion that Providence had called him to protect Tsardom against every enemy and lurking heretic. And it was to remain so for the whole rest of his life. For the Thunderer, as Feoktistov put it, the truth was so evident—his own truth, of course—that it could have been ignored only by people with sinister designs; he immediately suspected bad feelings, anti-Russian activities or intentions. His old vices—inability to accept a compromise, hatred and contempt for everybody who held an even slightly different opinion from his own—acquired monstrous proportions.[37]

The St. Petersburg "liberal-cosmopolitan" press organs—the *Golos* (Voice), the *St. Peterburgskiia vedomosti* and the *Birzhevyia vedomosti* (Stock-Exchange Gazette)—he assessed as the very embodiment of the "negative, separatist direction."[38] But his misgivings turned also against those Moscow Panslavs who raised minor reservations over the manner the Polish problem had been handled.[39] While he was willing to concede at least some personal integrity to the old Slavophiles, the Panslavs, "the epigones of Slavophilism," were in his vituperations mere "banknotes taken from circulation," with no idea to offer, intolerably soft to enemy and working in collusion with the Polonophiles of St. Petersburg.[40]

The Moscovite, though, would not confine his attacks only to those "second-raters." The foremost targets of his vigilance were—as he called them—the "bureaucratic, cosmopolitan secret enemies of Russia" in the ruling elite; first of all, the ministers pursuing the conciliatory policies.[41] This inevitably resulted in an open strife between him and the authorities.

Already in the summer of 1863, the organs of the censorship arrived at an understanding that the "insufferable egotism, arrogance and unspeakable haughtiness" of the Moscow publicist should be resisted. The Council for Press Affairs noted that his paper was imposing its views on the public and the administration alike "in a dictatorial manner" and that the government ought to cease the current praxis to "give it more freedom than to other papers." The Moscow censorship committee was directed by the Council to "curb the violence and unpardonable outbursts" of the daily.

"The government needs to keep a dog like Katkov to bark at thieves or at those who may be suspected of thieving. The dog is to be chained, though," wrote Academician Nikitenko, a member of the Council.[42] For quite a long time, however, no statesmen would dare to make an attempt at chaining. The editor grew too formidable an enemy for that.

Society in the old capital, Senator Lebedev observed, was "with rare exceptions in favor of Katkov." Another high official, Sukhotin, recorded in his daily: "The influence of Katkov impells so strongly upon our predominantly noble society and our young politicians have so greatly imbibed his ideas and opinions that in all private talks and debates they just serve as mouthpieces for the *Moskovskiia vedomosti.*"[43] The Orthodox hierarchy led by Philaret had, since the uprising, recognized the Muscovite as its spokesman too.[44]

So, the public could observe with some astonishment that while Aksakov and his *Den* suffered hard persecution, the Strastnyi Boulevard was left untouched and "everything is allowed" to its master.[45] True, since the winter of 1863-1864, the enthusiasm at Court over his editorials cooled appreciably and Katkov started to complain about ill-feeling against him in "higher spheres,"[46] but in principle no change in this relationship occurred. The dignitaries preferred to appease the Muscovite, although "he throws curses around like a drunken muzhik." Valuev[47] and Gorchakov continued to offer him secret information on important issues; their colleague Golovnin, the Minister of Public Instruction, proposed to subsidize his daily; the Governors General in the sensitive Western provinces, Bezak and Kaufman, made calls on Strastnyi Boulevard to ask for direction.[48]

The publicist's spirit leaped with growing arrogance. Valuev was in his eyes "little better than an agent-provocateur";[49] and he accused Golovnin of being in collusion with "Palmerston, Mazzini, and with all our enemies and breeders of European revolution."[50] "If we offered any service to the Ministry for Public Instruction," he wrote later, then it was "only in an unrelenting struggle against it."[51] He attacked Finance Minister Reutern and his deputy Bunge for their allegedly "anti-national" policy of loose credit, foreign loans and reluctance in using domestic sources in financing railway construction.[52]

* * *

Alerted by rumors of rising hostility between the publicist and the authorities, his admirers hastened to assure him of their undiminished support. And it may be assumed that the influx of collective letters in late 1864 emboldened him to make an entirely open challenge: recalling his loyalty to the highest state interests, he asked that his extraordinary position be formally recognized and his daily exempted from general censorship control. The request was backed by the Moscow University council, where Professors Liubimov and Sergei Soloviev, the well-known nationalist historian, stood as his staunchest auxiliaries. The council suggested that the daily be subjected only to academic supervision.[53]

This time Valuev finally lost his patience and wished for a showdown. But the majority of the government, facing demonstrative gestures of solidarity with the editor—banquets were given in his honour and an assembly of Moscow nobility delivered him a formal address, "something usually reserved only for the Emperor"[54]—refused to join their colleague. Some even openly took Katkov's side: Gorchakov proclaimed him "the only safeguard for conservative and national opinion"; Baron Korff, a Baltic German in charge of the Second Section, praised him as an "embodiment of Russia's views."[55] The proposal put forward by Moscow University was turned down; the Ministerial Council resolved, however, that the censorship organs ought to treat the *Moskovskiia vedomosti* with particular benevolence.

The outcome, inevitably, invited only further troubles. Encouraged, the publicist went on in his vendetta, making his disobedience a matter of principle. Raising the dispute on a quasi-theoretical level he asserted that there was a distinction between an "ideal" government protecting the interests of the state and concrete persons who at the moment exercise governmental functions; a situation could arise, he added ominously, when governmental posts are held by unworthy people exposing these vital interests to peril.[56]

"Success has blinded him completely and has made him arrogant to the point where he has lost all sense of decency," Nikitenko condemned the Muscovite; "no matter what government is in power, it cannot tolerate the existence of any force that attempts to steal its reins."[57] Count Stroganov, the protector of Katkov from his early university years, advised him to cool down; another ally, Tiutchev, admonished him—presumably in Gorchakov's name too—to seek an armistice with Valuev. The publicist, though, declined both to renounce his pretentions and to accommodate a man "who has appropriated enormous influence and has been using it openly to wreck the Russian cause." His militants were equally self-confident. They spread rumors that the government would not dare to deal with the Strastnyi Boulevard with a tight hand; and if it did the old capital would present "some kind of rebellion."[58]

Thus, in the spring of 1866, what proved to be the final contest between the Interior Minister and the Moscow editor took place.

It was brought to a head by an article written by the prominent journalist Charles de Mazade in the *Revue des deux mondes*. Like Schédo-Ferotti before him, de Mazade denounced Katkov as a man "of despotic and extremely suspicious nature," who obtained his prominence "not so much by merit as by his vehemence and his rage." Firmly persuaded that the attack was again performed on the orders of the "cosmopolitans," the Muscovite responded on 2 April by a vitriolic editorial in which he accused his foes in the establishment of "using all possible means to introduce into our state organism principles of national disunity," cherishing "plans for some kind of impossible federation destined to change Russia into nothing else than a personal union of many separate states."[59]

Valuev reacted to the charge by issuing an official warning. The publicist, however, hurled it back "in an unbelievably defiant manner."[60] He repeated the words of Muraviev that "the roots of rebellion are not in Paris, Warsaw or Vilna but in St. Petersburg" and made it clear that he would honor the authorities only in his peculiar interpretation:

> With all due respect for governmental officials, we do not consider ourselves their subordinates and we are not obliged to conform to the personal views of one or another of them. Above statesmen, as above everybody else, rises the supreme authority.[61]

In another act of defiance Katkov refused to publish the warning and chose to pay a fine instead. Two further warnings followed in short sequence at the end of May, which—if the press regulations made in law in 1865 were applied—would have been followed by the suspension of the newspaper for three months.[62]

In the heat of the contest, the Moscovite unrolled both his stubborness and inventiveness.[63] After a short pause in publication, the *Moskovskiia vedomosti* reappeared under the purely formal editorship of his trusted Professor Liubimov; and, at the same time he directly approached Alexander by asking him to take a stand in the dispute. The wording of the letter to the Tsar was judged to be a tactical blunder, mainly because of the boastful phrase that he would "need a year or two to mold public opinion completely."[64] Still, the essential calculation proved to be sound.

From the outset, Alexander had been unwilling to cow the Thunderer. First, when the latter applied himself with Muraviev in whipping up the anti-Polish hysteria, he had defended them as "useful nuisances." Later, he recognized the Hangman as an outrage and relived him from the Vilna post, but would not touch the Muscovite although he openly questioned his authority.[65] And when the Interior Minister pushed the conflict to a razor's edge, he recoiled again.

The attempt of the revolutionary Karakozov on the Tsar's life (on 16 April 1866) furnished the publicist with a formidable trump-card. The "patriotic" fever rose to new heights and Alexander would not dare to defy a man considered by too many to be the most authentic guardian of his reign. Student crowds demonstrated on Strastnyi Boulevard in favor of the daily and its editor. In St. Petersburg, the Tsarina and her entourage, Miliutins and the newly appointed "strong men," Minister for Public Instruction Count Dmitrii Tolstoi and Count Peter Shuvalov, the chief of gendarmes, pleaded for returning the Muscovite to his rights. In vain the party of the Interior Minister—as Feoktistov informed Katkov— asked for his transfer to another official post "to prevent you staying at the head of public opinion and going against them."[66]

When the Tsar arrived in Moscow in June, he sent Shuvalov to Strastnyi Boulevard with the mildest possible admonition. The message allegedly ran as follows:

> In the first period you defeated Herzen; all Russia applauded you. The second period was that of the Polish question. You sized up the situation. In the third you went before the government, proclaiming a national policy. You captivated everyone; and, willy-nilly, they followed you. In the fourth, you engaged in the struggle with the government. Since you had been victorious in everything else there was cause here to fear that you might also win a victory by discrediting the government. . . .

The publicist could remain unbending. He was supporting the government, he repeated his usual argument to Shuvalov, but the only way to do so must be to require the elimination of everyone opposing national unity. The audience which Alexander granted him on 2 July, confirmed his victory. According to Katkov's testimony, retold by Liubimov, the ruler patiently listened to the harangues against his ministers, and, although disapproving of the tone of the campaign, assured the guest of his full confidence:

I know you, I believe in you and I consider you devoted to me.
Hold your sacred fire . . . . You don't need to be worried. I am
closely following the *Moskovskiia vedomosti,* I am reading them
regularly. I trust you completely.[67]

Although a historian may wonder whether the Tsar said that, whether
he was frank and above all, whether the latter Katkov's statement that he
received supreme protection from then on tallies with the truth,[68] the
results were nonetheless unmistakable. The Muscovite was restored to the
rights while the Interior Minister had to acknowledge "the weakness of
the government" and his own impotence. "A complete triumph of Katkov" was also the universal judgment.[69]

CHAPTER 6

SCENTING THE "GERMAN DANGER": THE KATKOV-SHUVALOV CONTEST AND THE BALTIC QUESTION (1866-1869)

The *Moscow Gazette* is the *Times* of Russia in one sense, but not in another. It is the first paper in the Empire, but it leads rather than follows public opinion. The *Times* changes with the times. The *Moscow Gazette* adheres to its own views. The *Times* is impersonal, anonymous. The *Moscow Gazette* is Mr. Katkov, and Mr. Katkov is the *Moscow Gazette*.
Novikova

Ministers asked me for advice, Governors General in crucial positions entrusted to me their proposals and problems, foreign politicians were forced to take me into their account. . . . My name was equivalent to a political programme.
Katkov

At that time our higher administration cringed according to the positive or negative reactions of Katkov. And if Katkov on any issue expressed his disapproval, our dignitaries. . . were in terrible confusion.
Zalesov

70

The Polish uprising and its chauvinistic aftermath had not immediately stiffled the post-Crimean course. The educational reform (1863), the introduction of the elements of self-government in local administration (the so-called "zemstvo" reform), the judicial reform (1864) as well as the new press regulations,[1] all the qualifications notwithstanding, were enormous improvements in comparison with Nicholas' regime. In the comment of Senator Lebedev, "the nation has been recognized mature, ripe, deserving of full confidence and capable of control in its thinking, opinions and words."[2]

Katkov had still professed sympathies for these reforms and had even been considered one of their leading proponents. While his future accomplice in this police blanket."[5] On has Kindly, persecution."[10] ready branded them as "the noise of cheap and shallow fantasies," the publicist castigated "the enemies of the great privileges granted to the Russian people, which introduced them into the family of civilized nations."[3] He took an active part in the discussions on them and held often positions reminiscent of his liberal period. He presumably approved Valuev's "constitutional project" put forward in 1863 proposing to reorganize the State Council and include into it elected representatives, as well as the Slavophile idea that the historical "Zemskii sobor" (Land Assembly) should be resurrected and replace bureaucracy as a communication channel between the supreme power and the population.[4]

Yet, as it has been noted, the prevailing mood pointed in quite opposite direction. In Herzen's words, a deeply frightened society wished for nothing else than to find sanctuary under the "old, dirty, but familiar police blanket."[5] On 14 December 1864, Pobedonostsev wrote to Anna Tiutcheva:

> You will not believe how disgusted we are with the reforms, how we have lost faith in them, how much we would like to stop at something stable, so as to know at last which wheel is turning and where each worker stands. . . .[6]

Diaries of influential contemporaries testify that Herzen was correct and that in this aspect Pobedonostsev rather than the Moscow editor gave tongue to the "true Russia." Their writers perceived "choas pervading every area," "patent scorn for law and order," "general dissoluteness," "lack of safety for people and property." "One feels the inevitability of revolution in the air and the conviction that it is coming grows stronger and more widespread," Nikitenko lamented. "We stand at the brink of anarchy; in fact, it has already begun."[7]

Most tragically for the country's future, Alexander II also succumbed to this spirit.

In many ways, and primarily because of his "humane and understanding outlook on life,"[8] the "Tsar-Liberator" may be distinguished among Russian rulers. Kindly, compassionate and generous, he had been moved to an honest attempt to alleviate the sufferings of his people. It was the natural goodness of his heart no less than political calculation which animated him in the strife with the ultraconservatives resisting to the abolition of serfdom and general liberalization. However, he had always stayed a man with traditional convictions, who had given faith to the inviolability of the autocratic principle just as much as to the duty to keep Russian rule in Poland intact. Like too many statesmen before and after him, he had been possessed with the fixed idea that if a constitutional system were introduced, the Empire would relapse into anarchy and fall to pieces. The traditionalist trait deprived him of elasticity and clearer prescience so badly needed in the dramatically changing situation Tsardom experienced after the Crimean War. Moreover, life in the shadow of the overbearing Nicholas attenuated in him the foremost quality of a successful ruler—to enforce his will in a proper manner.

In the finest hour of his reign—the peasant's emancipation—Alexander displayed "greater decisiveness and truer idea of his own power than his father,"[9] but incessant disappointments stripped him both of self-confidence and confidence in people in general. His approach to the "Katkov problem" disclosed a diminishing courage to resist openly persons and groupings he might inwardly detest. He grew more and more distrustful, double-faced, nervous and prevaricating; and like the majority of his politically-minded subjects, he abandoned hope in reform as the means to solve Russia's problems.

The shots fired by Karakozov marked the watershed. In Herzen's words again, "the hardly awakened public opinion plunged into wild conservativism and enforced its participation on (decisions concerning) the affairs of the state by pushing the government to terror and persecution."[10]

Old mild men had to go. Most importantly, Prince Dolgorukov, accused of turning the Third Section into a "temple of smiles"[11] was replaced by his young deputy Peter Shuvalov whose name was to rise into a symbol for the forthcoming freeze of the reform effort.

Like his close friend Prince Bariatinskii, Shuvalov was a perfect product of his milieu. A scion of one of the best aristocratic families, intimate with the Tsar from their boyhood, elegant, handsome, with accomplished manners, he easily achieved prominence at Court. And his astuteness, vitality and extraordinary gift in handling people coupled with a thorough absence of scruples predestined him to a meteoric career.

In the debates on the peasant question, Shuvalov won overwhelming "planters" sympathy. Also in literature he has been characterized as a "profound reactionary, who for most part of his life had been doing his best to undermine his sovereign's reform operations."[12] In fact, his actual position after he had reached the apex of power was much more intricate. He was too European and too clever to only look backwards. Together with Bariatinskii, he favored abolition of peasant commune, wisely pointing out that without this measure economic progess was hardly possible. His intentions included change in the political system: at first, he wished just to enlarge the rights of the zemstvos, later he even proposed to adopt the parliamentary model. However, his personal ambition was the only thing he truly cared for. Jockeying for preeminence, he would have neither antagonized the Tsar nor the "planters" who had rallied behind him, by pressing the demands they did not like.

Shuvalov perfectly adjusted his steps to the overriding craving for order and tranquility. Exaggerating with utmost dexterity the revolutionary danger, he made himself and his police force indispensable. Before long, the elite commenced to call him "Peter IV" or "Arakcheev II."[13] He tamed prominent reactionaries into his stooges and packed them in the highest positions. After Tolstoi, who had replaced Golovnin as Minister for Public Instruction, Count Pahlen took over the Justice Ministry and finally, in 1868, General Timashev, another old-timer, moved to Valuev's post. In the government, only Miliutin survived from the reform era and his situation has been described by a sympathetic biographer as that of "Daniel in the lion's den."[14]

Katkov felt endangered by the new upstart. In the Karakozov affair he saw a proof that St. Petersburg remained the "centre of sedition" (kramola) and claimed that the Nihilism of 1861-1862 and the cosmopolitan conservativism of 1866 were of the same origin; Shuvalov, a prefect prototype of the latter category, obviously striving to thwart the "patriotic spirit," appeared in his eyes an enemy no less harmful than Valuev.[15]

Compared with the latter, operating under the strained conditions created by the Polish uprising, the new gendarme chief and his group had a visible advantage. After a brief upsurge sprouted by the attempt on the Tsar's life, the militant mood began to wane. It showed also in the diminishing interest in the *Moskovskiia vedomosti;* its circulation dropped to only 6000 copies.[16] Yet, until 1870, the change was not perceptible enough either to curb the nationalist press campaign or embolden the government to set out for another tug-of-war with the Strastnyi Boulevard.

The Muscovite stuck to his old tactics: haranguing against every possible enemy, he assaulted almost indiscriminately the entire St. Petersburg establishment[17] as well. And there was still a battlefield, where he could hit the "cosmopolitans" hard—the question of Russian security in the western borderlands. The advances of German unification exacerbated the public's sensitivity on the subject. Moreover, as the military scum streamed into the Asiatic Eldorado, the scum of officialdom —"the legions of Khlestakovs and Chichikovs," in the words of a letter to the editor alluding the famous prototypes created by Gogol—flooded the western gubernias. Most of them were Katkov's nominees or people who put their stakes on him; in the local administration, said a testimony, the reading of his daily was considered equal to a service duty.[18]

In terms of quantity, the themes of "Polonism" and "Ukrainophilism" continued to tower in his editorials. But, owing to close ties between Shuvalov and the Germans, the prevailing Prussian orientation in St. Petersburg and Prussian ascendance in Europe, the Baltic problem clearly appropriated paramount significance.[19]

The publicist reopened his campaign in early 1867,[20] by several articles criticizing privileges enjoyed by Dorpat University and other schools in the region and easily succeeded in creating an atmosphere propitious to his goals. Heartened by Prussian triumphs, Baltic Germans responded with defiance. Concurrently, the nationalist pamphleteers in Germany rose to defend their kinsmen. They often used arrogant words about Russian backwardness and German cultural superiority. The Russians' always lurking temper leaped accordingly. That the Baltic "barons," in contrast to the Poles, could present almost unblotted record of loyal service to the

Tsars and that Alexander stood visibly on their side, made little difference. The Russian press, with rare unanimity—the ultraconservative *Viest* (Report) and the *Novoe vremia* (New Times) being the sole exceptions—joined the *Moskovskiia vedomosti* in prolonged outcry against their alleged separatist proclivities.

Aksakov's *Moskva* had been most shrill in its utterances.[21] In April 1867, the Interior Ministry suspended its publication for three months for "incessant efforts to castigate governmental actions," but as soon as the limit expired, Aksakov was "throwing himself with open eyes onto knives." On the liberal side the *Golos,* so often scorned by Katkov for national nihilism, also overshadowed the main Muscovite organ in ferocity. Since the autumn of 1867, an open fight raged between the press and the authorities.[22]

That the Thunderer opened his second campaign against the "sedition" of non-Russian peoples with complaints about the conditions in schools was by no means an accident. The control over the educational system grew into his virtual obsession: "we have given our whole souls to this struggle," he wrote.[23] German schools should be changed into Russian ones with Russias as the first language.[24] Furthermore, the publicist called for abolition of the Baltic Germans' traditional privileges, introduction of the Russian-type local administration, judiciary system and land ownership, pronouncing these innovations necessary requirements for attaining the goal of "sole political nationality." The expression of "German," he affirmed, had not only ethnographic but also political connotations; a Russian subject could not be at the same time a German, a Frenchman, an Englishman.[25]

Not surprisingly, Russification was proclaimed a fulfillment of the dreams cherished by the local population. The Baltic peoples, oppressed by the Germans, Katkov assured his readers, wished only to be united with the great Russian nation; the problem rested merely in St. Petersburg's unability to recognize this patent truth.[26]

* * *

Alexander was profoundly annoyed by the campaign and accused its culprits—meaning above all the man from Strastnyi Boulevard—of sowing disunity in the Empire. "I spit on the press which tries to put you on the

same level as the Poles," he told the representatives of the Baltic gentry.
"I respect your nationality and will be as faithful to it as you are. I have
always maintained that it is ridiculous to criticize someone because of
his origin."[27]

In an effort to stop the strife, the government attempted both to
appease and intimidate its main instigator. On the one hand, a decree
was promulgated promising to enforce the law from 1850 on obligatory
use of Russian as the official language in the three Baltic gubernias. On the
other hand, the *Severnaia pochta* (Northern Post), the organ of the Interior Ministry, issued a statement condemning the Katkovian abuses; and the
publicist was given a "confidential signal" of the Tsar's displeasure.

In late 1867 Gorchakov assured Prussian Minister Prince Reuss that
now all the polemics would cease and the Muscovite be brought to his
senses.[28] In reality exactly the opposite happened: in 1868 the crusade
of the Strastnyi Boulevard and the rest of the press competing with it in
the exhibition of patriotic fervour, reached its climax. An additional
impulse was provided by the publication of the first part of Samarin's
book "Okrainy Rossii" (Russian Borderlands).

In it the author, an old hand of the Moscow party, customarily imputed
to the Baltic Germans a design to establish a separate "Osstee state," a
"new Baltic Finland." In accord with the Katkovite arguments, he demanded a profound change in the official approach: the Germans should
be deprived of their privileges and compelled to recognize that "the Baltic was not the advanced post of Germany. . . but a western, maritime
borderland of Russia, and, therefore, to recognize entirely, unconditionally and for all time. . . that they are bound now and in the future to the
destiny of the latter."[29]

In order to avoid censorship the volume was issued in Prague; and before he confused authorities could prevent it, the leading newspapers
managed to quote its key paragraphs.[30] Alexander and Shuvalov fumed,
and the new Interior Minister, Timashev, was given as his principal task
the fettering of the press. Still, the episode had usual sequel. Prince Dolgorukov, the Moscow Governor General, was ordered to summon Katkov
and Aksakov and demand "avoiding sharp polemics." The two men put
the blame squarely on Germany pamphleteers, promised more moderation and then went on in their tirades.[31] Eventually the *Moskva* was
closed down for good but Katkov's paper remained unharmed.

Indeed, every effort to restore internal peace seemed to stop before the Strastnyi Boulevard fortress. In vain Grand Duchess Helen, an early admirer of Katkov and now the leader of the "German party" in the Winter Palace, admonished the Tsar and the ministers to adopt a more determined stand.[32]

If the highest dignitaries were scared, then the officials serving in the Western and Baltic provinces saw no reason to put their loyalty to the sovereign above that to the Muscovite. The case of General Potapov, Governor General at Vilna, taught them enough. Potapov volunteered to silence the campaign and hoped to be awarded for his achievement by appointment as the Interior Minister; however, Katkov's venomenous assaults at the end forced him to retreat.[33] So, almost everybody in the area preferred to treat the Moscow editor with utmost reverence and parrot his views.

With an air of astonishment, a Soviet student relates to us the report of Colonel Moller, the correspondent of the *Moskovskiia vedomosti,* to his chief.

In Reval, Governor Galkin complained to him that his work had been ignored by the paper; at this Moller responded sternly that the Governor must first distinguish himself to deserve Katkov's notice.[34]

To this we may only add that Galkin took the lesson very seriously and had to be later recalled for his extreme Russification policies.

Big changes had to happen on the international scene to induce the Muscovite to at least a temporary truce on the issue.

CHAPTER 7

TIMIDITY IN THE WEST, BOLDNESS IN THE EAST:
THE INTERLUDE OF 1863-1866

The Asiatics respect only armed forced. The
slightest vacillation and indecisiveness, and
especially any concession. . . will be taken
by them for weakness and thus not only will
the aim not be attained but it may have a
disastrous effect on the regions newly conquered by us, on our steppes and our former
lines.
A joint instruction of Gorchakov and
Miliutin

It has constantly been said that for the glory
of Russia, for the raising of her prestige, it
is necessary to take some stronghold or
other, or to smash the Asiatic hordes in the
field. Strongholds have been taken one after
another, the hordes have been utterly defeated, good borders have been attained and
then it has invariably turned out that one
more stronghold is lacking, that one more
final victory is necessary, that the really perfect frontier lies somewhat farther off, that
our prestige is still not sufficiently raised by
our former successes.
Stremoukhov

Although the Western "war of démarches" came to nothing, it disclosed Russian vulnerability in the continental power system and compelled St. Petersburg to reaffirm with great emphasis the principles espoused after the Crimean War. "All the endeavors of our policy are at the moment directed to make it possible for Russia to eschew activities abroad," wrote Gorchakov; "European affairs are for us in every respect but of secondary consequence."[1]

On the Eastern Question, the harm done by the Polish uprising was perceived with particular intensity. The French Second Empire, which according to the earlier calculations ought to assist in effecting Russian plans, reappeared as the arch-enemy; and the Crimean spectre, never to be forgotten, glared at the St. Petersburg statesmen. In Asia, on the contrary, the fears were sensed far less acutely or its "soft" areas even held as suitable for exercising pressure to keep the West in check.

During the uprising there was a highly significant initiative. Prompted by the possibility of war with the English, General Khrulev set forth another variant of his southern march:

> Two columns—35,000 troops—were to perform a pincer maneuver through the Central Asian khanates, Persia and Afghanistan and in 3-4 months cross the Indus near Attok. The Afghans would 'welcome the long expected Russian armies,' turn against the English and fight 'for their independence and faith.' In virtue of the Asiatic venture, the world balance would be reversed—Great Britain driven to isolation, Napoleon induced to change 'from enemy to an ally' and Europe forced to recognize that 'we are not anywhere as powerless as she would like to believe.'[2]

Although the scheme bordered with madness, Miliutin and Ignatiev were anxious to put it at least partly into effect. General Zalesov, considered most experienced among the Orenburg military, was entrusted with its organization. "In case of war we cannot harm England in Europe; there remains only Asia," the War Minister told him. The action, even if not powerful enough for the invasion of India, would "at least draw off English strength from Europe and cause their commercial interests as much harm as possible."

The top secret instruction for Zalesov envisaged that with the outbreak of European hostilities, two detachments would advance on Kabul:
one, headed by Colonel Mikhail Cherniaev, along the Amu-Daria; the other
commanded by Khrulev from the Caucasus across Persia and Herat.[3]

The war scare quickly passed and there was no actual preparation for
the adventure. Even when the spirits cooled down, though, the principal
trend held. Naturally not the Indian chimera but the more feasible objective—the establishment of "secure frontiers" vis-à-vis the khanates—
reappeared in the foreground.

Most of the former obstacles were removed. Whereas in the Caucasus
only a limited number of forces were needed for mopping-up operations,
at least part of the resources thus spared could be employed beyond the
Caspian Sea. The Kirghiz steppe was now more or less pacified and the
khanates, weak and combatting each other, opened for an attack from the
north and the east. Also the climate on the Neva became exceptionally
propitious. The government's prestige after the Polish troubles required
a fillip; so, despite usual admonitions to caution, daring deeds would be
tolerated provided that they were successful.

Small wonder that enterprising officers, chasing after promotions,
fame and money were not slow to profit from this situation. Among them,
the name Cherniaev—like Khrulev, he was a member of the Moscow
Committee—grew into a true symbol.

In May-June 1863 Cherniaev penetrated with his column into Kokand,
captured the fortress of Sudzak and proclaimed it a Russian possession.
Albeit the raid was unauthorized, Miliutin praised it without reserve:
"we ought to particularly value the occupation of this region, which will
bring us closer to the northern frontiers of India and facilitate access
to that country."[4]

The Sudzak event spurred further advance. Previously, the pleas of
Miliutin, Ignatiev and Bezak had been vetoed by Gorchakov and Finance
Minister Reutern. Now the Tsar interposed and acceded to the thesis
of the War Ministry "on the impossibility of a strictly peaceful policy
in contact with the half-wild tribes." The unification of the frontiers,
i.e. closing the 500-kilometer wide gap between the forts on the Syr-
Daria and those in the valley of Ili (Semirechensk), was acknowledged
a security priority and Cherniaev ordained to perform the task.

After capturing the town of Turkestan and thus achieving the purpose
given to him, the fiery officer again felt free to exceed the instruction

given to him by the conquest of another Kokandese fortress, Chikment. Familiar with St. Petersburg ways, he volunteered to explain the advance to the English as assistance to the Uzbek population, oppressed by the Kokandese: "We can dress ourselves in the clothing of defenders of an exploited people."[5] On 3 October 1864, Chikment was stormed.

The repeated act of disobedience slightly discomforted Miliutin. He recognized the implications: "Fine, but who will guarantee that after Chikment he (Cherniaev) won't deem it necessary to take Tashkent and then Kokand; and what will be the end of it?" However, the Tsar was only jubilant about the affair. And it was symptomatic that Cherniaev's superior, the Governor General of Omsk Duhamel, who had earlier invariably sided with the moderates, found it politic to profess his "exceeding pleasure" that "in higher governmental circles they appreciate this glorious exploit."[6]

Cherniaev was made General, given the command in the so called "New Kokand line," awarded the most prestigious St. George's Cross and finally appointed Military Governor of the Turkestan region. His and similar cases, together with financial bonuses for service in remote parts of the Empire, incited military men of most dangerous kind to go to Central Asia. The dignitaries in the capital were often to complain about this "scum," but it was the official attitude which had helped to create such conditions.

* * *

In November 1864, Gorchakov and Miliutin submitted to Alexander what the framework for the future policy in the area ought to be. The document proclaimed the seizure of Tashkent contrary to Russian interests, because it would lead to risky and costly adventures and eventually to "serious international consequences." The new frontier established by the closure of the gap between the two fortified lines should be considered permanent and any advance beyond it "not in accordance with the views of the government."[7]

The Tsar concurred and on 3 December 1864, the Singers' Bridge dispatched a circular to assure the Powers of eminently peaceful Russian intentions.

At first glance, the note seems to be just a guarantee for the future wrapped in flowery Gorchakovian verbiage; and a historian cannot doubt that the Vice-Chancellor conceived it as a logjam for the extremists. Seen through the prism of the subsequent events, though, an Indian scholar has been reasonably right when characterizing it as 'perhaps one of the most representative manifestos of imperial expansion in the annals of history of mankind.'[8]

It announced that Russia had entered on the same path of civilizing mission as 'France in Algeria, Holland in her colonies, and England in India' had done; and that she, like all the others, had found herself 'on the horns of a dilemma: either to abandon the struggle which renders security and civilization possible, or indulge in expensive repression.' Retreat was out of the question, the note read, 'for Asiatics respect only visible and palpable force'; but with the present stabilized frontier, Tsardom would be able to eschew the dilemma and neither be involved in 'distant and expansive expeditions at frequent intervals' nor pursue a 'career of conquests and annexations such as gave England her Indian Empire.'[9],[10]

There was, however, no firmness or will in St. Petersburg to enforce the programme in its restraining connotations. The formula that Russia was performing a civilizing mission among peoples who "respect only palpable and visible force" provided the extremists with convenient excuse. And so did conditions in Central Asia: apart from being unable to understand and react properly the threat facing them, the khans were merciless, greedy and bloodthirsty despots, and the Turkoman tribes cruel robbers and slave-drivers. There was plenty of room left for playing the perennial Russian farce described by Cherniaev as "dressing ourselves in the clothing of defenders of exploited people." What Gorchakov and Miliutin in their joint memorandum bashfully described as "the influence of temporary circumstances and the personal, sometimes one-sided views of local commanders," was to remain the general pattern in Russian conduct.

Showered by promotions and awards, Cherniaev proceeded in his exploits. On the pretext that the new borderline could not be secure until "order was established" in Kokand and "the plans of Bukharan Emir forestalled," he led his troops anew across it—on Tashkent, the main trade center for the whole of Central Asia. In May 1865 he stood under the formidable walls of the city manned by 30,000 defenders; although desperately outnumbered—his column counted about 1,200 soldiers with 12 guns—he managed in the night of 26-27 June to force the entrance; and after two days of fierce fighting in barricaded streets obtained unconditional surrender.

"Tashkent was taken by General Cherniaev. Nobody knows why and what for," Valuev noted down the common complaint raised by the moderates.[11] This, however, was not quite the truth. At the time, the Gorchakov-Miliutin programme had already been consigned to oblivion. The Vice-Chancellor retreated with misgivings; the War Minister, albeit annoyed with Cherniaev personally and bent on replacing him by a man he could rely on, quickly rejoined those canvassing the bold course; Alexander, as usual, rejoiced over the "glorious affair" and bestowed the "Lion of Tashkent" with a golden sabre with diamonds. Prolonged deliberations were devoted only to the query as to whether to proclaim the city as an "independent khanate" or annex it outright. By its incorporation into the Empire (in August 1866) a formula coined by Cherniaev won the day that no natural frontier existed in the area and for that reason "it ought to be dominated militarily (as a whole)."[12]

* * *

Unlike Central Asia, there was no chasm between words and deeds in the policies pursued on the continent and on the Eastern Question. Such, indeed, was an emphasis on the status quo in them that Russian conduct appeared devoid of any vigor or perspective. In "no issue has the voice of Russia been heard and it looks as if she has lost her place in the general councils of Europe," Katkov heaved a sigh.[13]

The difference was essentially due to the Tsar's attitude: in Asia he sided with the generals; on the big traditional issues, intrinsically paralyzed by the Crimean complex, he entirely subscribed to the dictum formulated by Gorchakov that "under the present conditions in our state and in Europe in general, the main endeavour of Russia must be consistently chanelled to the accomplishment of the work of our internal development and all her foreign policy subordinated to it."[14] The Vice-Chancellor put it neatly in saying that the very existence of a Ministry for Foreign Affairs was for his master, for the time being, a mere "object of luxury."[15]

In conversations with diplomats, Alexander stressed his disapproval of the Panslav idea. "As to the fear of Panslavism, from my side I am a Russian rather than a Slav," he told an Austrian Minister; Turkey, too, had nothing to worry about, because his government acquiesced in her existence as a "sad necessity."[16]

A scholar analyzing Russian foreign policy in this period made a correct observation that the Tsar and Gorchakov "became, for a time, defenders of all treaties, not excluding the one primarily directed against Russia herself" (i.e. the Paris Treaty).[17]

The Russian statesmen objected to the notion that they had been proceeding along the detested Holy Alliance path; nonetheless, there was a perceptible trait of it, not only in the loudly proclaimed "sanctity of treaties" but also in the tendency to respond to the "nationality principle" of Napoleon III by the methods of Nicholas and Nesselrode. The enmity towards the Rumanian emancipation effort and Prince Alexander Cuza, the man who unified the so called Danubian Principalities and initiated a programme of social overhaul, may be pointed out as the most outstanding manifestation of conservative rigidity.

Since 1859, Tsardom had striven to hinder the unification process and prop the boyars and Greek Orthodox clergy against the rising nationalist forces. Cuza had to wrestle all the time with a vast Russian-inspired intrigue. Ignatiev, who in 1864 took over the diplomatic mission at Constantinople, worked hard to instigate the Turks against him and foment the opposition among his subjects.

Katkov and the Moscow party were in complete accord with this policy. In notable contrast to the Greco-Bulgarian Church dispute, the publicist was entirely "pro-Phanariot" when it concerned Cuza's government and the Greek hierarchy. In his judgment, the Rumanian leader was but a "Napoleon's prefect in the Danube Delta," a "foe of Russia and Orthodoxy."[18]

In February 1866, Cuza was overthrown in a coup d'état. Buoyed by it, the *Moskovskiia vedomosti* and the *Russkii invalid* brought the Russian wishes entirely into the open demanding that the unification be abrogated, because it, according to them, only exposed the populace to "disorder, violence and general impoverishment"; and, again in the name of the "well-being of the people," they called for full reestablishment of Ottoman suzerainty, i.e. for the return of the system whereby Moldavia and Wallachia had been ruled by Phanariot "hospodars" appointed by the Porte.[19]

However, nothing but disappointment awaited the Russians. Despite their frantic protests, Charles of Hohenzollern-Sigmaringen, considered a French-Prussian candidate, was recognized as the new Rumanian Prince. At the conference in Paris dealing with the problem, the St. Petersburg initiative for the return to the status quo ante singularly failed; and neither did Turkish intervention, earnestly wished by Katkov and most probably advised to the Porte by Ignatiev, materialize. Again, experiencing painful diplomatic isolation, Tsardom had to backstep. In June 1866 Ignatiev informed the Turks that "he had an order to abstain in the future from any counsel and keep an attitude of observation."[20]

Inevitably, the timid, unimaginative status quo approach could not endure unchallenged. The disappointing Rumanian settlement coupled with rising European tension in 1866 gave the impetus for an overall criticism and new extremist initiative.

The first appeal for a radical change was issued by Field-Marshal Bariatinskii:

> The Austro-Prussian war will break out soon and then, after their victory, the Prussians may take on a dominant position in the continent, in detriment to Tsardom. In order to prevent the unfavourable shift in the power balance, St. Petersburg should make a deal with Berlin to enforce the division of the Habsburg Monarchy. If the Austrian Slavic provinces were acquired, the Eastern Question would also be solved 'without any trouble and complication,' because the 'way to Tsargrad lies in Vienna.' If, however, St. Petersburg were to go on being a mere observer of events, then a very high price would have to be paid in the future.[21]

The essential idea canvassed in Bariatinskii's memoir—that "advantage must be taken of the present moment" and the peril menacing in the Prussian prepondence be responded by a vigorous forward policy—was shared by the whole Moscow party. "The proximity of mighty Prussia threatens us with danger," wrote Aksakov. "We have to encounter its might with our might, German unity with our unity. Parallel with Prussia's vocation to gather the scattered parts of the German world into a whole, we can and must emerge with our own vocation, the unification of the Slavic world." Along with the leadership in the emancipation of the Balkan peoples this should imply the drive to "restore the boundaries of the Crown of St. Vladimir and reunite to Russia the Russian tribes in Hungary, Bukovina and Galicia."[22]

Katkov elaborated on those themes at considerable lengths.

Since the Hohenzollern prince had surfaced in Bucharest, his comments on Rumanian affairs had essentially altered in emphasis. Although still hostile to the unification and the "French intrigue," he visibly recognized the stance taken by both St. Petersburg and himself to be shallow and ineffective:

> Instead of vain protests, events should have been interpreted as the beginning of the dissolution of the Ottoman Empire; the Rumanian violation of the Paris Treaty should have been used to get rid of the obligations imposed in 1856. Of the treaty, 'only the stipulations directed against Russia remained intact'; 'has not the time come when we should finally revoke our signature to an act which de facto and de jure has no more international bearing? . . . Indeed, nobody would have expected from us such curious demeanour when we performed as defenders of a treaty designed against us . . . and of our free will restrained ourselves from prosecuting our traditional policy.'[23]

The Austro-Prussian conflict exacerbated his worries. Under the impact of what he perceived as approaching catastrophe for European balance and grave threat for Russia's great-power status, the publicist for the first time directly attacked the Singers' Bridge and preached an offensive course pure and simple.

Already before the war of 1866, his comment showed mounting anxiety. He predicted that victorious Prussia would change into a restless and increasingly dangerous neighbor and that defeated Austria would look for compensations in the Balkans.[24] Then, with the sombre forecast coming true, his message grew more and more unswerving:

> By 'all the forces of history . . . Russia was being called into action.' Unwillingness to listen to his command is futile—'we will be summoned.' The arguments of unpreparedness 'are nothing but a continuation of Nihilism.' 'Bold feats would always provide the means. Is it possible, anyway, that Russia would be incapable of procuring resources in a matter where not only her dignity but also her whole future is at stake?'

Tsardom could not afford the luxury of lagging behind in the competition; if it faltered then 'out state would not only lose its position as a Great Power but would be driven entirely out of Europe.' The frontiers must be improved and other measures taken 'to safeguard our vital interests.' People in Galicia and the Balkans 'wait with impatience and hope for some decisive Russian deed.' Further delays would be unforgivable because 'the conditions at the present time are more propitious for action than they may be in the future.'[25]

Yet, the governmental reaction to extremist exhortations was unequivocally negative. In the war of 1866 and in its aftermath, St. Petersburg was hardly more than a "mere observer" and no substantial change was contemplated either. Any great conflict appeared to Alexander to be just a "general misfortune of which only revolution, the common enemy of all of us, could profit."[26]

The evaluation he and the leading statesmen made on economic and military potential was wide apart from the Muscovite's nonchalance, and quite deservedly so.[27]

Ten years after the Crimean disaster, recovery had still been painfully slow. Suffering by serfdom's heritage, agriculture and industry wrestled with formidable problems. Technological backwardness and labor productivity were appaling. Railway construction, proclaimed the first priority, lingered far behind the needs and the progress made by potential European rivals. As to the army, its mobility and armaments had not improved perceptibly since the Nicholas' time. Conservative vested interests, deep-rooted old routines and permanents financial troubles hanged like a millstone round Tsardom's neck. No wonder that Miliutin, otherwise closer to the hawks than any of the ministers, required to "postpone by every means the moment of our participation in an European war."[28]

A secret committee set up by Alexander to examine Bariatinskii's proposals, decided against the Field Marshal; and an Extraordinary Council, held sometime in September-October 1866, also refused to run the risk and undertake a diplomatic action against the Paris Treaty.[29] The Eastern Question should be left frozen: his country, Gorchakov told Reuss, would not abandon the present course despite its "contradition to traditional policy."[30]

CHAPTER 8

TEMPTATIONS AND REALITIES:
THE "PANSLAV" CHALLENGE OF
1866-1869

The historical move of Russia from the
Dnieper to the Vistula was a declaration
of war to Europe which had broken into a
part of the continent which did not belong
to it. Russia now stands in the midst of the
enemy's lines. Such a condition is only
temporary: she must either drive back the
enemy or abandon the position.
Fadeev

Sooner or later, whether we wish it or not,
a battle with Europe (or at least a significant
part of it) is inevitable—over the Eastern
Question, that is, over the freedom and
independence of the Slavs, over the possession of Tsargrad, over every thing that,
in the opinion of Europe, constitutes the
object of illegal ambition of Russia. And
in the opinion of every Russian worthy of
the name, this is the necessary demand
of Russia's historical destiny.
Danilevskii

Not unlike the Nicholas-Nesselrode era, the cleavage between St.
Petersburg and the "patriotic" opposition to it commenced to take on

primarily the form of a contest between the chief of the Foreign Ministry and his critics.

In 1866, Prince Gorchakov could not dispute the argument that conditions for active Russian participation in international affairs had considerably improved. Great Britain was absorbed in her own problems, Austria shattered by military defeats, the two great continental rivals— France and Prussia—entangled in mutual confrontation. Indeed, in the annual report the Singers' Bridge went as far as to state that in its consequences, "the German crisis has liquidated the hostile alliance against Russia which had originated in the Crimean War" and that "today it is impossible to repeat the situation of 1854, when two European Powers were against us."[1] Nonetheless, the Prince insisted, in the Near-Eastern sphere no real change had taken place; a "big confrontation on the Eastern Question would be detrimental to our essential interests" and the status quo there "might be solely altered to our disadvantage."[2]

That this impossible position in the eyes of the "patriots" had not yet led to a total breach between them and the architect of the official foreign policy, was due to the stance the latter had taken on the other crucial issue, the option between Prussia and France. While Alexander, after the Polish uprising, considered Prussia the only trustworthy Power and possible ally, Gorchakov countered this proposition with the demand that Russia must determine her stance strictly on the non-alignment basis, his formula reading as follows: "to uphold certain balance between Prussia and France, which would preserve the element of hostility without driving them into a conflict" and, profiting from this rivalry, "foster our own Russian purposes."[3]

After his disappointments with the French since 1856, the Prince had to be on his guard in dealing with them and repeatedly assured the Tsar that Napoleon would not enlist him for the anti-Prussian cause. In fact, however, he along with Katkov and Russian society veered back to the old hope, anticipating that because of the gravest threat rising from beyond the Rhine, the Second Empire would be now more than ever anxious to strike a bargain. The price for Tsardom, of course, would be paid on the Eastern Question. Underestimating the prestige and economic motives in the Napoleonic policy, Gorchakov assumed that for the French Emperor the East was "only a trifle (un appoint) which he would be willing to sacrifice on behalf of his European objectives."[4]

The alliance between the Moscow publicist and the Prince may be pointed out at this juncture as a very significant factor on the Russian scene. After the diatribe at the time of the Austro-Prussian war and immediately after, the former returned back to political realism: he recognized that Russia could not attend to her aims in the Balkans and the Straits while disregarding the European balance and eventually put forward the rapprochement with France as the absolute priority.[5] The main difference between the two men was that whereas the Prince had always taken pains to parade loyalty to his august master, the editor refused to care much about Alexander's displeasure.

Katkov's increasingly unequivocal campaign for a comprehensive understanding with France[6] had been a logical augmentation of his national-interest concept; and such also had been his crusade on the "Ostsee question" and his laudatory comments on Gorchakov's effort.

Yet, not even the cooperation between the Singers' Bridge and the Strastnyi Boulevard, much discussed and approved by society, could save the Prince from impetuous criticism from the other "patriotic" quarters. His stance on the Eastern Question was branded as "thoughtless, careless and lacking in foresight." "Prince Gorchakov," wrote General Ignatiev, "aimed also at the destruction of the Paris Treaty, but there was a radical variance in our viewpoints. He believed in Europe, he was fond of conferences and congresses, cared more for eloquent phrases and brilliant writing than for truly diplomatic action."[7] The process which ended in the total rejection of the old man and his system had already been well in progress.

* * *

While Bariatinskii stepped aside and devoted his zeal to the contest with Miliutin on military problems, Ignatiev emerged in the second half of 1866 as the leading "Panslav" in the elite.

Historians may wonder whether his convictions were genuine or whether they were just a by-product of his egregious ambition to obtain the post occupied by Gorchakov. There cannot be any doubt, however, that in Russian diplomacy, Ignatiev's activities and attitudes most distinctly represented the extremist alternative to the policies of the Prince; and that it was with good reason that in Europe nefarious Russian designs were primarily connected with his name.

Missions in the East and service at the head of the Asiatic Department provided Ignatiev with the necessary experience and at the same time proved his extraordinary abilities. In 1864, only thirty-two years old, he was appointed to the top diplomatic position at Constantinople. From this stronghold, first as a Minister and then, from 1867, as Ambassador, virtually independent of the Singers' Bridge, he could start his big gamble in earnest.

Before coming to the Turkish capital, the ascending young diplomat had formulated a three-point foreign-policy concept. The first point, to achieve the destruction of the Paris Treaty or at least its revision in the articles concerning the Black Sea and Bessarabia, corresponded with the official goal. The second and the third contained the gist of the extremist blueprint: (2) to obtain mastery in the Straits "either by assuming an exclusive influence over the sovereign and existing authorities" or "if Europe works against us and the local government is unyielding, by annexing the place"; (3) to unify the Slavs "by a slow process," starting with "the help of a common language," then through alliances against the Turks and finally by marshalling them "under a joint diplomatic and economic direction."[8]

Once entrenched on the Golden Horn, Ignatiev set out to turn these objectives into a reality. He described his endeavors to the effect that

> I entered into close relations with the Sultan, I paralyzed the Anglo-French-Austrian accord of 1856 directed against us, I supported one embassy, then another against the rest, trying to sow seeds of discord between our antagonists. . . . The subversive actions against the Paris Treaty and also against Western and in general foreign influences on the Bosphorus and especially against Turkey herself and Austria, had to be continued until the increasing strength of Russia and favorable events would permit us to work out an independent solution of the Eastern Question in Russian sense, that is by the forming of units of common blood and common religion, tied to Russia by indissoluble bonds and by achieving the transfer of the Straits.[9]

Documentary evidence indicates[10] that the Russian envoy was well alive that the Slavs and Greeks were still unable to effect a collapse of

Turkish power, but this would not prevent him challenging Gorchakov's course. When the Austro-Prussian conflict broke out he joined in the extremist appeals, asserting that "our chief enemies have been de facto paralyzed."[11]

Aside from Prince Michael's renewed effort in forging the anti-Turkish coalition, the Greek uprising in Crete offered him and his alike in Russia the latitude they were looking for.

The latter event was triggered by increasing taxation on the island, but behind this local dissatisfaction lay the growing national aspiration of the Greeks, who, inspired by Italian and German examples, heard the hour strike also for them to put into a life their "Great Idea" of the unification of all territories inhabited by the "Hellenes" into one empire. In the sequel of the first skirmishes on the island, a Cretan assembly convened in the Sfaxion mountains announced its resolution to "destroy Ottoman rule forever" and reunite "with mother Greece under the sceptre of George I, the King of the Hellenes"[12] (September 1866).

Prompted by Gorchakov's request for detailed information on Balkan conditions, Ignatiev composed a memorandum (dated 27 December/ 8 January 1867) which should according to his opinion constitute the "new governmental programme on the Eastern Question instead of purely passive attitude in which the leading role was renounced for the sake of European views."

The envoy did not openly dispute the official keyword that "we must avoid any external conflagration, because of the precarious state of our finances, lack of strategic railways and the incompleteness of our reforms." But just as Katkov had said six months ago, he maintained that "events do not wait for our economic and military preparedness" and that if the peoples of the area "fall under Western sway," a situation "incomparably more disadvantageous for Russia" may arise. Then "our ill-wishers and enemies" would take over the position "we have been deprived of due to our passivity and our concessions." The new generation of Balkan Christians had been corrupted by the West; "they will never be able to win freedom and throw the Turks out of Europe" alone without a Russian lead. Therefore, without formally renouncing its neutrality, Tsardom must direct their efforts; and assist the conclusion of a Serbo-Greek alliance.

Although the Greeks ought to be granted moral encouragement, absolute preference should be given to Serbia and Prince Michael "who promises quite exceptional guarantees and on whose devotion we may fully rely." "All our art must consist in keeping in our hands the threads of every possible movement in the Balkans" and channel it to the common purpose; this purpose being the Balkan federation with its capital at Constantinople and under Russian protection. No opportunity should be missed; religious hatred between Sunnites and Shiites, hostility between the Armenians and the Kurds, Turco-Persian border dispute, should be incited and exploited. Similar tactics were to be applied to European rivalries in the area. Thereby a situation were to emerge where the "concern for the new state of affairs on the Bosphorus would seem to be of secondary importance."[13]

The policymakers on the Neva were greatly discomforted by Ignatiev's memoir. Even Miliutin, who was soon to be tempted by the Balkan possibilities, rejected it as a scheme aiming at a general war and Russian involvement in such a disaster.[14] If, however, confidential proposals could be put aside, the mood of society, developing in the "holy mission" vein, was somewhat to be appeased.

The educated layer laboured under the strain of "Polish qualms." After atrocities, pillage, executions, mass deportations and confiscations—all of which were loudly applauded—there was an acute need to prove Russian magnamity, altruism and civilized behaviour; and the defence of Cretan Orthodox brutalized by the Moslems offered a splendid opportunity for the purpose. The heroic tragedy of the convent of Arcadi, where the besieged Cretans blew up the powder magazine and perished in the ruin together with their wives, children and about 500 Turks (on 21 November 1866), spurred a campaign for humanitarian assistance to the Greeks. In Moscow, offices of the *Moskovskiia vedomosti* and *Moskva* became the collecting centers.

The Tsar and his court ostentatiously joined the action in an obvious bid for swerving the mood into this uncontroversial channel. Yet society would not settle on altruism alone. Philaret's manifesto which inaugurated the campaign was understood by it as "the opening of a political initiative," too. A Moscow Senator wrote:

> The time is ripe. The existence of Turkey is incompatible with the dignity of Europe.... Furthermore, we need to destroy the treaty of 1856. It has become imperative to settle Eastern affairs and give proper shape to the importance of the Danube and the

Black Sea basins. . . Russia ought to expand to the Danube, Serbia
should be extended to the Balkan range; beyond it and in the
Aegean will be Greece. . . . True, we are not ready either with new
weapons or railways, but these are secondary matters. The shame
of the Paris Treaty is the main thing.[15]

While Katkov returned to more subdued tones, Aksakov's *Moskva* took
the lead in advertizing the bold course and castigating the Foreign Ministry. Its writing also tells us more about the contacts between the old
capital and the clique of hawkish Balkan diplomats with Ignatiev at its
helm. Some of the key editorials published in *Moskva* were dictated
by Mikhail Khitrovo, propably the most adventurous among the envoy's
lieutenants:

We must first of all realize that our main foreign policy objectives are centered in the East. This time our Ministry (for Foreign
Affairs) has definitely failed to comprehend and size up that fact.
Our most vital interests in the East have been sacrificed because
of some dubious consideration of utility in relation to our interests
in the West. . . . We should at last take into account that financial
questions and criteria of economy must not hamper our political
activities if these are being required by force of events. We cannot
create circumstances according to our will; we must be able to take
advantage of all possibilities.

The fiery Aksakov used the same Ignatievian verbiage and went as
far as asserting that "the Ministry for Foreign Affairs neither satisfies
Russian public opinion nor the expectations of the Christians; and neither
does it command the confidence of the West-European governments."[16]
The blame that the Singers' Bridge was prosecuting "the policy of laissez-
faire, laissez aller" also appeared in the "non-Moscow" press.[17]

Meanwhile, the Vice-Chancellor and the moderates in St. Petersburg
had to register still more serious signals: the Serbian and Greek official
guests at the Tsarevich's wedding apprised their hosts that Athens and
Belgrade planned to start war against the Turks in the course of the next
spring.[18]

Put into a quandary, Gorchakov nonetheless remained unbending
in his resolve to insist on a purely diplomatic approach. Heartened by the

reports of Ambassador Budberg from Paris, assuring him that the Second Empire was ripe for a deal, he proposed to the French (on 28 November 1866) a common initiative to achieve the unification of Crete with Greece or at least the autonomy of the island. Later on identical suggestions were also made to the other Powers; and, in view of the expected Balkan upheaval, the Singers' Bridge called for noninterference on behalf of the Turks. No other steps, though, should be taken beyond these confines.

The annual report of the Foreign Ministry for 1866 contained verbal rather than salient concessions to its opponents. The document conceded that the course aiming at the mitigation in the antagonism between the Porte and its Christian subjects fell short of producing palpable results; the patience of the latter had been exhausted and "any attempt to stop them would be barren," merely bringing about the loss of the sympathies they cherished for Russia. The maxims enumerated in the report, however, simply reworded earlier statements:

> 1. To take over the moral leadership of this movement (of Balkan Christian peoples). . . . 2. To prevent, if possible, or at least localize a general violent conflagration. . . . 3. For this purpose, to reach an agreement with the (Great Powers') cabinets on certain principles for either pacification through collective mediation or at least for the localization of the struggle . . . and prevent Europe to suppress it. 4. . . . To use the legitimate rights of Russia . . . in order to fulfill her historic mission in the East, . . . but to avoid involvement in complications which would jeopardize the success of our internal work, as well as the risks of renewal of the now destroyed and weakened coalition hostile to us.[19]

Whilst Ignatiev's memorandum established the extremist programme, the four points of Gorchakov were destined to remain the official Russian line until the great Eastern crisis ten years earlier. The peculiarity of the situation in 1866-1869 lay in the fact that both the Panslav expectations and those of Gorchakov for a diplomatic breakthrough failed to materialize. Another painful retreat was to be the inevitable net result.

* * *

The first eight months of 1867 were decisive for the failure.

At the beginning of the Cretan crisis Lord Stanley, the British Prime Minister, assessed the Ottoman Empire "worn out and unable to defend itself"; and, consequently, the traditional doctrine of the integrity of Turkey as impossible to uphold. If public opinion pronounced itself for the cession of the island, he told the Austrian Ambassador, "he could only yield the pressure." No such pressure emerged, however. Even in the Liberal party, traditionally pro-Greek, the Duke of Argyll found "conscience dead and apathetic."[20] Moreover, the Turks proved militarily capable to cope with the revolt. Thus the London cabinet could reappear in its usual role and it affected the position taken by Austria and ultimately by France too. The power constellation of the Greek struggle for independence in the 1820s was not to be resurrected; instead Russian diplomacy was confronted by increasingly arrogant Turks, an uncooperative "European concert" and worst of all—by the French rushing back to the old "Crimean" fold.

For both Gorchakov and Katkov—their axis had never been so firm as in 1867[21]—the new disappointment with France presented the hardest blow.

First, they were buoyed by the pledge made by the Foreign Minister de Moustier to assist Russia in the backing of the Greek and Serbian claims. Then, they expected a dramatic change, when Napoleon III triggered the so called Luxemburg crisis. Finally, they hoped that Alexander's summer visit to the World Exhibition in Paris would bring about at least some commitment on the Eastern affairs. However, instead of the Tsar, who was shown cold shoulder and on top of all was fired on by a Polish exile, it was to be the Sultan who returned from a similar trip triumphant. Soon afterwards, the meeting of Napoleon III and Francis Joseph I at Salzburg filled Gorchakov's and Katkov's cup of frustration to the brim.

> In a spell of dispair, the editor suggested watching the French-Prussian rivalry dispassionately, like a mere 'fight of two gladiators.' Without exposing itself to the perils of European war Russia should be truly concerned solely with the movement for Balkan emancipation. Nobody but the peoples of the 'Greek-Slavic world,' he now agreed with the traditional proponents of the 'historical mission' were true allies and only they, after setting up independent states, could assist Tsardom to counterbalance the 'colossal power... created by Prince Bismarck.'[22]

* * *

Judging from the complex international situation, the Russian elite should have remained immune to the extremist appeal. Moreover, the sympathy for the Greek cause was quickly cooling down, with the Panslavs detecting in the "Great Idea" serious danger for its aims. In the *Moskva,* Aksakov put it in plain words: in the bid for the resurrection of a Hellenic Empire the Greeks could "turn from friends to our worst enemies and so, however great are our sympathies, we cannot sacrifice to them either our Slavic brethren or our Russian interests."[23] The intensity and effects of the Greek-Bulgarian Church dispute sounded the alarm[24]; there also Katkov, who had otherwise evaded any anti-Greek utterance, joined the pleas that Bulgarian, Slavic cause must not be sacrificed to the Phanariots.[25]

All the warning signals notwithstanding, however, in just the first eight months of 1867 there was a symptomatic development revealing the intrinsic impact of expansionist tradition. Since the Luxemburg crisis the conviction had been overriding that a big European war and with it a Slav-Orthodox general rising would flare up soon; and for the Russian such a perspective was too tempting to resist. Even in the hitherto very cautious policy-making group a strong tendency to exploit the unique moment unfolded.

Next to Franco-Prussian tensions, the Serbian Prince again gained head in the calculations. Incited by the Turkish and Austrian troubles, Michael with renewed ardor set out to rally the Balkan forces, keeping simultaneously close contacts with St. Petersburg, Moscow and the Ignatiev faction. On 5 October 1866, a Serbo-Montenegrin alliance treaty was signed; it obliged Prince Nikola to go to war with the Turks and after a presumed victory to integrate his country into the Belgrade-led federation. Similar negotiations were conducted with Croat national leadership Bishop Strossmayer and Bulgarian émigrés. Most significantly, a political and military pact between Belgrade and Athens was concluded on 26 August 1867.

Unfortunately, we are in no position to assess fully the extent of Russian involvement in Michael's endeavours in organizing anti-Turkish forces; and this applies to both the "Moscow" and the "St. Petersburg" side.

Over and above the activities of Ignatiev's and Slavic Commitee's agents, including Panslav-oriented consuls and Ministers (Novikov in

Athens, Ionin in Ragusa, Khitrovo, Dendrino etc.) are opened to speculations.[26] It may be taken for sure, however, that none of them was directed by the official Singers' Bridge line as formulated in Gorchakov's four-point programme.

Ignatiev himself not only 'offered marked sympathy to the leaders of the Slavic movement,' but 'gave advice to the Serbian government on the questions of military readiness and ordered . . . military attaché at Constantinople, Colonel Francini, to prepare the project for the whole campaign.' The envoy entrusted the most sensitive political tasks to Ionin and Khitrovo. On his orders the former secretly observed the Cretan events from a Russian warship; then, together with Novikov, led prolonged negotiations in Athens which probably paved the way for the new Serbo-Greek alliance treaty. Ionin also helped to organize the guerillas in Epirus and Thessaly, and with his friend, 'Mercurius' Khitrovo, tried to incite risings in Macedonia and Albania.[27]

As to the zealots from the Moscow Committee we know that its military expert, Colonel Raevskii, took part in the talks between Serbian emissaries and Bulgarian exiles in Bucharest, together with Consul General Offenbach. Later on, under Ignatiev's auspices, he elaborated a plan for the guerilla war in Bulgaria.[28]

Concerning the attitudes in St. Petersburg, a Soviet scholar has mentioned a highly interesting anonymous memoir from that time. According to it, Gorchakov, Shuvalov, Reutern and Valuev formed the "moderate" or "conservative" party, while Miliutin and Prince Gagarin, the chairman of the State Council, led the "war party of Panslav democracy," ready to take risks should the European war and the Eastern crisis break out. Being "between two fires," the document affirmed, Alexander hesitated to take a firm stand.[29]

Other sources also indicate that Miliutin was prone to forget his own cool judgment on Russian military and economic capabilities. A special commission of his ministry headed by Colonel Leer, the future leading strategist, departed for Belgrade to supervise Serbian preparations. In the depots of Nikolaevsk 46,000 rifles and a large stock of ammunition were ready for immediate shipment in case of a Bulgarian rising. And there is a sufficient evidence that the War Minister persuaded the Tsar that the eventual Austrian action in Bosnia-Hercegovina must be responded to by the invasion of Galicia.[30]

Undoubtedly, the moderates laboured under heavy pressures and Gorchakov conceded to a material support for the expected Serbia-led action. "The Ministry (for Foreign Affairs) has decided to subordinate all its further endeavours," he wrote in his instructions to Offenbach for the Bucharest secret talks, "to his plan of the arming of all the Slavic peoples in Turkey."[31]

* * *

For the Panslav-nationalist party these were its first truly great days. The Slavic Congress held in Moscow in June 1867, at the time of an ethnographic exhibition, manifested for the whole of Europe its powerful position in society no less than its inflated ambitions. The Congress, wrote a Soviet authority on the subject, became the occasion when the "Slavic Committee finally revealed its true character and political framework."[32]

The Austro-Hungarian "Ausgleich," which established German and Magyar hegemony over the Slavic population in the Habsburg Empire, created an exceptionally favourable atmoshere. Apart from 12 representatives of Serbia, two Montenegrins and one Bulgarian, 63 delegates came from the newly reconstructed Dual Monarchy—27 Czechs, 16 Serbs, 10 Croats, 4 Ukrainians, 3 Slovenes and 3 Slovaks; and even the moderate Czech leaders, affronted by the Vienna's option, were now willing to look on Tsardom as the sole hope for their nation.

Alexander and Gorchakov were evidently unhappy about the gathering. But, cornered by overwhelming public enthusiasm, they and other dignitaries had to meet the Slavic guests in audiences and allow the press to indulge in almost unbridled propaganda for Panslavism in both its anti-Turkish and anti-Austrian connotations. "They say that the existence of Austria is a necessity; that if she had not existed, she would have to be invented. Well, . . . would it not be (now) better to invent something else?" wrote Katkov.

The Moscow editor used the opportunity to exhort again the government to emulate the French and Prussian examples. As France had taken over the protection of the Romance peoples and Prussia the unification of Germany, Russia had equal obligation towards the Slavs and Orthodox. 'The task is noble and free of all egotism. It is beneficial, for it will complete the triumph of the nationality principle and provide solid ground for the modern equilibrium of Europe. It is worthy of Russia and her greatness and we are firmly convinced that Russia will fulfill it.'

True, the publicist was prudent enough not to overdo the plea. "Fear of a world-wide Slavic monarchy is deprived of any foundation," he assured; Russian national interest does not require annexations, but the protection of independent Slavic and Orthodoxy peoples.[33] At the Congress itself, however, his and his kinsmen's demeanor disclosed their genuine intentions.

The measure of tactlessness displayed may astonish us even today. The Russians welcomed their guests in St. Petersburg with Glinka's chauvinist opera "A Life for the Tsar" (renamed under the Soviets "Ivan Susanin"). Then the opera ballet performed Slavic folk dances; and while the distinguished audience wildly applauded the Russian ones, it hooted the Polish mazurka. Similar scenes took place in Moscow. The conciliatory speech of Rieger, the Czech spokesman, soliciting for the Poles "the right of their own national existence as a branch of Western Slavs," entaled only harsh Russian rebuttals. Cherkasskii contended that the Poles had irrevocably forfeited the liberties granted to them by Russian magnamity and that "no power on the earth" could change that; they might be forgiven solely if they repent meekly and acknowledge the present conditions. Katkov, to nobody's surprise, was equally inexorable. Foreign Slavs, he put it bluntly, are uncapable of judging the problem in a "proper way"; as a political term, a Pole is natural and implacable enemy and must be handled accordingly.[34]

Equally distinctly, Panslav-nationalist extremism was spelled out in the demand that the Slavs ought to give up their "dialects" and accept Russian as the universal literary language. Haughtily underrating the renaissance of non-Russian languages, Professor Lamanskii described them as a "token of servile polition and spiritual slavery" and Shebalskii as a remnant of "the feudal or appanage period." On this occasion, Katkov avoided disparaging words; still, he insisted on the same requirement as a "condition sine qua non of Slavic unity."[35] Expressing the wish to deprive the Turkish and Austrian Slavs of the very symbol of their national

identity, the Congress brough to the light that the Russians recognized
their right for an independent existence in appearance only. So, particularly in this context, the Moscow editor's words that "the Russian eagle
will closely watch every inch of the Slavic lands"[36] must have been met
by more thoughtful delegates with apprehension rather than by elation.

The Slav guests, an American scholar summed up,

> got more and more the impression that by Panslavism their
> Russian hosts understood a Pan-Russianism, the acceptance of the
> Russian language and the Orthodox faith by all other Slavs, a Russi-
> fication of the Austro-Hungarian and Balkan Slavs similar to the
> processes then operated within the Russian borders. . . .[37]

The chance given by the Austro-Hungarian "Ausgleich" was wasted;
the Congress turned for Tsardom's image in a liability instead of an asset.
Not surprisingly, no such gathering would convene again, despite promises
to the contrary. For the Muscovites' domestic purposes, though, the
event was an indubitable triumph. It attested that the Panslav-nationalist
current represented much more than several hundred exalted nobles,
professors, literati and officers. The public eagerly followed the proceedings in the press and wholeheartedly approved the reasoning of their
spokesmen. "The greatest, the best result of the Slav visit is that the Slavic
question has penetrated the mind and the consciousness of Russian society.
It has passed from abstraction into active reality," Aksakov could claim
with full justification.[38] Equally importantly, the Russians had begun to
conceive the "Slavic question" in the Katkovian interpretation. The
liberal *Vestnik Evropy* put it plainly:

> The Slavs may unite with us, but it must be understood—and it
> has been in fact understood—that the frontiers of the union will
> not be Slav, but Russian again. . . . We are born Slavs, yet we
> became Russians after centuries-long endeavours and strides. That
> is why no one can demand that in politics we should be first Slavs
> and then Russians.[39]

* * *

In July 1867, an Extraordinary Council chaired by the Tsar settled
for a more determined Balkan commitments. It was believed that the

awaited "conflagration in Western Europe could be of immediate benefit
to the Christian population" in the sense that it would inspire a general
rising."[40] Actually the whole calculation proved completely wrong.
After the Luxemburg crisis, continental tensions temporarily abated and
the growing Russian isolation on the Eastern question cooled down
Prince Michael's fervency. As in the crisis of 1862 he fully realized that
his armed forces were inadequate,[41] and the Salzburg Austro-French
summit learned him that he would have, apart from the Turks, also the
hostile Great Powers to cope with. Instead of running risks, he again
decided for modest gains—an agreement with the Porte on the final withdrawal of the Turkish garrisons from his Principality.

Gorchakov was not slow to diagnose the new situation. "Although
in our general policy we feel no isolation, in our efforts to bring about a
serious improvement for Eastern Christians we are alone," he wrote
in a memoir in September 1867. Without sufficient resources, "we neither
wish nor can declare war on Turkey." Because of this, Russia must reduce
her activities solely to "moral support" and "preventing harmful outside interference."

Both Alexander and Miliutin approved the analysis.[42] They were still
resolved to respond to Austrian military action in Bosnia-Hercegovina by
an invasion into Galicia—a "natural frontier" in the Carpathian Mountains
was a generally recognized strategic desideratum—but would not go
beyond the protection of immediate state interests. There was again an
overall consensus in the elite that until the railroad netword had been
substantially improved in the southwestern and western parts of the
Empire, an active policy in the Balkans was next to impossible. When
Greek King George came to St. Petersburg to marry Grand Duchess
Olga, Alexander administered a hard lesson to him insisting that he must
fetter his hotheaded subjects, pouring into Crete as volunteers and attacking the Turks in Thessaly and Epirus, and not expect any direct assistance
at all.[43]

The Russian Chancellor contrived to cover the retreat by issuing a
declaration of non-interference into the disputes between the Porte and
the Christians; and he dispatched the trusted Tiutchev to the old capital
with a plea for support.

The message the poet-diplomat delivered to the Muscovite leaders
allegedly maintained that the declaration would give the Balkan peoples

the necessary boost for their rising.[44] The latter could not possibly have been so naive as to believe in such an outcome. It rather appears that they consented to take part in the deceit. After Prince Michael had retracted, they must have abandoned their sanguine hopes; the Greek ordeal in Crete hardly moved them much. The intensity of the "Ostsee campaign" indicates that they, like society in its overwhelming majority, accepted the Katkovian view conceiving the Prussian danger to be the absolute priority. Likewise, the energetic participation of the Strastnyi Boulevard in the debate on strategic railways[45] allows us to surmise that the current it represented acknowledged that the progress in this field was a necessary precondition for a forward Balkan policy.

At any event, when the declaration was formally published on 30 October 1867, both Katkov and Aksakov uttered their approval. It remains, wrote Aksakov, "to wash our hands and free Russian diplomacy for all responsibility for the consequences of Turkish policy."[46] The departure of the Russian military mission from Belgrade after Michael had dismissed Garašanin (on 14 November 1867), put the policy of "washing hands" into its proper context. So did the overall approach of Tsardom to the Eastern Question in the following months.

* * *

Gloomy predictions that the non-interference declaration would be ensued by humiliation and loss of prestige proved only too correct. Needless to add, no great conflagration took place and both Turkey and Europe made the Russian retreat even more painful than expected. England and Austria refused to adhere to the Russian diplomatic action; France formally joined it, but in practical steps drifted further towards the Anglo-Austrian bloc. "France, England and Austria now form a compact grouping here," Ignatiev reported from the Golden Horn, obviously relishing Gorchakov's discomfort.[47]

Taking advantage of the aborted action, the Ambassador attempted in the extraordinary councils held in January-February 1868 to save something of his concept: a policy of close cooperation between Berlin and St. Petersburg should be inaugurated; then, troop concentration on the Galician border would suffice to regain the initiative and change the Balkan situation. Stremoukhov, the Director of the Asiatic Department, and Ambassador Budberg backed the scheme but the prevailing opinion was decidedly against it. "If somebody pronounces a different view (than yours), Reutern told Gorchakov, "send him to me. I shall show him the impossibility (of an active policy) based on facts which nobody will be able to dispute."[48] Alexander and Miliutin had already been convinced.

Indeed, the old course reintroduced by the non-interference declaration was to be pursued with such consistence that it led to almost total Russo-Greek estrangement.

After the King's Russian marriage the Greeks had desperately clutched to the hope that Tsardom would come to their rescue. Nothing, however, was more distant to the intentions of the St. Petersburg dignitaries: they, and the Moscow party evidently with them, had simply written the Greeks off. "Public opinion in Russia does not care any more for them," said Tolstoi, and "no one voice will be raised" on their behalf. Alexander declared that "peace is more important than the fate of a handful of Greeks"; and Gorchakov angrily dubbed the Boulgaris cabinet which had embarded upon a militant line "un ministère d'harlequins." It may be safely assumed that Ignatiev talked with the Turkish ministers in much the same way.[49]

Perfectly assured, the Porte could engineer the conclusive showdown. Using the manifestations in Athens and the departure of a new group of volunteers for Crete as pretext, it announced on 2 December 1868, the rupture of diplomatic relations with the Kingdom and the expulsion of all Greek subjects from the Ottoman Empire. On the Powers' insistence, the execution was postponed, but on 11 December an ultimatum followed dictating that any aid to the dying revolt must cease, volunteers be disbanded and the "Enosis," the last ship still carrying men and supplies to the island, prohibited from further voyages.

Upon a desperate appeal for salvation, St. Petersburg arranged only a conference of the Paris Treaty Powers. For public showing, Gorchakov promised to be "the spokesman for Greece," but every diplomat who took part in the gathering (on 9-20 January 1869 in the French capital) knew where the Russians stood.[50] Necessarily, the plea of Tsardom's representative, Stackelberg, for more leniency met deaf ears and the declaration produced in the end just repeated in somewhat milder terms the wording of the Turkish ultimatum.

In the measure of their indifference, the Russians perhaps surprised even their Western opponents. Stackelberg was advised that the St. Petersburg government found the outcome of the conference "very satisfactory"; and the Singers' Bridge instructed Minister Novikov to warn King George that any obstruction in complying with its verdict "would be attended with serious consequences and expose Greece to dangers against which it would be impossible for the Tsar to afford any protection." Talking to the Prussian envoy, Alexander reiterated that he held the Greeks mostly responsible for their predicament and that he "does not cherish any sympathy whatever for that corrupted and incompetent nation."[51]

The effects for the Russian position in the area were too overwhelming to be ignored. By her duplicity, Novikov grieved, Russia had been losing "the future allies obedient to her command" and turned them into "foes sold to the West."[52] After the Paris dictat, the Greeks might be well put on the enemies list. In Belgrade, following the assassination of Michael (on 10 July 1868), the tendency to look for Austrian rather than Russian guidance became manifest. "Being discredited in the Cretan eyes, no longer so terrifying for the Turks and inciting suspicions in Western Europe, we were deprived of all the former means on which our strength rested in the East," ran Ignatiev's indictment.[53]

Still, except when connected with the "Prussian theme," Katkov and the Russian press had since the autumn 1867 raised no serious objections to the official course; the thesis reiterated in the annual report of the Foreign Ministry for 1868—"at the moment when in Europe the effort is directed to save peace and when neither Russia nor the Turkish Christians are ready for decisive struggle, any (bold) move in the East would be untimely and dangerous"[54]—now expressed the almost universal opinion of both society and the elite. Commenting on the anniversary of the naval battle at Chesme (1770), a hallmark in Russian military advance in the area, Katkov went as far as accepting the St. Petersburg maxim that the "solution of the Eastern Question depends at present not on military force but on the internal development of Russia."[55]

The Moscow publicist had not overlooked the loss of the Greek ally and agreed with Ignatiev that "lessons must be taken."[56] However, he understood the "lessons" above all in general preparedness on the western and southwestern frontier—he called for construction of fortresses, communications and modernization of armaments[57]—and in a correct position in the Franco-Prussian contest rather than in the customary "Panslav" framework.

* * *

Taking into account the meager results achieved, the Moscow Congress (1867) and Panslav hopes brought about substantial advances to the Slavic Committee's movement.[58]

Rather than the growth of the committees, however, the writings of their ideologues was the most significant symptom testifying the rise of the militant Muscovy spirit. Besides the already mentioned Samarin's opus on the Russian borderlands, particularly the book by Nikolai Danilevskii, "Russia and Europe" and two pamphlets of Fadeev on the Russian army and the Eastern Question ("Armed forces of Russia"/Vooruzhenye sily Rossii/ and "Opinion on the Eastern Question" /Mnenie o Vostochnom voprose/, all published at the end of the 1860s, were with full justification taken abroad as the quintessence of the Moscow politico-military programme.[59]

Both Danilevskii and Fadeev preached an unabashed Machiavellism in the name of state interest, as did Katkov since 1863.

The basic laws of politics, wrote Danilevskii, are not different from those of nature. The criteria of morality may be applied to individuals with immortal souls; but as principles of state they are meaningless:

> An eye for an eye, a tooth for a tooth, a severe law, the Benthamian principle of utility, that is of a properly conceived self-interest—that is the law governing foreign policy, the law of international relations; there is no room in it for love or sacrifice.[60]

Fadeev expressed the same idea in soldiery terms. Countries like Sweden, where the army is not a "full guarantee of national security" do not have identical rules of political life with a first-class Power like Russia:

> A first-class Power is a nation or a political body existing independently of any rights and agreements and maintains these rights by its own force.[61]

Whereas Danilevskii's goal was to revitalize the old dream of Russian world dominance by giving it a modern, quasi-scientific coating, Fadeev's writings were primarily composed for the immediate military and foreign policy objectives and plans pursued by the Bariatinskii group. The General wrote to the following effect:

> Since the early 19th century 'we have only postponed open contest with Europe by . . . entering into her service, sacrificing all our national interest and almost ceasing to be Russians in a political sense.' Now, when Russia has thrown away the Holy Alliance burden, she 'must be ready for every consequence resulting from the resurrection of her historical individuality.' She cannot solve her problems by a mere domestic reform and neglect her great-power role. 'Decline, even temporary one, in external might is instantaneously reflected in social apathy or social strife.' In this sense, the 'decade of self-isolation' after the Crimean War has further 'accumulated the debt which ought to be repaid without delay and with a high rate of interest.'[62]

The situation in the non-Russian parts of the Empire made the task even more imperative. The borderlands "will drain the greatest sacrifices from the government and society, until decisive events persuade them that they are ours for good and beyond recall of destiny. The first successful war will radically change our present conditions; then a mere fragment of current effort will be more effective."[63]

The existing frontiers are in the long-term indefensible and Tsardom "must either extend its preeminence to the Adriatic or withdraw beyond the Dnieper." The great tasks cannot be accomplished by the seizure of the Straits and the Turkish possessions in the Balkans alone, the main battles are to be fought on the Vistula, because there stands the enemy, "the German race with its excessive demands."[64] As to the Constantinople goal, neither the Turks nor the Western Powers are a serious obstacle. But the Habsburg Monarchy presents a real problem: it has to be disposed of first inasmuch as it is bound to oppose Russia and it would be committing suicide to act otherwise. "The Eastern Question can be solved only in Austria, not in Turkey; the way to Tsargrad goes through Vienna."[65]

So, the Eastern, Polish and Black Sea questions are to be conceived as inextricably woen into each other. The annexation of Galicia ought to be the first step in the correct direction, owing to the fact that "this advanced position of the enemy within Russia's natural frontiers "both hinders her contacts with the Slavs and can be used as a springboard for an attack through Poland.[66]

Russia must take the initiative first, before her enemies, and establish her control over the whole eastern part of the continent. "In the present divided Europe, there is no place for a handful of petty nationalities . . . ; liberated Eastern Europe needs firm unifying ties, a common head with a common council, the direction of international and military policy in the hands of this head, the Tsar of Russia, the natural leader of all Slavs and Orthodox." There will be not a few opportunities to accomplish this great purpose; it should only be remembered that it has to be done in the near future and by means of force.[67]

The pamphlets of Fadeev, an American scholar observed, had "the power of a hammer-blow in its simplicity"; the book of Danilevskii, with its pseudoscientific stamp, provided the Moscow doctrine with a "sense of greatness and of confidence in the inevitable triumph."[68]

A specialist in botany and agriculture, inspired by Socialist theories, the author of "Russia and Europe" depicted the forthcoming mastery over the world as a logical result of a natural-historical process. Applying the principles of biological development to the development of mankind, he explained it as a cyclical course of growth, maturity, decay and death of successive cultural-historical (civilization) types. And "owing to God's will," he maintained, it would be crowned by a Socialist civilization created by Russia; a civilization which would make true all the aspirations ever cherished by Man, and which would be founded on an authentic economic democracy, not on a political democracy produced by the "Germano-Roman" civilization type.[69]

The conflict between civilizations being both key and highly positive phenomenon in world history, war is not only essential but a healthy precondition for the triumph of progress and inner recovery:

> We consider the very process of this inevitable war, and not only its desired results, salvatory and beneficial. For only this fight can sober our thought, can raise the popular spirit in all levels of our society . . . . We are not preaching war . . . we are merely asserting . . . that the struggle is inevitable and we submit that, though war is a great evil, there are much greater evils for which war can be just the cure . . . . [70]

Since the 18th century, the Germano-Roman civilization has entered into the phase of decline and decay and ought to be replaced by the Slavic one. So far, this has been prevented mainly by the Ottoman and Austrian empires, keeping the Slavic peoples subjected to them on a level of mere ethnographic material. Thus, both these empires must be destroyed first; they lost their raison d'être anyway and should be disposed of "for hygienic reasons, as any other corpse."[71] With the rest of Europe and the world, "peaceful co-existence" is possible, but only if Russian-Slavic rights are fully acknowledged; and that contingency is highly improbable. Consequently, the new Slavic civilization may come to flower only after the final solution of the Eastern Question, Russian military triumph over the West and the establishment of a Slavic federation under the leadership and hegemony of Tsardom—the "Panslav Union", consisting of the Russian Empire, the Kingdom of Bohemia, Moravia and Slovakia, the Kingdom of the Serbs, Croats and Slovenes, the Kingdom of Bulgaria, the Kingdoms of Rumania, Greece, and Hungary, and Constantinople as the capital of the federation. "The Panslav Union is the only firm foundation on which an authentic Slavic civilization can grow; it is an indispensable precondition. . . . And thus for every Slav. . . after God and his Holy Church the idea of Slavdom must be higher than any earthly good."[72]

Russia is strong enough to achieve this historical goal. Discipline, obedience, readiness to sacrifice rather than money and military organization will decide. Her cause is the just one and once war will "loose the bonds of diplomatic complacency," all Slavic peoples will rise in response to her appeal. "And thus will begin a new, Slavic era in world history."[73]

For the foreign-policy concept of Russian nationalist extremism, Danilevskii's and Fadeev's writings were something of a "manifest destiny." They disclosed what Katkov would never have considered wise to pronounce openly—that in the ideology promoting permanent national vigilance, an unrelenting struggle against any foreign opposition and internal dissent, war and expansion leading to a world-wide supremacy were the clue and the ultimate objective. Much more directly than the Strastnyi Boulevard, they made attractive the overall offensive.

There was, however, a big paradox in these appeals. At the time they were presented to the reading public, domestic and external realities offered far less glamorous outlook.

CHAPTER 9

KATKOV "IN OPPOSITION":
RUSSIA BETWEEN THE PRUSSIAN AND
THE FRENCH OPTIONS
(1868-1871)

> Can Europe remain indifferent while one of
> the Great Powers is being crushed and al-
> most abolished? Can her right to participate
> in the settlement of the fate of so important
> a member of her system (as is France) be
> disputed? No, if Europe is a reality, one can-
> not stay aloof at the sight of a catastrophe
> of such consequences (as is the Prussian vic-
> tory) and she cannot abdicate a right to
> interpose without her becoming a mere
> empty name.
> Katkov

Since early 1868, to an even greater extent than before, the Russian debate on Balkan policy unfurled into that concerning foreign policy in general and the attitude to the Franco-Prussian contest in particular.

There, the divisive lines somewhat shifted. While the Thunderer and the Muscovites became virulently anti-Prussian, some extremists in the elite (Ignatiev, Stremoukhov[1]) veered in the opposite direction. The basic pattern, the broadening chasm between the official stance and public opinion, however, was even more pronounced. Almost the whole of society followed Katkov's path. Gorchakov, Miliutin, Grand Duke Konstantin and probably many other high dignitaries were in sympathy with it, but the St. Petersburg line increasingly appropriated the traditional Romanov-Hohenzollern taint. At Court, the pro-German faction led by Grand Duchess Helen,[2] in the government the Shuvalov group uncompromisingly connected the Prussian with the conservative monarchical cause. And above all, Alexander had, after the Paris experience of 1867, been firmly convinced that his old option had been correct. Unlimited confidence in King William, always paramount in his reasoning, now grew into a dogma: "he can count upon me as I count upon him," the Tsar stressed.[3]

Katkov's judgments, as indicated in the context with the "Ostsee problem," were at war with those of his sovereign. Whatever disgust he might have felt for the French Emperor, it paled by considerations he assessed as substantial. With the Balkan development taking an unfavorable turn, he conceived the understanding with the Second Empire even more imperative: "no other alternative is available for Russia. . .in the present state of affairs, her whole task rests in escaping subservience to German policy through Prussia."[4] And since he found the fundamental national interest jeopardized by the Tsar, he did not hesitate to enter into an almost open polemics with him.

The German party on the Neva had its most persuasive argument in the undisputable French unreliability. To ward it off, Katkov and the Muscovites counteracted by giving to the question "to whom may we trust" opposite, anti-Prussian connotation.

In January 1868, the *Kreuzzeitung* by denouncing Panslav ventures and calling for furthering the "German mission" of Austria in the Balkans, delivered the excuse to sharpen the polemics precisely in this vein. Without delay, in two boldly formulated editorials, Katkov set out for an attack, broaching the thesis of Prussia's duplicity and at the same time identifying the St. Petersburg position as that of "subservience to alien goals" against which he had so earnestly warned:

> Only 'extreme blindness and brainlessness could induce her (Russia) to seek the solution of the Eastern Question's secrets in an exclusive alliance with Prussia.' There is 'only France which (still) could be Russia's natural ally.' Because the 'shadows of misunderstanding do not allow us (so far) think of separate alliance of (these) two nations, a free-hand policy remains to sole possible course to pursue.'[5]

Just before the editorials were published, Gorchakov and Prince Reuss had met (on 11 and 17 January) to discuss the press polemics and the "Katkov problem."[6] Thus, as a token of good will, the *Pravitelstvennyi vestnik* (Governmental Messenger) reacted on the fresh invectives by a statement containing a rebuke to the Moscow daily, but, reasonably enough, the Prussian diplomat did not envisage any change. The publicist, he wrote to Bismarck, "knows the power he possesses and is quite well aware that it covers the architect of Russian foreign policy, too."[7] Such, indeed was the situation in a nutshell.

The Strastnyi Boulevard and the Winter Palace continued to go their separate ways, with the Russian Chancellor in covert sympathy with the former. Alive to the effect his campaign produced—German diplomats reported "animate debate on Prussian enmity"[8]—the editor could reject the official statement and dwell on his opposition to the St. Petersburg-Berlin axis.[9] And when Bismarck responded evasively on the Tsar's alliance proposal of 4 March,[10] Gorchakov obtained a quite considerable latitude to support the Katkovian plea.

The annual report of the Singers' Bridge, written some time in the first half of 1868, argued on the pivotal continental issue as follows:

(1) to keep the door open for rapprochement with France in the event that she would deliver positive and clear-cut proof of her plain dealing;

(2) to uphold good relations with Prussia on a basis of mutual interest, without limiting, with this intimacy, one's own liberty of action;

(3) to maintain an equilibrium between France and Prussia, taking, at the same time, advantage of their rivalry to further Russian goals by all possible means.[11]

Meanwhile, Katkov had been steadily broadening the scope of his criticism. So he attacked deviation from the traditional principle of supporting lesser German dynasties and maintained that unification would have an inevitable consequence in the drive for annexation of all territories with a German population, i.e. also Tsardom's Baltic provinces.[12]

Turning upside down the main argument raised by the German party, the publicist blamed the one-sided orientation on Prussia for the manifest lack of French interest in Russian friendship; and persevered in the claim that despite everything, the Tuileries would in the end stop their foolish game with the Polish question and with the Crimean bloc and pay the requested price for favorable neutrality. Then he went even further:

> The St. Petersburg government had no reason whatever 'to value Prussian friendship higher than that of any other Power.' Russia should 'disappoint all our enemies and without delay offer to France an alliance treaty.' 'The genuine, correctly conceived interests of Russia and France are by no means mutually contradictory; there is no point on the globe where they could not be harmonized and where Russia and France would not be able to help each other.'[13]

* * *

By late 1868 Bismarck found his patience with the Russian press exhausted. "For a long time we have learned to be used to hostile feelings from these quarters, but the current attacks exceed all measure in their unreasonableness and shamelessness," he wrote to his diplomatic mission in St. Petersburg and directed it to purchase a "special Russian organ" which would neutralize the campaign and promised adequate financial means for the purpose.[14]

The Prussians on the Neva realized, of course, that it would be next to impossible to succeed in such an undertaking and that the only chance lay in corrupting the Thunderer. Already two years before, in October 1866, the military plenipotentiary Schweinitz had advised King William on the role of the publicist and his daily: "regarded by the hundreds of thousands as an oracle," the *Moskovskiia vedomosti* has become in terms of its impact probably "the most influential in the world."[15] Now, in January 1869, Reuss made a similar observation. Katkov's "national Russianism" acquired such a popularity that nobody could stop him; every other newspaper had incomparably lesser authority and none could discharge the task demanded by Bismarck; society might be swayed solely through the Strastnyi Boulevard.[16]

Schweinitz, empowered to negotiate with the Muscovite, asked Feoktistov and Count Apraksin for mediation. But the attempt, apparently half-hearted, misfired as badly as could have been presumed. With relish, Katkov turned down the bait and later ridiculed it in his editorials; a rumor even circulated that he had complained to Gorchakov and threatened to expose Schweinitz publicly if he were not to leave his post.[17]

The affair just animated the editor in his crusade. The Paris conference on the Greko-Turkish crisis provided him with another convenient pretext. He contended that the Prussian representative had sided with Russia's enemies and so once again it had been confirmed that the option for Berlin was all wrong; the government should use the opportunity when Prussia "anew demonstrated her true self" to correct this mistake. No ties whatever ought to be recognized with a Power which had deserted Russia and delivered Greeks to the mercy of foes.[18]

* * *

In the months preceding the Franco-Prussian war the course solicited by Katkov and, albeit with more caution, by Gorchakov appeared to be winning ground.

Vienna moved to improve the Russian connections. The meeting of the two Chancellors, Gorchakov and Beust, at Ouchy was visibly inspired by the common will to contain Prussia. In November 1869, a new French Ambassador General Fleury arrived at St. Petersburg with the determination to bring about a dramatic improvement in the chilly atmosphere existing between the two courts.

Also Alexander seemed to be motivated by the wish to preserve peace rather than to further the Romanov-Hohenzollern solidarity. Although he again affronted society by bestowing on King William the Grand Cross of St. George (December 1868), he left enough latitude to his Chancellor's undertakings and even assisted them. While earlier he had on matters of German unity "talked the language, pure and simple, of Prussian diplomats and newspapers financed by Berlin," now he implored William and Bismarck to uphold tranquility and order in international affairs and respect the independence of the German states south of the Main River.[19]

In the meantime, the Moscow editor exuded undiminishing pugnacity. He wrote that his programme "does not require diplomatic agreements and treaties . . . only . . . that France should in everything pursue French policy and Russia Russian policy," but in fact considered an understanding which would prevent Germany being forged into a "fifty-million strong military Power" a task "dictated by the force of things."[20] And, because Gorchakov lacked the courage to engage the German party in a full-fledged confrontation in this matter, he commenced to be increasingly impatient even with him. In vain Jomini, one of the Chancellor's deputies, and Feoktistov assured the publicist that the Foreign Ministry did not intend to "throw itself into the Prussian embrace"; the Singers' Bridge was changing in his vigilant eyes into a "Foreign Ministry for Russian affairs."[21]

While observing that weariness took hold of society and Shuvalov group tightened its grip over it, diplomatic reports continued to describe the Strastnyi Boulevard as a "power which nobody would dare to assail." The "secret understanding" between the editor and the Chancellor was believed to be still in force and getting the upper hand over the German party; the sensation created by the booklet written by Katkov's well known lieutenant Colonel Moller, in which the bid for the Russo-French alliance appeared in especially aggressive formulations, probably originated precisely in these beliefs.[22]

The recurrent expectations that the St. Petersburg friends of Prussia would be driven to defensive and isolation, however, proved ill-advised.

Gorchakov's endeavours met obstacles that could not be overcome. Although Vienna paraded willingness to conciliation, the German party prevented a fresh start. Only full Austrian compliance in the Polish and Balkan questions, Shuvalov told Minister Chotek, might bring it about. Vienna, naturally, would not pay that price. Nor did the French mission of Fleury produce any tangible effect, when the Winter Palace and the Tuileries manifested just their usual obstinacy.[23]

Poised to the attack, the gendarme chief moved to fulfill the promise he had given to the Prussians that the repeated official protests would in the end sway the prevaricating Tsar to shackle the Moscow trouble-maker and also get rid of the "half-childish vain fool" Gorchakov.[24]

The long-awaited tug-of-war between the governmental majority and the Strastnyi Boulevard was opened by the memoir "On abuse of the printed word," circulated by Interior Minister Timashev.

Like earlier documents composed on the theme, it stated that the *Moskovskiia vedomosti* had ignored all warnings and had not ceased to spread suspicions and intolerance, inciting the "still unripe public opinion"; that it had been perpetuating "systematic agitation" with the purpose of compromising "high governmental personalities." Its editor, General Timashev summarized, "cannot be left room without the prestige of the government being irreparably injured."[25]

The memoir was discussed (probably in the first days of January 1870) in an Extraordinary Council chaired by Alexander. The debate and the conclusions taken were pronounced strictly confidential, but it transpired that despite a "terrible row" raised by Shuvalov and Timashev, Gorchakov managed to persuade the participants that "in the view of the present situation, it is important to have an independent press."[26]

For a brief moment it looked like the very repetition of the Valuev-Katkov contest in 1864-1866. The editor flew at the pro-German faction in his most impetuous assault so far, repeating the keyword that "the center of the conspiracy does not rest in Warsaw or Vilna, but on the banks of the Neva." He asserted that now "all the parties of evil" were "united in an action openly directed against both Russia and the present reign"; and that to "stop them became almost impossible," because the values and principles of sound government have been "insulted and shattered."[27]

Then, however, the affair unfolded in a manner which neither contemporaries nor historians could explain.[28] When on 20 January the Interior Ministry responded on the diatribe by a formal warning, Katkov, in surprising contrast to his previous conduct, without delay accepted the verdict and conceded that the gloomy picture he had just drawn was incorrect.[29]

It seems that the Muscovite was well alive to the difference in the "vigilant spirit" in 1863-1866 and in the sulking, passive dissatisfaction with the "anti-national" trend in St. Petersburg now; and that he decided to make this concession to preserve his press tribune for the crucial battle on Russian option in the momentous test of continental balance. But there also lay the limits of the just described first victory of the government over the publicist, however important it might have been per se. On the Franco-Prussian issue, Katkov would not retract.[30] In fact, his opposition to the policies identified by the public with the Tsar's person had never been so flagrant as in the forthcoming war crisis.

* * *

While Napoleon and his ministers, preparing for the fatal confrontation, continued to blunder,[31] Bismarck played perfectly on Alexander's susceptibilities. "Would Russia permit the destruction of Prussia and French armies in Berlin and Posen?", he asked in a message sent on 14 July 1870. The Tsar responded by promising that he would hold Austria back if need arrived—this time with 300,000 men; and in another token of goodwill, he agreed to cede the guns recently ordered at Krupp's.[32]

Informed earlier about the Tsar's intentions, Katkov had written two warning editorials. This time, his reasoning was somewhat at variance from the usual. The Russo-French entente was not alluded and the conflict presented as an "entirely alien matter" from which Russia should be fully detached. Nonetheless, the meaning was unmistakable: any undertaking, "for example, to form an observation corps to bind Austria to prevent her in joining the war," would be a futile and harmful measure.[33]

The efficacy of the armed demonstration on the Austrian border was also questioned inside the government. Still, when France declared war to Prussia on 19 July, only a minor concession was offered to public opinion: Tsardom declared its non-armed neutrality "as long as Russian interests are not impaired."

Unhappy about the course events had taken, Katkov resorted to the hope that France would be victorious.[34] From the very outset, however, the progress of military operations revealed that he—like most observers, including Russian and Austrian statesmen who had calculated with a long struggle and/or French preponderance—grossly erred. Almost overnight, Europe was faced with the prospect of victorious Prussia ordaining her destinies.

The consequences of the final breakdown of the post-Crimean power balance on Russia were necessarily both instantaneous and far-reaching. At no time after 1856 had the contradictions in her policy been revealed in such a dramatic way and never had the winds in St. Petersburg changed so rapidly.

* * *

In the first phase up to French capitulation at Sedan, military preparations against Austria[35] were coupled with diplomatic action with an opposite purpose.

Alexander had his moment of afterthought. True, he felt emotionally elevated by the Prussian triumphs which he somewhat perceived as revenge for the Crimea and which promised him safety in Poland. Bearing the responsibility for Russian great-power status, though, he could not overlook the broader implications which had been so often stressed by Gorchakov and in still more downright manner by the Muscovites. So, he engaged himself fully in his Chancellor's effort to create a diplomatic front of Russia, Austria-Hungary and England, interpose in the conflict and save France and the continental balance.[36]

The press vehemently sponsored the diplomatic initiative. Katkov coined the thesis that since Alexander I the existence of a strong France had been the key desideratum in continental policy; a claim which was to appear frequently in Russian statements after 1871. The comments of the Moscow editor, however, were not those of a loyal subject approving the authorities. He castigated the Winter Palace's fear of the "Polish spectre" and other beliefs which according to him had led to the present disaster: neither would French victory have been harmful to Russia, nor would it lead to another Polish crisis. Abandoning his former judgment he now claimed that the real culprits in the troubles on the Vistula had been the English, not the French; the latter "had been deceived like us." Once more, he ridiculed as "extreme simplicity of mind" the hope that Prussia would help to solve the Slavic question.[37]

The Prussians were greatly annoyed. Reuss accused Gorchakov openly of complicity with the Strastnyi Boulevard, of turning into a "mere instrument of the Old-Russian party."[38] Nothing, however, would induce Bismarck to yield. Holding, in military victory, the trump-card nobody could beat, he was resolved to deny any interference in the peacemaking process. Moreover, the German party at the Romanov court furnished him with an important means of leverage.

On 10 August, Grand Duchess Helen apprised Berlin that she and her friends would attenuate the effort to harness Prussia by raising the Paris Treaty issue. Two weeks later, Bismarck joined the maneuvre by a formal proposal to include Russian demands in the German peace terms. Followed by the French surrender at Sedan (on 2 September), this produced another shift on the scene.

* * *

In Russian society and the press, the despair over Sedan was enormous.[39] Before the event, Katkov had called for the turning of non-armed neutrality into an armed one; now, he insisted that there must be a swift intervention in the imbroglio, "because tomorrow everything may change and the balance problem become an anachronism" in a Europe dominated by Germany or by an Anglo-German bloc. In the crucial editorial commenting on Sedan, he coupled a frantic interventionist plea with a scarcely veiled attack on the Romanov House policies. King William, he argued, demonstrated how a dynasty should identify itself with the "common national idea and common patriotic front";

conversely, a sad fate was in store for those dynasties which descended into "instruments of alien interests."[40]

For Alexander, on the contrary, Sedan was a "revenge for Sevastopol"; and, instead of making him more circumspect, the public dissatisfaction drove him along the path the German party and the Prussians pointed him in: he chose the Paris Treaty revision as the device to rally society behind the throne. On 27 October, at the meeting of the Ministerial Council at Tsarskoe Selo, he announced his intention. No serious complications would arise, he asserted, if Russia would get rid of the humiliating clauses: Prussia promised her support, the other Powers would acquiece in the end and even the English opposition would be vociferous only in the terms of "war of pen and ink."[41]

On 31 October, the Chancellor dispatched an official circular on Russia's restoration of her rights on the Black Sea to the Powers and on 15 November let it be published in the press.

Envisaging, despite Alexander's assurances, a serious crisis, the government exerted itself in the effort to procure a positive public response. Timashev assembled St. Petersburg's editors and administered stern warning to them:

> We must be prepared for every eventuality and the duty of the press is to behave according to the gravity of the moment. Above all it should be kept in mind that the 'big step made by Russia' has been rendered possible because Prussian sympathy and that assistance from this quarter is also expected now. Thus, the 'ultrapatriotic excesses' which have inflamed the Ostsee question must not be repeated. The Tsar cannot tolerate 'even the slightest insult of a friendly Power. If you continue in a hostile tone against her, then bear in mind that the government will not only use threats but apply strict sanctions.'[42]

The Moscow editor was handled separately and with circumspection. The Interior Minister sent to him an appeal through a special emissary (Veselago) to "tune his lyre to merry music" and "not incite national feelings."[43]

But neither society nor the Muscovite reacted in the way the authorities had hoped; nothing was reminiscent of the spirit of 1863 when

Europe was defied in the "war of démarches." Albeit the return to the Black Sea "pleased the much injured Russian selfindulgence,"[44] the worries about the consequences obscured it. The stock exchange was in panic and rumors on military preparations in the south furthered overall nervousness. More importantly, while in St. Petersburg the assembly representing the populace obediently passed the required loyal resolution, in Moscow a defiant mood again took the upper hand.

Katkov's editorials took a marked exception from the St. Petersburg action:

> Instead of building first a naval force on the Black Sea and then confronting Europe with the accomplished fact, a merely inexpedient and futile gesture was made. The risks undertaken is not commensurate to the purely formal significance the circular bears. 'Why was it necessary to impose the word before the deed?'
>
> Moreover, 'our politicians' are all wrong in the assumption that 'after defeating France, Germany will help us to solve the Eastern Question.' Not St. Petersburg but Vienna will profit from the situation; whilst Russia has not even asked for Southern Bessarabia, Austria may, with Bismarck's connivance, tighten her grip over the Balkan Slavs and perhaps annex Rumania.[45]

These comments roused a formidable echo. On the Neva too, a correspondent reported, "after the first minute of instinctively felt joy," the opinion whowith shifted to embrace Katkovian arguments.[46] The Court elite raged against the publicist. Also his high-placed sympathizers—the Tsarina, Tiutchev, Stremoukhov—condemned his stance and the last named publicly attacked it in the *Golos*.[47] Soon the affair took on still bigger proportions when the Moscow city duma capped the defiance. Its members signed an address to Alexander composed by Aksakov, containing strong protest against the system introduced by the Shuvalov clique. It asked for more political and religious freedom, return to the reform policy. The people, the address read, "persist in seeing in You the reliable protector of liberties . . . and expects only from you the crowning of Your noble intentions, above all in giving space for (free) opinion and the printed word . . . ."[48]

Fortunately for the Russian establishment, Europe reacted to the renunciation of the Black Sea clauses in the manner Alexander predicted.

True, Austria facing her foreign policy in shambles, responded with unexpected ire and on 29 November, Beust instructed his London Ambassador to remove any doubt whether Vienna considered itself bound by the tripartite alliance treaty of 1856. In the British press and public too, there was a genuine war outcry. But nothing was to come out of it.

The London cabinet had no intention to go beyond diplomatic presure. Gladstone, the Prime Minister, was particularly determined on that point. "We have a highly inflammable and susceptible state of the public mind to deal with," he wrote to Foreign Secretary Granville, so it would be "an immense responsibility to take any military measure whatever at such a period." With emphasis, he even rejected a proposal for a "little strengthening of the Mediteranean fleet."[39] This stance, of course, forced the Austrians to prudence. "Situated as we are between Russia and Germany, with a very explosive Slavic element on our southern frontiers, we are to be very careful and we are able to take a firm stand only if we are certain of being seconded and supported," Ambassador Apponyi summed it up.[50] The last Power which might have resisted by force, Turkey, was still less inclined to take the risks. The Porte, in fact, was enormously relieved when Ignatiev assured it that Tsardom did not contemplate any further steps.

Consequently, Bismarck's formula "a conference before hostilities" easily won the day; and the conference itself (on 17 January-13 March 1871, in London) confirmed the obvious. Tsardom's diplomatic victory was only partly offset by granting the Sultan the authority to open the Straits in case of emergency to "vessels of war of friendly and allied Powers." Overjoyed, Alexander ordered "Te Deum" to be sung in the Winter Palace and bestowed Gorchakov with the title of the "most illustrious Prince."

Perhaps wishing to spite them both, Katkov wrote on 24 March still another provocative editorial about "a cheap service" obliging Russia to bear "the heavy burden of gratitude" towards Berlin.[51] Nonetheless, at that time the restive mood had finally evaporated. Resignation mixed by relief that the country had escaped war allowed Shuvalov to discipline also the Muscovites: Prince Cherkasskii, the extremist head of the city duma, had to resign and the terrified body adopted a new address to the Tsar in customary servile wording.[52]

Tsardom entered the Armed Peace era in a spirit portrayed by Turgenev in his "Smoke." For several years before the "Slavic question" was to shatter it again, inertia seemed to permeat every public sphere. In it, even the vitriolic Thunderer "went downhill" and his daily appeared in many eyes to be but the main governmental mouthpiece.[53] Moved by the Turgenev novel, a contemporary drew a sombre picture:

> Nothing can surpass the banality that exists among us today. A passion for gain, for the acquisition of money, is the most glaring and outstanding feature of contemporary society. In everything else, either complete apathy reigns or there are momentary outbursts of noble decisions and inclinations which all go up in smoke.[54]

PART TWO

SOWING THE WIND AND REAPING THE WHIRLWIND:
TRIUMPH AND FAILURE OF PANSLAVISM
(1871-1881)

CHAPTER 10

BACK IN THE FOLD:
THE THREE EMPERORS' LEAGUE
(1871-1873)

> Since the fall of Napoleon, nobody has
> threatened the European peace so exten-
> sively as Slavophile Russia.
> Bismarck

> If I would accept the thought that I might
> have at any time to turn into an enemy of
> the Tsar and Russia, I would consider myself
> a traitor.
> Bismarck

> I flatter myself at having been the first in
> Europe to break with the old tradition with
> which the Western Powers have innoculated
> all the cabinets, namely, that Constantinople
> in Russian hands would be an European
> danger. I consider that a false idea and I do
> not see why the English interest must be an
> European interest. As for the interests of
> Germany, they will decidedly not be affect-
> ed by that eventuality, and I believe, on the
> contrary, that the Russian nation will be-
> come more converted to the cause of peace
> when their ambition has at least reached its
> goal. . . .
> Bismarck

> You too often lose sight of the importance
> of being one of three of the European chess-
> board . . . . All politics reduces itself to this
> formula—to try to be one of the three, so
> long as the world is governed by the unstable
> equilibrium of five Great Powers.
> Bismarck

It has been widely accepted that the peace illusion after 1871, that "blindness of almost everyone in the Western world,"[1] was mainly due to Bismarck's genius. Historians, however, may with good reasons subject this view to critical scrutiny. Unquestionably, the great Chancellor considered Germany after the victory over France and unification a "saturated" Power; and, resisting the appeals of the military as well as his own allurement to finish France for good, he devoted his consummate skill to create an alliance system and manipulate local balances and tensions with the purpose of not only safeguarding the preeminent position of his Reich in Europe and isolating the beaten western rival, but also of preserving general stability. Yet, however clever he might have been in his moves, the net ultimate results were negative and his effort with full justification described as a "gigantic exercise in wishful thinking."[2]

There were, of course, enormous objective obstacles on the Chancellor's path. Still it appears that it was precisely his failing genius after Sedan which was essential cause of his troubles to come. Although he remained an unparalleled master in diplomatic maneuvre and political tactics, in the crucial strategic decisions taken from the Franco-Prussian war onwards he based his judgments often on oversimplified or entirely wrong propositions which inevitably kindled opposite or at least ambivalent effects; and his options with immediate positive results unfurled in the longer perspective into evident liabilities.

Owing to the manner in which he treated France, Bismarck could not be trusted as a peacemaker: he "had about himself an European credibility gap."[3] Statesmen and public opinion everywhere perceived in him a new Napoleon craving for Germanic dominance in the world. Professor Medlicott fittingly characterized him as a victim of both his personality and repute, who failed in his new role of a man of peace, "because the memories evoked by his great name were too strong; partly, however, because his nerves and mentality did not allow play it with any real conviction."[4]

Bismarck decided to build up his system on traditional foundations of the three conservative Empires. There he expected to find the elements firmly attached to the monarchic cause of "order and civilization" which would be eager to help him in his efforts. Taking this option and pursuing its stubbornly, he at the same time proved overly prejudiced to put German relations with the French and English on sounder footing. Intermittently intimidating and humiliating the former, he narrowed his elbow room still more by carelessly handling the latter; his occasional attempts to counterbalance Russian hostility by an agreement with London were half-hearted and "drained into sand the moment Bismarck was certain that he had organized his relations with Vienna and St. Petersburg to his liking."[5]

Although perhaps less conspicious, nowhere were the limitations of the Chancellor and his system of greater consequence than in the Eastern Question. Bismarck neither understood nor really tried to understand it. "Everybody who would wish to teach me about the Eastern Question is a deceiver," he proclaimed.[6] He conceived the complex process of disintegration of the Ottoman Empire from a very limited standpoint, only in the old confines of diplomatic game, underestimating vitality of national movements and the impact of conflicting great-power interests on European stability. "It would be a triumph of our statesmanship if we succeeded in keeping the Eastern ulcer opened, thereby jarring the harmony of the other Powers in order to secure our own peace,"[7] ran his most fallacious idea.

True, the Chancellor did not subscribe to it entirely. But, owing to it, he considered the Russian drive towards Constantinople and the Straits propitious to his scheme of local tensions and balances and was ready to encourage it. The commitment of Russia in what he regarded as a periphery would in his opinion bind her hands and entangle her in a drawn contest with England: "If a conflict between Russia and England breaks out, it would do us no injury whatever. . ."; they "can do each other little harm and we may remain calm observers of the struggle."[8] Furthermore, he believed that by encouraging Russian aspirations he would earn gratitude and strengthen his hands of the friendly St. Petersburg moderates against the Moscow party.

This focal calculation proved completely wrong. Always dissatisfied with the measure of German support on the Constantinople and Balkan issues, the Russians only grew more distrustful of the Chancellor's designs. Worse still, unable to channel Russian restive spirits exclusively towards Constantinople or another sphere of Anglo-Russian contest, Central Asia, Bismarck had to see the weakest point in his system, Austro-Russian rivalry, fatally exposed.

After the formation of the German Empire, the tendency of the Dual Monarchy to seek in southeastern Europe the confirmation of her great-power status, compensations for prestige losses and an outlet for her commerce grew in prominence. For obvious reasons, well predicted from 1866 by Katkov, the Chancellor sponsored the Austrian drive. He realized that it would put the cooperation of the three monarchies under heavy strain, yet cherished another unsubstantiated hope—that owing to their financial difficulties and military weakness, Vienna and St. Petersburg would ultimately agree to settle on dividing the "Turkish heritage" into their respective spheres of influence. What could have been perhaps achieved in the time of Catherine II and Kaunitz, however, now turned out to be an outright impossibility. Nobody would be able to draw a line of division which did not injure some substantial interest. The Russian tradition of historical mission, the Austrian economic claims in the directions of the Danube and Salonika, and the Hungarian determination to resist both the Russian presence in the Balkans and the integration of additional Slavic territories into the monarchy's orbit occurred as incompatible elements. Tensions stemming from the emancipation efforts of the Balkan peoples, were constantly shaking the supreme edifice of the Bismarckian system, the Three Emperors' bloc, and by no device could the Chancellor stop or at least mitigate the process for a longer period. Each of these crises roused intense anti-Austrian enmity in Russia and vice versa. Worse still, the contending partners required from Berlin a clear-cut stance; no proclamation of German disinterestedness and impartiality could liberate Bismarck from the horns of the dilemma. "If one joins Austria, then he has in Russia an implacable foe and French ally; in the other event, Russia will grow exceedingly powerful," the Chancellor summed up his fatal "Optionfrage" for the eventuality of a Russo-Austrian war.[9]

D'Oubril, the Russian Ambassador to Berlin, rated Bismarck "too good a mathematician" to back the weaker side, i.e. the Habsburg Monarchy.[10] Many shared this judgment; and, indeed, the Chancellor seemed sometimes to stand on the brink of the Russian option. Franco-Russian entente was the worst of the coalition spectres haunting him, and this was the way to escape it. Besides, he probably trusted the Tsars and the St. Petersburg elite more than Francis Joseph and the Vienna Catholic aristocratic circles.[11] Ultimately however, both domestic considerations—"public opinion in Germany would not permit us to go against Austria in her war with Russia"—and those of general power balance—"only as long as Austria exists can we keep Russia in check"[12]—pushed him in the opposite direction.

This, of course, made the gradual estrangement between St. Petersburg and Berlin inevitable and with it, the emergence of the dreaded "unnatural alliance" of Tsardom with republican France a logical consequence. Katkov's quest for a "true national policy" was to proffer the most revealing part of the whole story.

* * *

The extremely harsh conditions imposed by Bismarck in the Frankfurt Treaty (10 May 1871), shocked Russian society and made its revulsion towards the new German Empire if possible even stronger than that felt earlier towards Prussia. The ostentatious gestures of the Tsar who showered the triumphant Hohenzollerns and their generals with congratulations and decorations were deeply detested. "Never before," Feoktistov wrote in his memoirs, "had our government appeared in such a contradiction to public opinion than at the time when the Prussians crushed France.[13] Even the imperial family was badly split on the issue.[14]

The Russian press with Katkov at its helm poured forth defiant feelings. The Moscow publicist snubbed Alexander for ascribing too great a value to mutual devotion with Emperor William and for expecting German gratitude:

> Between states and peoples, gratefulness is an empty word. There, nobody bothers about personal relations. Persons change, states remain . . . the force of facts overcomes the individual will. No personal friendship can alter the fact that German supremacy on the continent imposes upon our motherland the most grave dangers.[15]

In vain, though, the Muscovite and all opponents of "Alexander's line" looked for an alternative; except from complete isolation, there was none left.

For awhile they might have still pinned their hope on Vienna, where the so-called fundamental articles (September 1871) seemed to inaugurate a policy of federalization and reconciliation with the Slavic element. In a laudatory account, Katkov envisaged a new era in the Habsburg Monarchy when a "Slavic policy" would prevail both in domestic and external affairs; and in order to encourage it, he made repeated assurances that Russia had "abandoned the path of war and entered that of peaceful action and moral rapprochement."[16]

But the good omen passed quickly. While there was a violent reaction that Austrian Germans and Magyars against the fundamental articles, a dramatic turn in foreign policy had already taken place in the direction precisely opposite to that wished by the Russians. On 18 May, Chancellor Beust in a memoir to the Emperor recognized that his anti-Prussian course had failed; to find a new balance, he proposed to make a bidding to Berlin, which would prevent the "unnatural" Hohenzollern-Romanov alliance and retain the perspective of aggrandizement in the Balkans. The meetings of German and Austrian leading statesmen at Gastein, Ischl and Salzburg (September-October) demonstrated that the new trend had been set in motion. The Singers' Bridge evaluated the entrevues as a "possible alliance, albeit without final and definite aims"[17] and the further events only furthered the Russian uneasiness. On 25 October, the "federalist" ministry of Hohenwarth fell amidst the wild enthusiasm of Vienna's crowds and on 8 November the former Hungarian revolutionary, Count Gyula Andrássy, replaced Beust as a joint Austro-Hungarian Foreign Minister.

Panic-stricken by the prospect of a hostile Germanic bloc, the Moscow party was in disarray while St. Petersburg hastened to accentuate still more Russo-Prussian solidarity. On the occasion of the visit of Prince Frederick Charles and Marshal Moltke, the Tsar hailed in his toast the "fighting brotherhood of our armies" and the "closest friendship uniting us" as eternal values and the "best guarantee of peace and lawful order."[18]

In the editorial of 26 December 1871, Katkov himself bowed before the hard realities. In marked contradiction to his prior statements, he portrayed Russia and Germany as two stalwarts of peace:

> In the good relations established between them, there is no reason to see anything like the Holy Alliance; they are 'serving only as the

safeguard of general peace, presenting no menace to anybody'; their cooperation is 'necessary to their mutual interests as well as to the interests of Europe.'[19]

The statement completed the publicist's temporary retreat to a more modest, in a way less independent position, first hinted in his repentance in January 1870. True, he would not renounce his ambition to be the arbiter in the matter of national policy or depart from his basic concept. Speaking to Prince Frederick, he stressed that everybody must respect the essentials of the "national direction," i.e. that "Russia alone should be the judge of what was in her interest." Yet, he was ready to conform in his writings and ventures to the changed conditions; a blind anti-German hate would not be the leading motive determining Russian conduct, he assured the Prussian guest.[20]

So, in domestic policies, the editor was going, until the end of the "Shuvalov era" (1874), to act in accord with the pro-German gendarme chief; and, until the death of Alexander II (1881), he was to abstain from discussing the potentially anti-German theme of Russian borderlands. In external affairs, he threw away the French card as useless and commenced to look for an arrangement which would harmonize national interest with the existence of the Bismarckian system.

* * *

Owing to the absence of an alternative, so distinctively mirrored by Katkov's volte face, it seemed that "Alexander's line" would now prevail in undiluted form. In fact, the actual development was to unwind at considerable divergence from this notion and the Katkovian realism was to remain a minority option. Even in the establishment, although in subdued tones, the pro-German course continued to be questioned by many as one "founded on personal sympathies between monarchs, not on (real) interests of both the states."[21]

There were in particular two centers where the enmity towards the powerful Reich had never been restrained. The first was in the Anichkov Palace, the seat of the their apparent. There, the future Alexander III attracted a motley of "patriotic conservatives" more or less connected with the Moscow party.[22] The second may be identified with the Miliutin faction. The War Minister, as Reuss reported in 1872, was firmly convinced that Russia would "sooner or later be attacked by Germany," because "Germany had crushed all her other neighbors and must do the same with Russia in order to freely give her orders to Europe."[23] In virtue of the absolute predominance of this view among the General-Staff's "professors," the military planning went at cross purposes with official guidelines. Thus, in the midst of the Russian honeymoon with the two Germanic powers, in 1873, a war plan against them was elaborated by Miliutin's chief aide, General Obruchev.[24]

Gorchakov's almost paranoic jealousy of his German rival was another important factor. It sufficed that someone would name Bismarck simply "the Chancellor" for the old man to explode: "What Chancellor? There are two chancellors—Bismarck and me!" People around him claimed that he "lived in his thoughts in Berlin rather than in his ministerial cabinet."[25] Most certainly, the Prince craved to injure his foe wherever he possibly could; and the latter accused him quite deservedly of being motivated in his deeds "by personal ill-will, which was stronger than his cognizance of responsibility towards Russia."[26]

Katkov censured this "policy of feelings";[27] but again German diplomats had to observe with dismay that injured Russian pride which could not stomach Prussian ascendancy, left the "most illustrious Prince" enough room to play.[28] Alexander II himself, despite all the manifestations to the contrary, was obviously not free from the misgivings that a country, which had been, during the reign of his father, considered a mere Russian vassal, now itself played the role of European schoolmaster. His position towards Germany evolved in much more contradictory way than it had earlier been towards Prussia. On the one hand, the Paris Commune made his faith in dynastic solidarity and its Romanov-Hohenzollern keystone as firm as ever. The diktat of Frankfurt, on the other hand, allowed him to rationalize the hurt self-indulgence into intense distrust of the "new Napoleon" in Berlin. And it was this qualm above all, which granted Miliutin the freedom in his planning and Gorchakov in waging the "war of the two Chancellors."

As a result, the Bismarckian system had been, from the Russian side, exposed from the outset to considerable strains.

* * *

Stressing the necessity to close ranks against the perils presented by the Commune and the Internationale, Bismarck from the first postwar months appealed to St. Petersburg and Vienna to adopt a corresponding policy.

For Andrássy, the optimal European constellation would have been an entente between Germany, Austria-Hungary and England, with an Anglo-Austrian axis as the backbone, but the German Chancellor would not yield to such an anti-Russian scheme. Although he wished to cooperate closely with the monarchy, he repeatedly told Austrian diplomats, he would never sacrifice Hohenzollern-Romanov amity to that goal; and he advised them that Panslavism could be held in check only through the favorable disposition of the Tsar.[29] Also in Vienna, the powerful military-aristocratic "Hofpartei" disapproved with the Foreign Minister's concept; in its name, Archduke Albrecht rejected it as the perpetuation of "ingratitude to Russia," which since the Crimean War much contributed to Austrian military-political disasters and Prussian triumphs. Francis Joseph I stood close to this opinion and at the secret conferences held on 17-19 February 1872, he reminded the Hungarian that he had to adapt his policies to the views of the army leadership as he had promised it when taking over his office.[30] So, Andrássy was forced to play a double-game. While still making futile overtures to London, his talks with Minister Novikov went in a much different vein. He gave sweeping assurances: he "considered annexation of the Slavic provinces (i.e. Bosnia-Hercegovina) ruinuous," he absolutely trusted to the Tsar's opposition to the Panslav schemes, and, consequently, he assumed that the two Powers might easily assent to the upholding of the status quo.[31]

Novikov, who had come to Vienna cured, after the Balkan experience, of the Muscovite doctrine, solicited for rapprochement. He would not dispute Andrássy's anti-Russian predilections, but assessed him an "honest rival," who, "because he cannot wage a successful war against us and is forced to peace, will do it with good-will and loyalty."[32] Gorchakov, vastly relieved after the previous dangerous symptoms, warmly approved. "But this is exactly my programme," he exclaimed over the Hungarians' proposals. "For eighteen years already I have been advocating an identical policy here." He instructed Novikov to inform the Ballplatz that guarantees concerning Bosnia-Hercegovina would dispel all the mistrust.[33]

Deprived by advanced age and the inordinate jealousies of the elementary statesmanlike endownment—correct evaluation of people and situations—the Russian Chancellor commenced to see in Andrássy more than a 'honest rival''; the latter became in his eyes "his man, a younger incarnation of himself, exclusively concerned with the consolidation of monarchy,"[34] who would help him to disarm the arch-foes, Bismarck and Ignatiev.

When on 3-11 September 1872 the three Emperors and their chief ministers met in Berlin, the tactics Gorchakov decided to pursue was demonstrated with crystallic clarity.

Bismarck planned to stage the entrevue as a demonstration of dynastic antirevolutionary solidarity which would simultaneously reveal French isolation. On the first point, his Russian rival would not oppose: like everybody else he called for common struggle against Internationale. On the second, though, the German stateman was to learn where his future troubles would lie. Gorchakov managed to persuade Alexander that they have to show their concern for European balance too. They granted audiences to the French Ambassador to hearten the Paris government, naturally worried about the Berlin meeting. Speaking on then much discussed French army reorganization, the Prince stated that "on this question Germany has no right to impose any requirements on you." "Proceed as you deem necessary," he continued, "we need a strong France."[35]

Besides the protection of the republic, the incumbent of the Singers' Bridge also believed that he had scored a major victory in his second main objective—Austro-Russian rapprochement, counterbalancing German supremacy.

Andrássy confidentially revealed to Ambassador Russell that the alliance with Great Britain was "the dream of his life";[36] in his conversations with Gorchakov, however, he repeated the pledges he had given to Novikov. His often quoted statement, in which genuine conviction was mixed with basic deceit, ran as follows:

> With regard to the East, I emphatically declare that all the rumors that have been circulating as to our ambitions in Bosnia and Hercegovina are without a shadow of foundation. Accessions of territory, if such were possible, would benefit neither Austria nor Hungary . . . . The dualistic system is the main feature of the organization of Austria-Hungary . . . . Austria-Hungary therefore inevitably becomes a 'defensive' state unable to indulge in any territorial aspirations.

. . . Hungary especially is so overloaded with rights and privileges that the Hungarian vessel would sink under the slightest addition to her cargo. . . whether of gold or mud. Hungary can undertake no additional burden.

"So, we may be perfectly sure that the cabinet of Vienna does not cherish any canting idea concerning the East," Gorchakov wrote in a memoir for the Tsar; and in his enthusiasm for the "younger incarnation of himself" he promised that any official evidently involved in the Panslav propaganda would be punished.[37]

Apart from the "Gorchakovian angle," the Berlin meeting also tells us the story of the Emperors' bloc before its split in the Eastern crisis (1875-1878) in a nutshell: There were to be demonstrations of unity, impressing upon Europe a notion that the Holy Alliance was back and alive. In this—but almost only in this—sense Bismarck's effort was successful. Behind the impressive façade, even in these "best years," deception, jealousy, mistrust and both open and back-stage counter-maneuvre were at work, reflecting more than just accidental personal feelings.

* * *

After Berlin, the visit of William I to St. Petersburg (April-May 1873) manifested "Alexander's line" in its untarnished form. The police made it sure that the city had flags and portraits in abundant display; generals had to change their red trousers because they seemed to resemble the French uniforms; and the united brassband of the Guard—about 1800 musicians—welcomed the German guests by the "Wacht am Rhein" and the so-called "Parish march," played first in 1814 when Russian and Prussian troops had paraded in the French capital. And so it went on.

Bismarck was obviously carried away by the atmosphere no less than the old Emperor. In the talks he professed his faith in the "close entente with Russia as the only rational policy for Prussia," his "contempt for England" and "indifference to Austria." Closeted with Gorchakov and Stremoukhov, he promised that Berlin would discharge all the influence it possessed in the East to the benefit of Russia, the Power whose good will he considered "dear and necessary to us."[38]

Yet no more than words and passing feelings resulted from the visit.

True, Field Marshals Berg and Moltke signed on 6 May a military convention by which both sides obliged themselves to help the other with 200,000 men if attacked by a third Power, and the Emperors immediately ratified it; their Chancellors, though, discreetly carted it away by imposing a condition that they would countersign the document after Austria-Hungary joined the undertaking. Neither of them wished to see the military alliance disturbing his own plans: Bismarck would not allow his Austrian policy to be impaired by it, and Gorchakov also wanted a free hand to play the Austrian card as well as the French one.

The convention was forsaken in the way they had expected. When the Tsar visited Vienna a month later, in order to make the alliance comprehensive, the Austrian statesmen declined to follow suit with the excuse that such a secret commitment contradicted the constitutional rules in the monarchy. Only a vague so-called Schönbrunn Convention of 6 June was to serve as a treaty basis for the now formally established Three Emperors' League.[39]

Alexander felt hurt that Francis Joseph had rejected the forthright alliance; Gorchakov, on the contrary, rated the Schönbrunn Convention as a highly satisfactory arrangement and the Vienna visit a further step to Russo-Austrian intimity. According to a Singers' Bridge summary, the state of mutual relations "permitted to forget the unpleasant past. . . . The spectres of Panslavism, Pangermanism, Polonism and Hungarian-Danubian state were reduced to a minimum. These problems will no longer appear in solving practical problems."[40] Those also were the hopeful expectations of the St. Petersburg moderates. No one viewed the Schönbrunn document as an adequate instrument to cope with a crisis situation; but with France reduced to impotence, England isolated and the Muscovy hotheads tamed by failure no emergencies were envisaged.

In general, temporizing appeared to offer the statesmen of all European Great Powers the best outlook: everybody was in need to improve military, economic and political conditions of their states first. This tendency, natural in any post-war period, however, did not just buttress the new stability; within the framework of internal consolidation, important shifts took place detrimental to it. Such contradictory processes could be distinctly observed in Russian domestic policies, in the disputes to which Katkov and society directed their main concern.

* * *

At first sight, the system masterminded by Count Peter Shuvalov appeared an undisputable triumph and the position of its chief proponent impossible to challenge. Although dubbed "Peter IV" or "Arakcheev II," the names reminiscent of limited martinets, Shuvalov played his game almost faultlessly. He was adroit enough to avoid a too open display of power, impressing the others by patience, tact in listening and asking questions, contempt towards petty intrigues permanently brewing at Court, as well as by self-assured handling of affairs. Valuev himself, whom the gendarme chief ousted in 1868, returned to the government in 1872 in a modest capacity as Minister for State Domains, ready to praise his leadership.[41] Also Katkov, albeit retaining influence which dwarfed any publicist in Russia or elsewhere, abandoned the feud with Count Peter and made a "pactum" with him which he had earlier refused to other politicians.

European statesmen welcomed in Shuvalov an ideal partner to deal with: "good looking, civil and intelligent, as pleasant a Russian as I have met," Lord Granville portrayed him.[42] They expected him to get rid of the tiresome Gorchakov and finally contain the restless ones disturbing both internal and external peace. Yet the man whose outlook was perfectly fitted to the spirit of the time and the broader concept of Bismarckian order met in Miliutin an opponent he failed to match.

The mild, unpretentious War Minister became for liberal society the symbol of the earlier reform effort and it centered on him the hope that this quest would be resumed. Moreover, without being a flunky, Miliutin was able to convince the Tsar that his loyalty and service was more valuable than Shuvalov's. His unblemished "patriotic" record proved at the end stronger than the assets of the police chief.

Two big political battles culminating in the opening years of the 1870s —on educational system and army reform—mirrored the gradual dissipation of Shuvalovian rule. In the first Katkov, Tolstoi and others, working hand in hand with "Peter IV" to affirm the conservative supremacy, won their case. In the second, although his foes seemed still more powerful and numerous, Miliutin already scored a victory which in its consequences made him the dominant figure in the government.

* * *

Under the liberal guidance of Golovnin, the Russian educational system had vastly improved. The minister proclaimed the rise of cultural standards "the most urgent need in our time" and by the statutes promulgated in 1863-1864, opened secondary schools and universities to "all classes and faiths." A new type of secondary school, the real gymnasia, was introduced to provide instruction in the hitherto neglected natural sciences. The burdensome supervision exercised by the Holy Synod and other governmental agencies was relaxed, universities granted a broad autonomy.

Even there, however, the shots fired by Karakozov interrupted a promising development. "You know my deep convictions that classic education has to be the basis for everything," Katkov directed Tolstoi, the newly appointed Minister for Public Instruction. The "classicist crusade" for the return to the old system of Uvarov was to evolve into the most symptomatic feature of the whole anti-reform era and depressing demonstration of the enormous sway the Muscovite had over Russian public life. The ministry was virtually demoted to the Strastnyi Boulevard's agency, its chief officials—Delianov, Feoktistov, Georgievskii, Gezen, Markevich—competing in obsequious service to the editor, whom they in their reports called the "grand master" (bolshoi khoziain).[43]

The secondary schools were to suffer first. There, Katkov and his lieutenant Leontiev affirmed, lay the root of the evil; and they announced the intention to "give all our souls" into the battle against it, "decisive for the future of our nation."[44]

Initially, they had been cautiously advertizing their programme as the adaptation of the best principles tested in the more advanced European schools. The immature young people, they had asserted, are incapable of studying natural sciences properly; in the curriculum, furthermore, too much time is devoted to history and geography and there are some subjects in it, like economics and rhetorics, which are utterly superfluous and even harmful. Allegedly in order to cast off these errors, they had contended for a curriculum based on Latin, Greek and partly on mathematics. "The European school is a classical school reposed on the study of the two languages of classical Europe," sounded their keyword. The real gymnasia, where natural science had priority, were to be replaced by the so-called real schools oriented on narrowly conceived "practical needs" and their pupils ought not to be permitted to continue their education at universities.[45]

In order to prove the advantages of his concept and marshal the elite behind it, Katkov founded in 1866 the "Lyceum of Tsarevich Nikolai." The institution enrolled sons from some distinguished families,[46] but the overwhelming response was distinctly negative. Count Stroganov, an influential sympathizer, warned the publicist against undue haste which would only intimidate society, "rouse opposition in all its layers," and antagonize the Tsar. Tolstoi himself, although a classicist par excellence, hesitated to push hard the issue and jeopardize his career in the process. "I cannot conform to everything that has come to the head of a journalist," he used to complain.[47]

Still, "a journalist" only warmed up; and the stance taken by the minister showed the strength of his power. Conscious that the Muscovite distrusted him and let his acolytes spy on him, Tolstoi was more fearful of his wrath than of the educated public. So, in the end, he had always obediently "conformed to everything that had come into his head."

The famous case of the revolutionary extremist Nechaev (later immortalized by Dostoevskii in "The Possessed") brought the decisive breakthrough. Now Katkov could reveal the meaning of his classicist counter-reform with complete frankness:

> Where 'the interest of science is at stake, the government must yield no concession, otherwise it will perish and together with it all the great interests entrusted to its protection.' After 1849, the gymnasia 'consistently corrupted the cream of Russian youth' and reared Nihilism as their 'entirely natural product.' Consequently, 'the auditoria of the universities were filled by a mass of half-wild, semi-educated adolescents,' prone to 'hasty, premature conclusions'; and 'science was trampled into the mud.' Only an uncompromising return to the system prevalent under Uvarov could repair the damage: the 'lower trading classes' should be given elementary schooling, the 'better-off trading classes' the real school education, and the universities almost exclusively opened to the 'upper class which decides the fate of nation and charts the future.'[48]

Prompted by the Nechaev case, Shuvalov cast his weight on the scales in favor of the Katkovian plea. Reasoning from a similar "police angle," he managed to persuade the Tsar and the rest of the imperial family that the widespread hostility to classicism sprouted from "all sorts of revolutionary derangement."[49]

When in early 1871 Tolstoi presented the draft of the new gymnasia statute to the State Council, the opposition led by the Miliutin faction raised an "awful storm." According to a common belief, the approval of the project was to be followed by a full-fledged reaction; whereby the feud was transformed "from a pedagogic discussion into a symbolic conflict about the nature of the Russian future." In both the State Council and the special commission set up to review the draft, Tolstoi's motion was thwarted by an overwhelming majority. However, Alexander had already taken the side: due to his intervention, the new gymnasia statute was promulgated on 20 June 1871.[50]

The statute for real schools (15 March 1872) offered the same sad story. Its critics maintained that the country badly needed education in natural sciences for the sake of its economic progress and military preparedness; the Katkov-Shuvalov-Tolstoi coalition continued to insist that the new type satisfied better the requirements of the urban population "exclusively concerned with practical everyday affairs." Once again, the draft was outvoted in the State Council and the special commission, but the Tsar endorsed it nonetheless.[51]

The Katkovian concept triumphed. The principal purpose of the secondary schools was openly admitted to be to "discipline the mind" rather than to raise the standard of knowledge.

This time, in glaring contrast to his previous campaigns, the Muscovite could not command a broad backing for his cause. But that by no means dampened his fervor. For some time, he had already learned that his maxim—to keep public opinion in permanent state of alert, to marshal it constantly behind his lead—was impossible to achieve. On the other hand, the authority he had attained in the elite, no matter whether founded on fear or approval, remained relatively stable even in times of weariness; and he discovered that owing to it he could effectively apply alternative tactics —to prosecute his aims with aid "from above," through groups and personalities allied with him. From that aspect, the portentous test he underwent on the classicism issue must have brought him prodigious satisfaction and self-confidence for the future: even when confronted with overwhelming dissent, he was able to carry the day.

* * *

In the second great dispute, that on the military reform, Katkov's position was much more complex. Two contradictory motives visibly clashed in him: patriotism and intense fear of Prussian might made him alive to the requirement of radical improvements in armed forces; rising conservatism drove him close to those who sensed in the reform dangerous democratic elements.[52] Only in 1873 did the latter impulse prevail and his stance may be perceived as the logical continuation of the "classicist" crusade. Then tactics, too, were identical: he allied himself with the Shuvalov faction and acted mainly through Tolstoi.

It is to be recalled that the bid for the modernization was set out by new system of organisation initiated by the Caucasus Army. Successfully tested also in Poland, this system introducing relatively independent military districts was instituted into the whole army.[53] A mere administrative reshuffle, though, could not provide remedy for the main ills and solve the essential problem—to improve efficiency and raise the numbers of men trained for war at a time when the shaky state of finances dictated stringency in expenditure.

Miliutin, the spiritus agens of the reform, warned that under the traditional system of recruitment and "in view of the huge armed forces which are being formed in all the European states, not excluding Turkey" Russia would be inept to conduct a big campaign either on her western frontiers or in the Balkans.[54] The formation of a mass army with adequate reserves (i.e. also with educated reserve officers) he proclaimed an urgency and the adaptation of an Prussian model of universal military service the only way to satisfy it.

His initiative set into motion a violent confrontation.

In it, the struggle between liberal and conservative groupings was interspersed with a clash of different military schools and personal ambitions, and the resistance of the traditionalists of the serf army once again revealed the main antagonism of post-Crimean Russia, that between the ruling bureaucracy and the nobility defending its remaining privileges.

Ambassador Schweinitz noted in his diaries that Shuvalov perceived "Miliutin's system disastrous for the dynasty, and consequently, used every means to prevent its introduction."[55] But, similarly to his conduct during the educational dispute, the gendarme chief eschewed a too open involvement and resorted to his favorite manner of underhanded manipulation. He let first Tolstoi and then also Katkov perform as his front;

and, above all, supported his friend Field Marshal Bariatinskii and General Fadeev, who, owing to pure and simple ambition and hostility to Miliutin turned from modernizers into the advocates of the serf army tradition.[56]

Confronted by formidable opposition, the prospect of reform looked quite bleak.

The shock administered by the Franco-Prussian war brought about the first reckoning. Miliutin found an unexpected ally in Valuev, who during his European sojourn observed the swift German mobilization and after the return presented to the Tsar a memorandum confronting him with the dilemma: either the system of all-class conscription were adopted or Russia would have to recognize the unfavorable power balance as permanent. Impressed by the document, Tsar Alexander ordered a discussion on the implementation of the War Ministry project (on 15 November 1870).[57] Yet, the initiative still belonged to the opposition. As it showed in the debate on the gymnasia statutues, the Nechaev case made the elite very sensitive to the revolutionary peril; and the argument that social status quo in the army must be uphold bore more weight than any other consideration. In the State Council and the commissions discussing the project, the heir and his influential former tutor Pebodonostsev joined Tolstoi's diatribes clamouring for the protection of the officer corps against the unreliable elements from the universities. Indirectly, raising the financial stringency issue, Gorchakov and Reuterm supported the anti-reform camp. In the meantime, Fadeev and Cherniaev set out to discredit the War Minister in their *Russkii mir* (Russian World): an educated Russian soldier was but a whim of "writing desk officers," they claimed; an army "which expanded Muscovy into an empire covering half of the globe" needed no more than discipline, morale, firm commanding authority.[58]

The strife culminated in 1873. For Miliutin, the whole year "passed like a dark cloud." Never before, he complained, "did I endure so much unpleasantness, annoyance and failure. The intrigue begun long ago against me grew to full maturity and unfolded in all its ugliness."[59]

In March, Shuvalov summoned Katkov to the effect that the *Moskovskiia vedomosti* ought to "take a more active part in the now burning question of "to be or not to be" of Miliutin's military system.[60]

So far, the gendarme chief must have been highly disatisfied with the publicist's performance. Although a sort of understanding between the

Strastnyi Boulevard and the Bariatinskii-Fadeev group had existed since 1864 and although in the debate its daily supported the thesis that the levies were more suitable for Russia than European-type reserves, the comments were overwhelmingly in favor of the modernization drive: even in 1871-1872, when Miliutin emerged as the leading spirit in the uproar against "classicism," there was no substantial change in this attitude.[61] Now, however, the Muscovite seems to have been convinced that the anti-reform coalition would certainly win the contest and joined its bandwagon with noise adequate his repute. Not only did the *Moskovskiia vedomosti* compete with the *Russkii mir* in trumpeting "the salvation of the army's soul," but its editor also bombarded leading dignitaries with memoranda written in the same vein.[62]

Observing the work of commissions paralyzed by Bariatinskii and his stooges, the State Council poisoned by Katkovian exhortations and the "peevish, jaundiced, obstinate disputes" of Tolstoi, Miliutin dispaired; and when in November 1873, Katkov and Pobedonostsev were invited to attend debates in these bodies in person, he visibly dreaded that his reform and perhaps his career as statesman were doomed.[63]

Yet, suddenly the whole situation underwent a sudden twist. The Tsar who after the Nechaev episode had seemed to be swayed by Bariatinskii and Shuvalov, and praised the "new" arguments in the *Moskovskiia vedomosti*,[64] decided that the War Ministry's project must be adopted without change. We know nothing about the circumstances which led to this volte-face; in any case, the notions of military efficiency and the great-power status prevailed over the worries concerning the possible negative social effects of the reform. In January 1874, the law on universal military service was promulgated.[64]

This shattering setback for the Shuvalov faction was to bring about far-reaching political consequences. German diplomats correctly pointed out the most weighty one for the destinies of the Bismarckian system and future Russian foreign policy in general: the military reform speeded up the process of the disappearance of the old officer corps still nurtured by the tradition of Russo-German "brotherhood in arms" and anti-revolutionary solidarity; with Miliutin increasingly powerful in top decision-making, the mood of the younger officer cadres, in which the inferiority complex towards the hated Prussians strangely intertwined with enhanced aggressivity, took the upper hand.[65]

CHAPTER 11

ON THE LION'S PATH:
THE SUBJUGATION OF THE
CENTRAL-ASIAN KHANATES
(1866-1873)

For fifty years back my clear belief about
the Russians has been that they are a good
and even noble element in Europe. Ever
since Peter the Great's appearance among
them, they have been in steady progress of
development. In our own time they have
done signal service to God and man by
drilling into order and peace anarchic
populations all over the world.
Carlyle

I shall not touch those who cherish the
friendship of the great Russian land, but
(I shall bring) misery to those who will not
appreciate the beneficial, peaceful views
of the White Tsar. The troops of His Majesty
are always ready to punish on my order an
unruly neighbor and there are no fortresses,
no fortifications which could save the culprit.
Kaufman

I am an outspoken opponent of any extension of Russia whatever; but I can do nothing
against the ambitions of our generals.
Gorchakov

For some time, although a war plan against Germany and Austria-Hungary was ready in 1873, no army or other extremist pressure exposed the St. Petersburg government to the demand for "secure frontiers" in the west and the southwest. Prussian military performance against France intimidated even the most staunch adventurists; and they readily acceded to the old argument that Russian armament and communications in Poland and the Western provinces were still inadequate. Moreover, so far a quite satisfactory outlet was opened for them in the East: in the advance in Central Asia they could proceed almost unhindered and the formation of the Three Emperors' League which accentuated English isolation made conditions for them even more propitious.

The great thrust in the early 1870s was well prepared by the earlier development. The highly controversial "Cherniaev episode,"[1] instead of putting St. Petersburg on alert, strengthened the aggressive trend.

True, the moderates as well as many Muscovites including Katkov carried on in their opposition against the zealous Asiatic military. In the councils on Asiatic affairs, apart from Gorchakov and Reutern, the director of the Asiatic Department Stremoukhov, the Chief of General Staff Heyden and Chief of Staff in the Caucasus Svistunov were particularly determined in their criticism, proclaiming seizures beyond the Caspian Sea financially wasteful and essentially harmful to Russian interests; in the last resort, however, they were almost invariably on the losing side. Alexander and Miliutin continued to give they helping hands to Cherniaev's successors and rivals who promised to hold the opinions on the Neva in due respect while being steadfast in their service to Russia's power and glory. That the official instructions were often ambiguous made no difference: the conquest went on with gathering momentum.

First, the Emir of Bukhara, blinded by Cherniaev's failure, became overconfident and delivered the military hawks the excuse they were looking for. The time has come, wrote Kryzhanovskii in his plea for action, to teach the Emir that "Russia is not Khiva or Kokand and it is impossible to insult us."[2] He got a green light.[3]

In the spring of 1866, General Romanovskii inflicted a heavy defeat upon the Bukharan army and took the Kokandese fortress of Khodjent, controlling the fertile Ferghana valley. Being a moderate, scrupulously following the official proclamations on Russian restraint, he considered this to be a sufficient lesson for the Emir; such a proposition, however, only revolted Kryzhanovskii who craved to "fight anybody not matter whom."[4]

Then an organization of the conquered territories into a separate Governor Generalship of Turkestan was discussed in St. Petersburg and Romanovskii, successful on the battlefield and mild in handling the local populace, seemed the best choice to lead the new administration. Yet an extremist intrigue prevented the nomination. General Konstantin von Kaufman, a favorite of Katkov and a "merchant from Miliutin's shops" as they dubbed him for his basic allegiance, got the Turkestan appointment and with it a free hand to complete Russian predominance in the area. In a special decree (on 29 July 1867) Alexander granted him plenary powers to "decide on any political, frontier and commerical affair, to send to the neighboring territories trustworthy persons for the conduct of negotiations and the signing of conventions"; and, moreover, obliged himself to "accept anything that will be signed and concluded by virtue of the above mentioned plenary powers."[5]

The new satrap soon obtained the chance to assert himself. Hard-pressed by unruly clergy and begs the Emir of Bukhara declared, in April 1868, holy war against the Russian infidel. Although suffering from the customary ills of bad supply and the hardships of a steppe campaign, Kaufman's troops found no match in the undisciplined and poorly armed Bukharan host. It was all over in less than two months. Samarkand was occupied, the subsequent week-long rising of its populace drowned in blood. And, as a warning to all those who would dare to resist him, the Governor General let loose his soldiery for two days of murder, pillage and arson in the ancient center of Central Asian civilization.

With the peace treaties signed during the summer of 1868, both Bukhara and Kokand ended their independent existence. The strategically and economically most valuable parts, including Samarkand, were—despite the frantic protests of the Singers' Bridge—incorporated into the Turkestan Governor Generalship. What was left became Russian dependencies, their rulers recognizing the Tsar's protection.[6]

Triumphant, Kaufman could from them on fully enjoy "both the prerequisites and the substance" of his elevated status. The ceremonious display of power, the rigid etiquette by which he surrounded himself in Tashkent, coupled with the military might he had at his disposal, so much impressed the whole of Central Asia that people there started to call him the "Yarim Padishah" (Half-Emperor).[7]

* * *

Gorchakov's opposition to the Asiatic adventures had always been bred by fears that there would be a forceful British response to them; and in view of the then brewing European complications he considered the Kokand-Bukhara enterprise highly untimely. Indeed, this time the London cabinet, forced by mounting criticism of the "masterly inactivity" doctrine,[8] did react to events north of the Indian possessions. Peaceful and earnestly engaged solely in internal problems as they were, Gladstone and his colleagues had to look for guarantees against the further moves of the Bear. But the subsequent Anglo-Russian diplomatic hagglings only showed their ineptitude in dealing with the threat.

In 1869, Foreign Secretary Clarendon approached St. Petersburg with the suggestion to recognize "some territory as neutral between the possessions of England and Russia which should be the limit of these possessions and be scrupulously respected by both Powers." The overture led to the meeting of Clarendon and Gorchakov (in September 1869 at Heidelberg) and further prolonged exchange of views. To characterize them in brief, irresolute English representatives were found by Russian counterparts to be soft bargainers. Alexander and his Chancellor repeatedly professed absence of ambition for territorial gains and agreed with the principle of division but they rejected the Amu-Daria as the demarcation line and insisted on retaining a free hand against the khanates. Moreover, they urged that Afghanistan ought to be a neutral zone, which implied equal English and Russian status there. What has been in diplomatic exchange and historical literature called the "Anglo-Russian agreements of 1872-1873" was a strange sort of understanding indeed. While the English recognized Russian supremacy over Bukhara and Kokand, the Russians only obliged themselves to respect Afghan integrity without, however, any clear delimination of the northern Afghan frontier.[9]

Still more significantly, while the negotiations were in progress and the Russian policymakers showered the English with assurances, their military enjoyed true heydays. Katkov spelled out the universal opinion when he read the parleys and their results as a "passive consent by England to the subjection of Central Asia to Russian influence."[10] Small wonder that the Tsar saw no reason to keep his word and discipline his generals.

Unable to give to public opinion any satisfaction other than Asiatic triumphs, he probably even heartened them. "Take Khiva for me, Konstantin Petrovich," he allegedly implored Kaufman.[11]

* * *

It was not to be the Turkestan "Yarim Padishah" alone who would try to make the best of the situation; the same rosy prospects propelled both Orenburg and Tiflis into fierce competition with Tashkent. Particularly the Caucasus military group, led by Grand Duke Mikhail, pushed vigorously to the area of conquest.

For years the ambition of Tiflis had been to establish a base on the eastern shores of the Caspian Sea and from it to subjuge the vast territories inhabited by the Turkoman tribes; but it had been effectively staved off by the Foreign Ministry's claim that such an venture would impair good relations with Teheran, drive it into the British embrace and unduly complicate even the Russian position vis-à-vis Turkey. After the Heidelberg meeting, these arguments seem to have lost their credibility. Already at the end of 1869, units from the Caucasus landed in the Bay of Krasnovodsk and installed their springboard there. From that moment onwards, Tiflis was to become "as much a thorn in the flesh of the British as Tashkent,"[12] or to be more exact, their rivalry was to spur them to what already instituted a direct threat to the British security zone.

Jockeying for preeminence, Kaufman probably hesitated between two options: he could either crown the drive against the khanates by an invasion of Khiva or to take advantage of the unrest in the northwestern Chinese province of Sin-kiang, where Yakub-beg, a former Kokandese officer, set up a semi-independent state.

At first, the Chinese variant must have greatly tempted the Turkestan warlord. Advertizing it as the punishment of Yakub-beg for his revolt against lawful authorities, he dispatched General Kolpakovskii with substantial forces to seize Kuldja and the valley of Ili on the old Silk Road (summer 1871). Then, he toyed with the idea of an expedition to Urumchi, and, as he wrote to Stremoukhov, treading into the steps of the famous Cossack ataman Ermak "to press even farther, in a more daring manner."[13] In the end, however, the enterprising Caucassians made him decide for the westward move: Colonel Markozov, a brutal and reckless hawk commanding the Krasnovodsk detachment, had already in his raids penetrated deep into the Turkoman steppes to procure camels for the Khivan expedition. Thus, in June 1872, the Chinese action was stopped by a semi-protectorate treaty with Yakub-beg and at the same time Kaufman raised in St. Petersburg the issue of "safety" on the upper Amu-Daria.

The debate took the familiar pattern. Stremoukhov maintained that there was "no urgent need to fight" Khiva and ridiculed the military who invented fables about anti-Russian intrigues spun by its Khan; General Heyden urged that operations in the area ought to be avoided "till the last extremity"; and the most determined opponent, General Svistunov, even called for the withdrawal from Krasnovodsk and the whole of Central Asia. In the decisive Extraordinary Council on 16 December 1872, Alexander again said that his "strict guiding principle" was that "under no circumstances would he welcome the extension of borders" and Shuvalov himself then departed for London to inform the Liberal cabinet to this effect.[14] Despite all of that, a green light was given to the attack on Khiva. In fact, the question was no longer whether the army extremists would have the upper hand but which of the eastern groups would snatch the fame.

The Tiflis command requested that the operation be entrusted mainly to its toops; and the General Staff, probably because of the backing the Viceroy, Grand Duke Mikhail, had in the elite, endorsed their scheme. But Kaufman again managed to sway Alexander on his side. All the three rival centers—Tiflis, Tashkent and Orenburg—were to participate equally and their column proceed according to a timetable which would assure their simultaneous appearance under the walls of Khiva.

The Grand Duke and his new Chief of Staff Sviatopolk-Mirskii, another member of the Moscow Committee who replaced the reluctant Svistunov, still attempted to beat Kaufman by ordering Markozov to start the advance before the others; but fortune turned against them. Markozov badly muddled the action and his column had to return back, while the Turkestan troops performed their task without excessive trouble. The Khivans put up but half-hearted resistance and by early summer Kaufman held the Khanate in his grip. The Orenburg contenders presented him with the last difficulties, when their units, most experienced after decades of fighting in the steppe, advanced more quickly and on 9 June, feigning misunderstanding in communications, General Verevkin with his

Siberians stormed the city of Khiva. Still, the final satisfaction was to remain in store for the "Yarim-Padishah": it was to be him who in the capitulation ceremonial in the garden of the Khan's palace sat on a raised platform like a big Oriental conqueror and the Khan knelt by his feet.[15]

The epilogue of the campaign was perhaps most symptomatic for the Russian "civilizing mission" in the East.

The dispositions from St. Petersburg directed Kaufman "to demonstrate to Khiva her vulnerability and weakness." He understood it not only in terms of breaking the morale of the Khan and his entourage but primarily as "teaching a lesson" to the Turkomans. Thus, an enormous tribute impossible to pay was imposed on the tribe of Yomuths, to provide a pretext. On 19 July, General Golovachev was ordered to move into the Yomuth lands and "give over their settlements and their families to complete destruction and their herds and property to confiscation." Three days later, when killing, burning and looting was already in progress, a second instruction came from Kaufman, "at the least attempt to migrate, carry out my order for the final extermination of the disobedient tribe." Because the desperate Turkomans naturally tried to "migrate," Golovachev saw the task quite simply: "This expedition does not spare either sex or age. Kill all of them!", he told his subordinates. Like in the Caucasus, there were no qualms of conscience.[16]

Scared out of his wits, the Khan signed on 24 August 1873 a treaty by which he proclaimed himself an "obedient servant" of the Russian Emperor and promised to conduct his policy under the guidance of Tashkent. Near his capital, the Russian fort of Petro-Alexandrovsk was erected to serve as a "sentry" watching him. In flagrant contradiction to all declarations and assurances to London, territories on the right bank of the Amu-Daria were incorporated into the Turkestan Governor Generalship. On 10 October 1873, the Bukharan Emir had to sign a protectorate treaty similar to that imposed in Khiva. And to please also the Tiflis group, a separate Trans-Caspian military district was established for the future offensive in the Turkoman lands, including northern Persia and Afghanistan.[17]

Indeed, in their bid for "secure frontiers," the eastern militarists would not concede to the St. Petersburg moderates even a short respite.

CHAPTER 12

LOOKING FOR A POLICY
(1873-1875)

Russia feels herself squeezed and stifled
in the Black Sea. She must have a way out
through the Straits as a direct or indirect
guarantee of security for the commerce
of the South and also for (other) political
and economic considerations. Russia cannot
do otherwise than be a master there, either
by assuming an exclusive influence over
the sovereign and existing authorities at
Constantinople or by annexing this place . . .
Ignatiev

The Austrian and Turkish Slavs must be our
allies, the weapons of our policy against
the Germans. In order to attain this objective,
Russia may make sacrifices for their liberation and consolidation; but to sacrifice
Russian interests exclusively, taking the
means for the end, only to have in view
the liberation of the Slavs and to leave them
afterwards to follow a policy hostile to us,
and to content ourselves with the humane
side of our successes, would be unreasonable
and criminal.
Ignatiev

The eastern militarists most certainly disturbed Gorchakov in his sleep; yet, General Ignatiev was undoubtedly the one whose image plagued the old man at the Singers' Bridge more. There was a good reason why the latter asked the Ambassador whenever he met him in St. Petersburg: "Are you coming to depose me?"[1]

During the first half of the 1870s, Ignatiev had not only entrenched himself at the Golden Horn and demonstrated his outstanding diplomatic talents ("diplomatic" in the sense the Russians had always understood it) but also, just as in the preceding period, he had masterminded a concept which was totally at variance with that of the ministry. While Gorchakov sought to establish a system reposed on understanding with Austro-Hungary, the Ambassador fought Austrian influence wherever he could and insisted that preponderance instead of status quo must be the Russian goal.

Already before 1870, Ignatiev had been recognized as the best informed man in the Turkish capital. "When darkness fell, adventurers, political intriguers or simply spies" were according to his subordinates sneeking into the Ambassador's residence, bringing news from the Serail, ministries and provinces; mostly they were Greeks and Armenians, whose he payed and protected against punishment.[2] It was also among non-Turkish nationals where his enormous power had been first seen.[3] However, he had never forgotten that the Turkish elite might supply him with the winning card in the game; and once his hopes for a Balkan upheaval paled he promptly shifted from the "Slavic" to the "Turkish" alternative. So, when the catastrophe of 1870-1871 removed the French, hitherto the mightiest influence, from the Constantinople scene, he could fill the vacuum. As he himself put it,

> Our relations with the Porte between 1871-1875 could have never been better, and they kindled jealousy of other European Powers. The Sultan had complete confidence in the Russian Ambassador and in this way we were able to take preparatory steps for the revival of our brothers and co-religionists, in readiness for the moment when it should be in Russian interest to raise the Eastern Question. We were ultimately vanquished, compromised and weakened on the Bosphorus not by the frank struggle . . . but by the agreement with Germany and Austria, by the Dreikaiserbündnis.[4]

Although the Turkish dignitaries had always contested the allegation that the Porte through Ignatiev "gave itself up to Russia,"[5] this was what nearly happened. The Ambassador's contenders used to explain his power by the exorbitant financial means at this disposal, but that was not the whole truth. The adroitness with which he took advantage of the generally favorable conditions—English passivity, German support, the death of the three strong men of the Porte (Grand Vizier Ali Pasha, Foreign Minister Fuad Pasha and War Minister Omer Pasha) as well as of the succession problem[6]—was at least equally important. The Turks feared him and called him "Father of the Lie" (Yalan Pasha, Menteur Pasha) for his unashamed cheating; still, they grudgingly recognized him as a "vice-Sultan."[7] The Ambassador could with good reason look forward to the moment when he would dominate the Porte completly. Then, he envisaged, Russia would "allow the Sultans to complete their lives" at Constantinople, but the Straits would be in her hands and the Balkan nations her docile allies.[8] No wonder that Gorchakov and European statesmen perceived in him, in Gladstone's words, "both fox and firebrand," a man who "will yet I fear make a war in Europe before he is done."[9]

* * *

The "danger of Ignatiev," nonetheless, has to be seen in its correct proportions. While towering at the Golden Horn, the Ambassador was in 1871-1875 rather a lone challenge to the official line. The St. Petersburg elite watched him with suspicion as unrelenting schemer and warmonger. And, his concept of cooperation with the Turks, albeit recognized as useful under the circumstances, could scarcely incite enthusiasm and serve as a rallying point for the extremist cause.

In general, the return to the fold of the three monarchies and clouded Balkan conditions deepened disarray and loss of perspective in society and the Moscow party traditionally oriented towards the Slavic mission. Aksakov's lament well expressed this state of mind:

> Austrian policy has become active, offensive and we have taken over the thankless task of policy of containment and restraint, looking for a compromise. We are losing respect, Austria is winning it . . . . The 'sick man' (i.e. Turkey) will die when it suits the West, not us.[10]

Also Katkov, though hostile to the "Foreign Ministry for Russian affairs" and increasingly convinced of Gorchakov's incompetence,[11] visibly lacked a clear-cut proposition of what should have been done in the "Russian national interest." His comments on cardinal foreign-policy themes must have left the diminishing number of his readers bewildered or bored: he either reproduced the official formulae or in the vaguest terms reiterated the advantages of non-alignment.[12]

The insipid and sporadic criticism of the course personified by Gorchakov in the *Moskovskii vedomosti* well testifies the absence of any "patriotic" alternative; and for that reason, rather than because of a more stern censorship, there was no true foreign-policy debate in the Russian press at that time. This, naturally, ensured basic security for the Chancellor.

True, neither abroad nor at home did Gorchakov command much respect. European statesmen held him for scarcely more than a "fluent if ineffective liar in the theatrical yet boring Russian manner"[13] and the St. Petersburg elite made him an object of almost daily gossip and ridicule. The belief was widespread that "his weakened will could not cope with the infirmities resulting from old age," that "egotism, megalomania, passion for publicity, greed and lust, which were always present in the Prince's nature . . . now, no longer controlled . . . wholly possessed him and obscured his inborn clear outlook." Shuvalov despised him deeply, hoping, no less than Ignatiev, to get his office.[14] Yet, even if he too most certainly joked with all the others about the frequent amorous escapades of his aged aide, Alexander still considered him useful; and, as it has been pointed out, the anti-Bismarckian and anti-Prussian bent of the "most illustrious Prince" fitted to the mood and complexes of his kinsmen. Moreover, the European situation after the power-shift in Paris in 1873 unwound in a way exceptionally propitious just for Gorchakov's approach, and rendered a broad space for his maneuvres.

* * *

Bismarck's mentality clashed with cool political reason demanding patience: he assessed the replacement of Thiers by Marshal MacMahon at the helm of the French state as a "substitution of weaker, non-militant, anti-clerical and isolated France by a stronger one, militarist, ultramontane, capable of winning allies"[15] and when the Catholic bishops raised protests against the discrimination of the Alsatian and Lorrainian co-religionists, he reacted in familiar, bullying manner—by war threats. Simultaneously, he set in motion a campaign against the Catholic Church in Germany, accusing it of fostering separatism in the southern and western parts of the Reich. This again roused the Tsar against the man who, as he told Miliutin, like Napoleon "after each war without delay looks for a pretext to start a new one."[16] In December 1873, undoubtedly with supreme consent, Gorchakov could repeat to the French Ambassador earlier assurances:

> The feeling of sympathy for France has not changed . . .it is in our interest and our hope that she will anew, and as soon as possible, hold that important position in Europe which rightfully belongs to her . . . . Bismarck, acting against the moral conscience of Europe, cannot force a war upon you.[17]

Then, in February 1874, the visit of Francis Joseph and Andrássy to St. Petersburg still more buttressed the Prince's stand. The fact that almost a hundred years after Joseph II, a Habsburg Emperor had again descended on the banks of the Neva and that he bowed before Nicholas' grave demonstrating apology for past "ingratitude," led many to believe that the long-delayed reconciliation was finally achieved and would develop into a stable factor in the European situation. Furthermore, Francis Joseph showed how repelled were the Catholic ruling circles by Bismarck's heavy-handed conduct. Andrássy had to follow Gorchakov to the French Embassy and express the monarchy's disapproval of the Berlin policies.[18]

This brought additional confusion into the Moscow party. Next to Pogodin's recantation, Katkov performed another volte-face and, professing the innocence of Panslavism, promised that Austrian Slavs would be left to their fate:

> Russian interests should never be connected with the disintegration of Austria . . . . Russian sympathies with the Slavs have always had the most unambitious, ethnographic and literary character . . . . Russian policy feels no compulsion to interfere in Austro-Hungarian internal affairs . . . . Whatever nationality prevails there is no Russian concern . . . . Any attempt by Russia to spread her state sphere to the west would raise the whole world to arms against her . . . . By

introducing new bodies into her structure she would not strengthen but enfeeble herself. . . . The unification of all Slavic nations under one scepter or in one state is a political nonsense . . . . [19]

Also the most significant events in domestic politics at least indirectly helped Gorchakov: his mightest foe, Shuvalov, first lost the crucial battle on army reform and then all his power. While benevolent to the short-comings of the aged, docile Chancellor, Alexander became obviously tired of the formidable "Peter IV" and when the latter badly slipped—forgetting his proverbial caution, he ridiculed the liaison of his master with Princess Dolgorukaia—nothing could save him. In the summer of 1874, a much surprised society learned that Shuvalov was appointed Ambassador to the Court of St. James. The rise of Miliutin was an asset for the Chancellor. Although critical of him, the War Minister did not covet his office, and above all, shared his dislike of the Prussians and their leader.

* * *

Bismarck had not indulged in exaggerated optimism as to the state of the Russo-German relations. Even after the triumphant St. Petersburg visit he considered the good will of the Tsar the only stable factor and did not expect any real improvement because "Prince Gorchakov would not serve the German policy of his sovereign with his whole soul." The contra-dictory stances taken by St. Petersburg and Berlin to the crisis in Spain—the former supported the clerical-monarchist forces, the latter the republi-cans—only deepened his scepticism. Similarly, he feared that the "Hof-partei" would prevail in Vienna. According to Ambassador Odo Russell, the German statesman was carried away by a spectre of Russo-French-Austrian entente which would alter the commanding position of his coun-try into an isolated one. [20]

Nonetheless, he would not reconsider his tactics. Despite the adverse effect hitherto produced by the anti-French and anti-"ultramontane" campaign, the tension on the Rhine was escalated. And, by sending at the same time Radowitz, the head of the Eastern department in the Foreign Ministry, with a special mission to St. Petersburg (February 1875), the Chancellor made almost everybody believe that he was after a big bargain which would give him a free hand against France in exchange for the same opportunity for Russia in the Near East. Not surprisingly, his opposite number at the Singers' Bridge did his utmost to further precisely this interpretation. He let it transpire that Radowitz, "in the talks with Russian dignitaries indicated quite distinctly that Germany was ready to pay for benevolent neutrality by supporting all her (Russia's) stances in the East"; but that "we replied that we have nothing in mind save tranquility in the East as a factor of world peace" and "we did not go beyond this thesis."[21]

Opinions have always been split in the vast debate among the historians concerning both the Radowitz mission and Bismarck's ultimate intentions in 1875.[22] Whatever the purposes of the German Chancellor might have been, though, the fact remains that by perpetuating a counter-productive policy[23]—on 8 April, the Conservative *Post* published its famous article "Is war in sight?"—he invited the opponents of his system, particularly the Russian ones, to exploit it in full.

Finding the Tsar highly annoyed with Bismarck, Miliutin presented the alarmist Obruchev's memorandum of 1873, predicting general conflagration in the near future and Gorchakov persuaded the ruler to assist him in buttressing the diplomatic counter-offensive started by the French Foreign Minister Duke de Decazes. Besides new assurances offered to the Paris government, Alexander agreed to go to Berlin as a mediator of peace.[24]

Already before the Tsar and his Chancellor arrived at the German capital (on 8 May 1875), Bismarck had evidently resolved to retreat. But his further imprudent utterances on the advantages of a preventive war, like those of Moltke and Radowitz, allowed Decazes to keep the atmosphere conveniently warmed up and Gorchakov to advertize his master and himself as saviours of France.

"The peacemaking effort of Russia was easy to accomplish. Both the Emperor William and Mr. Bismarck have evidently peaceful intentions," Alexander announced after his talks with the German statesman.[25] In the circular of 13 May, however, Gorchakov gave a different emphasis to this statement; and, moreover, the well-known communication mistakes[26] changed Russian informations into outright insults.

German isolation was to be only temporary. During the forthcoming Eastern crisis, Bismarck reestablished his stature in Europe beyond any doubt. The 1875 episode, though, was never to be forgotten and forgiven and the "war of the two Chancellors," in one form or another continuously straining the Russo-German relationship, remained the most auspicious token of Bismarck's failure to organize the bloc of the three Empires according to his wishes.

CHAPTER 13

PARADING IMPOTENCE: ST. PETERSBURG AND THE OPENING OF THE EASTERN CRISIS (1875-1876)

Be not false to thyself, Great Russia
Trust no strangers, my native land,
Trust not their false wisdom and
their insolent deceit
And, like St. Cyril, do not forsake
The great mission of serving the Slavs.
Tiutchev

Briefly, this dreadful Eastern Question constitutes almost our whole future fate. Therein lay, as it were, all our tasks and what is more important—our only exit into the plenitude of history. Our final conflict with Europe is also involved in this question, and our ultimate communion with her but only upon new, mighty and fertile foundations. Och! How can Europe at this time grasp the fatal and vital importance to ourselves of the solution of this question?
. . . No matter what may be the outcome of the present, perhaps indispensable diplomatic agreements and negotiations, nevertheless, sooner or later, Constantinople must be ours. . . .
Dostoevskii

> The Emperor Alexander received me . . . in
> an extremely gracious and friendly manner.
> First, he pointed to his breast, where he was
> wearing Austrian and German decorations,
> and said: 'Here is my programme!'
> Andrássy
>
> What do you want? There is no programme!
> Jomini

In contrast to the strange Russo-German friendship, the relations between Russia and Austria-Hungary achieved by 1875 a degree of cooperation—and tolerance from the Russian side—unparalleled in the whole
Armed Peace era.

As far as it can be ascertained from the scanty evidence on the talks in
1873-1874, there had been a complete understanding to abstain from annexations and actions injurious to the other side. Andrássy had not only
reiterated his former pledges; he also promised that if a crisis were to arise
between the Turks and the Christians, the outcome would be left to its
"natural development." On behalf of Russia, Gorchakov had warned that
the principle adopted on the Neva in 1866—to consider Austrian military
intervention in Bosnia-Hercegovina a casus belli—was still in force; concerning peaceful consolidation of influence in the area, though, he had
apparently granted to the Dual Monarchy a considerable leeway. A Singers'
Bridge survey put it as follows:

> If Austrian influence develops in these countries where our influ-
> ence dominates, we shall not see in it a danger for the future of the
> Eastern Christians, nor an attack on our prestige and interests. . . .
> The ties of faith and race which unite us (with the Balkan Slavs)
> are a (sufficient) counterpoise to the too great ascendancy of Aus-
> tria-Hungary.[1]

The "Panslav" opposition to the Gorchakov-Novikov concept continued to be on the wane. Even such hawks like Stremoukhov and Ionin
deserted Ignatiev; as the Ambassador complained, "they imagined that it
was not Austria who had been our eternal Balkan rival, that Austria has
been transformed."[2] He might as well accuse Katkov of the same sin.

When in the autumn of 1873 the Ballplatz intervened into the conflict between Bosnian merchants and Turkish authorities, the publicist had still considered it an encroachment into the Russian preserve. The "new era" in the Habsburg Balkan policy, he had admonished, "could cost the unfortunate Turkish Christians dear"; and he had even attacked Ignatiev, asking "what is our representative at Constantinople doing and why is he leaving this case to the others."[3] In early 1875, however, commenting on Vienna's interference in the Turkish-Montenegrin clash at Podgorica, the Moscow editor already praised this initiative as proof of the advantages proffered by "that good understanding between the three Empires now considered by everybody to be the best guarantee for European peace."[4]

But the shaky stability in the Balkans could not last for long. The aspirations of its peoples, governments and rulers, as well as the Austrians and the Russians, were too explosive to be dulled by any status quo agreement. Above all, St. Petersburg's complaisance emboldened the Vienna elite in excess.

Two concepts of active Balkan policy had evolved there since 1866. The first one had been designed by Chancellor Beust and his diplomatic agent in Belgrade, Count Kállai, and aimed to combine forceful economic penetration with the tactics of winning the Balkans Slavs by satisfying their "inexpensive demands"; the second, canvassed by the military, had demanded that the strategic position of the monarchy in the area must be improved by territorial acquisitions.

Although his effort had been marred by his own class, the Hungarian nobility and its allies, who rejected any Slavic connections for political and/or economic reasons, Andrássy sought to develop the Beust-Kállai line. Originally, he had been ready even to buy off Serbia by letting her take Bosnia-Hercegovina; learning that this would not be allowed either in Vienna or at Constantinople, he at least protected the Serbs, Montenegrins and Bosnians in their minor strifes with the Turks.

Profiting from the Austro-Russian entente, this policy promised big gains. But the annexionist-oriented "Hofpartei" craved for more: it insisted that Bosnia-Hercegovina had to be seized as soon as possible to procure the hinterland for the exposed Dalmatian coast. Thus another historical paradox took place when pro-Russian or pro-Slav aristocrats and generals (Archduke Albrecht, Rodić, Beck) were instrumental in triggering events ultimately leading to a new estrangement.[5]

Although the Vienna debate as to Tsardom's plans concerning the Dual Monarchy and the Balkans had been inconclusive,[6] the "Hofpartei" must have felt quite certain of St. Petersburg's benevolence; and Francis Joseph was easily persuaded by it. The arguments soliciting for the Bosnia-Hercegovina action seemed convincing, indeed: after two hungry years, the population of the provinces was exceedingly irritated by heavy taxation and the tyranny of the Moslem begs and administration; guerilla warfare had already been in progress and following the Podgorica incident, a Turco-Montenegrin war appeared imminent. So, at the Crown Council held on 29 January 1875, Andrássy had to yield. He approved that "when a situation which justifies our intervention" arises, then the Dual Monarchy "cannot afford to let such an opportunity to pass"; and that the government "need have no fear of foreign opposition, not even from Russia, for our relations with her are based on the necessity to maintain (general) peace."[7]

The tour Francis Joseph made to Dalmatia in the spring was visibly staged by the generals to bring about the crisis they wished; and in this respect they succeeded perfectly. In July, a revolt broke out at Nevesinje and quickly spread first to the whole of Hercegovina and then to Bosnia. As to the broader perspective, though, the Vienna planners proved badly mistaken: the revolt activated radical tendencies of all kinds and instead of a local Austrian police action, reopened the Eastern Question in the most dramatic form.

Conscious that the blueprint charted by the "Hofpartei" failed to materialize, Andrássy anew switched his position. Now he put his stake on the calculation that the Turks "would crush the rebellion before a local matter became an international one"; in the meantime, he intended to arrange a diplomatic solution which would more or less reestablish the status quo and elevate Vienna into a position of arbiter between the contenders.[8]

The initial phase of the crisis still left him some hope for keeping the development under control. Francis Joseph, flabbergasted by the situation he had not expected, gave him a free rein. And, above all, the Russian entente paid its dividends: scared by the Balkan complications, St. Petersburg recognized the Austro-Hungarian Foreign Minister's initiative and leadership.[9] Yet, he had to wrestle with odds ultimately impossible to overcome. In order to hold back the aroused nationalist forces on both the Turkish and the Christian side, a perfect unity of all outside influences and a common realistic programme would have been necessary. In fact Andrássy could not even discipline his domestic opponents. He might in angry words reject a proposal for a joint Austrian-Serbian-Montenegrin action in the provinces forwarded by General Rodić, but not prevent him and his administration in Dalmatia from supporting the uprising. More importantly, no entente between Vienna and St. Petersburg could restrain the Moscow party and its allies for long. The feverish activity of Austria's implacable foe Ignatiev signalled that it was only a question of time when the conditions, almost ideal for the "Panslav" purposes, would propel them into the foreground.

* * *

Naturally, the stance taken by the Singers' Bridge stirred Ignatiev's blood. He still valued his Turkish assets higher than the Slav ones and would gladly see the rebellion stopped; but he insisted that the Austrian initiative must be "paralyzed" and "Count Andrássy, our sworn enemy and rival" prevented to arise as the "master of the Eastern Question." So, he resolved to ignore the instructions and, using his enormous sway at the Porte, started his own ventures. He managed to persuade the Sultan that in order to avoid foreign interference, concessions must be offered to the Christians and that a man dedicated to conciliatory policies—who happened to be his stooge Mahmud Nedim Pasha, dubbed "Mahmudov"—be nominated the new Grand Vizier. Finally, he obtained from Abdülaziz a pledge to conclude with Russia a secret treaty if the Tsar obliged himself to shield the Empire against "official collective pressure."[10]

The Tsar and his Chancellor were painfully alive to the vulnerability of the position dependent on Austrian goodwill, yet would not wage to take the initiative themselves. The sick man on the Bosphorus was agonizing, Alexander proclaimed, but "I do not want his corpse." Gorchakov too, as Ignatiev complained, "decidedly rejected the idea of direct agreement with Turkey and preferred to follow blindly the fantasies and plans of Andrássy."[11]

It can be judged both reasonable and understandable that the Ignatiev-Abdülaziz project was not taken in earnest; the Ambassador peddled a gambler scheme containing incalculable risks for Tsardom—international isolation, total estrangement with the Balkan Slavs and uproar in Russian society. The trouble, however, lay in that fearful paralysis which took hold of all leading advocates of moderation and which eventually allowed the extremists to prevail. Jomini, who had been during Gorchakov's frequent absences in charge at the Singers' Bridge, put it most succintly:

> We are profoundly convinced of our powerlessness and weakness as we face the immense task opening before us like an abyss. We are convinced it will devour the purest Russian blood to no purpose and exhaust our forces. Pray God that he may take this goblet away from us. Believe me, we prefer any outcome which would render it possible to avoid this abyss. That is what we cannot openly admit. . . . [12]

When Kartsov, the Consul General in Belgrade, came at the end of 1875 to St. Petersburg to ask for clear-cut dispositions, Gorchakov just snapped his fingers: "This is our programme." Taken aback, the diplomat turned to Jomini, but got the same reply: "What do you want? There is no programme!"[13]

Although rebuffed, Ignatiev could do as he pleased. Thus even before the Panslav spirit was aroused to its heights, foreign observers in the crisis area had been unable to distinguish "who represents Russian policy." The Ambassador at Constantinople Sir Henry Elliot was certainly close to the truth when he suspected that the "Father of the Lie" had "pretty nearly carte blanche" and that "his government does not wish him to keep them too well informed about his doings. They allow him to work with the Slavic Committees and it is more convenient to be left in ignorance of what goes on."[14]

It was much the same story with the attitude to Andrássy's contrary initiative. Gorchakov warned the Ballplatz about the rising doubts on whether the Austro-Russian "marriage of reason" was sincere and useful; if it were to survive, there should be "more frankness, less despotism and more respect to our viewpoints";[15] but in reality he simply plodded along. When the Austrian plan for settlement was finally formulated in the so-called Andrássy note (30 December 1875), the Russian Chancellor proclaimed it a perfect expression of his own notions and advised Ignatiev to adapt his actions to it.

True, Andrássy's proposals were quite far-reaching, providing for religious freedom, changes in taxation and the tax-farming system and for local self-government in the two provinces. But being devised only—as Austrian secret documents openly admitted it—"to break the Russian moral protectorate over the Christian population" and "prepare the ground for annexation"[16]—it contained no guarantees or sanctions; and because of it, could never have been accepted by the insurgents.

So in their different ways, the maneuvres of Ignatiev and Andrássy and the timidity of official Russian policymakers spurred rather than restrained explosive Russian and Balkan nationalism.

* * *

Most acutely, the Vienna-St. Petersburg axis was burdened by Serbian and Montenegrin policies.

In Serbia, the elections in summer 1875 brought a sweeping victory for the Liberal party of Jovan Ristić, canvassing a bold course. And Prince Milan, in comparison to his predecessor a very mediocre ruler, always vacillating and scared of being overthrown by the Karadjordjević family, soon confessed to Kartsov that he felt unable to handle the situation to the Powers' satisfaction: "only one remains to me—to give way to the universal enthusiasm and take lead of my people."[17]

In Montenegro, Prince Nikola lacked neither determination nor authority; but precisely because of this, he would not let the opportunity pass.

At first sight, the restraining pressures exercised by the Ballplatz and the Singers' Bridge achieved tangible results. In October, in a passing moment of courage, Milan ousted Ristić from the government; and Nikola hinted his readiness to play ball provided that he would be rewarded by some Hercegovinan districts. Yet the both principalities were aiming all the time for conflict and there were few doubts that if the revolt in the provinces were not suppressed soon they would join in the fray. After his aborted attempt with the secret Russo-Turkish treaty, this was also the bet on which Ignatiev gradually shifted his stakes. Diplomatic reports observed that Austrian influence in Belgrade and Cetynje decreased considerably and that counsels offered by the Russian "vice-Sultan" were more weighty than the admonitions coming from St. Petersburg. The Serbian ruler allegedly had "not taken a single step without consulting that Ambassador" and the "military preparations carried on here" had been undertaken according to his "regular and strong recommendations." The links between Ignatiev and the Prince of Montenegro were even firmer.[18]

Moreover, it was precisely the perspective of the Serbian and Montenegrin action that had awakened the "Panslav spirit" in Russia.

In the first months of the crisis, society and even Slavic committees had been almost listless and it seemed as if only the notorious court nuissances—the Tsarina and her ladies-in-waiting—were truly engaged in sponsoring the Slavic cause. Alexander permitted to collect contributions for civilian victims of the Turkish repression, but the immediate resonance fell short of expectation and the Moscow businessmen, presumed to be the main source of help, were visibly unwilling to open their purses. The press had docilely observed the official line, Cherniaev's *Russkii mir* being the only exception.[19] Katkov had advised against "the system of procrastinations and postponements for tomorrow," clamoured for collective pressure on the Porte, and, most significantly, for the autonomy of the Christian areas; at the same time, though, he had not questioned the Austro-Russian cooperation in the settlement and even conceded that the reservations the other Powers might raise against dramatic changes ought to be taken into account.[20]

In October, with the expected direct involvement of the two principalities, the great turn commenced. In a letter to Cherkasskii, Aksakov charted the new prospects:

> I am sure Serbia and Montenegro will not stay neutral—the cup of patience is brim-full so that the slightest drop will cause it to overflow. What then? Can Russia allow Austria to occupy Serbia with her armies? That would be the beginning of Russia's fall. So unless diplomacy can maintain the status quo, there will be thunder and lightning. Now it is very essential to excite public opinion here in Russia.[21]

Using, after the ban of the *Moskva*, the *Russkii mir* as his mouthpiece, Aksakov admonished St. Petersburg that neither Serbia nor the other South Slavs ought to be intimidated by Vienna and that no consideration ought to stop Tsardom in assisting them. Since October, this was no longer to be an isolated voice; the other dailies took up similar arguments.[22] At the same time Aksakov could see how his hope for exciting public opinion began to surpass his wildest dreams. "The money for collection flows in, in a steady stream, despite the paucity of funds, the absence of interest from the government and its diplomatic stand in the matter," he noted proudly. It was above all the allegedly completely ignorant "dark people," the "overburdened simple poor," who responded to the appeal.[23]

Although the Red Cross and the Holy Synod participated, the whole of the credit was ascribed to the committees. They were invigorated and enormously increased in authority. New branches were opened in Kharkov, Ekaterinoslav, Kazan, Warsaw, Samara, Orel, Saratov and elsewhere. For 1875, the annual budget of the Moscow Committee had been envisaged as a mere 7000 rubles; in fact, only for the short period between the middle of September and the beginning of November it received 750,000 rubles and spent 400,000 rubles.[24]

The restraining efforts of the government—it prohibited the raising of money in churches and private houses and the participation of state employees and zemstvos in the collection—had rather the opposite effect. Equally resented was the demand that the funds should be used as the Tsar ordained it, i.e. on a strictly humanitarian basis; there was overriding consent that the money ought to be spent on weapons and Russian volunteers, not on "maize and medicine."[25]

The mission of the Hercegovinan leader Veselicki-Bojidarović to Russia in January 1876 produced the first important extremist breakthrough. While Gorchakov tried to persuade the emissary that the insurgents had "to accept these Andrássy reforms and subordinate themselves to the will of Europe," the heir and the representatives of the committees advised the opposite, and, as it seems, Alexander yielded to them. Veselicki was given 90,000 rubles to buy arms and the same probably happened with at least a portion of the 360,000 rubles delivered in the following months to the Balkans. On 26 January, Gorchakov's deputy Giers informed Kartsov that the Tsar concurred to Serbian war preparations and that he might hint to the Belgrade government to get ready for the event if Russian peaceful desires proved barren. "Thus," wrote Giers, "your hands are untied. You will of course not neglect to observe that caution and foresight which are indispensable in such a delicate case."[26]

When Schweinitz returned in March 1876 to St. Petersburg, this time as the German Ambassador, he reported that he had found no "war party" in the elite, not even "a single statesman or general wishing to disturb the peace."[27] Nonetheless, the concessions already made indicated what would be the consequence of Alexander-Gorchakov's policy, or, to be more precise, the absence of policy.

* * *

Russian passivity in the initial stage of the Eastern crisis coincided with increasing commitment in Central Asia: a new drive for "better frontiers" on the approaches to India and China had been in progress and the Moscow party commenced to be largely engaged in the enterprises of their military associates beyond the Caspian Sea.

Earlier, the attitude of the Muscovites to the Caucasian and Asiatic ventures had been ambivalent, with the apprehension that the "holy mission" might have been abandoned for the predominantly steppe, desert and mountainous regions with hostile Moslem populations looming in their thoughts. Katkov, although much less Slav-Orthodox conditioned than most of the others, had been particularly unenthusiastic. Commenting on the last phase of the Caucasian conquest, he had advised a firm policy of colonization and integration into the Empire, but warned that this effort must not detract Tsardom from the vital tasks in Poland and the Western provinces.[28] Concerning Central Asia, his judgments had been pronouncedly negative. He had hinted that the generals were performing in detriment to the national interest, swerving the government "from the solution of the problems with which the importance of Russia as an European Power is connected." The English benevolence merely gave him an additional reason to be wary: he suspected behind it a sinister design to entangle Russia in a "distant, wild country."[29]

Since the end of the 1860s, there had been a general turn of the tide as far as Russian public opinion was concerned. Senator Lebedev observed that while even the greatest events in the Caucasus had passed almost unnoticed, the triumphs east of the Caspian Sea incensed the press and society.[30] Also seemingly one-tracked Aksakov and Dostoevskii proclaimed Russia's "Christian obligation" to spread civilization and liberate peoples subjected to British rule.[31] But Katkov was still reluctant to join the trend. Stressing the needs of Russian commerce and industry, he saw them in contradiction with territorial aggrandizement in the area. "Our merchants have the right to expect (from the government) safety of travel and improved communications, (but) without unreasonable sacrifices," he wrote at the end of 1872.[32]

It was to be the expedition to Khiva, followed by the *Moskovskiia vedomosti* with keen interest, which marked the watershed. Albeit still admonishing St. Petersburg to eschew "expensive and for us tiresome permanent occupation," and to limit its objectives to the establishment of a military base in the mouth of the Amu-Daria and by opening the river to trade,[33] the publicist already broached ideas which were to identify him in the future as the foremost advocate of Asiatic expansion. He subscribed to the extremist maxim that military advance was an unavoidable precondition for economic preponderance. Because of this he pleaded for the strategic "Great Central-Asian Railway" planned by Lesseps;[34] pronounced the "introduction of order in the Turkoman lands" as the immediate task;[35] and recalling the "vast trade connections" of the Moscow and Siberian merchants with China, he started to request active policy in the Chinese-Pacific sphere, including the build-up of a powerful Pacific fleet.[36] No less significantly, the Moscovite adhered to the principle that the English should be dealt with sternly: no guarantee ought to be offered to them, no concession made, no neutralization or a buffer zone which would deprive Russia of a free hand. Firmness, he assured, would induce London to be more accommodating in Europe, to cease its "insulting interference . . . into purely Russian affairs" and even to enter into an economic partnership with Tsardom in Asia.[37]

Sensitive like everybody else to the Thunderer's campaigns, Ambassador Loftus in the dispatch of 29 October 1873, already proclaimed him as a man steering Russian Asiatic policy.[38] A closer insight, however, reveals that this did not fully match reality. Despite the shift just described, the editor wished that doors should be kept opened for Anglo-Russian understanding to counterbalance the Dreikeiserbündnis commitments;[39] while St. Petersburg saw no reason to abandon the established pattern. Mostly due to the clumsy and timid British approach,[40] the official policy leaned to the hawkish principle "action instead of negotiations" rather than to the Katkovian "action to ease negotiations."

A new drive was precipitated by the crisis in Kokand, where the rule of Khudoiar Khan stirred up enormous discontent. Entirely servile in obeying Kaufman's orders and feeling secure under his protection, the Khan imposed upon his subjects a system of terror and extortionate taxation exceeding by far even Oriental standards.

In August 1874, St. Petersburg recognized Khudoiar's position untenable and advised the Tashkent warlord to abstain from military action in case of a change on the throne. Kaufman, however, took no heed of it: in view of the strategic value of Kokand had for possible thrust against India and China, he looked for an excuse to annex it into his Turkestan fief. Events favored him. In the capital, a palace coup engineered by the local "Russian party" was expected; in reality, unrest exploded in summer 1875 into a general uprising, Kokand was proclaimed independent in its historical frontiers and the insurgent army penetrated into Russian-occupied territories. Having his hands untied, the "Yarim Padishah" of Tashkent left no stone unturned. Not only did he put the valley of Ferghana, the "pearl of Central Asia," under sword and fire, but also dispatched his most enterprising general, Mikhail Skobelev, to the Pamir, to provide the best strategic argument for the conquest.[41]

Indeed, in the debate on the Kokand affair, the Eastern military paraded their full strength. Already preoccupied by the explosive Balkan situation, Miliutin sided with the rest of the ministers and opposed the annexation; in Central Asia, he maintained, the British "are watching our every step" and therefore, the Turkestan and Caucasus authorities should "avoid offensive actions as much as possible and abstain from trespassing existing border lines." But Alexander shared the view of his hawks, correctly predicting that London would just watch and do nothing. Even before Russian troops invaded the khanate, a council presided over by him had decided to dismiss eventual protests and Ambassador Shuvalov had been instructed to proceed as usual: to utter soothing words, but not give binding guarantees "for the future, in case of new circumstances." And when it came to the "new circumstances" the Tsar, in Miliutin's words, "in five minutes, without any deliberation" approved the proceedings of Kaufman. On 19 February 1876, the city of Kokand was taken and on 3 March the annexation was formally announced. Renamed "the Ferghana region," the khanate became an integral part of the Turkestan Governor-Generalship and Skobelev appointed its military governor.[42]

Boosted by the autocrat's benevolence, the Tashkent clique was all ready to go even further. Skobelev had returned from his Pamir expedition in the highest spirits: the old Indian plan was quite feasible, he reported, particularly if the drive to Kashmir were performed simultaneously with the advance along the Astrabad–Herat–Kabul route. On these grounds, Kaufman pleaded in St. Petersburg that the acquisition of the mountain area should be unfurled into an "effective demonstration" on the Indian borders; such an action, he peddled the familiar formula, would give Russia substantial advantage in the Balkans, preventing the English in helping their Turkish friends.[43]

Albeit already in the midst of intense war preparations on the Armenian border, the Caucasus command also indulged in similar schemes. Grand Duke Mikhail and his staff proposed first to occupy the Turkoman centers, Akhal-Tekin and Ashkhabad, and then develop this move into a large-scale advance into Persia and Afghanistan.[44]

Katkov was mightily inspired and, in the boldness of his demands, quickly catching up the Eastern hawks. The Merv oasis, considered a part of Afghan territory, he proclaimed the "key to the peace in the Turkoman steppes and Central Asia," which must be obtained forthwith.[45] Beyond it, the Russian sphere of influence should embrace all territories north and west of the Indian border and, furthermore, include the northeastern Chinese provinces. Exhiliterated, he even for a while abandoned his main concept. The talks with the English on Central Asia, he wrote, "are closed forever"; they have "no right to dictate how Russia should deal with her restive neighbors, and their further encroachments in this quarter will naturally be met with energetic resistance."[46]

In the meantime, however, the crisis in the Balkans had already entered the stage where the Asiatic initiatives were entirely overshadowed by it. The inflated "Panslav spirit" turned the Moscow party and the public exclusively to this sphere. In the ensuing fatal three years it was to be the only area which really mattered; also some leading militarists who had won their laurels in Central Asia (Cherniaev, Skobelev) were to appear beyond the Danube carrying with them their inflated ambitions.

* * *

The exceptionally hard winter of 1875-1876 brought a temporary lull into the Balkan fighting. For the Russian statesmen, though, this offered no relief.

Pressed by Ignatiev and facing financial bankruptcy, the Porte would perhaps gladly settle on some compromise. But the Christian rising roused a powerful wave of Moslem fanaticism both in the Balkans and at Constantinople, which was to aggravate the crisis still more. In eight months the only concession the Bosnian Moslems had allowed was the ringing of a small bell on an Orthodox church in Sarajevo; maybe, a British diplomat commented with bitterness, "now that a beginning has been made, the Turks will get accustomed with the sound, and make no opposition if eventually a larger and more sonorous bell be used."[47]

Under the circumstances, the Andrássy note was doomed to remain but another document for the annals of diplomatic history. The attempt to negotiate on its basis (on 4-7 April at Sutorina) failed. According to a Russian report, Christian leaders expected "if not complete liberation. . . then at least European guarantees; and when they discovered that the Andrássy note contained no such a thing and left them to uncontrolled Turkish rule, they resolved to continue the revolt."[48]

The deepening stalemate deprived the St. Petersburg policy of all its rationale. In this conjunction, the position taken by the *Moskovskiia vedomosti,* heretofore more circumspect than that of the rival dailies, was very symptomatic.

Until January 1876, the Katkovite organ had claimed that the line prosecuted by the Three Emperors' League—'first to help appease the agitated spirits and then dwell on removing the reasons which had created dissatisfaction'—was correct. Its editor had even gone as far as rejecting the doubts raised by the press and shared almost by the entire society: 'Russia has not changed (her traditional) policy,' he maintained, 'on the contrary, her unchanged policy has become the common policy of the whole of Europe. Her opinions concerning the Eastern Christians have been taken up by everybody. What she has been earlier saying alone, is now being repeated. . . also by her former foes.'[49]

After the Andrássy note, the Muscovite sharply swerved to a radical stance. He immediately disclosed its essential weakness—the absence of guarantees—and introduced his counter-programme. Albeit repeating that the Eastern Question was not yet ripe for a 'genuine solution,' he nonetheless proposed an arrangement very close to it—either full autonomy for the insurgent provinces or their annexation to the other 'vassal dependencies of the Porte,' i.e. to Serbia and Montenegro.[50]

While advertising a settlement in total divergence to Austrian aspirations, the publicist joined the chorus of Gorchakov's opponents who affirmed that Vienna should not be trusted. He still exculpated Andrássy and put the blame on 'diverse currents which are at work around him and behind him'[51] but this was only a temporary dispensation: the time for leniency was over and more direct indictments would ensue.

Alexander and Gorchakov muddled through the crisis more and more resigned, wondering whether it would not be better to let the "bloody drama" expected for the spring take its course. The consent the Tsar had given to Serbian war preparations was a sign of it. Also his Chancellor, although still taking part in the Austrian threats to Belgrade, assented that probably "European diplomacy would not succeed in holding back Serbia, Montengro and perhaps Rumania, from open interference in the struggle" and if that were to be the case the best policy would be to "leave both sides to the dictates of fate, when the arms decide which of them will triumph."[52]

Inevitably, such a resignation could not but encourage the forces wishing to cut the Gordian knot—the Serbians, Montenegrins and the Russian extremists. Few among the South Slavs would believe in the warning that Tsardom would not help them; in fact, they expected it to take the lead. Metropolitan Mihailo wrote to Moscow:

> Russia, which has twice borne conflicts with Europe, must clash with it a third time. And we hope, we pray to God, to aid her to emerge victorious in this desperate struggle. . . . Please, solve the Eastern Question as soon as possible, later it will be difficult for us both.[53]

While Prince Milan showered Vienna and St. Petersburg with "satisfactory assurances," the preparations for war went on undisturbed. Since February, an alliance treaty had been negotiated with Montenegro, where Nikola was similarly veering to the bellicose option. As he put it to Ionin, it was unpleasant for him to lose European sympathy; yet together with Milan they would rather take that risk than let themselves by "roasted on a small fire."[54]

Again, no historian will ever be in a position to assess fully the measure in which Russian hawkish diplomats and Slavic committees,

deliberately wrecking the efforts of their Tsar and their government, inspired the South Slavs to boldness. The Singers' Bridge
issued to its Balkan consuls a strict order prohibiting 'Panslav'
agitation; thus, they had to be extremely cautious in their reports.
Also the essential decisions taken   by the leading groups in the
committees were kept strictly secret. 'We did not blaze away about
them, we did not note them down in protocols,' Professor Lamanskii volunteered. According to Nikitin, the best Soviet authority
on the subject, the first official emissary of the committees, Prince
Vasilchikov, was concerned only with humanitarian issues and the
amrs deliveries were organized by the correspondent of the Katkovian press, Monteverde. It appears though, that among manifold activities the main one was connected with paving the way
and then supporting the mission of the 'Lion of Tashkent,' General
Cherniaev.[55]

Cherniaev, a man with a suitable heroic record and well established
contacts to the heir of the throne, had from the very outset loudly advertized his intention to go to Serbia, become a Balkan Garibaldi and
by his deeds "wake up Russia, that sleeping Tsarina." And when he
escaped police surveillance and surfaced on 28 April in Belgrade, all
ceased to doubt what the outcome would be.[56]

In the meantime, Russian extremist heralds stepped out with their
big plans. The autonomist scheme elaborated by Katkov was the most
modest among them. The rest chiefly originated or were given impulse
by the unrelenting Ignatiev, whom the rapid change at Constantinople
depriving him of his grip over the Porte induced to switch back to his
old "Panslav radicalism." Now he and his lieutenants were going to solicit
a large-scale solution where diplomacy would be replaced by Tsardom's
military might. The first step in this direction had been undertaken in
December 1875 by the chargé d'affaires of his Embassy, Alexander Nelidov.[57] Later on, Ignatiev himself, together with military attaché Colonel
Zelenoi, composed several project for a campaign, all of them based on
the idea that the main strike would be delivered by a strong army group
formed on the Armenian border.[58]

Although disdainful about Ignatiev's strategic concept, the General
Staff group had also been caught by his warlike fire. That Alexander

strongly objected against even "preliminary preparations" did not matter. The war planning was well under way, officers were lectured about it and in April Miliutin already submitted to the Tsar Obruchev's memoir on the political aspects of the mobilization as well as the results of a topographic survey secretly carried out in Asiatic Turkey. In the elite, the Tsarina was particularly ostentatious in her approval for military readiness and publicly criticized the "passivity of our diplomacy," i.e. de facto the policy of her husband.[59]

The government was quickly approaching the point where the manifold pressures would force it to cease the hide-and-seek game.

* * *

Bismarck followed events with growing apprehension. The new emphasis given by St. Petersburg and Vienna to the Emperors' League unity did not elate him. He would not believe a word of the Russian and Austrian peaceful assurances[60] and feared that the two partners might at any moment come to blows.

At first, he tried to postpone the dreadful "Optionsfrage" by enlisting English help. But Lord Derby declined the take pary in what he believed to be just another mischievious ploy and compelled the Chancellor to go back to his old partners and arguments. Discussing the crisis with Ambassadors d'Oubril and Shuvalov—"with the face of a nice man with the best of intentions," Miliutin remarked with irony[61]—he proclaimed the moment most propitious for Russia "to settle accounts with Turkey according to her notions." To d'Oubril, he suggested a large-scale agreement with the other Powers on the division of the "Turkish heritage" and offered his mediation. With Shuvalov, his most intimate friend among the Russians, he went even farther. According to the Ambassador's report, he promised—albeit only as "Bismarck the nobleman, not as Bismarck the Chancellor"—that the Reich would pay back its debt of honor for support provided in 1866 and 1870 and that Tsardom might "unconditionally count on it"; if divergencies were to occur between Russia and the Dual Monarchy "his vote would be in our favor and he would put at our disposal, in case of need, the German army."[62]

Bismarck's feelers coincided with a highly significant initiative from the Strastnyi Boulevard.

It is to be recalled that after 1871 the Moscow editor gradually re-interpreted his 'free hand policy': he ceased to regard France as the 'natural ally' and departed from the Gorchakovian concept of the European balance more or less based on it. In early 1875, he modified also his idea of an Anglo-Russian understanding: for England, he affirmed, no other way remained than to leave her 'splendid isolation' and join the Bismarckian system. The value of the Emperors' League, moreover, he pictured not just in terms of 'best guarantee for European peace,' but also as the instrument providing 'the possibility to pursue an unanimous policy' in the East; and explained this unanimity in a rather peculiar way, as 'freedom of action on questions not related to European peace.'[63]

The Radowitz mission must have furthered Katkov's conviction that Berlin had grown ripe for a deal which would ensure Russia a protective umbrella for pursuing freely her aims in Central Asia and in that part of the "Turkish heritage" where Austrian interests were not directly involved. Gorchakov's concept of a strong France was, of course, entirely incompatible with such vistas and it became only a question of time when the publicist would enlarge his earlier hints by a full-fledged appeal for a change. Whether he learned about the Shuvalov-Bismarck parleys or not, the appeal came in their wake, at the end of March (1876). The arguments used were remarkably similar to those repeated in the "option debate" in 1866-1871, if only a reader would replace "France" for "Germany" and vice versa. They ran as follows:

> The republican regime established west of the Rhine is an 'arti-
> ficial plant' and those politicians who 'speculate on the French-
> German antagonism' and would give Russian support to France
> are 'devoid of rational thinking.' Reasons of national interest ask
> for the cultivation of German friendship, because there is no real
> contradiction between Tsardom and the Reich; and their aims,
> 'if not identical in everything, can nonetheless be reconciled.'[64]

Yet, as the editor blamed the St. Petersburg policy-makers in the great indictment written before his death, they let the fateful opportunity "to test German friendship" slip away.[65] The Bismarckian soundings met the same response on the Neva as on the Thames. Gorchakov accused his rival of being the "great tempter," who "strove for nothing else than to isolate France"; but, he added, "the Tsar will not be seduced to the conquest of Constantinople."[66]

Indeed, both the German Chancellor and the Moscow publicist chose a wrong moment for their initiatives. Mounting pressures forced Alexander to abandon his passive stance and plunge together with Gorchakov into a feverish diplomatic activity. The dominating motive of his conduct, however, was still identical with his moderate ministers: it was the desperate search for a way to escape the dreaded war abyss.

The Russian leading statesmen hoped to find the new point of departure at the forthcoming League summit in Berlin. There, their partners should be won over to a more effective common programme based on the formula of "complete autonomy."

This was the solution Gorchakov had suggested already the previous autumn and Katkov had canvassed since then; and which, as the latter made clear in his 10 May editorial, could solely be accepted by the Russian public as its compromise with Europe:

> The Turkish Empire is no more a 'sick man,' it is a 'dead man' already. . . . In the interest of all Europe, in order to safeguard general peace, the obsolete construction of the Ottoman Empire cannot collapse instantaneously . . . ; it remains bolster it for the time being. . . but merely as the principle of the Sultan's suzerainty, not as that of Turkish dominance over the Christians. Therefore, the Powers must. . . insist on full equality for the population. And because this is impossible to achieve under Turkish administration, the autonomy of the provinces appears inevitable.[67]

In a memorandum for the talks, Gorchakov went perhaps even farther. In a visible effort to placate both Russian hawks and the "Hofpartei," he requested that the autonomy programme should be secured by a naval demonstration near Constantinople and by Russian military presence in Bulgaria and Austrian in Bosnia-Hercegovina.[68]

Dramatic events just in progress in the area seemed to supply the Alexander-Gorchakov duo with the most persuasive arguments. On 6 May, rising Moslem hatred against the raya led to riots in Salonika: German and Franch consuls were among the victims. Three days later, demonstrations broke out at Constantinople; "Mahmudov" had to resign and the new government was composed of determined opponents of conciliation. Moreover, first reports were coming in of an anti-Turkish rising in Bulgaria. Instead of a new start, however, the Berlin entrevue turned out to be just an embarrasing epilogue.

Andrássy arrived in the German capital irritated by his failures and tired of pretending to be Russia's friend. To the Germans he spoke his mind with brutal candour:

> This unnatural thing which calls itself the Three Emperors' League comes from Germany. It is you who made the Russians so great and it is no business of ours to take the consequences. When it begins to rain into this miserable shed of a League, we shall take our umbrellas and walk out. You have crowded us out of Germany—to our advantage. A state of 36 million inhabitants (Austria-Hungary) cannot have its centre of gravity outside its own territory. But a state must have a mission and ours lies in the East.[69]

In the talks with the Russians, he dismissed Gorchakov's proposals in equally unmistakable terms.

Terrified by Igantiev's telegrams announcing imminent upheaval in the Ottoman Empire and appalled by the possibility that this might happen simultaneously with the breach in the monarchic bloc, the Tsar panicked and agreed to "eliminate all you oppose." In the end, the Hungarian Count himself dictated what was to be another still-born programme of the League. This so called Berlin memorandum (13 May 1876) asked merely for an armistice and continuing negotiations; only if the hostilities should break out again, some arrangement among the Powers concerning "effective measures . . . to arrest prevailing evils and prevent them to grow" was envisaged.[70]

Somber re-examination after the Berlin shock warranted the Russian statesmen but one conclusion: that they had been all the time saving the formal understanding at the too high price of prolonged stalemate, and that the entente with Andrássy, on which they had built their Eastern policy since 1871, "albeit still alive . . . turned barren."[71]

CHAPTER 14

PANSLAVISM AT LARGE:
THE SERBIAN EXPERIENCE
(1876)

Instead of diminishing, unrest is growing day after day. It is increasing in strength, because there is no notable governmental action. It seems to many that the government, conscious of its external and internal weakness, is immersed in some sort of apathy. Everyday brings new, confused and vague news and rumours. . . . No wonder that under such circumstances, together with unrest, dissatisfaction and mistrust arise towards the authorities which take no clear and firm stance. . . . This state of mind is very dangerous. Forces which are in the ascendant in all layers of Russian society are of such a nature that the government must necessarily take some decision. . . . It has become imperative to take hold of this popular movement; or else it will spread further, violently, in a wrong direction, outside the control of the government, distrustful and even hostile to it. Then it will be bad, very bad. . . .

Pobedonostsev

> Everything points to the beginning of
> action. Whether this is beneficial or not,
> results will reveal. We cannot retreat because
> we have gone too far . . . and you, if you
> leave us to our fate, know well that it is
> your own case.
> Metropolitan Mihailo in a message to Moscow

> Serbia cannot stand at the helm of Russian
> society and in no way should Russian public
> opinion trail behind Serbia . . . . Only the
> Russian stock, or rather only Russia, has a
> political future. The other people can
> exist solely in a close association with Russia
> in a form not yet determined by history.
> Our task is to liberate them and give them
> an opportunity to live and grow; it is our
> task to take away their national egotisms,
> which are detrimental to the common
> Slavic idea.
> Aksakov

After the May Berlin experience, Alexander II must have realized
that the dam was irreparably broken and he would have to swim in the
torrent whether he liked it or not. There was to be no moment of respite
for him, and the "revolutionary" and "Crimean" spectress always haunting him would now loom as large as ever.

Interrupting the long era of vacillations and concessions to the Russians,
Disraeli reintroduced the "British danger" into the game. He rejected
the Berlin memorandum outright and under a curious pretext of preventing Russian seizure of the Ottoman fleet, he got the consent of his cabinet for a naval action. On 26 May, British vessels arrived at the Besika
Bay, close to the Dardanelles.

The London resolve had immediate repercussions in the Turkish capital. In the night of 29-30 May, a military coup deposed Abdülaziz; and
the both groups now forming the government—traditional Moslem conservatives and the liberal-nationalist New Osman party of Midhat Pasha—
made it clear that they would accept external guidance and support from
the English only. Everything that the "Father of the Lie" had achieved by

intrigue, corruption and cajolery was lost and he himself conceded it: "the steeple-chase between us is no more possible and I voluntarily resign on the price," he said to Ambassador Elliot.[1]

Ignatiev, of course, ascribed this "complete fiasco" to the official policy which "had bound our hands and feet" by subservience to Austria-Hungary.[2] And others supported his demand that the British action should be countered without delay by an even more forceful move. Using partly Katkov's reasoning, General Fadeev claimed, in a memoir composed in June, that because of the obvious sterility of the pacific course, only one was left to Russia to preserve her great-power position—to strike a bargain with Germany and helped by the South Slavs, to establish her control over the Straits and the Balkans.[3]

Soon the proponents of war received from the Balkan nations the long-expected most weighty instruments to corner the government. The first one was delivered to them, though in a rather peculiar way, by the Bulgarians.

* * *

The Russian policymaking elite reacted on the coming reports on growing Bulgarian unrest[4] and the extremist moves to encourage and exploit it with the usual mixture of countermands and benevolence. Fadeev, the conspicuous leader of the Bulgarian-oriented faction with the same Garibaldi-like proclivities as Cherniaev, was closely watched by the police, while less notorious but equally firey men (brothers Kireev, Colonel Kishelski, Ivanov) might more or less freely operate a "private help" including deliveries of weapons.

The more responsible Panslav leaders hesitated. "To incite poor, defenseless Bulgarians to insurrection when they lack arms and when neither Serbia nor Russia has promised them aid, would be to condemn them to inevitable destruction," warned Prince Vasilchikov. The émigré "Old Party" also pleaded unpreparedness. But among the radicals of the "Young Party," the revolutionary fever ran high; and their view was summed up by the poet Christo Botev to the effect that "if there are no cannons and rifles, let the people rise with scythes and cutgels."[5]

Always optimistic about the mood of their kin, the exile hotheads also this time read the situation incorrectly, by ignoring the fact that the peasants and artisans, albeit now yearning for national liberation, were still reluctant to offer their property and lives for it. Their Panslav friends were equally irresponsible. The Vice-Consul at Plovdiv, Gerov, had according to a British report done "more mischief than anybody": he incited a local rising, claiming that Russian troops were already crossing the Balkan Mountains.[6]

When the insurrection broke out permaturely on 1 and 2 May at Koprivshtitsa, Panagurishte and Klisura, the most terrible awakening ensued. The rest of the country did hardly stir. And, although most all the Turkish troops were deployed in Bosnia-Hercegovina or on the Serbian borders, the irregulars, Turkish, Circassian and Pomak (islamized Bulgarians) "bashi bazouks" were strong enough to overwhelm the dispirited defenders of isolated townships; and, at the same time, joined by Moslem and Gypsy rabble, roamed at large over the greater part of the country. In the sanjak of Plovdiv alone, more than 60 localities were burned down and about 12,000 people murdered. The secretary of the British Embassy Baring, sent in July to make an unbaised observation, reported that he had been confronted by "the most awful sight that could present itself to the eyes of man." On Batak, where 6,000 of its 8,000 inhabitants were massacred, he wrote:

> The first thing I saw was some twenty or thirty dogs devouring human bodies, and in the place they were feasting I counted 62 skulls in about 20 yards. . . . The whole of the main street was a mass of human remains, but the most fearful spectacle was the church and its enceinte: here the corpses lay so thick that one could hardly avoid treading on them. . . . . Altogether, I can hardly describe the horror of the scene.[7]

Insignificant and even harmful for the extremist cause as the uprising might have been on its own, the atrocities committed were bound to have far-reaching repercussions favorable to Russian war advocates. Already before the world press got hold of the ghastly information, Ignatiev had demanded in their name to "stop the bloodshed" by a gigantic pincer movement of the Tsar's army across Bulgaria and along the route Alexandropol-Erzurum-Bosphorus and crush the Ottoman Empire.[8] Later, every gory detail gave them for months an effective instrument to the emotional mobilization of the public against the government. At the same time, they had also received what was believed to be their ultimate trump card: the Serbian and Montenegrin war against the Turks.

* * *

The predicament of Consul-General Kartsov in Belgrade well mirrored the cul-de-sac of the official Russian Balkan policy.

Earlier, Kartsov had hesitated between the opposite courses embodied by Ambassadors Ignatiev and Novikov; but seeing Cherniaev at large and the "action ministry" of Ristić reappointed, he fully realized the fatal implications. By renouncing the principles Russia had espoused in the recent years, he wrote to Ignatiev, she would probably rouse against herself a European coalition and "the disaster of 1853 would be repeated"; therefore, "our direct and holiest interests demand that we, as far as possible, should distance ourselves from solidarity with the Slavic movement."[9]

The diplomat, however, in vain sought for unambiguous support by the Tsar and Gorchakov. After visiting them in May, he must again feel very depressed, indeed. While Alexander ordered him to ignore Cherniaev and sternly warn the Serbian government, the Chancellor cautioned him: "Despite everything, do not forget that although the Tsar is opposed to war, his son, the heir, stands at the helm of the (pro-war) movement."[10]

And so it went on as before. Kartsov threatened, but Ignatiev, Cherniaev, and their associates effectively counterpoised his and other restraining voices.

Taking advantage of the wavering St. Petersburg stances, Ignatiev misinterpreted them entirely: "How can you expect that the Tsar should tell you his secret wish straight-a-way? Naturally, he cannot do that. Yet I repeat to you: as soon as you declare war, Russia will follow you without delay," he was reported as saying to a Serbian military plenipotentiary.[11]

Cherniaev's impressions from the Principality were far from encouraging. He observed, and Milan acknowledged it to him openly, that the pro-war exaltation was limited to the nationalist intelligentsia, while the peasant majority and the army rank-and-file felt differently. Privately, he informed Aksakov that troops were unprepared and the financial situation deplorable. Still, his original beliefs were unshattered: the Serbs "must be given a shove or else they will just talk without taking action." The financial problems should be solved by a Russian loan organized by the Slavic committee, which—with mines and forests as collateral—would also serve for making the Principality Tsardom's economic dependency; military deficiencies ought to be offset by a massive influx of Russian volunteers and by a general insurrection in Bulgaria, where, as he still spuriously asserted, "the population merely awaits a signal from Serbia" to begin war. With about 40,000 men, he claimed, he would reach Sofia in three days.[12]

Kartsov fittingly observed that in the extremist purposes, the Serbian war with the Turks "became a sort of decoy; the true struggle was conducted against (official) Russia or rather against the Winter Palace."[13] It must be added, however, that there were two concepts of this struggle. The first one was personified by the "Lion," who wished to be the hero who almost single-handed, without any participation from the treacherous St. Petersburg, would perform the task of liberation; and only then Russia, "the sleeping Tsarina," would wake up and punish her traitors.[14] Ignatiev and Aksakov, on the contrary, pursued the sole objective in forcing the government to war. However large-scale might be the participation of the committees and volunteers, the latter insisted, they could not warrant that the Russian mission would be accomplished. Serbian victory and Slav liberation would be inexpedient and even harmful save with the participation of Russia "in its entity, as a state, with the government at its head." Later, castigating Cherniaev for his Garibaldi-like dream, Aksakov wrote:

> By equipping and sending you to Serbia, and then by supplying you with volunteers, I had in mind provoking the official Russian involvement. Never have I believed in the possibility of solving the problem by the action of the committees alone. You cannot do practical things with lyricism.[15]

The Tsar and his Chancellor were keenly alive to the extremists' intentions; and they also knew the risks they exposed the reign to by giving them way. But they were too disheartened by the prevalent restive "patriotic" mood to put up effective resistance. When on 2 July the day Serbian and Montenegrin forces crossed their borders, and the Lion issued a manifesto announcing the crusade "for the holy cause of Slavdom," for the "Orthodox cross" and for the "unity of the Balkan peoples," Russian policymakers saw their hands tied.

To be sure, they were now feverishly active in establishing Russian diplomatic initiative in the Eastern Question. But still without a clear concept, "not in calm deliberation but under the influence of immediate, often accidental impressions,"[16] they were just prisoners of events and forces they were unable to control. And, all the time looking in vain back for escape from the abyss, they trailed along the path indicated to them by the extremists.

* * *

Wrestling with their dilemmas, Alexander and Gorchakov conceived, quite naturally, the foremost task in putting the relations with Vienna on a new footing. On the one hand, the most urgent demand to liberate Russia from Andrássy's tutelage was to be met; Katkov undoubtedly aired the view of almost the entire society when declaring that "from Russia's side, further sacrifices of her interests are out of the question."[17] On the other hand, equally weighty criticism of Miliutin—"our diplomacy is conducted so that in case of war we will be inevitably isolated"[18]—had to be responded to. "We are not willing to continue in the present sterile attitude," the Singers' Bridge conveyed to the Ballplatz.[19]

The new undertakings should include both a different formula for the non-intervention principle and more precise arrangements for the eventual dissolution of the Ottoman Empire. The pro-memoria of 2 July stated it as follows:

> The St. Petersburg government cannot proceed on the course which 'respects the wishes of Count Andrássy . . . in extreme'; now, inasmuch as 'events tend to violent solution,' different framework must be agreed on if 'this (Austro-Russian) understanding were to be more than an empty word.' The non-intervention principle has to be recognized 'an obligation between the cabinets,' yet not in the sense of impartiality and laissez-faire, but in the context of 'humanitarian feelings and Christian faith . . . the interests of the neighboring states and general power balance.' So, in the case of a Turkish victory in the war just starting, the programme devised by Andrássy might remain in force; whilst in the case of Christian triumph, the breakdown of the Ottoman Empire should be envisaged

and the two cabinets be ready with a scenario preventing 'political and revolutionary anarchy.'[20]

Owing partly to exceptionally lucky coincidences, it seemed for a brief moment that the Russian statesmen would get the desperately needed maneuvring space.

Andrássy would gladly respond to them as in Berlin and join the English. Another rebuttal from London, though, suddenly revealed his weakness: it left him no argument against the Emperor and the "Hofpartei," who lost patience with his game, wished to safeguard the seizure of Bosnia-Hercegovina and strike a deal with Tsardom to this effect. Thus the Russian pro-memoria supplied a point of departure for the talks Alexander, Gorchakov, Francis Joseph and Andrássy held on 8 June and which entered into the history of diplomacy as the "Reichstadt agreement."

No official protocol was signed at the summit and each side only subsequently noted down its own version of the agreement, with essential divergencies in points concerning the expected partition of the "Turkish heritage."[21]

Yet, contrary to Andrássy's interpretation[22] it may be affirmed that for the consent to the occupation of the two provinces the Tsar and his Chancellor bought the acknowledgment of their non-intervention formula and their initiative in the settlement.

The indisputable Russian gain was further mightily strengthened by the imbroglio in England, where during the summer and autumn the government was virtually paralyzed by the shattering effect of the Bulgarian massacres.

Disraeli (now Lord Beaconsfield) had desperately tried, first to conceal, and then to minimize, the ugly truths; by doing so, he only spurred his rival Gladstone, "the old hunter once more sniffing the scent," to take up the issue.[23] [24] In September, about 200,000 copies of Gladstone's pamphlet "Bulgarian Horrors and the Question of the East" were sold; and the popular outcry over the Turkish atrocities escalated into an overwhelming movement. Confronted by huge public pressure, the cabinet was not only unable to continue the diplomatic offensive started in the spring; it underwent a profound split. While the Prime Minister was driven by the campaign into an intransigent anti-Russian and pro-Turkish stance, most of his colleagues—above all Lords Salisbury, Derby and Carnavon—tended to the opposite position.

The lucky turn, however, unwound soon in a fashion scarcely wished by the St. Petersburg statesmen. Before the "Bulgarian horrors" outburst, the fear of the Anglo-Austrian coalition and the Crimean experience exuded its magic even upon notorious expounders of the forward policy; it also undoubtedly lay behind Katkov's thesis about Europe being "unripe for a proper settlement." Now, the fears receded and the government was to be exposed to exacerbated criticism for indifference, for missing favorable chance to intervene when England was lame by internecine strife.

While the English campaign against Beaconsfield and his Eastern policies put an additional feather in Katkov's and the Moscow party's cap,[25] the policymakers were castigated for the unability "to see the patent truth." "I cannot look at our useless and stupid policy without profound indignation," Cherkasskii wrote in a private letter.[26] Katkov in his editorials, of course, had to be less outspoken, yet he too clearly dissociated himself from the official line. On the communiqué of the Reichstadt, announcing that "the best understanding has been achieved,"[27] he responded by a redoubled anti-Austrian harangue; the reports on the Bulgarian massacres led him to question the value of any dealings with the European concert;[28] and, most significantly, he gradually retracted from his original approval of the non-intervention principle. The transpiring truth about the "Cherniaev war" made him together with the other dailies claim with increasing insistence that a mere volunteer action would not suffice.

Indeed, it was the harsh Serbian reality above all which was rapidly pushing the extremist-moderate contest to its climax.

* * *

In different ways the war of the two Balkan principalities with the Turks turned out to be close to a disaster for Russian moderates and their extremist opponents alike.

The Montenegrins fought as it had been expected. Although their initial push on Mostar had been repulsed, the victorious frontier battles at Vrbica (July) and Podgorica (August) upheld their prestige and morale.

The Serbs, on the other hand, signally failed. Their leaders had been too much carried away by nationalist fervor to see the realities; as did their Russian instigators, they underestimated Turkish military prowess, wrongly read the Bulgarian situation after the massacres, and took it for

certain that the Tsar would help them.[29] At the beginning even the sceptical Kartsov praised their "patriotic enthusiasm which seems to unite all
hearts";[30] then his reports became gloomy and disdainful. "Serbia was
like a duelist who had informed the police about the duel but arrived at
the duelling ground to discover with horror that the police were not
coming,"[31] he wrote forgetting somehow that it was his kinsmen—Ignatiev, Cherniaev and tutti quanti—who had done their utmost to create
this fatal illusion.

In Bosnia, the Turks easily thwarted the drive on Sarajevo; worse still,
Colonel Despotović, who was sent to organize and lead local insurgents,
behaved true to his name and caused serious estrangement. In the east
Cherniaev in vain awaited the Bulgarian popular explosion which should
sweep the enemy from his route to Sofia. (Turkish terror had not only
paralyzed the Bulgarians; they blamed their radical intelligentsia and
émigrés for the sufferings they had to undergo.) Beaten on 18 July at
Veliki Izvor, the Lion ingloriously returned to Serbian territory; and only
further disasters were in store for him there.

No less far-reaching than the military defeat were to be the political
consequences of the volunteer action, when after the Moscow Congress
(1867), Russian Panslav nationalism again revealed in it its true face.

Undoubtedly, among those who responded to the committees' exhortations, many were inspired by lofty motives and fought and died
with proverbial Russian gallantry. Yet, as a whole the volunteer movement operated in a manner strangely fitting to the selfish and unscrupulous aims its organizers and leaders tried to conceal. Possessed of airy
hopes, wrote Meshcherskii, "we did not notice or rather did not wish to
notice what a riff-raff had entered the volunteer ranks, and in what a
minority were the decent people . . . ."[32]

According to estimates,[33] about 4,500-5,000 men signed up. but only
about 2,500-3,000 actually took some part in the combat. The rest remained in Belgrade; and while the "most elegant and well-to-do" spent
their nights in the palace and let "gold flow in a stream" in card-playing
with the Prince, the low-grade parasites invaded cafés and inns and plagued
and insulted the Serbs with the boorishness and overbearance congenital
of their stock.

Russian observers[34] have left us a shattering picture in which the volunteers parade as constantly quarreling, drinking and whoring scum, who,

"when asked to pay their bills, slap the Serbs in their faces for the affront—as they say—to demand money from their saviours." Small wonder
that the populace soon viewed their alleged benefactors as "worse than
the Turks" and "prayed to God to relieve them of these pushing guests."[35]

The Lion and the military around him were a liability of another type.
"All of us, from generals to sergeants, were little Pompadours, adopting
the role of dictators and we did not hesitate to dominate the Serbs," a
honest volunteer stated it bluntly.[36] Limited, impulsive Cherniaev entirely lacked competence in commanding larger units in modern warfare. His
numerous opponents accused him of wasting human lives and favoring
minions willing to buttress his wild schemes.

In order to manipulate Russian public opinion and advertise himself as
a great warrior he established his own propaganda office, the Correspondence Bureau. News was sent out from it about victories which had never
taken place; while the setbacks, if mentioned at all, were explained by
treacheries and conspiracies, like large-scale diversions of Austrian troops
in Turkish uniforms. "Not a single honest line could reach the Russian
press from the battlefield," wrote *Golos;* "the Bureau was really a weapon
of political blackmail of the most criminal kind. By means of lies and
deception, it hoped to involve Russia in a war with Turkey."[37]

Consciously or not, the *Moskovskiia vedomosti* fully participated in
the fraud. Its correspondent in Serbia, one of the few privileged at the
Bureau, duly reported fairy tales and Katkov's editorials had been, until
August, tuned to highest optimism. When the official *Pravitelstvennyi
vestnik* published correspondence from Constantinople on the Serbian
defeats, the editor accused it of being the "most Turcophile in Europe."[38]

Even after the truth could no longer be concealed, the Moscow party
considered it politic to uphold the Lion's and the volunteers' heroic image
at any price. Katkov later refused to publish the final part of "Anna
Karenina" in the *Russkii vestnik,* because of Tolstoi's truthful description of the volunteer action.[39]

Among the many scandals by which the General antagonized the Serbs,
the attempt to perform a military coup, abolish the parliamentary system
and proclaim Milan a king gained the widest notoriety. He explained his
vistas to Aksakov as follows:

> This way, 'the influence of Russia upon Serbia would be real
> and rest on firm foundations. The chief of state and the entire

people (!) sympathize with Russia. The ministers could be gradually named from Russians. Hostile parties would disappear and the Principality become de facto a Russian province.'[40]

On September 15, the Lion opened his gamble with a telegram to Milan to the effect that the "spontaneous movement" to proclaim Serbia an independent kingdom "could not be restrained." Misinterpreting the report of the Correspondence Bureau, the *Moskovskiia vedomosti* announced the coup as an accomplished fact and even affirmed that the Assembly approved it by all but two dissenting voices.[41] Actually, the affair unwound to Cherniaev's detriment. Neither the ministers nor the Assembly were willing to commit political suicide and Milan, albeit probably sympathetic to the scheme, was forced by pressure from Vienna and St. Petersburg decline his participation too.

* * *

In the meantime, confronted with the Turkish advance deep into Serbia and the growing probability that Belgrade would sue for an armistice, the whole Moscow party escalated its quest for preventing the "disaster of peace" by Russian direct military intervention. The Panslav wave in the summer of 1876 seemed to give it all the chances for success.

The press, describing universal exaltation, compared it with the mood during the Napoleonic invasion in 1812. Meshcherskii recollected that "everything else was put aside and only the Slavic question preoccupied all minds to the point where there was no place in Russia in which it would not be a burning issue."[42] True, in the well-to-do and liberal layers many disapproved of the Panslav hypocrisy. "Those who really love Russia should comprehend that she needs peace and only peace," read an annonymous letter to the authorities. "Start a collection for national education instead. . . . Be consistent. If you behave humanly to the Serbs, behave in that way to the Poles too!"[43] Still, the initiative belonged entirely to the other side. The activities of the Slavic committees took on a scope and intensity vastly surpassing all the former or later efforts and achievements. The financial donations amounted by October 1876 to three million rubles; the contribution in kind, 500,000 rubles. Most of it, again, was not "wasted" on humanitarian help but employed on transportation and maintenance of the volunteers. The committees also mediated a big war loan to Serbia from Russian banks.

The portentous trait of the situation, the capitulation of the government before public opinion, grew in prominence.

Surely, there was no one minister favoring war. They were visibly annoyed at Alexander, who, true to his natural disposition, sought escape in palliatives, allowed the army officers to join the volunteers and on the matter of a war loan for Belgrade "waved his hand" and said "do whatever you want if only the government is not involved officially."[44] Observing that the Tsar let his son, the heir, turn the Anichkov Palace into a "centre for agitation running entirely counter to the accepted foreign policy," Miliutin complained that "with such a duality there cannot be any definite system in our actions or any clear plan."[45] Yet, though only too keenly aware of the huge risks involved in a new crusade against the Turks,[46] neither the War Minister nor the Chancellor, the two men with crucial influence on decision-making, were free from similar double-facedness. When on 9 August the *Novoe vremia* raised the question whether Tsardom was prepared for war, Gorchakov claimed that the only reason for his caution had been the bad state of the army; upon which Miliutin responded angrily that "Russia's military forces have never been prepared to such a degree as they are now."[47]

The concessions granted continued to irritate rather than appease. The press criticism showed but the tip of an iceberg. After a journey in several gubernias, an anonymous official reported to police chief Trepov:

> Respect for the Tsar's person is diminishing everyday . . . . The insensible, indifferent attitude of the Russian Emperor to the Slavic brethren in the Balkan peninsula . . . the demonstrations in favour of Prussia and Germany in 1870-1871—all this proves that our great Tsar is inwardly an alien. The contempt a Russian feels to the current policy of his ruler is limitless . . . .[48]

Disloyal undertones occurred even in the message the usually servile Holy Synod sent to Cherniaev. There was virtually no place where Alexander could find peace. "You are destroying the dynasty," his wife accused him.[49]

Because of their overt appeals to military involvement, the *Grazhdanin* and the *Russkii mir* were temporarily suspended in August; but others stepped in their place.[50] It was at this juncture that the *Moskovskiia vedomosti* reemerged as the leading extremist organ.

When the summer Serb defeat by Alexinac induced the Singers' Bridge to join international action to arrange a truce on a status quo basis, Katkov cried wolf. At first, he dismissed the truce as a part of an "European intrigue" and on 1 September implored the Tsar to prevent this "most dangerous and disgusting maneuvre" by acting "in accordance with the unanimous feeling of his people."[51] Then, facing Turkish advance into the Morava valley, he assented to an international understanding on the cessation of hostilities, but insisted that Russia must refuse further participation "in this strange deception called European action," request the presence of her "volunteer troops" in Bulgaria and full autonomy for the whole of European Turkey. Any other settlement should be regarded unacceptable and military intervention be the only response:

> War is a calamity. Every country wishes to remain in peace—but the peace has to be in harmony with her substantial interests, honor and dignity.[52]

* * *

Taken more and more prisoner by the overwhelming mood, Alexander finally succumbed to it. The transformation expected by the moderates with trepidation, had come true in the deliberations held from 9 September at Livadia.

The fatal dilemma "war or chaos," looming large over Russian dignataries assembled in the Tsar's Crimean summer residence,[53] was forcefully stated by Pobedonostsev, in his message to the heir:

> The moment is now crucial, not only for foreign policy. If this ends in some dirty peace, to our shame and to the satisfaction of our so called allies, all the exasperation which has so far been directed abroad, will turn inward and such a deep strife may occur between the government and the people that will be without parallel in history. For Russia nothing is more disastrous than such strife. Our whole system has been upheld by one thing only—by national faith in the force ruling the country. There is no other basis and cannot be in this vast Empire.[54]

The Muscovites worked skillfully on softening Alexander that way. They sent to Livadia merchant Porokhovshchikov as "representative of the Russian people"; and the man apparently succeeded in impressing upon the ruler that the aroused mass "might enter the war outside the control of the government, without waiting for a decision."[55] At any rate, Ignatiev could in the memoir[56] he presented hammer out extremist projections. The heir assured Pobedonostsev that the document "dispersed the uncertainty":

> The Tsar is (now) convinced that he can achieve nothing without war and hence he has decided in favor of war. He wants to clear the decks as soon as possible and the sole question remains—how to achieve it.[57]

The only voice of protest was raised by Reutern, who submitted a very pessimistic analysis on the economic consequences of mobilization and war. He could not even conclude his statement, being silenced by Alexander's outburst: "we need deeds now, not words." The Finance Minister returned from the Crimea deeply shaken. "Except for Adlerberg, everybody there is mad," he unburdened himself to a friend.[58]

It was agreed that the focal task of the running diplomatic action would be to create conditions where "Turkey will not be supported openly by any Power." Russia should take part in the conference due to meet at Constantinople, but "simultaneously prepare for war" and "once the futility of the negotiations is established, without delay resort to arms and wage war independently, unrestricted by any previous conditions and agreements." Gorchakov summed up the debate:

> It may be stated that in no period of our wars against the Turks we were in such a favorable position and had such a possibility of achieving swift and, with relatively limited resources, decisive results.[59]

On 15 October, Obruchev set forth the plan for the Balkan campaign; on 23 October, the formation of the Danube Army was announced, with Grand Duke Nikolai (Nikolaevich), a brother of the Tsar, as Commander-in-Chief; on 26 October, Reutern was ordered to prepare finances for war.

* * *

In historical retrospect, the Livadia deliberations represent a distinct watershed. In the immediate conjuncture, however, the extremist victory was still far from complete. Gorchakov speculated with delays which would enable in the end a diplomatic settlement; Miliutin allied with him in opposing Ignatiev's demand for immediate military action; and the doubts about the position of the two partners in the League, particularly Austria-Hungary,[60] helped them to withhold the now inflammed Tsar. The situation remained extremely complex.

Suddenly entangled in the Panslav web, Alexander now lived in a strange state of feverish exaltation and allegedly dreamed that not only the Balkan co-religionists but also Jerusalem would be liberated.[61] This buttressed the extremist design that a convenient pretext be found to circumvent the Livadia resolutions and push him to start the war without passing through the shifty grounds of diplomatic dealings.

Katkov stood in the lead of a massive press campaign aiming to obviate the trap of a negotiated settlement. "Diplomacy is finished. Diplomatic notes are now superfluous, only swift, energetic measures are wanted," sounded his keyword.[62]

On the official mission to Vienna he responded by a summary attack in which the whole development was depicted as an enormous plot staged by Andrássy and Beaconsfield.[63] No credibility should be given either to the anti-Turkish campaign in England or to the efficacy of the Dreikaiserbündnis. The debate behind the Channel should not be "taken seriously"; Beaconsfield remained in the publicist's analysis in full command and the Liberal opposition but an unadulterated hypocrisy. As to the Emperors' League, it had "proved to be lacking in any creative force" and (its existence) brought no positive results; it invalidated Russia in all that should constitute her direct historical mission."[64] Once again, Bismarck appeared in his reasoning as the only statesman worthy of dealing with; and for the sake of the deal, he hinted, France should be offered as the price.[65]

By the end of October, the opportune moment seemed to have arrived. After a temporary lull, the fighting was resumed in the Morava valley and on 30 October news reached Livadia that the Turks had stormed the key position at the Djunis heights, inflicted heavy casualties on the Russian volunteers and turned Serbian units into havoc. In a dramatic debate over the desperate telegrams coming from Belgrade and Cherniaev's headquarters, the heir and Grand Duke Nikolai demanded a war declaration and the Tsar was willing to sign a mobilization decree.

But, in a cunning maneuvre, Gorchakov (probably backed by Miliutin) spoiled the extremist hope. He persuaded the others that Europe should not be challenged "while the negotiations are still in progress." Thus, only an ultimatum was dispatched to the Turkish capital demanding the cessation of hostilities within twenty-four hours; upon which the Porte immediately yielded.[66]

In a frantic effort to save the game, Ignatiev—at that moment already back on his post at Constantinople—urged Livadia to send another ultimatum requesting the proclamation of autonomy for Bulgaria, Bosnia and Hercegovina. The Turks were in panic, he asserted, and could be forced to give up without mobilization and war; in fact, his calculation undoubtedly was at the opposite—that the Porte would refuse and thereby oblige the Tsar to start military action.[67]

Alexander was willing to proceed according to the Ambassador's advice. Yet another setback in the Russian diplomatic quest for allies—on 1 November, after a long silence in Berlin, Schweinitz delivered evasive reply to soundings on German assistance[68]—obviously checked him and induced to accept the reasoning of Miliutin, Gorchakov and Adlerberg that it was untoward to use a direct threat "almost every day" and "after one Turkish concession to ask immediately with raised fist for another one."[69]

At first sight, the way Tsardom prevented Serbian final disaster appeared as a final extremist victory. Not even the Muscovites understood the implications. Katkov conceived the ultimatum equal to a war declaration and recognition of his thesis that Russia "has no reason to be more afraid of isolation, she has to be more afraid of cooperation with the other (so-called European) friends."[70] Alexander behaved precisely as the Panslav-nationalist party wished it. He rejected every thought of a peaceful outcome as an "insult to Russian honour and dignity," Austrian and German evasion making him only more defiant; "in his considerations, there is just one essential idea—to mobilize as soon as possible and cross the Russian border," Miliutin observed.[71] Most significantly, in his famous Kremlin address, the ruler identified himself before the whole world with the Muscovy programme (on 11 November 1876):

> I know that all Russia joins with me in taking the deepest interest in the sufferings of our brethren by faith and in origin. For me, the

true interests of Russia are dearer than anything, and I would do my utmost to spare precious Russian blood being shed. That is why I have striven and am continuing to strive to achieve, by peaceful means, a real improvement in the life of all the Christian inhabitants of the Balkan peninsula. Deliberations between the representatives of the six Great Powers are shortly to be begun at Constantinople . . . I much desire that we will reach a general agreement. If it is not attained . . . , then I firmly intend to act independently and I am convinced that in such an eventuality all Russia will respond to my appeal, when I deem it necessary, and the honor of Russia requires it. I am convinced likewise that Moscow, as always, will set the example. May God help us to fulfill our sacred mission.[72]

While the moderates were shocked—Interior Minister Timashev, who knew how much the Tsar loathed the Panslavs with their sacred mission, could not believe that he had pronounced such a speech—Katkov and Aksakov now put Alexander on the pedestal beside the greatest builders of the Empire—Ivan III, Peter I and Catherine II.[73]

On 13 November, mobilization was ordered. Yet, Ignatiev's exasperation over the lost October opportunity was well-grounded. Not only the chance of starting war under what he conceived, and what probably were, the most propitious circumstances, had been missed. Soon after the Kremlin address, the very war perspective became blurred again.

CHAPTER 15

BETWEEN PEACE AND WAR:
THE LAST TESTS
(1876-1877)

> How is this winter going to pass? What will it
> bring to us? How much time has been lost?—
> those are the sad questions. I fully share
> your opinion that it is time for the govern-
> ment to take all the Slavic Benevolent com-
> mittees' (movement) into its own hands; for
> otherwise God only knows what is going to
> come out of it and how it may end.
> Pobedonostsev to the heir

The October ultimatum saved Russo-Serbian relations from the worst,
but mutual psychological estrangement could not be repaired.

Katkov and most of the press had already taken strong exception to the
Belgrade government and its army when their clashes with Cherniaev became public.[1] Then it was the return of the volunteers which exacerbated
the resentment. In Aksakov's words, "instead of brotherly love" they
spread "brotherly hatred"; and in consequence, the contributions to the
Slavic committees now bore the inscription "only not for the Serbs."
Aksakov himself raged with calousness endemic in his kind:

> The blood of thousands of Russians sacrificed . . . demands loud
> satisfaction and exemplary punishment. The Serbs must justify
> themselves before Russia. One needs a truly Russian patience and

magnamity to avoid spitting in the face of the Serbian government
and intelligentsia and leaving them to their fate.[2]

True, liberal organs criticized the scandalous demeanour of the Lion;
yet public opinion in its entirety would not stomach the fact that their
kinsmen met no docility. Deeply hurt in their overbearing arrogance, the
Russians willingly accepted the sole explanation of the failure in Serbian
cowardice, "calculation, self-indulgence, ambition, petty thoughts of
egoistic, cool reason." The Tsar in his Kremlin speech echoed the mood:
while he praised the Montenegrins for being "as always, the heroes in this
inequal struggle," he chided the Serbs that "it is impossible to say the
same about them . . . despite the presence in their ranks of our volunteers,
many of whom paid with their blood for the cause of Slavdom."[3]

The effect might have been disasterous for extremist purposes. After
reaching its peak in the days immediately following the Kremlin address,
the Panslav wave visibly decreased never to regain its summer and autumn
intensity. The announcement of an internal war loan of 100 million
rubles met feeble response. In a gloomy letter to Cherniaev, Aksakov
despaired that "Russian society is losing faith in . . . its independent
activity."[4]

Not surprisingly, upon his return to St. Petersburg the Tsar emerged
in an entirely different atmosphere from that in Livadia and Moscow.
General Mezentsev, the head of the Third Section, reported considerable
divergencies in opinions, apathy among nobility and merchants; he cautioned that "outside the (Great-) Russian and Ukrainian gubernias a recourse to war would not be responded by sympathy and willingness to
sacrifices; and, on the contrary, in gubernias with numerous Polish and
Moslem inhabitants "strengthened surveillance" would be imperative.
According to the Austrian Ambassador, even notorious hawkish groupings in the Winter Palace and the army were bent to peace; the ministers
"expressed themselves quite openly to the strangers" in the same vein.
Again in heavy doubts, Alexander wondered whether he "had not fallen
victim to Bismarck's game."[5]

Not surprisingly either, Gorchakov saw in the changing winds his
chance. The mobilization had substantially narrowed his elbow-room, but
he made it clear to Western diplomats that if satisfactory arrangement
could be agreed on, Russian military action still might be avoided. Like

every moderate, he pinned his hope on the forthcoming Constantinople conference; and, indeed, much pointed to the optimistic prognoses that the gathering would be a turning point to peace. There were particularly strong reasons to believe that the English and the Russians would meet halfway.[6]

Russian programme for the diplomatic gathering in the Turkish capital was elaborated by Ignatiev. He knew nothing about the Reichstadt agreement, but in order to secure Austrian benevolence, put the sensitive Bosnia-Hercegovina issue aside and centered his plan entirely on Bulgaria and Macedonia. In its maximal variant, it asked for full autonomy guaranteed by external force; in its minimal variant it envisaged a gradual transformation to autonomy. The Ambassador, now uncertain about the war prospect and eager to reassert himself as superb diplomat, obviously wished the conference to succeed. Hence, the draft was so moderate that Gorchakov applauded it.[7]

Ignatiev and his wife again displayed their peculiar talents. Their attention, of course, was focused on Salisbury, who arrived in Constantinople after an European tour convinced as ever "of the deplorable folly of the Crimean War." According to Onou, the secretary of the Russian Embassy, the Ambassador led his spouse to tame the English Lordship in the same manner which had in the past proved so effective on Ambassadors Zichy and Corti. When Onou cautioned her before attempt to seduce a virtuous Puritan, Countess Ignatieva dismissed it lightly: "I shall make use of virtue to seduce him." And she allegedly bore away the bell. Ambassador Elliot, the second British delegate, saw himself outmaneuvred again by the Russian pair, "both absolutely unscrupulous . . . to the extend that defies underlying," as he complained.[8]

Due to the Ignatiev-Salisbury intimity, the delegates quickly approved the reorganization project for European Turkey.[9] On 21 December, the triumphant Russian Ambassador delivered it to the Porte and Salisbury ordered British warships to depart from Besika Bay to Athens as a token that the times when London protected the Sultan were over and issued a stern warning against obstruction.

Yet the last card belonged to Elliot and Beaconsfield behind him. Encouraged by them, Grand Vizier Midhat Pasha wrecked the conference: when it formally opened its proceedings on 23 December, there was some gunfire and Savfed Pasha, the Foreign Minister, announced to the surprised representatives of Europe that the new Sultan, Abdulhamid II, had just granted to his subjects a constitution giving everybody equal rights and that henceforth the discussion about the improvement of the Christians' position had become superfluous.

Both loud protests—Salisbury condemned the "unworthy comedy staged beforehand by Midhat," naming the Grand Vizier and Elliot the "biggest pair of liars to be found"[10]—and considerable reduction of the original project produced no effort whatever. On 18 January 1877, Midhat summoned about 300 handpicked "delegates" to what he called a provisional National Assembly; and this organ proclaimed any external interference inadmissible. Two days later, the conference broke up and its participants left Constantinople in protest.

While presenting another severe diplomatic setback for the moderate, compromise-seeking Russian statesmen, the Constantinople failure poured oil on the flames of the Thunderer's campaign, in which any negotiations —save a secret deal with Bismarck, of course—were proclaimed a harmful pastime.

In the sequel of the Kremlin address, the publicist affirmed, time should not be wasted: "any minute, the occupation of Bulgaria becomes a pressing need."[11] Neither Salisbury's smiles nor threats pronounced by Beaconsfield in the Guildhall speech, should cajole or intimate Tsardom; even if England entered war, she would just exhaust herself.[12] The very idea of the Constantinople conference was not only "fundamentally false," it was a ploy invented to protect the Turks against Russia and deliver the city on the Golden Horn to the British.[13] The only European position which might have been considered satisfactory was that of a complete break with the Porte; "then military occupation could be performed peacefully" and "Russian troops march to Bulgaria as the troops of Europe to fulfill her decisions."[14]

In the course of his warlike harangues, the editor used the unsuccessful demonstration staged by the revolutionaries before the Kazan Cathedral (on 18 December) to revive the doctrine of permanent vigilance. The patriotic spirit, so persuasively demonstrated in the previous months, was the best remedy against all domestic ills, he postulated:

Now everybody can observe that the negative occurrences on the surface of our society, which attracted our youth, were not a symptom of some deep inner evil. We fooled because of boredom, because of doing nothing.[15]

Although less distinctly than Danilevskii and Fadeev, Katkov indicated to Tsardom's elite that a "patriotic war" would be that magic wand relieving it from the revolutionary spectre.

Equally importantly, this was the occasion when he formulated in unmistakable terms his concept of Russia's strategy in world affairs. Bismarck's declaration in the Reichstag on 5 December, containing only customary assurances, was sufficient for him to ask that Russo-German friendship should be given a solid basis, a "more precise form" of an agreement on freedom of action on the Eastern Question and on the Rhine:

> Now the crucial moment has come when 'even the other Powers should reconsider which combination would best suit their interests.' As for Russia, further undertakings with Vienna are worthless; if she have to deal with enemies, then contacts with London would be 'more direct and simple.' Only an understanding with Germany 'is a natural combination which is being opened to our policy'; and only Russia and Germany can establish a sound European peace by disposing of the two focuses of unrest. 'Europe has been sick by two crises: not solely by the Eastern, but by the Western as well.' If Berlin would fully support Russia in handling the first, it could expect the same service in the second.[16]

Swallowing his pride, Katkov even travelled to the capital to call at the Singers' Bridge and win its chief for his concept. Only more intense hatred resulted from it, however. In his later testimony the publicist claimed that he had found the old Prince immersed in his obsession "which of the two Chancellors is the biggest"; that he had not only refused to "test German friendship" but had defended his stance by a foolish argument that European "freedom of conscience," challenged by Bismarck's feud with Vatican, must be protected.[17] The former associates, whose alliance had been during the 1860s such an essential feature of Russian policy, parted never to meet again.

* * *

The idea of the Russo-German European con-dominium was not without a rationale. The designs of the Berlin Chancellor in the period preceding the Russo-Turkish war had left a large area for guesswork and the historians have never ceased speculate on the theme.[18] At the time of the Gorchakov-Katkov meeting, however, the possibility of a "big deal," if it had ever existed, already passed.

It appears obvious that after the initial hesitations and soundings, Bismarck resolved to oppose peaceful settlement and the Austrian tendency to hinder the Russian drive to the Straits. Beside other considerations, he must have been intensely worried about the growth of the Panslav spirit, believing that only military victory could save Tsardom from serious troubles harmful to the conservative-monarchic cause, and conceiving this victory, despite the inevitable consequence for the Austro-Russian rivalry in the Balkans, as a lesser evil than to have a destabilized, frustrated Great Power on the German border looking for a scapegoat and prone to alliance with France. On the other hand, he decided not to give Russian statesmen the promise to go with them "through thick and thin," especially not in the case of a conflict with Austria-Hungary.

When he conveyed Bismarck's stance in early November at Livadia, Schweinitz put it to Alexander perhaps more frankly than his chief intended—"a warlike intervention against England on our part is completely excluded and a permanent weakening of Austria contrary to our interests"—but this was precisely the true German position; and when Gorchakov in the talks declined to warrant Russian guarantees for the Rhine frontiers,[19] there was nothing that could have changed it.

The relations between St. Petersburg and Berlin being now, contrary to Katkov's notions, again heavily tainted by mutual distrust,[20] Russian policymakers simply had to conceive arrangements with Vienna and London their priorities: either concessions ought to be obtained there to save "Russian dignity" and give excuses for the demobilization, or at least some assurances procured that no Crimean War situation would emerge with the outbreak of hostilities.

In the negotiations with Austria-Hungary, they managed to clarify the most pressing issues connected with the implementation of the Reichstadt agreement. By the resulting Budapest conventions of 15 January and 18 March 1877, Russia confirmed the right of her partner to occupy at any time Bosnia-Hercegovina and promised that (a) she would limit the actions of her troops on the territories east of Serbia and (b) in the final settlement she would not strive for the "establishment of a great, compact Slavic or other state" in the Balkans.[21] Andrássy advertised this outcome as his triumph. In fact, the arrangement fitted the Russian immediate offensive objectives quite well. In the sequel of the Serbian disappointment, these were centered almost exclusively on Bulgaria and the Straits; and the conventions gave good reason to assume that if the operations were swift and successful as expected, they would prevent effective common Anglo-Austrian countermoves.

This was unquestionably a big step on the war path, and so were the results of the crucial Councils held on 20 and 24 February at Tsarskoe Selo.

There, the moderates were in a strong position, being represented by Gorchakov, Reutern, Timashev, Valuev and on this occasion even supported by Grand Duke Konstantin. However, their too straightforward plea for a pure and simple retreat—if the Porte refused to cooperate, Russia should abandon the European concernt, demobilize and "leave the Ottoman Empire to its fate"—was effectively countered by Ignatiev and Miliutin.

The Ambassador conceded that Russia had missed her best moment for attack but insisted that it was imperative for "financial and economic reasons to finish with the Ottoman Empire (now and) forever." This was not time for pessimism or excessive modesty, he maintained, inasmuch as the first shots on the Danube would incite the lust for spoils in Russia's rivals and awake "the slumbering, unconscious forces of the East."

The War Minister, in a memoir which he composed together with Obruchev and read at the first council, presented the arguments in favor of armed action even more persuasively:

> Internally and economically, 'Russia is in such a phase that any external entanglement may lead to a prolonged disruption in the state organism. Not one of the initiated reforms has been completed. The economic and moral forces of the state are far from being balanced with its requirements . . . . War in such conditions will be a great misfortune.'

But a retreat before Turkish obstinacy could turn into a long-term plague for the Empire, 'injuring its dignity and material interests, perhaps up to the point where the last remnants of our influence in the Balkan peninsula are uprooted. . . . We need peace, but not a peace at any price, (we need) a honourable peace even if it has to be achieved by war. However terrible war may be, there exists a chance to wage it swiftly towards the desired goal. Our army is prepared and organized as never before. The Three Emperors' League can at least in the first period make our rear safe. . . ; even England has proclaimed solemnly that she does not intend to go either with Turkey or gainst her. . . . The early and determined success of our army can strongly influence European opinion and wrestle from it such concessions which are at present unthinkable.'

Alexander approved the Miliutin-Obruchev analysis as "fully expressing his views and beliefs"; "there are moments in the life of states and individuals, when it is imperative to forget everything save the defense of honor," he observed. On this ground, the Council agreed on 27 February on a tactical plan which should clear up the situation. Ignatiev ought to visit European capitals in the last attempt to enlist assistance for a tolerable settlement. If the reaction would be positive, Russia could demobilize and declare the crisis a collective responsibility; in the case of failure though, an ultimatum with terms roughly matching those envisaged by the Constantinople conference should ensue; and if the Porte turned it down, war would be declared.[22]

* * *

Despite the Budapest conventions and the outcome of the February councils, the peace party still had a fair chance. While in Moscow the fighting spirit had not abated perceptibly, in St. Petersburg and the provinces, there was not much will left "to spill blood for Turkish Christians."[23] The "folly of mobilization" was loudly deplored and Gorchakov already felt safe enough to take what he certainly believed to be the first steps back to normalcy. When Prince Charles of Rumania procrastinated in the negotiations on the passage of Russian troops across his territory, the Singers' Bridge instructed its representative not to press the issue;[24] and Nikola of Montenegro was admonished to conclude a peace treaty with the Turks.[25] The protocol drafted for the Ignatiev mission was also with good reason described by Miliutin as "very mild, even excessively modest."[26] Indeed, one must be surprised by what the Tsar considered compatible with the honour he cherished so much. Recalling the reform decree recently issued by the Porte,[27] the St. Petersburg draft merely requested its speedy implementation, conclusion of peace with Serbia and Montenegro and the demobilization of the Turkish army.

Small wonder that the Panslav-nationalists watched the development with a renewed air of intent disapproval and were virtually mortified by the notion that the English and the Turks might settle on such a Russian disgrace. Perturbed, Katkov stepped up his campaign.

Already before Ignatiev departed on his European tour, the editor hurled upon the government new accusations: when the mobilization had taken place, he reiterated, all diplomatic actions should cease and the war operations start while the Balkan Slavs were "still filled with unshattered confidence in us"; the arguments (of Miliutin) against the winter campaign were fallacious because Russian troops would certainly cope with the climatic conditions better than the Turks.[28] The news about the Ignatiev mission must have made him trembling with rage and anxiety that the St. Petersburg "anti-Russian party" retreated back into the old quagmire. Almost every day he condemned in his editorials the very principle of dealing with Europe and once again, only the Germans were worth talking with:

> Agreement with England is impossible. There is no point of knowing what the views of France are or whether they exist at all . . . . With Austria, our relations are unclear . . . . Solely with Germany . . . are the elements for a fruitful understanding at hand.[29]

Meanwhile, the Ambassador's travels finally tipped the scale finally in favour of the war advocates. Briefly, while the English foolishly refused to give the St. Petersburg government their helping hand, the outcome of the mission warranted that Tsardom could now start war without running immediate risk that an European coalition would be formed against it.[30] The peculiarity of the moment, though, lay in the fact that the Panslavs knew nothing about their victory. What they knew was that Shuvalov and Derby reduced the Russian draft in the so called London protocol (31 March) into a mere appeal to the Turks to demobilize and commence to reform their empire. And such a prospect raised their worries to utter desperation. Novikova, the Katkovian "deputy for Russia" in England, who had at that time visited her native country, recollected later:

> Those who lived in the very heart of the national movement can never forget the terrible foreboding of these dismal days. We all moved under the pressure of a great dread. Was it to end thus? Were all our sacrifices to be sacrificed? Was the blood of our martyrs split in vain? Was Holy Russia no more, but a mere appendage of cosmopolitan St. Petersburg? . . . And the sky grew dark overhead, and we went about as if in a chamber of death, speaking in low accents and oppressed by a terrible fear of that national dishonour, strange as it may appear to some people, dread even more than death.[31]

It is true that in these "dismal days" Gorchakov, Adlerberg, Valuev, Reutern, Timashev and Grand Duke Konstantin tabled for "unconditional approval of the English revision,"[32] but it may be safely assumed that after the rejection of the St. Petersburg protocol Alexander would listen no more to the moderate governmental majority and that he felt like the Moscow editor who denounced the document set forth by Shuvalov and Derby as a "comedy staged by both ours and the English friends of peace."[33] Although extremist pressures on him almost disappeared, and he did his utmost to escape war, the Tsar was well alive to the long-time implication of the eventual "national dishonour"; and he undoubtedly shared the view of Miliutin—or Bismarck for that matter—that there were bigger issues at stake than the economic consequences of war. That much he had already shown in the February councils.

In the end, the Turks made everything very simple. Like their English supporters, they let themselves to be carried away by a blind anti-Russian hatred and, moreover, while overestimating the momentary preponderance of the "cosmopolitan St. Petersburg spirit," they took lightly the long-time impact of the "spirit of Muscovy." Hoping to see what the Muscovites were so afraid of—total capitulation on the Neva—they resolved to refuse the unquestionably mild terms offered and proceed in the hazardous game. When the Porte turned down even the empty shell of the Derby-Shuvalov protocol, the Panslav nationalists could breathe out freely. On 11 April, the highest dignitaries gathered in St. Petersburg and with no dissenting voice approved additional mobilization, the breaking off relations with Constantinople and a declaration of war within two months.

CHAPTER 16

THE LESSONS OF PLEVNA:
THE FIRST PHASE OF THE TURKISH WAR
(1877)

Arise, O Rus! The hour is near!
Arise to do Christ's service!
It is not time, while crossing yourself,
to ring Byzantium's bells?
Tiutchev

First, Te Deum would be officiated in
the St. Sophia Church; thereupon the
Patriarch would consecrate it anew; by
that time, I believe, a bell would have been
brought from Moscow; the Sultan would
be sent to a proper place—and this would
be the end of everything.
Dostoevskii

On 24 April 1877, on a muddy field near Kishinev, Alexander II read in front of assembled troops the war manifesto.

After all the hesitations, the wildest exaltation had evaporated; nonetheless, there was still enough crusading spirit and drunken optimism to hail the last imperial march on Constantinople.[1] "War in our time," Dostoevskii wrote, "is a necessity: without war the world would become a sort of slime, an ignoble mire, poisoned by decomposed crayfish."

Moreover, "this war is an unprecedented one for the weak and the oppressed, a war to give life and liberty, not to take them away. It is ages since the world has seen such a war." So, "split blood is a great thing."[2] Almost every politically-minded Russian hoped that his dreams would some-how come true. While the conservatives connected the expected victory with the return to stability and order, the liberals divined an era of liberty; a rumour circulated that Valuev had already been empowered to prepare a constitutional project.[3] And, of course, the belief that Russia would rise to the apex of world power was overwhelming. The war loan was subscribed without difficulty and more contributions came from every part of Tsardom; in Moscow, where the frenzy nearly approached that of the previous autumn, the merchants alone offered one million rubles for the families of killed and crippled on the field of glory. Only the St. Petersburg "cosmopolitans" endured in their scepticism.[4]

The army exuded inflated conceit too. "Everybody is sure that the war will be won in one strike and that in September we will be back home," General Hasenkampf noted down.[5] Alexander himself departed to the front to participate in the historical triumph. Speculating on a walkover, titles, orders and advancements, scores of court parasites joined his suite or flooded the staffs of the commanding Grand Dukes. No one would consider the Turks a serious obstacle, although they had more modern rifles and guns and their navy controlled the Black Sea; nor did anyone bother much about possible European interference.[6]

Even the war plans which had been worked out earlier by Obruchev under the supervision of the usually sober Miliutin, had been tainted by sanguine vistas.

In the first project, dated 13 October, 1876 the liberation of Bulgaria was proclaimed the only aim and the Maritsa valley the main battlefield. Still, the real, thinly veiled goal lay on the Bos-phorus. The army, the document stated, must be ready to 'attack Constantinople itself'; there it would have 'with all probability' to fight the English, but once the Turkish capital were taken and declared free city, Europe would gladly accept the outcome. The preparations were to be performed with "extraordinary speed,' to prevent the overstraining of resources and larger international repercussions. For this reason the attacking Danube Army ought to be, at least in the initial stage, relatively small: 7 divisions and 10 Cossack regiments. Only if 'events obliged us to go to Constantinople' should these forces be strengthened accordingly, in order to attain 'unconditional superiority against the Anglo-Turkish troops which we have to face on the Bosphorus.' The whole campaign was to last no more than 3-4 months.[7]

On 13 April 1877, an improved war plan was set forth, in which the true aims were already stated with complete frankness. 'The circumstances have entirely changed since the autumn,' and thus the objective 'cannot be other than a full, final solution of the Eastern Question and unconditional liquidation of Turkish rule in the Balkan peninsula.' Consequently, the destination of the march must be 'more than ever Constantinople itself,' because the seizure of Bulgaria alone would not properly cover long-term strategic needs.

The plan conceded that the Turks had in previous months considerably improved their military potential. It maintained, nonetheless, that the Danube Army, raised to 300,000 troops and divided into two groups—one performing the offensive task, the other protecting the rear—would be able to take the Straits quickly and prevent the English influencing the outcome.[8]

The Russian military machine hitched from the very first day. It took almost two months before troops could be concentrated on the Danube and set foot on its southern bank. Not even proper maps of the Balkan peninsula were available.[9] Nonetheless, nothing could shake the generals in their self-confidence.

Already before the first shots were fired, they had won a signal political victory over "diplomats" who had attempted to "put a harness on their action"[10] and reduce Russian war objectives.

When on 6 May Lord Derby notified the Singers' Bridge of British interests on the Eastern Question—to keep the Suez Canal open, to prevent occupation of Constantinople or change in the Straits' status, and to protect the Persian Gulf—the moderates in St. Petersburg used the note to persuade the Tsar that the army should advance only to the Balkans range and Russia be satisfied with a "little peace" which would guarantee Bulgarian autonomy. Yet the move aroused a virulent outcry in the extremist press[11] and in the midst of it, at the deliberations which took place on 6 and 11 June at Ploesti, Ignatiev and Cherkasskii (the latter came to the headquarters as a "representative of Moscow" appointed to preside the future Bulgarian civil administration) advertised and enlisted full backing for these identical to those of Katkov: Tsardom should not let the chance slip away to create a Greater Bulgaria from the Danube to the Aegean, turn Constantinople into a free city, establish military bases in the Straits. Alexander, who had succumbed in the councils held in May in St. Petersburg to Gorchakov's and Shuvalov's arguments, now also used the words of the *Moskovskiia vedomosti,* denouncing "those of our statesmen whom the fear of war induced to scream for all the world about our powerlessness."[12]

Henceforth, the "political bashi bazouks," as Jomini called them,[13] were to be almost exclusively in charge. Gorchakov, after Ploesti, retreated to Bucharest, where he devoted his attention to the local ladies of easy virtue. Apart from the Tsar and the military, only diplomats with a pronounced extremist record—Ignatiev and Nilidov, named as the head of the diplomatic chancery of the Commander-in-Chief—were to take part in policy-making.

After the Danube was crossed (on 26-27 June), Russian conceit received a further huge boost. The inactivity of the Turks, who decided to hold only the fortresses and postpone the decisive battle, created a false notion that they would not fight at all. Eager to prove his martial qualities to all who considered him incompetent—"uncle Niki has always been a fool," the heir, himself not exactly a brilliant mind, used to say[14]—Grand Duke Nikolai set out for an even bolder war plan than that elaborated by Miliutin's "professors." Probably inspired by the feat of General Dibich in 1829, he wanted to reach Constantinople with a small force in the shortest possible time. Thus, while the Eastern detachment under the heir's command (75,000 men) was assigned with the task of infesting the four northern fortresses of Silistra, Ruse, Shumen and Varna, and the Western detachment of General Krüdener (35,000 men) with taking Nikopol and Plevna, General Iosif Gurko, leading a mere 12,000 troops, was directed to cross the Balkan mountain range and penetrate farther to the south.

At first the scheme appeared to be working perfectly, when Gurko and his Forward detachment performed in the best tradition: on 7 July they took Tamovo; on 15 July found their way into Southern Bulgaria through the unprotected Hain-Köy Pass; on 17 and 23 July occupied Kazanlik and Stara Zagora; on 19 July stormed the key Shipka Pass from the rear. In the meantime, the Western detachment overpowered the defenders of Nikopol. Everywhere, Turkish resistance was negligible. "But where is the enemy?", Emperor William asked in one of his congratulatory messages.[15]

"Only additonal brass bands are requested on the Danube" and "ladies at Tsarskoe Selo babble about Constantinople," Valuev characterized the atmosphere. Observers compared the situation with the flashy maneuvres near St. Petersburg: delirious and stubborn in his wish to be on the spot when the banner with the two-headed eagle was to be hoisted over the Turkish capital, Alexander with an enormous suite and hundreds of carriages followed closely to the front.[16]

The Tsar's presence at the war theatre was to have an essential consequence for the decision-making: in the words of Meshcherskii, there were to be "two currents, two influences and two wills directing the whole campaign." In what the Russians then called "the Grand Dukes' war," the animosities which had surfaced during the debate on the army reform, reappeared in new form. While the headquarters of the Danube Army nursed the old grievances against Miliutin and his "liberals and revolutionaries," the ruler's entourage, where the War Minister was the towering figure, seethed with suspicion and disrespect of Nikolai and his two deputies of Polish origin, Generals Nepokojczycki and Lewicki.[17]

The harm incurred by this duality was to be revealed sooner than the jubilant Russians could have expected.

* * *

The reports on setback suffered on the Asiatic front, where the Turks repulsed the invading force of Grand Duke Mikhail and even landed on Russian territory, prompted Miliutin to warn about the reckless concept of the Balkan command, but this could not prevent the disaster. The enemy had at last succeeded in transferring its best units to the main battlezone: the 40,000-strong corps of Suleyman Pasha, hitherto fighting the Montenegrins, was thrown against Gurko and the equally numerous corps of Omer Pasha streamed from Vidin to the fortress of Plevna to bar the war for the Western detachment. This immediately altered the whole picture. On 21 and 30 July Omer warded off Krüdener's attempts to storm Plevna, with shattering effect. "The retreat was reminiscent of a rout. Panic spread far beyond the Danube," General Zotov recollected.[18] Russian losses were terrible—15,000 killed and wounded. Hard-pressed by Suleyman, Gurko too had to pull back from Southern Bulgaria.

Haughty self-confidence turned overnight into its very opposite. Everybody now complained about bad coordination, inertia, weakness.[19] Is this the second Sevastopol?", the shocked Tsar exclaimed;[20] and in desperation ordered on 1 August to summon to the Balkans the cream of the Russian army, the Guards, something his late father would not have done in the worst days of the Crimea.

The next day, Miliutin released to circulation a memoir flatly stating that the concept of a blitzkrieg had floundered and that war must be waged in an entirely different way if a calamity was to be evaded. The minister enumerated the bitter truths:

> There were no reserves left, the army was split into small units dispersed over a vast area; the enemy was better armed and capable of effective defence in fortified positions. Consequently, until the arrival of the reinforcements, the offensive operations should be stopped, troops reorganized and entrenched in several strongholds; above all, the insane waste of human lives ought to cease. 'If we continue to rely upon the endless will to sacrifice and upon the patience of the Russian soldier, we are going to destroy our magnificent army.'[21]

The Danube Army leadership, however, was both unable and unwilling to follow the War Minister, "the writing-table general." So, the perennial defects of Tsardom and its armed forces were revealed in the most drastic form. In the first weeks following the crossing of the Danube, the supply problem had not been acute. In Bulgaria, the Russians found abundance of grain, cattle, fodder and the officers of intendance a veritable bonanza for personal enrichment. Used in a highly wasteful manner, though, the resources in the regions close to the front were quickly exhausted. With soaring corruption and theft and with the work of transportation being all the time close to breaking point, this had the effect that the soldiers had to suffer unbelievable deprivations.

Worse still, the traditional "serfdom" approach to the muzhik in uniform did not change as well as the blind trust in bold action.

Thus, although according to Miliutin conditions became so critical that only exaggerated Turkish fears of engaging the Russians in a great battle prevented the ultimate disaster,[22] the Grand Duke, desperately wishing to wipe off the shame, decided for the third assault of Plevna as soon as possible; and Alexander, probably emboldened by the endurance and courage of the 7,500 defenders of the Shipka Pass, who in the August heat, without water and amidst thousands of rotting corpses repulsed the attacks of 27,000 Turks, this time agreed with his relative against the War Minister. The both Romanovs resolved to use the Rumanian and Serbian help which they had unceremoniously refused before[23] and once the Guards and the Rumanians were amassed before the fortress—there was 85,000 men altogether—they moved to "restore Russian honour."

The die was cast on 11 September, the jubilee day of Alexander's coronation. The Tsar's observation post was well supplied with champagne for celebration and the painter Vereshchagin stood ready to immortalize the event. The Turks, however, did not waver and in the evening the Grand Duke had to stop the slaughter. Only Skobelev, commanding the left flank, manned some fortified positions and even these were taken back in a counterattack next day.

The Russo-Rumanian casualties amounted to more than 30,000 men; the elite units of Skobelev and Prince Imeretinskii lost half of their officers and under-officers.[24] At the war council on 13 September, Alexander in the deepest gloom suggested a retreat from Bulgaria; the Grand Duke and some others assented, predicting a simultaneous Turkish charge from Plevna and the northern fortresses, after which Suleyman Pasha would have but to "pursue our beaten units." Miliutin, however, kept his head cool and in the end convinced the Tsar that the retreat would be suicidal for the dynasty and the Empire.[25]

The principles stated by the War Minister in his August memoir were recognized as a guideline for further conduct in the campaign; and the old, experienced, cautious General Todleben, the hero of Sevastopol disgraced because of his opposition to the Turkish adventure, was invited to direct the siege of Plevna.[26]

* * *

Even with this outcome, the effect of the "third Plevna" upon the Russian public was devastating. The same feelings which took hold of the

Danube Army spread into Russia. "This battle," wrote the liberal *Vestnik Evropy*, "brought about a great change in the spirit of society; the boundless self-confidence, initiated by the first successes, altered into equally exaggerated frustration." Official silence about the reversal provided fertile ground for the worst rumours. Besides the Jewish company of Greger which had contracted the food supply for the Danube Army, the Tsar, the government, inept generals and also the Moscow party were blamed; the advertized crusade was now no more than a "Grand Dukes' war" or a "Moscow war." A new loan was subscribed up to a mere 30 percent and in Odessa, an unparalleled incident took place when the crowds hissed the Guards passing the town on their way to the front.[27]

Pobedonostsev complained to the heir:

> We are in a terrible state of mind here, in unimaginable excitement and dread, owing to the unexpected failure before Plevna and especially as a result of the persistent silence of the army, of an absolute lack of news . . . . Suddenly, the confidence to this (supreme) power was shattered . . . . Imagine, what can happen if—God forbid—the army in Bulgaria were to suffer a great disaster. Already now, the popular mass is terribly agitated. Then, there might be an explosion . . . .[28]

Katkov, albeit with a preceptible reluctance—how could he ignore that his postulates were belied?—joined the overall lament. His innuendos were transparently directed against the War Ministry, but he also put the blame on those who had at the beginning rebuffed Serbia and Rumania, Russia's "natural allies in the East."[29] The greatest concern of the publicist, though, lay elsewhere. Despite repeated allegations to the contrary, his editorials after the "second Plevna" indicate that he took an imminent Anglo-Austrian stab in the back almost for certain.[30]

This was not just another expression of Katkov's anti-Western paranoia. The exaggerated manner in which the warlike tendencies in London and Vienna were perceived was to grow into an overwhelming factor influencing thinking and decisions of the Russian elite until the very end of the Eastern crisis. But never throughout the whole period were Katkov's and Russian fears emanated from the Crimean experience less substantiated than at the time of the Plevna setbacks.

Gurko's lightning advance greatly disturbed the London cabinet. On 30 July, it tabled for the return of the fleet to Besika Bay and on 21 July for intervention if the Russians attempted for permanent occupation of the Turkish capital. However, when Beaconsfield and his allies asked for more—landing in the Persian Gulf, attacks in Central Asia and on the Black Sea coast—the reaction in the government was distinctly hostile. Most of the ministers were against military preparations and some even dwelled on the Gladstonian thesis that Russian mastery in the Straits could be tolerated. Salisbury wrote:

There is 'nothing in their (Russians') history . . . to explain the abject terror which deprives so many of our military party here, of their natural sleep. . . . Their finances, never good, are now desperate. Their social condition is a prolonged crisis threatening. . . socialist revolution. . . . And yet we are asked to believe that their presence in the Black Sea or the Bosphorus would be a serious menace. . . . We cling to the shread of an old policy after it has been torn to pieces.'

The Queen, being in full sympathy with her Prime Minister, deplored a 'miserable cotton-spinning, milk-and-water, peace-at-any-price' approach, but Ambassador Shuvalov, who had in Lady Derby a first-class source of information, received an assurance that 'the other ministers do not look favorably on this conspiracy of a half-mad woman with a minister who once had genius but has degenerated into a political clown.'[31]

The British ambiguity, as always in a crisis situation, had a signal bearing upon Vienna. And when dismayed by the 'second Plevna' Alexander reaffirmed former Russian pledges—'there is only Austria-Hungary with whom we have precise engagements . . . we will be faithful to their letter and spirit'—the Emperor and the military party turned against mobilization projects canvassed by Andrássy and the Hungarian Premier Count Tisza. As with Shuvalov's telegrams, the Russians could have felt relieved by Francis Joseph's message that 'whatever happens and whatever turns the war may take, nothing can induce me to recede from my given word; England has been informed in a decisive manner that she cannot count, in any event, on an alliance with Austria.[32]

* * *

Seeing his bid frustrated, Beaconsfield put the hope entirely on a single-handed Turkish victory. The Russians' losses are so terrible, he encouraged his admirers, they they could scarcely escape a complete breakdown; and the winter-campaign in Bulgaria would bring about a similar catastrophe to that which the Napoleonic Grande armée had suffered in 1812.[33] Indeed, this contingency seemed highly probable; and this also was the reason why Alexander turned into a wretch who "only prays and weeps."[34]

From the end of September, with the coming of rains and nightfrosts, the conditions the Russian soldier had to live in were—at least in terms of European standards—unbearable. The officers of the XI Cavalry Corps complained to Pobedonostsev that their unit was left "without boots, shirts, trousers." At the vital Shipka position, General Radetskii sat safely sheltered, played cards and reported to the headquarters with his famous "all quiet of the Shipka front" while his subordinates had to live in caves, without fire and warm food and clothed in rags. In the three months after the "third Plevna" only 700 were killed in fighting, but 9,500 died of disease and cold. Although numbers of sick were enormous, only a few sought medical help, being afraid of the overcrowded field hospitals with myriads of lice and raging typhus.[35]

With the greatest apprehension, the commanding staffs observed symptoms of rapidly deteriorating discipline: there was visibly better order in Rumanian and Turkish positions than in those manned by Russian regiments. "The murmuring took the form of general dissatisfaction," Miliutin noted down. "People grumble aloud against the army leadership and also against the ruler himself."[36] Worse still, the Tsar and his entourage must have been possessed by the anxiety about the situation at home. The information they had been receiving could not have been different from the alarming letters Pobedonostsev was writing to the heir or Ambassadors Schweinitz and Langenau to Berlin and Vienna, that the country was "moving towards a powerful convulsion, unless the situation is ameliorated in time." The Panslav and left radicals alike attacked the government and the assassination of the Third Section's chief General Mezentsev was perceived as a dreadful omen.[37] So, the hawks of yesterday now craved for peace at almost any price. The headquarters discussed Nelidov's proposal "to accept even the most modest conditions," the autonomy of Bulgaria north of the Balkan range being the only desideratum which should save at least some vestige of Russian honour.[38]

Just then, however, the fortunes of war changed again, and the proponents of the historical mission received a boost they had already ceased to hope for.

From the middle of October, good news was coming from the Asiatic front: the Turks suffered a heavy defeat near the border; on 5 and 16 November they lost their main strongholds, Erzurum and Kars. A new perspective emerged also for the Danube Army. General Todleben declined impatient pleas for the fourth assault on Plevna, but the fortress, tightly infested and exhausting its resources, could not last long. When on 6 December the Tsar opened a "Supreme Council" at Poradim to discuss the peace terms, the altered conditions were aleady evident. Ignatiev, who reappeared from a political sick-leave, and Nelidov, recovered from his spell of panic, enlisted support for demands dramatically

* * *

at variance from those contemplated in the days of gloom. They provided for an autonomous Greater Bulgaria "within the limits of Bulgarian nationality and in no case small than those agreed upon at the Constantinople conference"; similar status for Bosnia-Hercegovina with the special position of Austria-Hungary; independence and territorial changes for Serbia and Romania; a new status in the Straits. Russia should receive a big war idemnity, Southern Bessarabia and part of Turkish Armenia.[39]

In Russia, the announcement that "in both war theatres the moment of a decisive turn is near"[40] had to Katkov's considerable chagrin failed to arouse public enthusiasm. In early November, the *Pravitelstvennyi vestnik* had to warn against "hostile rumours" of new military reversals[41] and even in the following weeks reports were still to plague the Tsar that in St. Petersburg the alleged defeats were hailed with "malicious triumph as if it were the enemy troops" who had suffered.[42] But the seasoned Muscovites had already regained their courage as had their counterparts on the front. Ambassador Langenau depicted "collosal chauvinism" which took hold of them: they requested that Russia power be completely dominant in the whole Black Sea region, in the Straits and reach as far as Mesopotamia.[43]

Indeed, the "lofty aims" were again in sight.

CHAPTER 17

THE BITTER HARVEST:
FROM MILITARY VICTORY TO
POLITICAL DEFEAT
(1877-1878)

It was not rumbling rumour in our people
The news was not born in our generation
An ancient lofty voice pronounced it: 'The
fourth of the ages already is closing!'

When Byzantium is restored to us
The ancient vault of Saint Sophia
Will shelter the altar of Christ anew.
Kneel before it, O Tsar of Russia—
You will arise all Slavdom's Tsar!
Tiutchev

In the morning of 9 December 1877, Russian peace terms were sent
to Emperors William I and Francis Joseph I. Only several hours later,
the impatiently awaited final scene before Plevna began to unwind. Osman
Pasha threw the garrison against the encirclement and when repulsed by
well-entrenched and superior forces, surrendered his sword to the Tsar
the following day.

With Plevna also fell the last obstacle hindering the full recovery of the
extremist spirit. Although the situation in Russia was different, in the
army the atmosphere was strongly reminiscent of the very beginning

of the campaign. Before Alexander, now relieved of his worst fears, would return to St. Petersburg, another round of deliberations in Poradim (12-13 December) settled on bold tactics which were to be pursued in the coming stage: Europe should be surprised by a vigorous winter campaign and then faced with accomplished facts, above all in terms of Russian control over the Straits and Constantinople.[1]

The wish to wipe out the recent debacles and "purify himself before Russia" made Grand Duke Nikolai again advocate of a most reckless advance. According to his new plan, Gurko with 75,000 troops was to cross the mountains, engage Suleyman Pasha in Southern Bulgaria and thus open, for the equally strong detachment of General Radetskii, the route to the Turkish capital.

Considering climatic conditions, difficult mountainous terrain, and the state of troops—in every regiment on Shipka 1,000 men lay sick and rations were reduced to one pound of dry bread per day—the scheme bordered on madness. Even such adventurists as Skobelev dreaded the possibility that "we will be stopped behind the Balkan slopes by some new Plevna" and recommended a more simple march on Sofia instead.[2] Yet, the Grand Duke remained adamant on his gamble resting on a single card—the tenacity of the ragged, barefoot Russian soldier; and he almost succeeded. The dog-tired, hungry, sick and freezing Danube Army had after the fall of Plevna miraculously recovered its morale and in fifty days performed one of the most spectacular feats in the history of "pre-mechanized" warfare. Forcing through the ice-bound Balkan range, destroying the Turkish units to its south, the Russians advanced nearly 500 kilometeres to their great goal.

Only two weeks after Asman Pasha's surrender, on 25 December, Gurko started in a snowstorm and bitter cold on his march and on 4 January 1878, he had already captured Sofia. He found huge reserves of flour and ammunition there, which helped to alleviate at least temporarily the supply problem. The next day, Radetskii moved to break through the passes in the central Balkans. On 9 January, 36,000 Turks laid down their arms on the Shipka. Then, during one week, Skobelev overwhelmned the corps of Wessel Pasha, while that of Suleyman ceased to exist as a fighting force under Gurko's further blows. On 20 January, the advance cavalry units entered Adrianople.

In the meantime Russia's allies Montenegro and Serbia (Prince Milan joined the war anew on 13 December 1877) took full advantage of Turkish distress; the Montenegrins captured Nikšić and Antivari, the Serbs Niš.

When on 19 January, Turkish plenipotentiaries arrived at Kazanlik to beg the Grand Duke for an armistice, the Russian position looked more formidable than ever. Yet, in the following crucial weeks—crucial not only for the outcome of the Eastern crisis, but most certainly for the development of world affairs and the fate of Russian Empire too—Tsardom's politico-military leadership in its majority refused to take the ultimate risk. The fundamental feature, characteristic of the whole post-Crimean era, reappeared in crystallized form. Decisions of enormous consequence were made under contradictory pressures. On the one hand, the extremist groups pleaded for the final push; on the other hand, the fear that the occupation of Constantinople and the Straits would lead to a war with an European coalition favored the proponents of a compromise. Although pure chance played an enormous role in events, the state of public opinion was probably the essential background factor. In the pre-war phase the extremists commanded an overwhelming popular support and could thus force the Tsar and the government to follow them; now, although the Tsar was more or less on their side, they lacked this broad backing and the arguments of their opponents—the same which had been gradually rejected in 1876-1877—were to reappear and prevail.

Only in the first phase of this fateful contest, until the middle of January, was the trend seeking for the final solution clearly predominant. Only then it had been taken for granted that in the army, rushing towards the Golden Horn, as well as in society, any concession to Europe would be perceived as an intolerable treachery; while at the same time, there was no palpable evidence that Europe would be willing to fight.

England in particular, whose stance was to be the main external factor influencing the Russian option, had so far reacted feebly, the fall of Plevna and the subsequent Turkish rout producing there more panic than militancy. On 13 December, Shuvalov was given a memorandum containing only 'polite and conciliatory warning' that the conquest of Constantinople might incite public feeling to 'call for measures of precaution' and 'endanger seriously the good relations happily mantained between the two countries.'

This wording mirrored exactly the unending division when, in the words of Beaconsfield, 'in a cabinet of twelve members there are seven parties or policies.' As before, Lords Derby, Salisbury and Carnavon solicited for 'facing realities' that the Ottoman Empire was 'breaking to pieces past all remedy' and that among the electorate 'very few people now look back with satisfaction' on the Crimean War episode and 'nobody is insane enough . . . to desire a repetition of it.'[3]

The Russian Ambassador, with whom Lady Derby regularly confided 'every resolution of every council', could report on a complete stalemate both in the Whitehall and in the Anglo-Austrian negotiations. Moreover, Andrássy himself in a parliamentary exposé on 10 December promised not to oppose a temporary occupation of the Turkish capital.[4]

In this condition, even the bases for peace tabled at Poradim—especially in accepting Austrian rights in Bosnia-Hercegovina—were frowned upon. Pobedonostsev declared any concession to Venna a "disastrous thing for us and our moral weight in the East which threatens to generate terrible difficulties for the future."[5] The Tsar had been swayed by it. Although he had toasted to "his best friend, Emperor Francis Joseph," in his instructions of 29 December had modified the Poradim terms on two essential points: first, the allusion of the Austrian special position in Bosnia-Hercegovina was omitted; second—the Sultan should agree with a commitment concerning "Russian rights and interests in the Straits." Moreover, he stipulated that enemy could be granted an armistice only if these new terms were accepted. Gorchakov, who had returned from Bucharest to be a statesmen instead of a mere women-chaser again, also followed suit. In the reply on the mild British memorandum he declined to give any promise; "if you want war, say it, you can have it," he told Ambassador Loftus.[6]

From the middle of January onwards, however, the European scene underwent a change. In Austria-Hungary, Andrássy's suspicions that the Russians would break their promises, got hold of the Emperor, too; and, although the military party persisted in rejecting it, the possibility of an armed action in the Balkans was opened to intense debate and the Foreign Minister obtained much larger latitude in dealing with London. Still more significant shift took place there, following the opening of Parliament on 17 January: the trend personified by Beaconsfield and the Queen gradually prevailed over the one soliciting from the departure from the traditional defense of Ottoman integrity. In Tsardom, as a consequence, the always present Crimean complex again loomed large, bringing about the exactly opposite tendency, with the St. Petersburg moderates reasserting themselves and diplomacy seeking a compromise within the European concert.

That, of course, was to be a very complex process. Until the Great Powers met at the Congress of Berlin for the final settlement, Russian conduct had appeared as a maze of contradictory moves and a big confrontation probably often hung on a thin threat of pure accident. This complexity had firstly been due to a peculiar position Alexander took between the contesting hawks and doves, and secondly to the existence of an alternative decision-making centre in the headquarters of the Balkan Army (as the Danube Army was now to be called); enormously boosted in his self-confidence by the December-January march, Grand Duke Nikolai resolved to ignore the muddlers on the Neva and take care of Russia's fate himself.

The whole development "from military triumph to diplomatic capitulation" may be divided into four phases. After the initial one just described, the second covered seven weeks to the preliminary peace at San Stefano (3 March); the third nine weeks to the opening of the Berlin Congress (13 June); the fourth the Berlin summit itself.

* * *

The second phase had its most auspicious feature in the apparent divergence between the conciliatory diplomatic moves towards the two potentially hostile Powers, Austria-Hungary and England, and the tactics to confront them from the position of strength by forceful military actions and by a separate peace dictated to the Turks. It was inaugurated on 15-17 January, by Gorchakov's dispatches to London and Vienna and by new instructions to Nikolai. Responding to strong protests from both the capitals—Francis Joseph and Andrássy openly accused St. Petersburg of deceit—Gorchakov promised that the Balkan Army would not occupy the Gallipoli peninsula (i.e. the Dardanelles) and that Europe would be spared a fait accompli; while the dispositions for the Grand Duke directed him to proceed with undiminished vigor in the advance without, however, presenting the Turks with peace terms until the stances of the partners of the Three Emperors' League were clarified.[7]

Gorchakov's interference annoyed the Commander-in-Chief. According to his advisors, Hasenkampf and Skalon, he was "virtually possessed" by the great design to take Constantinople and force the Turks to capitulation. This way, he believed with the hawks, Beaconsfield would be prevented from using his fleet, while with the Austro-Hungarian statesmen "there was no need to talk much." Vis-à-vis St. Petersburg, this should "create the accomplished fact before it could be prohibited." Thus he threw away the instruction and allegedly even ordered—wishing to prevent further meddling in his moves—the telegraph lines with the capital to be cut. On 20 January, he forwarded the peace bases to the Turks and when they faltered before their harsh terms, announced to the Tsar his resolution to disregard other considerations and push for the ultimate triumph:

> Troops are exhaused, they have neither boots[8] nor guns or ammunition, but their morale is splendid; therefore his 'most steadfast conviction' is that 'it has become imperative to go to the centre, i.e. to Constantinople, and there complete the holy cause You have undertaken.'

On 24 January, the Grand Duke asked for formal permission to procure "that valuable security," Constantinople and the Straits, "to prevent their acquisition by alien hands."[9]

The position of the Tsar too, made the ambiguity of the Russian stance transparent and necessarily increased the suspicion of a double-cross. Perceiving the appeasement of Russian society—or, in his terms, the upholding of Russian honour—as his first duty, he marred the effort of Gorchakov and Miliutin, who, as so often in the crisis situations of the past, joined again their hands to work for a compromise with Europe. The letter Alexander wrote on 19 January to Francis Joseph, when compared with the Chancellor's message, shows clearly the different approach and explains why London and Vienna must have been alerted. He used "almost acrimonius, peremptory language" insisting that the establishment of Bulgaria as a big autonomous unit[10] and its two-year occupation by Russian troops was a conditio sine quo non for any future settlement; "every other transation would be bastard, fradulent and illusory," he claimed.[11]

Due mainly to the ruler's sympathy, the decisions adopted during the almost permanent sessions of the Council on 20-24 January buttressed the hawks. True, the Chancellor and the War Minister managed to impose some restrictions on their utlet: under no circumstances should troops enter Gallipoli and if the British landed at the Golden Horn, the Commander-in-Chief ought to "avoid clashing with them and keep units before the gates." But Nikolai was again encouraged to "continue the offensive in the Constantinople direction" and, in addition, advised to soften the Turks by the threat that different, much harsher terms would be imposed upon them "under the walls" of their capital. The task of negotiating the preliminary peace was entrusted to Ignatiev. Although the final settlement should be achieved "together with the whole of Europe," the Ambassador received a disposition to seek for "the radical solution of the Eastern Question." The Turks were to be forced to deliver their six modern warships—which should shift the naval balance in the Eastern Mediterranean—and sign a secret treaty on "joint defense" of the Straits.[12]

At first sight, no force was yet able to match the extremist initiative. On 23 January, Beaconsfield wrestled from his colleagues an order to Admiral Hornby to "sail at once for the Dardenalles . . . and Constantinople" and his opponents Derby and Carnavon tendered their resignations, but the next day the order was cancelled and Derby returned to the government. Consequently, Gorchakov's warnings about the imminent breach produced little effect,[13] especially when losing hope of English help, the Porte decided to yield. Its plenipotentiary Namik Pasha, who had only a few days before said to the Grand Duke that "it is better to die under duress than to sign," now professed total resignation: "Your arms are victorious, your ambition is satisfied; Turkey is lost; we accept whatever you wish." On 31 January in Adrianople, he and his colleague Server put their seals on the armistice documents and on the peace bases.[14]

While London dwelled in procrastinations,[15] the Moscow party exhorted society against the "diplomats" prone to "waste everything achieved by the army." Even the armistice was disapproved of, and, according to police reports, the old capital was out for a war with England.[16]

Katkov, as it could hardly have been otherwise, orchestrated the outcry:

> The proclamation of war for a rightful cause was met . . . with an
> enthusiasm impossible to describe; the news about the conclusion of
> peace, despite the great victory, is being expected by trembling fear.
> All the complications were caused by those who let the opportunity
> for a German deal pass while Bismarck had 'kept the doors half-
> opened,' and who now were 'more concerned about European bal-
> ance than about Russian interests, which they do not take into ac-
> count because they do not know them.' The presence of the British
> fleet in the Marmara Sea must be responded by the 'seizure of
> Gallipoli or at least of the forts commanding the entrances to the
> Black Sea.' This will provide Russia with a 'material guarantee' that
> the other Great Powers would not deprive her of what had already
> been delivered to her by Turkey.[17]

As to the general outlook of the Tsar, the publicist's mind might have
rested in peace. If the fatal dilemma were to occur, Alexander was determined to go to a new war. Highly sceptical about the gains of the Adrianople act, he repeatedly requested that the army be kept in "full preparedness" to "renew and even extend the fighting." Although he gave
way to Gorchakov's and Miliutin's insistence that some assurance ought
to be given to London and Vienna, and was perhaps willing to retreat in
the Straits Question, the issue of Bulgaria he took for a matter of principle where "we cannot afford any concession." "We must stand in readiness because in this age of (so-called) progress only force prevails," he
wrote to Nikolai. The British naval action made him only more resolute.
When informed about it, he immediately, on the evening of 9 February,
summoned the Council and announced that "this deliberate insult"
forced him to "take the decisive step—send troops to Constantinople";
then, rejecting the objections raised by Miliutin and Gorchakov, "on his
own responsibility, before God and nation," dictated a disposition to the
Commander-in-Chief to that effect. The next day, the War Minister managed to persuade him to alter it somehow—the action should ensue only
if the British attempted a landing—but in further communications with
the Grand Duke and the Sultan, Alexander was persistent in urging for
the Russian "protection of Christian lives and property" on the Golden
Horn and for the control of the Bosphorus.[18]

Notwithstanding the symptoms of almost unchallenged extremist vogue, however, the anxieties transpiring from Katkov's editorials were well founded. The nervousness and uncertainty which had since the middle of January taken hold of the Russian elite grew despite the vacillations in London and inadequate military preparations both in England and Austria-Hungary. The concessions wrestled by Miliutin and Gorchakov might have still appeared as mere devices to lull Western vigilance, but further development disclosed their considerable significance. On 29 January the Dual Monarchy was offered an assurance that it could count on Tsardom's consent if the Ballplatz convoked an international conference to discuss the final peace terms. Then the Russians assented that the delimitation of frontiers would be subjected to the debate and that neither bases in the Straits nor free-city status of Constantinople be demanded by them.[19]

Most importantly, what the Tsar and the hawks wished was already thwarted by the complete twist in Nikolai's stance. While earlier the Grand Duke had served as the main, albeit unconscious instrument for the extremist bid, now he helped the peace party in the same manner; that he hated Gorchakov and Miliutin no less than Ignatiev made no difference in this context.

Nikolai perceived the contradictory instructions he had been receiving from St. Petersburg as "heavy, spirit-scrippling harnesses" and by imposing upon the Turks the Adrianople terms his warlike spirit was almost spent. Such was even more the case in his entourage, including Nelidov, who had earlier emboldened him most. The possibility of English action, heretofore dismissed as a mere Gorchakov's invention, and general weariness took its toll. Pleading exhaustion of troops, an inadequate striking force owing to extended communications and lack of heavy weapons and supplies of all kinds, the Balkan Army command asked for a speedy return home. When Ignatiev on 8 February arrived at Adrianople to secure an optimal preliminary peace, he discovered to his utmost dismay that only the notorious hawks Gurko and Skobelev were in accord with him that at least the heights controlling the Bosphorus should be taken to procure "securities for the future." If the Tsar's telegrams had been delivered before the armistice, they would most certainly have initiated the fateful last thrust. Now, the Grand Duke responded on them evasively: the seizure of Constantinople was no longer "so easy and possible as two weeks ago."[20]

Seemingly, Ignatiev and the cause he represented still stood a fair chance. The dispositions sent from St. Petersburg on 15 February gave him considerable latitude: he was to speed up negotiations, obtain for the forthcoming European summit "as many accomplished facts as possible" and "stand firm on everything pertaining to Bulgaria."[21] The Grand Duke complied at least half-way to the Tsar's requirements, when he conceded to intimidate the Porte by moving his headquarters to San Stefano, some 12 kilometers from Constantinople, and by sending limited detachments to the Aegean Sea and the Bosphorus.

Yet, the way to the ultimate "accomplished fact" was effectively barred. Although from the heights near San Stefano he could see the cupola of St. Sophia and on 24 February telegraphed the Tsar that "the presence of our units at the very gates of the Turkish capital is finally reposing the destiny of the Ottoman Empire in our hands," Nikolai was firmly resolved to check the only too transparent gamble of the Ambassador—to exploit the recurrent stalemates in the negotiations, break the armistice and force the army to go ahead. "You are mad. You just wish to drag us into a new war with England. That is where your schemings are directed!", the Grand Duke shouted on the troublesome St. Petersburg's plenipotentiary in one of their frequent quarrels.[22]

The Commander-in-Chief was after a single aim: to make the Turks sign the preliminary peace treaty and get thus his achievements confirmed. And that, too, turned out to be the result of the San Stefano episode. The diplomatic haggling followed the pattern set at Adrianople.[23] The Porte, more terrified by the prospect of renewed Russian advance than hopeful of British assistance, in the end yielded and on 3 March its representatives signed the dictat.

Ignatiev appeared before assembled troops holding the document triumphantly high in his hand; but, as a witness says,[24] his face was sombre and gray. Indeed, there was no victory in it either for him or his kin.

* * *

If this were the final settlement, the San Stefano treaty would have been a quite impressive crowning of Russian military triumph. Although the main war aim was not achieved—the treaty avoided the issues of Constantinople and the Straits—the terms satisfactorily covered other essential political and military-strategic objectives:

Tsardom would receive 310 million silver rubles in war indemnity and territories both in the Balkans and Asia Minor (Southern Bessarabia, Ardahan, Kars, Batumi and Bayazet). The Porte recognized Serbian, Montenegrin and Rumanian independence within new frontiers; autonomy for Thessaly, Epirus and Albania; promised reforms in Turkish Armenia. And most significantly, the stipulations on Bulgaria, on which St. Petersburg abode so strongly,[25] were confirmed: an autonomous principality, tied to the Ottoman Empire only by a payment of annual tribute and occupied for two more years by Russian troops, was to stretch from the Black Sea to the Lake of Ohrid and from the Danube to the Aegean.[26]

"When I asked you (in Livadia) about the goal I should seek to attain, You replied laconically: 'Constantinople'; and now, after 16 months, I, with the whole Guard regiment prayed on our knees before Tsargrad for the victories granted and the magnificent peace," the Grand Duke wired to the Tsar.[27] Big words, though, could not move Alexander. He knew like everybody else that his predicament had not ended; in fact, he expected that conflict with the English and possibly the Austrians would break out any minute. Indeed, the weeks following San Stefano brought the tension to a boiling point and, as a historian put it, it has often been a "cause of amazement that some untoward act did not precipitate war."[28]

Thus, the pattern remained unaltered: while Miliutin, Gorchakov and the Grand Duke played the waiting game, the Tsar went on insisting on the necessity to "prepare for final confrontation."

Orders for the occupation of the Bosphorus were to plague Nikolai until the middle of April and his reluctance to comply totally spoiled the relations between him and his august brother.[29] In the heated discussions in the extraordinary councils, dealing since 13 March about the "placement of forces and the conduct in case of war with England and Austria," Alexander also showed unusual impatience with his Chancellor. "Now, after bloody and victorious war, we cannot, under any circumstances acquiesce to reducing Russian prestige vis-à-vis the English," ran the Tsar-imposed crucial conclusion. It was recognized intolerable if Russia were to be exposed to humiliating demands at the forthcoming peace congress in Berlin; and from this aspect the conduct of the London cabinet was denounced as a permanent recourse to deliberate provocations making armed response unavoidable.[30]

It appears that most of the Romanov family and the elite still considered the bold course against the West the sole remedy against the mounting domestic tension, and harangued Alexander perhaps no less than the press, where, as always since the autumn of 1876, Katkov's opposition against negotiated settlement had been paramount.

The very idea of the congress was for the Moscow editor a product of collusion between Europe and domestic traitors sitting in the government. Heretofore, he had scrupulously avoided attacking Bismarck; but when the Chancellor announced his willingness to interpose as an "honest broker," he joined the chorus accusing him of devious intention to rob Russia of her gains.[31] The Russian ministerial and diplomatic schemers, of course, were to be blamed first: "Why accuse England and Austria? We invented European supremacy, we invented the congress!"

Russian participation at the Berlin gathering would be permissible only if the terms of San Stefano—according to the publicist they constituted the absolute minimum still compatible with national dignity—underwent a revision in the sense of an improvement. In that event, "a piece of land in the Straits of Constantinople would be more valuable to us than thousands of square verstas of Turkish Armenia."[32]

Commenting on Anglo-Austrian war preparations,[33] the editor contended that the both Powers were only looking for spoils, and if Russia wanted to obtain that to what she was entitled and to make herself secure, the seizure of the Bosphorus would suffice. There would be no new war if the government were "to act in accordance with our national honour and the greatness of our state and ignore the rest."[34]

Alexander himself felt constrained to rebuke Katkov for his incisive formulae, but to no avail.[35]

Apart from the Strastnyi Boulevard's campaign, the activities of Pobedonostsev were symptomatic for the fire-eating mood in the nationalist part of society. He tried to organize research and procure the means for inventing "ultimate weapon" to punish the British—a submarine capable of destroying their navy and an aerial bomb to hit London. More practical was his so-called Volunteer Fleet scheme. For the funds collected among the public, cruisers should be bought abroad and serve to block British shipping on the high seas. The heir, Prince Dolgorukov, Count Stroganov, Aksakov, Samarin, businessmen Günzburg and Morozov and other figures with the same inclinations joined the initiative.[36]

In this atmosphere, Miliutin and Gorchakov could only confront the Tsar with severe realities and keep him from rash, irreparable decisions, not forcefully state their views.

So, in the instruction to Nikolai (11 March), the War Minister followed Alexander's and Katkov's line of arguments, requesting the seizure of the Bosphorus and thus "make us invulnerable vis-à-vis England,"[37] while in his diary he reasoned to the effect that

> However much we wish to get hold of the Bosphorus and prevent enemy's fleet entering the Black Sea, it is doubtful whether we can achieve it with the forces at our disposal. Furthermore, the abrogation of the Congress implies war not only with England but perhaps with half of Europe . . . ; it is impossible to cherish hopes for a fortunate outcome in the present conditions when our military forces and resources are exhausted.[38]

Similarly, Gorchakov had to reject with great emphasis the proposition that Tsardom would make any substantial concession to the West. His dispositions sent to Shuvalov between 14 and 25 March read as follows:

> We grant the others full liberty of action and claim for ourselves the same liberty. We do not understand the English imperative 'yes or no' . . . ; the Russian position must be that we leave the others the freedom to raise at the congress such questions as they think fit, while reserving to ourselves the right to accept or refuse discussion.[39]

* * *

The continuing tendency to defend and even enlarge the war gains was to have its most notable and long-term consequences on the Russian army. The English warlike moves in the wake of San Stefano injected new stamina into the hawks. Planning for the "second round" enlivened the General Staff gamblers led by Obruchev; broke the brief stupor which took hold of the Balkan Army before the Golden Horn; and untied anew the hands of the Caucasus and Central Asian military.

The Asiatic repercussions were of particular significance. The dramatic escalation near the Straits gave a powerful boost to the dogma that the

English opposition in the Near East could best be attenuated by a thrust into the Indian defence perimeter; and the hard-line course inaugurated since 1876 by the Indian viceroy Lord Lytton on the Afghan question supplied another argument that Russian action there must be speedy and vigorous.

At this juncture, the "Bariatinskii heritage" found its foremost ex-pounder in General Mikhail Skobelev, whom the Turkish war catapulted among the leading military-political figures in Tsardom. In the letters and memoranda written in 1876-1878 and addressed to Kaufman, Katkov,[40] Cherkasskii and to his powerful relatives at Court, the General postulated:

> Turkestan cannot be seen in any other way but as an 'operational base' for deeds 'indicated by Providence.' The conquest of the khanates demonstrated that no serious obstacles exist. 'In our pre-sent knowledge, having courageous and—according to my assess-ment—considerable means at our disposal, there is nothing in Asia which could really prevent us fulfilling the most far-reaching strate-gic intentions.'
>
> If the Turkestan and West-Siberian military districts muster an expedition southwards, it can administer a 'decisive blow' to the English and undermine their European position. If the expedition-ary corps were 18,000 men strong it would make the enterprise 'risky but feasible'; with 50,000 men, there would be "no risk at all.' In any event, the risks will clearly be exceeded by the advan-tages: 'mais, enfin, Paris vaut bien une messe.'
>
> As a first step a mission should be sent to Kabul, with a detach-ment of 12,000 following in its path. The mission should conclude a treaty with the Afghan Khan Shere Ali providing for a common offensive against India; in case of Ali's refusal, Abdurrahman Khan, living in Russian custody in Samarkand, is to be recognized as the ruler, tribal war incited and Persia encouraged to join the melee. Whatever course events in this 'very short' initial phase will take, they should be climaxed by an attack of a 'massed Asiatic cavalry . . .in the name of blood and spoil' on India and by an anti-British uprising there. As to the Russian expeditional corps, the optimal variant would be an advance on Benares; but a seizure of Afghan-istan is a more realistic alternative. Another corps dispatched from

the Caucasus across Persia to Herat would make the new Russian position steadfast.

Unless Central Asia was used for such 'politically and strategically correctly directed demonstration,' which would in its turn enable Russia to 'conquer Tsargrad in good time,' all the earlier triumphs in the area would remain barren. 'A knowledge of this region and of its resources inevitably leads to the conclusion that our presence in Turkestan is justifiable solely if the Eastern Question were to be solved from this quarter. Otherwise, the hide is not worth the tanning, and all the money sunk in Turkestan is lost.'[41]

In the weeks of suspense, when the anti-British hysteria was running high and the outbreak of hostilities expected any day, Skobelev's pleas exerted visible influence on the military-political debate and decisions.

In a way British diplomatic reports claiming that Cherniaev had been ordered to take over the command and march with 50,000 troops on Kabul and Peshawar[42] were exaggerated. The Extraordinary Council held on 20 April settled for a somewhat different course. In prolonged debates, only Governor General Kryzhanovskii and Baron Tornau canvassed a scheme identical with that advised by Skobelev; while a majority judged that such a venture would turn Afghan and Persian rulers against Russia, and that, moreover, military and financial resources must be preserved for the expected confrontation in Europe and the Near East. For Central Asia, a scheme set forth by Kaufman was recognized as best suited to the circumstances. It included only the least risky part of Skobelev's proposal: the military districts in question should prepare their forces for an offensive, and, in the meantime, a mission be dispatched to Kabul to enlist the cooperation from the Khan.[43]

However, British anxieties were far from unsubstantiated. Although he sided with moderates in the April councils, Kaufman opted de facto for the "Skobelevian solution." The expeditionary corps, which had been organized in the strictest secrecy since April, was given ambitious tasks indeed: its first column, under General Trotskii, was to proceed from Kokand through Kashgaria; the second (General Abramov) from Samarkand through Kabul; the third (Colonel Grotenhelm) from Khiva and Krasnovodsk through Merv, Herat and Kandahar.[44] While Miliutin all the time advised extreme caution—"friendly relations with Shere Ali

will terrify England more than any troops movement," he wrote[45] —the
Turkestan "half-Tsar" directed the mission to Kabul in his own, bold way.
In the instruction of 7 June to General Stoletov, appointed to lead the
mission, he ordained:

> Propose the Khan an alliance treaty, military assistance in the war
> against the English and promise Beludjistan as a spoil; use every
> means to foster Russian influence and anti-British feelings both in
> Kabul and among the tribes; make logistic preparation for the arrival
> of the expeditionary corps; and if Shere Ali would agree with he
> treaty, take over the control of the Afghan army.[46]

* * *

In the Balkans, or, to be more precise in Bulgaria, the second, even
more explosive centre of extremist forward policy had been taking shape.
There, the alliance between the Moscow party and the military was to
parade itself in all its complexity, exposing Tsardom and European peace
for many years to recurrent tests.

The importance of Bulgaria as the key politico-military object, so clearly
stated in the San Stefano treaty, had been stressed in Russian documents
and deliberations since before the Turkish war. Two big disappointments
—first, the estrangement with the Serbs and then the failure to conquer
Constantinople and the Straits—had the decisive bearing upon this emphasis.

On 19 September, 1876 Aksakov—a man personifying, from the late
1850s onwards, the Serbian orientation in Panslav planning—distinctly
formulated the new approach. Recalling Fadeev's earlier analyses on
Balkan strategy he now asserted that neither Serbia nor Montenegro
could, for different reasons, "fight for all-Slav or Russian interests in the
Straits" and to help in solving the Eastern Question. Montenegro was too
small, backward and isolated to do the job. Serbia, too, apart from being
unreliable, could not serve to bring about the dissolution of the Ottoman
Empire; "cutting the Serbian lands from Turkey is a simple amputation."
The path to the great goal lay only through Bulgaria, "the very body
and marrow of Turkey."[47]

The Russian war plan of October 1876 indicates that this concept fully
corresponded with the viewpoints of the War Ministry and the Tsar.

Alexander, moreover, at that time incensed by Panslav exaltation, had named Prince Cherkasskii, the notorious Muscovite, as head of the future Bulgarian civil administration and gave him a general directive that "beyond the Danube we must do something similar to what was done in the Polish Kingdom."[48]

Judging from his memoranda, one would believe that the Prince wished to build Russian supremacy without resorting to arbitrary methods and clearly perceived the dangers ahead. He advised Alexander and Miliutin against the tendencies of the military to apply the methods lately used in Central Asia. Paraphrasing the Tsar's directive, he warned that the army must not resort to "introducing beyond the Danube something in the manner of the Turkestan situation"; instead, Russo-Bulgarian relations should be founded on "broadmindedness rather than on petti-fogging and irritating interference in internal affairs."[49] But with his imperious mentality—Pobedonostsev deservedly held him for a "man without heart, cruel and haughty"[55]—and with his mind tainted by the unsavory police experience in Poland, Cherkasskii proved himself exceedingly prone to act in the Turkestan style. The Bulgarians were soon to call him "the man of steel" (Celik Pasha).[51]

The Prince found the Turkish administrative system satisfactory and attributed its shortcomings only to the incompetence of the officials operating it. Thus, the administrative units were just given Russian names ("gubernia," "okrug," "uezd") and the important positions in them entrusted as a rule to Guards officers. The few Bulgarians in higher offices were people with long-standing Russian allegiance, a record of Russian service or graduates from Russian schools and seminaries. On the lower levels, those who served the Turks—nearly all of them the well-to-do "chorbadjii" alienated from their kin—were left at their posts.

Needless to add, the administrators imbibed in the Russian tradition behaved in the same way as their chief. One of them summed up their views as follows:

> The liberation of Bulgaria needs a whip. I know that I am detested by our so-called 'little brothers' but I couldn't care less. It is a miserable nation that it has to be treated harshly. Now they are afraid of me because they know that nothing is to be pardoned. Anyone found guilty will be thrashed. Let them be afraid of me![52]

For decades Panslav propaganda painted life in Bulgaria in the blackest possible colours. So the Russians suffered a veritable shock when they saw how the fields were tilled with care and affection, prosperous villages with plenty of cattle, schools, libraries—all this in sharp contrast with Russian reality. Nonetheless, the relatives of Gogol's Derzhimordas and Saltykov-Shchedrin's "Gentlemen of Tashkent" began to teach the population "to do it better, as we do." Nemirovich-Danchenko, later a well-known novelist, wrote with bitter irony:

> They ordered the cultivation of the soil in the Russian way, and the clipping of rams in winter; and they themselves clipped the population not only in the winter, but also in spring, summer and autumn.[53]

The conduct of the Danube Army was another outrage. The soldiers stole, plundered, pointlessly destroyed. As a representative of the Slavic Committee observed, "they exceeded the limits of patience, even for the patient and obedient Bulgarians." Among their superiors, the callousness towards a small nation was sometimes pushed to extremes. "It is a shame that the Turks did not annihilate them to the very last one . . . ; half-measures never pay," said a general at an official banquet attended by many of those who "should have been annihilated."[54]

The Bulgarians attached to the Slavic committees were horrified by this development. One of the Odessa leaders, the wealthy businessman Palauzov, warned Aksakov:

> If this is not to be stopped, his kin may soon 'turn into Poles or Rumanians.' Cherkasskii and his entourage do not realize that 'what has recently been practiced in the Polish Kingdom cannot be applied towards the liberated Bulgarians.' People are already comparing the Russians with the Turks and this comparison is not always favorable to the former. Russia should 'predominate in everything and everywhere,' but this has to be done 'cautiously, step by step.'[55]

Aksakov and Katkov felt the same. The *Moskovskiia vedomosti* accused the administrators of "in fact preparing the ground for the Turks to return" and required that the Bulgarians themselves should take over responsible positions and be only under general Russian supervision.[56]

In early 1878, almost everybody gave countenance to the plea that the thoroughly impossible Cherkasskii must go and his system—in a situation where wholehearted Bulgarian support was needed for the expected "second round"—be altered.[57] The Prince's timely death (on 3 March, the day of San Stefano) made the change smooth. The novel man in charge, Prince Dondukov-Korsakov, the sponsor of the Kiev Slavic Committee, proved outstanding abilities to attain hawkish goals by political manipulation rather than by coercion. As to the essentials, though, no one could have doubted that the Russians considered Bulgaria their vital war gain and would act accordingly.

* * *

In the midst of great words and new war preparations, Miliutin and Gorchakov managed to persuade Alexander that diplomatic action should be undertaken to isolate Beaconsfield and that for this purpose some accommodation with the Dual Monarchy ought to be attempted. Thus at the end of March, Ignatiev surfaced in Vienna with a carte blanche to agree on changes in the San Stefano treaty to placate the Austrian elite.

Despite the advancing rapprochement between London and Vienna, the Russians appeared to have an axe to grind there.[58] But hopes connected with this, what proved to be the last history-making mission of their ace diplomat, were badly disappointed. Aristocratic high society treated him well; he had to learn, however, that Andrássy was still the man with the power to decide. And the Hungarian displayed unconcealing hostility: if St. Petersburg would not yield on the two essential points in the San Stefano terms concerning Bulgarian boundaries and the Russian two-year occupation, then there would be a war and a Polish uprising.

The effect on the Neva was shattering; "the requirements of Count Andrássy exceed the worst expectations," Miliutin noted. At first sight it gave Katkov and the others denying any diplomatic compromise, the winning card. In the Extraordinary Council on 11 April, both the Tsar and the War Minister proclaimed that no accommodation should be sought with the Austrians in the future. On 24 April, Alexander signed a war plan, envisaging the formation of three armies for combatting England and Austria-Hungary in Europe and the Near East as well as of a corps for the expedition to India.[59]

In fact, however, Ignatiev's failure distinctly marked the turn of the tide in the opposite direction. Although the April war decisions were partly based on a memoir circulated by the Ambassador,[60] his advice had lost its former weight. And the ascendency of his moderate rival in London, Shuvalov, indicated that the Tsar and the elite had abandoned the proposition that to go to war for upholding prestige was a safer course than to accept a compromise and then to face mounting domestic troubles.

We are in no position to assess all the factors that finally tipped the scale and damaged the heretofore at least outwardly predominant extremist tendency. Nonetheless it appears to be beyond any doubt that the April public trial of Vera Zasulich—she had attempted to assassinate the police chief General Trepov, but the jury acquitted her and first the courtroom audience, composed largely of high society, and then almost the whole press applauded the verdict—unnerved Alexander and those who had spirited him to the bold course (including Katkov) so profoundly, that they ceased to believe in the basic loyalty of the upper classes.[61] To be sure, the Tsar let the vigilance campaign of the Volunteer Fleet[62] and the preparations for the action in Central Asia go unhindered; yet in his inner circle Miliutin, Gorchakov and later Shuvalov could not only freely state their viewpoints but also decide and act.

Besides domestic considerations, the peculiar development in the Balkan Army, where the disobedient Nikolai was relieved of the command and replaced by Todleben, had unquestionably been of a signal import. But Sumner's opinion that it was the memoir of Todleben sent to St. Petersburg on 9 May what decided about "the defeat of the war party,"[63] cannot be accepted. If we look for a new point of departure, then it were the councils of 27 and 30 April, which tabled to "sacrifice the unity of Bulgaria and consent to her division" and raised Shuvalov to the position of the negotiator with Europe; the alarming Shuvalov's telegram of 28 April—that the English were ready to occupy the Straits and land 60-70,000 troops in Batumi and Poti—probably functioned as the proverbial last straw.[64]

* * *

After being deposed from his police post, Count Peter Shuvalov waited impatiently for the opportunity to reassert himself as the leading statesman.

"They used me as an unripe fruit, and when I ripened they threw me away," he complained.[65] The role he was now assigned suited him perfectly. He blamed the Tsar and society led astray by the "phantasmagoria evoked by the Panslavs" for the lamentable state of Russian affairs;[66] at present, he believed, they had already sobered up and would permit him to take advantage of the excellent connections he had in London and Berlin and make a reasonable settlement.

Following intense negotiations with Salisbury, who took over the Foreign Office after Derby, the Ambassador was in St. Petersburg on 12-18 May and returned to London on 22 May to conclude the bargain. On the Neva he still noticed disquieting symptoms—Alexander remained convinced that the English were only after war, the Volunteer Fleet campaign was in full swing, Field Marshal Bariatinskii strove to rally the army opposition against Miliutin's conciliatory effort[67] and the government was unwilling to test its strength by curbing the extremist agitation—but his prevailing impression must have been positive. Assisted by the War Minister and the Chancellor, he won over the ruler at the Extraordinary Councils of 14 and 17 May for the proposition that it was "preferable to yield concessions to England than to clash with her or to bow before the improper, brazen demands raised by Count Andrássy."[68] The changed stance of the Strastnyi Boulevard also indicated that his essential calculation was correct. Dispirited no less than the Tsar by the Zasulich affair, the Moscow editor stopped his exhortations against "our diplomats" and gave free rein to his hitherto suppressed fear of the Crimean situation. "Pray God that the result will be beneficial and bring us peace we all wish," he hailed on 10 May the Ambassador's action. "The name of Count Shuvalov" suddenly became a warrant for him "that the talks will be serious."[69]

The councils agreed that Bulgaria was not to stretch either to the Aegean Sea or to Macedonia; and should be divided into two parts by the Balkan range—an autonomous principality in the north, an autonomous province under a Christian Governor in the south. This arrangement also supplied the basis for the Anglo-Russian protocol signed in the Foreign Office on 30 May, and, indeed, for the whole settlement achieved at the Berlin Congress.[70]

In the now predominant mood of resignation even the Balkan Army presence before Constantinople was recognized as a strategic liability. When the Extraordinary Council met on 29 June to its final pre-Congress deliberations, Alexander himself "against all expectations" expressed the peace party's reasoning in its extreme:

> It is entirely obvious that we have against us not only England but the whole of Europe and that we cannot expect support from anybody. If the matter is put this way we have no choice. We must agree with everything, retreat in everything.[71]

* * *

In the Russian political mind, the Congress of Berlin (13 June-13 July 1878) was to become a trauma almost as overwhelming as that of the Crimean War. The Russians were to perceive its results in the manner Katkov and the Moscow party had taught them—not as the inevitable consequence of the political, economic and military weakness of their Empire but as that of a monstrous conspiracy engineered by the West in collusion with alienated St. Petersburg cosmopolitan diplomats.

Undoubtedly, the Shuvalov-Gorchakov duo representing Russia made a very bad partnership.

The Tsar and the whole elite had felt that the "most illustrious Prince" should have stayed home; that he had "outlived himself," "his head had stopped functioning" and he had "finally relapsed into a state of childhood"; and that, moreover, his presence would antagonize the German Chancellor whose sympathies for the Russian position had been considered essential. Owing to Gorchakov's illness, also, Alexander had originally named Shuvalov the main Russian plenipotentiary. But when the Prince quickly recovered upon receiving the news, and when he insisted that he must "make his last sacrifice for Russia," the ruler lacked the courage to refuse him.[72]

So, while Shuvalov was to be praised by the other participants for a superb performance—he again impressed as a model diplomat, perfectly informed, looking for compromises and at the same time infatiguable in defending his country's cause—in Gorchakov they found the familiar vain, jealous nuisance; and Bismarck, who had promised to Count Peter "on the whole, his sincere support," was not anxious to help his old foe. "I won't allow Prince Gorchakov to climb a second time on my shoulders in order to make a pedestal," he said recalling the 1875 episode.[73]

Nonetheless, these were only second-rate factors which could perhaps have influenced details but not substantial issues. Miliutin stated in plain words Russian impotence and isolation when he told Shuvalov: "You, Count, must sacrifice your personal position and self-respect and give way in everything rather than let things end in a new war for which we are sorely unprepared."[74] Nothing could have saved Tsardom from losing a great deal of its San Stefano gains.

Of course the Turks, like the other "little ones" (the Serbs, Rumanians, Montenegrins and Greeks), counted in Berlin for nothing. But under Bismarck's presidency the Russians faced their sworn enemies Beaconsfield and Andrássy, now backed to the hilt by Salisbury, who had since early 1878 abandoned his former stances one after another, and often also by French and Italian Foreign Ministers, Waddington and Corti. Russian hope for English connivance did not materialize. There had been just before the opening of the Congress another outcry behind the Channel, engendered by reports of Kaufman's schemings in Afghanistan; and the leak of the secret Shuvalov-Salisbury May understanding to the press as well as the commitments they accepted towards Austria-Hungary[75] and Turkey[76] pushed the British delegates to utmost intransigence.

Apart from the territorial acquisition in Asia Minor and Southern Bessarabia, the task of the Russian plenipotentiaries rested in safeguarding as much of the San Stefano Bulgaria as possible. Not surprisingly, the discussions on the Bulgarian settlement were to take about a half of the congress' time and drive the gathering to the verge of a breach. By the Shuvalov-Salisbury protocol, the division had been accorded beforehand; but it remained to draw the boundary line between the future autonomous principality in the north and the autonomous province (for which the name of "Eastern Rumelia" was invented) in the south, and determine the rights of the Sultan in both of them. The British wished that the congress would allow the Turks to occupy the Balkan range and incorporate Varna and Sofia into Eastern Rumelia. In order to weaken Russian resistance, Beaconsfield repeatedly used the threat to leave the German capital and quite succeeded in the blackmail. In the resulting quasi-compromise, Varna and Sofia went to the Principality, but the Turks were empowered to reestablish their rule in Macedonia and keep their garrisons in Eastern Rumelia; while Russian troops and the Russian Imperial commissioner were to stay in Bulgaria for only nine months.

After the Bulgarian debate was closed on 26 June, the following ones, dealing mostly with the complex of problems connected with the territorial and political changes in the western Balkans and Asia Minor, brought further harm to Russia's position and prestige.

In accordance with the Anglo-Austrian convention of 6 June, Salisbury pleaded Vienna's case in the Bosnia-Hercegovina issue: "like a schoolmaster with cane in hand"[77] he taught the Turks that it was in their interest to be deprived of the two provinces by the Dual Monarchy, not by the Slavic states. On 28 June, the congress duly approved Austrian occupation and administration. That was, however, not the only item on Andrássy's list. Aiming at preventing Serbia and Montenegro from achieving a common frontier on the Lim river (provided by the San Stefano treaty) and open the road to Salonika, the Hungarian demanded the sanjak of Novi Pazar, too. Despite verbal protests, the Russians again did not feel strong enough to let the skirmish develop into a major strife and on 13 July Gorchakov signed a secret agreement pledging his country to "raise no objections," if Austria-Hungary were to occupy the sanjak "like the rest of Bosnia-Hercegovina."[78]

For this, the Montenegrins were at least partly compensated by the Hercegovinan border districts, Podgorica and the port of Antivari; while the Serbs, already badly disappointed by San Stefano, got only minor acquisitions at their eastern border (Mali Zvornik, Pirot, Tsaribrod, Trno), and even those were obtained against resistance of the Russians, unwilling to see further diminution of their future Bulgarian preserve.

So, by its territorial changes in the Balkans, the Berlin Treaty was mostly to further Russia's estrangement with the states of her crucial sphere of interest. First, Rumania turned decidedly hostile because of Southern Bessarabia, for which Dobrogea was not adequate compensation. Second, feeling deceived by Alexander and Gorchakov, Milan of Serbia opted to look for protection and support in Vienna only. Third, even the division of Bulgaria, evolved in the end into a Russian liability.

In comparison, the delimitation of the Asiatic frontier was but a trifle and has been remembered mostly as an exercise in hypocrisy and incompetence, with both the Russians and the British bluffing and blundering.[79] Still, there too the latter, confronted by Beaconsfield's talks of breach, were forced to return Bayazid and a territory of about 90,000 inhabitants to the Turks and promise to declare Batumi a free, solely commercial port.

On the top of all, two days before the final signature, Salisbury read out a declaration that his government recognized the principle of the closure of the Straits merely as its obligation to the Sultan. This meant that Tsardom, after failing to attain its focal war aim, the control of the Bosphorus-Dardanelles waterway, could not even safeguard its moderate, defensive modification; that, once invited by the Turkish ruler, the English were free to intervene militarily and enter the Black Sea. This way, the ingrained Russian security complex was drastically enlivened and the dissatisfaction with the diplomatic settlement, steadily growing during the congress' proceedings, received the ultimate push.

In this context, Katkov's comments were unmistakable. On the eve of the summit, still laboring under the "Vera Zasulich shock," the publicist had been too sacred to continue his agitation; and he apparently hoped that the English would more or less approve the San Stefano terms or perhaps agree on a deal in which they would obtain the Dardanelles and Russia the Bosphorus. So, he promised to be reticent and "made no predictions."[80] The uproar in the English press about the Shuvalov-Salisbury understanding, however, drove him quickly back to the old path.[81]

The usual disclosures of Western conspiracy would not suffice. With growing ferocity, he developed the familiar theme that the St. Petersburg elite was incapable of defending the national interest. He blamed Russian diplomats for the Bulgarian division, for the deliverance of the Eastern Rumelia to the Turks, for selling Serbia, Montenegro and Bosnia-Hercegovina to the Austrians.[82] Neither Miliutin's "liberal military bureaucracy" was absolved from the responsibility for the Berlin disaster: they, the Muscovite hinted, contributed much to it by badly preparing the army for war.[83] Finally, Salisbury's statement on the Straits convinced him that St. Petersburg's blunders made the ultimate disaster imminent —that the English would occupy Constantinople and the Bosphorus and establish their protectorate over the whole of the Ottoman Empire in the bargain.[84]

Summing up, Katkov found the cardinal fault in the elite's unwillingness to comprehend and follow his advice:

> . . .we shall always be isolated if we remain without firm alliance based on real interests. . . . The only reason for our diplomatic setbacks undoubtedly accrued from our (merely) platonic relations

with Germany. Germany paid us for our services with friendly words, but lacked interest in our success. We must blame ourselves for this: we had no concrete political programme. Neither Beaconsfield nor Andrássy caused our misfortunes; our concessions were directed by the policy of the (disinterested) German Chancellor.[85]

In the present moment, cooperation within the Bismarckian system had lost its whole purpose—so read the first part of the concluding message. The second part of it, at least for the time being, had even larger bearing: "our enemies celebrate a great victory, but nobody believes that this peace will endure"; congress had been only an "empty, miserable joke," a "mere breathing pause."[86]

Truly, at the very moment when, on 13 July, the Berlin treaty was signed[87] there was but a dim hope that European peace would escape further test.

CHAPTER 18

THE "SECOND ROUND" ISSUE
(1878-1879)

It is unfortunately true that people here are
simply afraid of the nationalist press. . . .
The Tsar, too, notwithstanding the fact
that the entire activity of these papers is
actually directed against the existing regime,
is averse to any attempt to subject them to
strict control. . . . Ever since the nationalist
tendency has come so prominently to the
fore, and particularly since it succeeded
in prevailing, against all better advice, on the
question of going to war, the so called
"nationalist party" has become a real
power, especially since it embraces the
entire army . . . . Behind many of these
papers stand the military. Everyone knows
that the sympathies of the army are with
the nationalist press; and the military
entourage of the Tsar takes care to see
that it receives excellent and favorable
treatment.
Kálnoky

As far as the press is concerned, the Russian
government is worse off than any in Europe.
Shuvalov

No, we are not afraid of a coalition, which
by political common sense ought to be
instantaneously discovered as impossible.
No, we are much more afraid of those
"friendly" plans proposed to us, allegedly
in order to forestall the war danger.
Katkov

Katkov's comments indicated what had happened in the course of the Berlin summit, once the dreaded European supremacy became manifest. While the moderates insisted that there was no better alternative left,[1] for the extremists the "second round" again appeared preferable to the conditions accepted by the Russian representatives; and by the outcry of humiliated pride, their press largely inflammed public opinion.[2]

In a passionate speech delivered at the Moscow Slavic Committee session, Aksakov threw down the gauntlet:

> Is it you, victorious Russia, who has voluntarily condemned
> herself? Is it you who like a criminal in the dock has to repent
> for bringing about a sacred action, who has to beg for being for-
> given for your victories? . . . The Western Powers led by Bismarck
> have been knocking down your laurels of victory and putting the
> cap of fools on your head . . . . Who is guilty of this shame? Western
> injury to Russia is an historic axiom which has been ignored only
> by Russian diplomats belonging to St. Petersburg's governmental
> sphere. The Russian people will never forget the dubious service
> rendered by their own diplomats . . . .[3]

The authorities dissolved the Moscow Committee and banned Aksakov from the old capital. The gesture, though, could neither intimidate nor convince anybody. In a letter to the heir, Pobedonostsev described the words of the Panslav leader as "very persuasive and true" and warned that "people would hold this peace for an insult." Predicting "pernicious and painful consequences for internal tranquility," he recommended to his former pupil to look for guidance in Katkov's daily. There "the indignation is manifested every day" and the fact had been established beyond any doubt that "Russian conscience can at no price admit that Bulgaria proper, Russian Bulgaria, might be sacrificed by the Russian government to the Turks."[4]

Alexander felt both cheated and cornered. Before the congress he had obviously hoped that the Bismarckian system, "the programme of 1872," would aid him to stabilize Tsardom's external position. Now, upon his arrival to St. Petersburg, Shuvalov found him labouring under the impression that in Berlin "an anti-Russian coalition headed by Prince Bismarck" had been at work. Together with the whole elite, moreover, the Tsar feared that the Turkish return to Eastern Rumelia would result in massacres and that domestic pressures would force him to reopen hostilities regardless of the terrible odds. Katkov's editorials and Aksakov's speech made it obvious that the extremists would not spare him the ordeal.[5]

* * *

In the diplomatic observations, the bonds between the Muscovites and their military associates, cemented during the Eastern crisis, had already been identified as the key pattern.[6] Exploiting Alexander's pessimist outlook and the press agitation, the hawks in the Balkan Army as well as their Asiatic counterparts set off to destroy "that miserable peace." The inglorious Austrian invasion of Bosnia-Hercegovina, started on 31 July, largely buttressed their purpose;[7] the Moscow-military bloc could in addition to injured Panslav feelings present the affair as undisputable proof that the Dual Monarchy was too effeted to engage in a major confrontation.[8] And if the massacre factor is taken into account, then one may well understand the recurrent euphoria. Even the old, cautious General Todleben for a while joined the chorus; his adjutant, the historian Shilder, remarked with irony that his chief would sooner be a janitor at Adrianople than go back to Russia. On the first occasion, the Balkan Army should turn against the Turks, the Bulgarians proclaim their unity and join or start the struggle. Several scenarious for the "second round" were in circulation. The most important one for future events ran as follows: the Bulgarians would invade Macedonia, the Turks respond by massacres and these would be used if no better then at least for a prolonged occupation.[9]

Owing to the extremist initiative, both parts of Bulgaria reminded observers of a bustling military camp. While in the south the generals were distributing tens of thousands rifles to the populace and under cover of gymnastic societies trained them in combat, in the north the Inperial commissioner Prince Dondukov-Korsakov organized the local

Land Army and encouraged the formation of guerilla "chetas" for the raid into Macedonia. To the great discomfort in St. Petersburg and indignation of Europe, Dondukov, Skobelev and other militarists publicly agitated against the Berlin Treaty.[10]

During the Turkish war Skobelev became a symbol of Russian military virtues. In white uniform, astride a white stalion, he seemed to appear in every dangerous spot and perform acts of bravery there. The hostility showed against him by Grand Duke Nikolai and his entourage of old-timers, only enhanced the prestige of the 'White General.'[11]

Due to this as well as his Bonapartist proclivities, Skobelev rose in the first post-war years into a leading figure among the new, egregiously nationalist-minded officer corps. In the 'second-round' contexture of 1878-1879, though, his bearing was dimmed by that of Prince Dondukov.

The Caucasus militarists, St. Petersburg's traditionalist 'mazurka-dancers' no less than the Moscow party considered the Prince their associate. Together with his first protector, Field-Marshal Bariatinskii, he resigned in protest in 1863. But when his other friend, Timashev, took over the Interior Ministry, he appeared in the top echelon of the state service, as a Governor General in Kiev. Because of considerable personal ambition and inclination to lie and hypocrisy, high society nicknamed Dondukov "Ignatiev the Second'[12]; nonetheless, excellent connections secured him a prominent position and the Bulgarian appointment reflected this fact.

In private conversations, the Prince held the Bulgarians in contempt.[13] But in his official capacity he behaved much differently and managed in a short time to repair the harm done by his predecessor, Cherkasskii. He agreed with the latter that Bulgaria required an iron hand; however, he pointed out that the hand ought to be in a 'velvet glove.'[14] Displaying 'American-presidential-candidate's' talents and energy, in Bulgarian uniform and traditional kalpak, Dondukov toured through the whole country, kissed children, shook hands with the elders and delivered innumerable speeches on the common Russo-Bulgarian cause; for the young intelligentsia, including the radicals viewed by most Russians with paramount suspicion, he arranged banquets and skillfully played on their hopes of getting the highest positions once the new Principality was formally established. In brief, probably spurred by the hope of acquiring the Sofia throne, Dondukov simultaneously succeeded in moulding the overriding resentment against the Berlin treaty and the anxieties about the return of the Turks into an almost perfect tool for his schemes.

It seemed as if the Tsar and his entourage were swayed by the arguments and projects canvassed by Dondukov and the forces he represented. Orders were given for speeding up the formation of the Bulgarian armed forces; on 29 September, at an Extraordinary Council at Livadia, two moderates—Todleben and Prince Lobanov-Rostovskii, the new Ambassador to Constantinople—pushed through the hawkish demand for a troops increase in the Balkans; and it was tabled that a peace treaty with Turkey and a military retreat from the area should be postponed for an "unspecified period."[15]

The extremists were also able to uphold the spirit of confrontation in Central Asia.

In the eve of Berlin, Kaufman received instructions that "in view of altered political circumstances," the detachments organized for the Afghan-Indian expedition should be disbanded.[16] This, naturally, made the mission to Kabul unpractical too, but General Stoletov, presumably with the Tashkent warlord's connivance, refused to be stopped.[17] On 21 August, the Russo-Afghan treaty was signed[18] and while the rest of the mission waited in Kabul, Stoletov brought the document to Kaufman. Not surprisingly, the latter was delighted and his message to Livadia requesting endorsement reverberated earlier Skobelev's memoranda:

> We can hardly threaten England in any other way than by opening a safe route from the Amu (-Daria river) to the Indian frontier; from this aspect the Central Asian theatre of action takes on a first-rate importance. . . . If we are unable to administer England a decisive blow in Asia, then we run the risk that the Eastern Question, when the time comes to its solution, will again stalemate, or, if some European combination occurs there, will be solved to England's advantage and not to ours.

The "half-Tsar" of Turkestan asked for considerable reinforcements—
2 infantry divisions, 4 Cossack regiments—to make "our protectorate
over Afghanistan" secure.[19]

* * *

In London and Simla, Stoletov's presence in Kabul produced a storm.
Katkov's editorial published on 6/18 July was quoted in Parliament as
the most signal proof of Russian sinister designs:

> The time has come for Russia to establish her influence over the
> whole of Central Asia, and this is all the more easy as the ruler of
> Afghanistan is not on good terms with England, our foe. . . . The
> concentration of our influence on the frontiers of the territories
> of the Indian Empress would be a natural response to the English
> seizure of Cyprus. . . . Such may be the inobtrusive, even peace-
> ful object of the military operations undertaken by the troops
> of the Turkestan military district. . . . In Asia there are two Powers
> confronting each other, and they must inevitably come into col-
> lisions. England wishes to be Russia's nearest neighbour in Asia
> Minor, and it is only natural, therefore, that Russia, in her turn,
> should desire to approach somewhat nearer to the English frontiers
> in India.[20]

The cabinet would perhaps have preferred to settle the matter with
St. Petersburg through diplomatic channels; but Lord Lytton would
not let the golden opportunity slip away. He ordered General Chamber-
lain to go to Kabul with an imposing military convoy and demand an
alliance treaty; and when Shere Ali showed reluctance to grant entry,
he proclaimed it as an act of hostility. On 21 November, the breach was
formally announced and British troops invaded Afghan territory.

No less seriously, Prince Dondukov-Korsakov and his lieutenants
moved in the meantime to create a crisis in Macedonia and thereby start
the "second round."[21] Despite St. Petersburg's repeated warnings, on
17 October a "cheta" led by Cossack Captain Kalmykov attacked the
Turks near Kresna and in the following month penetrated deep into the
Struma valley.

However, the adventure proved equally counter-productive for its
hawkish organizers as did the Stoletov mission. While the Macedonian

population remained passive, the expected massacre did not materialize and the Turks easily overwhelmed the isolated invaders, there was a
wave of protests from Constantinople and the European capitals, again
accusing St. Petersburg of breaking the peace.[22] Instead of inducing
Tsardom's policymakers to an open identification with the "anti-Congress"
line, Kaufman's and Dondukov's initiatives made them fully realize the
risks inherent in such a position.

"This is a repetition of the earlier encroachments of Moscow Slavophiles from the time of the Serbian revolt. The same volunteers, the same
lack of (sober) deliberation in deeds, the same calculation to involve the
Russian government into a new war," Miliutin aired his indignation over
the Macedonian venture. Alexander was equally affronted. He declared
Dondukov's conduct "inconceivable and unforgivable" and asked for
"the most strict measures to prevent any high-handed action under the
pretext of Bulgarian national unity." Russian military governors in the
area were ordained to stop the actions of the committees, to impede
their contact with supporters in Russia and sent home officers involved
in the hazard.[23]

At the same time, Kaufman was admonished to utmost caution and
the Kabul mission recalled. Shuvalov received instruction for another
peace mission: first of all, he should "make an attempt at renewal of the
former friendly understanding with England concerning Central-Asian
affairs"; and on his way to London, he was also to sound Vienna and
eventually Berlin on the possibilities of restoring the Three Emperors'
League.[24]

The Moscow-military bloc, of course, conceived this as a perpetuation
of the moral turpitude paraded at the Berlin summit and challenged
it vigorously. Katkov again declared St. Petersburg alienated from Russia,
"in many respects having common interest not with her but with foreigners" and refused to "disarm." Tsardom was facing a Western plot designed
to deliver the Straits to the English and drive it out of the Balkans; from
this, he enunciated the old dogma, "the fall of Russia as a Great Power"
would accrue and it has hence to be resisted by all means.[25] The Berlin
Treaty, he reiterated, must not be put into effect in the sense in which
Europe understood it; driving his arguments ad absurdum, he declared
the establishment of Greater Bulgaria a "consequent fulfillment" of the
document signed in the German capital.[26]

The Balkan military, too, stubbornly adhered to their vistas. Why not "refuse to elect a Bulgarian Prince and demand instead a continuation of Russian administration in the form of protectorate?", Dondukov wrote; a revolution will break out soon on the Golden Horn, the Eastern Question be reopened and then Russian troops in the Balkans and armed Bulgarians fighting for unity will supply the strongest cards for the game. Even Todleben, in a memoir "On the preparations of the Bulgarians for their self-defence" (6 November) still abode to the same idea: "Never will such a favourable opportunity occur again as at the present moment when everything depends on our decision."[27]

Yet, the Russian elite was swayed by differnt impulses. Although the splendour of the court life in the winter of 1878-1879 reminded a French diplomat of a "mixture of the century of Louis XIV and the century of Harun al-Rashid," he found high society "filled with dread and anxiety." Indeed, the ultrapatriotic Tsarina herself wrote:

> The maintenance of the army (in war preparedness) will ruin us completely; our internal condition, with the total devaluation of money and the prospect of new taxation which is helping the underground work of the Socialists, is most dangerous. The burden resting on the Tsar is almost superhuman . . . . [28]

All the hurt pride, the fears of antagonizing nationalist public opinion and the army notwithstanding, it was recognized imperative to win a breathing space. The Shuvalov mission pointed to the same conclusion.[29] So, in a conversation with Schweinitz, Alexander confirmed his intention to respect scrupulously the terms of the Berlin Treaty and end the crisis provoked by "Dondukov and his comrades"; and he empowered Miliutin and acting deputy Foreign Minister Giers to use his name in imposing new stern rules on Todleben, Dondukov and Kaufman.[30] This development also produced two months later, on 8 February 1879, the final Russo-Turkish peace treaty.

For the détente in the Balkans, the efforts of the British Ambassador to St. Petersburg, Lord Dufferin, were of key significance. Against the Moscow-military bloc and their press campaign, Dufferin advised to his government, London should make way for

Alexander's 'sincere desire to get out of the Balkan peninsula' and to 'strengthen Count Shuvalov's hand as much as we can.'[31] He correctly earmarked the 'East-Rumelian liberties' as the issue in which concessions to Russian susceptibilities would produce the best effect. Indeed, when he proclaimed the Turkish presence on the Balkan ranges 'a fiction,' the Tsar and his entourage were enormously relieved and negotiations could proceed to a satisfactory conclusion. At first a mixed occupation of Eastern Rumelia seemed to be the answer, but in the end it was agreed that when free of Turkish garrisons, the province might be kept quiet by the local militia alone. According to the understanding signed by Shuvalov and Dufferin on 9 April, the Turkish military presence was 'provisionally' limited to the Rhodope mountains.[32]

With the immediate Russian desiderata largely satisfied, the opposition to the Berlin Treaty lost much of its credibility. Todleben and Lobanov now produced optimistic reports. The former estimated the number of armed Bulgarians in Eastern Rumelia at 70,000 men; and, "our influence in the country is unlimited," he wrote to Gorchakov. In the north, in the future Principality, it was to be still more so; about 500 Russian officers and officials were to stay and control the army and the higher administration.[33]

The Dondukov group struggled until the very end against the settlement. Its grip over the Bulgarian nationalists had been overwhelming, and, if the population were given a free choice, it would undoubtedly elect the Imperial Commissioner or Ignatiev as their Prince.[34] The backstage schemings, however, were in vain. Both Todleben and Lobanov, who had earlier been in sympathy with his views, advised St. Petersburg that the man in Sofia, instigating unrest and compromising Russia in both Turkish and European eyes, must go; "nobody has any confidence to Prince Dondukov," Miliutin observed.[35] Neither the unrelenting press campaign against the withdrawal, orchestrated by Katkov,[36] made any difference. On 29 April 1879, Alexander of Battenberg, a twenty-three year old relative of the Tsar and a "candidate of Europe, was acclaimed by the Bulgarian National Assembly at Tarnovo as the Prince. On 7 May, General Obruchev announced from Constantinople that the Porte had accorded to leave Eastern Rumelia without its garrisons. In summer, the Balkan Army evacuated the peninsula.

The extremist gamble for the "second round" was over.

CHAPTER 19

FEARS, ANGERS AND SUSPICIONS
(1878-1880)

> Russia looked like a country hit by the
> fire of a terrible revolution. . . . It seemed
> as if at any minute there could be an er-
> ruption, compared with which all the
> horrors of the French revolution would
> pale.
> Katkov

Contrary to the hopes of the St. Petersburg elite, the Balkan settlement brought it no respite. The press outcry against Bismarck's alleged
treachery at the Berlin Congress initiated a serious crisis in Russo-German
relations.

Irritated by the attacks, the Chancellor responded in early 1879 by
what has been described as a "pin-pricks policy." Rigorous quarantine
measures to protect Germany against the plague which had hit the Volga
region were generally viewed as a transparent maneuvre to injure Russian
agricultural exports; and so was the new tariff introduced soon thereafter. The uproar sprouted by these actions in Tsardom was, according
to Schweinitz, equal to a "complete volte face in the attitide of the
Russians to the Germans."[1]

The St. Petersburg newspapers which had previously opposed the false
interpretation of Bismarck's role at the Berlin summit, now joined the

chorus; and so did the Moscow Thunderer, after the years of champion-
ship of the Russo-German "natural alliance." Their common view, as
enunciated by Katkov, read to the effect that the German economic
sanctions were invented as the device to drive Russia out of the Balkans
and that by it Bismarck started a novel policy with the aim of substituting
the Three Emperors' League by a Germanic alliance designed to prevent
the unity and liberation of the Slavs and subject them to exploitation.[2]

This way a feud had arisen which has sometimes been rated simply
as a continuation of the "war of two Chancellors."[3] In fact, much more
then before, the tension revealed profound antagonism lying beyond
mere personal animosities. Because of his advanced senility and frequent
absences from places where the Tsar and his inner circle took their decisions, Gorchakov's role had become almost immaterial. Bismarck himself, although attacking his old foe, knew that Miliutin was "the minister
who is now exercising the decisive influence upon the Emperor" and
considered him to be the chief troublemaker.[4]

Miliutin's advices on the issues of general policy were mostly in favour
of moderation. However, the post-Congress anti-German mood prompted
him to implement the military doctrine of "concentration in peace."

> The doctrine emerged as the almost inevitable product of the
> most serious handicap inherent to the Tsar's army—its inability
> to perform a swift mobilization. In a memorandum circulated
> in 1872, the War Minister pointed out that 'no human endeavour
> is capable of overcoming the disadvantage of our geographic po-
> sition' and that, regardless of some progress in railway construction,
> 'we cannot compete with the Prussian and even with the Austrian
> in the speed of concentration of our forces.' Soon afterwards, this
> reasoning was enlarged by Obruchev in a memoir called 'Delibera-
> tions on the defence of Russia.' In case of war with Germany,
> it stated, the Russian army would be mobilized and concentrated
> in 54-58 days; the enemy was able to do it in 20-23 days. In case
> of war with Austria-Hungary, the corresponding figures were 63-
> 70 resp. 30-34 days to Russia's disadvantage. The obvious deficien-
> cies, above all in the railway system, would 'give a decisive pre-
> ponderance to our enemies, even if they were to fight separately.'
> The both authors envisaged, as the only remedy, that the bulk of

the army would be already in the peace-time deployed in six military districts on the frontier, with an especially heavy concentration of cavalry and artillery units in the Polish Kingdom.[5] Now, in 1879, they took on to effectuate their concept.

Consequently, a permanent source of friction emerged on the Russo-German border. The economic contradictions, dramatically revealed by Bismarck's sanctions, were to be the second factor infusing in the relations between the two Powers a constant element of vexation.

Up to the Eastern crisis, satisfaction had prevailed over the evolution of mutual trade. From the second half of the 1860s, Russian agricultural and particularly grain exports had entered into a new phase of rapid expansion; and while earlier England had been considered the best market, now, due to her free-trade policies, Germany absorbed almost 35 percent of Russian exports, whereas the German share in Russian imports amounted to almost 45 percent.

With the deepening of the world recession after 1873, however, protectionist forces were gradually taking over in both countries.[6] Bismarck's heavy-handed measures were the hallmark, and the same may be said about Katkov's reaction to them.

Already during the anti-Prussian crusade in the 1860s, the Moscow publicist indicated diminishing enthusiasm for free trade and argued against the policies pursued by the "Germans" in charge of the Finance Ministry, Reutern and Bunge; but only "after the plague" he really commenced to consider Russian and German economic interests incompatible and became the leading advocate of (a distinctly anti-German conceived) protectionism.[7]

* * *

When additional units, mainly cavalry regiments, were moved from other parts of Russia to the Vistula in the winter of 1878-1879, Prussian generals for the first time declared openly that confrontation was imminent and inevitable. In April 1879, Moltke set forth a two-front war plan.[8]

Undoubtedly, Bismarck's pin-pricks actions were not inspired by the wish to provoke an armed conflict. Such an eventuality was for him a "grave, useless calamity" and in this respect he had always substantially differed from his military "semi-Gods." He rather hoped that when driven on the defensive and into isolation, St. Petersburg would be compelled to "renounce Slavic chauvinism" and the "conservative and well-to-do classes" could reappear there as the "centre of gravity" in the decision-making process. But, Bismarck told Schweinitz, Gorchakov's "constant coquetry" with France, Miliutin's "endless armaments" and deployment of troops, as well as the violent language of the Russian press convinced him that also Alexander might not be relied on as before; consequently, he decided—and there Katkov and his alike were right—to give priority to closer understanding with Vienna and London and develop it into an "organic relationship."[9]

Russian nervousness, in the meantime, grew near to hysteria.[10] The Katkovian thesis on the alleged sinister German designs in the Near East were supported by alarming reports from the international commissions working on the implementation of the Berlin Treaty; Ambassadors Lobanov and Novikov, both staunch anti-Muscovites, were among those who warned in the same vein as did the editor.[11] Under the strain of real and imaginary menaces, Alexander committed a serious blunder, when on 15 August, "ab irato, without consulting anybody," wrote to Emperor William an emotional letter full of complaints and accusations against Bismarck and his policies on the Eastern Question.[12]

It looked like an irreparable Russo-German rift. The warning of "fatal consequences" for mutual relations, pronounced by the Tsar, seemed furthermore to imply a departure for a free-hand policy, again vigorously pleaded by Gorchakov and the Moscow party. Katkov admonished the government to act fearlessly, "without appeals to Europe, without dispatches and conferences, to decide alone about our interests in the East"; Russia, he affirmed, was capable of matching the Austro-German or any other coalition.[13]

Not unlike the "second round" issue, however, the actual outcome was vastly different. At this critical juncture, both Alexander and Miliutin assessed the break with tradition as an impermissible risk and resolved to go counter to the emotions running high in society and the press.

The impulse for critical re-examination was given by a memor of Pavel Saburov, the Minister to Athens, who had recently held long discussions with Bismarck at Bad Kissingen. The diplomat proclaimed isolation suicidal; and on the question "to which Power ought we to ally with in order to establish anew the equilibrium?" he furnished a clear-cut answer: "Often in politics the old ideas are the best. Close friendship with Prussia is one of them, and whatever the misunderstandings of recent time, they have but little weight in the balance of the advantages which this close understanding assures to us."

In the words of a Singers' Bridge survey, the document submitted by Saburov had "thrown a new light on the situation"; and Alexander eagerly espoused its reasoning.[14]

Accompanied by his War Minister, the Tsar rushed to meet William (at Alexandrovo, on 3-4 September) and to pledge his devotion to peace and the Hohenzollern-Romanov solidarity.[15] More than that. In the ensuing deliberations at Livadia (on 21-23 September), the Russian statesmen—in the absence of Gorchakov—adopted the course Katkov had been canvassing during the Eastern crisis. Saburov was directed to depart for Berlin and offer the Germans a free hand to deal with France in exchange for help on the Eastern Question against Austrian and English menaces.[16]

William I, enormously relieved by the Alexandrovo meeting, would gladly let bygones be bygones. Bismarck too, was willing to accept conciliation: the anger that St. Petersburg "behaved towards its only friend like an Asiatic despot for whom a servant had not run quickly enough on the stairs"[17] and the words about re-orientation on an Anglo-Austrian axis notwithstanding, he had preferred the three Empires system. Yet, the episode had still to have far-reaching consequences. A military-political bloc with the Dual Monarchy appeared to the Chancellor now, when Andrássy, compromised beyond repair by the inglorious occupation of Bosnia-Hercegovina, would have to leave the Ballplatz, to be a top priority; and not even the Russian promise of a free hand against France could sway him to change his mind.[18] As he put it:

> I consider Russia a dear friend who had lost his senses during a promenade with me. Therefore, I sprinted home and returned with a gun. Thus secured, I wish to continue on the friendly walk.[19]

The Austrian alliance was to be precisely that gun against the "dear friend." So, the proposals brought in by Saburov pleased him rather as a proof that his brow-beating tactics were correct. Although Russia was now ready to change her posture, he wrote to the Emperor, the "ambitious Slavic elements" remained untamed and only Austro-German unity could steer her to the path of peace and break the spell wielded upon the Tsar by the "warlike and revolutionary Panslavs and namely by the minister Miliutin."[20] William could but forget the tradition and give way. On 7 October 1879, the anti-Russian secret treaty of Dual Alliance was signed in Vienna.

* * *

The debate inaugurated by Saburov's memorandum unwound into one of the most significant polemics on Russian foreign policy strategy and tactics. The number of its participants was strictly limited and hardly a dozen persons were fully informed about the commitments made during its course. (Even Gorchakov was left in the dark, considered by the Tsar and his closest advisors too biased and out of touch with reality.) Regardless of the narrow confines and a strong dose of personal ambition and rivalry, which especially in the opening stage somehow blurred the contours, however, the main currents influencing the decisionmaking in the "time of the Thunderer" can be traced in the disputes.

The hawkish viewpoint was personified by Saburov.[21] He was obviously far from the traditional Muscovite creed in his outlook and he also disliked the outside pressures and deplored the government's weakness in handling the press.[22] But suddenly inflated aspirations led him, like so many others, to put his stake on the extremist horse and seek support from Katkov and his kind. Even then he would neither pretend sentimentality over the "holy mission" nor conceal his hostility to Panslav tenets: he may well be described as an outstanding example of how after 1878 Russian nationalism had progressively abandoned its former veneer. For Saburov, the task of obtaining the Bosphorus "key to our house" eventually became the only substantial goal; and in order to attain it, he called at the latter stage of the debate for a departure from the offensive policy in Asia and for funnelling financial resources to the expansion of the Black Sea naval force. In the sphere of diplomacy, St. Petersburg ought to accommodate Germany, espouse the Bismarckian plan for the division of Turkey and, in order to win Austrian consent with the seizure of the Straits, even let them dominate the Balkans.[23]

Until the death of Alexander II (1881), Miliutin stood as the central figure in the debate—as it corresponded with his pivotal position in the government—and Saburov's main opponent.

The conduct of the War Minister has always been too complex, his already mentioned inner conflict between a sober scholarly brain and a traditional "Russian heart" was too strong and his aloofness too pronounced to provide clues for a completely satisfactory biographical study. Looking for general formulae pertaining to the discussion it may be said that he considered Saburov's big Bosphorus dream a dangerous lunacy; the experience of the Turkish war had convinced him that the closure of the Straits for warships, to provide safety for Russian Black Sea coast, was the sole realistic objective. Furthermore, he considered the formation of a Balkan federation as the most promising prospect and, again in contrast to Saburov, would not compromise it by an deal; his calculation rested on the firm hold of Bulgaria and patient building up of influence in the area, preventing Austrian and German ascendancy.

Rather than taking his own initiative, Miliutin backed Nikolai Giers, the acting Deputy Minister for Foreign Affairs, in the debate. Thus, first outwardly and then, when Miliutin left the government and Giers became the Foreign Minister (in 1881, resp. 1882), directly, the Giers-Saburov contest stood in the foreground. Until 1882, the two men competed for Gorchakov's succession; in 1882-1884, after Giers got the appointment, he had to defend his position against relentless attempts of his rival to depose him.

While Saburov pleaded the hawkish cause, Giers was both by his nature and experience a convinced moderate conservative, hostile to adventurism, particularly that in the Eastern Question. Like his opponent, he favored allegiance to the Bismarckian system; in cooperation with the two traditional allies, though, he saw not a spring-board for gains but the best warrant for the status quo established by the Berlin Treaty. Rather than striving to impress with big schemes he aimed at the upholding of the fragile balance jeopardized by "Panslav" intrigues, Austrian expansion and by the national aspirations of the Balkan peoples.

* * *

The Russian foreign policy debate started amidst intense internal crisis.

"After returning from the Crimea, I found St. Petersburg in a strange mood," wrote Miliutin. "Even in higher governmental circles one may hear talk about an imperative radical reform. The word 'constitution' is pronounced. Nobody believes in the stability of the existing order." Grand Duke Konstantin, Valuev and Miliutin himself headed impressive groups of officials and courtiers who affirmed that stability could be attained only through broadly-based liberalization.[24]

On the other hand, there was a dangerously rising wave of reactionary dissatisfaction with the weak, vacillating government, both in the elite and amongst the general public. While the "dark people" remained loyal to the Tsar and the upsurge of revolutionary terrorism made this loyalty only more steadfast, in the eyes of high-placed conservatives, the ruler was the main culprit. In a private letter, Pobedonostsev poured out his disdain:

> Of the master himself it is no use talking. He is a lamentable and unfortunate man and there is no going back for him. God has afflicted him. He has no strength to rise and control his movements, even though he imagines that he is alive and active and powerful. It is obvious that his will has gone. He does not want to listen, does not want to see, does not want to act. . . . [25]

To nobody's surprise, Katkov spearheaded this reactionary current. The Zasulich trial spurred on the venom he had felt towards the revolutionary and liberal intelligentsia, to new heights. The fact that all the St. Petersburg and Moscow press except the *Grazhdanin* approved the acquital convinced him that sedition was at large and perhaps worse than in 1863. He spelled it out bluntly:

> This so-called intelligentsia is our plague from which we must liberate ourselves at any price. Only an iron-hand rule, combined with mass vigilance would bring about the remedy: 'the debilitating fear of dark forces can be conquered merely by salutary fear before the legal authority.'[26]

Letters of approval, coming to the Strastnyi Boulevard from persons belonging to all social classes, and the beating the radicals received from the St. Petersburg crowd on 12 April, bolstered the publicist's convictions.[27] "Everybody without exception, from a big noble landowner to the lowest peasant, expects from the government stern measures and will perceive them as acts of beneficence," he was assured from the provinces. And, of course, his best placed acolytes and allies—Pobedonostsev, Prince Urusov, Counts Delianov and Stroganov, General Kireev, Feoktistov, etc.—agreed with him too, that a new Muraviev-Vilenskii was the solution; condemning at the same time the Tsar for his unwillingness to resort to the Hangman's methods.[28]

Following Soloviev's April attempt to kill Alexander, temporary military Governors General were appointed in St. Petersburg, Moscow, Kiev, Odessa and Warsaw. On ministerial level, a special commission operated with the same task of combatting sedition. This, however, would neither appease those sharing Katkov's views, nor temper the liberal dissatisfaction. The overall malaise condemned the government to fight its desparate battle with the handful of terrorists in frightful isolation,[29] paying dearly for its short-sighted retreat from the reform course and innumerable other follies.

On the international scene, Tsardom fared no better. Apart from the tensions with Germany and Austria-Hungary, exaggerated fears of English designs cast a dark shadow: the Shuvalov-Dufferin understanding bred no lasting détente.

The Katkovian press had been especially prolific in sowing distrust, alerting the Russian public on the allegedly impending British naval action in the Straits. Also Miliutin felt victim of his chimera, claiming that London had already appropriated de facto mastery over Constantinople and would soon send its fleet there to make it permanent.[30] First the invasion of Afghanistan, crowned by the semi-protectorate treaty of Gandamak (26 May) and then Salisbury's November speech in Manchester, in which he hailed the Austro-German alliance as "good tidings of great joy" added cogent impulses for Russian anxieties and irritation.[31]

The expedition against the Turkomans[32] obtained thereby a highly prestigious, pronouncedly anti-British bias with far-reaching consequences, its net result being the nearly senseless sharpening of the tension with London[33] and a humiliating setback at the moment when Tsardom was in almost desperate need of some success.

A quite impressive force had been assembled for the Turkoman expedition—12,000 troops with cavalry and 34 guns. This should suffice

more than enough to smash the Tekke tribesmen[34] who were almost without firearms, and conquer Akhal-Tekin as well as Merv. The action for
which the Caucasus military looked with unbounded optimism and Katkov
hailed as "return to Peter the Great's heritage,"[35] however, ended in the
greatest defeat in the history of the Russian Central-Asian expansion.
General Lomakin underestimated not only the difficulties of terrain and
climate but also the Tekke's ability to resist. The decision came on 9
September 1879, when he led his columns against Denghil Tepe, a fortress
erected at the foot of the Akhal-Tekin hill. The defenders counted only
15,000 men and at the beginning it seemed that everything would go in
its usual way: several hundred Tekke's were killed by gunfire, thousands
of their women and children trying to escape from the oasis mercilessly
slaughtered. But in the final assault the famous Caucasus regiments sorely
failed; worse still, panic broke out in their ranks and they simply fled,
leaving 400 dead and wounded, 600 modern rifles and some of their guns
on the battlefield. The trek back to Krasnovodsk became an additional
calamity, when the expedition lost almost all its camels.[36]

The scope of the setback appeared even more overwhelming in comparison with the British capture of Kabul (on 30 September). Besides the
highly adverse impact upon the public, general unrest and increasing English pressure in Central Asia, war with China[37] and, once again, the formation of European anti-Russian coalition, were intensely feared.

All this inevitably left a strong imprint upon the foreign-policy debate
in the Tsar's Crimean residence.

* * *

Despite his anti-British outbursts, Katkov intensely admonished against
a course which would bind Russia again to the Bismarckian system:

> During the Eastern crisis we have for one reason or another opted
> for the liberty of action. It has been left to us as our sole consolation,
> as the sole advantage we have gained from our failure. We could safe-
> guard our interests in the Bosphorus, we could retain the San Ste-
> fano treaty, we could at least prolong the occupation. Yet we have
> renounced all this, and in consequence we are not committed to
> any bargain . . . . Our liberty of action worries Prince Bismarck. We

have bought it dearly—and now they propose that we should sell it for a song.[38]

In Livadia, though, his voice roused no perceptible response. Both domestic and external troubles made the policymakers believe that an entente with Germany would somehow bring them deliverance. Even the visibly discomforted Miliutin conceded that "it became imperative to renew our friendly relations with Germany, if only ostensibly . . . we have no ally in Europe."[39] But because of suspicions, remorses and rivalries, this awareness alone would not suffice for a truly new departure.

From the second round of his conversation with Bismarck (29 September-1 October in Berlin), Saburov brought back limited results. The Chancellor professed his readiness to cooperate exclusively within the old three Empires framework. And he would not commit himself to assist Russia in the matter of her crucial interest: "the question of Constantinople has been left to future events." All Saburov could produce was a draft of an understanding on three points:

> First, in the event of war between England and Russia, Germany was to remain neutral and prevent 'by force if need be' any other Power joining England.
>
> Second, Russia would assume identical obligations if there were a French-German conflict.
>
> Third, Russia was to respect the territorial integrity of Austria-Hungary provided that the latter would 'not extend her sphere of action in the East beyond the boundaries laid down by the Treaty of Berlin without preliminary agreement with Russia.'[40]

Initially, even this outcome was conceived by the Tsar's inner circle as "more favorable than it could have been expected,"[41] but the alleged English menace soon entailed the first divergences. Miliutin and Giers returned to the "key-to-our-house" problem. They argued that the Bismarck-Saburov draft, if implemented, would be more favorable to Germany than to Russia: because no less than 15-20 years would be needed to build a force capable of transporting 20,000 troops to the Bosphorus in the moment of crisis,[42] at least the principle of the closure of the Straits must be guaranteed to give an essential security to the Empire in the meantime. "The Straits question is the most substantial, perhaps our sole interest, the safeguarding of which may compensate us for the obligations taken vis-à-vis Germany," the War Ministers affirmed.[43]

Saburov put up a stout defense of his deal. Bismarck could not help Russia save by the obligation "to deprive England of the ability to contract continental alliances," he reasoned; it would be unwise to complicate negotiations with Germany "by demanding from her services she would not be in a position to render to us, even if she had the good-will to do so." Asked for opinions, Ambassadors Lobanov, Novikov and Shuvalov approved the obviously sound argument of their colleague. But excessively preoccupied by the possibility of a surprise attack or of a sudden shift of power balance in the Near East, Miliutin would not retract and Alexander in the end gave him the countenance. Under these circumstances, the new parleys with the German Chancellor (on 31 January-7 February 1880) just made the stalemate more apparent. Outwardly understanding, he would not step back an inch from his position: solely the reconstructed Three Emperors' bloc would be the solution, even for enforcing the principle of the closure of the Straits.[44]

Hence, the St. Petersburg policy stood after months of intensive negotiations still empty-handed and isolated and the relations with Berlin were scarcely better than those with Vienna and London. Both governments —and the press even more so—got engaged in mutual recriminations on the military preparations in the border areas; moreover, there were unending Russian accusations of German plotting in the Balkans.[45] On 10 February, Alexander approved a memoir on army mobilization in case of conflict, set forth by Obruchev; and albeit he professed his hope for peace, the common belief was that such a conflict would certainly break out "as soon as the Emperor (William) dies and possibly before that contingency." From his side, Bismarck again commenced to hesitate on whether a bloc with Austria-Hungary and England would not be after all a better implementation of his dogma of "three against two in the greatpower balance."[46]

Then, the situation changed almost overnight to Tsardom's advantage. The victory of Gladstone in the 1880 elections made all the difference.

CHAPTER 20

THE MOMENT OF RELIEF
(1880-1881)

> I have no fear myself of the territorial ex-
> tension of Russia in Asia; no fear of them
> whatever. I think such fears are only old
> women's fears.
> Gladstone

> Progress, the rise and growth of Russia
> demand increased power and intensified
> action by the government. Languor, in-
> ertness would lead to decay and decline.
> Katkov

During the months of the British electoral campaign, the framework
of Russian conduct remained unaltered.

True, the defeat at the Akhal-Tekin oasis subdued the warlike tone
in the press and the ministries for foreign affairs and finance could again
openly plead for prudence, but the Eastern militarists and their associates
retained the initiative. Though for different reasons, the hawkish stance in
Asia, the kernel of anti-British animosity, was as strongly motivated as
before. After the Turkoman debacle, "the news of the reverse spread
through Central Asia, shook Russian power in the entire area" and it was
felt that "if prestige was not regained at once, Russia's new empire would
be in danger of crumbling." Also the effect of the army's humilitation in

the eyes of both the Russian public and Europe, it was argued, required a speedy remedy.[1]

Giers warned Ambassador Dufferin "at the possibility of his own views being overriden by a military clique."[2] In fact, that had already happened. English troubles in Afghanistan, where the population rose en masse against the invader, provided the "clique" the leverage they needed. Miliutin and Kaufman persuaded the Tsar that Abdurrahman, the son of Shere Ali (the Khan himself died on the flight to Turkestan) waiting in Tashkent, ought to be sent to northern Afghanistan to lead the struggle; that way, they assured him, a separate khanate under Russian tutelage would emerge between the Hindu-Kush and the Syr-Daria and the lost initiative and authority would be restored. In December 1879, supplied with large funds, Abdurrahman "fled" from Kaufman's custody. And, immediately afterwards, the Caucasus command issued an appeal for a new Turkoman expedition, which would push the boundaries of effective control to the Hindu-Kush watershed.

The motion was discussed in several extraordinary councils in February-March 1880 and resulted in an overwhelming victory for the extremists, represented there by Miliutin, Obruchev and Skobelev. Reutern and the Chief of Staff Heyden, who spoke up for an agreement with London, met deaf ears. The old ploy justifiying Asiatic conquests by the search for secure frontiers again sufficed. Until the Turkoman territories were under control, the argument ran, the Caucasus and Turkestan would be dangerously exposed to British designs; "owing to the verve and dash of the English, it is impossible to stop the advance."[3]

In the meantime, the group led by Pobedonostsev and the heir busily worked on the Volunteer Fleet scheme. The collection of funds centered in Moscow and the Anichkov Palace, produced a considerable sum of more than four million rubles. Six ships were bought in the West within a short period and officers and sailors recruited for the force. While the Moscow merchants were promised that the fleet would eventually be used to futher connections with the Far East and other regions of commercial interest, the main objective rested unmistakenly in the military sphere. In April, a Council attended by the heir, the grand dukes and the ministers of war and navy recognized the Volunteer Fleet to be "the main instrument for our struggle against England."[4]

* * *

For Gladstone, who was returned to Downing Street in the spring of 1880, all fears of Russian designs in the Neas East and Central Asia were just "old women's fears" and a "Russian bogey."[5] Neither clear symptoms of Russian hostility nor the consistent overtures of rapprochement coming from Vienna could alter his belief that not Tsardom but Austria was the universal "enemy of liberty" and in his famous Midlothian pre-election campaign he several times gave vent to this conviction.

In his fourth Midlothian speech he proclaimed:

> Austria has been the steady, unflinching foe of the freedom of every country in Europe. Russia, I am sorry to say, has been the foe of freedom, too, but in Russia there is one exception—Russia has been the friend of Slavic freedom. . . . There is not an instance, there is not a spot upon the whole map where you can lay your finger and say 'There Austria did good.' In the Congress of Berlin, Austria resisted the extension of freedom and did not promote it.[6]

Bismarck saw in Gladstone's come-back a very serious menace. He had always taken the "people's William" for a "crazy professor," who together with Gorchakov, Gambetta and Garibaldi formed "a revolutionary quartet on the G-string," jeopardizing the European order with their extravagancies; now, he expected an Anglo-Russian as well as Anglo-French rapprochement as the consequence of his new premiership. If he had recently contemplated the English option, then at this moment the revival of the three empires bloc appeared to him as urgent as ever. At the Ballplatz, too, though with utmost reluctance, the fact had to be acknowledged that the course pursued by Andrássy and his successor, the present Foreign Minister Baron Haymerle—to isolate Russia and hold her in check in a common front with Germany and England—lost ground.[7]

To St. Petersburg, on the other hand, the development brought an enormous relief. "The change of government in England strongly modified the overall relationship among the Powers and rendered a substantial improvement in our standing," Miliutin summed up.[8] The Singers' Bridge was ready to explore the opening prospects. In the instruction to Lobanov, Shuvalov's successor at the Court of St. James, Giers aired his hope for a "good understanding": "It will be assured the moment we have succeeded in smoothing the differences of the two governments in the Near East and in Asia. That must be our immediate objective."[9] Following the directive, the Ambassador talked on 30 April with the Foreign Secretary Lord Granville and his suggestion for an agreement met warm approval; without delay, Gladstone put down guidelines for the proposed deal.[10]

At the same time, a much more confident Saburov confronted Bismarck with the request for a speedy implementation of the three-point programme elaborated during the earlier talks. He reported:

> I told him that it was above all necessary to make Vienna feel the inevitability of seizing the opportunity before it has gone . . . . It may be that Gladstone is the enemy of Austria, but he is not our enemy! And if the conclusion of the triple alliance happened to encounter obstacles, it would perhaps be too late to return to it when we shall have found a modus vivendi with England which is agreeable to us.[11]

After many years the Russian statesmen felt again free to take any option they wished.

* * *

The dramatic change in the international position was accompanied by a substantial improvement in the domestic situation too.

Khalturin's dynamite charge which exploded in the Winter Palace on 17 February 1880, marked the peak of internal malaise. An English journalist recollected in his memoirs:

> The result of the explosion in St. Petersburg was a state of public feeling that rapidly grew towards panic. The air was filled with alarming rumors and reports of all kinds, originating no one knew how, spreading with inconceivable rapidity, inspiring the more timid with absolute terror. I had personal knowledge of people who barricaded their rooms at night, kept loaded revolvers by their bedsides, and seemingly expected a repetition of the horrors of the French Revolution.[12]

In the disarray encompassing the whole upper crust, Katkov's plea for a dictatorship which, backed by the witch-hunting "regeneration of the national spirit of 1863,"[13] would bring a remedy by suppressing any dissenting view, commanded an overall conservative approval. On 20 February, at the insistence of the heir and Pobedonostsev, Alexander set up an emergency Supreme Executive Committee and bestowed at its head, General Count Loris-Melikov, broad plenary powers. As the followers of the Muscovite reported to the Strastnyi Boulevard, in his statement on the necessity to "concentrate power," the Tsar "almost verbatim" repeated the editorial of the *Moskovskiia vedomosti.*[14] "So, your idea . . . has materialized," wrote Feoktistov.[15]

When the new "dictator" without delay made a "pactum" with him,[16] Katkov must have been convinced that Russia would henceforth be administered according to his rules. Loris-Melikov, the conqueror of Kars, however, was a man with deep insight into his country's ills and introduced the very opposite course. Owing to him, the last year of Alexander's reign was to be remembered as that of rising optimism and sharp decline of "Katkovshchina."[17]

In a profound analysis submitted to Alexander, Loris pointed out the close connection between the social unrest and frustrated reform hopes. He rejected as iniquitious the approach relying on police methods and directed against every form of opposition. His programme included more tolerance for the press and the liberal malcontents as well as broader possibilities for the nobility, towns and zemstvos to participate in both decisions on governmental policies and their realization. "In the support of society I see the main force capable in helping the cause of renewal," was his keyword.[18]

In this conjunction, the "dictator" saw the dismissal of Tolstoi as a matter of principle; "by his cruel, imperious and entirely clumsy conduct," he wrote, the Minister for Public Instruction carried the brunt of responsibility for the gap dividing the educated stratum and the authorities.

Katkov made a desperate effort to save his associate from the anti-reform battles; he described him in a letter to Alexander as a devoted, unbending servant of the autocracy, disliked not for the blunders committed but for the consequent performance of his duties. After some hesitation, though, the Tsar yielded to Loris' reasoning. The minister was fired amidst common jubilation. "Everybody is saying: he is no more. The man succeeded in forcing everyone without exception—or, with very rare exceptions—to hate him," noted the wife of General Bogdanovich, who ran a much frequented St. Petersburg salon.[19]

In the ensuing governmental reshuffle, Loris took over the Interior Ministry; and liberal-oriented grouping gained additional positions by the appointment of Abaza to the Finance Ministry and Saburov, a relative of the Ambassador, as Tolstoi's replacement in the Ministry of Public Instruction. (The conservative circle in the Anichkov Palace, on the other hand, ought to be appeased by the nomination of Pobedonostsev as the new Director General of the Holy Synod.)

Going ahead with the fulfillment of his programme, the Interior Minister dismantled both the "dictatorial" Supreme Executive Commission and the detested Third Section; the latter was transformed into a mere police department in his ministry. Most of those imprisoned and banished for political offenses were set free; and in what may be named the first press conference in Russia (in October 1880), Loris made public his intention to curtail police arbitrariness and stop undue interference in the journalists' work.

Frustrated in his hopes, the Moscow publicist dubbed the new system a "dictatorship of the heart," but the educated public began to appreciate it. The Katkovian press with its badly concealed hostility found itself in growing isolation. Even Pobedonostsev, while deploring that except from the Thunderer's organs "all periodicals applauded Count Loris-Melikov," advised the Strastnyi Boulevard to be "more cautious." "At least for some time it seems necessary to avoid fully legitimate sharp accusations against the official intelligentsia, inasmuch as they arouse (only) irritation."[20]

Pressures coming from the ultraconservatives made the task of the minister still enormously difficult and he had also to face the enmity of many courtiers and politicians who could not stomach the fact than an "Armenian outsider" had become second after the Tsar; but he certainly succeeded in reopening the dialogue between the government and society and made more real the prospect that Russia might return to a reform effort.

* * *

In the meantime, due to a pronounced pro-Russian tenor in London, Tsardom might truly enjoy a free hand in foreign policy decisions.

In the talks on the Asiatic issues, the Liberal government offered substantial concessions. Granville agreed to accept Abdurrahman, "Russia's
man," as the Afghan ruler and promised that the London cabinet
would respect his independence; simultaneously, Ambassador Dufferin
mediated in the Russo-Chinese boundary dispute.[21] Almost unparalleled
cooperation was established in the Balkans: in the crisis initiated by the
Greek and Montenegrin claims on Turkish-held border regions, English
diplomacy went hand in hand with the Russian, much to Austrian and
German annoyance. "It remains to us only to wish a long life to the Gladstone cabinet," Miliutin observed, praising its "loyal and honest conduct."[22]

Relieved from fears kindled by isolation, and then enhanced by the
energetic engagement of London in the Balkans, the Russian press and
society were even more positive. And so did the Moscow editor. Before
the Liberal victory was secured, he had professed his indifference to the
electoral returns: "we may watch the struggle for votes with complete
disinterest," he wrote.[23] With Gladstone's take-over, however, his position underwent a notable change. Not only did he conceive it as a marked
proof that the free-hand course was the one which suited Russia best; he
admonished for "new alignments in international politics":

> From the Austrians and the Germans, Tsardom may expect no-
> thing save hostility, including naked force; her financial crisis not-
> withstanding, Vienna is mobilizing its resources for 'unknown
> military aims.' 'Friendly and honest' Anglo-Russian cooperation on
> the Near-Eastern issues, on the contrary, evinces that 'what ap-
> peared so far impossible,' an understanding on common policy in
> Asia, can be achieved.[24]

Nonetheless, the debate at the apex of the government would not detract from the pattern it had developed in the second half of 1879. Rather
than looking for the "new alignments" suggested by the Strastnyi Boulevard and by the liberal St. Petersburg organs alike, the policymakers resolved to improve the old ones on their own terms. Saburov was particularly emphatic in the matter:

> Bismarck learned his lesson, abandoned his previous reticence and
> 'saw no objections to the realization of Russia's boldest dreams, on

the sole condition that she lets Austria subsist and does not contend
for her sphere of influence in the western part of the Balkan peninsula.' The new combination should be exploited in order to re-
construct the three Empires' bloc on that basis. 'No combination of
European alliances would be able to assure a more advantageous
situation for us on the day when we shall be ready for action. It will
be the glory of the present reign to have prepared for it.'[25]

In their conversations, Saburov and Bismarck agreed that drawing a line
in the Balkans which would divide it into Russian and Austrian spheres of
influence was the best basis for future cooperation. That Foreign Minister
Haymerle was singularly unenthusiastic did not matter; the Balkans were
but a "Poland of today," the Chancellor asserted; "Maria Theresa had not
wished it either and yet Austria has been holding (a portion of) it firmly
until now." Ending her contest with the Habsburg Monarchy, the Ambassador suggested, Russia should embark on a forceful anti-English
policy; no friendly gesture from London should detract her, "because
Gladstone is a mere shining meteor—a meteor which will pass."[26]
Saburov's main opponent, Giers, hated the talk about "Russia's boldest
dreams" and in general favored a more balanced approach. He considered
the English friendly disposition highly useful for dealing with the Germans as equals and wished to bolster it with an Asiatic settlement. But
he too concurred that it would be imprudent to exchange "permanent
advantages" secured by the German alliance, for "temporary ones, created
by the favorable attitude of the present English cabinet to us."[27]
Undoubtedly, mainly due to the Central-Asian situation, Anglo-Russian
relations were in such a state that, however Gladstone might have wished
it, there was hardly a true perspective for long-term understanding. A
senior Singers' Bridge official wrote:

> Even those Russians who had been in no way enthusiastic about
> the conquest of Central Asia were gradually induced to embrace the
> idea that a confrontation with the English on the banks of the Indus
> and in the heights of Hindu-Kush has been unavoidable, prescribed
> by immutable natural law.[28]

After a brief period of rejoicing over the escape from isolation and
exaggerated hopes in Gladstone's services, the trend unwound in full force.

From late 1880, Katkov too cooled down in his pro-English plea. With the united front in the Greek and Montenegrin issues achieving only limited results and the agreement on Asia being nowhere in sight, his editorials shifted in emphasis. Because of the mounting Irish problem, he envisaged the fall of the Liberal cabinet and, therefore, recommended to proceed in the advance towards Akhal-Tekin and Merv without delay.[29]

On the British side, similarly, the suspicions about Russian designs could not have been subdued. Kaufman's letters to Shere Ali, found after the seizure of Kabul, as well as the much advertized new expedition against the Turkomans and the construction of the Trans-Caspian railroad, described as "a sword of Damocles perpetually suspended above the Shah's head," gave additional impulses to them. Neither the exhortations coming from the *Moskovskiia vedomosti* and the *Novoe vremia* (the latter even overshadowed Katkov's organ in bold talk) were ignored; if compared with them, the official soothing words that Merv "was in no sense the object of attack" sounded as unconvincing as ever.[30]

* * *

If he knew for certain what had been in the meantime discussed at Livadia, in St. Petersburg and Berlin, Katkov would have most certainly been horrified. In fact, there was undoubtedly no one noteworthy group in the three involved empires, either in their public or in their elites, which would have wholeheartedly supported the renewal of the Emperors' alliance. Particularly the Bismarckian proposition that Tsardom and the Dual Monarchy should again join hands in the Near East, seemed under the impact of recent experience obnoxious. Even those who professed to be led strictly by the motives of raison d'état, raised strong objections: while Miliutin considered Austrian conduct "outright hostile" and the Bismarck-Saburov projects intolerably favourable to Vienna, Haymerle maintained that it would be unwise to trust a government "in which such a weak man as Giers only writes and decisive influence is being wielded by the great revolutionary Miliutin."[31]

Yet, in the specific sphere of the "high policy of the cabinets," hidden before everybody save a few, it was to be the forceful stance of the German Chancellor which would decide after all. Taught by the Gladstonean episode, he was now prepared to offer to the "Livadia circle" the assurances concerning the Straits and mercilessly hammered the Ballplatz to cease its obstruction. Since his September talks with the Austro-Hungarian Foreign Minister at Friedrichsruh, it might have been taken for certain that the latter would eventually give way. Albeit still protesting against Panslav intrigues and complaining that "we risk turning permanently into the dupes of Russian diplomacy," Haymerle promised to seek an agreement with the Singers' Bridge, first on problems like the Straits question and then on a general basis.[32]

Thus, when the Russian foreign policy debate reopened in late 1880, the query was no more whether to enter the coalition or not, but whether offensive or status quo course should be prosecuted within its framework.

After an initial phase of moderation and realism, Saburov put his stake entirely on a big deal with Bismarck which, in exchange for the recognition of Austrian Balkan rights, should make Tsardom master in the Bosphorus.[33] The Tsar and his inner circle, though, were seeking for sorely needed tranquility rather than for a springboard to conquest. With Gladstone at Downing Street there was no more worry about the English offensive moves; they might expect time to work for them. And, above all, domestic problems gave no room for extremist impatience. After a bad harvest, hunger and big budgetary deficits were presaged; the overriding belief was that only drastic reductions in military expenditure could provide relief.[34] So, the status quo concept in Europen and Near-Eastern policies, solicited by Miliutin and Giers, won easily.

The War Minister set forth his reflections in a memorandum "Thoughts about the possible solution of the Eastern Question in case of the final breakdown of the Ottoman Empire." In it, he argued that

> The collapse of 'that shabby building,' the Turkish Empire, must be expected 'in more or less near future' and European diplomacy should settle for its substitution by a more healthy organism. This ought to be found in the Balkan federation, formed by independent states and territories with a special status (Bosnia-Hercegovina under Austrian control; Constantinople, thé Straits and the vilayet of Adrianople under international control). The Straits were to become a neutral waterway.

Although he adopted a slightly modified Panslav nationalist stance, Miliutin's essential intention was to oppose immediate expansionist plans aired by Saburov. He even explicitly dismissed the conquest of the Straits "under favorable circumstances in the future," which he had canvassed a year ago in Livadia; now he stressed that Russian direct control was only a "dream." In order to evade further disasters, Tsardom should reduce its effort on strengthening its authority within the projected federation and consider the closure of the entrance into the Black Sea for all warships, a satisfactory settlement.[35]

Saburov desperately tried to save his gamble and keep the Bosphorus issue at a boiling point. In the proposals he forwarded on 14 February 1881, he feigned accord with the War Minister but interpreted his memoir in an opposite sense: Austria-Hungary should be offered the leading role in the federation in return for agreement on a Russian military presence in the Straits. Simultaneously, in a private letter to Giers, he asked for the speedy formation of a special secret committee which would prepare the seizure.[36]

Not surprisingly, however, the acting Foreign Minister stood firmly on Miliutin's side; and, the prevailing temper in the government allowed him to state frankly his own views.

Giers' profession d'foi, "The bases of agreement between Russia and Austria" (9 March 1881), approved by the Tsar, then gave the negotiation of the renewal of the three Emperors' bloc and Russian policy in the Near East an entirely different direction than that wished by the Ambassador:

(1) The two Powers consider the maintenance of the present status quo in the (Near) East (necessary) . . . for as long period as possible. (2) They will enter into an agreement to uphold this status quo against attempts to break it . . . . (3) As long as the status quo exists both Powers will . . . endeavor to maintain the Christian peoples within the framework of the Berlin Treaty . . . . (4) For that purpose both Powers will direct their representatives and agents in the Balkan countries to avoid all personal competition . . . . (5) Both Powers will agree that the growth of their trade interests and resulting political influence . . . should not lead to mutual antagonism . . . . For this purpose they will agree upon a rational frontier beyond which each Power will refrain from actions directed against the other . . . . (6) If the existing state of affairs is threatened . . . the two governments will enter into consultations concerning the principles . . . as

well as the spheres within which each will act. (7) The principles affirmed during the Reichstadt agreement with regard to an eventual collapse of the Ottoman Empire shall apply to the following points: the creation of independent states in the Balkan peninsula; their federation in their own interest; neutralization of Constantinople and the Straits; an European guarantee of these agreements. (8) Having agreed not to accelerate this plan prematurely, both Powers ...(will strive to carry it out) if the decisive crisis should take place....(9) Should events take a different turn...both Powers will...consult each other to find a solution best suited to their mutual interests.[37]

Apart from being a perfect expression of the mood which led the Russian elite into the Three Emperors' Alliance, the nine heads also constituted the general guideline for policy-making in the forthcoming years. Needless to add, the course it instituted was unacceptable to the extremists and thus destined to be vigorously challenged by them.

* * *

The year 1881 opened for Russia full of promise. First of all, after worried expectations, good news came from the Turkoman steppes, where General Skobelev "restored the honor" of Tsardom and his army, so badly mauled by the Tekkes in 1879.

Perhaps the White General had a different notion of what should be done in Central Asia. Immersed in his Napoleonic dreams, he observed the "military-bureaucratic" colonial methods applied there with patent distaste. To his high-placed friends he wrote:

The sooner the military despotism and military terror in the rear is stopped, the more advantageous will it be for Russian interests. ...Let's not irritate the local population by empty expeditions... and organize the Bukharans, the Khivans, even the Turkomans and the Afghans against England instead, before it becomes too late. And when the time comes, raise a hundred-thousand strong cavalry force and move it, in the name of blood and spoils, to English India.[38]

Whatever reservations he might have had, however, Skobelev performed his task with skill and brutal efficiency, his ambition being, obviously
to reassert himself before the army and the public as the military leader
Russia had been in need of. The disposition signed by Alexander gave him
everything he wished for the moment—the overall command in the Trans-
Caspian region and the right to take any decision without asking permission from any quarters.[39]

Before leaving the capital, the General received a briefing from Miliutin: "the military operations were not the goal but only the means to the
pacification," and therefore he should not "seek for a fight."[40] He would
not pay heed to this, though: he looked for a bloodbath, not for a capitulation. If Russia had been failing to win the peoples in the area "to relive
Tamerlan's time," then the fate of the Tekkes should drive them to resignation and their paralyzing fear soften the ground for further advance.
In accordance with tradition, he interpreted the fact that the Turkomans
defended themselves in 1879 as an act of aggression[41] and his proclamation admonished the soldiers that "Russian honour demands vengeance
for our killed comrades."

He completed the preparations in nine months. The march through the
desert and steppe was equally swift.

Again, the Tekkes defended themselves in the Daghil Tepe fortress, and,
although plagued by epidemic, offered during a three-week siege a stout
resistance. Every night they raided Russian camps; simultaneously, Turkoman hosts attacked the rear of the expedition from Persian territory.
Meanwhile, nervousness grew in Russia. Rumours spread about failure
and General Popov was dispatched to assist Skobelev or—as it was believed—
to replace him. It was allegedly Popov's arrival to Krasnovodsk which
prompted the White General to assault. It took place on 24 January 1881
—the day of Paul I's famous order for the Indian expedition eighty years
before.

The "battle of Akhal Tekin" was over in three hours. Then, Skobelev
carried off his focal purpose. Artillery followed the tribesmen as they fled
from the oasis and "mowed them down, until darkness put an end to the
pursuit." Thousands perished in that way. More than 6000 corpses were
also found afterwards in the fortress, where the soldiers were given four
days to murder, rape and plunder. The booty was evaluated at 6 million
rubles; the precious Tekke carpets were sold by the marauders for 3-5 rubles,
i.e. for one percent of their value, or often for a mere glass of vodka.[42]

Skobelev later told a British journalist:

> I hold it as a principle that in Asia the duration of peace is in
> direct proportion to the slaughter you inflict upon the enemy. The
> harder you hit them, the longer will be quiet afterwards. We killed
> nearly 20,000 Turkomans. The survivors will not soon forget the
> lesson.[43]

No doubt, in this respect he attained both his immediate and long-term
goals. There was to be no sustained local resistance to the Russians in the
years to come.

* * *

The Akhal Tekin affair remained but another episode in the bloody
history of Russian empire-building. For a brief moment, though, it seemed
as if it could also serve a better purpose. After months of trepidation, the
public rejoiced;[44] and, relieved by Skobelev's victory and positively conditioned by the evident relaxation of the general atmosphere, the Tsar and
the establishment were more than ever open to a breakthrough on the
crucial issue of political reform.

The eclipse of the reactionary forces became apparent and included the
Moscow Thunderer too. Never before or afterwards had his authority in
society been so low. It even looked as if he would bow before the prevailing liberal current. He severed his relations with Tolstoi, did not risk openly challenging the Loris-Melikov course and moved towards conciliation
with those he had venomenously attacked in his "anti-intelligentsia fury."
At the Pushkin commemoration in June 1880, he delivered a highly
reasonable speech pleading for unity and forgiveness and toasted his known
opponents. (The novelist Turgenev was the only one who refused to follow
the mood "let bygones by bygones" and clink the glass with the Muscovite.)[45]

In different atmosphere, as usual, many changed their colours. Staunch
conservatives, such as General Fadeev, proposed to reform the autocratic
system. Shuvalov, the former head of the "planters' party," in a memoir
written in February 1881 advised the creation of a two-chamber parliament with advisory functions; the ruler of Russia, he argued, could not
refuse his Russian subjects the same right which the Balkan Slavs under
his protection or the Finns enjoyed.[46]

Loris-Melikov took full advantage of it. According to his projects, commissions should be created with the participation of "informed individuals" from zemstvos and society, to give their opinions on legislative proposals concerning improvements in local administration, the status of peasantry, fiscal policies etc. Besides, ten to fifteen best qualified representatives of the public ought to be invited to join the State Council.[47] The projects were discussed and approved at three top-level councils held at the Anichkov and Winter Palaces. Alexander himself concurred and ordered the chairman of the Ministerial Council, Valuev, to summon the body on 16 March; after the meeting, the official proclamation was to be issued announcing what might have been the opening of the constitutional era.[48]

The numerous warnings that the retreat of Katkov and the "Katkovshchina" were only temporary, seemed to be refuted. Yet, in so many times in Russian and modern world history, one type of extremism could deliver in crucial moment to another, opposite one, invaluable services: and this happened just now. Isolated and increasingly deprived of public sympathy, the left terrorists finally succeeded in their attempts on the Tsar's life. On 13 March 1881, on his way to the Winter Palace, Alexander II fell victim of Grinevitskii's bomb. The act of supreme political folly roused a public reaction of the worst kind; and the evil power of the Thunderer was catapulated to its peak in this terrifying backlash.

PART THREE

IN THE MISTS OF ERROR:
THE "KATKOVSHCHINA" OF 1881-1887

CHAPTER 21

ALEXANDER III:
A STRANGE NEW ERA

The main trouble accrues from the fact
that there is no firm governmental policy;
perhaps no governmental policy whatever.
Pobedonostsev

A wild, pre-Petrine element is prevailing
here . . . . It is not Teheran yet, but it is
no more St. Petersburg.
Valuev

The maintenance of peace in Europe is
in the present world situation to a large
extent dependent on the impressions received by Tsar Alexander, because it depends
on the personal will and temper of this
monarch whether the weight of the Russian
nation with its hundred million people
is thrown into the balance for a warlike
or a peaceful European future. As Your
Imperial Highness will have seen from
the newspapers, public opinion in Russia
is chauvinistic; that is to say favorable
to warlike undertakings, and only the

285

person of the Tsar maintains a counter-
balance. A simple move on the part of the
Tsar to the other side would awaken in the
Russian nation an unanimous enthusiasm
for war. . . .
Bismarck (to the Crown Prince Frederick
William)

The assassination of Alexander II disclosed that the Russians thought and felt in a Katkovite manner, far away from both the wishful thinking of the revolutionaries and the fears of the panic-stricken elite. The hysteria which took hold of the masses had only one, profoundly reactionary dimension. The authorities virtually suffocated under the avalanche of stigmatizing, witch-hunting appeals. "The denunciation mania has spread to all social classes. I receive anonymous letters with slurs on my servants for their abusive sayings about me," the former minister Golovnin complained.[1] The same stream, directed against every imagined form of dissent, also poured into Strastnyi Boulevard.[2] Worse still, the mob moved to punish those allegedly responsible for the revolutionary plague. Large-scale anti-Semite atrocities reminded the shocked Europeans of long forgotten times and made them aware that beneath the veneer of civilization, the Russian mind went on working in its own peculiar ways.

No substantial divergence can be traced between the obscure "representative of the poor," who clamoured for an overall purge to dispose of liberals, Jews and Poles,[3] and the educated and well-placed ones stirring up this mood. The Holy League (Sviashchennaia druzhina) groups, an embodiments of the Katkovite "popular militia" idea, were composed to a great extent of officers and officials; and they often organized and led the ostensibly "spontaneous demonstrations of outraged people" which turned into ugly scenes of pillage and murder.

Pobedonostsev and Ignatiev must be counted among the chief culprits, first of all because they encouraged the well-known anti-Semitism of the new Tsar and strove to exploit it for their own purposes.

In St. Petersburg, Ignatiev wrote to Alexander III, banks, the stock-exchange, the bar, the press and bureaucracy were under the thumb of a formidable Jewish-Polish alliance; it was this alliance and its associations which robbed the treasury, inspired sedition and silenced "any honest Russian voice." As the first remedy, he advised the ruler to seek at least temporary refuge in Moscow, where he would be "protected by devoted people."

The "Father of the Lie" himself joined the Holy League and later inspired the ill-famed "Temporary administrative regulations" (in May 1882), which allowed most of the Jews to settle only in the so-called Pale (Lithuania, Poland, the Ukraine and White Russia), prohibited them moving outside towns and townships in the Pale, purchase or manage landed property and trade on Sundays and Christian holidays.[4]

Katkov had never been an anti-Semite; still, the Stratnyi Boulevard has to be considered the focus from which the main inspiration to the reaction came. The assassination liberated the editor from the forced truce with liberal society and his pen could run wild. He explained, of course, the roots of the tragedy by the reform ventures which enfeebled autocratic principles:

> The evil has penetrated 'our official sphere,' 'our press,' 'our poor schools'; and both the liberals, 'the traitors of the nation' and the cosmopolitan 'rotten conservatives' in the St. Petersburg elite bear responsibility for it. It remains to the Tsar to leave the capital on the Neva, 'where evil was born and has been nurtured' and seek sanctuary in the old fortress of Russian patriotism; 'only from the Kremlin can Russia be cleansed of the revolutionary infection' and 'Russian state power demonstrated in its inshakable strength.'[5]

Moreover, personally and through his lieutenants, he extolled Pobedonostsev to stop lamenting and engage in a merciless battle with the 'evil spirits' still sitting in the government.[6]

Under the circumstances, the effort of the more farsighted statesmen to save the Loris-Melikov reform proposals were doomed to failure. The exhortations coming from Moscow inflammed the Director General of the Holy Synod, who, for his part, wielded decisive influence on his pupil, the new Tsar. "I arrive, we sit down together, I tell him everything, and I can hardly bear not to look upon him with tears of love and compassion," Pobedonostsev wrote about his almost daily talks with the ruler.[7]

Invited by his admirers, the Thunderer arrived in early May in St. Petersburg to orchestrate the battle. It was won on 11 May, when the

Tsar's manifesto composed by Pobedonostsev and published without consulting the other ministers, condemned the quest for changing the system and proclaimed the autocratic principle inviolable. "Like heavenly manna descended the word of the Tsar, so eagerly awaited by popular feeling. Here lies the solution: it brings the autocratic Tsar back to the Russian people," the Moscow editor ejaculated.[8]

"All this is the work of Pobedonostsev and Katkov," the liberals dispaired.[9] The resignation of Loris-Melikov and Abaza ensued without delay, that of Miliutin was to follow.

The Interior Ministry was given to Ignatiev. Again, in all liklihood, the two leading spirits of reaction manipulated Alexander's choice. Albeit with misgivings about his character and intentions, Katkov proclaimed the "Father of the Lie" the "symbol of Russian national policy in foreign affairs"; and Pobedonostsev recommended him to the ruler as a "statesman who still has healthy instincts and a Russian soul" and whose name "has a good reputation among the healthy portion of the Russian population."[10]

* * *

The dramatic Russian events aroused the gloomiest anticipations in Berlin and Vienna. The assurances the Ambassadors Schweinitz and Kálnoky received at the Singers' Bridge that the new Tsar would remain true to the policies designed by his father[11] could not assuage them; the long-term connections between the Anichkov Palace and the Panslav-nationalists were only too well known.

Already at the time of the extremist eclipse in 1880 the Austrian Embassy warned that in Tsardom the hatred against Bismarck was no less intense than in France in 1871 that the Muscovy way of thinking had "entirely permeated the blood and flesh of the nation as well as of its elite" and that therefore men of the future would not be Shuvalov, Valuev or Lobanov-Rostovskii but those coming from the "national Russian party of Katkov's colouring."[12] The somber predictions now appeared to come true. The spectacular ascendancy of Katkov, Pobedonostsev and Ignatiev was taken as proof that "Muscovite old beards" would decide on everything and that the already eliminated Gorchakov would be formally replaced by their nominee. There was allegedly also a peasant prophecy predicting that "as the first Alexander had delivered us from the Frenchman and the second from the Pole, so the third is destined to relieve us from the German."[13] In his dispatch of 9 April, 1881 Kálnoky suggested that in the view of the inevitably forthcoming Muscovy supremacy the consultate-general in the old capital should be entrusted with the tasks usually performed by the embassy.[14]

Moreover, some sort of revolution was acutely feared. Bismarck gave vent to his foreboding by an order to Schweinitz to telegraph him daily, morning and evening.[15] The episode of Skobelev's return from the Central-Asian expedition demonstrated that these anxieties were not entirely unfounded.

Though disliked by many in the elite—Meschcherskii described him as a "cynical spoiled child of destiny," Miliutin and Feoktistov as extremely gifted and equally dangerous condottiere[16]—the White General was a hero par excellence for both the public and the army rank-and-file; and the Akhal Tekin affair provided him an additional lustre. All the way to St. Petersburg, innumerable crowds welcomed him as the "savior of Russian honour."

After the gathering before the Moscow railway station, Governor General Dolgorukii noted with patent vexation: "I saw Bonaparte returning from Egypt."[17] And, indeed, much more than Field Marshal Bariatinskii before him, Skobelev represented that danger. Unscrupulous and intoxicated by mass worship, he differed from the Field Marshal and other similarly attuned Russian military in one very substantial aspect: he would not stop at the person of the autocrat, and even advertized his intentions. "Vous serez ma Josephine," he used to promise the women he courted.[18]

Sympathetic to the reform programme, the General had had perhaps some weak spot for Alexander II; not, however, for his son. And when, after extatic manifestations, the new Tsar met him and in a chilly audience—hinting at the massacre of the Turkomans, he put an embarrassing question "how was the discipline in your detachment"—Skobelev's hostility immediately surfaced. "He will be kicked off," he fumed. The capital simmered with rumours about "le premier Consul" and the fronde forming around him.[19]

Gripped by panic, Pobedonostsev with unusual candor reprimanded Alexander:

The times are such that extreme prudence in social contacts must be observed. God knows what events are in store for us and whether we will live in peace and security. One cannot deceive oneself: fate has predestined Your Majesty to pass a stormy, very stormy period, and the greatest perils are still ahead. . . . Circumstances have unwound, to our misfortune, in a way unknown in Russia. . . . Skobelev has become a big force and attained an enormous spiritual sway among the masses, i.e. people believe in him and follow him. This is terribly important, and more important than ever. . . .[20]

However tense the Russian conditions might have been, though, things did not come up as badly as Bismarck had expected. And the tactics he used to stave off the "Muscovy wave"—to appeal to traditional conservative predilections—again proved to be quite an effective one.

Katkov tried to resist it. While condemning France and England, "the hotbeds and sanctuaries for the revolutionaries," he warned against Russia being seduced by Holy Alliance talk about monarchic solidarity against subversive elements and serve as a German auxiliary:

Why should Russia feel called upon to put herself at Germany's disposal and perform as her voucher against France whilst at the same time abandoning the Turkish heritage to Austria-Hungary? . . . In Berlin they imagine that Russia will find her reward in the support she is receiving in her struggle against revolutionary propaganda. Do not our friends ask a high price from us for the measures they propose to take in the interest of their own safety?[21]

Yet, not only did Bismarck's exhortations find extensive sympathy in the elite labouring under the shock of the regicide. Alexander III himself was obviously tuned at the same wavelength and ready to respect the Romanov-Hohenzollern intimity as a part of the burden his father had left him. Thus, despite his inflated authority, the Moscow publicist failed to influence even the final stage of the debate on the conclusion of the Three Emperors' Alliance. The only challenge to the programme recently set forth by Giers came from Saburov, and from this side the German Chancellor had nothing to worry about.

Saburov's designs were transparent: to exploit the change on the throne and the uneasiness in Berlin for pushing through his formulae. The opening looked promising for him. In a dispatch, he wrote about the hope "to see one beautiful day the occupation of the Straits by Russia." Giers passed it to the autocrat with the remark that "this is going too far." Alexander, however, thought otherwise: "Perhaps not at the moment but in the course of time it will become inevitable," he commented.[22]

Probably apprised on the detail, the Ambassador rushed to the capital and on 7 May 1881, forwarded a memorandum which should win the ruler to his side. The document, a very significant piece of Russian neo-nationalism, postulated

> From the time of isolation in 1879, conditions have radically altered and the foundations of the Berlin Treaty have been shattered. The new Tsar has to take advantage of it, remembering that 'every Russian Emperor has to write another glorious page in his people's history.' This new page, however, should not be connected with the compromised Panslavism. 'As Russians, we can always find allies in Europe, as Slavs—never.' In Russian Near-Eastern policy, there has always been but one authentic goal, that of weakening the Ottoman Empire and acquiring complete control over the Black Sea and its entraces; the support given to the Slavs has been subordinated to this objective, and in the present conditions it has become imperative to throw this ballast away in order to safeguard the best international climate for the occupation of the Straits. 'The Straits question may occur at any minute as the most burning one'; and, consequently, the most pressing task must be seen in 'the strengthening of the Three Emperors' bloc and in obtaining German consent to the military action as well as the obligation to keep Austria neutral 'in the minute of the operation.'[23]

Saburov's frank statement, however, only bewildered the Tsar. Conditioned to Panslav arguments, the wording of the memorandum must have revolted him: "much truth, (but) much untruth, too," he noted down.[24] Writing on the margin of the document, he professed his allegiance to a "purely national and Russian policy," yet he was far from understanding it otherwise than in the traditional framework. Furthermore, feeling highly insecure, he would not enter any unexplored path, either by adopting a free-hand policy advised by Katkov or a Saburovian "big bargain" concept. Whatever might have been his aspirations concerning the Russian future in the Straits and in the Balkans, he craved for tranquility above all. For that, Giers' programme of status quo suited him best.

The Russian Ambassadors asked for their opinion also assessed it to be the best course, pointing out accumulated Austro-German power, its capability to throw two million troops across their eastern borders.[25]

Thus Giers was empowered to direct the negotiations in the way he wished it. Bismarck's verbal assurances that Germany would not attack France were recognized as a satisfactory guarantee that the European balance of power would not be impaired. Alexander just insisted that alliance must be kept strictly secret not to compromise him before his subjects, that no concessions should be made to both partners save those already granted and that the duration of the alliance should be limited to three years only.[26] This gave the "Dreikaiserbund" treaty signed on 18 June 1881 in Berlin, more or less a character of a mere "practical arrangement about the Near East without even a monarchical flourish,"[27] but after the fears enkindled by the assassination of Alexander II it still seemed to Bismarck and the advocates of his system as a satisfactory arrangement providing good prospect for the future.

Soon, however, events revealed what the trouble would be: albeit not threatened by revolution, the Russian "novum regnum" proved incapable of true stabilization.

* * *

With his mentality and personal experience, Alexander III, now thirty-seven years old, was predetermined to cling to peace, order and inertia. This giant, a "splendid example of the old-fashioned, God-fearing Russian type,"[28] who used to bend iron bars and straighten horseshoes with his bare hands, was inwardly—particularly in the first period of his rule—an extremely diffident man. And neither his imperious conduct nor the language of gutter in which he unburdened himself even when writing on the margins of important state papers, could conceal this want of confidence. Although feared for his fits of rage by the entire imperial family and by the highest dignitaries, he was himself afraid of tackling the most burning problems. Because of this, rather than for security reasons or his well-known distaste for the court life, he preferred seclusion in the Gatchina Palace. There, he diligently read a mass of documents, poured his feelings forcibly on paper, but when the moment of decision came he, as a rule, escaped into comforting inactivity, which some wrongly identified with laziness.

He sought for tranquility, but was incapable of giving his quest any positive purpose. Such also was the problem with the men who emerged as the leading ministers of his reign—Pobedonostsev and Tolstoi. None of them possessed true statesmanlike qualities.

In accordance with his ally Katkov, Pobedonostsev proclaimed from authority and resolute governmental action the supreme need. Yet, he himself was 'anything but a man of action, who had neither the stuff nor the breath of a dictator"; or, as the Moscow editor complained, he "could move at ease only in the pure ether of principles." He applied his considerable knowledge and energy in the totally negative manner of a fanatic. "Under the impact of unsurmountable fears which dominated him, he was disposed to do everything. . .he stopped before nobody and nothing (yet solely) in repressive measures," wrote Feoktistov; he closely followed even the most obscure local sheets to detect in them a source which might contaminate the public mind, and from the same aspect, he scrutinized every administrative and legislative project. No dissent, no deviation was to be tolerated—in the political, cultural or religious sphere.[29]

Tolstoi, another old reactionary, was not unintelligent and uneducated either. Being a cold, dry, ambition-driven bureaucrat, however, he was equally unable to provide leadership. His dismissal in 1880 had revealed that society intensely disliked him as a "man narrow and stubborn, who sees no one except St. Petersburg circles, who hates any independent movement or the appearances of freedom, and is, in addition, devoid of all moral convictions. . . ." Ambitions aside, his conduct was determined solely by immediate pragmatic expediency. Condemning the reform policy—according to him, it produced but a "a ruined, impoverished, drunk and dissatisfied peasantry and an equally ruined and dissatisfied nobility, courts that continuously interfere in the working of police, and 600 zemstvo gossip parlors"—he saw the solution in a pure and simple return to the Nicholas-type system, in a "paralysis of every opposition to the government."[30]

The rest of the government was composed mostly of unprincipled and/or mediocre bureaucrats. Those who aimed for improvement in the limited field of their responsibility—Minister for Public Instruction Baron Nikolai, Justice Minister Nabokov, Finance Minister Bunge, Minister for Foreign Affairs Giers—were almost constantly on the defensive, struggling for political survival. Paralyzing fear of Alexander's or Katkov's wrath, mutual jealousies and permanently brewing intrigues deprived the highest executive body as a whole of true authority. With a patent gusto, the Moscow publicist stressed this "irreparable weakness of the government." "No, gentlemen, you indulge your hopes in vain. Nobody believes that you can do anything in earnest," he once told the assembled dignitaries.[31]

So, a highly abnormal situation developed when the Strastnyi Boulevard's "great master" commanded more respect from the Tsar and the country than the Tsar's own ministers. Katkov's arguments, Miliutin despaired, "were accepted by our vile public . . . nearly as evangelic truth"; and Alexander recognized him as a genuine intermediary between the throne and the people.[32] With good reason the Muscovite might boast that the Russian press was now more free than its counterparts in Western Europe, because—he was, of course, judging it from his own position—it experienced the conditions and responsibilities in which it could "achieve pure independence."[33]

Among the publicists, the enormous sway of Katkov upon the autocrat was being rivalled, in a different and limited sense, only by Prince Meshcherskii.

An "enfant terrible of the reaction,"[34] Meshcherskii had moved in the 1860s from St. Petersburg to Moscow and had turned into a true Muscovite vastly inspired by the Strastnyi Boulevard.[35] His power lay in the long-time intimacy with Alexander III. (Before marriage, Alexander had been enamored of the Prince's sister.) His daily, the *Grazhdanin*, enjoyed like the *Moskovskiia vedomosti* the supreme protection against censorship. Meshcherskii repaid it—as well as the regal subsidies he received from the Gatchina Palace—by underhand information or rather denunciations of prominent personalities. Society believed that the Prince's advice decided most appointments and promotions; thus, although he was universally despised for homosexuality and called "the Prince of Sodom," his

Sunday matinées became "gatherings of high-placed ones, seeking for protection and support."[36]

The whole "reactionary quartet"[37]—Katkov, Pobedonostsev, Tolstoi and Meshcherskii—preached on behalf of Alexander III a slightly modified version of the old "Autocracy-Orthodoxy-Nationality" doctrine, emphasizing the political obligations instead of the political rights of the Tsar's subjects.

Katkov postulated that parliamentarism was a "vile doctrine, which has everywhere lost its credit," that the "Russian model" of the highly-centralized, dictatorial-type government represented the most advanced type of state organization. He admonished the ruler to exercise his prerogatives, the Church to cultivate the spirit of obedience, and the people to follow their commands:

> We are obliged to respect authority. The Church teaches that authority comes from God. We are bound to respect authority not only out of fear but also our of persuasion; both our conscience as citizens and as Orthodox Christians commits us to this.

In his idea of government (tsarstvo) there was no room for any public participation in the direction of the state; any quest for it should be considered but a product of that liberal-revolutionary "plague from which we must free ourselves at any price."[38] He even dreamed about the revival of the famous Third Rome idea:

> The Russian Tsar is more than the successor of his ancestors; he is the successor of the Ceasars of Eastern Rome, of the builders of the Church and its Councils. . . . With the fall of Byzantium, Moscow was elevated to the grandeur of Russia. Here is the secret of the deep peculiarity which distinguishes Russia from the other nations of the world.[39]

All that suited well Alexander's inclination to see his realm and the world around him in the same way as the old-time Muscovite rulers were used to. But the system could not work. The haughty Katkov's challenge, thrown into the face of educated Russians at the beginning of the "novum regnum"—"stand up, gentlemen, the government is coming, the government is returning"[40]—had never materialized. Neither the best intentions

nor the great deal of common sense the new autocrat possessed could substitute the absence of vision and initiative. Perceiving incompetence,
hypocrisy and corruption around him, Alexander became increasingly
authoritative in a clearly negative manner. A trait of his mentality, which
an American scholar named "denseness" (tupost') gradually bulked into
a "kind of obstinate self-righteousness most difficult to deal with."[41] It
sprouted into an additional obstacle to a more rationally-founded policy
and, in the end, also hit Katkov himself.

True, from the conservative viewpoint it looked like a substantial
improvement in comparison with the era just passed. Manifestations of
opposition subsided, society was tamed into submission. Students who
had spat in a collection box for a wreath on Alexander II's grave, now
threw their coats on the mud just to make it comfortable for the imperial
family to walk from their carriage to the University building. But Russia
was going to pay dearly for her docility: Alexander III's era made a huge
contribution to the conditions nurturing future catastrophes.

* * *

The impact the new Tsar wielded on Russian foreign policy was much
more complex and contradictory than that of his father. The simple,
puritan Alexander III, "the most honest man in Russia," as a foreign
diplomat characterized him,[42] disliked the libertine St. Petersburg society
and in his general outlook was undoubtedly more "Muscovite" than any
other Romanov on the throne since they had moved their capital on the
Neva. His tutor Pobedonostsev had taught him to value highest the ideas
originated in the city under the Kremlin walls and read the *Moskovskiia
vedomosti* as the only "responsible" newspaper. In his letters and quite
frequent visits, which the editor had commenced to pay him as soon as
Alexander became the heir apparent,[43] he was learnt that "any deviation
of our thought beyond the confines of the good of the state . . . willy-
nilly leads it astray, onto a wrong path which ends with voluntary or in-
voluntary treachery and encourages the enemies."[44] And the Tsar's utterances show convincingly how deeply he imbibed the Strastnyi Boulevard
sermon:

> I understand only one policy: to exact from every situation all
> that is needed by and is beneficial to Russia; and to do it with as

little inhibition as possible; and to act in a straightforward and resolute manner. We ought to have no policy other than that which is
purely Russian and national. This is the only policy we may and
must follow.[45]

Alexander wished to apply this principle above all on the Eastern Question. "One cannot save a man who is looking for death. Turkey is a finished country and only lazy ones do not pick up the remnants," he affirmed.
The Russians should seize Constantinople and the Straits in order to
"establish ourselves for good there and to be sure that they will forever
remain in our hands." "When we shall be strong enough in the Black Sea,
we won't need to be worried about England." As to the Balkan peoples,
complete Russian supremacy "must be inevitably achieved."[46]

Nevertheless, as the consent to enter the Three Emperors' Alliance indicated, the Moscow editor and the other extremists who expected too
much of "their man on the Neva," had to go through mounting disappointments. Once he took over the supreme responsibility, Alexander
showed a marked want of alacrity to act as it had been charted for him.
As it has already been stressed, there was to be a considerable variance
between his "ferocious pen" or talk and his deeds. Though verbally
extolling the absence of inhibition and praising the will to go ahead
directly and with the greatest determination, he had, fortunately for his
rule, never dared to do that himself.

Giers observed that the peace and dignity of Russia were the values
the Tsar cherished most.[47] The dignity in traditional interpretation,
coupled with the choleric nature and growing obstinacy of the autocrat, helped the extremists in their plea for "direct action." Yet, they
were in the last resort hindered in their aims by his peaceful leanings, on
which the advocates of moderation could always appeal in their countermoves.

Bitter lessons from the Balkan battlefields were undoubtedly paramount in cooling Alexander's Panslav-nationalist ardor. He put it very
well himself:

I am glad that I have taken part in actual warfare and seen with
my own eyes the horrors which are inevitably connected with a military action. After such an experience, not only will a ruler never

desire war, but he will employ every honourable means of sparing his subjects the trials and terrors of armed conflict.[48]

Observing the shadowy sides of Russian military organization, the Tsar turned with disgust from the Romanov habit of playing with soldiers. The mania of parades, endless exercises and maneuvres, the whole "exercise-ground tradition" (platsparadnaia traditsiia)[49] lost supreme favor. The abolition of the May parades as well as the operetta hussar and hulan regiments, were with some justification conceived by observers as an indication that the army no longer had that enhanced position it still enjoyed under Alexander II.

This, together with the Tsar's strong attachment to the monarchic principle gave the Bismarckian system a certain perspective. "The Tsar has not much intelligence, but he is immovable as a rock. He wants peace —firmly, persistently, absolutely," General Cherevin, perhaps the closest friend of the autocrat, told the German diplomats. Giers gave them equally weighty and correct advice: "The Tsar does not like the Germans, but he does not like the French and the English better. On the other hand, he likes monarchies and detests republics. This is your chance; you should profit from it." Balancing all the pros and cons, Bismarck himself soon recognized Alexander as the most important bulwark of general tranquility among the Russians.[50]

The Tsar demonstrated his peaceful predilections also in the choice of the Foreign Minister. Though exposed to unrelenting pressures to appoint a "genuinely Russian representative," he entrusted the position to Nikolai Giers, a pronounced conservative moderate, and let him keep it throughout his whole reign. Still, the peculiar relationship between the ruler and his minister, the limited authority the latter enjoyed and the latitude conceded to Katkov to scorn him and the programme he represented revealed in a signal manner the basic contradiction of Russian foreign policy under Alexander III's scepter.

In a way, Giers was no less typical a figure of the era than were Katkov or Pobedonostsev on the opposite side. A descendant of non-Russian ancestors, lacking money, noble status and connections at Court, he might scarcely have expected a remarkable career at the Singers' Bridge. But his diligence helped him. Gorchakov, lazy and enamoured of the worldly life, needed people who would take care of boring paperwork.

Giers, a bureaucrat by nature, grew thus into an invaluable asset for the old Chancellor. After the Berlin Congress, he also took over his chief's place in the Tsar's councils and—as it has been noted—proved the capacity to advance broader concepts. Even then, however, he remained something of a pariah, acquiesced to the "modest role of a secretary" who polished directives and met foreign diplomats to assuage their suspicions.[51]

The ministerial nomination in 1882 only changed the form of Giers' dependence. With a big family to support, he trembled for his post and consequently scarcely ventured to engage the extremists in an open contest; and, naturally, he would never have contradicted his august master. He was panic-stricken before every audience at the Gatchina Palace and his closest friend and collaborator in the ministry, Count Lamsdorf, rushed on these occasions to burn a candle and pray for him in church.

"I am only a little fish swimming against the current; that is my fate," the minister lamented.[52] Alexander, afraid of displeasing the "patriots," would not bolster his authority by bestowing him a higher order, a title of count or give him money which would free him of material worries. The poor man, stooped, with a slanted forehead and long ears reminded his ill-wishers of a scared hare whom they could insult at will. At a banquet, in the presence of hundreds of prominent guests, Prince Naryshkin, the Marshal of Court, could call him contemptuously to order: "But, my dear minister, you cannot use our fork like that!"[53] In consequence, in his relationship to ministerial colleagues, foreign diplomats as well as to his subordinates, Giers was, to an ever greater extent than his predecessors, devoid of the authority connected in normal circumstances with such an office and his replacement was a matter of frequent gossip.

In broader lines, the Foreign Minister represented a continuity of traditional policy with the emphasis reminiscent of Nesselrode's rather than of Gorchakov's approach. He considered the nationalist extremists to be "our enemies" who would eventually "bring about the fall of the dynasty" and a revolution compared with which "the Commune of Paris would look like child's play." He wished to live in peace with everybody, but linked the stability almost unequivocally with the Bismarckian system. In the German Chancellor he appreciated the "sound perseverance in pursuing an eminently conservative and pacific course" and argued that "if there is a Power for which such a course should be suitable, then it is Russia."[54]

For a short time and within limits, Giers was able to uphold his concept. The ideas of anti-revolutionary monarchic solidarity were shared by Pobedonostsev, Meshcherskii, the leading diplomats, the "German party" at Court (Shuvalov, Grand Duke Vladimir, etc.) and by the Tsar himself. Katkov tolerated the minister and his achievements in patching up the serious frictions with Berlin and Vienna propped up his position. From the very outset, however, he was unable either to curb the militarists in Asia or the extremists schemings in the Balkans, the area, which he with good reason regarded equally fatal for Tsardom as medieval Italy had been for the German emperors.[55]

The international crisis in 1885-1887, triggered by events in Bulgaria, marked the watershed. Suffering one setback after another, the Russians put the blame squarely on Bismarck's and Giers' shoulders. The stances of the Tsar, Pobedonostsev[56] and Meshcherskii shifted accordingly, while Katkov was incited into his final crusade against the Bismarckian system and the "traitor" at the Singers' Bridge. Even then, the Tsar refused to surrender to the hawkish call for a military solution and the dismissal of the Foreign Minister. But the course the latter represented was to be in principle exchanged for the one clamoured by his Moscow foe and by the public.

CHAPTER 22

THE AKSAKOV-IGNATIEV-SKOBELEV "INTRIGUE" (1881-1882)

> In (the present) governmental paralysis
> everything is possible.
> Katkov

In September 1881, Alexander met Emperor William at Danzig, and pleading his loyalty to the Three Emperors' Alliance, he allegedly repudiated the Panslav-nationalist current. Although nothing in this sense was made public, the very fact that the entrevue took place sufficed for comments assessing it as a point of departure for a new era of a traditionally-styled monarchic policies. But soon thereafter, the prognoses again underwent a change. The Danzig visit namely fanned afresh latent anti-German freelings, subdued somewhat by the shock of the regicide. The extremist groupings and the press resumed their usual diatribes.[1]

Already on 25 August, an Extraordinary Council summoned to discuss the future of the Russian army returned to the "Bosphorus theme" and by proclaiming the building of a mighty Black Sea naval force and preparation for a landing operations as the most pressing tasks carted away the moderate concept of Miliutin.[2] Probably informed about the outcome of the council, Katkov in the editorial of 24 September requested a more daring approach which would strive for an undisputed control over the Black Sea entrances and also for a dominant position in the Far East.[3] Simultaneously, he reopened the highly sensitive issue of security on the western borders of the Empire, demanding that the Germans should be deprived of their rights in the strategic Libau-Romny railway.[4]

Thus poised for the attack, the Moscow editor responded on the Danzig meeting by an unveiled warning against German alignment. There, he spelled out his key postulates:

> In past years, the Bismarckian system had been 'set in motion precisely at the moments when Russia's most material interests were at stake and when it became imperative to divert her from the correct path. . . . What the other Powers take for an isolated position, the one which they are afraid of, that is for Russia safer and better than all the alliances. The greater freedom she retains, the stronger he international position and the more authentic the national character of her policy will be.[5]

It was to be, however, the more sensitive Russo-Austrian relationship, where Katkov and the whole nationalist camp centered their challenge; and there too, the recently concluded agreement between Tsardom and the two Germanic powers proved sorely vulnerable. The affair of the Serbian Metropolitan Mihailo opened a new period of intense and unconcealed friction.

From the 1850s onwards, Mihailo had been the most reliable Russian tool in the Principality. In the publicist's words, "the Russian people trusted to Serbia only in the person of the Metropolitan, and the assistance from Russia came chiefly through him."[6] Naturally, both King Milan and Vienna saw in the ecclesiastic a serious obstacle to the pro-Austrian course inaugurated in Belgrade after the Berlin Congress and when a dispute over the taxation of church property offered in autumn 1881 a suitable pretext, the King removed him from office.

The dismissal created an uproar in which the whole Russian press participated. The Moscow editor fulminated about an "obscure government, which born yesterday, may well disappear tomorrow" and suggested that the Russian diplomatic representative be recalled from Belgrade and official contacts go through the Austrian Minister instead, "as with a vassal country, openly subordinated to Austria-Hungary." More importantly, he made it an occasion for the broadening of his criticism of St. Petersburg's policymaking, which in his view had been forfeiting the big opportunity to abandon the concept proven totally wrong:

Does not this establish the truth that since the Berlin Congress Russia's authority in the East has been in decline and that the designs of her opponents, the foes of Orthodoxy and Slavdom, have been successfully carried out?[7]

Ignatiev joined the outcry with similar purpose. Aspiring no less than Saburov to inherit Gorchakov's post, the Interior Minister could so far injure Giers only by insulting gossip.[8] Now, an opportunity emerged to reaffirm his stature as the custodian of the Russian cause and denounce his Singers' Bridge foes. He wrote to Pobedonostsev:

The removal of our trusted ally Mikhailo is an irreparable blow inflicted on our influence by the Hungarians and the Germans. . . . I had continuously supported him for fifteen years against various enemies and intrigues. At one stroke, they have been able to shatter this firm foundation. We are now harvesting the fruits of the Berlin agreement and of our humiliation.

Pobedonostsev willingly presented the affair to the Tsar as another example of Catholic, liberal and Austrian conspiracy; and the latter, although concurring only to a diplomatic remonstrance in Belgrade, seems to have been persuaded to the same effect.[9]

If the Mihailo case supplied the extremists with a convincing opening, then the revolt in Bosnia-Hercegovina delivered them a veritable boon. Prompted in late 1881 by the introduction of military conscription, the revolt signalled a singular failure of Austrian rule, Vienna's inability to satisfy national, religious and social groups in the recently acquired provinces. Irritated by burdensome taxation, haughtiness of the officialdom and, above all by unwillingness to alleviate the dead weight of the begs upon the peasantry, Orthodox joined Moslems in common enmity to an alien regime. Moreover, the uprising brought in train large-scale agitation in the neighboring lands.

* * *

Katkov's vitriolic language on events in Bosnia-Hercegovina was noted both in Russia and abroad with considerable apprehension.[10] In this case, though, it were the old Balkan conspirators, Aksakov and Ignatiev, who together with General Skobelev were the pivotal figures in the new Panslav-nationalist quest for change in Tsardom's policies. Aksakov collected a large sum—allegedly 200,000 rubles—and through his Hercegovinan aide Buradžić and the notorious Khitrovo, now diplomatic agent in Sofia, organized deliveries of arms and a volunteer action.[11] Meanwhile, a dangerous split, typical of crisis situations, appeared to be taking place in the St. Petersburg government. While the Foreign Ministry wielded pressure upon the Montenegrin Prince to divert him from the usual temptations, the Interior Ministry under Ignatiev let the press free to whip up the emotions. Panic-stricken, the Austrian Embassy on the Neva feared that conditions like those in 1876-1877 might soon emerge and gradually force Alexander III to intervention.[12] The Bonapartist ambitions of Skobelev invested the most explosive element into the imbroglio.

During his sojourn in Europe after the unpleasantness with the Tsar, the White General appears to have looked for any partner who would go with him either against the "German peril" or the "dynasty which had lost its prestige." He had allegedly negotiated even with the revolutionary émigré Lavrov; and back in Russia, he continued his search, working hard at the same time on advertizing his popular image. Already on the battlefield he had paraded an extraordinary talent for it, being, in Feoktistov's words, "ready to offer his life, but always as an accomplished actor calculating on effect."[13] He now flooded the country with his portraits—full face, in profile, on foot and on horseback—on chocolate, scent and soap boxes. "You must get them worked up. You cannot do anything without publicity. Glory is a whore. She requires it and you know that I mean to win her," he told his friends. "I want to possess her exclusively. Yes, everything or nothing."

Imprudent utterances brought Skobelev an admonition from the new War Minister, General Vannovskii, but no one could stop him. "The show is going to hell. There will be nothing left.... Dynasties collapse and change, the nation often benefits thereby. The Bourbons almost ruined France. Napoleon saved her and made her greater than she had ever been before," he declared before Generals Cherevin, Dragomirov, Dukhturov and Vorontsov-Dashkov, all belonging to the highest establishment.[14]

The political reasoning of the White General may be summarized as follows: Both the liberals and the revolutionaries are too weak, without roots in the masses. In Russia, there is only one force capable of over-throwing the government—the army. For this, two preconditions are necessary. Firstly—a popular pesonality whom every Russian would follow. Secondly—a mobilizing slogan which would appeal to everybody. The personality in question would be himself, the slogan—war with the Germans, for unification of the Slavs.[15]

Soliciting for support among the powerful, Skobelev described an anti-German crusade and the solution of the Eastern Question "in the sense of all-Slavic, that is to say Russian interests" as "the only means to improve our economic and political situation," the only way to "the external grandeur and the internal prosperity." If the present course were not to be stopped, then "the consequences would be disastrous."[16]

Aksakov and Ignatiev joined forces with him. Certainly, neither of them would favor a military coup and a quasi-republican pronunciamento; but, as the White General wished to use them, they wished to use his enormous popularity to achieve their own goals. Aksakov dreamed of breaking up the bureaucratic rule and remodelling Russia according to Slavophile principles. Ignatiev planned to obtain "the direction of Russia's foreign affairs in succession to Prince Gorchakov"; or better still, to become a "wielder of Russia's destinies," in the capacity of an "all-powerful (prime) minister," presiding over a cabinet "composed of ministers of the same opinion, i.e. subservient ones," and over a "strong regime based on nationalist ideology."[17]

In Skobelev's plans, a dramatic anti-German appeal followed by radical rapprochement with France was to be the key. How far the other two members of the triumvirate were involved, a historian may merely speculate.[18] At any rate, in early 1882 the three men started their action with each of them in a special role.

Aksakov and Skobelev prepared a speech word by word, which the latter delivered on 24 January 1882, at a St. Petersburg banquet organized to commemorate the first anniversary of the Akhal Tekin victory. Using the mauling of the Turkomans as evidence of Russian military valours, he pounced on the ruling elite, "paralyzed by some strange timidity" at the very time when the Austrians were "pointing their guns against Slavic, Orthodox chests." Despite this sad condition, the General promised, "the time of retribution must come" and the Russian soldier "remembering our brotherhood in arms" would perform his duty for the "sacred Russian and Orthodox cause."[19]

Then, while Aksakov in the column of the *Rus* escalated the anti-Austrian call to arms, the General departed for France. The tour was prompted by his French admirer, Juliette Adam, a woman with an ambition to be the second Madame de Staël; an ardent revanchist—she had published since 1879 the ultrapatriotic *La Nouvelle Revue*—and on the most intimate terms with Léon Gambetta, Adam believed that after the electoral victory of the Republic Alliance (1881) her country was also ready to depart radically from the timorous policy hitherto observed by moderate republicans.

In Paris, whether with premeditation or not, Skobelev without delay fired his biggest political bombshell. On 17 February, meeting a group of Balkan students, he allegedly pronounced the following words:

> I am bound to tell you the reason why Russia is not always equal to the discharge of her patriotic duties in general and to the fulfillment of her mission as a Slav Power in particular. It is because at home as well as abroad Russia has foreign influences to combat. We are not masters in our own house. Yes, the foreigners are everywhere and everything in Russia. . . . And I shall tell you the name of that intriguing intruder. . . . You all know him. It is the author of the 'Drang nach Osten.' I repeat it and I entreat you never to forget it: the German is the enemy. A struggle is inevitable between the Teuton and the Slav. It cannot be long deferred. It will be long, long and terrible, but I entertain the faith that it will culminate in a Slav victory. . . . [20]

The next day, in an interview for the *Voltaire,* the General repeated the anti-German diatribes and assured that the future would belong to a French-Slavic alliance. By virtue of it, Russia would "recover her lost independence" and France her great-power position.[21]

Although Bismarck reacted to the Paris scandal with studious nonchalance, its impact on German opinion was considerable. The speculations on a Russo-German war reappeared with new intensity[22] and there was widespread speculation on possible repercussions in St. Petersburg—that either the Tsar must punish the popular hero and thereby dissociate himself publicly from the "patriotic forces" or that he would succumb to them. However, no dramatic change ensued.

On the one hand, Alexander ordered the General to return home immediately, yet would not dare even to reprimand him. Remembering Pobedonostsev's warning, he let Cherevin and Vannovskii arrange a conciliatory audience. "The Tsar loves Skobelev and is in sympathy with his national orientation," the War Minister announced.[23]

On the other hand, although a British journalist claimed that the "hero of Plevna had risen to a height of popularity that few men in any country have attained" and even such an experienced statesman as Valuev dreaded the possibility that the Russian would-be Bonaparte and the Interior Minister concealed behind him would prevail in imposing their will upon the enfeebled government, it soon became obvious that the "intrigue" had misfired. There was not that sort of a response on which the triumvirate had speculated. True, the Paris speech obtained broad approval in the public and partly even in the army and the press. Skobelev was inundated with addresses of sympathy; several regiments toasted him; in the *Istoricheskii vestnik* (Historical Messenger), Colonel Krestovskii repeated his sharpest formulae in an article with the ominous title "Our future war." Yet, the prevailing reaction in society was that of grave concern rather than enthusiasm. A great deal of the press censured "Muscovite provocations"; the business interests protested that the warlike noises exacerbated troubles for Russian credit already harmed by the anti-Jewish atrocities; the higher officer corps took exception to the venture.[24] Ignatiev himself was obliged to play a double game. He assured his confidants that "we will have war in the spring," but to Pobedonostsev he found it politic to write that Skobelev had "profoundly saddened me with untoward speech."[25]

Katkov's attitude was most instructive. He accused "the intelligentsia" of misinterpreting the General's noble intentions and the French press of distorting the content of the speech; he also blamed German armaments and Austrian conduct in Bosnia-Hercegovina for the irritation in Russia. But he made his stance completely clear: by its infatuation with the effeted, corrupted France, the triumvirate indulged in a dubious game. As he wrote later to Alexander, he considered at that moment the direct anti-German agitation "non-sensical" and therefore moved to "sober up public opinion."[26] Using the birthday of the Emperor William, he announced, "to everybody's surprise," "the end of rumors about the alleged cooling off between Russia and Germany" and spelled out formulae incongruous in their spirit with those he had pronounced after the Berlin Congress:

> Both Powers cherish no aggressive plans and need mutual good-will, friendship and alliance. Only Russian diplomacy should be held responsible for the disappointments of the Turkish war and the Congress. 'Prince Bismarck tried by all means to reach an understanding with us on the basis of common interest . . . ; we, with the same intensity . . . eschewed agreement with him.'[27]

In the following weeks, the editor continued to castigate Austria-Hungary, but in the same breath emphasized peace and stability as the fundamental principle Russia would and must observe.[28] Growing anxiety that the destabilized Tsardom might plunge into an armed conflict with a German-led coalition, was to overshadow all other considerations.

* * *

So, while putting the public and the army circles in Germany and Austria-Hungary on the alert and strongly influencing even their governments, in its Russian domestic connotations the Skobelevian initiative simply petered out. Furthermore, the same reasons which had brought about this failure also sealed Ignatiev's fate. Ambassador Thornton, otherwise a quite undistinguished observer, correctly evaluated the situation:

> That Count Ignatiev had previous knowledge of General Skoelev's intentions and even inspired his inflammatory speeches, I cannot doubt. But the country does not seem to have appreciated his language as the Minister of Interior expected, and the feeling that the latter should be replaced by some more pacific statesman is certainly gaining ground.[29]

Already Ignatiev's nomination to a key ministry was commented on in the upper stratum with much scepticism. A too transparent thirst for power and elementary dishonesty were his insurmountable handicaps. Feoktistov compared him with Nozdrev, the anti-hero in the "Dead Souls": he "lied as easily as a bird sings or a dog barks, at every step, without the least need or calculation, and even to his disadvantage." The conduct of the former "vice-Sultan" in the ministerial position only confirmed these misgivings; he proved to be much less successful than on the Golden Horn.

Entertaining his own "little court" and seeking to please everybody, Ignatiev apparently aspired to emulate the Shuvalovian pattern and form a powerful faction; instead, his maneuvres brought him rather new enmities. "You fancy being another Arakcheev. It is a false system. You irritate everybody," Grand Duke Mikhail told him. While in the liberal circles the "Father of the Lie" was identified with the pogromist hoodlums and adventurous Panslav escapades, the ultraconservatives accused him of continuing the work of his constitutionalist predecessor: the State Secretary Peretts called him a "red-haired Loris-Melikov," and Dondukov-Korsakov denounced him as a "cheat playing with false cards."[30] Katkov complained that the Interior Minister was "showing himself as liberal to (that part of) the press which corrupts society and favours treason, while his smile disappears (when he is dealing) with that part of the press which is disposed to obey the call of duty."[31]

The critically exposed position would have induced a more prudent statesman to keep a low profile and wait. Too sure that Alexander would back him, however, Ignatiev persisted in tempting fortune. After the uproar created by Skobelev, he advertised the Slavophile project on the ressurection of the traditional Land Assembly (Zemskii sobor), elaborated by Aksakov and Golokvastov.[32] In his conversations with the Tsar, the minister reasoned as follows:

> There are three options for Russia. The first is that of intensified repression, which cannot get positive results; the second, that of constitutional concessions, would be yet more dangerous. Thus only the third road remains, the return to the past, to the 'historical contact between the autocracy and the land.' The Land Assembly (which had last met in 1613) would be convoked during the coronation and include all the members of the State Council, the Senate, the Holy Synod, all ministers and high ecclesiastics, marshals of nobility, mayors of important towns and elected representatives of landowners, merchants and peasants. In this way, the Tsar would be directly informed of the needs of his subjects and 'consult' with the best of them.[33]

Presenting the draft of the Land Assembly manifesto in late May, Ignatiev committed his final blunder. According to his subsequent claim, the Tsar was ready to concur, but Katkov and Pobedonostsev swayed him. A historian cannot be sure of the Tsar's attitude; on the other hand, there is no doubt at all that the two evil spirits of his rule were mainly responsible for toppling the minister, whom they had only a year ago helped to get the post, and for killing the last attempt at a very modest reform of the autocratic system before 1905.

Pobedonostsev was appaled by the draft; any concession to the constitutional principle, he warned the ruler, would be "a revolution, a ruin of the government and ruin of Russia."[34] Then, alerted by Feoktistov and Ostrovskii, the Moscow editor intervened forcefully in the same vein. Already on 23 April, he had openly attacked Ignatiev maintaining that "political sedition has never spoken so brazenly" as at the present and that Loris-Melikov's "dictatorship of the heart" has only been exchanged for a "dictatorship of a complacent, all-embracing, smiling little joke."[35] Now, although the authorities admonished the press "to be silent on the issue," he ignored it and in the editorials published on 23 and 24 May accused the whole government of passivity amidst the dangers surrounding it and demanded personnel changes in it:

> The Land Assembly project is a 'triumph for the forces of sedition,' because the same idea has been fostered by the most dangerous revolutionaries. Nechaev and Zheliabov. People sharing such views must leave. 'If our government seems to be weak, in a need of an assembly . . . would it not be more proper to see the source of this weakness in the incompetence of its accidental representatives?'[36]

Those who took part in the Extraordinary Council summoned on 8 June to Peterhof to discuss the affair all turned against Ignatiev. Katkov's ally, the Minister for State Domains Ostrovskii, led the censure. Alexander himself affirmed that his confidence in the minister—for a long time 'full and unreserved'—had ended. In vain the accused argued that the Land Assembly would be a mere "decoration' to appease the educated public. On 11 June, he was recalled and replaced by a man who personified bureaucratic rigidity pure and simple—Count Tolstoi.[37]

Four days later, the Muscovite commented on these events in one of his most famous editorials, in which he both bluntly stated his special position in the establishment and victory of his concept:

> Our 'enemies are mistaken when they look upon us as being some-times in opposition and sometimes in power. We are always in power and always in opposition. Personnel changes do not concern us and do not alter our position.' Our strength is derived from an unflinch-ing defence of the 'major formula that A is equal to A', i.e. that Rus-sia and autocracy are fully identical and no pluralist deviation is permissible.[38]

* * *

Tolstoi's nomination was again credited to be a choice made by the Katkov-Pobedonostsev duo. The admirers of the publicist were far from universally happy about it. "Even from him you were able to make a statesman; and you are responsible for his name entering into history. Quite an incredible tour de force," Feoktistov wrote to his "great master." "Only you are capable of making something out of him. Otherwise, no-thing good can be expected." But, neither Katkov nor Pobedonostsev saw an alternative. Although the former in a letter to the Tsar blamed Tolstoi that "in the last years he ignored all (my) admonitions and distanced him-self from me in the hope of appeasing his foes, to placate them with in-activity," his and the Holy Synod's chief's conviction still was that, despite "enormous weak points," the Count "at least represents a whole pro-gramme and his name is a symbol of a certain direction."[39]

The members of the defeated faction dispaired. "One may meet no-thing by apathy, petty egotism, chasing after posts and the complete triumph of mediocrity," Khitrovo complained.[40] Rumors circulated that great events were still in the offing, that during the forthcoming corona-tion the White General would perform a coup d'état and take over as Michael II;[41] but there was to be no more of the "Skobelev problem" for Alexander and his government.[42] Less than one month after Ignatiev's fall, the would-be Bonaparte ended his life under circumstances of a strange irony—he died from heart failure in the company of a German prostitute, in the Moscow bordello "England." Katkov allegedly rushed to the place to arrange the discreet removal of the body from such compromising surroundings and a convenient popular explanation quickly spread that the worshipped had been poisoned on German orders.[43] A huge funeral with a display of Russian public sorrow safely closed the first, transitory period of Alexander III's reign.

CHAPTER 23

KATKOV IN POWER:
TRIUMPHS AND THEIR LIMITS
(1881-1887)

Behind the writing table of a journalist, Katkov elevated himself almost to the position of the ruler of Russia. Ministers trembled before him, second-rate officials he used as lackeys.
Chicherin

Katkov's political ideal is as follows: the Russian Tsar is sitting on the throne and Katkov is beside him. I do not know to what degree this is in harmony with an autocratic government which desires firm rule.
Polovtsov

My paper was not simply a newspaper. It was an organ of state activity. In it the affairs of the government were not merely reflected but decided. My work was a state service without salary, decoration or court uniform.
Katkov

They say that Russia is deprived of political liberty. They say that although the Russians

are granted civic liberties, they have no political rights. Russian subjects have something
more than political rights, they have political
obligations. Every Russian is bound to stand
a guard over the rights of the supreme power
and care for the benefit of the state.
Katkov

"So, Russia is being commanded by Katkov and by the mad Pobedonostsev," Aksakov grieved after Ignatiev's dismissal.[1] The "normalization" of the autocratic regime could now set out in earnest.[2] In this process, the impact wielded by the Strastnyi Boulevard on public opinion was
perhaps less intense than during the whirlwind period of 1863-1866, but
in what has been called the "governmental sphere," Katkov's authority
unquestionably reached its apex.

In influencing the Tsar, the Muscovite was most effectively served by
Pobedonostsev and Feoktistov. The former persistently advertized him to
the autocrat as the only responsible, properly educated representative of
the press.[3] The latter, who headed the Main Administration for Press
Affairs, on the one hand kept the publicist perfectly informed on Alexander's attitudes and moods, on the other hand helped him to sway them;
his duty being to prepare for the ruler a private "svodka" (Imperial Review) of press comments, he used almost exclusively the materials printed
in the *Moskovskiia vedomosti* or those elaborating on their views.[4] And
where the Director General and the press lord seemed to him unsatisfactory, Katkov as before intervened with letters, memoranda and visits
to the Gatchina and Anichkov Palaces.

For nurturing and spreading the "Katkovshchina," the ministries for
internal affairs and public instruction were of particular importance.

Although the personal relations between Tolstoi and Katkov were quite
strained, there was no change in the pattern. Handled mercilessly by the
Strastnyi Boulevard grouping, as a mere "corpse deprived of all will," Tolstoi had never dared to free himself from the grip.[5] In addition to many
known acolytes of the editor, furthermore, the ministry had been since
1885 under an effective control of his new recruit, Pazukhin; and Pazukhin, too, had grown into the main figure in the preparation of the counter-
reforms.[6]

The Ministry for Public Instruction was in even greater degree an outright Katkovian agency. When a vast intrigue against the minister, Baron

Nikolai, resulted in the nomination of Count Ivan Delianov as his replacement, Miliutin heaved a sigh: "It is almost the same as if Katkov himself were to be appointed . . . Poor Russia!" The publicist haughtily acknowledged the strange character of their relationship. "It is not secret to me that Ivan Davidovich is a helpless man and that everything falls out of his hands. But my eyes will watch him closely; as long as I am here, he is not going to venture any step without turning to me first," he wrote. The actual direction of the ministry, at any rate, continued to belong to Georgievskii, whom Tolstoi called the "âme damnée de Katkoff."[7]

Besides Pazukhin, two other relatively fresh upstarts became prominent in the Katkovian "party of order"—Mikhail Ostrovskii, a brother of the famous dramatist, and Ivan Vyshnegradskii, a scientist with somewhat shadowy record of stock-market speculation, who was first appointed to the State Council and then took over the Finance Ministry.

According to State Secretary Polovtsov, the "Katkov court" composed of ministers or their acting deputies (Pobedonostsev, Delianov, Ostrovskii, Pazukhin, Vyshnegradskii) and presided by the publicist discussed and decided on the dismissal of the highest government officials as well as on the main issues of domestic policies.[8] This may be an exaggeration, but the fact is undisputable that through his clique the Muscovite could effectively assail everything that remained from the reform period.

* * *

Not surprisingly, the man from Strastnyi Boulevard centered his main retrograde efforts on wiping out the remnants of the liberal heritage in the educational system, i.e. on the abolition of university autonomy. And it was to be a depressing repetition of the "classicist dispute," where his power paraded and triumphed over the educated public.

For a long time it looked as if universities could be protected against Katkovian designs. During Miliutin's supremacy (1874-1881), the editor stood in almost complete isolation on the issue, when even his two main allies in the anti-reform drive, Tolstoi and Pobedonostsev, refused to follow him. The former, albeit wishing to establish a rigorous control over higher education, had been again afraid to engage in a contest where odds were heavily on the other side; the latter saw in Katkov's concept a debasement of universities such as he could not assent to. Consequently, in the commissions set up to discuss the new statute, the pliable lieutenants of the Strastnyi Boulevard—Georgievskii, Liubimov, Delianov—were just a fringe group.

Changed conditions after 1881, however, gave the publicist the winning card in what seemed to be a lost game. First, he could effectively appeal to the Tsar, arguing the necessity of suppressing the sedition entrenched in the universities and the incompatibility of their autonomy with the very essential principle of autocracy.[9] Second, after the removal of the two foremost opponents of the counter-reform, Miliutin and Nikolai, Tolstoi revived his spirits.

When Tolstoi and Delianov introduced the draft, elaborated under Katkov's supervision, to the State Council in December 1882, there was still stubborn resistance. The protests focused against the requirement that the examinations should be entrusted to the state-appointed commissions instead of the professors; this way, as Valuev and Golovnin put it, universities ought to be turned from "temples of learning" into "higher police-educational institutions" where both teachers and students would be "subordinated to the abuses of administrative power." Pobedonostsev too went on warning against the strong emphasis on "punitive measures" and refused to support the draft. "In the new statutes I see no benefit but harm for the very principle (of "normalization" at the universities) which has motivated the reform," he wrote to Katkov.[10]

Despite Pobedonostsev's defection, though, the "party of order" proved to be better organized, more determined and, above all, having more influence upon the Tsar than the majority of the State Council. After several direct appeals from the Strastnyi Boulevard, Alexander invited to the decisive deliberations on the issue—the Extraordinary Council held on 24 August 1884, at the Ropsha Palace—only those more or less allied with the publicist. (Of the opponents of the draft, nobody save Pobedonostsev was present.) Thus, except for some minor alterations, the editor pushed through the counter-reform as he wished to have it.[11]

By the new university statute promulgated on 4 September 1884, autonomy was substituted for its very opposite—complete administrative control exercised through the Ministry for Public Instruction and its agents —inspectors, curators and deans. The system introduced was similar to the one in force under Nicholas and Uvarov: deans and rectors were appointed, not elected by professors; inspectors were empowered to supervise every student activity and curators bossed the whole of the university life. In the most symptomatic token of return to the old conditions, students were again obliged to wear uniforms.

"Russian youth was sacrificed to Katkov's personal aims," Professor Chicherin voiced the universal lament in the educated stratum.[12] Students this time came to Strastnyi Boulevard not to applaud but to catcall; yet, the days had long been gone when the "watchdog of autocracy" cared for their sympathy.

* * *

The Moscow publicist could also score irrefutable gains in two other areas which had been attracting his crusading spirit since the 1860s—on the Russian "state nationality" question and on the economic issues.

Unlike Alexander II, his son was all for the Russification of the border-lands; and thus many of bureaucrats who would otherwise have hesitated to subscribe the unsavoury Pobedonostsev-Katkov principles, lost their scruples or docilely followed the official line. The case of moderate Niko-lai Bunge, the Finance Minister, is perhaps most instructive. The man who had been persistently plagued by Katkov for alleged "German cosmopolit-anism," in his memoir "Notes from the grave"[13] obediently parroted the Muscovite doctrine:

> The Emperor Alexander III justly recognized that in Russia the Russian state system should predominate—that is, Russian state power and Russian institutions. . . . Further, the Russian nation-ality should hold sway. . . as should the Russian language as the general state language. Finally, respect for the roots professed by the Russian people and its sovereign should have primacy.[14]

Bunge manifested how he understood it chiefly in the paragraphs where he dealt with the Polish and Baltic questions.

As a method of fighting Polonism, he asked for "the expulsion of the surplus population to the West to the broadest possible extent, while not confusing it with considerations whether it will be good for the immigrant in the new location. We should not forget that immigration has very fre-quently been accompanied by sacrifice and deprivation, and that it would not be wise to display more sympathy for the Polish immigrants going to America than for Russians going to Siberia."[15]

Concerning the development in the Baltic gubernias, the praxis prevalent under Alexander II was condemned, since it allegedly "fostered the awakening of the Eatonian and Latvian nationalities and the creation of a more intellectual class among them, in opposition to the Gemans"; this "proved opposed to the general interests of the state." Only Alexander III again, "was the first to take a firm hand in the matter of the Ostsee question . . . ; in five years the Russian language was made the dominant one in the schools, in business, and in dealings of the local institutions with the local and central authorities."[16]

Aside from the anti-Semitic laws promulgated in 1882, the inspection in the Baltic area ordered by Ignatiev and performed by the keenly nationalist Senator Nikolai Manasein (1882-1883) can be marked as the point of departure. Manasein was not a Katkovite, but in his report, a crucial document on the issue, he closely followed the Muscovite's lead, requesting the government to apply its "firm will" in order to make the use of Russian obligatory and exclusive in administration within two years. Moreover, his recommendations repeated the old desiderata of the Strastnyi Boulevard concerning Church affairs, courts and schools, notably Dorpat University.[17]

Manasein's requirements were embodied in the decree of 14 September 1885—"the most extreme language measure applied to Estland, Livland and Kurland."[18] Simultaneously, Pobedonostsev exhibited his zeal at his worst. Orders concerning mixed Orthodox-Lutheran marriages (obliging their children to become Orthodox), pressues exerted upon the population to change their religion, and expropriation of lands for the Orthodox Church were denounced in the State Council and obtained bad notoriety throughout Europe; Alexander himself sometimes disapproved their brutality.[19] Nothing, however, could stop the fanatic ardor of the "party of order" and its numerous following in the Baltic provinces' apparatus.

In economic policies, too, the slogan "Russia for Russians" had been steadily winning ground; and, yet more importantly for Katkov's authority, his arguments and campaigns not only strongly appealed to the Tsar and the public; it also assured him political and financial support of the powerful business interests. The man who at the outset of his career knew next to nothing about economics, rose even in this field into a leading nationalist ideologue.[20]

The publicist was in principle at one with the government that there was a close correlation between efficacious foreign policy and economic preparedness; and that railway construction was the key to the rise of Tsardom into a modern state capable of competing both militarily and economically with its more advanced rivals. This, however, by no means implied a benign approach to governmental effort. The finance ministers in particular had to suffer constantly as whipping boys in the Strastnyi Boulevard's campaigns against the cosmopolitans allegedly leaving the foreigners to expropriate Russian wealth, to keep her poor and backward, an exporter of grain and importer of manufactured goods.

The railway theme served most often as a point of departure for such a criticism.[21] The editor proclaimed the existing system, when railway companies thought more about speculative profit than about national interest and when the practice of the state subventions favored this, an unhealthy development. Eventually, he pronounced Russia ripe for adopting German model of state-owned railways; that, he claimed, would lead to that optimal state in which "rails coming just after bayonets would accomplish political integration."[22]

Fervently advocating industrialization and particularly the development of heavy industry as the means of national liberation, and at the same time demanding better conditions for peasants, craftsmen and small entrepreneurs, Katkov had after 1878 assailed the Finance Ministry under the banner of radical protectionism.[23]

Urgent fiscal needs following the Turkish war and government's action to reduce the budget deficit helped the Muscovite to tilt the balance in his favor. Confronted by massive criticism, Bunge tried to check it by more liberal taxation policies and better conditions for agricultural credit; three times after 1881 he also raised tariffs on imported goods. But he wrestled with a situation he could not master. State debt amounted to six billion rubles in 1881 and to almost six and a half billion in 1886; the debt payments itself constituted a burden which made financial stability impossible. The Finance Minister was blamed for an unsatisfactory rise in import duties, cuts in expenditures of the war and navy ministries, the abandonment of the paper ruble and heavy borrowing abroad. Finally, the dramatic fall of the ruble and the difficulties of Russian bonds on the international stock market in late 1886 sealed his fate. Bunge's replacement by Vyshnegradskii was generally recognized as both a momentous personal victory of Katkov in a long feud and the triumph of his economic programme.[24]

* * *

Contemporaries had often passed the judgment that in 1881-1887 Katkov was omnipotent and the opinion has been more or less sustained by Professor Zaionchkovskii, an authority undoubtedly possessing the best knowledge of primary sources on Russian domestic policies in the Armed Peace era.[25] Yet, all this must be understood in its proper contexture. There were, naturally, quite distinct limits of the Muscovite's power. He had been terribly effective in expressing and creating the overall mood and in that sense, his activities have left a fatal imprint upon his time and beyond it; he could even prevail upon in matters of crucial significance without broader backing. Yet, he was unable to win the elite for his purpose or silence the liberal criticism; still less could he enforce and animate a consistent totalitarian system.

An important stronghold of the opposition against the "Katkovshchina" survived above all in the State Council with its quite resolute anti-Muscovite majority (Miliutin, Loris-Melikov, Abaza, Nikolai, Polovtsov etc.). Affronted by the constant charges hurled by the Strastnyi Boulevard, State Secretary Polovtsov, with biting irony, suggested to Pobedonostsev that he be replaced by a "person designated by Mr. Katkov" and that the whole Council should be supplanted by the editorial board of the *Moskovskiia vedomosti*[26] [27]; but neither he nor the body he represented were willing to act as a rubber-stamp. Though too weak "to press forward any positive programme of its own or to fill the vacuum that seems to have existed in the government," the State Council managed to hold in check both the Tsar and the "party of order" and reach at least a stalemate of sorts in the battle over the counter-reforms.[28] Defeated on the university statute matter, it succeeded in stemming the ultrareactionary vogue in the contests on the judiciary and zemstvos issues; there, despite almost identical contours of the debate, the final results were different.

In its effort to destroy the judiciary statute of 1864,[29] the Strastnyi Boulevard was again buttressed by Alexander and Tolstoi, who both deeply disliked the principles of an independent bar, trial by jury and the permanent tenure of judges. But the Minister of Justice Nabokov, assisted by the State Council, ably and firmly "declined Katkov's orders"[30] and contrived to preserve the essentials of what the publicist himself had once praised as a great step on the path of modernization of Russia. In his draft of the new statute, Nabokov somewhat limited the rights of the judges and enlarged the power of the ministry in supervising the court, but left the substance of the 1864 reform unimpaired. In a frantic appeal to subvert the proposal, the editor visited the Tsar and prompted Ostrovskii to set forth a counter-project. Finally, Alexander dismissed Nabokov and named Manasein in his place, but on 1 June, 1885 confirmed the original draft.[31]

In the quest for curbing the prerogatives of the zemstvos, the "party of order" had not fared much better.[32] Pazukhin's initiative was effectively seconded by Tolstoi, while Pobedonostsev and Ostrovskii backstepped. The key idea of the Katkov-Pazukhin plan—to appoint a land captain in every district, as a representative of the government with almost dictatorial powers in peasant affairs—was approved only after the publicist's death and in a substantially mellowed form.[33]

The Thunderer could not even unite the ultraconservatives. Already when they were still on friendly terms, Katkov, Pobedonostsev and Tolstoi reminded an observer of the goose, the pike and the crayfish in the Russian fable: Katkov would get excited and loose control, arguing that they had to be more energetic; Tolstoi would not know how to start and continue the affair; the Pobedonostsev would only lament and raise his hands to the sky.[34] Now only the Katkov-Pobedonostsev alliance remained more or less intact, which, however, did not mean that the latter would support the former in some of his crucial battles. Tolstoi assisted the "party of order," but hated its leader, proclaiming him "the sort of swine I don't admit into my presence."[35] Alexander, too, contrary to the widespread opinion, was far from being Katkov's tool. The more self-righteous and obdurate he grew, the more irritated he became over the inroads into the external policy matters which he regarded solely as his own preserve.

Infuriated by Pobedonostev's admonition that he was overshooting the mark and that the "adverse party" should not be constantly provoked by vituperative raids, the editor made all the dignitaries of the "novum regum"—not excluding the ruler—responsible for the incoherence of the policies and the generally unsatisfactory state of affairs. "The adverse party is nothing but a shadow projected by the incompetent government," he contended.[36] He would never have recognized that it was the content of his totalitarian vision itself what even more than the opposition of the liberals and "cosmopolitan" conservatives or pre- varications of his allies posed the decisive limits upon the effectiveness of his sermons.

CHAPTER 24

THE "BOSPHORUS THEME" REVIVED
(1882-1883)

> From the viewpoint of Russian state in-
> terests, there is only one satisfactory solu-
> tion of this question, the one formulated
> in his historic saying of the Tsar Nicholas,
> "We must have the key to our house."
> This key alone will be able to give us com-
> plete security on our southern frontiers.
> A single fortification at the mouth of the
> Bosphorus will take the place of a fleet,
> of an army, of a whole line of fortresses
> necessary today to maintain our coasts
> on the Black Sea in a state of defence.
> Saburov

After the Skobelev affair settled down, foreign observers could note some promising symptoms on the Russian scene. The Tsar made it clear that he took the task of financial recovery in earnest and that the army would not be extempted from the general stringency programme; compared with 1880, military expenditures were reduced by 15 percent.[1] In May 1882, in a patent gesture to placate the disturbed allies and re-affirm the moderate course, Alexander finally appointed Giers as Gorchakov's successor. Soon, however, it became obvious that the extremist initiative had not been ended by the abortive Aksakov-Ignatiev-Skobelev "intrigue."

Two phenomena were pointed out as most telling about the situation. Firstly, the Katkovite ascendancy made the national interest concept more pronounced. In Valuev's words, "Russian principles, Russian strength, Russian people" made the slogans of the day; or, as Ambassador Wolkenstein put it, instead of the Panslav vogue, a "specific Russian, Pan-Russian or Moscow-Katkovite trend" took over in almost absolute mastery."[2] Secondly, in the personal reshuffles following the change of reign, many key positions were taken or re-taken by the extremists.

The enhanced role of the army group, led by the newly appointed Chief of Staff Obruchev, was perceived as being of particular significance; it confirmed that neither the retreat of the mighty Miliutin nor the death of Skobelev had interrupted the rise of the younger, anti-German and adventurist-bent officer generation.

For moderate, conservative St. Petersburg Obruchev was another embodiment of the dangerous, democratic and republican spirit introduced into the armed forces by Miliutin.[3] Before he became the main figure in politico-military planning, Obruchev's past had been much too colourful for traditionalist tastes, indeed. As a young Guards officer, he had belonged to the "Land and Freedom" secret left organization; in 1863, then a Chief-of-Staff in a Guards division, he had refused to take part in the suppression of the Polish uprising. Even when he changed views and turned into a "patriot," reservations against him did not subside. The strong streak of political adventurism sprouted in a restless quest for Russian military triumph at almost any price and risk. He was blamed for "complete diregard" for the catastrophic state of the finances[4] and suspected that by his pronounced pro-French leanings and insistence on achieving more "secure" frontiers (primarily on the Carpathian Mountains) would carry Tsardom to another disaster. Both Alexanders shared this distrust. But Obruchev was protected first by Miliutin and now by his successor, General Peter Vannovskii, who valued him as indispensable for his energy, organizational talents and experience.

Among other military-political appointments, those of the pro-French Admiral Shestakov as Minister for the Navy, Prince Dondukov-Korsakov as Viceroy and Commander-in-Chief in the Caucasus and no less notorious General Cherniaev as Governor General in Turkestan were registered with patent apprehension.[5]

In the Asiatic department of the Foreign Ministry, the cautious Melnikov was replaced by the former Minister in Teheran Zinoviev, a man without scruples, "a veritable villian from a tabloid melodrama," who had been getting on in the world through his allegiances to the Moscow Thunderer and the Asiatic military. When he presented his opinions for the first time to the Ministerial Council, Counts Lamsdorf and Kapnits, Giers' deputies keenly hostile to the extremists, walked out in protest.[6]

* * *

Diplomatic reports from St. Petersburg suggested that even the moderates recognized that they could "draw the sting" of the nationalist pressures solely by "successes in foreign policy." Giers himself indicated to Ambassador Thornton that the governmental would be bound to apply the old tactics of channelling the military fervor to Central Asia.[7] That indeed took place, and we shall dwell on this theme later on. But, the extremists looked for yet more daring enterprises. Only the revision of the Berlin Treaty, Prince "Nicki" Dolgorukii, the military plenipotentiary in Berlin told the Germans, could "preserve the Russian dynasty and save Russia from the otherwise inevitable Panslav or Nihilist revolution"; Eastern Rumelia must be united with Bulgaria and, above all "the two fortresses on the northern end of the Bosphorus" must be given to Tsardom.[8]

The already mentioned Extraordinary Council on 25 August 1881, had given the first clear signal. What was started as a plea for a powerful Black Sea fleet[9] evolved into a renewed bid for mastery in the Straits. This purpose united several hawkish groups—the "General Staff chauvinists,"[10] the Muscovites and the anti-Giers faction in the diplomatic corps.

The Strastnyi Boulevard provided if not the guidance then at least essential inspiration. Comparing English, Austrian and French strivings for acquisition of Ottoman territories—this was the time when Tunisia and Egypt were changing masters—with the meagre gains and passivity observed by St. Petersburg, Katkov revived opposition against the Berlin Treaty system asserting that "if this were to go on, we may well witness the moment when the whole of Turkey will be in alien hands."[11] Commenting on the Egypt crisis (1881-1882), he praised the London cabinet for ignoring European protests and proceeding unflinchingly along the track of conquest. This should be Tsardom's position too: instead of bothering "about that really impossible European concert," it ought to be concerned solely about its own vital interests.[12]

The editor explained what he had in mind in an editorial devoted to Skobelev's demise (on 20 July 1882):

> In the steppes of Central Asia, the White General was 'animated by the thoughts of Bosphorus.' In his letters, he admonished his kinsmen that if Russia failed to 'take the Eastern Question in her hands,' all the sacrifices in Asia would be in vain, since her greatness, security, prosperity, expansion of her trade and industry depends on the control of the Bosphorus. This heritage must be honoured. The Russian frontier is still opened to an attack, the Polish question 'keeps us in a state of siege'; only after the conquest of the Bosphorus may a Russian say in confidence 'finis Polaniae.'[13]

The shift in power balance engendered by the occupation of Egypt, Katkov persisted, could not be counterbalanced in Central Asia only; and the advantage must be taken from the fact that while the London Liberals would not tolerate Austrian encroachments against Turkey, they would certainly be willing to strike a bargain with Tsardom on the Straits issue. The 2 August editorial put it as follows:[14]

> Unquestionably, the Egyptian question cannot be solved separately from the Eastern Question. If England regards this moment convenient to bring to a head her intentions in the Nile Valley, then she will undoubtedly realize that the Bosphorus question has ripened for a final settlement. Mr. Gladstone, by the way, never concealed his belief that the time has come to finish with Turkish rule. . . . With the transfer of Egypt and the Suez Canal into her hands, the Bosphorus has lost its importance for England. And whereas an agreement between Austria and Germany and Mr. Gladstone's cabinet is inconceivable, one between England and Russia is possible, as it was stressed thirty years ago by Emperor Nicholas.

* * *

In December 1882, the issue became the main topic in a top-level foreign policy debate. It was kindled by the traditional extremist hotbed, the Constantinople embassy,[15] when chargé d'affaires Nelidov presented his memoir "On the occupation of the Straits."[16] He argued to the following effect:

> 'The complete and perhaps sudden disintegration of the Ottoman Empire' is already under way and the policy striving for upholding the existing status quo lost its justification; such being the case, Russia is bound by political, military and trade considerations to deliver the fatal blow and occupy the Straits.
>
> Among the three eventualities always contemplated in conjunction with this historical task—(1) war with Turkey, (2) a surprise attack, (3) a peaceful agreement with the Porte—the second appears to be the most feasible. A pertinent military plan has already been elaborated by Lieutenant-Colonel Protopopov in the General Staff; the task of diplomacy now is to make its execution easy and determine the best moment. Preparations 'must start as soon as possible, in utmost secrecy and with the maximum of caution; and the widest contingencies and the most unfavourable and unforeseen circumstances must be computed.' 'A convenient pretext can be found or created at any minute . . . anything can serve as an excuse for intervention'; yet the invitation to Russian troops by the Sultan would be the best outcome. For it, clashes inside the Serail furnish plentiful opportunities; or the Embassy itself can 'prepare such an occasion and so, without much commotion or sacrifice the most valuable trump-card may be put into our hands.' No means are to be spared and the united efforts of the ministries for foreign affairs, war and navy are imperative. It has to be steadily kep in mind that gains will be enormous: after the occupation of the Straits, the Turkish capital and other 'semi-independent remnants' of the Ottoman heritage will be under Russian protectorate, and the Eastern Question be settled for good by a 'free unification of all Slavic nations with Russia.'

Alexander reacted in the most encouraging way. "Everything is written in a very matter-of-fact and persuasive manner. God allows us to live to see that happy and exalting occasion. I am not losing hope that sooner or later it will and must happen. What is most important—not to waste time and miss the opportunity," he noted on the margin of the document.[17] Nelidov was soon promoted to the ambassadorial rank.

The military and diplomatic hawks seemed to be unleashed. Generals Obruchev and Gurko pushed for the action and Vannovskii parroted their pleas. The Navy Minister Shestakov and his crony Modest Novikov, the commander of the Black Sea squadron, were allegedly even more active. "Modest Dmitrievich will conquer Constantinople, will be rewarded with a million, then he will lose this million in a card game and will have to ask for another million—but Constantinople will be ours," Shestakov was supposed to have boasted.[18]

Not unexpectedly, Ambassador Saburov, who had made the seizure his programme, did not stay aloof. So far, his plea—(1) "the Three Emperors' Alliance should be strengthened in order to obtain German consent to the occupation of the Straits and the obligation to keep Austria neutral during the operation," and (2) Austrian neutrality should be cemented by a special agreement on the division of the Balkans[19]—had found no real prop. Suddenly, however, he seemed to receive it from the most important, Strastnyi Boulevard quarters: after a period of emphasis on the Anglo-Russian understanding and cool reserve towards the Austro-German bloc,[20] in the editorial of 11 January 1883, Katkov again praised German loyalty to Russia and, more significantly, criticized St. Petersburg's hesitations to profit "in national interest" from Bismarck's goodwill.[21] We may assume that this was precisely the impulse which, besides the Nelidov memoir, spurred Saburov to a fresh departure. He approached the Wilhelmstrasse with a quite transparent proposition. In the spring, he told the Germans, the Russian leadership would gather at the coronation festivities in Moscow and that would be a perfect occasion to set out for the renewal of the 1881 alliance treaty; a German initiative would be appreciated in this matter, particularly if connected with a statement on the intention "to satisfy Russian ambitions in the East."[22]

The German Chancellor understood the hint perfectly. But while in the past he had often encouraged the Russian Ambassador, this time he reacted with circumspection. The Skobeley episode could not be forgotten; for that, the rising hawkish spirit coupled with the ascendance of such openly pro-French and/or anti-German military figures as Obruchev, Gurko, Shestakov as well as unabated military preparations on the western frontiers created too evident obstacles. Furthermore, during his recent visit Giers spelled out distinctly his wish to keep the Eastern Question frozen. The enquiries made at the Singers' Bridge by Schweinitz confirmed the suspicion of a personal machination. Giers apprised Berlin that Saburov and Nelidov were trying "to awaken the Tsar's interest in the dissolution of the Ottoman Empire and win him for a programme which he would not otherwise have considered." To prevent untoward development, the Foreign Minister suggested, "let sleeping dogs lie" would be the best policy. To this Bismarck and the Austrian statesmen, who were also consulted, readily concurred.[23]

Contrary to all appearances, Saburov failed to muster any significant help. In St. Petersburg, too, the extremist offensive alerted all those favoring a cautious policy. The familiar pattern reappeared: while in Asia the hawks could enjoy a considerable latitude, the prospect of a new Near-Eastern adventure roused a pronounced wariness. Although the evidence is scanty it appears that—apart from a great deal of personal and group rivalries preventing a concerted hawkish front as, for example, that between the Volunteer Fleet organizers and the navy command led by Shestakov[24]—extensive pressure had been exerted upon the Tsar and the armed forces leadership prior to the decisive "coronation confrontation."

Russia had been in serious troubles. Concurrent with failing agricultural exports and industrial depression came the consequences of the anti-Jewish atrocities. The French Rothschild group and the London stock exchange took a lead in what the world called a "Jewish revenge": Tsardom's borrowing abroad was blocked, its securities and ruble exchange rate suffered. It looked like an approaching financial collapse.[25] So, the moderates could argue with much persuasion that military play with fire might "not only be followed by bankruptcy but by the decomposition of the state."[26]

The seemingly overwhelming hawkish bloc disintegrated. "Concerning the naval operation, we are not yet ready. It appears necessary to wait—for one or two short years," Obruchev told Kartsov, when he came to St. Petersburg to solicit the case of the Constantinople clique. Vannovskii and Nelidov intimated the same to him and also his visit at the Strastnyi Boulevard ended in disappointment.[27]

The course followed by the *Moskovskiia vedomosti* in early 1883 confirmed that the editorial of 10 January had been misleading as to the immediate concern and priorities of the Thunderer. His favourable treatment of Germany and the castigation of Russian press organs writing about the possibility of a war between the two Powers[28] were occasioned by the same motives that induced him to intervene against the Aksakov-Ignatiev-Skobelev "intrigue," i.e. by the awareness that Tsardom was in a too desperate state, both politically and economically, to indulge in any risky action. The Bosphorus theme lost for him all its attractiveness. What made him anxious at that moment, apart from security considerations, was the obvious decline Russian influence was undergoing in the Balkan principalities. Reviewing unfavourable developments in Bulgaria and Serbia, he had to come to a painful conclusion that only the tiny, isolated Montenegro could be rated as a trustworthy ally[29]; and, against this alarming trend he recognized a sole remedy—combating Austrian policies.[30]

The position taken by the Tsar lay near to that of the Moscow editor. While he had approved Nelidov's memoir with its arguments close to his heart, Saburov's reasoning again mostly irritated him. "That is definitely impossible," "that we cannot permit," he wrote commenting on the proposition to divide the Balkans.[31] If the Three Emperors' Alliance were to be renewed, then it should be done solely in its negative, status quo meaning. So, Giers might announce that "it is imperative to avoid anything that excites nerves and raises suspicions of our intentions, which remain unchanged."[32]

* * *

Saburov succeeded in just one thing: the Tsar assented that the Moscow "coronation debate" would take place. But only five persons—Giers, Jomini, Miliutin, Lobanov and Saburov—were invited to participate; and this selection was scarcely propitious for the extremist plea.

In the discussion held on 1 June 1883, Saburov completely reversed the premises he used in 1879-1880. Now he maintained that "this entente was more favorable to Germany than to Russia"; and "for that reason a renewal of the treaty ought not to be brought about except on the basis of perfect equality, . . . on the condition of giving both Powers entire freedom, the one in the East, the other in the West . . . ." Germany as well as Austria-Hungary should recognize Russia's right to dominate the Straits and agree in advance "to our acting according to our own desires in the East."

All the other participants, however, objected that Bismarck would never give his consent to such a modification and urged for upholding the treaty on the former status quo basis. Lobanov proclaimed it the best guarantee of peace; Miliutin emphasized its utility in preventing Austrian expansion. As to the Straits question, Saburov was reminded by his opponents that the preconditions stipulated in Livadia in 1879— i.e. financial equilibrium, adequate Black Sea naval force, German and Austrian favourable neutrality—were still unfulfilled. They argued:

> Without sufficient funds for war and without a fleet...shall we be able...to finish with Constantinople and the Straits, in the face of European hostility? And if we could not do it simultaneously (with the German war 'to finish with France')...would Germany at any later time aid us, in good faith, to realize our Eastern programme?

Ostensibly a compromise, the conclusion of the "coronation debate" purported a victory for Giers: "if we contented ourselves with renewing our arrangements for three years, we should be gaining time, indispensable for our preparations and we should be fortifying the status quo...."[33]

"Saburov is the most enterprising of all our diplomats. But otherwise, the affair is postponed. From the military viewpoint, we are not ready," Nelidov confirmed the setback to Kartsov.[34]

The disintegration of the extremist camp aggravated in the sequel. Many beat a hasty retreat, including Nelidov himself. A depressed young hawk exasperated:

> He was disposed to win easy political laurels and please Katkov. But he would not risk his position for the sake of that. When he saw, during the coronation, that Giers managed to persuade the Emperor that it was premature to think about the Bosphorus, Nelidov changed colours, ordered us to conceal the dangerous memoranda...and under various pretexts turned his back on those with whom he had only yesterday shared his views.[35]

To make their despair even deeper, the failure in the Bosphorus scheme intertwined with the mortifying defeat which the proponents of a Near-Eastern offensive suffered in the crucial Balkan position—in the Bulgarian Principality.

CHAPTER 25

THE BULGARIAN DISILLUSION:
THE FIRST PHASE
(1879-1883)

> I shall not enlarge on this subject, but I
> know that by no means should we expect
> gratitude from the Slavs; we should prepare
> for this in advance. . . . To begin with,
> they will unfailingly announce to them-
> selves and convince themselves—tacitly if
> not aloud—that they owe Russia no gratitude
> whatever; that, on the contrary, at the time
> of the conclusion of peace, they barely
> saved their skin from Russia's ambition
> by the intervention of the European concert,
> and, had Europe not intervened, Russia,
> having taken them from the Turks, would have
> promptly swallowed them with a view
> of expanding her borders and creating
> a great Panslav Empire in order to make
> Slavs slaves of the greedy, cunning and
> barbaric Great-Russian race.
> Dostoevskii

> Prince Alexander, as it seems to us, is
> quite correct in understanding and de-
> termining the relations of his country

towards our homeland. By doing so, he also distinguishes himself sharply from his neighbor, the Serbian King Milan. It remains only to wish that the salutary endeavors of the Bulgarian ruler be frankly supported by the Bulgarian and our governments and by the public of both countries.
Aksakov

It is difficult to accept that I am a foreign creature. It is difficult to be one. A Russian diplomatic agent, a Russian minister in Bulgaria—they are in fact the Prince's gouvernants and uncles. But de jure the first of them is only a representative of the Russian government, the second a servant of the Prince. This double role requires extraordinary tact. The Prince is to be governed but he has not to feel it.
Aksakov

The Black Sea, the Bosphorus and the Dardanelles must be ours; there lies our future. Bulgaria is (also) our case. If the Prince will not follow the correct path, he is going to be overthrown in six months. We must fight against Austria for our existence.
Domontovich (a high-ranking Russian officer in Bulgaria)

Your Highness, you take everything too seriously. No Russian officer is looking upon you as on the supreme commander. We are the outposts and fight only for Russian interests. Your displeasure is the best recommendation I can have in Russia.
Timmler (another high-ranking Russian) to Prince Alexander

In its first years of existence, the Bulgarian Principality was generally considered a safe Russian preserve.

The protectorate-like control was most apparent in the armed forces. Owing to an unwritten understanding, the post of the War Minister was reserved for a Russian general; and Russians also held every commanding position down to company, cavalry squadron and battery levels. Less auspicious, but still weighty was their presence in the civilian apparatus. The young Prince Alexander of Battenberg, a grateful and devoted worshipper of his Romanov uncle, was viewed as a mere tool destined to act in accordance to the wishes of the Russian military and diplomatic representatives; and so were the ministers, often people with a long record of Russian service, connections and education. Concerning the populace, there was a well founded notion that the gratitude would overshadow any ugly experience, such as that undergone during the Cherkasskii administration. Indeed, this was still the time when a Bulgarian considered any anti-Russian idea sacrilegious, regarded Alexander II a deputy of God on earth endowed by a special grace, and when he could not imagine the existence of the Principality without its Slavic saviours.[1]

However, it was precisely in Bulgaria where the process of disillusion already observed in Greece and Serbia, took its most dramatic form.

Dostoevskii, disturbed by the conduct of Russian administrators and soldiers, cautioned his kinsmen before what he called "the Slav's ingratitude":

> If Russia wanted to escape the fatal conflict, she 'must never think of enlarging her territory at the expense of the Slavs, of annexing them politically, of carving Russian provinces out of their lands,' because 'even now all the Slavs, much like all Europe, suspect her of such aspirations. Only by providing the Slavs from the very beginning with as much political freedom as possible, by withdrawing herself from tutelage and supervision of any kind . . . may (she) thereby rid herself of the dreadful troubles and commotions of enforcing this tutelage and her political influence and keep the prospect of ultimate unification around her alive for the future.'[2]

Despite the bad crop harvested by Cherkasskii, though, the warnings of the great novelist were ignored. It took less than two years and Petko Karavelov, the deposed Prime Minister, denounced Russia exactly as Doestoevskii predicted and by 1883 her prestige already lay in shambles.

Aside from the deeply-rooted reflexes in handling "liberated peoples," the absence of a clear-cut policy, or rather the existence of two different policies, reflecting Russian inner divisions, accelerated the process. The military headed by Miliutin advocated an orientation toward the "Young," now unified in the Liberal party; the Ministry for Foreign Affairs and the bulk of the Moscow party, suspicious of the radical Bulgarian intelligentsia, urged support for the Prince and the Conservatives, the successors of the "Old."

Due to the authority Miliutin enjoyed in the last years of Alexander II's reign, the pro-Liberal course prevailed. Autocratic Tsardom had been instrumental in introducing the so-called Tarnovo constitution, one of the most "republican" in the 19th century Europe. A nationalist diplomat explained the rationale of this move as follows:

> The constitution was noted for an unfettered radical and democratic character, putting the executive power into full dependence on a one-Chamber Assembly elected by universal suffrage. Yet that was precisely its utility from our Russian standpoint. The decisive influence of the National Assembly stood for the assurance that the German Prince would not bring Bulgaria into a junction with the West.'[3]

But the system would not work. The two Bulgarian parties were engaged in a violent power struggle, paralyzing the administration; and instead of operating as a stabilizing and mediating force, Russian personnel merely exacerbated the tensions by behaving as if in a conquered country and treating Alexander of Battenberg with few scruples. "The scum of the whole of Russia has. . .taken refuge here and has tained the entire (life of the) country," the latter complained[4] and such also was the feeling of an increasing number of his subjects.

Observing the Russian misdemeanor and the strange situation where the diplomatic agent Davydov assisted the Prince loyally while the War Minister Parensov and the military attaché Colonel Shepelev used the Liberals to undermine his position, Western statesmen tended to explain it simply as a continuation of the "second round policy." In Bulgaria, Haymerle affirmed,

> the Prince is left to the mercy of officials and improvised politicians who receive their instructions from other sources than from the

Ministry for Foreign Affairs . . . . The conspiracies of the Moscow Panslavs and certain military men who went in former times to seek their fortune in Serbia, recommence there under another form.[5]

This, however, did not exactly reflect the true condition; at least not yet. When the Prince appealed to his Romanov uncle against the liberal-constitutionalist trend, both Katkov and Aksakov unreservedly stood on his side. The Thunderer castigated the Miliutin party:

Why was it necessary to raise the question of limitation and the weakening of (the Prince's) power in a country where this power had heretofore been absent and should rather be established and strengthened? By providing the Principality with the farce of a constitution and of a National Assembly, and not by a strong monarchical authority, the St. Petersburg officials (i.e. the War Minister) must carry all the blame for the Bulgarian troubles.[6]

Alexander II was quite annoyed with the cul-de-sac and inwardly must have shared the reservations raised by his nephew and the Muscovites; nonetheless, he let Miliutin deal with the problem. So, although the latter eventually recognized that the drunkard Parensov behaved as an "utterly tactless and prejudiced man"[7] and the three leading Russian representatives —Parensov, Shepelev and Davydov—were replaced in early 1880 in quick succession, the system remained unaltered. To change it, the military maintained, "would mean to play into the hands of the Austrians and other enemies of the Slavs and ourselves"; and they even impressed upon the Tsar that the Bulgarian stalemate was engendered solely by the feud between the Conservative-led government and the Liberal-controlled Assembly and that it would disappear once the Liberals were given governmental responsibility.[8]

Contrary to these allegations, neither the Liberal cabinets of Dragan Tsankov and Petko Karavelov brought more stability into Bulgarian politics nor made the Russian elite any happier. They drastically purged the state apparatus of their opponents and gave some positions to their friends from the Russian revolutionary emigration; they proposed to replace the army by a militia with elected officers and "commanded" by a commission of the Assembly; and, because of the conservative allegiances of most ecclesiastics, they turned against the Church. As a result, the Holy Synod appealed to the Tsar to protect Bulgarian co-religionists against "Nihilists, terrorists, Jacobins," the Moscow press continued its sharp polemics against "unnatural" constitutionalism and the Singers' Bridge moved to investigate émigré activites in the Principality. The split among the Russians on the spot did not cease either; now, while the new political agent Kumani followed Miliutin's line, Parensov's successor General Ehrnrooth, a conservative Finn, sided with the Prince and affirmed with him that the root of the evil lay in the constitution, which must be modified "in order to put an end to this intolerable state of things."[9]

* * *

In early 1881, tensions culminated in a Liberal proposal of constitutional amendments, which, if implemented, would have deprived the Prince of all political power. "Now, when I have realized that a crisis is bound to come, my aim must be to bring it about as soon as possible," wrote the young man on the throne. The assassination of Alexander II provided him with a perfect cause. When they met after the funeral, the new Tsar clearly showed his dislike for Miliutin's experiment; and travelling from St. Petersburg through Berlin and Vienna, Battenberg even received direct encouragement. "I also consider it necessary to find some remedy against the existing licence and the predominance of the radical parties, if the Principality is to exist. Why not risk a coup d'état, if you can rely on your troops?" Bismarck told him.

Back in Sofia, the Prince abandoned his last doubts. Ehrnrooth threatened to resign if the Liberals were not routed. So, on 9 and 23 May 1881, proclamations were published announcing that the constitution had been suspended and an interim government led by Ehrnrooth appointed to prepare elections to the Grand National Assembly; in case this body were to refuse his conditions—including extraordinary powers for seven years—he would abdicate, the Prince warned.[10]

In the name of conservative Russia, Katkov hailed the "decisive attempt of the Prince to fulfill the obligation he had accepted with the Bulgarian crown" and announced the end of a course which had left the Principality "unprotected against our liberalism." The constitution, he reiterated, was yet "another blunder of Russian diplomacy"; copied from "vile textbooks," it brought into existence "political parties alien to the national spirit," and their "furious and senseless struggle" produced but chaos.[11]

That the Bulgarian Liberals tried to appeal for help not only to Russian "friends of the Slavs" (Aksakov, Ignatiev, Katkov), but also to the leading European anti-conservative politicians (Gambetta, Gladstone), put them in the eyes of the Tsar in the worst possible light. "These Liberals are nothing else than Socialists," he wrote: "the Bulgarian people will, I am sure, support the Prince." And he decided that Tsardom ought to interpose to that effect. A governmental proclamation issued on 11 June condemned the "lust of dangerous agitators" and exhorted the Bulgarians to "keep their unbreakable bonds with the Prince," who is a "warrant of true well-being." The notorious Khitrovo, appointed a head of the Sofia agency, received a directive to assist Battenberg "without reservations."

Khitrovo duly accompanied the Prince on his electoral tour and harangued the populace to rally behind the new regime; while Ehrnrooth divided the Principality into five military districts each under a Russian commissary who had to strictly supervise the voting. The Bulgarians, obedient to the Tsar and the Prince and obviously tired of Liberal misrule, voted for the Conservative candidates backing the programme of extraordinary powers. On 13 July 1881, the Grand National Assembly convened at Sistova and unanimously and without discussion endorsed it.[12]

* * *

Despite the goodwill of the Tsar and the Muscovites toward the Prince, and the anti-liberal character of the "novum regnum," the old divergencies reappeared soon. Khitrovo had dutifully accomplished his task given to him for the electoral campaign; but after the Sistova assembly he dispatched a memorandum clearly indicating that he would resist the policies just inaugurated. Although their methods were distasteful, the agent claimed, the Liberals served Russian purposes better than their opponents would do; so, Tsardom should quickly escape from the "abnormal and dangerous position" in which it had been entangled by backing the coup.[13]

In order to enforce the dissolution of the "abnormal and dangerous" bonds, Khitrovo activated the highly controversial railway question.[14]

Knowing that the Conservatives, connected with the well-to-do merchant and landowning stratum pinned their hopes on the economically advantageous Austrian project (the Vakarel-Tsaribrod line), he alerted the leading Russians in the Bulgarian administration—acting Interior Minister Colonel Römlingen, War Minister General Krylov and others—to push hard for an exclusive concession to be granted to their kinsmen, Struve. And despite the fact that St. Petersburg disapproved his action, creating serious complications for Russo-Austrian relations, and in spite that the Prince and the Conservatives begged him for a compromise, he would not relent. Because General Ehrnrooth had been recalled, the agent could for some time proceed unhindered.

It again showed that the intense anti-German and anti-Austrian feeling, centered on the person of Battenberg, had not been limited to the "patriotic" Russian officers only. Whatever the young man might do, he was a "German" and thus a suspect. Returning to the worst practices from Parensov's time, Khitrovo used every occasion to insult, slander and intimidate him. His "brutal rudeness and ruthlessness even shocked and disgusted many Russians serving in the Principality"; as an Austrian diplomat remarked ironically, he could not think of a better ally to work against Tsardom's cause.[15]

With the open involvement in the Bosnian insurrection (1881-1882)—he was the main organizer of the anti-Austrian "volunteer action" besides Aksakov[16]—Khitrovo turned an utter liability for St. Petersburg. Worse still, he made the split of the Moscow party on the Bulgarian issue, that peculiar feature of the period 1879-1883, as visible as ever. When Battenberg arrived in May 1882 in Russia to enlist support against the hostile clique, the old capital gave him an enthusiastic welcome. In the Kremlin, he was visited by many delegations, and Katkov and Aksakov hailed him as a "wise leader of the Bulgarian people," a "living symbol of Russian victory over five centuries of Bulgarian bondage." Alexander III too demonstrated that he trusted his cousin more than his own subjects operating in Sofia. So, Khitrovo, Römlingen, Krylov and other officials and officers most compromised in the intrigues against the Prince had to leave their posts.[17]

* * *

Although so much pointed to the opposite, however, the pattern set by Parensov and Khitrovo was soon to prevail completely and unify the Muscovites with the military and diplomatic hawks on that basis. On the other hand, the fateful condition was irrevocably created against which Dostoevskii had warned so earnestly: not only were the Russians deeply involved in Bulgarian domestic affairs, but by their heavy-handed interference condemned themselves to antagonize each of the major political forces in the country. While increasingly hostile towards the Prince and the Conservatives, they were unable to reestablish a workable alliance with the Liberals, harmed beyond repair by the 1881 coup.

During his Russian talks, the Prince wished to have back the loyal Ehrnrooth, but Katkov and Aksakov, on whom Giers prudently shifted this sensitive matter,[18] made a different choice. They entrusted the task of "establishing law and order in Bulgaria" to two generals with Central-Asian experience, scarcely suitable for the Balkan principality—Leonid Sobolev (as the Prime Minister) and Alexander Kaulbars (as the War Minister). Nothing is known of the motives and circumstances which determined the choice; at any rate, Sobolev in particular, who had served in Bukhara and then led the Asiatic department of the General Staff, went to administer Bulgaria as if with the intention of making it just another khanate.

Shortly upon his arrival in Sofia, the General had a highly illuminating conversation with a French visitor. Pointing at a dossier on his table, he confided: "You see, this is a collection of laws and directives I issued when I was in charge of organizing (the protectorate in) Bukhara. So I have at hand everything I need in the Principality. I never expect any trouble to occur. . . ."[19]

Sobolev started precisely where Khitrovo had stopped—by reopening the railway question.

The Bulgarian Conservatives still strove for a compromise. In a proposal set forth by them in June 1882, they suggested that both the "Russian" and the "Austrian" line be built simultaneously, but, because of the enormous burden the first one would impose on the half-empty Principality's treasury[20] asked St. Petersburg for financial assistance. The chasm, however, could not be overcome. While the Russian government, itself under enormous financial strain, would not help, Sobolev resolved to go ahead with the "Russian line" at any price, i.e. to squeeze the necessary funds from Bulgarian taxpayers.[21]

When the National Assembly convened in December 1882, the feud between the generals and the Conservatives was brought into the open. Sobolev blocked the budget and demanded that a new Ministry for Public Works, with responsibilities covering railway construction, be set up under antoher Russian, Prince Khilkov; the Conservative-controlled Assembly and State Council responded by calling for the abolition of the universally detested dragoon corps, a mounted gendarmerie organized after the coup along the Russian (Cossack) model and commanded by the Russians. Then, two events took place which drove the contest to a razor's edge and prompted the Prime Minister to look for a Bukharan-type solution: in February, the Ministry for Public Works was established, but instead of Khilkov, Conservative leader Nachovich got the post; in March, Exarch Iosif in the name of Bulgarian Holy Synod removed the pronouncedly pro-Russian Metropolitan Meleti and replaced him by Grigori, an ally of the Conservatives.[22]

Determined to destroy his opponents and become the master of the country, Sobolev had two powerful cards to play with. The first was offered to him by the Liberals, blinded by their lust for power and the thirst to punish the Prince and the Conservatives for the 1881 coup; although the General had earlier struck them with a draconic electoral law and had proclaimed his task to be to "put an end to their odious intrigues," a vague promise to reintroduce the Tarnovo constitution seemed to suffice for their complicity.[23] The second card delivered the Prince by his timidity.

The conduct of Battenberg had been all the time mainly moulded by the fear of being accused in St. Petersburg and Moscow of ingratitude. Whatever he might have thought about them, he had almost always sided with the generals: he had sponsored Sobolev's rail programme, tolerated Kaulbars' purge of "unreliables" in the army, left the dragoon corps intact. Over Bulgarian protests and warnings, he had responded to the effect that "Russia is the only country that has shown kindness to Bulgaria and continues to show it."[24] By yielding to the generals, he finally (on 12 March 1883) induced the three leading Conservatives—Nachovich, Stoilov and Grekov—to resign from the government.

Thereby, Sobolev could see his essential purpose attained. The new, "non-party" cabinet he formed was with full justification characterized as that of "Governor General with a group of puppets";[25] three Russians (Sobolev, Kaulbars and Chilkov, who got thus at last the Ministry for

Public Works) were seconded by four Bulgarians known as mere Russian clients.

* * *

So, the sad net result of the "extraordinary powers regime" introduced by the coup was that the Prince gave himself up to the mercy of foreign protectors. In a long memoir the three resigned Conservative ministers captured well the harsh realities of the "dictatorship of the two (generals)":

> Every Bulgarian who has dealt with them resents the fact that these two aliens venture to behave in their homeland with scorn towards everything that patriotism holds great and sacred. The open preference for everything that is Russian and everything that comes from Russia, the appointment of Russians to such duties which Bulgarians could perform better, the sending of our young officers to Russia while (new) Russian officers are brought in daily—these are the reasons of the constantly growing dissatisfaction with the Russians.
>
> 'The arrogance they display towards Bulgarians is so irritating that persons who have to deal with them hate them and this hatred can easily be directed towards the whole nation they represent. . . . The generals wish to introduce a Russian-type administration, with officials educated in Russian-tradition; . . . to proceed to the construction of the projected railway without asking the Assembly for consent . . .'; they try to take over every branch of the state administration and already have all the armed forces under their control; they intend to drive the Prince into a position where he will be compromised before his subjects and thus make him fully dependent on their will.

The triumvirate agreed that the "national ideal" of unification could not be achieved "without Russian help and vigorous cooperation." They affirmed, however, that the present moment imposed different priorities. The situation could be saved if the Prince discontinued the policy of permanent retreats, called the Assembly into session, took over the lead of the national movement and—in the event the generals refused to renounce their dictatorial role—demanded their resignation.[26]

Battenberg was well aware that the establishment of a protectorate-type government would only encourage Sobolev to go further, to have a sort of Bukharan khan on the throne, yet resorted to his usual device: during the forthcoming coronation festivities in Moscow he hoped to obtain similar assistance as he had received against Khitrovo. "It is natural that the Bulgarians wish to get rid of Russian or any other kind of slavery, but a burning hatred now flared up and they forgot how much she (Russia) had done for them," he maintained.[27] And in order to make himself blameless in the eyes of the alleged benefactors, he entrusted the regency for the time of his absence to Kaulbars.

The young man headed for a truly hard lesson. No more fanfare awaited him in the Russian old capital. Among dozens of celebrities present at the coronation, he was treated as the proverbial poor relative. Worse still, whereas Sobolev and his clients were received by the Tsar without delay, he in vain asked for audience. This proved to be a part of an open complot against him. During his absence, Kaulbars had organized municipal elections in Sofia in a way which had assured Liberal victory. Now Suknarov, the newly appointed mayor, came to Moscow with a "counter-deputation" which demanded that a new ruler be given to Bulgaria—Prince Waldemar of Denmark, another Romanov relative. The official delegation led by Metropolitan Simeon was told by Giers that "the Conservative party has disappointed the expectations of the Russian government and hence cannot count upon our support." The Foreign Minister, according to Schweinitz's testimony, considered Battenberg written off and found it politic to side with his enemies; and when the Prince protested against the preference given to the "deputation of revolutionaries" he told him in a rage: "You no longer have the rigth to give orders in Bulgaria, Kaulbars is the regent!" Visiting the Strastnyi Boulevard, the Prince had to learn that he could not expect further favors from that quarter, either.[28]

To be sure, not every boat had yet been burnt. In his editorials, Katkov was still circumspect. He confessed lacking orientation "in this chaos" and conceded that "Russian generals are good in war but whether they are so good in peace we simply do not know"; having obviously in mind the Serbian experience, he advised that "petty misunderstandings between the Bulgarians and some Russians in the Bulgarian service should be forgotten."[29] This, most importantly, turned out to be the Tsar's attitude too. When the Prince in the end of the sojourn "forced his way unbidden" to his suite, he showed him allegedly even more than the usual benevolence.

According to Battenberg's account, related by Corti, the Russian ruler "assured the Prince of his goodwill and was so encouraging that the latter poured out unreservedly his story of the troubles caused by the generals in Bulgaria. Alexander III listened quietly, appeared to agree with him, and finally they came to an understanding whereby the generals were to stay on, but, on the Prince's own request, Ehrnrooth was to be appointed as his Adjutant General and adviser. In addition, the Prince was to convey the Tsar's orders to Kaulbars and Sobolev to moderate their behaviour and was once again to entrust a Conservative cabinet with power."[30]

Nonetheless, the action set off by Sobolev was going on. Two moves were undertaken to assure Bulgarian financial enslavement. The first one —the transfer of the whole reserve fund of the Principality into a St. Petersburg bank—failed owing to desperate resistance of the Prince. The other, an agreement on the so-called occupation debt, however, could not be prevented. Signed on 16 July 1883, it obliged the Principality to pay for its liberation more than 25 million francs, in two-million annual installments. Sobolev wrote in triumph:

> The occupation fund 'will be the material tie which will for twelve and a half years, in a certain degree determine Russo-Bulgarian relations. And then it will be Eastern Rumelia's turn. When it is unified with Bulgaria, the Russian government will forward new demands, for another 25 million francs . . . .' The money obtained will be used for furthering politico-military objectives: establishing secondary schools where an entire generation will be educated in Russian or rather Panslav spirit'; sponsoring the journals and literary works propagating these ties between the two countries; building up a strong Black Sea fleet—'briefly, to create a (Russian) force near the Straits.'[31]

Instead of Ehrnrooth, the Tsar was persuaded by Giers to send to Sofia another hawkish heavyweight, Ionin, as an extraordinary envoy to secure a proper settlement.

* * *

Heretofore, Battenberg had been contemplating abdication rather than resistance to the Russians. But when, in summer 1883, he returned after a long absence to Sofia, he appeared to be ready to espouse the national cause. What swayed him most we do not know: it might have been the disgrace he had recently undergone in Moscow followed by the Tsar's unfulfilled promise to end Ehrnrooth; or his recent talks with Austrian statesmen, who intimated him that a broad front to resist Russian encroachments had been in the offing; or the tumultous welcome the population, tired of the Russians, had given him; or the rapprochement between the Conservatives and the Liberals on an "anti-Sobolev" basis.[32] At any rate, bitter experience had finally taught the young man that it would be less humiliating and safe for him to return to constitutional rule than to live under tutelage and hope just for the protection of his imperial cousin. He made the move which the Conservative leaders had recommended him in their March memorandum: he summoned the Assembly to an extraordinary session. The retification of the agreements of the occupation debt and with Austria-Hungarian railways,[33] as everybody knew, were a mere pretext: the body ought to vote non-confidence in the generals.

Alexander III was undoubtedly honest with the Prince and his letter written on 14 July testifies that he had conceived the Ionin mission as that of appeasement:

> I need not assure you that I have your interests at mind and I consider them inseparable from those of Bulgaria and Russia. . . . I hope we shall have your cooperation in working out a clearly defined and decisive policy, from which all personal intrigue and misunderstanding will be excluded and that we may in this way achieve your objective. That is (the task of) Ionin's mission which has a definite time limit. I think that it will meet your wishes and I count on your loyal cooperation. I beg of you, my dear cousin, to believe in my sincere, cordial feelings toward you.[34]

But, being too simple-minded to understand the implications of his subjects' constant schemings, the Tsar quite naturally perceived the convocation of the Assembly as a brazen abuse of confidence and his rage was boundless. The incident inevitably had enormous consequences. From then on, it was to be his unshakable belief that all the troubles were due to a "base intrigue" of Battenberg; and the almost neurotic hatred of him was to serve as the most powerful instrument the extremists had at their disposal.

It immediately found its resonance in Ionin's Sofia performance,[35] which turned out to be "something unseen and unheard of in the annals of diplomacy.[36]

Shortly upon his arrival, on 24 August, the extraordinary envoy delivered the Prince an "energetic protest" from the Tsar, who condemned the convocation of the Assembly as an "overtly hostile act towards Russia and a direct insult to his person." Then, in a form of an ultimatum, he demanded what constituted the gist of the Russian plan for the settlement: that save the approval of the budget and recently concluded conventions "no further debate of any kind would be allowed"; that the rule of the generals would be retained in its present form for at least another year; and that a commission would be set up to prepare a revision and re-introduction of the constitution. Ionin said

> The 'Tsar gave you extraordinary powers and it is he who now takes them away, because you made wrongful and fraudulent use of them.' The ultimatum must be accepted without delay; there will not be and cannot be any consession. 'If anyone has to leave it will not be the Russian ministers, but, if necessary, Your Highness. . . . Do not try to draw Europe into the affair. . . . With Europe, we have innumerable methods to deal.'[37]

Unfortunately, we are in no position to depict adequately the following dramatic days. This concerns above all the complex stance of the Liberal leaders, men with inordinate personal ambition and conceit, who fancied to play the umpires between the Russians and the Prince/Conservative bloc. Undoubtedly, being approached by Ionin and impressed by his dictatorial conduct, legitimized by the Tsar himself, also those among them who otherwise would be willing to go against the generals again hesitated in their choice. It showed in the second audience the envoy had with the Prince on 30 August. Any attempt to remove Sobolev and Kaulbars, the Russian said, would be responded by 125 Liberal bureaus ready for counter-action. "In that case I will not be a Prince here; if I cannot order my ministers I had better leave Sofia," Battenberg protested. "As it pleases you," the diplomat retorted.[38]

Highly pessimistic about the Liberals, the young ruler had in the meantime sought to appease St. Petersburg and/or win Western support. But he failed in both. From the capital on the Neva, his emissary Stoilov returned empty-handed; London, Vienna and Berlin, despite the promises obviously given to the Prince during his many visits there, preferred not to irritate the Tsar and remained non-committant.[39] So, on 1 September, feeling deserted and scared that Kaulbars would engineer an army coup, Battenberg capitulated and accepted the ultimatum. As he told a British diplomat, he obliged himself moreover "not to sanction any law, not sign any decree without the consent of their (Russian) ministers, not refuse any measure which they may consider necessary."[40]

While Battenberg recognized the Russians to be "the masters of the situation," however, something went very wrong in the negotiations betweem them and the Liberals. Allegedly, Sobolev imprudently disclosed to Tsankov that their real aim was not to reintroduce the constitution but to establish a ten-year protectorate. In any event, the leader of the moderates came to a conclusion that it would be safer to go with the Conservatives and the Prince after all, because the Russians would make Bulgaria their province and the West might condone it.[41]

Although the Prince feared a Russo-Liberal trap and did not believe Tsankov's assurance that he would administer the generals a "death blow," the counteraction was eventually agreed on the night of 15-16 September[42] and the key man in the game honoured his promise. When the Assembly opened its sessions on 16 September, the Russian ministers were exposed to repeated shocks. First, the newly elected Liberal deputies took the oath which implied that they recognized the extraordinary powers of the Prince. Then, on 18 September, a joint Conservative-Liberal commission was entrusted to compose the answer to the throne address; and the answer, already prepared was read immediately:

> We, the representatives of the people, animated by the most humble devotion to the person of Your Highness, request to restore the Tarnovo constitution by means of a manifesto and to indicate at the same time which points are to be examined and altered.

Sobolev and Kaulbars in their government banks were "speechless and white with rage." They found their voices only after Tsankov rose and expressed his approval. "Rascals! Swines! Perjured rabble," they shouted, leaving the chamber amidst the general amusement of the deputies. The whole Assembly then went to the Palace and the Prince solemnly promised to comply with the plea.[43]

The brave generals suddenly lost their courage. They nearly begged for forgiveness and Ionin in vain exhorted them to stay firm.[44] On 19 September they tendered their resignation upon receiving corresponding instructions from St. Petersburg. Frantic though they must have been about what was clearly the most signal Russian political defeat after the Berlin Congress, the policymakers on the Neva were at that moment too intimidated by the tension on the western frontier and by threatening financial catastrophe to contemplate any swift revenge.

CHAPTER 26

NEW FEARS: THE TENSIONS OF 1882-1883

At this minute the essence of the Eastern problem comes down to an alliance of Germany with Austria, plus Austrian seizures in Turkey which are encouraged by Prince Bismarck. We can, and, of course, will protest only in some extreme cases. However, so long as these two nations are united, what can we do without incurring very grave risks? . . . In a word, let us only wait and refrain from meddling—even if we are invited to meddle. Just as soon as their discord comes to a crash, the "political equilibrium" will crack, and then the Eastern Question will at once be solved. We should only have to chose the opportune moment, like at the time of the Franco-Prussian slaughter, and we should suddenly declare, as we then declared concerning the Black Sea: "We do not wish to recognize any Austrian seizures in Turkey." And all seizures will instantly vanish, perhaps together with Austria herself. In this way we shall catch up with everything which ostensibly, for the time being, we let slip.

Dostoevskii

In a circular of 18 August 1883, another highly significant programmatical document elaborated at the Singers' Bridge in the post-Crimean
era, Giers set forth the principles which should guide Russian foreign
policy in the years to come and make the victory achieved over the extremists in the "coronation debate" of a durable character.

Both Alexander II and Alexander III, wrote the Foreign Minister, proclaimed internal improvement and peace the fundamental political principle. But these principles were not applied consistently, albeit the experience after 1856 confirmed their soundness and indicated the path
which ought to be followed:

1. We should not interefere actively in European affairs and instead
   let the dissensions and rivalries develop, which have been inevitably surging between the Powers as long as they are not united in
   their common hatred against us.
2. While waiting, we should expand our internal forces to be in
   readiness to act at any moment, either to prevent European complications altering the balance dangerously for us, or to profit
   from these complications to satisfy our proper interests.

Proceeding from this moderate interpretation of Russian national interest to current tasks, Giers stated that the present reign had "the sole aim
of maintaining the state of peace as long as possible"; and from this viewpoint, he also explained Russia's allegiance to the Three Emperors' Alliance:

That is why the Imperial government has joined the entente established between Germany and Austria. Our adherence has given it a
negative and defensive character which has blunted the edge that was
ultimately directed against us and made it, for the moment, a guarantee of peace. In other words, it guarantees us against Germany
and protects us from immediate conflict with Austria.

Although the Vienna cabinet "obliged itself to slow down its march
of conquest in the Balkan peninsula," the minister recognized the contradictory character of Austrian and Russian interests. Nothing can prevent
Austria's "commercial and industrial pressures as well as Catholic propaganda"; and "the railroad construction to Constantinople and Salonika

she (Austria) pursues . . . will be a powerful means of influence." He also stressed the dangers which the Serbian and Bulgarian questions presented for the relations between the two Powers. Nonetheless, Giers maintained, there was no other way to safeguard Russian position save in the "development of our commercial ties with these countries . . . fostering the bonds of sympathy which unite us with the (Near-) Eastern Slavs, and in bringing the Sultan to a rapprochement with us." The mutual frictions rendered it impossible to establish intimacy between St. Petersburg and Vienna, but the trend towards confrontation should be barred. "The status quo of the Berlin Treaty remains the sole basis on which the two cabinets may unite in preventing conflicts. We intend to maintain it as long as Austria will not abandon it."[1]

In response to this status quo declaration of faith, Saburov made still another attempt to deprive the Foreign Minister of the triumph achieved in the coronation debate. Giers was willing to go with Berlin and Vienna under any circumstances, he advised the Wilhelmstrasse, but the Tsar and the statesmen gathered in Moscow felt mostly different. If Germany wished to prevent the renewed alliance treaty being devaluated into another dead letter, she should offer "positive proposals," which could lead into a "far-reaching understanding of the three Empires" in a way envisaged by the Reichstadt agreement.[2]

The overture, however, only revealed that the Ambassador was progressively losing his touch with realities. By the summer of 1883, the conditions were pronouncedly unfavourable for any "positive" remodelling of the Three Emperors' system. In fact, the Chancellor at that time doubted perhaps more strongly than ever whether a Russian alliance had any perspective at all.

* * *

In his biography of Bismarck, Crankshaw has made a thoughtful observation that the treaty concluded in 1881 was the Chancellor's last move "forming a part of a calculated pattern." "Henceforth, he ceased to act positively and was limited to reacting to changing circumstances or the actions of others"; and although these actions were often "bold and brilliantly ingenious," he himself must have realized that "he was now almost permanently on the defensive."[3]

True, since late 1881 Bismarck could organize his common policy with Vienna on a better personal basis, when uncooperative Haymerle died and the ministry at the Ballplatz was taken over by the former Ambassador to St. Petersburg, Count Gustav Kálnoky, who shared his views on Tsardom and the necessity of good relations with it.[4] Their wishes, however, were effectively offset by what was in their countries believed to be Russian psychological and material preparations for war. And they themselves could not cease wondering whether the unholy alliance of the military and the Muscovy "old beards" might be prevented of disturbing European peace by the alliance device only.

In April 1882, impelled by massive anti-Austrian agitation in Russia, the heretofore cautious Chief of General Staff Beck produced a project for a preventive war in the east: after armies and railways were put to readiness, concerted operational plans prepared and agreements with Italy, Rumania and Turkey concluded, the action should start in spring 1883. His German colleagues, Moltke and Waldersee, under the fresh impression of Skobelev's speech, were all for it.[5]

While rejecting the rash conclusions of the military, in the predictions about the future Bismarck hardly differed from them. Only financial difficulties, he reasoned, hindered the extremist trend to take the upper hand in St. Petersburg:

> Owing to the mood which is prevalent in Russia and namely in the Russian army, and owing to the difficulties which the government has to face, one must be afraid that as soon as they have money they will move to war—first of all against Austria-Hungary.[6]

Giers conciliatory mission to both allied capitals engendered but temporary and limited relaxation. In December 1882, three weeks upon the Foreign Minister's departure, Bismarck agreed with Waldersee that a forceful press campaign should be conducted to injure still more tottering Russian credit on the international money market.[7]

German and Austrian preoccupation with Russian military preparations and the inflated role of Obruchev in political decisions continued throughout almost the whole of 1883. Waldersee might claim that a sort of "shadow government" led by the Chief of Staff existed in St. Petersburg and that the danger of attack was greater than ever.[8] The talks Bismarck had with

Kálnoky in September at Bad Gastein were overshadowed with scepticism and uncertainty. The conduct of the Russian generals in Bulgaria was taken as another proof of large-scale expansive intentions. Both statesmen agreed that Giers must be helped and the Three Emperors' treaty prolonged; yet the reasoning was not unlike that voiced by the participants of the Moscow coronation debate. The treaty was evaluated solely in its utility to "either moderate or localize" Russian aggressive tendencies. Pointing out armaments and troop concentrations taking place in Tsardom, the Chancellor reiterated his fears that Giers was being kept in office merely as a veil which would fall once the chance for a successful war would appear.

In order to meet the emergency, at least a part of the military desiderata were acknowledged in the proposition to "broaden our league of peace with Italy to the east[9] and thus procure a firm basis for the policy of Rumania and eventually for Serbia and Turkey too." This led to the Austro-Rumanian alliance treaty on 30 October 1883, soon joined by Germany. Though envisaged as the implementation of the tactics which the Bad Gastein parleys settled on—that the task of containing Russia should be left to "other opponents whose interests are more menaced than ours, or equally menaced"—the explosive implications were unmistakable.[10] By this important concession, as Medlicott put it, Bismarck agreed to regard action by Austria in defense of a Balkan country as a casus foederis under the Austro-German alliance and had thereby conceded the point urged so vainly by Haymerle.[11]

In Russia, too, apprehensions about the reckless fantasies perpetuated by the Obruchev-Vannovskii set had been widespread.

From Polovtsov's diary we know that the moderates in the elite had set out to expose the military clique in spring 1882, when, in addition to Skobelevian escapades, they had learned that a top secret army gathering had decided and then prevailed upon the Tsar to speed up the transfer of troops from the Far East, Southern Russia and the Caucasus to the western frontier as well as the build-up of strategic railways (1500 kilometers within three years). This, together with the Bosphorus affair, was also the occasion when they accused the generals of bringing about financial bankruptcy, secretly working for a Russo-French alliance and thereby preparing dissolution of the Empire. In foreign policy, Shuvalov articulated the anti-hawkish opinion, Russia had no other option than to do nothing and wait. Only after Bismarck's death, internal conflicts in Germany may offer the chance to use the French card and "escape the deplorable position in which we have emerged."[12]

Among the educated public, Katkov persevered in his plea for a less emotionally motivated approach. His cautious and outwardly even friendly comments on German policy included such a highly controversial theme as the formation of the Triple Alliance. Albeit visibly surprised by the proclamation of Italian Foreign Minister Mancini on the adherence to the Austro-German bloc, he did not resort to the familiar alarmist outcry. On the contrary, he anew condemned the newspapers for spreading a war scare, claiming that Russia might stay a "distant observer" of a conflict in the West which purportedly was of no consequence for her.[13]

With the rising suspense in the autumn of 1883, the editor redoubled his effort. Highly symptomatically, he used the anniversary of Sedan to identify Russian national interests:

> Its peaceful intentions are drawing Tsardom nearer to Berlin and Vienna, because Bismarck and Kálnoky 'undoubtedly follow the aim of upholding peace. If France has lost her former commanding position in Europe, permanently threatening Russia, what madness would induce the latter to shed her blood in a vile attempt to assist her enemy against her eternal ally, loyal to her in the most substantial matters of European policy?'[14]

On 19 October followed an explicit approval of the Chancellor's current actions:

> That Germany has undertaken to form a comprehensive alliance system is a quite natural consequence of her elevated international position; and the endeavours to enlarge it further are no less legitimate. Russia ought to support this system, which is a guarantee for peace. To withstand it by rapprochement with France 'would undoubtedly be tantamount to a preparation for war.'[15]

The Muscovite must have been terribly upset by the reports on Rumanian and Serbian integration into the German bloc and by the repercussions the Chancellor's lashes had on the Russian financial situation, if he went as far as accepting German continental hegemony.[16] So were many others.

"Bismarck has encircled us by an iron ring," Shuvalov observed somberly. In September, the Tsar ordained Nikolai Dolgorukii to go to Berlin with his personal message for William I which should have ensured a détente. In November, when an armed conflict was viewed as "more and more probable," Vannovskii himself had to rush to the German capital with another appeasement mission.[17]

At first the Germans refused to be impressed. Also the usually accommodating Schweinitz, when Giers presented him Katkov's editorials as the best proof of Russian good intentions, professed his disbelief. "The most beautiful articles of Herr Katkov are immaterial as long as your cavalry and mounted artillery is moving menacingly on our borders," he said.[18] In the end, however, the last Russian pilgrimage to Bismarck in 1883, made by the Foreign Minister, produced a breakthrough.

A huge stroke of luck blessed the Russians—the illness of the eighty-six year old Emperor William and the expected ascendance of Crown Prince Frederick William. Friendly to German liberals and pro-English, the Crown Prince was known by his scarcely heeded hostility to the Chancellor and the policies he designed; and his wife, a daughter of Queen Victoria, even more so. The virtual obsession of Bismarck that he must take every precaution "against the death of William I and the 'Gladstone cabinet' which . . . the new Emperor would appoint"[19] not only enormously alleviated Giers' task but caused what was soon to be discerned as portentous reversal in the Chancellor's approach. Firstly, it drove him to an energetic anti-English colonial policy.[20] Secondly, it pushed him to stubborn pursuance of the pro-Russian course in general and on the Bulgarian question in particular. (The intimacy of Prince Alexander with the family of the Crown Prince made Bismarck his sworn enemy, willing to buttress the Tsar against him to almost any length.)

* * *

Bismarck wished to take the fresh opening with Russia as sweeping as possible. He showered Giers with both assurances and proposals. Though "he had not always been rightly understood," his arguments ran, "he had during his whole career favored alliance with Russia" and still "considered the entente with Russia as of more import than all the alliances with Austria and Italy." Then he "dwelt long on the proposition of understanding with Austria to determine the spheres of influence in the Balkans."

Taken by surprise by this overture, the Russian guest deemed it necessary to dampen somehow the zeal of his host. Because "the situation in the three Empires did not appear very propitious," he suggested that "it would be better not to go too fast and for the moment simply renew the treaty." As for the essential, however, both statesmen were in perfect accord.[21] And, seeing that the theme of Balkan division remained for Giers an unpleasant remainder of the rivalry with Saburov, Bismarck offered more attractive tokens of goodwill: he ordered backing the Russians in Sofia, lifted the sanctions upon their credit and sent his son Herbert to the capital on Neva.

The mission of the younger Bismarck completed the change.

Of course, after two years of frictions there was at the beginning still tension in the air. While the notorious Germanophiles like Adlerberg and Shuvalov supplied the emissary with optimistic information,[22] other talks—on 20 May 1884, he also met Katkov[23]—made him apprehensive. He admitted that the Tsar "wants peace at any price," yet judged the extremist trend "stronger because of his apathy and other shortcomings." He also advised his father that financial boycott was the only means to hold the "Panslav-republicans" check and prevent them engineering an assault on Austria. As the time went on, however, and his contacts with the Tsar, Tsarina and Court became more relaxed,[24] Herbert Bismarck not only lost his doubts about the benefits of the alliance but, as will be shown later, turned into a proponent of a line even more pronouncedly pro-Russian than was the one chosen by the Chancellor.

For Giers, this was perhaps his finest hour.

When he was in Vienna to amplify the Russo-German détente by that with Austria, Saburov hurried to St. Petersburg "to outline his programme with the Tsar." Instead of undermining the minister's position, the Ambassador finally compromised himself as being "a mere petty intriguer." The audience with the ruler led nowhere and a powerful phalanx which rose against him—Adlerberg, Bunge, Dolgorukii, Shuvalov etc.—soon achieved his recall from Berlin, where a more trustworthy Prince Orlov came as the replacement.[25]

With his main extremist rivals Ignatiev and Saburov relegated and Shuvalov out of the autocrat's favor, Giers could at the same time observe diminishing troubles with the Russian press. After unending anti-Austrian tirades,[26] Katkov inaugurated the year 1884 in an entirely different tone. "Everything is turning out propitiously in our affairs. . . . Everybody is looking for our friendship and nobody feels the need for quarreling with us. . . ." Not only did he again put the whole blame for earlier "misunderstandings" with Germany on "mistakes and confusions in Russia's previous policies," but mentioned with approval the more positive Austro-Russian relations. Quoting the assurances uttered by the *Neue Freie Presse* that "Austria renounced the intention to be Russia's rival in the East," he characterized it as a signal for the promising future.[27]

Later, the publicist would sometimes criticize Austrian policies in Galicia or Bosnia-Hercegovina[28] and point out the difference between Russo-German and Russo-Austrian relations—"between Russia and Germany, only misunderstandings produced by random personal accidents occured; between Russia and Austria, substantial reasons for disagreement, detrimental for both sides can emerge"[29]—yet other aspects were stressed as decisive. Katkov recognized that "the Habsburg monarchy seeks to enter into direct, honest rapport with Russia" and that the common anti-revolutionary front safeguards the European order.[30] Moreover, vastly impressed by the German colonial initiative, he demanded that Russia should emulate the example and look for new greatness in non-European territories and seas.[31]

Accelerated Russian expansion in Central Asia, albeit far from convenient to his eminently peaceful, conservative nature, must have appeared to Giers at this juncture as a minor evil furthering the main objective of his programme—upholding the status quo in Europe and the Near East by cementing the ties between the three empires.

CHAPTER 27

THE ASIATIC BRINKMANSHIP:
THE AFGHAN CRISIS
(1881-1885)

Skobelev's victory resounded all over Asia
to her remotest corners: "Another fierce
and proud people bowed before the White
Tsar!" And let this rumor echo and re-echo.
Let the conviction of the invinciibility of
the White Tsar and his sword grow and
spread among the millions of these people—
to the very border of India and in India
herself.

After General Lomakin's failure there
must have spread doubts throughout Asia
as to the invincibility of our sword, and
Russian prestige was unquestionably jeopardized. This is why we must not stop on this
road. The peoples may have their khans
and emirs. In their imagination, England,
whose strength they admire, may stand
as a menace. But the name of the White
Tsar must soar above those of the khans
and emirs, above the name of the Caliph
himself. Such is the conviction that must
prevail in Asia! And, from year to year,
it has to spread there. We need it because
it prepares them for the future.
Dostoevskii

If the English would only throw aside
their misplaced pride and study a little
deeper the foundation of Russia's rule
in Central Asia, comparing it with their
own, they would soon see plainly why the
name of Russia has such prestige in Asia,
and why the natives of India hate the
domination of England, and set their hopes
of freedom upon Russia. . . . As to our
antagonism in Asia, England herself threw
down the gauntlet at Savastopol and if the
Russian flag now floats over Merv, the
English have themselves to blame. We
accepted their challenge, it now only rests
with them whether there is to be a Russian
invasion in India or not. But we hope that
time has come when English strategists
will take into consideration the 200,000
troops of the Caucasus, and the 100,000
in reserve in Turkestan and Western Siberia,
besides another army of half a million
behind in European Russia, and will look
on the map and see what must happen if
a Russian corps of 200,000 men, accompanied by another of 100,000 of splendid
irregular cavalry, pass through Herat and
Balakh into India, and proclaim the independence of the native population. Let
England think well of the consequence
of Russia deciding to take up arms against
her.
Sobolev

Of course it is possible—all things are possible
to a good general—but I should not like to
undertake the task, and I do not think
Russia would. Of course, if you enraged
Russia, if by your policy you excited her,
if you made her wild, we might attempt
it, even in spite of all the difficulties. For
my part, I would only make a demonstration
against India, but I would fight you at Herat.
Skobelev (to Marvin)

> We are told by the late government that
> the danger they wished to guard against
> was the danger of a military base to be
> formed by Russia on the Caspian. I hold
> that to be one of the wildest dreams ever
> entertained.
> Duke of Argyll

Like the rest of the extremists, Skobelev considered the seizure of Akhal-Tekin just for curtain-raising: now the Great Game on the approaches to India should start in earnest. On 30 January 1881 he took Ashkhabad and requested that his plenary powers be "temporarily" prolonged "in view of the many questions of supreme (state) interest which ought to be solved in the nearest future"; in other words, as Terentiev explained, he asked for carte blanche to go without delay to Merv and Herat.

The White General was denied the possibility of effecting his design. In his 7 February directive, Miliutin prohibited actions east from Akhal Tekin or infringement of Persian territory "under any pretext."[1] Under the new reign, however, Skobelev's successors soon regained the same leeway as in their earlier heydays. With the Ministerial Council debased and the moderates in the elite centered on preventing adventures in the Near East, they could take full advantage of Alexander's sympathy for bold deeds. Moreover, their cause was furthered by two quite sound premises: firstly, that the peoples in the area, scared by recent massacres, would not dare to put any serious resistance; secondly, that the British, with Gladstone at Downing Street and hands tied on the Nile, were incapable of firm opposition either.

There was a complete unity between the military and the Moscow party in fundamental approach, as enunciated by Katkov. Although praising Gladstone's determination on the Egyptian question, the publicist at the same time encouraged the widespread opinion that Great Britain was a "finished country." Behind the goodwill in London lies the impotence to fight against strong rivals, he stressed; and so Russia has only to act with determination to establish a "scientific frontier" in the Hindu-Kush and to appropriate a forceful position in the Persian and Afghan glacis.[2]

From the military's side, those themes were elaborated at considerable length in a treatise by General Sobolev, published in St. Petersburg in

1882.[3] The ill-famed dictator of Sofia, then still in the capacity of the chief of the Asiatic department in the General Staff, reasoned to the effect that

> There can be hardly any doubt that Afghan Turkestan will detach itself from Kabul . . . (and) also that the whole of the northern Afghanistan from the Amu-Daria right up to the Hindu-Kush will become included, by the force of circumstances, into the direct sphere of Russian influence. England herself occasioned this state of affairs as consequence of which Russia will receive in Central Asia a natural scientific frontier.[4]

Sobolev's analysis of the last Afghan war aimed to prove the contention broached by the War Ministry that "despite all recent reforms, the English army is not puissant enough to protect English possessions (even) in time of peace." Once Herat was seized, the General assured, the broadest vistas might come true:

> There is no place more important from military point of view than Herat. Asia Minor, the Caucasus, Persia, Turkestan and Afghanistan, Beludjistan and India—all are connected one after another by this town. . . . Through Herat runs the sole road traversable by a large army. Between it and lower India no natural barrier whatever exists. . . .[5]

This was not just the extremist wild talk. Politico-military preparations were well under way.

The convention of 21 December 1881, forced upon the Persian government by Zinoviev (he was then still the Minister in Teheran) obliged the Shah to permit the passage of troops through his northern provinces; and this, as Zinoviev pointed out, cleared the path for planning "high aiming actions." Indeed, after two generals, Grodekov and Lessar, had performed reconnaissance of the Herat routes, the first named was ordained by Obruchev to draw up a scheme of the march. Thus, another "Indian variant" was elaborated, envisaging this time that a corps of 50,000 men would use Persian supply bases and proceed along the route Akhal Tekin—Shirwan—Meshed—Herat.[6]

Simultaneously, the War Ministry undertook—under the guise of a trade caravan of Moscow merchant Konshin—a venture designed to facilitate the seizure of Merv. The caravan, led by Captain Alikhanov and young Turkoman traitor Makhtum Kuli-Khan, was not only to be a spy mission collecting data for a military move but also an instrument to create by bribes and threats the "Russian party" among dispirited local chieftants and arrange a suitable decor for the occupation. Quite transparently, Katkov's daily hailed the enterprise as a part of the great intent "to overtake Akhal Tekin, Merv and Khorasan markets, otherwise condemned to fall into English hands."[7]

In the assessment of the English response, Katkov and the army hawks proved once again entirely correct.

The Russo-Persian convention, the construction of the Trans-Caspian railway, the military bases in Akhal Tekin and Ashkhabad constituted hard facts which the Liberal "anti-alarmists" could scarcely dispute. In 1863, the Russians were separated from British India by nearly 2,500 kilometers of steppes, mountains and deserts; now, the distance was reduced by half, and, though the Trans-Caspian railroad was incomplete, regiments posted in southern and even central Russia—not counting those in Turkestan, Siberia and the Caucasus—could be deployed on the approaches to Herat at a relatively short notice.

Nonetheless, despite the stir aroused among the colonial and military circles by the discoveries of Lessar[8] and despite diplomatic reports from St. Petersburg already announcing the move on Merv impending, Gladstone refused to commit himself.[9]

So the established pattern remained unaltered when Ambassador Thornton heard from Giers "the familiar chant that the Tsar had no intention of extending the frontiers of Russia,"[10] while his soldiers worked to the very opposite purpose.

Furnished by Alikhanov's optimistic reports on the conditions in the Merv oasis, the hawks dominated the two summer (1882) extraordinary councils on Asiatic affairs. The gatherings agreed that Merv, being "the sole serious obstacle on the road connecting our Central Asian posessions with the Caspian Sea" ought to be appropriated notwithstanding the pledges given to London.[11] It was not at all the fear of the British response but the serious situation on Russia's western frontiers which delayed the move considered to be the last step "to the gates of Herat."

* * *

While another period of British inactivity seemed to be in the offing, Central Asia assumed in Russian grand strategy an enhanced role.

On numerous occasions, perhaps with greatest emphasis in Skobelev's memoranda, the Russian statesmen and military portrayed Central Asia as an auxilary sphere of action subordinated to the aims in the Eastern Question. Many outside observers took it for granted. As Thornton put it,

> My impression is that their real objective is always Constantinople and that their threatening attitude towards India through Afghanistan is merely a detail and intended to induce us to send as many troops as possible to India and keep them there far away from the real object of their ambition.[12]

In reality, however, the Central-Asian theatre of contest had in the early 1880s taken on a specific significance and its relationship to developments in the Near East had been much more complex.

From the viewpoint of prestige, so prodigious in the whole Russian tradition, the failures in the "Slavic question," particularly those in Bulgaria, as well as military incapability to perform the Bosphorus operation, raised Central Asia again to the only stage where unruly extremist energy was expected to bring palpable compensations without exposing Tsardom to undue risks.

From the economic viewpoint, the importance of the areas east and south of the Caspian Sea vastly overshadowed southeastern Europe in the Russian eyes. While their inferior industrial products stood no chance on the Balkan markets easily accessible to Western exports, and almost nobody believed that this could be altered, Central Asia and northwestern Chinese provinces still promised viable prospects. In this contexture one should bear also in mind that the heavy economic crisis tormenting Russia from 1882 onwards was to a considerable degree bred by relative overproduction. The bumper crop of 1884 provoked an outcry of desperation; and industrial commodities overflooded the narrow internal market too.[13] That is why Russian business interests hailed Katkov's fierce campaign clamouring for opening up Persian and other Eastern markets for the salvation of hard-pressed industry,[14] for optimizing the effect of the Trans-Caspian railway by turning it on Persian territory[15] and against the transit of foreign goods on the Poti-Baku line[16] as the greatest service to the state.[17]

* * *

The fundamental foreign-policy statement, Giers' circular of 18 August 1883, is a persuasive testimony of how much latitude the St. Petersburg moderates were willing to bestow on their opponents in order to detour them from Galicia, the Balkans and the Straits to Central Asia.

> A firm position has been established 'by our operations in the Turkoman steppe. We have been continuing in consolidation and development. It is a purely defensive effort and we have no interest in menacing England in India. But it provides us with an operational base which, if need be, may become an offensive one. . . . So long as the struggle for influence rests on permissible limits, we are going to apply the same (inoffensive) means. However, when English officers incite, arm and organize the Mervans against us, we intend to remind the London cabinet that liberty of action and reciprocity is the foundation of our relations.'[18]

Since the argument about the English "inciting, arming and organizing" the Merv Turkomans was a vast exaggeration, the implications were at hand: the Singers' Bridge fabricated excuses to justify an action already in progress.

In the meantime, while Katkov was advertizing the Caucasus as the key region for "taking advantage of the dominance on the Caspian Sea and in Central Asia,"[19] a corresponding shift in the rivalry and relative importance of regional military groups had taken place. Kaufman, stricken by paralysis, had ceased to exercise his enormous power; and when he died in 1882 his successor, the prematurely aged "Lion of Tashkent" Cherniaev, proved unable to enliven the Turkestan Governor General-ship's administration to its former vigor. The initiative and indisputable priority thus returned to the Caucasus, ruled by more adroit and virile Prince Dondukov-Korsakov.

The pivotal role in the forthcoming ventures was assigned to General Alexander Komarov. Appointed in April 1883 to the commanding post in the Trans-Caspian region, Komarov was presumably empowered by Dondukov and/or by the General Staff to explore both alternatives of an advance on Herat—the Persian one proposed by Grodekov and the Mervan one advised by Lessar. We are in no position to establish what conclusions he made in the Persian case: we know only that he departed forthwith to meet the Shah in the Khorasan province and that—although a brass band accompanied him to prove friendly intentions—his true purpose was to "study the main routes to Meshed and other towns."[20] On the other hand we may be sure that the Turkestan rivals launched a counteraction which evidently induced Komarov, the Tiflis Viceroy and their allies in St. Petersburg to take the Mervan option.

Though worn-out and handicapped by an obsessive strive to destroy everything connected with Kaufman's name,[21] the Lion could still be a big nuisance for them. Often by-passing Vannovskii and Obruchev, he appealed directly to his long-time admirer and protector, the Tsar, urging him to follow the rather chaotic projections he devised. These, most importantly, included the commitment of Bukhara and Khiva in Merv and then a full-fledged war with the Afghans. In the spring of 1883, Khivan representative was installed in the oasis as a "Governor"; later, reports commenced to reach Tiflis and St. Petersburg that a movement of a combined Turkestan-Bukharan force to Afghanistan was imminent.[22]

So, the War Ministry and the Caucassians had to strike back without delay. While they set off a massive intrigue on the Neva to remove the Lion from his post—it succeeded in March 1884—two persons who had exhibited their talents in the Konshin caravan, Alikhanov and Mukhtum Kuli-Khan, appeared in Merv and required acceptance of Russian suzerainty. Only a small Cossack group convoyed them, but a part of the Trans-Caspian detachment under Colonel Muratov awaited the results in the near-by Tedjen oasis.

The Merv population, swelled to about 250,000 by refugees from Akhal Tekin, had lived in the shadow of Skobelev's bloody lesson; and the Russian column at Tedjen, according to Muratov, engendered among them "confusion equal to panic." The general tribal assembly thus yielded to Alikhanov's thinly veiled threats and on 13 January 1884 motioned to enter "voluntarily" under the scepter of the White Tsar.[23]

A month later, on 12 February, a delegation of four Turkoman khans performed the formal act of allegiance at Komarov's headquarters at

Ashkhabad. The General then led in person troops into Merv. Only a small minority obeyed their religious leaders exhorting for a holy war against the infidel. On 14-15 March, the attack of about 2,500 men, mostly armed with mere sticks and scissors for sheep-cutting, was repulsed by guns and cavalry.[24] And that was to be the end of the Merv question, for so long looming large in Anglo-Russian relations.

* * *

In views of many British proclamations and many Russian pledges broken, St. Petersburg naturally expected a fierce reaction. Ambassador at the Court of St. James Mohrenheim apologized to Lord Granville and affirmed that the Tsar had been no less surprised by the seizure of the oasis than Whitehall. Similarly, Giers intimated to foreign diplomats that he had been left in the dark about the whole venture.[25] For a short time, the proponents of expansion kept also low profiles. In soothing words, Katkov assured that the last conquest had been but "the epilogue of the Tekin expedition" and should solely assert Russian supremacy over the already subjected peoples; the next steps were to be of a strictly economic nature, like the completion of the Trans-Caspian railway.[26]

The London cabinet could have scarcely believed in assuaging Russian explanations. The Embassy in St. Petersburg had incessantly poured out their warnings. It reported on the activities of the Tiflis and Tashkent military, about distinct indications coming from the Singers' Bridge that they would not be harnessed, as well as about the press comments discussing the importance of Afghanistan and the feasibility of the drive to India. Thornton advised Granville that Russian policy in Central Asia "has been that she has valued each fresh annexation of territory not so much for its intrinsic worth than for the advantage it possesses as a stepping stone to further and more important conquests"; he also brought to the Foreign Minister's attention the fact that the Russian War Ministry had published a map in which the boundaries of Tsardom were already stretched almost 300 kilometers beyond Merv, to the vicinity of Herat.[27] Nonetheless, the Liberal ministers stubbornly maintained their opposition to "alarmism." While Lytton had once described the Merv oasis as "the most important spot in Central Asia," they took a refuge in a contrary exaggeration, claiming that the place was entirely worthless, just a "few mud hovels in the desert."

So, the sequel of Komarov's undertaking was but a "mild flurry of activity in London." Granville expressed to Mohrenheim his "real surprise" that the Russians had forgotten their promises, and that settled it. In Parliament, the Secretary for India Duke of Argyll ridiculed the public outcry as "Mervousness."[28]

The Gladstonian languishing encouraged the Russians to proceed in the same manner as they did in the early 1870s.

Commenting on the supine response, Katkov reiterated his familar proposal for a broader Anglo-Russian understanding in which England should recognize "the question who keeps Constantinople relegated to secondary importance" and thus buy for herself the security of her Indian possessions.[29] Giers, perceiving the Anglo-German colonial disputes and the Sudan ("Mahdist") uprising as unmistakable tokens that London would have no option but to pay the price,[30] instructed the new Ambassador, Baron Staal, to the same effect (in June 1884):

> Our august master does not nurture any hostile intention towards England, neither in Asia nor in Europe. On the contrary, His Majesty believes that in Asia the two Empires can live in peace, each in its natural sphere of influence and action. . . . The course of events has considerably modified their respective interests. Those of England are particularly directed to Egypt and the Suez canal. Ours are centered rather in the Balkan peninsula and in the Straits; not because of ambition but in an effort to procure a guarantee for our security and our (other) interests. The situation is favorable to an rapprochement between the policies of the two countries.[31]

In order to forestall further "uncontrollable actions," the Singers' Bridge and the Foreign Officer came to an understanding to set up a joint commission for the delimitation of the Central-Asian frontiers. (Generals Lumsden and Zelenoi were appointed to lead the British, resp. the Russian part of the commission.)

On all this, however, the army hawks responded only with their usual arrogance. To wait until concessions were obtained through diplomatic deals was, as always, in principle unacceptable to them. Observing only prevarications and lack of mettle on the opposite side, they saw no reason to pause or depart from their highly effective tactics of direct challenge.

Giers was only too correct when predicting that some lucky strike would inspire Dondiukov-Korsakov and his Caucasus grouping to seek for "another piece of Afghanistan."[32] The news about the joint commission they dismissed with scorn. "Well, let them (the English) work, let them fry in the heat and shiver in the cold. We shall be unperturbed and achieve precisely the border on which we have decided already a long time ago!", General Terentiev put it bluntly.[33]

The Moscow publicist also hardened his tone. Impatient that the "finished Power" was not eager to strike quickly a comprehensive bargain and angered by the establishment of a commission—in his eyes, it was yet another device to hinder Russian advance "to our part of the Himalaya Mountains"—he released the cat out of its bag in the editorial of 4 June. Merv was no longer the final chapter, but a mere episode. Only the conquest of Herat "could in a dignified manner conclude our expansion in the Afghan direction." The rest of Afghanistan should enter into "proper" treaty relations—Khiva being a model, we may add—and the English be driven back to their "natural border, beyond Himalaya and the Indus."[34]

Hence, instead of narrowing the space for friction, the frontier delimitation only spurred Dondukov and his faction. Upon Viceroy's orders, Zelenoi simulated illness and stayed in Tiflis; meanwhile, Komarov dispatched his detachments into the strategically most valuable areas expected to be disputed. When Lumsden arrived on the spot in the autumn, they had already gone half-way in performing the task to "secure the border we wished."[35] That they could not accomplish even more was due to a countermove of Abdurrahman Khan. The Afghan ruler, who had spent years at Kaufman's "court," knew the Russian intentions only too well and in order to thwart them, posted his troops in the key Penjdeh area.

* * *

In a letter to Jomini, Ambassador Staal implored that "les exaltés de la cause" should not force the Foreign Ministry's hand.[36] He was to be badly disappointed. However honest Giers might have been in the effort to handle the affair within tolerable limits, he would not dare to antaganize the "exalted ones." And, it is also more than a matter of curiosity to note how strongly the official reasoning ressembled that of the *Moskovskiia vedomosti*. Firstly, the border settlement was connected with the recognition of Russian "security interests" in the Straits, the Balkans and even in the valley of the Euphrates. Secondly, albeit ostensibly taking into account "the difficulties Mr. Gladstone has to fight against," the dispatches to Staal insisted on "material assurances" which included Russian territorial demands; and these were based on the so called "ethnographic principle," i.e. that the northern Afghanistan inhabited by the Turkoman tribes should be ceded to Tsardom.[37]

In vain the British statesmen admonished St. Petersburg that the "deliberately unacceptable stance" had "excited many susceptibilities both in India and England."[38] Accusations of intrigues were hurled at them in response. True, the moderates in general deplored the fact that "we have got imprudently involved" and affirmed that Russia lacked the means for any major confrontation. However, the prevailing opinion in the elite was close to Katkov's and the army hawks: that there was no risk at all of such a confrontation; that "England is in full decay" and "one does not to be overly scrupulous with her." The mirage of promotions and medals tantalized the courtiers and generals alike. When the wife of Vannovskii cautioned her husband about excessive provocations, he retorted with astonishment: "Why, don't you want to be a Countess?" Also the Tsar was visibly intoxicated by the Caucassians and the Obruchev-Vannovskii clique. Highly perturbed, Gier's deputy Vlangali apprised his friends from the peace party about the remark the ruler had written on the report about English complaints: "It is useless to have more talks with them."[39]

The extraordinary councils on Central Asian affairs, summoned on 4 November 1884, and on 12 January 1885, were entirely dominated by the hawkish military (Vannovskii, Obruchev, Zelenoi, Dondukov-Korsakov and his aidés Kuropatkin, Lessar and Shepelev attended). The latter gathering resolved that the English proposals, "encouraging Afghan pretentions" and "injurious for Russian prestige among the Turkoman population," must be rejected. A resolution set forth by Dondukov was adopted, envisaging that the new frontier line should run "at least" 100 verstas from Herat" and deprive the Afghans of the strategically crucial Penjdeh oasis and the Zulfagar Pass. If London refused to assent, then "England must bear all responsibility for a rupture," and in view of that contingency, "military measures should be taken without delay," including the occupation of further strategic points and communications. Two special detachments were to be formed to assist troops in forward positions.[40]

Komarov was given virtually a free hand to cope with emergencies. In a telegram of 10 March, the War Minister advised him to act "with prudence, but in accordance with Russia's dignity." Dondukov-Korsakov was more explicit. He promised the General that he would in no way limit his initiative and, if need be, protect him against criticism: "You know that you will always have my support and readiness to take much on my own responsibility. It remains only to achieve success and thereby uphold the honour and dignity of the government. The matter calls not for bureaucratic correspondence but for immediate solution."[41]

Thus, amidst intense rumors that Herat was the real objective and the conceited pronouncements of high ranking officers that "our frontiers are marching with us,"[42] on 30 March an event took place which changed the tension into an acute crisis. Komarov assailed the Afghans in their positions on the left bank of the Kushq river, and killing and wounding several hundred of them, overwhelmed the whole valley of Penjdeh. The Russians now stood, as the council tabled it, 100 verstas from Herat.[43]

* * *

Since January 1885, the English public had laboured under a severe shock produced by the fall of Khartum to the Mahdi and the death of General Gordon killed by the rebels. In this atmosphere, if he wished to survive politically, Gladstone could not continue—at least not openly—his "anti-alarmist" policy. The Penjdeh affair seemed to be the proverbial last straw. The press most certainly expressed the overriding opinion when demanding a forceful response. "One word more and only one is needed. That is, a declaration of war," wrote the Conservative *Standard.*[44] So, in his address to Parliament on 22 April, the Prime Minister characterized the Russian attack on the Afghans as "unprovoked aggression" and asked for 11 million £ of war credit, the largest sum required for that purpose since the Crimean War. Army and militia reserves were called out; the Indian government was ordered to send 20-30,000 troops to Quetta; the Far East fleet entered Port Hamilton in Korea, a well-known object of Russian designs; and there were also speculations about pressure on the Porte and the forcing of the Straits.

From the capital on the Thames, Staal damned "our chauvinists," "les enragés" who "pretend that the road to Constantinople passes through Herat"; he proclaimed them "our worst enemies" and suggested that their "most fatal error" be repaired by at least temporary withdrawal from the sensitive area.[45] This, however, hardly corresponded with the mood dominating both society and the elite. In letters written in April from Moscow, Novikova advised her English friends to the effect that

> People here, including *Moscow Gazette*, are indignant. It is England who invents pretexts for gaining time; we are ready. It is England who had been threatening and insulting us; 'we kept our word —we have not been sending and instigating agents wherever we could' (they say). Russians are now quite eager to punish England for all her insults. . . .
>
> I have been busy trying to calm Katkov and the others who are as indignant with the English press as they can be.
>
> . . . Russians say . . . that we ought to prove that war is not dreaded now. Just the opposite. We cannot seize India, but we can do no end of harm to England, and reduce her to the position of a second-rate Power.[46]

Alexander sided with the hotheads and Giers was too faint-hearted to contradict him. The proposals forwarded by Staal were declined on the usual grounds of "our interests and our dignity."[47]

Only when the intensity of British war preparations seemed to indicate that Gladstone had capitulated before his hard-liners, did at least a partial shift take place. The moderates were spurred into fierce opposition to Komarov and the forces he represented. In an emotional plea to the Tsar, written on 20 April, Polovtsov implored him to prevent a disaster which "a dispute for several inches of desert" might bring upon the country:

> None of the persons who have access to You dare to remind You of the dimensions of the catastrophe threatening to inflict new suffering upon the miserable, backward Russian people. Russian interests are not jeopardized from Afghanistan; . . . the happiness of the

people entrusted to You is dearer to You than the self-indulgent delusion of those who by their recklessness have led us too far.[48]

The military became somewhat sobered. Scared of the expected attack
on Vladivostok, an expedition to the Caucasus and a landing at Odessa,
Vannovskii conceded that his colleague from the navy, Shestakov, had
been right in the proposition that "we are definitely not prepared."[49]
Similarly, Katkov appears to have lost the impetuosity described in Novikova's letters. He let her publish in the *Moskovskii vedomosti* articles advocating conciliations and his own editorials, too, were quite ambiguous.
Though he would not abandon his allegation that the English were militarily weak to be afraid of, he stressed the necessity of peace and confidence in Gladstone, "the eminent statesman. . . with great wisdom and
feeling of justice." The "misunderstanding" should be settled by "agreement instead of a breach"; "it appears to us that between Russia and England not only a more or less tolerable modus vivendi but a friendship
profitable for both can be established."[50]

It was neither the intention of Whitehall to start a war nor even strive
for diplomatic humiliation of the aggressor playing the injured party; after
saving its face before the country, the cabinet offered a settlement through
international arbitration, providing thus enough room for "Russian honour" and the endeavours of the St. Petersburg peace party. Nonetheless,
when an Extraordinary Council assembled on 11 May to discuss the English move, it was still a true touch-and-go affair.[51]

Alexander himself had undergone the gravest doubts,[52] yet his emotions drove him to extremes.[53] When, at the council, Vannovskii appealed
for the "preservation of our military dignity and national self-respect," he
agreed with him. According to Bunge's testimony it looked like a war
declaration would result from the meeting. Giers was silent. But Shestakov
"by a courageous speech saved Russia from the greatest calamity." He flatly stated that Russian coastal defences were in an "extremely unsatisfactory shape" and could not withstand an attack. Then, Bunge and Grand
Duke Vladimir joined the plea for peace. The former at great length sur-
veyed the disastrous consequences the last war had on Russian financial
stability. The latter ably soothed the autocrat's susceptibilities; the success
of Russian troops, he said, had raised military and political prestige in Central Asia and rendered it possible to grant concessions, in order to help

Gladstone appease the aroused emotions in his country. In the end, the gathering assented that arbitration was the best outcome.[54]

* * *

The emergency was over without, however, harming the extremist cause. Not unlike the tactics of Grand Duke Vladimir had applied in the crucial council, the basic compromise—the Russians should retain Penjdeh, the Afghans Zulfagar Pass—was advertized as a big victory and the public readily accepted this explanation. Bülow, the future Chancellor then serving at the St. Petersburg Embassy, reported that the Russian soldier was once again pronounced the best in the world and society fancied that this quality would be manifested soon both in Asia and the Near East.[55] With the mood of arrogance untamed, the military cliques could persevere in toying with national dignity[56] and Katkov, free from worries, to return to the old formula on the Anglo-Russian understanding in its offensive interpretation.

The idea of a buffer zone, which the English had solicited for years, he again discarded as a "fantasy" and insisted that the other side must "forget all about Herat and the Afghans"; only an agreement which would fully recognize Russian rights in the area could render British India safe. A purely diplomatic arrangement, he wrote, was "highly unpopular in Russia"; and although her "main task had become the consolidation of the conquered territories," she must still consider the question of defensible Asiatic frontiers "opened to natural development," until London recognized Afghanistan as lying outside its sphere of influence.[57]

The unabated venturesome spirit may perhaps be best illustrated by the "Ashinov episode."

Ashinov, a typical hazard-prone Cossack ataman, presented a memoir proposing that the long-term support provided by the Russian Orthodox Church to Abyssinian Christians could now be ensued by further steps eventually leading to the establishment of a colony. Taking this part of Africa under her control, he affirmed, Russia "could always duly impress the English and other enemies." "Not without reason all the European countries are ready even risk war in trying to secure an important hold on this world route. Why should not Russia seize one? We need it even more, if we wish to develop our trade with the East as well as (connections) with

Vladivostok. Abyssinia is the key to the whole of Egypt and Africa and those who rule Abyssinia will also hold the main (commercial) artery," he wrote.

During the spring of 1885, Katkov and Aksakov introduced the Ataman to their high-placed and similarly versed allies—Generals Obruchev, Dondukov-Korsakov, Richter and Ignatiev, to Grand Duke Sergei, to Metropolitan Isidor and Pobedonostsev. None of them doubted that the Cossack was a mercenary pure and simple, yet they were eager to bolster him. As Pobedonostsev put it, "as a cutthroat, he can be useful in a war."[58] With their blessing, Ashinov departed for Africa.

All this, in its complexity and contradictions, put the imprint on the Russian position vis-à-vis the Bismarckian system.

CHAPTER 28

A PAUSE IN THE NEAR EAST:
THE PASSING "SPIRIT OF SKIERNEWICE"
(1884-1885)

England is our bad-tempered cat, Germany is
our good-tempered tiger. . . . Germany's
conduct towards Russia in all matters is perfect. She will at any time go out of her way
to oblige us. She will not abandon her interests to serve us, but those of her friends and
allies she will sacrifice with enthusiasm to
avoid annoying us. In all our enterprises, Near
East and Far East, or anywhere else, we can
count upon German support as confidently
as we can count upon English opposition.
Lessar

I need hardly reaffirm that Austria-Hungary
would not adopt a policy and become involved in enmity with Russia merely of sympathy with the Prince. But the Peace of
Berlin did aim at a certain stability in the
Balkans and therefore, as Foreign Minister
of Austria-Hungary, I cannot remain indifferent to a change of rulers and consequentl y
unrest in the whole of the Balkans. . . . Should
Austria . . . give Russian influence a free
hand in Bulgaria, it would mean giving Russia carte blanche in the whole of the Balkan

peninsula. The work of the Congress would
be defeated the day that Austria's influence
disappeared from both the Bulgarias and
these became Russian provinces.
Kalnoky

Bulgaria serves as an arena for the performance of our military and civil clowns.
Novikov

We were unable even to determine the goal
which we could have and should have attained. Therefore, we were confused in the
choice of means; each of our agents worked
out his own plan of action and destroyed the
work of his predecessor . . . ; Russia has not
justified the hopes of the Bulgarian people
and its intelligentsia instinctively leaning to
her. . . . A permanent change of views,
people and systems, the shift from the
Tarnovo constitution to a slightly veiled
despotism confused the minds and shattered our moral credit.
Ionin

On 27 March 1884, Bismarck and Ambassadors Orlov and Széchenyi
signed the documents which renewed the Three Emperors' Alliance treaty
for another three years. Soon thereafter Prince Dolgorukii, a man close to
both Alexander and William, proposed that the warmth of friendship, con-
spicuously absent in relations between Russia and her allies, should be injected by the familiar device of an imperial summit. The idea met the
highest approval and the monarchs, accompanied by a host of dignitaries
including Bismarck, Giers and Kálnoky gathered on 15-17 September at
the Skiernewice Castle near Warsaw.

After six chilly years, the believers in the Bismarckian system were once
again in high spirits. From St. Petersburg, Bülow wrote on the "surprisingly good impression" the summit had produced; Katkov too, he pointed
out, espoused the view that not only Germany and Russia but also Russia
and Austria had to tolerate each other.[1]

Indeed, the crisis in Central Asia induced the publicist to ascribe much
more value to the configuration created by the Chancellor. While his

favorable utterances made in 1881-1883 had been more or less motivated by fear, they now obtained a positive content; he visibly acknowledged the alliance as a framework for Russia's policies, ensuring her safety in the west and a free hand in the east.[2] As in the 1870s Bismarck stood high in his personal esteem.[3] Apart from appreciating his stance taken during the war scare of 1885[4] and on the Bulgarian question, he was mightily impressed by his daring moves overseas. It was at least partly this aspiration which in 1884-1885 gave Katkov's interests truly world-wide ramifications: he clamoured for the railway and naval build-up in the Far East[5] and as the Ashinov episode indicated, the African "scramble," too, tantalized his mind.[6]

In the St. Petersburg elite, the same tendencies were in the ascendancy. The Afghan episode deprived Giers, the main proponent of the Bismarckian system, of much of the credit he had gained by a patient work to repair the damages caused by the extremists; he was blamed for cowardice towards the Tsar and for giving extensive elbow room in his ministry to Zinoviev.[7] But the German party at Court, headed by Grand Duke Vladimir and Shuvalov, recruited many adherents who wished to see no more of Skobelev, Ignatiev or Obruchev-type nonsense.

Not unlike similar periods in the post-Crimean era, however, these occurrences were to remain only of passing consequence. Due mainly to the "public opinion factor," the alliance of the three Empires could never be more than a marriage of reason; and, devoid of any firm long term ties except those of dynastic solidarity, it was always likely that, heavily dependent on the circumstances of the moment,[8] it would be shipwrecked on the rocks of well-known antipathies and conflicts of interest. With the "spirit of Skiernewice," it was to be the same story.

Also Katkov, the essential approval of the system notwithstanding, deemed it imperative to reiterate his former reservations. Probably apprised at that time by Zinoviev of the existence of the secret "Dreikaiserbund,"[9] he delivered in his editorial of 30 September 1884, an unmistakable message on the subject. He hailed the "rapprochement of the three Empires" as vital for "preventing European wars, upholding internal peace and strengthening the monarchic principle," but along with it stressed that the free-hand policy still had to be conceived as the most suitable for Tsardom, mainly because "real reaons of disagreement" may arise between it and the Dual Monarchy. "God protect us against alliances which have no foundations in common national interest," he added ominously.[10]

The bulk of the Moscow party and society in its entirety, never attracted to the advantages of the Bismarckian realpolitik, were visibly unenthusiastic about the Skiernewice prospects. The most outspoken Aksakov rejected them outright, and the views he repeated undoubtedly reflected the prevalent public attitude:

> Only one condition has been agreed upon—to uphold the status quo. For Russian diplomacy status quo means to keep up a passive, negative policy; for Germany and Austria, it is expressed in continuous, unrelenting activity. Our friends have magnamiously granted us the freedom to abide to our status quo, the freedom to rest in inactivity and there is no reason to be afraid that they will restrict this our privilege. . . . We fully recognize the great importance of the Russo-German alliance, yet this alliance has been bought by us for too high a price, a price which is higher than the value of the alliance itself and thus puts it on shaky grounds.

The "coquetry with Germany," according to Aksakov, was permissible but for a limited period, until "our fortresses in Poland are ready." Instead of self-imposed constraint, he required such conduct as would prove that Russia was "capable and would dare," that she was "not scared of war."[11]

Bismarck, intensely alive to the fact that without viable common interest the alliance could not survive, pressed Vienna hard to the division of the Balkans or at least to the recognition of Bulgaria as an exclusively Russian domain. But the Austro-Hungarian statesmen, even the accommodating ones, would not be a part of this scheme. If Russia were allowed to do in Sofia as she pleases, Kálnoky argued, then she would want to have it that way in every Balkan state, and "gradually all these countries would be governed by Russian creatures." Owing to his St. Petersburg experience, the Foreign Minister would not assess the Skiernewice episode as more than a truce.[12] While the Chancellor, haunted by the fear of William's death, was resolved to ignore Russian military preparations and offer as far-reaching concessions as possible, his Austrian colleagues would not and could not go beyond the status quo formulae of the renewed treaty.[13]

Before long, German diplomatic reports had to state that the Austro-Russian détente, however promising it might have appeared, lacked a stable footing. Even in St. Petersburg court circles relatively immune to the nationalist sermon, Bülow had to note hostility to the "Skiernewice spirit." The Tsar was leaning towards a "loyal armistice" with Vienna, he was told, but the Russians would not let him leave the great tasks to the next generation; irritated as they are by the ingratitude shown by the Balkan peoples and constant retreats, they will not tolerate supineness in those matters from anybody, not excluding their ruler.[14]

Much friction emanated from the Galician issue where the long-term requirements of the military for "natural frontiers" in the Carpathian Mountains intertwined with the religious zeal of Orthodox vigilants and the political aims of the Moscow party in the Polish question.[15] Yet, the main source of trouble, as Bismarck correctly judged it, was in Bulgaria.

* * *

Acute Russo-Bulgarian tensions lasted until late 1883, prolonged by the so-called army crisis.

The repeated bad experience proved that with a Russian War Minister and a Russian officer corps responsible to him rather than to the Prince, no stability could be achieved. Thus Battenberg used his victory over Sobolev and Kaulbars and demanded that his constitutional rights as Commander-in-Chief be formally recognized by St. Petersburg; that the War Minister be entrusted solely with administrative functions and—again in accordance with the constitution—be responsible to him and the Assembly. Furthermore, he asked the Tsar for his consent that the loyal General Lesovoi be appointed in Kaulbars' place. Alexander responded (on 24 October) by ordering Lesovoi to depart for Russia within 48 hours, upon which Sofia retaliated by the dismissal of Colonel Rüdiger, the interim War Minister, and other compromised officers.[16]

Emboldened by the protracted conflict, Ionin in two telegrams to Giers (on 25 October and 2 November) proposed what may be identified as the blueprint for the extremist programme in the years to come. The envoy wrote:

> It would suffice to send to Sofia a general, who in the name of the Tsar would take over the command of all Russian officers and

their troops; and support him by dispatching there four batallions —or at least three warships to Varna—in order 'to make clear our wishes and goals and hereby clarify the condition to the Bulgarian people confused about our intentions.' Such a fait accompli 'would also give us a firmer position in talks with Europe, because we would have a hostage—a country.'[17]

This too was the occasion when the Strastnyi Boulevard emerged as the champion of the anti-Battenberg hardliners.

In the concept of the Muscovite, the "strengthening of order" in Bulgaria had always been connected with the cementing of the Prince's ties with Russia. The highest obligation of the ruler was not towards Bulgaria but towards Russia and her "Slavic policy":

Alexander of Bulgaria must be a Bulgarian Slav and at the same time a Russian deep in his heart . . . . The Bulgarian nationality does not represent a world of its own; her future is possible only as a part of a broader unity, only as a planet in a system in which Russia is the centre of gravitation and the source of light and warmth. The Bulgarian national feeling must be simultaneously a Russian one.[18]

Hitherto, Katkov had never openly accused the young man of any failings in performing these duties. As late as 1 November 1883—still pleading lack of trustworthy information—he blamed but the "greedy proponents of predatory intrigue", i.e. the Conservative leaders "misusing the confidence of the Prince."[19] A week later, however, came the fateful turn. Battenberg was proclaimed an enemy, the entire previous policy on the Bulgarian question was condemned and a direct Russian rule in the Principality was recognized as the sole remedy. Now, the arguments ran to the following effect:

The St. Petersburg government made the gross blunder of establishing a base monarchy, deprived of all dignity. Because it could not trust the Prince, its tactics had been reduced to pretence: limit his powers, harness him with various tricks, hinder him of enjoying the liberty to act, push him into antagonism with his own nation, create a system of mutual deceit—all of which had necessarily led to the present stalemate.

A distinctly different approach became imperative. The Prince must be prevented by every means from controlling the army which like Bulgaria itself is a Russian creation; no token of support must be granted to his rule; and the twelve million francs in the Bulgarian treasury belonging to Russia must be used as a security against any accident.

The sole natural solution rests on the liquidation of the base monarchy and its two parties-caricatures. As in Russia, there can never be political parties in Bulgaria except one—the Russian party; and the system suited her best should be a local administration controlled by Russia and headed by a Governor General.[20]

In their obstinacy, the Russians could not recognize the real reasons for their failure. "Governmental circles, the press and politically-minded society are equally excited about the Bulgarian developments, about what they call the ingratitude of the Prince," Alfred von Kiderlen-Wächter, another future leading German diplomat, reported from St. Petersburg.[21] In the government and at Court, though, nobody stepped forward to associate himself with Ionin's and Katkov's hazardous propositions. Preoccupied by culminating tensions with Germany and Austria-Hungary—one has to remember that this was still the year 1883—they opted for retreat instead.

Above all Giers realized that it was impossible to leave the initiative on the Bulgarian question to the Muscovites, as he did in 1882, when he let Katkov and Aksakov select the Prince's Russian generals,[22] and at the same time seek improved relations with Berlin and Vienna. Although he remained profoundly prejudiced against Battenberg, he moved towards a policy of circumspection and restraint. On 10 November Baron Nikolai Kaulbars, the military attaché in Vienna, who in contrast to his brother, the scheming general, was known for his opposition to the "barren and unpolitical" hostility, came to Sofia to negotiate a statute for Russian military personnel.

The convention eventually signed was a distinct concession to Bulgarian susceptibilities. Russian officers were to serve only in the army and navy, not in gendarmerie, police or in administrative posts; their service was limited in time (three years) and they were subjected to Bulgarian military code and made responsible to Bulgarian authorities. The document stipulated that they would not "interfere in any form in internal political affairs." The Tsar had the right to appoint the War Minister, but the latter became equally responsible to him and to the Sofia Assembly.[23]

On 1 December, in a joint instruction to Ionin, Giers and Zinoviev summarized the new line as follows:

> We accept the fait accompli . . . ; we do not intend to expose ourselves to any responsibility with which constant interference into internal affairs . . . is associated; we leave it to the Bulgarians to deal with their internal problems . . . ; we shall use just moral influence to put a brake on harmful passions . . . .[24]

Prince Cantacuzène, who took over the Sofia War Ministry, may be indicated as the personification of this line. He promised to consider himself but one of the ministers and restrict his activities to purely military matters, and, whatever his personal views might have been, he kept his promise. His prudence, politeness and administrative abilities were highly appreciated by both the army and the Prince.[25] Also Ionin's successor at the head of the Sofia agency, Alexander Koiander, a standard bully from the Asiatic Department, felt constrained to observe caution. "Work on discrediting the Prince as much as you can; but don't overdo it, be careful. Here we are not in Russia," he admonished his subordinates.[26]

* * *

After several hectic years, the Bulgarian problem appeared to be relegated to a second-rate issue. The Russian press turned its rancor from the Balkans and the Dual Monarchy to the English; Katkov stopped commenting on Bulgarian events. For the seasoned extremists, however, the modest position in a country considered crucial for their grand strategy, was a retreat impossible to tolerate for long. In fact, the programme of the "Governor Generalship" had never been completely abandoned. Its proponents had their greatest asset in the Tsar's enmity towards his cousin; and neither the complexities of the Bulgarian domestic scene nor Bismarck's altered stance were of minor consequence.

Before departing from Sofia, Ionin had made a very clever move. He had invited Karavelov, the leader of the "radical Liberals," to come back from his Rumelian exile and promised him that the Russians, despite the insults he had hurled upon them after the 1881 coup, would help him to attain his former power. Karavelov had been during his student years in Russia a convinced Nihilist and still kept some contacts with the revolutionaries; at the same time, he was undoubtedly a sincere patriot. Nonetheless, now he became in many ways a useful tool in the extremist game, by helping to perpetuate the Bulgarian internal split and particularly by accepting and spreading the debilitating thesis that "without Russia we cannot succeed." His agitation led in 1884 to the dissolution of the Tsankov-Conservative coalition and induced Tsankov himself, the most unscrupulous of power-seekers among Bulgarian politicians, to backstep to the Russian fold. When in late 1884 Karavelov got the premiership, the harmful proposition seemed already to predominate, that it was just the "dynastic question," i.e. the person of Battenberg on the throne, which after all prevented the relationship with the sobered "Power-liberatrice" being organized on a sound footing.[27]

The Prince, always distrustful of local party leaders, resorted to his stereotype: confronted by danger, he looked for external help. After his appeals to the Romanov relative for conciliation led nowhere, he tried to make his position firmer by a marriage with Princess Victoria, the daughter of the German Crown Prince and the granddaughter of Queen Victoria. At first sight, this seemed a good bet; the English Queen and the family of Frederick William were very sympathetic to him and intensely anti-Russian. In fact, however, the young man multiplied his troubles. Not only did the marriage project spur the Russians to countermoves and untied the extremist hands, but also turned Bismarck, almost paranoic with suspicion against the Crown Prince and the "Anglo-Polish plot," into a supporter of the "Governor-Generalship" settlement.[28]

As his first service to Tsardom, the Chancellor persuaded Emperor William to prohibit the marriage and in the interview with Battenberg (on 14 May 1884) faced him with the gloomiest perspective:

> If you wish to stay in Bulgaria you must submit to Russia for better or for worse and even adopt an anti-German attitude. In any case, I consider the permanent existence of a Bulgarian state problematical. Some day it will become an object of bargain, and sooner or later—but the day will come—you will sit by the fireplace and remember your stormy youth. In St. Petersburg, they know our

wishes. I therefore advise you to seize every opportunity to make peace with Russia.[29]

At the time of the Skiernewice summit, the Prince's international position was more precarious than ever. To be sure, Kálnoky sharply disapproved of Bismarck's approach and Queen Victoria admonished her ministers to come to the rescue of the young man. But the affirmation of Windelband is probably true that both the Austrian Foreign Minister and the English statesmen would watch Russian action without much protest under the pretext that the action made Tsardom's strategic position more vulnerable.[30] That contingency was not too remote. "The man is no good. I have come to this conclusion and do not think he will stay there much longer," the Tsar told Prince William (the future William II) who had brought him the message that "Germany has no interest in the Prince of Bulgaria or his country." Even Giers warned the Austrian Ambassador that albeit she "will for the moment play a waiting game . . . Russia will suffer no restraint where her legitimate sphere of influnce is denied to her."[31]

The activities of the Russian agency in the Bulgarian capital illustrated perfectly that things were heading fast towards a new crisis. Presumably emboldened by Zinoviev, Koiander and his people were increasingly brazen in their campaign against Battenberg. There was no lie which they could not invent in order to defame him: in the rumors they spread the Prince was alternatively a homosexual, impotent, a lecher who invited prostitutes to the Palace and suffered from veneral disease.[32] More seriously, they negotiated the "dynastic question" with the Bulgarian politicians[33] and when they could not obtain the measure of cooperation they expected, their attitude only hardened. In the analysis Koiander sent to Zinoviev on 16 June 1885, the extremist purpose was unveiled in all its overbearance:

> The Bulgarians are scarcely capable of finding their own means to combat the harmful elements. Among the so called intelligentsia there is not enough of the healthy forces which would render it possible to challenge the demoralizing ideas introduced into the Principality by the broad freedoms suddenly offered to semi-illiterate savages. It is my belief that they cannot manage without external help. . . .

The best solution would be our occupation of the Principality, the appointment of a Russian Governor General and the introduction of our laws. Another possibility is to replace Battenberg by a man fully devoted to us. Since the Bulgarians are reluctant to perform the operation, the best method to accomplish it would be to invite the Prince to St. Petersburg, where the Tsar would announce to him that he must not return; the new ruler would then suppress the constitution and thereby, bereft of public sympathy, become entirely dependent on Russia. A third eventuality would be the formation of a Russian government headed by Prince Cantacuzène and reconciliation with Battenberg if he approved it; the fourth—the recall of Russian military personnel, which would lead to chaos and in the end to occupation, because, plunged into anarchy, the Bulgarians would be impelled to beg the Tsar to reestablish order.[34]

Alexander III approved the analysis. "There is no doubt that the moment has come to bring to an end these problems in Bulgaria," he noted down in the margin,[35] blissfully ignorant of what burden the hard line would repose on his shoulders.

* * *

Koiander himself conceded that the drastic actions he proposed might "lead to complications or results contrary to those we expect"; nonetheless, he affirmed, the risk had to be taken inasmuch as "without radical steps we are in danger of losing Bulgaria in any case."[36] Indeed, the estrangement stemming from the antagonism between Bulgarian nationalism and Russian imperialism continued to grow. Despite the petty intrigues in which they indulged, the Liberal leaders themselves wanted to be masters in their own house. "Our liberators must forgive us, but concerning internal administration . . . we do not wish to be under anybody's influence," maintained their slogan, the *Tarnovska konstitutsiia*.[37]

The stance taken by Karavelov, a radical turned into a real-politician par excellence, provides the most revealing example. To support the Prince, he told a Czech guest, became an imperative in order to check "the adventurist policy of Russian careerists"; Bulgarians should neither fulfill the orders of "some little Tsar," nor exchange Battenberg for a henpecked person willing to perform such a service. In another confidential debate, the Prime Minister compared his feelings towards Russia with that of Potugin, the character of Turgenev's "Smoke": he loved Russian literature and those he considered fighters for emancipation; he hated the autocracy and corrupted society.[38]

Equally importantly, since the Sobolev-Kaulbars rule, the Prince had been identified by the bulk of his subjects as the symbol of the national cause. The slanderous campaign orchestrated by the agency proved counterproductive. Kartsov, at that time the consul at Vidin, recalled in his memoirs:

> To us who worked there it was evident that the Bulgarians would no longer tolerate the Russian protectorate and that the position of Russian officers had become intolerable too. The hope of I. A. Zinoviev and his satellites in Sofia . . . to overthrow the Prince with the help of the (Liberal) radicals was a hapless self-delusion. The Prince now triumphed on a large scale. The attempt of a foreign Power, i.e. Russia, to discredit him, brought about the opposite effect. It only elevated him as an expression of the national idea.[39]

Regardless Battenberg's fears that he would be foresaken by the West and his scheming politicians, these were to be the decisive factors in the approaching crisis. Rejecting a reasonable compromise, the Russians were striding towards a portentous bankruptcy of their "Slavic policy."

CHAPTER 29

THE GRAPES OF WRATH:
THE BULGARIAN CRISIS OF 1885

Poor Russia! On the throne, instead of
crowned heads, there are now only crowned fools.
Lamsdorf

It is difficult to come to any satisfactory
conclusion as to the real objects of Russian
policy. I am more inclined to believe that
there are none: that the Emperor is really his
own Minister, and so bad a Minister that no
consequent or coherent policy is pursued;
but that each influential person, military or
civil, snatches from him as opportunity of-
fers the decisions which such person at the
moment wants, and that the mutual effect
of these decisions on each other is determined almost exclusively by chance.
Salisbury

His Majesty's determination to avoid war
was one of the most solid facts of the present
situation. But . . . this determination is subject to the very important condition that no
direct affront, no direct challenge, the refusal
to accept which would involve national dishonour be offered him. In such a case I

> believe that there would be a sudden out-
> burst of passion, blind to all the conse-
> quences, unamenable to the dictates of
> reason, tearing down all before it.
>
> / Morier

In the summer of 1885, the European political barometer pointed high, promising a good time even for the future. The heavy clouds of the Anglo-Russian collision slowly dispersed and the continent east of the Rhine basked under the sun of the three Empires unity. The improvement in the weakest link in the Bismarckian system, the Austro-Russian relationship, appeared particularly auspicious. Commenting upon the Kremsier meeting between Alexander III and Francis Joseph I (on 25-26 August), Katkov welcomed it as the "completion of the work done at Skiernewice"; and a French diplomatic analysis asserted that a "new basis for European peace had been created and a guarantee given for a status quo based on mutual understanding," where "no one needs to be afraid of a clash between Russian and Austrual interests."[1]

Kálnoky arranged a visit of Battenberg at Franzensbad, where Giers was taking waters. The Prince, convinced that his value in the power game had diminished to the point of exposing him to any Russian attack, once again proposed conciliation. He promised the hold Tsardom's susceptibilities in the greatest consideration and above all, dampen the growing agitation for Bulgarian unity. The Russian Foreign Minister, though unmoved in his personal dislike, nevertheless seemed quite accomodating: the preservation of tranquility in the Balkans and the current happy mood in the imperial alliance were visibly his priorities.[2]

Like Giers and Alexander III—the latter departed for his usual sojourn in Denmark—most of European dignitaries left their capitals and places of assignments to enjoy the delayed vacations. No one anticipated that a new tempest would break out soon, this time the fatal one for the whole of the power balance, and that the unification of Bulgaria would initiate it.

* * *

It is true that the division of this Balkan country had always been perceived as a temporary arrangement, yet European diplomacy ceased to number it among acute problems. This was mainly due to the Russian attitude: much to the satisfaction of the other Powers, Tsardom's sympathy for Bulgarian unity manifestly cooled off. At first, St. Petersburg wished to uphold the status quo in order to eschew big international complication; then, with the disappointing development in the Principality, even the Moscow party became wary of a Greater Bulgaria. According to a common belief, the unification would be impending only after Battenberg's eviction, as part of the decisive "Panslav" assault against the Berlin Treaty system.

Events in Eastern Rumelia since 1879, no more encouraging for Russian purposes than those in the Principality, appeared to confirm this presumption.

The first Governor General in Eastern Rumelia, Aleko Pasha Bogoridi (Vogorides) had been expected to do Tsardom's bidding. Instead, being antagonized by the dictatorial manners of Russian consuls general, Prince Tseretelev and Krebel, he sought to encourage the opposition against the new tutelage. In 1881, he obtained important allies: after the coup, when Karavelov fled from Sofia to Plovdiv, the local Liberals turned against the "saviours."[3]

Coupled with the diminishing influence of the hitherto entirely predominant Unionist (Conservative) party, led by the obedient Geshov family, this naturally put the Russians on the alert. But, being unable to look for true explanations—Katkov, for example, discovered the reason for the East-Rumelian mishaps in Krebel's German-Protestant origin(!)[4] — and increasingly alien to the Bulgarian quest, they just changed diplomatic agents.

After Krebel, came the full-blooded disciple of the Katkovian lycée, Sorokin, who pretended to work earnestly for the unity while secretly dreading it. "We keep them (the Bulgarians) only because of the hope of unification," he spelled out the Russian dilemma. "Even now they don't want to respect us. Still less would they be willing to do so when unified."[5] So, even when Aleko Pasha was replaced (in 1884) by Gavril Krästevich, an old stooge of Ignatiev, "feeble and destitute of prestige,"[6] and Karavelov struck his bargain with Ionin and returned to the Principality almost tamed, there was no turn of the tide. Temporarily helped by Sorokin's machinations, the Geshovites were soon compromised like their mentor. Contemptuously dubbed by their kinsmen as "fake

Unionists," they had to leave the initiative for good to radical Liberals of markedly anti-Russian leanings (Zakhari Stoianov).[7]

Briefly, observers read the Rumelian situation in the wrong way, because they registered Russia's dwindling zeal for Bulgarian unity while ignoring the implications of her loss of grip over the nationalist effort. In early 1885, Stoianov set up a revolutionary committee with the programme of "protesting against the conditions in the Balkans with weapons and blood." The body was joined by an officer group of the local militia (Nikolaev, Mutkurov) which committed itself to organize a coup d'état; and the moment of action was eventually fixed on the maneuvres scheduled for September.

The same trend had unwound in the Principality, too. While Karavelov after his return to Sofia cautioned against "adventurist policies," Stefan Stambolov, the young chairman of the Assembly, commanded growing support for his proposition that a forceful pursuance of the main national goal would help to disentangle the web of the other complex problems facing Bulgaria.[8]

Learning from the emissaries sent by the Plovdiv committee (on 9 or 10 September) that the coup would be staged in the next few days, the Prince was put into a quandary. He was afraid to break the promise just given to Giers and thus incite again his cousin's fury. On the other hand, his closest followers advised him that in order to retain the loyalty of his subjects and check Zinoviev's and Koiander's schemings, he must remain a champion of unity as he had always been; according to Golovin, their reasoning was approved by Aksakov, who in his letters pressed to do "something big" and hereby win the hearts of the Tsar and all the Slavs.[9] At any rate, however strongly Battenberg might wish to at least postpone the action, it was already too late. Following half-spontaneous local risings, by 18 September the whole Eastern Rumelia was in the insurgent hands. The perfectly bloodless affair was reminiscent of a carnival rather than a revolution, its most spectacular episode being when Governor General Krästevich departed for exile in an open carriage guarded only by a local lady with a naked sword.

The leaders of the coup proclaimed the union of the two Bulgarias under Alexander of Battenberg and invited him to confirm the new status. Trapped by events, the Prince could not refuse if he wanted to stay on the throne. "The time of hesitation is gone by," Stambolov baldly confronted him with the dilemma. "Two roads lie before Your Highness—the one to Philippopolis (Plovdiv) and much farther God may lead; the other (back home). . . to Darmstadt." With heavy heart, Battenberg set out for Plovdiv and by this act, the fireworks of the Rumelian festival ignited the powder keg lying beneath the edifice of the Bismarckian system.[10]

* * *

In the months preceding the revolt, the Russians had received many warning signals and took both official and behind-the-scenes steps to prevent it. Nonetheless, the Rumelian events caught them unawares just like the other "big ones." The prolonged absence of the Tsar and the Foreign Minister from St. Petersburg made their first reaction even more confused.[11] On 20 and 21 September, the perplexity ended, however, when the Tsar and the Thunderer pronounced their verdicts. The latter wrote:

> In the San Stefano treaty, Russia had planned Bulgarian unity; but 'the meaning, the form of his unity and its timing—that is another question. Russia cannot be against unification, yet she can hardly remain indifferent to who, how and with what purpose will effect it.' From these aspects, events in the Balkans have to be denounced as a conspiracy directed from Sofia in favor of the Prince and hostile to Russia. 'Eastern Rumelia was better off under the Sultan than the Principality under Battenberg and his ministers.' Hence, the status quo ante has to be reestablished forthwith; and 'the unification will be desirable only when Russia liberates Bulgaria from chaos.'

Like Aksakov, Katkov pleaded for a forceful action, but his message—"to break with the policy of half-measures, which is destroying the country liberated by us and wrecking the Russian position in the East"[12]—pointed to an entirely different extremist course, to that solicited earlier by Khitrovo and now by Koiander.

Alexander sounded equally determined. Not surprisingly, he perceived the affair through his usual personal angle, as another insolence by his

Battenberg relative. On 21 September, he proclaimed the union illegal and—still from Denmark—ordered the resignation and recall of all Russian military personnel serving in the country. Also Giers, worried by the collapse of the Balkan status quo and deeply hurt by what he felt to be the Prince's calculated deceit, called for the convocation of an ambassadorial conference at Constantinople which would respond to the violation of the Berlin Treaty.[13]

Terrible perils suddenly loomed before the Bulgarians. The Russian reaction clearly indicated that the "liberatrice" would do almost everything to punish them for their disobedience and topple the Prince. On 20 September, the Porte approved the military plan for the occupation of Rumelia; reservists were mobilized and troops amassed on the frontier. Athens and Belgrade denounced the unification and started war preparations too.

In great historical decisions, nations and their leaders value most the hour of victory and are quite reckless as to the consequences. The Bulgarians were no exception. They were alive to Russia's negative stand; but they believed that she would not dare to jeopardize her prestige by resisting unification openly. They were equally optimistic about the Balkan responses, expecting a general anti-Turkish upsurge and the final Ottoman withdrawal from the area. No one of these calculations proved correct. Nonetheless, by a unique combination of sheer luck, immediate favorable circumstances and the effects of the previous developments, they escaped the seemingly unavoidable doom.

In the first hectic moments, Ambassador Nelidov unwittingly provided relief. Lacking directives and fearing that Turkish intervention would trigger an overall Balkan mêlée, he sternly warned the Porte against resorting to arms. Later, when the instructions to the contrary came from St. Petersburg, conditions had already changed. Sultan Abdülhamid, dreading the risks involved, dismissed on 25 September the warlike Grand Vizier Kücük Said Pasha and replaced him by Kiamil Pasha, an Anglophile moderate.[14] The shift was coupled with a resolute stance taken by the London cabinet on behalf of the Bulgarians.

Back in power in 1885, the British Conservatives had to cope with the painful Liberal heritage. Gladstone and his party, the new Prime Minister Lord Salisbury complained, "have at last achieved their long desired 'Concert of Europe'"; they have succeeded in uniting the continent of Europe—against England." This appeared particularly dangerous to him at this stage when, as he believed under the impact of the Afghan crisis, Russia was making intense preparations for armed confrontation.[15] So, he judged it to be his most urgent task to escape isolation, break the Three Emperors' bloc and stave off Russian pressures at sensitive points.

Already during the summer months, London had sought for closer contacts with Germany and Under-Secretary Currie had prolonged talks with the two Bismarcks, trying to change their views on Russia, the Bulgarian and the Straits problems. The results, however, were thoroughly disappointing. The Chancellor reiterated that if she would seize Constantinople, it "would do no harm to anyone except Russia herself, who would be weakened by the extension of her lines of defence and become more vulnerable." As possible aggressor, he alleged, Tsardom presented no danger at all; "the country was seething with revolution, steeped in corruption, militarily worthless . . . unconquerable in defence but despicable in attack."[16]

For all these reasons, the Bulgarian crisis emerged for the British Prime Minister as a God-sent opportunity.

Salisbury's initial opinion on the Rumelian affair, to be sure, had been negative. Expecting that after the bid in Central Asia Russia wished to revitalize her Near-Eastern policy, he judged the Prince's conduct "very ill-advised"; "if he succeeds, he would only be plucking fruit for Russia to eat." The angry reaction of the Tsar, however, prompted him to a swift turn. On 24 September he already proposed as "the best practical issue" a personal union of the two Bulgarians under Battenberg, the "institutions of each one remaining without change"; this way "both the stipulations of the Berlin Treaty and the wishes of the population would be respected." The British representative at the Golden Horn, White, was warned against taking part in any discussion on sanctions; and the Prime Minister publicly challenged the interventionist plea as a return to the Holy Alliance system, to "the policy of the Congress of Verona."[17]

The Turkish lassitude and the British opposition created considerable hindrances to Russian intentions. Over and above that, the stance taken by the Bulgarians themselves was to be of great consequence. On 3 October, an English diplomat reported on the conditions in Sofia:

Prince Alexander has become universally popular, and the Russians universally detested. His Highness, by placing himself at the head of the movement, has gained the hearts of all the Bulgarians, who will certainly resist to the very utmost of their power any attempt to destroy the union or to dethrone His Highness. . . .

The Russians here are open-mouthed against the Prince, and their violent abuse of His Highness is doing much to destroy the very little influence they still enjoy here. . . . It is evident that they believed that, as soon as it was known that the Tsar disapproved of the movement, the Bulgarians would have deserted the Prince and left His Highness in the lurch. They were amazed that this was not the case and that on the contrary Prince Alexander's popularity if possible increased.[18]

The Russian expectation of chaos in the Bulgarian army proved particularly fallacious. Almost everybody welcomed the withdrawal of the overbearing Tsar's officers and even looked upon the possibility of war with hope rather than with dread.[19]

All this echoed in the St. Petersburg elite. Although on the offensive and having the public behind them, the extremists were soon to wrestle with moderate resistance and counteractions. More importantly, in Alexander's mind, anxiety about consequences commenced to clash with the impulses of vengeful hatred. The net result was that almost incredible disarray in the decision-making process which so bewildered foreign statesmen.[20]

* * *

The extremists from the outset put their stakes on arousing the Tsar's "true Russian feelings." Katkov in his editorials clearly pursued this purpose:

The Bulgarian crisis was a long-premeditated intrigue concocted by Battenberg. Vienna and London and finally agreed on in the summer, i.e. at the time when the credulous autocrat was entertained by the Austrian Emperor at Kremsier. Because of this mischief, the deposition of the Bulgarian ruler and his replacement by a 'person devoted to Russia' had become a matter of principle, where the dignity of Tsardom was exposed to a supreme test. A failure to achieve this object would 'mean that a country liberated by Russia was sacrificed to the worst enemies of Slavdom' and hereby, her 'interests would be irreparably compromised.'[21]

It was not easy to handle Alexander III, though. At the horns of a dilemma, he had been prone to retreat to sulking inactivity; and he showed it already. Blaming the South Slavs for ingratitude, he wrote on 24 September to Obruchev:

> According to my opinion, we must now have one aim only—to conquer Constantinople in order to entrench ourselves in the Straits and be sure that they will remain forever in our hands. This is in Russia's interest and should also provide the direction for our further endeavours. Everything else (including what is) happening in the Balkan peninsula is for us of secondary import. There has been enough propaganda to the detriment of true Russian interests. The Slavs must now serve us, not we them.[22]

This must have heavily embarrassed the Chief of Staff. Venturesome as he was, he could not at this juncture think about taking Constantinople or the Bosphorus. Since the coronation debate two years before, Russian military potential in the Black Sea had not improved and neither were international conditions much better. Besides, he knew only too well about the discrepancy between Alexander's bold words and his hesitations when actions was required. The only thing Obruchev judged proper to do was to direct the Tsar towards a more feasible Galician alternative. In a memoir written in October, he argued as follows:

> The policy of 'false interference in European affairs' and 'the defence of the Slavs' must be abandoned, being but a 'net into which Europe has entangled us.' Instead, immediate problems of Russian security have to be solved: in the first phase, the Polish question should be closed for good by the annexation of Galicia and Bukovina; then, once the safe frontier has been established on the Carpathian Mountains, the great Bosphorus aim could be attained.[23]

Outwardly, Obruchev appeared successful. The idea of a drive to the Carpathians had been intensely discussed and reportedly found many sympathizers including Pobedonostsev.[24] Yet in reality this distraction rather revealed the fundamental weakness of the extremist camp. Devoid— in contrast to the Eastern crisis in 1875-1877—of massive, entirely over-riding public pressure and of sole unifying purpose, the Moscow party and its military allies were forced to accomodate to the changing mood of the Tsar; and, chasing several hares, they became less effective in the final impact.

Upon the return from Denmark, Alexander made his confused and thoroughly negativist stance known everywhere: apart from venom towards Battenberg and those allegedly using him to injure Russian honour, he had but one pervasive feeling—to be left in peace.[25] He would not give count-enance to the opinion held by a rapidly sobered Giers and other moderates that the altered situation in Bulgaria must be accepted somehow, including the elevated status of the Prince. His cousin, "cette canaille" had to be punished and got rid of. Nothing, however, would induce him to a full-fledged confrontation. A council summoned in the middle of No-vember to discuss "the extraordinary measures to be taken in relation to Balkan events" merely confirmed the apparent: instead of proposing the means of coercion, as the topic would suggest, the gathering "pro-duced a unanimous opinion of all responsible ministers" that "in view of the economic, political, military and financial situation . . . the final solution of the Eastern Question should be postponed as far as pos-sible."[26]

Well informed about the autocrat's mood, Katkov also found it ex-pedient to adopt more subtle tactics. He visibly acknowledged that noth-ing could be done for the time being except warm up old animosities and suspicions and wait for a propitious occasion to renew the inter-ventionist plea in full voice. So while continuously recalling Russian honour, he already on 29 September recognized that military involve-ment in restoring the Balkan status quo was futile and suggested reor-ganization "without armed interference provided that the unified Bul-garia will be led not by adventurists but by serious people."[27]

Deflected from applying armed power and reduced to the means of diplomacy, Tsardom could not achieve its purposes. The ambassadorial conference at Constantinople, opened informally in early October and formally on 5 November, brought about only further frustration and widened the gap between Russian wishes and actual developments.

To judge by appearances, the gathering was a mere repetition of dozens of similar hagglings in the long history of the Eastern Question, a "futile struggle with a hopeless task"[28] to find a settlement acceptable to all the "concert." However, there was a momentous variance. Nelidov, representing a Power which had been for two centuries intervening, at least purportedly, on behalf of the Balkan Slavs and Christians, performed as a champion of Turkey's treaty rights, thereby appropriating the role traditionally played by the British and French; whilst his British counterpart, White, vehemently vindicated the Bulgarians. Needless to add, this change was decidedly not furthering Tsardom's prestige in the area.

Moreover, due to headlessness in St. Petersburg, the Russians could not even confront the conference with a clear-cut proposal.[29] While Giers calculated with the triumph of a common Russo-Austro-German diplomatic front,[30] the Tsar and the extremists clung to the belief that by demonstrating anger they would somehow induce the Porte to a military action or the Bulgarians to capitulation.[31] So, on 7 November, against warnings pronounced by Giers, Vannovskii, Grand Duke Vladimir and the St. Petersburg Slavic Committee, the order of the day excluded the Bulgarian Prince from the Russian army list[32]; and, commenting upon the decision, Katkov made the implicit threat plain to everybody:

> Because Battenberg was the 'head of the revolutionary party,' Russia would be satisfied only with his removal together with 'the whole band' of her enemies; and if this ignored by the Turks and they failed to restore their authority, she would consider it 'distinct proof that the Ottoman Empire and the power of the Porte had ceased to exist.'[33]

None of the devices applied had viable effect, although Nelidov re-received backing from his German, Austrian and Italian colleagues, and the Sultan vacillated before manifold threats.[34] Salisbury would not let Tsardom to prevail and his firm position influenced Kálnoky's and Bismarck's stances. The former, naturally, was unwilling to assist to any move which would ensue in the dethronement of the Prince and a Russian protectorate over a united Bulgaria; the latter, despite considerable hesitations—his ideas "lost all coherence, he changes his mind overnight," Holstein complained—would not consider a Russian takeover unless an Austro-Russian understanding was achieved beforehand; and this contingency was, of course, next to impossible.[35] The abortive sounding between Berlin and St. Petersburg in November illustrated best that the state of affairs in the Three Emperors' alliance was ultimately favorable to the British and the Bulgarians.

On 10 November Bismarck proposed "in confidence" to Ambassador Pavel Shuvalov (a brother of Peter Shuvalov) who succeed Prince Orlov at the Berlin post, that an agreement ought to be sought with Vienna "on the question of Russian entry into Bulgaria in case the Bulgarians were to resist the conference's decisions"; and from his side he promised help "if only we were sure Russia was contemplating such a step." The Russian response, delivered on 18 November, brought him an inpleasant surprise. The St. Petersburg statesmen had obviously understood his hint as a counsel to immediate military action and turned it down on the grounds of possible English armed retaliation. The undertaking, Shuvalov told Herbert Bismarck, would be safe only if Germany took part in the intervention; this way, he added, every suspicion and antipathy felt towards the Germans in his country would disperse and any European counteraction prevented. The crux of the original proposal, the Austro-Russian deal, was ignored altogether. Small wonder that Bismarck was frantic: "We gave no advice . . . . And even if we, i.e. I personally, do give Russia advice, it is not with the intention of giving her armed assistance . . . . All we want is peace among the European monarchies."[36]

* * *

The confusion in Russian policies and the English stance made Bulgaria safe from military coercion; nonetheless, she could not escape a big conflict. Milan of Serbia set out to exploit the occasion and enhance his meagre prestige by territorial acquisitions on his Slav neighbour's account. Owing to back-stage maneuvres[37] the restraining pressures exerted by the Powers on Serbia were to remain futile. In the early morning of 14 November, the Sofia government received the Serbian war declaration.

According to general opinion, the Serbs possessed the trump cards. By the withdrawal of Russian personnel, the Bulgarian army lost its former higher and middle commanding staffs; and it seemed to be no more than a loose conglomerate of diverse units, which, moreover, were deployed mostly on the Turkish border, far from the war theatre.[38] The Russian extremists and their proxies in Bulgaria, too, based their calculations on Serbian victory.

Like the whole of the Russian press, Katkov had used Milan's war preparations to broach the explanation that Balkan events were a part of the devious Western conspiracy and had advocated Russian and/or Turkish police action as the redress.[39] Once Serbian troops crossed the borders he made his proposition entirely clear: because the invaders were to reach Sofia "almost without resistance," this would be a perfect occasion to evict the Prince and intervene.[40]

The blueprint of the Russian fifth column in Sofia was identical. "Bulgaria can exist only under Russian military protection; without it, she will collapse, alone she cannot save herself," Tsankov advised in the *Novoe vremia*.[41] On 18 November, while panic spread among the population of the capital, Cantacuzène announced that "everything is finished and by the evening the Serbs will be here" and Koiander summoned political leaders to appeal to the Winter Palace. About fifty persons assembled in the house of Metropolitan Kliment to discuss a resolution asking for the deposition of Battenberg and the proclamation of the Russian protectorate.

On 21 November, in a dramatic exhortation, Katkov proclaimed "the Three Emperors' Alliance powerless in Bulgaria and Serbia" and renewed his interventionist plea with full force: "the dignity of our state, our national honour . . . the most substantial and vital interests are in the gravest danger"; consequently, firm action to save Bulgarian integrity became unavoidable.[42] But, the publicist and his like had built just a miserable sandcastle: their every premise was belied by the facts. In St. Petersburg, as the already mentioned Bismarck-Shuvalov exchange indicated, the policymakers were not eager to get involved. In Sofia, even those who attended the gathering at the Metropolitan denied to participate in an open act of betrayal and Kliment himself allegedly "denounced the Tsankovite traitors."[43] Over and above that, the course the Serbo-Bulgarian war had taken was at total variance with the predicted outcome.

The main Serbian column proceeding along the Pirot-Sofia route was halted at the fortifications of Slivnitsa and defeated in three days of fierce combat (17-19 November). Prince Alexander with his equally young

Bulgarian commanders displayed unexpected talents and efficiency; the whole army overcame its inadequate armaments and organization by tenacity and courage. On the opposite side, on the contrary, when the sanguine expectations failed to materialize, morale plummeted, Milan panicked and the Serbian retreat from Slivnitsa turned into a rout. After another Bulgarian victory at Pirot (25-26 November) the possibility occurred that Alexander would march on Belgrade.[44]

The implications were at hand: instead of being toppled, Battenberg was to rise further in status. But extremist disappointment was not the only result. Official St. Petersburg policy, as enunciated and effectuated by Giers, was severely hit too, its most sensitive spot and the frailty of the Three Emperors' Alliance being again exposed in full.

If the Serbian attack opened the Austrian position to grave hazards, the reversal threatened to be a true disaster. Almost everything was possible—the fall of the Karadjordjević dynasty, uproar in the Slav parts of the Dual Monarchy, the loss of every position in the Balkans. Though alive to the consequences for the already strained Austro-Russian relationship, Kálnoky saw no other escape tan to bolster the tottering King by every means. Khevenhüller was directed to meet Prince Alexander and request and immediate cease-fire; and, in face of refusal to comply "with our friendly advice," he was to intimidate him by armed intervention.

The Austrian diplomat arrived at the Bulgarian headquarters on 28 November and presented the ultimatum in even harsher form than that intended at the Ballplatz. If the armistice were not granted on the spot, he declared, both an Austrian march into Serbia and Russian occupation of Bulgaria would entail. The Prince had to give up.[45]

By enforcing its will and saving Milan from the ultimate catastrophe, Vienna had upheld its image in the area. But for the Bismarckian system the working of the Khevenhüller ultimatum was a pure poison. With good reason the Chancellor lost his temper over Austrian demeanor, the Russians were in uproar and Giers warned the Ballplatz that mutual relations were on the verge of a breach.[46]

As Nolde put it, "for the second time since September Russia was faced in the Balkans with the accomplished fact." First, she had been relegated to the position of a mere observer of Bulgarian unification. Then, she was to see her rival having "the last word in a conflict of vital interest for the Bulgarians and the Serbs; in the eyes of Russian public opinion, this was an intolerable defeat."[47]

Alexander III breathed fire and fury no less than the Russian press.[48] Katkov, who had already before the event questioned Kálnoky's sincerity, could now without any scruples question the soundness of the Skiernewice course.[49] The annual meeting of the St. Petersburg Slavic Committee on 3 December, attended by Ignatiev, the Archbishop of Kazan and several generals including Cherniaev, turned into a full-fledged anti-Austrian demonstration. In his speech, General Durnovo, a man with a strong position at Court, repeated the accusations spelled out by the dailies that the Dual Monarchy was the main culprit responsible for the "fratricide war in the Balkans." On 4 December, a German diplomatic report advised that the Russian military were openly and hopefully talking about the forthcoming campaign in which Galicia would be invaded while 100,000 troops concentrated at Merv would hold the English at bay. The Tsar was allegedly in sympathy with such a "punishment" because the outcome of the Serbo-Bulgarian war convinced him that the Austrian army would be no match for his soldiers.[50]

* * *

At first glance, aroused anti-Austrian hatred and the Bulgarian triumph on the battlefield created a favourable atmosphere for reconciliation between St. Petersburg and Sofia.

General Nikolai Kaulbars, who had negotiated the compromise Russo-Bulgarian military convention in 1883-1884, took up the initiative for a fresh opening.[51] He received wide support. Many in the imperial family and in the policymaking elite—allegedly including Obruchev and Zinoviev—wished that the Tsar would "exchange anger for grace." From Berlin, Bismarck confidentially suggested to make it a hallmark for stabilization in the Balkans:

> By his courage and decision, the Prince of Bulgaria has won his laurels and obtained a position which is to be reckoned with; moreover, the majority of European Powers is on his side. . . . To pull Prince Alexander back to Bulgaria and Turkey to Eastern Rumelia is out of the question. Only one (solution) remains—allow the Porte to name the Prince the Governor General (in Eastern Rumelia).

Giers would have gladly settled on it, too; yet he would not dare to advance such a proposition to the unmollified Tsar. The initiative drained into sand.[52]

Alexander III made up his mind:

> Prince Alexander of Battenberg is an enemy of Russia, and as long as he governs his influence will be hostile to us. . . . Sooner or later he must be expelled. To support the unification under his sceptre, even if he were to become only a Governor General of Rumelia, would mean to reward him for all his mischief. He deserves punishment, not reward. . . . Within six months (anyway) the Bulgarians would be ready to get rid of him.[53]

This, naturally, gave ample elbow room to those who like Katkov wished to "introduce order" by armed force as soon as a suitable opportunity would be at hand.[54] For a while, the Muscovite put it in unmistakable terms, Tsardom would leave the initiative to the local "patriotic, healthy forces" and observe patience, without forgetting, however, that the Bulgarians were "unfit to decide their own destiny as they were unable to free themselves from the Turks"; then the time would come, when "one Russian regiment thrown on Varna" would make all the difference.[55]

There was to be no change in the established pattern: the more setbacks they suffered, the more obstinately the nationalist extremists stuck to the concept of "Governor Generalship," of Greater Bulgaria as a "mere geographically separated province of Russia, with a Dondukov-Korsakov or an Ignatiev (at the helm). . . and with an army on which Russia might rely."[56]

CHAPTER 30

THE HERCULEAN PILLARS OF ARROGANCE:
THE "RUSSIAN CONSPIRACY" OF 21 AUGUST AND
THE KAULBARS MISSION (1886)

The latest news from the East is extremely
confusing to public opinion—everyone is in a
state of anxiety and uncertainty. All feel
that events in the East are not only turning
against us but are aimed against Russia. All
have been thinking that under the shelter
and cloak of the Three Emperors' Alliance
there are concealed mysterious aims directed against Russia and Russian policy in the
East. They are perplexed and ask themselves:
Have we a clear and definite plan of action
in view of England's fervent participation in
intrigue directed against us, obvious to
everyone?
Pobedonostsov

The moment has arrived for fearing God
more than Europe, not only for the sake of
the well-being and redemption of poor Bulgaria, but also for that of our Empire. . . .
The time has come when Russia must take
action openly, fearlessly and firmly in the
name of the Church, Autocracy and im-
memorial traditions, and severing all connections with revolution, she must obtain

the mandate of Europe for re-establishing
order in Bulgaria.
Meshcherskii

The only immediate solution of the present
crisis appears to be the occupation of Bulgaria. Bulgaria does not need a diplomatic
representative at (her) unlawful government
but a commissary with dictatorial powers for
one year or two.
Katkov

Although Russian moral credit in Bulgaria had been shattered, the "Russian conspiracy" against the country remained throughout the whole of
1886 the focal element in the rapidly deteriorating international situation
and the final breakdown of the Three Emperors' Alliance.

The heroic, enthusiastic yet extremely exacting months of the unification crisis and war were not unexpectedly followed by those of weariness
and discord. Personal aspirations and unsettled accounts always surface in
such historical circumstances in newly formed structures and Bulgaria was
no exception. Due to the special conditions produced by the earlier developments, those dissatisfied in their ambitions inevitably found a rallying
point under the Russian banner; and for that purpose the occupation fund
supplied an additional and very alluring stimulant.

The case of Drangan Tsankov is most instructive. Progressively outmaneuvred by his younger rivals and heavily in debt, the old politician
turned literally into a full-time paid mercenary in the service of Russia.
In his request for "monetary assistance" from the occupation fund, he was
joined by two other prominents, Burmov and Balabanov. At first, the
Tsar rejected their high financial demands but later, captivated by his anti-
Battenberg obsession, became more accommodating. The Tsankovite
triumvirate was promised 40,000 francs in annual subsidy for "publication of a newspaper explaining to the Bulgarians their true interests." In a
written pledge, the recipients entered into an obligation "to follow in their
activities a line identical with the opinion of the Imperial government."[1]

It was very symptomatic that the Russian-subsidized Tsankovite organ,
the *Svetlina,* advertized as the "opinion of the Imperial government" the
views of the extremists. Russian occupation was canvassed as the "second
liberation" and the readers were exhorted to look forward to "that beautiful

day" when "the Don Cossacks would appear in Ruse and Varna . . . the Russian army band playing our national march" and when "people would breathe freely again, as in 1878, when liberated from the Turks."[2] No wonder that Katkov named Tsankov and his minuscule clique the "Bulgarian national opposition" against the "predatory, anti-national band which had usurped power."[3]

Among the others, who were bought in the same manner, the largest sums were, according to Ambassador Nelidov, paid to corrupted ecclesiastics.[4] But, for the developments, the recruitment of several dozen officers into the Russian fifth column was of the greatest consequence; and it was also in the army that the specific conditions of the post-unification period found its keenest expression.

While the Prince won overall respect by his leadership in the critical period, an important segment in the new officer corps turned against him. Some had already clashed with the ruler during the Serbian campaign over matters of tactics, some felt inadequately promoted and rewarded afterwards. The rivalry between the "Rumeliots" (i.e. those originally serving in the Rumelian militia) and the "northerners" (from the army of the Principality) introduced an additional element of friction. Hence, Colonel Sakharov, the Russian military attaché entrusted by his St. Petersburg superiors to organize the malcontents in uniform, could report promising progress.

Battenberg was in an uneasy position. The war had disrupted finances and deeply affected the whole economic life. Unrelenting Russian animosity forced him to seek escape from the diplomatic stalemate in a direct agreement with the Turks. Although the Turco-Bulgarian treaty signed in February 1886 was in the circumstances a reasonable compromise,[5] in many Bulgarian eyes it denigrated the very act of union.[6] Furthermore, in its final act the Constantinople conference (on 5 April 1886), approved Salisbury's original formula, but it confirmed upon Russian insistence only "the Bulgarian Prince" as Rumelian Governor-General, avoiding the naming of Battenberg.[7]

True, the prevailing mood was clearly in favour of national independence and against Russian interference; in the elections held in both Bulgarias, the Tsankovite opposition suffered a total defeat. Yet there was again, as before the unification, a dangerous hesitation among the politicians on whether the country should not seek accommodation with the Tsar and eventually sacrifice the Prince. In the Karavelov government,

Foreign Minister Tsanov and War Minister Nikiforov were directly involved in Russian schemings and the Prime Minister himself prevaricated.[8]

The Russians and their clients could indulge in subversion almost without constraint. Not only were the Tsankovites allowed whatever they wished and collect signatures for a petition asking Alexander III for a protectorate.[9] When Captain-Major Nabokov (the nephew of Russian Justice Minister) organized a Montenegrin band with a task of abducting or murdering the Prince, he could escape punishment: in May, the authorities found out about the plot and arrested the participants, but a stern Russian warning sufficed and the government, afraid to give a pretext to military intervention, released the main culprit.[10]

Battenberg tended to ignore the brewing conspiracy. "I do not wish to remain the Prince by force," he declared, "and if they don't want me, let them tell me so and I shall go voluntarily." In particular he would not renounce his German notion of a soldier's loyalty: Captain Gruev, the chief army plotter, was for him a "honest man and devoted officer," entitled to full confidence.[11]

* * *

The more European-minded among Russian statesmen and diplomats went on pleading for a cautious approach. "Any participation (in internal unrest) or external pressure can only unite the elements hostile to us and, helped by other influences, fortify the (Sofia) government," the sobered former hawk Nelidov warned from Constantinople.[12] But what the diplomatic reports named "the universal wish" was identical to that of the Tsar and the publicist: to "blow-up" the Prince and re-establish the "old tradition of Russia's Eastern policy."[13] In addition, the rising combativeness was not limited on the Battenberg issue only: the wrath of the "enragés de la cause" extended with gathering momentum on the usual big targets.

The launching of a new warship at Sevastopol evoked threatening noises well expressing the trend. The most outspoken *Novoe vremia* wrote:

> If a Prussian Prince were not reigning in Bulgaria, if none of the existing misunderstandings had arisen, the meaning and significance of the Sevastopol ceremony would be the same. It is with Europe that we had to deal in the Crimean War and it is with her and not

with any Prince of Bulgaria . . . that we have to deal in solving the Eastern Question.[14]

In Moscow Alexeev, the city mayor, greeted the visiting Tsar with an appeal in the same vein.

Giers visibly dangled in void, his person and policies being exposed to increasingly disparaging comments from the Strastnyi Boulevard and other extremist quarters. After a talk with the minister, Ambassador Morier observed:

> The episode of Moscow, I could see, has reduced him to despair. Yet here he was, the representative in the eyes of Europe of the foreign relations of Russia, unable to move a finger against the enemies who were making his entire diplomatic action an absurdity.[15]

Earlier, the British diplomat believed that even the reckless ones like Obruchev or Ignatiev "were quite determined not to risk a war as long as Emperor William is alive and Prince Bismarck by his side."[16] Now, he felt constrained to advise his government:

> I have no wish to indulge in pessimistic dreams. But living in this country . . . it is impossible for me to ignore the many political complications which may be in store for us and against which we should be wise to be forewarned and forearmed.[17]

Considering that Morier had since the 1870s vehemently advocated concessions to Russia and had been regarded by the Queen and the Conservatives as almost a Russian tool, this cannot be taken for an exaggeration. Also his Turkish colleague, Shakir Pasha, alerted the Porte that "the current was getting too strong" and that the Tsar and his ministers "might be carried away by it."[18]

Western observers mostly assumed that it would be the Straits or Asia, rather than the Balkans, where the extremists would trigger a major confrontation. And there were, indeed, serious signals to that effect. The British Embassy acquired copies of secret plans indicating that the danger threatening the Indian security zone might still be ahead. The most significant of these documents was the project of General Kuropatkin, who in

the name of the General Staff and the Caucasus command again proposed
a three-pronged advance on Herat and Kabul, with India as the final destination. The mission of General Shepelev, the chief of Dondukov's chancery, to Teheran, was another cause for British worries. According to an
intelligence report, the General brought to the Persian capital a draft of
secret convention which would enlarge the one concluded in 1881 and
assure Russia of an ally in a war against England and/or Turkey; if the
Shah refused it, the report asserted, the provinces of Mazendran and Gilan
were to be annexed.[19]

The anxiety about next developments in the Straits and east of them
were the reason why the London government reacted vigorously when in
July 1886 St. Petersburg, violating the Berlin Treaty, announced the abro-
gation of the free-trade status of Batum.[20]

In order to assuage the equally alerted Germans, Giers and Peter Shuvalov stimulated the "Straits-Asian" explanation. They claimed that the
Tsar considered his prime duty "to close the outlet from the Bosphorus
to the Black Sea with Russian forts" and "all his intentions were centered
on this"; and that also Katkov's recently begun anti-German agitation was
solely engendered by the intention of wrestling from Berlin the greatest
measure of cooperation for the Eastern enterprises.[21]

Nonetheless, it was still the Bulgarian theme, disastrous for the Three
Emperors' Alliance, on wich the extremists primarily centered their zeal;
indeed, it grew into an overriding obsession comparable with the anti-
Polish rancor, reaching "as far down as the peasant stratum."[22]

* * *

The final plan for the Bulgarian coup had apparently been agreed upon
in secret talks between Colonel Sakharov, the military attaché, and the
local army cabal. The Russian agency communicated to St. Petersburg its
essentials as follows:

> Rumors about an impending new war with Serbia will be spread
> to confuse the government and to provide the excuse for removing
> from the capital the units and officers loyal to the Prince; then Alex-
> ander will be seized and a provisional government composed of suit-
> able representatives of the political parties, will request an Imperial

commissary (Dondukov-Korsakov or Ignatiev) and invite Russian officers to take over command of the army again.[23]

The first stage of the scheme was put into effect without complications. After the elite First ("Alexander") regiment departed for the borders, troops controlled by the conspirators occupied, on the night of 20-21 August, a sleeping Sofia, took the Prince prisoner and dispatched him under heavy escort out of the country, into Russian custody. "Bulgaria is prostrated at the feet of Your Majesty," Tsankov wired to Alexander III. Metropolitan Kliment, proclaimed the head of the provisional government, exhorted a crowd of about 200 persons to beg the Tsar for forgiveness and led it to the Russian agency; there, the procession kneeled in ankle-deep mud in an act of obeissance.[24]

Europe did not stir. The press in subdued tones deplored the bitter end of the Prince but acknowledged that "Russian diplomacy has won a tremendous victory and Russian dominance has been established for good."

Ambassador Hatzfeldt informed the Wilhelmstrasse that "the English, convinced that the three Emperors have already settled the Near-Eastern question among themselves, dare not take action alone"; Randolph Churchill, a prominent figure in the Salisburg cabinet, told him that "he is decidedly in favor of agreement with Russia which he does not consider difficult, since the English can enter into any agreement provided that India is secured." It was also believed that Morier in St. Petersburg had already been at work on such an understanding which would, "in exchange for the Indian guarantee . . . turn over to the Russians the entire Balkan peninsula and Austria."

What looked like a total British retreat, undermined Kálnoky's resolve. On the parleys just taking place at Kissingen and Bad Gastein, he conceded, upon the insistence of Bismarck, that Russia should be allowed to remove the Prince from the Balkan scene.[25]

Bulgaria's destiny seemed to be sealed off and the Russian press was jubilant over the triumph. Buoyed by the supine European response, Katkov explained it as proof that regardless of the Berlin Treaty, the Principality had always tacitly been recognized as a Russian domain:

> The Prince who ruled Bulgaria was a lieutenant of Russia and all his rights derived only from his obligations towards the Russian

Tsar. The relations between Russia, Bulgaria and her Prince have been understood by everybody precisely in this manner and could not have been understood otherwise.[26]

These were, however, highly premature conclusions. In the moment of supreme trial, Bulgarian nationalism demonstrated its surprising vitality.

Already the formation of the new government disclosed the truth; nobody outside the notorious circle of politicians close to the Russian agency and the occupation fund would compromise himself by joining it. Then from the nationalist stronghold of Tarnovo Stambolov, the chairman of the Assembly, publicly defied the coup and set out to organize resistance. He found immediate response in the south where on 22 August the officers of the Plovdiv brigade headed by Major Mutkurov decided to launch a "march of liberation" on Sofia. Most of the garrisons and the First Regiment joined the action. In a manifesto issued by Stambolov and Mutkurov "in the name of Prince Alexander I and the National Assembly," the government of the Metropolitan was declared illegal and everybody assisting it threatened to be "sentenced and punished according to military law."[27]

The plotters were in total disarray and only direct Russian intervention could save them. But, notwithstanding big words pronounced and money delivered—Nelidov allegedly said that 300,000 francs were spent on the coup[28]—St. Petersburg was unprepared to step in.

From scanty documentary evidence it may be surmised that Sakharov was planning the action under Obruchev's direction and that the army had been inclined to prop it; but that Giers had given the promise of assistance only half-heartedly, out of fear of displeasing the extremists. The Tsar had been very sceptical. "I am afraid that nothing sound will come out of it," he noted on the crucial dispatch to the Sofia agency. Thus Zinoviev, the man who bore the direct responsibility, had also remained uncommited. "In such ticklish matters, we cannot avoid being extremely cautious," to have "means of escape" and eschew open participation which "could compromise us," he prevaricated.[29]

The two key persons on the spot, Sakharov and the acting Consul General Bogdanov, another disciple from Katkov's "Lyceum of Tsarevich Nikolai," had been left without clear instructions; hence, when the Metropolitan and Tsankov appeared on 21 August in the agency and asked for the Tsar's protection, they were offered only empty words. Neither the outcry of the Russian press and public, nor the resigned European response made Alexander III more daring. He agreed to advance additional 800,000 francs from the occupation fund to finance the pronunciamento, yet persevered in evasion on the main issue: the Bulgarians would be protected against external threat (nonexistent at the moment), but short of it, there would be no military move. He even declined Giers' advice to send Prince Dolgorukov to Sofia as the imperial commissary; he was at one with Nelidov who cautioned to "delay the departure of Dolgorukov in view of the emerging disorders in the country."[30]

In despair, Bogdanov turned to Karavelov, who had earlier refused to join the "Russian government" of Kliment, to help him out of the quagmire; and promised him that the agency would interfere no more in internal affairs, if only the Prince stayed out of the country. The caretaker government formed on this basis on 24 August, though, could not stop the loyalist action either. Stambolov would not let victory slip from his hands; and he knew that any authority could be upheld solely by the consistent identification with the legitimate ruler. Moreover, St. Petersburg muddled the Bogdanov-Karavelov effort. The impatiently awaited instructions came at last but they were completely out of touch with reality: the men who took over on 24 August were to be given hope for reconciliation without, however, being supported or trusted.[31]

His last hopes crumbling, Bogdanov wired on 27 August: "The situation is deplorable. I am powerless. I am deeply convinced that if I am not to be empowered to announce that the occupational corps is being embarked on ships, the proclamation (restoration) of the Prince is inevitable." The Tsar, however, dismissed it: "All this is nonsense and all those in Sofia, including Bogdanov, do not know what they are doing."[32] Of course, the diplomat knew only too well "what he was doing." When on 30 August Rumelian troops entered the jubilant capital, the restoration of Battenberg was considered a foregone conclusion. Only the latter himself weakened the overwhelming impact of the Russian debacle.

The Prince had been escorted by the conspirators to the Danube and then to Reni on Russian territory. He had been kept there briefly in custody and then the Tsar ordained to deliver him to the Austrian border.

Deeply shattered by the experience he had to undergo the young man wished only to find peace and solace in his native Darmstadt. On the way through Galicia, though, he received several important messages—from Queen Victoria, Crown Princess of Prussia, the members of the Hesse-Battenberg family, and, naturally, from Stambolov in the name of the population—which urged him to prevent Dolgorukov in establishing Russian dictatorship. Although with utmost reticence, the Prince changed his mind.[33]

Battenberg's return to Sofia developed into a huge demonstration, with Polish, then Rumanian and finally Bulgarian crowds giving vent to their anti-Russian feelings. The changing mood among European elites was fiercely articulated by Queen Victoria:

> My indignation and fury against your barbaric semi-Asiatic tyrannical cousin are so great that I can hardly trust myself to write about it. But thank God he has done himself very great harm in Germany, particularly also in Austria, and here naturally everyone is absolutely horrified. My government will make every effort to influence the Powers in your favor and against Russia . . . . [34]

Yet, full of misgivings against both Europe and the Bulgarian politicians who had so often relinquished him, the Prince was already lacking in the courage to resist "his tyrannical cousin." When the vice-Consul at Ruse and correspondent of the *Moskovskiia vedomosti* Shatkokhin, who pretended to be confided by Katkov with a "Balkan mission,"[35] approached Battenberg with a vague promise of conciliation, the latter made his ultimate mistake. He sent to the Tsar a telegram of politically suicidal content, offering "final proof of devotion": "As Russia has given me the crown, I am prepared to give it back into the hands of her sovereign."[36]

Appalled by the mess caused by the Tsar and the extremists, the moderates would have welcomed the reconciliation. The Singers' Bridge officials composed several memoirs on this theme, but the autocrat turned them down. In the end, he wrote the reply himself and ordered to publish it forthwith:

> I cannot approve of your return to Bulgaria in view of the disastrous consequences which may entail in the country so severely tried . . . I reserve judgment upon the course I am bidden to take

by the honoured memory of my father, the interests of Russia, and the tranquility of the East.[37]

"God be thanked!" The firm and mighty word of the Russian monarch, raising high the national spirit of Russia has put an end to this scandal," Katkov exclaimed.[38] The extremist cause, which appeared irreparably harmed by the August tests, retained its fair chance.

Instead of clarifying the situation and relieving the burden imposed by the prolonged crisis, the imprudent overture of Battenberg aggravated it still more. All those around him, and the Prince himself, regretted his folly; and they asked at least for "binding assurances" that the "independence of the nation would not be harmed," the constitution and the act of unity be respected and the country would not come "under the rule of a Russian governor."[39]

Literature on the subject has assumed that these guarantees were actually given.[40] Indeed, in the final proclamation of the Prince, issued on 7 September, the day of his farewell to Sofia, there was a sentence to the effect that "I have received from the government of His Majesty the Tsar of Russia the assurance that independence, freedom and the rights of our state will not be jeopardized and that nobody will interfere in its internal life."[41] But, on 20 September Staal notified the London cabinet as follows: "In the act of abdication. . .the Prince had stated that the Emperor had assured him that he would respect the independence and watch for the interests of Bulgaria. That statement was not exact. All that the Emperor had done was to direct the Russian agent to act in concert with any provisional government in Bulgaria which would be able to maintain order and liberty."[42]

The Tsar might have been tired of Bulgarian complications and willing to give the guarantees,[43] but if that was the case then the hawks made him change his mind. Katkov had severely reprimanded his lyceist Bogdanov for waiting for instructions and not acting at his own risk.[44] Now, the publicists and his alike were out to exploit Battenberg's blunder. As Morier reported, they were "anxious that no Prince should be elected at all. . .and that in the place of a foreign Prince either a Russian general or a native Bulgarian enjoying the confidence of Russia should be appointed as the 'administrator' of the country,"[45] i.e. the final solution was to be prepared when the Tsar accepted the Bulgarian crown and the territory beyond the Danube received a status similar to that of Finland or a standard Russian gubernia.

* * *

Katkov's total emotional involvement in "the matters of foreign policy connected with the Bulgarian question," dominating the last period of his life, was to bring about far-reaching consequences.

In the Muscovite's interpretation, Russian mishaps looked even worse than they were in reality. The Bulgarian unification in the form approved by the Constantinople conference he took for the final blow to Russia's traditional influence, a "kicking her off the Balkans":

> 'Prince Alexander obtained in full all that he has wished and the protocol of the conference is the protocol of his triumph'; by taking part in such a settlement, St. Petersburg's diplomacy has made an impermissible concession to the West and departed from Russian dignity and vital interests in a manner which could have been tolerated 'only after an unsuccessful war.'[46]

As for the "Western conspiracy," he for some time directed his wrath exclusively against England and Austria-Hungary. German conduct was questioned only indirectly, the implications hinted at, however, were significant enough:

> In one thing Lord Salisbury has succeeded. His Balkan policy has disclosed the secrecy everybody was alive to—the shrill disharmony in the concert of the three Northern empires organized by Prince Bismarck. . . . At any rate, Russia should not regret this success (of Salisbury), because owing to it she has regained the indispensable freedom of action.[47]

By the spring 1886, the last crucial twist came about in the editor's thought. He became convinced that they key role in the "plot" was played by the very Power "in whose good intentions Russia had trusted,"[48] that behind the failure lay a diabolic plan of the German Chancellor to isolate and mortally weaken her. From this angle, Katkov reinterpreted the whole crisis started by the Rumelian revolt. Summarizing the development in the first half of 1886, he affirmed:

> In the last six months, all the civilized world could observe a very strange picture. The main monarchical Powers of Europe tolerated the triumph of a predatory conquest. To the impostor (Battenberg) everything was forgiven and he was even encouraged openly to commit unlawful deeds. As a result, 'Russia has in fact been isolated and events had taken their course not only beyond her control but even dead against her.'[49]

The reports in the English press that a "league of peace" was in the offing, incited his sickly imagination. He obviously leaned to the proposition that an Anglo-Russian war might break out in which Germany would take the enemy's side.[50]

Inclined to respond on perils he scented by enhanced combativeness, Katkov intimated (in April) to his Paris confident Elia Cyon the new scenario of action: he had found Russia's breach with the Bismarckian system imperative and, in order to ensure the triumph of his free-hand concept and thwart the machinations of the Berlin schemer, he decided to work for a Russo-French rapprochement. He empowered Cyon to sound out the French and invited him to open a campaign in the *Moskovskiia vedomosti* for that purpose.[51]

Though a long-time partisan of the Russo-French alliance, the latter felt quite uneasy. There were, of course, considerable sympathies among the Russians for France and even some contact between the military, but since 1870-1871 policymakers on both sides had never seriously contemplated that alternative; the Muscovite himself, it is to be recalled, had many times condemned the idea as not only barren but self-destructive. Moreover, considering the actual state of mutual relations, such an initiative appeared particularly ill-timed.

The French elections in 1885 substantially strengthened the anti-Russian Radical party. In order to secure a parliamentary majority, the moderate republican leader Charles de Freycinet had to offer the Radicals four seats in his government and satisfy some of their demands. In January 1886, in a presidential amnesty for political prisoners, the notorious anarchist Prince Kropotkin was set free. The Tsar's annoyance scarcely subsided when Freycinet recalled Ambassador General Appert, a monarchist much liked by the imperial family. This time, the autocrat flared up: the "lousy government" in Paris was only a "bunch of scroundels" and the regime it represented "no longer a republic but a Commune." He refused to accept General Billot as Appert's replacement and ordered his Ambassador, Mohrenheim, to leave French territory. When in early autumn Freycinet, under Radical insistence, pushed through a law on the expulsion of the heads of families who had once reigned in France, the breach appeared irreparable.[52]

Nonetheless, in early May Cyon started his series of articles to prepare, as he put it, the ground for the Thunderer's heavy artillery. At first, alluding to the most pressing Russian distress, he accentuated French financial power as a factor which could alleviate the dependence on German banks. Then, probably prompted by the ferocious outburst of his master against "Western conspiracy" in the Balkans, he made his bid more daring. Because of increasing French military power and militant spirit, he claimed, Tsardom had nothing to fear from Germany: "she will not throw herself into any serious action against our plans as long as there is poised behind her back an army of one and a half million men, excellently armed and prepared to fall upon her with the genuine furia Gallica."[53]

When the French revanchist leader Paul Deroulède came to Russia for Aksakov's funeral, Katkov for the first time openly displayed his volte-face. While the official Russia frowned upon the demonstrative gestures of the unwanted guest—at a funeral mass, Deroulède appeared with a wreath dedicated to the "great Russian patriot, a friend of Skobelev" and decorated with the tricolor and the ribbons of Alsace—the publicist entertained him and uttered praise for what he called the "substantial change in the French attitude to Russia."[54] Then, on 30 July, he used the "heavy artillery" in his most famous editorial.

Commenting on the expected meeting of Bismarck with Kálnoky and Giers at Kissingen, the Thunderer started by comparing the "pilgrimages" of the Russian Foreign Minister to the German Chancellor with the "ancient voyages (of Russian vassals) to the Golden Horde." After this shocking opening, he challenged the very concept of Russo-German intimacy, claiming that it had been "much more a necessity for Germany than an advantage for Russia":

If Germany is so high, is it not because she has risen upon Russia's shoulders? . . . For whose good are these alliances, those accords? . . . Even now, Russia would have only to restore her freedom of action— to cease, in other words, to serve as a carrier of Germany—and the phantom of German omnipotence would dissolve in an instant. Russia would then take her place in the company of other states. . . . It is not natural that a Great Power such as Russia should remain, under the quise of friendship and alliance, . . . in a state of blind subservience to an external will, as though under hypnotism.

'What need do we have to secure European peace? Are we supposed to be the gendarmes of the European world? And what is the peace of Europe, anyway? It is enough for us to secure the peace of Russia, within the framework of her own interests.' Instead of serving as a pawn on the chessboard of the Bismarckian system, Tsardom should restore its independence and change 'from a slave into a real friend of those who are our friends.' 'We would like Russia to be in free though friendly relations with Germany, but we would like to see ourselves having similar relations with other Powers, and the same with France, which . . . is assuming more and more the position most appropriate to her in Europe.'

From the aspect of handling the Tsar, the final part of the editorial was a true masterpeice. The publicist expertly wrapped up a criticism of Alexander's emotional reaction to French domestic policies with sentences he could be sure the autocrat would approve:

'Why indeed should we quarrel with her (France)? And what need do we have to interfere in her internal affairs?' Tsardom must only look after its own interests, 'keeping a sharp eye on the march of events.' 'The others, while themselves grabbing everything not nailed down, charge Russia with a passion for acquisitions. Not being in the habit of starting things, we have no need of allies; but it would be strange on our part not to wish that our opponents had other opponents besides ourselves.'[55]

Paradoxically, never before had Bismarck striven so much to save the Three Emperors' Alliance by supporting Russian claims and was so near to the Russian option as at that time. That he posted his son Herbert, who wished to abandon the Dual Monarchy, at the head of the Wilhelm-strasse, made even some of his long-standing lieutenants agree with the Crown Prince's group that he had turned into a dupe. "For the first time in twenty-five years I mistrust Bismarck's foreign policy. The old man is led by his son, and the son is led by vanity and the Russian Em-bassy," Holstein wrote in his diary.[56]

But, as the critics had foretold,[57] the utmost zeal of the two Bismarck in pleasing the Russians made the Tsar and his subjects wide open to suspicions of German deceit and to its crystallized expression—the Kat-kovite outcry. The Chancellor himself could not ignore the tokens sug-gesting dangerous twist of the autocrat towards the Muscovite's position following the fatal editorial of 30 July.[58] On 11 September, Alexander signed the order to bestow Katkov with the highly prestigious St. Vladimir Cross, which the poor Giers had coveted for so long and so in vain; si-multaneously, he gave a green light to another extremist action in Bul-garia required by the publicist.

* * *

Stambolov and his followers who took over the reins of the govern-ment after Battenberg's departure knew only too well that their en-deavours had to be directed towards stabilization. All political groups except the utterly compromised Tsankovites were represented in the cabinet and nominations for ministerial posts were made in consulations with the Russian agency. On 10 September, the Tsar's birthday, the three regents (Stambolov, Mutkurov, Karavelov), Prime Minister Rado-slavov and other highest officials attended to Te Deum officiated by Kliment and then visited Bogdanov to express goodwill and plead the same from the Russian autocrat.[59]

The impression among diplomats in St. Petersburg was that after the fortunate outcome of the Battenberg affair the Russians would "for the present affect an attitude of extreme moderation"[60] and that the Regency regime had a fair chance. In fact, the confrontation course only hardened; and the decisive opinion was that just another push would suffice to achieve the aim envisaged. Katkov pronounced the new Sofia leadership "men without God and conscience, robbers and Nihilists" and went as far as to claim that, his big shortcomings notwithstanding, the evicted Prince was "in every respect more acceptable than Stambolov & Co." No internal force could save Bulgaria from chaos, the extremists reasserted; and because the international conditions were, according to them, still favorable, armed intervention ought to be "the best solution." Alexander III was in accord with them in what appeared at that moment most important: the Bulgarians were ruled by a "band of impostors," and to compromise with it would be a blasphemy.[61]

So, Stambolov's reluctance to set free several detained conspirators and then the announcement of elections for the Grand National Assembly— a body which according to the constitution was to decide on the new Prince—were taken as pretext for the non-recognition of the Regency; and, to the greatest satisfaction among the extremists, the Tsar resorted to the idea of an Imperial commissioner who would settle the matter.

At first glance, the person chosen for the task, the "compromise-maker" General Nikolai Kaulbars, promised that no heavy-handed action was contemplated. Also the instruction given to the General by Giers was obviously mild, directing him to "assist by his counsel...in bringing the present crisis to an end." Yet, albeit the Tsar affirmed to Prince William that he was "disinclined to interfere, because he could not expose Russian soldiers to the experience of being treated as enemies by the Bulgarians," the briefing of Kaulbars by him and by Obruchev, which took place at the maneuvres near Brest Litovsk, must have been at considerable variance with moderation. In the words of Tatishchev, the way the General subsequently behaved "could be explained by one calculation only—to create a justifiable excuse for occupation"; and we may at least assume that he was empowered to use any device to create a crisis and force the Regency to capitulation.[62]

Thus, as it happened, General Kaulbars by his mission "brought the theory of preferential Russian rights to the Herculean Pillars of absurdity."[63] Never had the true Russian "Slavic policy" and its bankruptcy been paraded in such a flagrant manner; even the deeds of Parensov, Khitrovo, Ionin and Koiander paled before it.

The determined Bulgarian stance was of decisive consequence for the failure. The Russian fifth column—or the "ruble party" as it was called in contrast to the "Bulgarian party" embracing all national currents[64]—revealed its isolation and incapacity for a large-scale action, so

badly needed by the extremists in order to win the Tsar for the "second
liberation." Nekliudov, another disciple of Katkov's lyceum now in
charge of the Sofia agency, had to concede that "unfortunately, the
opposition is not representing the people and influences the people less
than other parties."[65]

Kaulbars set out for the showdown already a day after his arrival
at the Bulgarian capital, on 26 September, by presenting the first of his
intimidating notes. He "advised" the government to delay the elections
"for as distant time as possible," to lift the state of siege and release all
those imprisoned for complicity in the August coup; any act of the Grand
National Assembly or an election of a new Prince would be considered
illegal, he warned.[66]

Bulgarian polite but firm insistence that the constitution must be
respected, only enraged the General. "The Tsar knows the Bulgarian
constitution better than you," he retorted to Stambolov. Further notes
followed, and, at the same time, Kaulbars made the feud public. Russian
claims and complaints were summarized in a long statement and distributed throughout the country. On 3 October, the commissioner appeared in person at a gathering in a Sofia square to harangue it against
the Regency. This was not only an encroachment upon diplomatic norms
but also a foolish deed bound to disclose the basic Russian weakness:
he was shouted down and the scandal made him ridiculous both in Bulgaria and Europe.[67]

Kaulbars, however, would not sober up. He resolved to go to the
province, in the hope of arousing a military revolt or at least inspiring
an overall boycott of the elections scheduled on 10 October. (The Tsar
applauded his resolution: "I agree with this and this is also necessary."[68]
So, after the "Sofia tour," he was to be administered another lesson.
On the streets of minor townships the same hostility—or indifference—
awaited him; and, above all, although there was considerable tension in the
garrisons of Shumen, Sistova, Ruse and Viddin, the unruly officers floundered, facing determined colleagues and subordinates loyal to the Regency.[69]

"The movement of garrisons, with which we had at one time connected
out expectations, has obviously been frozen," Nekliudov reported on
10 October. The elections took place despite Russian intimidations. In
vain, the agency's clients tried to disrupt voting at least at one of Sofia's

polling centers; outside the capital, the boycott tactics succeeded in only two districts. The National bloc unifying parties and groups supporting the government obtained 477 of 522 seats.[70]

In the meantime, Kaulbars had been losing the "war of notes" too. At the outset, he had seemingly followed Giers' instruction and only "advised." Then, he had thrown away even this vestige of diplomatic nicety and pronounced his "energetic castigation" to the government. The net effect was still more harm for the Russian cause. Sofia went on responding in courteous but determined manner. "Bulgarian ministers accept a castigation solely from the representatives of the nation, as is the custom in every constitutional country," Foreign Minister Nachovich replied.[71]

* * *

The members of the Bulgarian fifth column realized that nothing short of military intervention could save the Kaulbars mission. "Send here two regiments of your gallant army. Then we, with the Russian commissary, will be able to harness both your foes and ours," they appealed to St. Petersburg.[72] Katkov conveyed the same plea in much more resolute terms, angrily declining the official formula that the General should only "negotiate and advise":

> There must be no dealing with the regents 'deprived of dignity, unconcealed enemies of Russia and traitors of their people.' 'What Bulgaria needs now is not advice but an iron hand which will put to an end the prevailing lie, violence and anarchy . . . . In the Balkan peninsula what Russia deems necessary will now happen . . . the time of concessions has passed.' The abdication of the Prince was but 'the first step to a peaceful solution'; the decisive one should be to bestow Kaulbars with plenary powers and protect him, if necessary, by 'the occupation of the Principality by Russian troops.'[73]

When the *Russkiia vedomosti* and the *Odesskii listok* voiced the plain truth that "with some exceptions the whole Bulgarian nation has risen against Russia and almost universally hates her" and that the people supposedly craving for another liberation turned its backs on Kaulbars, the Muscovite denounced it as a seditious act of the "St. Petersburg intelligentsia."[74] The more apparent became the failure of the mission, the more were his editorials edged against own government:

> The General, 'the herald of the Russian Tsar-Liberator,' must be supported to the end, by 'uncharging the heavy duty' of occupation. There are no risks of international complications involved: England is 'in decline and powerless'; Austria-Hungary and Germany, too, cannot hinder the Russian 'forward movement in the East.' The sole obstacle lies in the lack of courage displayed in St. Petersburg: 'we go on postponing the occupation of Bulgaria' and this will have the result that 'we shall find ourselves obliged to declare war on her.'[75]

On the Neva, the elite had been increasingly embarrassed by the "great latitude" the Tsar had given to Katkov and Kaulbars and even more by the repercussions it entailed.[76] Morier admonished Giers:

> This participation by the friends and allies of Russia in one of the blackest political plots of the century had been boldly claimed by Mr. Katkov as a title of honour for its authors, and if the Imperial government now sought, through its agent, to shield the criminals, an indelible impression would be produced that official Russia has inspired herself with the views of the *Moscow Gazette* . . . . Do you not see how completely this attitude is at variance with the general character of your policy and the anti-revolutionary ideas which the Emperor and all Russian society with him, pride themselves?[77]

Nonetheless, two weeks after the Bulgarian elections, Kaulbars' dispatches and Katkov's harangues seemed to achieve their purpose. On 24 October, St. Petersburg announced that its warships were to arrive at Varna, purportedly to offer protection to the Tsar's subjects.

* * *

On 25 October, a Russian man-of-war, "Zabiiaka," anchored in the Bulgarian port; four days later, it was joined by another, "Pamiat Merkuriia."

Simultaneously, the Russian consul threatened the authorities that if his country's nationals were molested again, a bombardment would ensue; and Kaulbars in an ultimatum menaced that either his conditions had to be met or a final break was to follow. Since the Russians simply inveted the story of maltreatment, these moves were naturally conceived as a provocation signalling imminent invasion.[78]

Both the "realists" and the traitors among Bulgarian politicians urged capitulation. The commanders of the northern brigades negotiated with Kaulbars, the leaders of the Unionists (Geshovite) party in former Eastern Rumelia did the same with Igelström. On some places, Tsankovite secret committees were set up and their center delivered to St. Petersburg the scenario of "normalization," or "half-occupation" as Kaulbars named it.

It envisaged that the occupation would be performed by a "limited detachment of our (i.e. Russian) troops in brigade strength." The invading force should be landed at Varna, the local officers detained on Russian ships and the garrison itself mixed with Russian units. The same procedure should be applied everywhere until the country was 'liberated.' Then the normalization regime should decide all important matters— the election of the Prince, foreign policy issues, army reorganization— "solely in accord with the advice and directives given by the Russian Imperial government." The "abuses of democracy" were to be eliminated and the internal system based on Orthodox principles; "extremist elements" purged, above all from schools, and deprived of the possibility of influencing people.[79]

After a brief shock, though, Stambolov and his followers recovered and handled the emergency cooly and cleverly again. They set free the imprisoned plotters and by this concession demonstrated willingness to agree on a reasonable compromise as well as trust in the loyalty of the army and the nation. At the same time, they reintroduced the state of siege over the capital, lifted before elections, and resolved that the invasion would be met by force, with the Vidin fortress as the centre of resistance.[80]

Much of the Bulgarian determination sprouted from the proposition that a storm had been rising against the Russians in Europe and that by the threat of invasion the overall resentment roused by Kaulbars' uncouth demeanor would overflow. Indeed, this was what had actually happened.

The sharp British reaction, already noted in the talks Morier had with Giers, was yet more perceptible in the tone Foreign Secretary Iddlesleigh used in conversations with Staal. "With an animation which I have never experienced in our former meetings," the Ambassador reported, the British statesman protested against the affronts of the General, "who seems to treat Bulgaria as a Russian province, imparts to her the Tsar's orders and appears to ignore that other signatories of the (Berlin) Treaty also exist." Staal adminished St. Petersburg that the methods applied against a small Balkan country were, in London, not only "severely judged" but received "almost with satisfaction," owing to their adverse effect upon continental opinion.[81]

From that aspect, events in Austria-Hungary brought the greatest satisfaction.

Under the impact of Kaulbars' performance, the soft approach taken by Kálnoky after the August coup became untenable; and the warnings coming from Bismarck—that Germany would not protect Austria if she became involved in war with Russia provoked by her "Balkan ambitions"[82]—only increased irritation. "Sweeping interpellations" were forwarded in Hungarian Parliament, blaming the Ballplatz for cowardice and Germany for betrayal. This enforced the statement made "in agreement with the Ministry for Foreign Affairs" by Premier Count Tisza, that "the government stands firm in its repeatedly expressed opinion that, under existing treaties, . . . no Power is entitled to undertake any single-handed intervention or set up any protectorate in the Balkan peninsula."[83]

Also in Germany, both the politico-military establishment and the public showed keen resentment to the Bulgarian policy of the Chancellor. The Kaulbars scandal provided a convenient outlet to the bad feelings aroused by Katkov's and other press agitation, by the suspected designs of the Obruchev-Vannovskii clique and by the tariff strife. The both Bismarcks were blamed that their "unfortunate tendency to make every possible diplomatic concession" was the reason why the Russians and their press could treat Germany "with the utmost insolence and contempt, maintaining that our friendship . . . springs merely from fear." Even Emperor William, who had been tagging so long behind his Chancellor, became "outraged" by the Russian conduct in Bulgaria.[84]

To be sure, Russian diplomats delivered until the middle of October optimistic reports from Vienna and Berlin. The Austro-Hungarian government "would confine itself to a platonic protest designed to placate public opinion and the national-Hungarian parliamentarians," wrote Muraviev; he affirmed that both the Emperor and Kálnoky agreed with the two Bismarcks that Tsardom ought to be given free hand. Also Pavel Shuvalov, who met the Chancellor on 15 October, communicated that his interlocutor had warned against the risks of military intervention but that he would nonetheless consider it legitimate and expected only formal Austrian reservations.[85] Yet, the Tsar, though fuming at European reaction,[86] had already resolved not to be drawn into a large-scale crisis. Obviously, however much he might have emotionally approved Katkov's tone and Kaulbars' conduct, nothing short of restuaration of Battenberg would incline him towards the deeds they were championing. As his interview with Prince William at Brest-Litovsk indicated, he was quite conscious of true Bulgarian feelings and knew that the occupation would entail a complete loss of prestige among the Balkan peoples. Coupled with firmness in Sofia, the fear of a forceful European response made his resolution, at least for the time being, final.[87]

Also the army leadership, Jomini intimated to Morier, which had heretofore "advised the immediate dispatch of troops" panicked before the possibility of an "effective alliance between Austria and England" and was "strongly urging against the folly of such an undertaking."[88]

So, Giers could turn down the "normalization scenario" presented by the Tsankovites and his own memorandum was approved: St. Petersburg should leave it to the Bulgarian army opposition to untangle the knot; only internal forces were "ultimately to compel the Regency to bow before the demands presented to it." The Tsar, Zinoviev informed Kaulbars, considered military commitment in the Balkans an "exceedingly serious measure to which we may resort solely in case of extreme urgency"; "as long as an agreement is not attained beforehand from the Powers, nothing can be done."[89]

* * *

Despite the thundering from Strastnyi Boulevard, the warlike spirit of society dwindled too.[90] In the last phase of the Kaulbars mission, only the already tested weapons—local upheavals and diplomatic threats—could be employed.

On 5 November, the notorious Nabokov and his group made an abortive attempt at Burgas; two days later, a similar event took place at Sliven, with another Russian officer, Captain Belov, in the lead.[91] Finally, on 14 November, Kaulbars set off to use an incident at Plovdiv, where a crowd had beaten a Bulgarian employee of the Russian consulate, to present his last ultimatum: he required the dismissal of the local commanders, punishment of those involved in the incident and a formal apology in front of the Russian flag.[92]

The Russian emissary still hoped that if the Regency complied with the demands, it would be compromised in the eyes of loyal officers and the tide be turned at last. This, however, was a chance which the Bulgarian leaders were not constrained to offer. The immediate danger of invasion had passed and further encouraging signals were coming from Europe.

On 9 November, in the traditional Guildhall speech, Salisbury delivered his sharpest attack on Russian conduct.

Describing the Bulgarian events since 21 August, the Prime Minister denounced the men who "debauched by foreign gold," performed a "midnight conspiracy" and equally their foreign supporters, who resorted not only "to save those men from doom they had justly merited," but also for "further encroachments upon the rights of a free and independent people."

Salisbury, Staal complained, "had covered Prince Alexander, and the Regency that succeeded him, with flowers and had reserved all the rigor of his language against Russia." But an even bigger sin which the English statesman had committed was his direct appeal to Vienna: "The opinion and judgment of Austria must weigh with enormous weight in the councils of Her Majesty's government, and the policy which Austria pursues will contribute very largely to determine the policy which England will also pursue."[93]

More significantly still, the scarcely heeded admonition for a common Anglo-Austrian front was strongly echoed in the Danube Monarchy. Delegations had just met in Budapest to discuss financial matters, including defence spendings, and the Hungarians used the occasion to increase the pressure on the Ballplatz. Their press described the task of the gathering in re-establishing "harmony between governmental promises and facts, between that which the government proclaims as its programme and that which it tolerates." In a memorandum for Francis Joseph, Andrássy asserted that "if the Berlin Congress excluded Russia from the Balkan peninsula, my successors have brought her back again"; and that the policy of obeisance to Bismarck's vain effort to appease Tsardom would inevitably lead to the "abdication from our natural power sphere" and to "war as its consequence."

This compelled Kálnoky, in the foreign policy statement on 13 November, to a decisive shift of emphasis.

Responding to criticism, the Foreign Minister defended Bismarck's "advice and mediation" as the "most fruitful way for the peace of the world and our own interests" and still pleaded for settlement with St. Petersburg and a "middle road" on the Bulgarian issue. But the way he reacted to Salisbury's appeal made the final breakdown of the Three Emperors' coalition unavoidable:

> English declarations show that a profitable change of views has taken place in healthy public opinion . . . ; thus the identity of important interests and the wish for the maintenance of peace permits us to hope that England will also join us if it comes to a question of intervening for the upholding of the Berlin Treaty and the legal status created by it. The Austrian position would be that even a temporary single-handed occupation of Bulgaria by foreign troops, any appropriation of the self-governing powers . . . or anything approaching a protectorate be considered as a violation of treaties and in our opinion inadmissible.

"Nobody in Austria-Hungary wishes war. We all yearn for peace, but not for peace at any price," ran the gist of the message.[94]

The Sofia regency could be sure that Kaulbars and his protectors had been deprived of all their strong cards and that it could without running excessive risk turn down the ultimatum.

The Russians stood before Europe empty-handed and humiliated in their haughtiness. After a brief pause, the Tsar, the elite and society alike were in uproar.[95] For Katkov, Kálnoky's speech was a "war declaration" and final evidence of the Germanic conspiracy:

No more proof is needed that the upheaval in Bulgaria has been buttressed, encouraged and made powerful by the intrigue of the allegedly friendly and allied governments.[96]

Still, even he had to recognize that the occupation was at the moment impracticable and the sole hope remained that the Bulgarian fifth column itself would "ignite the fire in which the quasi-government would perish."[97]

When the limit of the ultimatum expired on 18 November, Kaulbars could afford no more than an empty gesture: the Bulgarian government, he announced, had completely forfeited Russian confidence; therefore, diplomatic relations would be broken off as long as it was composed of its present members. Two days later, he left the Bulgarian capital, with only a discouraged handful of Russians and Tsankovites bidding him farewell. In a spell of sobriety, Meshcherskii's *Grazhdanin* pronounced the verdict:

The chief result of General Kaulbars' long stay in Bulgaria is that the truth has thereby been discovered that all the talk about the sympathies of the Bulgarian people towards Russia is completely false, and that it is not the case that the regents are forcing their will on the Bulgarian people, but the people are giving their confidence and support to a Regency which acts against the advice and authority of Russia and will moreover continue to do so.[98]

CHAPTER 31

THE DOOM OF THE THREE EMPERORS' ALLIANCE
(1886-1887)

We should have understood long ago that all
our strength lies within us, that it is impossible to rely upon any of our so-called
"friends" and "allies," that all of them are
ready to hurl themselves upon us at the very
minute when our weakness or errors become
apparent. But we still cling to them, still
want to borrow from them—we are not
bothering to gather in ourselves our own
strength and prepare our remedies.
Pobedonostsev

There is no Russian territory in the Balkan
peninsula, but there is what the Russian
people hold as the most important for itself.
The (Near) East is dear to Russia because of
the bonds and unity and faith. . . . Russia
cannot share the Balkan peninsula with any
other power. . . . It must belong to her with
no exception of race . . . to form with Russia
one system, one world. . . . The integrity of
the East is hardly less substantial and less
dear to Russia than integrity of her own
territory.
Katkov

The Kaulbars mission, "second to nothing in past experience as a fiasco of Russian policy,"[1] overfilled the cup of Russian debasement. European satirical magazines ridiculed "General Sofiasco" and even the French press just trying to cajole Tsardom sneered at him. Moreover, the statements pronounced by Salisbury and Kálnoky accentuated the disruption of Russia's foreign policy system. "The identity of Austrian and English interests was recognized and noisily proclaimed. England has departed from its isolation and this is a fact of considerable importance. The basis on which European peace reposed has been imprudently shattered," Staal observed. Giers too had to concluded that the London cabinet "succeeded in its aim of downthrowing the Three Emperors' Alliance."[2]

Not unlike their earlier reactions, the Tsar, the Thunderer and the public responded by vengeful fury, the overwhelming condemnation of Russian demeanour being for them, as the publicist put it, but "an enormous spectacle where statesmen acted in common with Nihilists and robbers."[3] The ascendancy of Kaulbars and his collusion with Katkov were symptomatic of the Russian scene.

Despite his disasterous Bulgarian performance, the General more than retained the confidence of his imperial master. "You are a soldier obeying the orders of your superior officer; you have acted to my full satisfaction," Alexander repeated his praise. The "obeying soldier" laughed at by the whole of Europe, rose to the stature of the highest authority on Bulgaian affairs. Because of him, we have been told, the flow of "wildly written" resolution from Gatchina plagued the Singers' Bridge more than ever.[4]

Katkov and Kaulbars met in St. Petersburg in December; seconded by Metropolitan Isidor and two leaders of the August conspiracy, Benderev and Gruev, they declared hostility to Giers and to the turncoat Zinoviev and assented that a full backing must be given to the preparation of another coup.[5] Probably at the same time, the Military Council, the highest political consultative body of the armed forces, approved Kaulbars' programme for a "Governor-Generalship"-styled Bulgarian settlement. The programme, presumably confirmed by the Tsar, envisaged that

      (1)   no foreign Prince would be elected to the Sofia throne and that the Principality be placed 'under the supreme rule of

His Majesty the Tsar-Emperor and of a deputy (namestnik) appointed by his will';

(2) the government would be composed of the 'persons who would express in advance their readiness to discharge the demands of the Imperial government';

(3) Russian 'infantry and cavalry regiments and artillery' would be stationed in the Principality and the mixed Russo-Bulgarian army formed under Russian command.[6]

The chances of the Bulgarian fifth column, on which "les enragés de la cause" pinned their hopes, were negligible.[7] Some former interventionists closely attached to the Strastnyi Boulevard also acknowledged this. Kartsov, who possessed first-hand experience, tried to persuade the editor to abandon his delusions; he portrayed the émigré officers frequenting the St. Petersburg and Moscow salons as cheating, irresponsible men and suggested that Tsardom should leave the Principality "stew in its own juice." Tatishchev shared his view stressing that occupation would entail either war or negative consequences for Russian future in the Balkans even if the Great Powers were to remain passive observers.[8] Nonetheless, the St. Petersburg peace party had good reason to worry that the Katkov-Kaulbars duo might still sway the autocrat, newly aroused by "insults to Russian honour," to an adventure; as Grand Duke Vladimir intimated to German statesmen, the "Battenbergiade" made Alexander overly nervous and prone to incalculable deeds.[9]

The moderates correctly estimated that the sole escape lay in finding a Prince acceptable to the ruler as well as to the Bulgarians and Europe. Attempting to solve this difficult problem, though, they made an extremely unhappy choice in their candidate, the Prince of Mingrelia (Nikolai Mingrelskii).

The cunning Circassian bon-vivant living in Paris—Katkov scornfully dismissed him as "le boulevardier"[10] —managed to secure quite impressive backing in Russia by giving opromises of all kinds, yet outside Tsardom stood no chance. Kálnoky and Iddlesleigh refused to concur with this "bad selection, contrary to the intention of the Treaty of Berlin, inasmuch as the Prince was simply a Russian subject."[11] In London, moroevert, chargé d'affaires Butenev probably deliberately assisted the extremists by telling the English that the Tsar "had named the Prince of Mingrelia not because he had any special affection for him but because he knew that he could rely upon him to do the work which Russians wanted done . . . to establish in Bulgaria that preponderate influence which was her (Russia's) due."[12] The Bulgarians rejected the man outright. There was a weighty reminiscence overlooked by Russian statesmen: the Circassaians were universally hated throughout the Balkans for the cruelties they had committed in their service to the Turks.[13]

So, instead of retaking the initiative, the peace party imposed on itself by the "Mingrelian affair" only more embarrassment. Later on, it tried with the Prince Waldemar of Denmark and Prince of Oldenburg, both relatives of the Tsar, but the game had already been spoiled. The well-founded rumours that Vienna and London contemplated the restoration of Battenberg, and the emergence of Prince Ferdinand of Saxe-Coburg-Gotha as another card in the Austrian "Catholic intrigue"[14] added fuel to the extremist propaganda. Towering in the Russian debate, the Bulgarian imbroglio would not allow Bismarck and Russian champions of his system to check its dissolution.

* * *

Strange as it might have appeared, it was not the English with their obvious anti-Russian initiative, but the Germans and Austrians who were the main targets of the overwhelming fury. In the words of a diplomatic dispatch,

> It is characteristic of the present temper of Russian opinion, that, throughout the current crisis, the open antagonism of England has produced far less bitterness and irritation than the somewhat specious assurances of goodwill which the Russian government has received from its two Imperial Allies. For one outburst against the 'Cabinet of St. James' there have been ten sneers at the 'treacherous duplicity of Austria' or the Machiavellian designs of the 'honest broker.'[15]

The Three Emperors' Alliance, Schweinitz confirmed on 17 December, had ceased to exist.[16] Not unlike Katkov and visibly set astir by him, Alexander considered the Chancellor the evil man pulling the strings of

Western intrigues behind the scenes. "I only wish he would at least overtly proclaim himself to be against Russia; then we could respond and adapt our attitudes accordingly," he exploded at a dinner at Gatchina. "I can assure you," Shuvalov told the German Ambassador, "that the only reason why we did not proceed to the occupation of Bulgaria was that the Tsar though Bismarck wished to lure him into it."[17]

As to the military, they were "entirely permeated by chauvinism," maintaining that "everything that is against Russia" is unlawful and to be punished.[18] This concerned equally the Bulgarian Regency and the Powers allegedly responsible for its "impudence." A war against Austria-Hungary was anew under intense debate. The Obruchev-Vannovskii set contended that the ostensibly impending conflict on the Rhine would warrant a successful advance to the Carpathian passes. In order to overcome the moderates' objections, the War Minister asserted that Vienna would open hostilities the next year anyhow, before her alliance treaty with Berlin would expire; but actually, the secret schemes of the army leadership had calculated with Austrian military unpreparedness. "For those people," Polovstov sadly observed, "neither economic nor moral considerations exist."[19]

Yet more seriously, while the St. Petersburg elite strove to tune down the intensity of anti-German feelings, it would not do so where the Dual Monarchy was the target. Speaking with Bülow, the Tsar's aide Cherevin re-stated the earlier Katkovite formulae with complete bluntness:

> The understanding between Russia and Germany is easy to achieve, their interests are nowhere in contradiction...(but) Russia and Austria must sooner or later fight each other...because their interests clash everywhere.... How can one believe that the Turkish legacy could be inherited without a war between Russia and Austria, when each of them wishes to dominate the Balkan peninsula?[20]

On Shuvalov, Herbert Bismarck noted after their talk on 16 October that "his respect and his fear of Katkov has risen to an unbelievable level and besides this he is overcome only by limitless anger against Austria."[21] Just a few persons, like Grand Duke Vladimir or the Asia-oriented Don-dukov-Korsakov were willing to compromise with Vienna and "cross bayonets with England" instead. Schweinitz assumed that due to this mood an attack on Austria-Hungary could not be avoided or even delayed.[22]

The great purpose of the Strastnyi Boulevard—to swerve Russian foreign policy first towards non-alignment and then into the French alliance—thus gained an exceptionally favourable wind. Owing to the Bulgarian frustration, the German Ambassador summarized, Katkovite propositions pervaded the whole press and even the higher stratum; they "detected everywhere, except in France, enemies kindled by Bismarck" and made Giers, the defender of the alliance, the chief accomplice in the plot.[23]

* * *

Partly because the Thunderer's anti-German crusade coincided with his editorials dealing with the tariff problem,[24] the Russian Foreign Minister took on to assuage the injured party by the contention that the Muscovite prosecuted strictly personal aim being "involved in the enterprises and speculations of the ultra-protectionist industrialists."[25] There was, however, no more than a fragment of truth in his allegation.

Undoubtedly, Moscow capitalists had been for years lavishly awarding the man who had so effectively advocated their interests. Polovtsov, for example, claimed that the millionaire Poliakov had paid him an annual subsidy of 35,000 rubles; and Bunge handed over to the Tsar documents ostensibly establishing that the publicist was committed to "various shady deals."[26] But it would be wrong to believe that this was an essential impulse of his conduct; he had never been a venal man in the sense Giers ascribed to him and now, moreover, he was too rich[27] and too sick to care that much for money. If there was a dominant drift which spurred him to utmost recklessness in this final crusade, then it must be looked for in the torments of his fatal illness, cancer of stomach, which made him most painfully aware that he had not much time left. Bismarck himself had been conscious of the Muscovite's incorruptibility and in Augaust 1886 denied to sponsor another initiative of the St. Petersburg Embassy for buying him off.[28]

The economic motive behind the animosity of the Strastnyi Boulevard against Germany and her alleged agents Bunge and Giers should be taken into account but in terms of Katkov's conviction that in these quarters lay also the main danger for Russia's economic future.

The unending financial crisis of the post-Crimean Tsardom, originated in exorbitant military expenditures and nurtured by them—the Crimean War alone had cost 800 million rubles and the war of 1877-1878 1,000 million rubles—was further aggravated by general industrial depression and the fall of agricultural prices. As it has been stressed, these developments had had its most significant political consequence in the clash of economic interests between the two countries once considered almost ideal commercial partners. By 1885, something like a vicious circle emerged. On the one hand, facing rapid reduction in exports to Russia—its value fell from 300 million marks in 1880 to 200 million in 1886—and urged by Prussian junkers, Rhineland-Westphalian and Upper-Silesian industrialists, the Reichstag responded in May 1885 with a new tariff considerably raising duties on grain and wood, the main items of Russian export. On the other hand, probably due to Katkov's and Pobedonostsev's forceful intervention with the Tsar,[29] Bunge had to promise relatiatory measures in duties on pig-iron, iron, coal and agricultural machinery as well as a overall rise in import duties by 20 percent.

This confrontation effectively marred the main effort of the Finance Ministry, aiming to improve the Russian position on the international money market, particularly by operations of conversion which would have reduced the enormous among of loans concluded on varying terms, into several large ones with better terms of amortization and lower rates of interest. After the British government and the Rothschild group had virtually chased Russian securities from the London stock market, the dependence on German banks became nearly total and the Germans could re-retaliate on Russian protectionist drive by blocking the conversion operations as well as by the depreciation of Russian securities and the ruble.[30]

Terrified by the familiar double danger—a big budget deficit and troubles with foreign credit—the St. Petersburg government resolved in May 1886, on Giers' and Bunge's insistence, to postpone the tariff revision. This spurred Katkov and the protectionist groups he represented, to a shrill outcry that Berlin and its proxies in Russian ministerial position were in conspiracy against the "fatherland's industry."[31]

* * *

That the Moscow editor was bestowed with the St. Vladimir order at the very time when Giers waited in vain for such an acknowledgement and when the Germans were voicing their protests against the tone of the Russian press, was taken in Russian and in European elites already before the tempest roused by the Kaulbars mission as unqualified evidence that a major change in European power balance was in the air. The Strastnyi Boulevard, foreign diplomats duly noticed, was again a Mecca for great fortune-seekers; among others Ambassador Mohrenheim and "Nicki" Dolgorukii, aspiring on a top position in diplomatic service, were there to pay their tribute.[32] In October, allegedly as a result of Katkov's personal intervention, Alexander consented to resume normal diplomatic relations with France, receive her Ambassador and send Mohrenheim back to Paris.[33] Meanwhile Kumani, a diplomat close to the Muscovites, presented himself to Freycinet as a person empowered to discuss an eventual alliance; Paris was buzzing with a rumour that a "Tsar's confidant" had brought to President Grévy a formal offer and the fact that military figures including Obruchev dwelled at that time in the republic made the story quite plausible.[34]

Alarmed, the Chancellor strove to counteract by cajoling the Russians as much as he possibly could, reiterating that the Tsardom must be granted free hand in Bulgaria and the Straits and that the German obligations vis-à-vis the Dual Monarchy did not cover the eventuality of Austro-Russian war resulting from their rivaly in Bulgaria.[35] It was probably due to this initiative that Schweinitz, through Tatishchev, offered to "explain to Katkov the whole German governmental programme."[36] These tactics, again, could not have worked as far as the Moscow party and its helmsman was concerned. The latter looked solely for pretexts to attack the Bismarckian system and the Austro-German alliance. "Between Russia and those Powers," he postulated, "an undeclared war is in progress." Affirming that Russia must abandon the path on which it had "followed Berlin's commands, forgotten her honour and her vital interests," he even spread the dangerous lunacy that the German army had stagnated and would be defeated if confronted.[37] Indeed, it is probably not far-fetched to surmise that he speculated with the war on the Rhine in the same way as the Obruchev-Vannovskii clique did.[38] At any rate, while exasperating over the course of events in Bulgaria, Katkov must have been for the moment quite content with continental developments. The

Russian initiative for a rapprochement with France, occassioned by him, not only introduced an additional element of tension; largely as a consequence, another explosive pole emerged on the Rhine border. The Bulgarian crisis unwound into the so-called "dual crisis" of 1887.

After years of intense fear of German attack, the French were regaining their self-confidence. The spectacular rise of General Boulanger, a demagogue promising to bring back the lost glory, to a great extent reflected the process; and the prospect of obtaining a powerful ally or at least profit from mounting divergencies inside the Bismarckian camp redoubled its intensity. Yet more importantly, although the French establishment was far from eager to embark heedlessly upon the risk of a war of revenge and although its first reaction to Katkovite bidding was distinctly negative,[39] its utmost caution could not prevent escalation.

The Prussian military observed the French recovery with a strange mixture of resentment and concealed statisfaction. Reorganization and re-equipment going on in the rival army as well as Boulanger's pronouncements and activities in his capacity of War Minister, furnished them with a perfect excuse to canvass their favorite ideas. Moltke and Waldersee maintained that zero hour had struck and action to safeguargd German security—either against France or Russia or both—could not be postponed; the German army, they stressed, was still armed with better rifles, its artillery could obliterate French fortresses in the course of hours, and Russian armed forces were in a state of decomposition. Austrian military weakness supplied them with additional arguments: while Herbert Bismarck made it the reason why Berlin should abandon the Dual Monarchy and lean close to Tsardom, the military "semi-Gods" took it as proof that France and/or Russia had to be crushed before Berlin was confronted with its ally's breakdown. "After profound evaluation of every possibility, I reckon it best for us to provoke a war against France; it would be completely wrong to wait and let the enemies chose the moment which suits them," Waldersee summed up.[40]

Bismarck had never judged an offensive war against Russia other than madness; and no tension could have changed his mind. In the French case, he was at one with his generals that Boulanger must be stopped; but otherwise, he behaved with marked reserve. To those prone to adventure he used to explain his caution by the stubborn pacifism of the old Emperor and the political parties of the centre and left; in fact, he himself was unwilling to expose the Reich, the work of his life, to hazards. To be sure, the elimination of the republic from the great-power chess-board would not cease to tantalize him; and he had hardly doubted that from a purely military view this could be achieved. But, the Chancellor was too shrewd a statesman—and perhaps also an old, tired and sick man—to subscribe to one-track schemes. He had always held for one of his maxims that the confrontation in the West should not be chanced anew without a prior, firm obligation from the Russian side. And from this aspect, the development in 1886 made him as insecure as ever.[41]

The "ridiculous proceedings of General Kaulbars" and the Katkovite campaign shook him profoundly; he confided to a friend that he had "lost faith in the permanance of our good relations."[42] While still blaming London and Vienna for the Bulgarian cul-de-sac, he could hardly dis-pute the argument of his domestic critics that the more he craved for accomodating the Russians, the more irritated, suspicious and demanding they grew.

Under these circumstances, only a complete volte-face in St. Peters-burg could have induced him to play with the fire on the Rhine. Yet, precisely this highly improbable eventuality seemed suddenly to come true, and created a condition paradoxically serving to Katkov's purposes.

* * *

Scared by the rumours of Battenberg's return to Sofia, Alexander III appeared to be changing his mind. Commenting upon German support for the Mingrelian candidature, he aired the belief that he might eventually resort to force being sure of Berlin backing: "now one can really see that Germany is with us on the Bulgarian question."[43] The opponents of the Moscow party immediately moved to take advantage of it.

On 15 December, a government statement was published condemning the Katkovite campaign and exhorting traditional Russo-German solid-arity:

> Bulgarian events. . .induced our newspapers to discuss the political relations of the European Powers to Russia. . . .Their judgments not only deviate from impartiality, but often stand in flagrant contradiction to reality. Some articles dealing with German

policy (especially)...have this character....With Germany...
Russia is connected by many vital interests....Being firmly
resolved to observe proper German interests with due respect, the
Imperial Government has every reason to hold the conviction that
also Germany will continue to avoid any action which would injure Russian dignity as well as her commitments evolved in the
course of historical developments towards our Eastern coregion-
ists....[44]

Soon thereafter, a Romanov family council resolved to appeal to
Emperor William for help against the Battenberg restoration and Grand
Duke Vladimir managed to persuade Alexander that Peter Shuvalov,
"a great friend of Prince Bismarck," be sent to Berlin to arrange the
matter.[45]

The promise that the former Bulgarian Prince would be prohibited
from returning to Sofia was easy to obtain.[46] But, anxious to reassert
himself after long years when he was eliminated from participation in the
policy-making, Shuvalov wished to make his mission a hallmark. On 7
January, he tendered to Herbert Bismarck a suggestion to replace the
Three Emperors' Alliance, entirely unacceptable to the Tsar, with an
exclusive Russo-German alliance. Within twenty-four hours, he said,
he could persuade the Tsar to sign a formal obligation that Russia would
remain a passive observer "if you start a war against France, impose upon
her a 14-billion reparation levy or if you even name a Prussian general
the Governor General of Paris"; all this for a mere written guarantee that
Germany would not hinder Russia in conquering the Straits or in taking
"any measure to re-establish her influence in Bulgaria."[47]

Although the proposition of an exclusive Russo-German bloc in principle
contradicted his fundamental concept, as matters stood the Chancellor
could not but utter his "great satisfaction" with the conditions offered.
Schweinitz still advised him that Alexander might be safe if complete
German support on the Bulgarian and Straits question were promised
and this appeared to corroborate it beyond any doubt.[48] When the brothers
Shuvalov dined with him on 10 January, the formulae for a treaty were
easily found:

In favor of Russia (1) the 'exclusive right of influence in Bulgaria' and (2) 'friendly German neutrality' in the case the Tsar

deemed it inevitable 'to safeguard the closure of the Straits and retain in his hands the key to the Black Sea.'

In favor of Germany (3) the same friendly Russian neutrality 'in any conflict' on the Rhine.

Aside from that, Tsardom was to recognize essential German security interests vis-à-vis the Austrian ally and promise (4) to undertake 'nothing against the territorial integrity' of Austria-Hungary and (5) respect 'the independence of Serbia in the manner in which it existed under the scepter of King Milan,' i.e. Vienna's exclusive preponderance there.[49]

The next day, in a speech before the Reichstag, Bismarck dissassociated himself from those who called for a different policy towards Bulgaria (and implicitly towards Russia):

> Russian friendship is for us more important than Bulgarian friendship and the friendship of all Bulgarian friends in our country. . . . We stand in the same friendly relations with Russia as we did under the late Emperor (Alexander II); and under no circumstances will these relations be disturbed by us. . . . I also do not believe that the Russians are looking around for an alliance in order to attack us in company with others. . . .

German vigilance, so ran the second part of the message, must be focused on the western frontier. The present political leaders of the republic are not contemplating war, Bismarck affirmed, but they can be replaced tomorrow by the proponents of revenge; "the war with France may start within ten years yet it may break within ten days, too."[50]

In the sequel of these ominous words deeds ensued which rapidly raised tension into acute crisis. On 14 January, the Chancellor dissolved the Reichstag averse to his "septennate" bill providing for further increases in the army; and while the Prussian government motioned to ask its more pliable Diet for extraordinary war credits, the population was exposed to an intense campaign to persuade it of the peril allegedly lurking from beyond the Rhine. On 30 January, the *Post* published its famous article "Auf des Messers Schneide" and a week later, exercises of 73,000 reservists in Lorraine were announced.

Debating with foreign diplomats, Bismarck assured that there would be no war unless Boulanger became the Prime Minister or the President; Count Münster, the Ambassador in Paris, informed the French leaders to the same effect.[51] The latter, as well as many experienced observers,[52] hoped that the Chancellor was speaking the truth and that the warlike noises were made only to assist him in the electoral campaign in obtaining a more docile Reichstag. But the majority opinion in Europe was that the situation was as serious as in 1870, that a German outslaught on the still weak rival was impending and that a Russian drive to the Balkans and/or to Galicia might follow it. The Austrian statesmen especially were in trepidation.[53]

Whatever plans Bismarck might have had, the crisis in the West only dispersed the illusion—if he still had any—that he could organize the relationship with Tsardom according to his liking, and strengthened Katkov's hand.

* * *

On the Neva, the Reichstad speech of 11 January created a forceful impression. Alexander directed the Singers' Bridge to convey Bismarck his satisfaction[54]; and, unprincipled as they were, many in the elite adapted their stances to what they believed to be a new situation.

The conduct of Obruchev, regarded as stalwart of the French party and staunch enemy of the Germanic Powers, may best reveal the habit of grabbing the opportunity wherever it occured. The General fancied a truly thieving scheme. "For the sake of European peace," he suggested an agreement with Germany "on an instantaneous assault on England." This Power, he argued in the only too familiar style, was "so disorganized and enfeebled that it could be reduced to a second-rate state and forced to pay a multi-billion levy, badly needed by our and German finances." He was ready to go to Berlin, he declared, and to strike a bargain with the Chancellor on this affair.[55]

Giers, too, had his own, though more modest dreams. The German arrangement should bolster him to clear-up the Bulgarian mess, isolate the English and on the grounds of these achievements to consolidate his ministerial position shattered by the Katkov party. In an upsurge of optimism, he instructed the London Embassy on 17 January to prepare for a contingency when Salisbury and his colleagues would be confronted with new conditions. "Assured of the friendly assent of the Berlin cabinet," he expected that the Ballplatz would be forced to change sides and join in the pressure on the Sofia Regency; "then we shall see whether the cabinet of London wishes peace of whether it will persevere in inciting unrest."[56]

While at the Wilhelmstrasse the anti-Russian Holstein again dispaired,[57] Schweinitz, carried away by the mood of the moment, looked forward to a comeback of the good old times. He returned triumphant from the audience with the Tsar: the understanding between Russia and Germany is complete, he told Polovtsov, and the Russian press is the sole disturbing element.[58]

However, personified by the Thunderer, the "Russian press" represented a force too overwhelming to be invalidated. It was mainly due to this voice of public opinion that the winter flurry of renewed intimacy was transformed into an important episode in the advancing process of estrangement.

The Muscovite met the Germanophile challenge in the most belligerent mood. In December, he achieved another big victory, which made his grip over Russian policy anew apparent to everybody. Hounded by his wrath, facing the fall of the ruble and the prospect of another big deficit, Bunge had to leave his office to be replaced by Vyshnegradskii, a member of the Strastnyi Boulevard set.[59] So, the official statement of 15 December, condemning the anti-German press campaign, was for the editor just a pinprick rousing his acerbity. During his visit at the end of the year to the capital, he refused to meet his former ally Zinoviev, whom he suspected of participation in "this shameless affront." As to the Foreign Minister, he was to be crucified next. "I broke Nabokov, I broke Bunge, I shall tear apart Giers," he declared to his proxies.[60]

As it has already been mentioned, Katkov just made a deal with Kaulbars to that effect. Despite the seemingly changing winds, the both main contenders for Giers' position, Ignatiev and Saburov, volunteered also their services; they delivered, besides "their personal reminiscences even papers from their private files," i.e. documents concerning the highest secrets of the state.[61] Tolstoi, who had promised "not to let the swine into my presence," hurried back to the Muscovites fold too; and while he had earlier made it his principle to evade participation in the great foreign policy debates, he now pleaded with the Tsar for the "swine's" cause on this novel field. In a memoir of 7 January 1887, he wrote as follows:

> The Three Emperors' Alliance is to be viewed as a mere temporary arrangement, perhaps useful for the time of military unpreparedness and financial distress, but unnatural in its substance and founded on abnormal conditions. For long, 'Bismarck has dreamed of destroying (France) for good and he would probably be ready, in order to obtain that possibility, to offer us full freedom of action in the East. But, under different circumstances, we could procure such a freedom without creating on our flank the most formidable Power, without sacrificing our good relations with France . . . . On these grounds, it seems to me impossible to disagree with Katkov's claim that Russia ought to uphold her freedom of action without binding her hands with disadvantageous separate treaties.'[62]

* * *

Tolstoi, too, was instrumental in delivering to Alexander Katkov's memoir dated on the same 26 December 1886 (7 January 1887), a "weighty monograph of almost book length,"[63] probably the most substantial statement on Russian foreign policy written by him.

This time the Thunderer was not prepared to handle the autocrat softly. For that he was too poised to the attack by his recent victories and too conscious that his remaining life-span was short and the minute decisive. "I have to speak out with complete frankness," he stressed.

First, the Muscovite dealt with the governmental proclamation of 15 December, "that shameful mistake of our diplomatic office" (i.e. the Foreign Ministry):

> The Singers' Bridge, having as its purpose to prolong or conclude a new treaty with Germany, has delivered by it Russia to Germany and has alienated those who have their accounts to settle with Germany (i.e. France). More than that, the proclamation has produced a hitherto unknown example of official and open interference of a foreign Power in our internal affairs, by making the Russian government responsible before the other Powers for the opinions of the Russian press and has subordinated it to foreign control.[64]

Then, the publicist proceeded with an account of the whole conflict between him ("the Russian press") and the Singers' Bridge.

He hotly disclaimed the view that "Russia was driven into the last Turkish war by her press." The responsibility lay fully with Gorchakov, who refused to consider the sound advice coming from Ignatiev. "Our policy went along the track of half-measures. . . ; we missed all the propitious moments to deliver a crushing blow to Turkey, if we had wished to act; if we did not, then we lacked the determination to keep aloof from the fruitless European haggling."[65]

After this failure came the blunders on the Bulgarian question. He, Katkov, had first advocated intervention; later, when "the military occupation was not envisaged," he solicited for support of the "movement against sedition inside Bulgaria," i.e. for the army opposition. If Russia had followed his advices, then she could emerge triumphant and relieved "of the difficulties which have brought her so many troubles and threaten by new complications in the future." Instead, as in many other things, "our administration was more in accord with our enemies than with our political interests"; and its calculation of German assistance, as always, has been fallacious. Even if Berlin were really willing to help "to establish our rights," gains obtained through "alien charity" would "neither be secure nor durable."[66]

Also the Three Emperors' Alliance was a grave mistake from the very outset and recent events were just the "fruits of this strange combination." The substance of Bismarckian policy has always been to "force Russia into such a suicidal system, more perilous than war" and the Alliance has served his purposes perfectly. "Not even an unsuccessful war could cause us more harm than this alliance concluded for the safeguarding of peace. Step by step, we have been pushed from the Balkan peninsula and put into grave difficulties."[67]

In the situation, Katkov summed up, where Tsardom is still lacking "a clear-cut programme in international affairs," it has become absolutely imperative to remain "free of the obligations devoid of concrete objectives" and to "stand in equally good relations with France and with Germany." This position which implies meeting French effort for rapprochement halfway, would have been invaluable advantages in an eventual conflict with England, "the most formidable enemy," and in general serve to uphold European peace and "our interests everywhere" much better than the former arrangements.[68]

His two main themes—first, that the Bulgarian military fifth column had to be given full backing in order to establish unlimited Russian control over the Principality and thereby regain initiative in the Near East; second, that Germany must not be granted a separate treaty allowing her to attack France—Katkov broached also in another memoir to the Tsar, on 20 January.[69] In the meantime, he continued to harangue the public. Contrary to Alexander, his verdict on the Reichstag speech of 11 January was entirely negative.[70] And the subsequent German bellicose moves against France furnished him, like most of the Russian press,[71] plenty of ammunition for his barrage. Any special arrangement with Berlin, ran the keyword, would lead to a forthwith aggression on the Rhine and to the fatal shift in the power balance detrimental to Tsardom:

> To permit a new war breaking out . . . in the present isolated position of France, to deliver her to German, English and Italian retribution—such an eventuality would be in contradiction to both popular sympathies and the most substantial Russian political interests.[72]

The Katkovite furor destroyed the game of the pro-German moderates. Though much of what the Muscovite had claimed in the memoir of 7 January had enraged the Tsar—"All this is completely untrue! Lies!", he commented—he was alive to the Russian feelings" laying in the indictment and reacted accordingly. "Tell him that I have no doubt of his devotion and his desire to serve the interests of the motherland, as he understands them, to the best of his ability," he repeated almost verbatim what his father told Katkov in 1866.[73] On 17 January, Giers returned from Gatchina in the blackest mood. "Evidently," Lamsdorf noted in his diary, "the intrigues of Katkov or certain other nefarious influences have once again knocked the ruler off the track. His Majesty is not only now talking against the Three Emperors' Alliance but is even against a bilateral pact with Germany."[74]

Whatever Alexander might have said to Schweinitz, he sensed well the limits which he could not and presumably did not wish to tresspass. What he told Giers, throws the sharpest light on the role of Katkov and the public opinion in Tsardom's post-Crimean foreign policy-making:

> He knows that such an alliance would be unpopular and contrary to the national feeling of all of Russia; and he must confess that he is

afraid to disregard those feelings and does not intend to destroy the confidence of the country in his foreign policy . . . . Earlier I believed that this was only (due to) Katkov, but now I have learned that this is the view of the whole of Russia; and if the confidence of our public opinion in (my) foreign policy is lost, then everything is lost.[75]

On 22 January, the Muscovite obtained an audience with the Tsar and was given a promise that the latter would consider no German treaty without consulting him beforehand.[76]

Even before the meeting took place, Giers had cautioned Pavel Shuvalov that "the proposals submitted by his brother to Prince Bismarck were (but a part of) a private conversation between two friends which could not have an official character."[77] Now, the whole anti-Muscovite maneuvre had been effectively blocked in both its Bulgarian and German ramifications.

* * *

Despite his inordinately stubborn insistence on keeping the "Draht nach St. Petersburg" intact, Bismarck could ignore neither the domestic criticism nor the alarming reports on crumbling Russia's social fabric and the apparent political consequences stemming from it, which had been reaching him even from places as distant as Madrid.[78] According to the surveys written by Bülow on 20 January and 16 February, the St. Petersburg elite judged internal conditions extremely critical, when, as Tsarina Maria put it, "everybody in Russia complains and about everything.":

The Panslav-nationalist party—ruined landowners, liberal-inclined officials, ultra-Orthodox merchants, hysterical Petersburg's women, ambitious men in the General Staff has taken complete command of public opinion. Even local sheets spread chauvinistic and war propaganda, even the peasants see in war remedy for their troubles. Concernign the Tsar, he is in fact more scared of public opinion than his father ever was . . . he is afraid of Moscow, Katkov, newspapers . . . . Katkov's power has been inflated so much that he became a vice-Tsar. The army is entirely unreliable, infected by republican and democratic spirit and cannot be turned from the Austrian and German borders to the Golden Horn. Only a small fraction

—Dondukov, Zinoviev, Dolgorukii—is willing to pick up their laurels on the Indus River. General Kuropatkin proclaimed: 'We know only too well that the Tsar does not want war, but we will blow it up so that he will be driven to wage it.' The overriding feeling among the elite has been that if the press and the demagogues were not silenced, then mob would force the ruler to declare war to his allies as Louis XVI was forced to do by the Paris riff-raff.[79]

Also the newly discouraged Schweinitz admonished that "this scum will have a war." The official attitude taken towards Katkov after the state-ment of 15 December, he alleged, convinced the public that he "can put up open resistance to the Imperial Government." The Tsar was neither capable nor willing to a forceful step, the elite helpless and silent, Tolstoi manipulated by Katkov and Pobedonostsev.[80]

Bismarck himself was increasingly inclined to believe that Katkov, not the Tsar was the real master of Russia.[81] Whether he liked it or not, he had to look after balances and combinations which would at least partly re-pair the damage caused by Russian developments. He now ascribed a much higher value to the Triple Alliance with Austria-Hungary and Italy; and while earlier he had always emphasized that on the Eastern Question the English and the Turks would have to bear the brunt of responsibility in resisting the Russians, the growing willingness of the second Salisbury gov-ernment (1886-1892) to cooperate with Vienna[82] and Rome induced him to inspire the formation of an anti-Russian bloc by these three Powers.[83]

All this, of course, conferred a substantial benefit to the policies of the British Prime Minister. Salisbury nurtured no illusions about the Chan-cellor's motives and reliability; he suspected him of the intention to pro-voke a war between Tsardom and the Anglo-Austro-Italian grouping in order to obtain a free hand against France.[84] Yet his priorities—to accele-rate the dissolution of the Emperors' Alliance, encourage the Austrians to stand firm and to hold Alexander back before invading Bulgaria and/or Afghanistan—were obvious. Salisbury's view on Russian policy had since 1876-1877 undergone a dramatic evolution, indeed. How he saw it now, he revealed in a most illuminative letter to Morier, written on 2 October 1886:

> The forces which are pushing the Russian frontiers outwards are mainly two—the religious, and the military . . . . Working with it, is

the constant appetite for gain and distinction which animates the officers of a vast military organization, (and) which the Tsar cannot disregard even if he wanted to: for their fidelity is the one sure buttress of his throne. And when the religious dream is satisfied and St. Sofia is again a Christian church, the frontiers of Russia will not cease to expand. The military appetite will be as imperious as ever: and the frontiers must go expanding, wherever military distinction and advancement is to be obtained. Russia can promise nothing with respect to Afghanistan except that she will eat Constantinople first. When it is eaten she must go forward, with all the weight of her augmented mass, in the direction of India.[85]

The Prime Minister was determined, whatever the complacent "British Philistine" personified by Gladstone might wish, to let Tsardom "take as long on the road to C(onstantino)ple as we can possibly contrive"; "of course, such a policy ought not to be made needlessly unpleasant to Russia . . . but her goodwill is not worth of buying by concessions."[86] This stance, so much at variance with the past record, profoundly influenced Kálnoky's attitude to the "League of peace." However sceptical about Italy, "a country where the mob rules the sceptre," the personal warrant given to him by Salisbury—to stake his career on the British coming to the aid in the case the Dual Monarchy clashed with Russia—made all the difference.[87]

In several dispatches during the second half of February, Bismarck advised Schweinitz that he had lost hope of a positive response on the January draft; and that, because the attacks on Giers and Germany had not stopped and there was no indication of willingness to fight Katkov and the rest of the extremist press, the Ambassador should observe the strictest reserve.[88]

On 20 February, the Triple Alliance treaty was prolonged for another five years; and soon afterwards, its existence was made public. At the same time (February-March) England, Austria-Hungary and Italy concluded agreements for cooperation in maintaining the status quo in the Mediterranean, Aegean and the Balkans, which, as Salisbury envisaged, would hold St. Petersburg back and ensure Bulgarian security.[89]

Indeed, Morier's warning to Giers that "there will be no alternative left for England but to rally around her such allies as will be ready to go

with her and beat the Russian advance,"[90] had been taken very seriously
Faced by the existence of the "League of peace," Katkov too could not
connive in the hazards of the moment. First of all, he perceived the appeals coming from Vannovskii-Obruchev clique—"to take advantage of the
existing situation and assault Austria . . . which we could have already long
ago smashed with glory"[91]—highly irresponsible. With regard to the
main purpose of his campaign, though, he perserved in his combativeness.

* * *

A historian can only guess about the scope of the Thunderer's activities.
We may be certain, however, that due to Franco-German tension he managed, either personally or through his emissaries, to come to contact with
the key figures and agencies which could further understanding between
Tsardom and the republic—Grévy, Flourens, Floquet, Boulanger, General
Saussier and the General Staff, the Havas press bureau. Important information was being exchanged between the Strastnyi Boulevard and the French
Embassy in St. Petersburg. While Cyon and General Bogdanovich were
probably the main intermediaries on the Seine, Captain Moulin, the assist-
ant military attaché, and a certain Tolstoi served in the same capacity on
the Neva.[92]

Cyon, who was in February summoned by his master to Russia, found
him seriously ill but in fighting and optimistic spirit. The publicist now
thought it certain that the Tsar had become "absolutely resolved to persist
in his freedom of action and not let France be attacked"; that his stance
would force Bismarck to use the war scare solely in his electoral purposes
and then "fall back in the last moment"; and that Giers would be chased
from the Singers' Bridge and the "patriotic" concept finally recognized as
the only foundation for Russian foreign policy.

The diary Cyon kept during his sojourn testifies that the Muscovite
had already made up his mind as to what the future course would be. The
hostile campaign against Austria-Hungary would cease—Obruchev was
conveniently made responsible for the proposition that the Dual Monarchy
was the "natural enemy"—and a "direct agreement" sought with her. For
the sake of this agreement, which should untie Russia's hands in order to
prosecute a vigorous anti-German policy, the editor was apparently willing
even to recognize the principle of division of the Balkans, proclaiming it

"infinitely more profitable" for the two Powers than the arrangements of the "Dreikaiserbund."

As long as Giers stayed in the Foreign Ministry, there should be no truce with it. In vain Jomini, the man who had most consistently tried to placate the Moscow party, implored Katkov (and Cyon) to relax, because the triumph of the new orientation had "already been ensured" and the only divergence lay in tactical approach. The arguments that the change of policy could not be proclaimed "in such a provocative manner" as it was the one paraded by the Strastnyi Boulevard, indeed, might scarcely persuade the publicist. For him, Giers was "the traitor of his sovereign and his country," whose resignation became "a conditio sine qua non if Russia wished to repair the mistakes committed." He had also made his choice for the position: though Saburov perhaps made the strongest bidding for his favor, he gave the preference to the second big pretender—Ignatiev. Five years earlier he had portrayed the "Father of the Lie," the most dangerous influence and had been instrumental in his removal from the Interior Ministry; now, he pronounced him a "true statesman, the only one capable of putting into effect the policy inaugurated by Alexander III."[93]

CHAPTER 32

THE FINAL STALEMATE (1887)

> The heart of the matter is that aside from
> the lawful government of the state, a
> peculiar governmental force has emerged in
> *vedomosti* who is surrounded by acolytes at
> the highest levels of the administration—
> Delianov, Ostrovskii, Pobedonostsev, Vysh-
> negradskii, Pazukhin. This court assembles
> by Katkov. . . openly discusses which of the
> ministers should be replaced by another
> person, what policy should be pursued in
> this or that question; in short, it haughtily
> issues its orders, prints both condemnations
> and praises, and in the end achieves its aim.
> This state of things cannot be explained
> otherwise than by absence of ideas in the
> government itself; the government takes the
> ideas from Katkov and debases itself in the
> eyes of the nation.
> Polovtsov

The history of Katkov's and the Moscow party's bid for a "true national
policy" in 1856-1887 evolved in three big cycles with a similar pattern.
There had always been the "stage of shock" as the main hallmark—the end
of the Crimean war, the Prussian triumph in 1870-1871, the crisis of 1878-
1880, the failures of 1885-1887. After the "shock" had come the "stages
of stalemate," when the Muscovites were in disarray or gathered their

strength and looked for new options (1856-1862, 1871-1875, 1880-1881). Then returned their heydays, the "stages of assertion," when they had either to the great extent dictated the official policy or stood in sharp opposition to it (1863-1870, 1876-1878, 1881-1887), their initiative, however, invariably leading not to their final victory but to a new shock and a new stalemate. This was precisely the situation which Katkov, seemingly at the peak of his power, had to experience in the spring of 1887. More than ever, the same fanatical zeal, dictatorial manners and malicious manipulation of people which had helped him in achieving so many triumphs, created a condition where he was denied the ultimate one.

Fame, wealth, family life—there he ruled with the same patriarchal iron hand as in his office at Strastnyi Boulevard[1]—did not mellow the Thunderer; politics took a complete hold on him. In the testimonies concerning his private life, one meets the universal picture of a man possessed by a mission, in vigil day and night, relieved but by short spell of fitful sleep at his desk or in a carriage. Cyon, a physician by profession, was taken aback to see him, mortally ill and obviously in great pains in the cancer-afflicted stomach, to eat a meal of stale mushrooms. Physical torment, as mentioned, merely whipped up the man's intensity and impatience: he wished to accomplish his goal before the death would claim him. He kept his illness secret, speaking only about "abandoning the struggle he had been engaged in for thirty years" and leaving the country if he did not succeed.[2] His activities in the last months of his life were as hectic as ever. Besides the engagement with the French, he vigorously sponsored the cause of the Bulgarian army traitors, worked for the reopening of the Moscow Slavic Committee (closed down by the authorities in 1878), pleaded for Indian Prince Duleep Singh who deserted the English and for the Cossack Ashinov just back from Ethiopia with the rosy prospects of Russo-French cooperation there.[3] He knew no measure, no priority.

Not surprisingly, tactical niceties in handling actual or potential opponents never being his forte, the Thunderer also forced those in the elite who would have preferred a compromise with him to strike back. This time, moreover, he drove to a fierce hostility Alexander himself.

At first sight it seemed that the State Council's effort to stem the Katkovite tide was just a last-ditch stand and that, only lamenting over the debasement of the autocracy by the power of the publicist, the moderates in the government would deliver their remaining positions. The Tsar ordained Tolstoi to go to Moscow and prohibit the man from attacking the highest personalities, but the Interior Minister would not dare; he could force into silence any paper save the *Moskovskiia vedomosti*, he told Bunge. And the ruler himself would rather remove the ministers stigmatized by the "party of order" rather than to resort to an open tug-of-war. When Ostrovskii came from Gatchina triumphant and announced that Nabokov would leave his post, Giers commented sadly: "This is the perspective of each of us; I cannot be sure that coming home I shall not find a note of dismissal." Indeed, after Nabokov, Bunge became a "political corpse strangled by the Katkovite clique"; Baron Nikolai, disgusted by general poltroonery before the editor, decided to resign from the State Council in protest; and almost nobody doubted that Giers, the publicly branded "traitor," would have to go next.[4]

The Foreign Minister appeared to be quite resigned to his fate. He had never been respected in the elite; even those to whom the publicist became obnoxious hinted to him that they wished to see at the Singers' Bridge a figure acceptable to society. Except for the loyal Lamsdorf, the senior officials in his ministry—Jomini, Zinoviev and the rest—were too "for the most part hedging their bets, extending elaborate courtesy, when opportunity presented itself, to Katkov and his various envoys, taking at least in part what they believed to be the great editor's line, striving in this way to ingratiate themselves and protect their position for the future."[5] He "cannot expect any help from the censorship, because the censors themselves are Panslavs," Giers told his few friends, and neither can he win the contest with the Muscovite. "Katkov . . . will most certainly force the Tsar to make a change of foreign minister; I am thinking only about some dignified way of departing."[6]

That the "party of order" had been running the show and that Alexander was under its spell was the generally shared view; the Tsar and the Thunderer were conceived as co-rulers of sorts, the "Majesties" jointly responsible for driving the Empire into an abyss.[7] Yet, the only hope the moderates cherished—"ce Katkov, la tête commence à lui tourner, il finira par fâcher l'Empereur"[8]—came true in the end. Wrestling with time, the "dictator of Moscow" overreacted and by antagonizing the autocrat spoiled, at least in terms of immediate consequences, his cause.

* * *

Also at this stage, strange as it may appear, the Bulgarian issue remained the main clue to Katkov's conduct.

There was overriding consent in the governmental agencies, society and the press that a new forceful engagement in the Principality must be postponed until the German drive to the "destruction of the European balance" would be checked. The Anglo-Austro-Italian rapprochement and the obvious German initiative leading to it added another weighty argument for circumspection. Butenev warned from London that the favorable German stance towards Russian occupation had the sole aim "to see us engaged in an adventure which would prevent us wielding our influence in European affairs" and that Berlin wished only "to declare war against France and instigate against us collective action by Austria, England, Italy and Turkey." The extremist *Novoe vremia* wrote in the same vein.[9]

Seemingly, the Moscow editor did not differ. He recognized that military action would be the "most grave mistake":

> Germany has prepared the Bulgarian complications for Tsardom and it would be disastrous to fall into the trap. Russia has first of all to see what will happen in the West, 'knowing that the East will not escape her . . . . The Bulgarian imbroglio is symptom, not reason.' Particularly after the formation of the 'League of peace,' Russia should not concentrate her attention exclusively on the Eastern affairs and tie her hands; active policy ought to be resumed only when the danger passed and she will be sure 'not to meet victorious Germany on the road.' Now, the occupation would serve only to the purposes of the Western (i.e. chiefly German) plot.[10]

However, Katkov was too deeply emotionally committed in the overthrow of the Regency and the activities of the fifth column to observe the necessary detachment. Therefore his true stance continued to be identical with that of the clique which opted for the "Finnish model" of Governor Generalship and speculated on Alexander's wrath.

The "Tsar of peace," Lamsdorf complained, would not stop "playing with dynamite," dwelling in that blindness conveyed by the draft of the imperial manifesto of 23 November 1886, and by the government declaration of 10 December. There the Regency was proclaimed a bunch of "radical agitators," oppressing the people and making the country a "hotbed of anarchy, revolution and hostility to Russia"; and the duty of the St.

Petersburg government to be "to direct its efforts to the removal of this corrupting yoke and to re-establish in Bulgaria the rightful order."[11] The seething hatred, as before, blocked every moderate attempt at a new opening.

In the winter of 1886-1887, such an attempt had been initiated by Nelidov, a man who had since the coronation debate (1883) abandoned hawkish adventurism and consistently pleaded for a versatile approach. Now, he invited Tsankov and the representatives of the Regency to Constantinople and proposed a settlement which would give the Bulgarians formal guarantees against interference in exchange for Russian control of their army and foreign affairs. Stambolov was willing to negotiate rather than prolong the dangerous stalemate: he offered Tsankov Karavelov's place in the Regency and one or two ministerial posts. The leader of the fifth column, knowing about the prevalent St. Petersburg wind, however, would not settle on less than a full-fledged capitulation. Aside from the purge in the army and its complete take-over by the Russians, he requested all the crucial ministerial positions for the members of his group, the dissolution of the Regency and National Assembly and the revision of the constitution. "The main evil rests in the constitution; the only way to Bulgaria's salvation—in Russian occupation," he summed up. The talks inevitably broke down.[12]

Katkov impetuously denounced the Foreign Ministry for Nelidov's conciliatory effort as well as for its endeavour to find a new Prince; after the Mingrelian, he maligned also the candidature of Prince Waldemar as the "basest intrigue" inspired by Berlin, London and Vienna.[13] There was no other solution, he responded to Kartsov who had been vainly trying to bring him to reason, than a rule by a Russian Governor General serving as a deputy of the Tsar; and a new military coup would pave the way for it.[14]

Alexander appeared ripe for the gamble. "I'll send a brigade," he proclaimed. And when Giers reminded him of the sad end of Nicholas I, he dismissed it lightly: "those were different times."[15] That he had eventually promised to the moderates to avoid an open identification with the fifth column's venture, seemed but a trifle. So, when the Foreign Minister had instructed Khitrovo, who in his capacity as the Minister to Bucharest was to supervise the conspiring émigrés, to "oppose every risky act of the Bulgarian officers and their untoward enthusiasm," the latter simply dismissed it as follows:

The system in Bulgaria was imposed by violent methods and can be destroyed only by violence. The sooner this is achieved the better, because any procrastination merely incites that moral degradation and rising apathy from which the present masters derive their already too long existence.[16]

Khitrovo arranged with the Rumanian Prime Minister, Ion Bratianu, free rein for the plotters, and provided them with arms and funds. Russian steamers on the Danube delivered to Bulgaria leaflets and threatening letters to people loyal to the Regency. The Embassy at Constantinople was involved in a similar action in Adrianople, where a centre for an uprising in Eastern Rumelia had been established.

The revolt broke out on 28 February at Silistra; and when on 3 March a part of the garrison at Ruse joined it, Katkov in exaltation announced "the beginning of the end."[17] As on previous occasions, however, the victorious outcry was to be exchanged for laments and impotent anger. In both towns, most of the soldiers and populace turned against the insurgents; and the Regency, this time reacting with harsh determination, quickly drowned the risings in blood. Moreover, no scruple hampered now Stambolov and his followers to imprison their civil and military opponents in Sofia (including Karavelov) and execute the insurgent officers (on 6 March at Ruse.)[18]

Not unlike the situation after 21 August 1886, the hawkish calculation with the Tsar's emotions proved all wrong. Alexander remained true to himself: the stereotype was not to be altered, his aroused feelings would pour out solely in comments in the margins of diplomatic dispatches. And the conclusion he made was beyond recall: "It is terrible but we simply cannot do anything to protect the poor Bulgarians."[19]

The military and most of the press uttered just their chagrin, too.[20] More confidential resolutions were to appear on the necessity of the "Finnish model settlement,"[21] but Katkov must have been painfully aware that he would not live long enough to see the Bulgarian humiliation avenged.

In addition to his final disillusion with Alexander over the manner he had reacted to the "Western conspiracy" in the Principality, there were other impulses to that effect: the Muscovite undoubtedly blamed the Tsar for the hesitation to take more positive steps towards rapprochement with France and conversely for the resulting lukewarm Paris reactions,[22] as well as for the short-sighted refusal to back the banker Poliakov in the action aiming at establishing Russian control over the Persian and Balkan railways.[23] Thus, consciously or not, the dying man headed towards a confrontation with the autocrat.

Commenting upon the execution of Bulgarian officers on 7 March, he made sweeping accusations. The regents, he affirmed, are but puppets, "through them an Englishman and a German beat their Slavic slave"; events in Bulgaria are nothing else than a part of a Bismarck-led crusade against Russia; "all of them are talking about peace yet we are in war, though a concealed one."[24] The implications were at hand: to enter into any sort of agreement with Germany when the Emperors' alliance was to expire, would be both morally indefensible and politically nearly suicidal.

Then, on 19 March, came a true explosion which a diplomatic dispatch characterized as "something that does not much differ from political anarchy."[25] In the editorial published that day, Katkov hit at the Tsar's susceptibilities in the most provocative manner and on several levels. Firstly, he disclosed that he knew about the Three Emperors' Alliance treaty (or the "treaty of Skiernewice" as he named it) which was supposed to be the highest state secret. Secondly and worse still, he made this secrecy known to everybody. Thirdly, and worst of all, he identified it in unmistakable terms as a plot concocted behind the nation's back, detrimental to its essential interests.

He wrote to the following effect:

> In order to understand the present state of affairs it is necessary to know that just this month of March the tripartite alliance expires, so pernicious for Russia, into which she was lured for a period of three years, at the time of her national humiliation, and which was then secretly renewed, again for three years, in 1884. . . . It was because of this treaty that Russia's importance has shrunk and why, losing progressively the character of an independent country, she has been pushed, step by step, out of the (Near) East.

Portraying the "shameful conditions" imposed upon the country the Thunderer made Alexander, at least indirectly, both a vassal and an accessory, who allowed Germany and her partners to employ "deceit" and "psychological pressure," who tolerated the "cosmopolitanism of our diplomacy" and "lacked sofistication in the direction of our policy."[26] All this was much worse than the scarcely heeded January memorandum.

While the Muscovite continued to depict Germany as the sworn enemy of "Russia's independence and vital interests," striving for the "dictatorship of Europe,"[27] the Tsar raged over the insults he had been exposed to. "This is a highly disreputable article," he wrote to the police chief Plehve on the (no. 66) editorial:

> In general, Katkov forgets himself and tries to play the part of a dictator; he is forgetting that foreign policy is my business and that I am the one who is responsible for the results, not Mr. Katkov. I order you to give Katkov the first warning for this article and for the recent trend (of the paper) as a whole; his madness must be stopped and (he must learn) that everything has its limits.[28]

Furious over the indiscretions, the Tsar also asked that Saburov, whom he suspected to leak the state secrets to the Strastnyi Boulevard,[29] as well as General Bogdanovich[30] be deprived of their positions.

* * *

During his stay in Berlin at the festivities of Emperor William's ninetieth jubilee (March 1887), Grand Duke Vladimir discussed with the old monarch "primarily the Russian press, the *Moskovskiia vedomosti* and the danger which threatens our international relations from these quarters" and promised "in the name of the Tsar that stern measures would be taken."[31] He and other highly placed enemies of the Muscovite now hoped that his blunder and the resulting anger of the autocrat had created precisely the situation they had been looking for.[32] But the next days showed that Alexander was far from ready to detract from the established practice.

On 23 March, Pobedonostsev sent him a letter warning against an open condemnation of the editor:

> The telegraph will spread the news to all the corners of the world; it will be an overpowering political event, interpreted as a change of our policy. The stock exchanges will react to it, there will be

triumphant demonstrations in all capitals. . . . In Russia, it will produce extreme dissatisfaction and confusion.

The General Director of the Holy Synod demanded that Feoktistov be sent to the Strastnyi Boulevard instead, to transmit only an oral reprimand.[33]

The Tsar recoiled forthwith and recognized that "to give a warning to the *Moskovskiia vedomosti* is untoward for many reasons." "I have been convinced that you are right and that I, in the heat of the moment, acted inconsiderately . . . ," he responded to Pobedonostsev. In order to make Feoktistov's visit even less painful for the editor, he promised to grant the latter another audience.[34]

It looked rather like another complete rout by the Tsar and the elite before the Thunderer. Tolstoi, who was at the time of the "Feoktistov mission" in Moscow, prudently disappeared from the scene, in order to evade being connected in Katkov's suspicious eyes with the reprimand. On 26 March, an imperial decree announced strict curtailment of German and Austrian immigration in the strategically exposed regions of the Empire. "This time, all the newspapers without exception distinctly support the party of Katkov in its effort to prevent the renewal of the Three Emperors' Alliance when its time expires," a Belgian diplomat reported.[35]

While the adherents of the "party of order" felt as safe as ever, their opponents were stunned by the outcome. Most of them returned to the proposition that there was no other way to obtain at least some elbow room than by introducing to the Singers' Bridge a less vulnerable moderate, preferably Lobanov, Pavel Shuvalov or Staal. Giers himself, hard-pressed by Grand Duke Vladimir, was again on the verge of going to Gatchina and tendering his resignation.[36]

In fact, however, the situation settled into a stalemate. When on 29 March Giers "asked the Tsar to accept his resignation, or else, in some public manner, to prove to the world that his policy and not that of Mr. Katkov was the one adhered to by His Majesty," the autocrat revealed the position he wished to maintain. He would not have a showdown with the Muscovite, although he disliked him now profoundly,[37] he would not publicly identify himself with the Foreign Minister, but he would not drop him either. He allegedly declared that his confidence in Giers "had never been greater"; and, "were I accept your resignation, it would be putting Katkov in the right and you in the wrong."[38]

So, the Tsar's audience with the Muscovite which took place in early April and which foreign diplomats and Russian high society alike, in a state of extreme suspense, had expected as the ultimate test of "whether the Imperial will was to be directed by public opinion or not" and even whether there would be peace or war,[39] produced no new clues.

Because of the contradictory position of the ruler, both sides claimed success. From the publicist, his lieutenants learned that Alexander had assented to all the judgments he pronounced on the international situation. The opponents, on the other hand, affirmed that the Tsar had reprimanded the editor severely and ordered him to "stop the unbriddled violence of the *Moscow Gazette* concerning Germany and the policy of the German Chancellor."[40]

No one, Morier wrote to Salisbury, knows in which current Alexander "is at present swimming."[41] The Tsar, however, had made his mind where and how he would "swim" and the subsequent events only confirmed that he could not be swayed that or another way.

Katkov had to swallow the bitter pill that Giers would stay in charge of the Singers' Bridge. The Tsar told him about the minister:

> Under the present circumstances, he is most useful to me. If war breaks out some time, which I recognize as the greatest calamity, then it will be prolonged and merciless one. It would be a madness to risk it without necessary preparation. Willy-nilly, we must procrastinate, try to win time, and not create sores. Caution is his most valuable asset.

And the ruler used the same arguments to vindicate his intention to "remain in agreement with Germany."[42]

On the other hand, to the displeasure of the moderates, he would not wrangle with the publicist either. Cherevin intimated to Bülow that Count Sheremetiev, the marshal of the Moscow nobility, had just warned Alexander that the old capital "stands on Katkov's side and the country does too" and that the autocrat must direct his steps accordingly. "The Tsar will not antagonize public opinion, there are already too many malcontents in Russia," the General summed up. "We shall prevaricate."[43]

* * *

For the Tsar, the whole matter would be settled best if the Foreign Minister and the publicist were to arrive at some accommodation: for this reason, he asked for a meeting of the two antagonists. And, above all, there had to be no "scandal." "Nothing is to be allowed to ooze out into publicity . . ; this is to be arranged 'en famille'" he said.[44] But it happened so that the "scandal" continued.

While Giers found his master unwilling to offer him "that minimum of satisfaction which he deemed himself entitled to," he could, nonetheless, abandon his intense anxiety that "His Majesty might after all be encouraging Mr. Katkov" and count upon the basic safety of his position. This, coupled with the awareness that in the elite the quest for a tug-of-war with the Muscovite was stronger than ever, spurred the usually exceedingly timid man to a surprising resolution. When Katkov, fulfilling the promise he had given to the Tsar, called at the Singers' Bridge, the minister refused to receive him.[45] Humiliated and at the same time considering his hands untied, the editor sent on 12 April to the Tsar the last of his big memoranda.

He must have realized the error he had committed in his recent writings by questioning the wisdom and the integrity of the autocrat; he would not repeat it. But as it could have been expected, he pronounced a wholesale indictment of his foe in the "Foreign Ministry for Russian affairs"; and, moreover, connected it with the most direct appeal for a break with Germany and for a joining of hands with France. He argued as follows:

> Owing to Giers' conduct, the opinion has become widespread that Russia has two policies—one 'imperial' and one 'ministerial.' Our diplomacy 'performs more like an executor of an alien policy than an organ of its own country. It has spoiled everything that has been elevating the Russian spirit and cowing the enemies . . . .' Most distinctly this has been manifested in the Bulgarian question: the diplomats disapproved the course decided by the ruler and chosen the path of compromise; the Foreign Ministry disagreed with the telegram which led to Battenberg's abdication; the ministry castigated General Kaulbars 'in one voice with the organs of the foreign press.'
>
> Concerning the European situation, the Foreign Ministry, in contradiction to the imperial will, has refused to abandon the idea of German alliance, while at this moment no option remains for Russia but a defensive alliance with France. 'No victorious war can raise

Russian prestige as much as such a combination . . . . Peaceful, purely
defensive rapprochement between Russia and France will create that
element of force . . . which per se is capable of re-establishing the
now shattered Russian authority in the (Near) East, put at bay her
enemies, sober her rivals.'[46]

Although Alexander passed the document to the Singers' Bridge without comment, Giers and his devoted Lamsdorf trembled at the thought
that the "weak-minded" ruler might anew be swayed by this "disgusting
denunciation";[47] and they perceived it as the worst of omens that once
again the Foreign Minister was omitted from the traditional Easter distribution of decorations.[48]

High society and foreign diplomats alike, of course, did not fail to
notice the affair and draw their conclusion. Profiting from the unending
hysteria over Bulgaria, the dispatches asserted, "Katkov's position is the
strongest in Russia and, in any event, stronger than that of Mr. Giers."[49]
On 29 April, Bülow summarized for Bismarck conditions as the elite perceived it to the effect that the Muscovite had become more cautious, yet
he "upheld his independence towards the Tsar" and "in principle, had
given a lesson not only to Giers but also the Tsar."[50] The international
press, too, went on dwelling on sensational speculations on the approaching Katkovite victory in the French alliance issue and on the precarious
position of the Foreign Minister.[51]

The Muscovite himself appeared to be still indulging in the hope that
he could "break Giers apart" and enforce the pro-French orientation. He
was convinced that Vienna and Rome were in the process of disentangle-
ment from the Bismarckian system and that it must show in the St. Petersburg stance;[52] the renewed French-German tension, triggered in late April
by the so-called Schnebele affair, he believed, irrefutably proved his arguments and made his position "firmer than ever."[53]

Katkov's hopes and Giers' anxieties notwithstanding, however, this was
still a drawn game, as far as the personal contest was concerned. The
"weak-minded" Alexander would not move.

* * *

In terms of private feud, the immobility of the Tsar and the stalemate
ensuing from it, were a failure for the Thunderer whose time was running

out. In the longer perspective, on the matter of what principles the foreign policy of Tsardom should be imbued with, however, the cause he stood for could not be vanquished. The dictate of public opinion, personified in the autocrat's fear of the publicist, would not permit the perpetuation of the traditional conservative-dynastic course. This had been manifested when, taking advantage of Alexander's renewed preoccuption with the "Bulgarian disgrace," of his ingrained aversion against changing established stereotypes, and, above all, of his anger against the "dictator of Moscow," the St. Petersburg German party moved to preserve at least its essentials.

Only fragments are known about the maneuvre. What can be established is that four men—Grand Duke Vladimir, Giers and the brothers Shuvalov—were the main figures engaged in it and that they had resolved to repeat the attempt from January. Because of the total estangment between St. Petersburg and Vienna, the Three Emperors' Alliance ought to be substituted for a strictly secret, exclusive Russo-German alliance, and this bloc à deux should be based on the familiar formula—a free hand for Germany on the Rhine to be repaid in the Bulgarian and the Straits questions, in order to "deprive the Panslav press of its arguments."[54]

In sequel of tentative steps—Giers' interview with Schweinitz on 19 March and the simultaneous talks of Vladimir in Berlin—where silencing the Strastnyi Boulevard or at least keeping it in the dark were stated as indispensable precondition for new openings, the German party started its bid in earnest from the middle of April.[55] Speaking with German diplomats, the Foreign Minister made more or less formal proposals as follows:

> While Russia had earlier demanded assurances that Germany would not attack France first, now she was willing to guarantee 'unconditionally' her neutrality for that event. To assuage the Tsar's susceptibilities, however, 'real services' must be offered by Berlin on the Bulgarian question. The English opposition would be broken by sustained pressure in Central Asia, but German assistance was needed in forcing the Porte to cooperate with St. Petersburg in an arrangement which would include the replacement of the Stambolov regency by a 'temporary regent,' preferably the already tested General Kazimir Ehrnrooth.[56]

It cannot be fully ascertained how much Alexander was involved in the scheme. It appears nonetheless that he took his final stance to the German deal in the last days of April or the first days of May and that, under the impact of Katkov's recent memoir and the Schnebele affair, he refused to approve the proposition of unconditional neutrality in a conflict in the West. At any rate, the instruction for Pavel Shuvalov, entrusted to negotiate the treaty, was short of the promise Giers had given to Schweinitz as late as 29 April. Written on 3 May it stated that "our obligation to observe neutrality in the case of war between Germany and France cannot be interpreted as our indifference if a death-blow were to be inflicted on one of the parties in the conflict."[57] (Furthermore, on the grounds of Russian military unpreparedness, German support for the Straits action was not to be asked for if Bismarck were to connect it with some concession; such an obligation from his side would be considered "very useful" solely if given with no strings attached.)

The formula considerably narrowed the Ambassador's elbow room. And if he wished to ignore it—as his brother had done in the January deal—then the course of his talks with the Chancellor, started on 11 May in Berlin, made it impossible. The very first clause of the St. Petersburg draft, obliging "both contracting Powers to benevolent neutrality and endeavors to localize the conflict in the case of a war of either of them with a third Power," revealed the basic imcompatibility in military-political objectives.

It is to be recalled that Bismarck accepted the fact that the Three Emperors' Alliance must be replaced by an exclusive Russo-German accord with profound discomfort, and, moreover, keenly aware that now even the staunchest supporters of the Russian orientation, such as his son Herbert or Schweinitz, recognized that "no matter what we do, the Russians will always be dissatisfied."[58] So, haunted by doubts, he perceived the draft as a device to procure a free hand for a war with Austria-Hungary (as, indeed, at least the Obruchev-Vannovskii clique had planned it); and, proclaiming it contradictory to the German obligations, he read to the astonished Shuvalov the text of the Dual Alliance treaty of 1879.

For the Ambassador, no other way remained than to turn back to his instructions and state that, if this were the case, Russia could not promise neutrality in an eventual German war against France; the recognition of the great power status of the republic, he added, remained for the

St. Petersburg cabinet the condition sine qua non of any Russo-German agreement. And that was the end of it.

Driven, no less than his brother, by the ambition of "demonstrating to the Tsar that he had succeeded in obtaining from the Germans more than Giers had even asked for,"[59] Shuvalov later attempted to give more value to his performance and wrestle from his partner a comprehensive pledge to take over the initiative in imposing Russian rule over Bulgaria. This, however, also met a flat refusal: Bismarck would not commit himself to more than diplomatic and "moral" assistance.[60]

The resulting so called Reinsurance treaty (Rückversicherungsvertrag), signed in the German capital on 13 June,[61] did not even create a pause in the contest. The Germans evaluated it just as a brake or sorts, slowing down Russian pace towards war and revolution; and which, in case of a Franco-German war, might delay Russian intervention for some 4-6 weeks.[62] Bismarck himself, highly displeased with the manner in which St. Petersburg and its Ambassador stuck on their peculiar concept of cooperation, in fact hardened his stance in the aftermath—on economic matters, on the press war, on Near-Eastern affairs.

* * *

It cannot be doubted that the Thunderer's shadow loomed over the abortive attempt for settlement. "This is all Katkov's fault," Bismarck remarked to the Russian complaint that he had changed his position on the Bulgarian issue.[63] Also the fact, Kennan suggests, that the Chancellor produced the text of the Dual Alliance was "one may suppose, his response to the repeated hints in Katkov's editorials that the day would come when the German-Austrian treaty would expire and when Russia could then take after the Austrians with impunity."[64]

Nothing of it, however, could be of any solace for the Muscovite in his last days. Oblivious of the aborted effort his Russian foes had made in Berlin, he underwent both the terminal torments of his dying body and the frustration of what he must have perceived as his final personal failure. His complex manipulations with the French, without producing the speedy results he had expected, made it possible for Giers to hurt him badly.

Contrary to the hotheads like Generals Boulanger and Saussier, the Paris government refused to play according to the Strastnyi Boulevard's script. It desired the tension on the Rhine to cool down; Russian rapprochement, advantageous as it might be, was not to be of such a nature as to spur the Germans to the violent response demanded by the heralds of preventive war. It therefore sought to cultivate Alexander's goodwill by taking a studiously pro-Russian stance on the Bulgarian question and simultaneously stressing in diplomatic communications with St. Petersburg its peaceful intentions. France is preparing to meet an aggression which may come tomorrow, President Grévy said to Mohrenheim, but her "regrets for Alsace-Lorraine would never lead to a new war to conquer it, (because) we are resigned to it."

Concurrently, France would not officially take stance showing its sympathy with Katkov's combatting the German party. On 14 April Foreign Minister Flourens directed Ambassador Laboulaye to maintain contacts with the publicist, but not get involved in his feud with Giers which "the French government regretted."[65]

In the situation where the Tsar was happy with the state of Russo-French relations as they were and the Moscow editor could do nothing about it, the latter learned (on 28 May) from Tolstoi about a disastrous telegram from Mohrenheim which had just reached the ruler. It read to the effect that in the government crisis unwinding in the republic—the purpose was to outmaneuvre General Boulanger, who became too much of a liability—the Radical leader Floquet, one of the candidates for the premiership, surprised Grévy by a letter of Katkov in which the publicist announced that Floquet's ministry would be welcomed in Russia and that the St. Petersburg government would make a declaration about it to Laboulaye.

Most probably, the publicist was entirely innocent in this particular case and the whole matter originated in an intrigue engineered either directly by Giers or by his son, then serving as an ambassadorial secretary in the French capital; but his earlier underhand dealings made Mohrenheim's story look highly plausible, and, needless to add, abundantly sufficed to arouse Alexander's temper again to the boiling point—over the Muscovite's meddling in the conduct of Russian foreign policy as well as against the "scroundels" who surrounded him, Cyon, Tatishchev and Bogdanovich. On 30 May, the last named was formally dismissed from the state service.[66]

True, neither did this episode alter the basic trend. Although the lash administered to Bogdanovich was considered a symptom of Katkov's

weakness, Schweinitz warned Bismarck that he could not count on a firmer stance from Alexander against the extremist press and, more importantly,
that nor he could count on Russian neutrality in a continental war.[67]
Propelled by Bulgarian events and by punitive measures undertaken
by the Chancellor against Russian credit, the anti-German campaign
continued without respite and the internal stalemate left speculations
on the theme of the Strastnyi Boulevard—Gatchina—Singers' Bridge
triangle to run free.[68] But for the Thunderer this was all of little consequence. By the April-May scandal, his enormous will was spent. He
took to the death-bed at his estate at Znamenskoe, where the latest
disastrous news hit him: he had to learn that on 7 July, the Bulgarian
National Assembly elected the Austrian candidate, the Prince Ferdinand
of Coburg, as the new ruler and that St. Petersburg would do nothing
about it.[69] After suffering a stroke, he died on 1 August 1887.

CONCLUSION:
THE HERITAGE

Historical development is enacted always
and everywhere through human personality
and this explains why the history of every
nation resembles a combination of the
biographies of individuals.
Belinskii

I believe that history will pronounce a
stern verdict on Katkov. God gave him
(enormous) talent, but what has he used
it for?
Chicherin

When one ascribes to any nation a monopoly
of absolute truth, then nationality becomes
an idol the worshipping of which is based
on falsehood and leads first to moral, and
then to political catastrophe. . . . For a true
and far-sighted patriotism, the most essential,
even the only essential question is not the
question of Russia's might but of Russia's
sin.
Vladimir Soloviev

"The death of Katkov is an event, the importance of which goes far beyond the boundaries of our country," Ambassador Staal wrote to Giers.[1] The less Russia and the world knew about the true state of the publicist's health, the stronger was the reaction.

The emotional outburst of a common Russian could only be compared with the demise of another popular hero, Skobelev; and, as in the case of the White General, rumors immediately sprouted that he had been poisoned by his enemies. All the way from Znamenskoe to Moscow, peasants carried the casket with the deceased on their shoulders; in the outskirts of the old capital, workers and artisans took over. Perhaps few of them had ever read the *Moskovskiia vedomosti* but "they knew" in that terrifying manner which has made evil so well entrenched in the vast empire they have helped to erect.

Russian newspapers proclaimed the dead man as one of the greatest personalities their state had ever had and compared his role with that of Bismarck.[2] Non-Russian politicians, diplomats and the press were scarcely more reticent in their judgments and it took several weeks before the story of the Thunderer ceased to be the major theme.[3]

The commentators with more thorough knowledge of Russian conditions emphasized again what had been registered in that or another way by many since 1863. That not only had the *Moskovskiia vedomosti* been read in every group of Russian society and in every gubernia, but that its editor had also had numerous supporters and propagandists of in all educated layers and in all parts of the Empire; that the measure of identification with him had always culminated in the times of crises— its peaks being in 1863-1866, 1870-1871, 1876-1879, 1881, 1885-1887; and, most importantly (the episode of his funeral manifested it distinctly), that his name had entered somehow and in some degree into the consciousness of the masses.[4]

Except for the French, of course, the European reaction on the Muscovite's death was at considerable variance with that of the Russian public. "For Europe and the world as a whole, the loss of Mr. Katkov is not a calamity. We may admire the man, the writer, the patriot. . . . But the interest of Europe consists of seeing Russia internally free to be able to pursue a pacific foreign policy, the *Standard* put it quite transparently.[5]

The English Conservative daily characterized the deceased as a "revolutionary unconscious of it."[6] The Russian elite felt the same and reacted accordingly. Although the highest dignitaries of the Church, representatives of the nobility and big business attended the Moscow funeral and in Warsaw Governor General Gurko ordered the Orthodox Archbishop to officiate a special mass in Russian cathedral,[7] there were few tears shed in the upper stratum. Alexander, alive to the sorrow of his "dark people," sent a telegram to Katkov's widow with solemn words proper for the occasion,[8] but he most certainly thought otherwise.[9] The official obituary, published on 3 August in the *Journal de St. Pétersbourg* was wholly centered on the early scholarly exploits of the editor in philosophy and philology.[10] The absence of the representatives of his former fortress, Moscow University, at the funeral ceremonies, was no less telling.

* * *

Katkov died a frustrated man; the "party of order" did not survive his demise and the elite made every effort to reduce him to a "non-person." But the heritage was too powerful to be buried with the body.

As Tatishchev noted triumphantly, "soon after the eagle closed his eyes, the dream changed into a reality."[11] The disciple of the late Thunderer, of course, meant the fateful victory of his master's foreign policy concept, which was at the same time the most momentous and paradoxical triumph of Russian public opion over the autocracy. Society fully espoused the Katkovite postulate that the traditional dynastic policy, as embodied in the adherence to the Bismarckian system, was "more perilous than war" and that "not even an unsuccessful war could cause us more harm than this alliance for the safeguarding of peace."[12] And, in the opening years of the 1890s Alexander III and Giers, though with marked loathing, also bowed before it irrevocably, entering the French alliance. The end is known to everybody: the new path led to an "unsuccessful war" and to the breakdown of Imperial Russia.

It might have been considered proper and uncontroversial to the subject matter of this book to stop here without drawing further conclusions. It appears, however, to the writer of these lines, to be his duty as a historian to stress the links between the Katkovshchina, a totalitarian and aggressive ideology amalgamating the worst of Russian tradition with "modern vistas," and the present time. The duty is dictated, above all, by the sad fact that the assumption of the Russian European-minded educated stratum that "history will pronounce a stern verdict on Katkov" proved to be all wrong. While in his native land there has been a strenuous effort to obfuscate the phenomenon he personified,[13] an eminent Western scholar may today still miss the whole meaning of his impact.[14]

* * *

True Russian intellectuals gave their kinsmen sufficient warnings as to the consequences of the Muscovite teachings.

Analyzing the development of Russian nationalism, the greatest philosopher of the late Imperial period, Vladimir Soloviev, already in the 1880s described it as a progressive degradation back into the barbarous Muscovy past, as that of retreating from common European-Christian civilization and values to the "cult of a strong state power," with law and justice being replaced by "the fist and the power stick." In the first phase, wrote Soloviev, the Slavophiles indulged in pure fantasy, worshipping their own people as a vessel of universal truth; in the second phase, Katkov (and Danilevskii), mixing fantasy with realism, put the nation on pedestal as an elemental force, independent of justice and morality; in the third phase, "the new obscurantists" were to take over, "realists devoid of any fantasy but also of any shame," who would bring "the worshipping of historical anomalies and national particularism which separates one's own people from civilized mankind" to its logical end.[15]

In the Moscow publicist, the philosopher perceived the "Nemesis of Slavophilism," the innovator of the "Islamic" feature always present in the Muscovite faith, where humility before God had been substituted by the resignation before the power of the state. "With genuinely Moslem fanaticism Katkov believed in the Russian state as the absolute incarnation of national strength . . . (where) one is obliged to recognize it unconditionally and without recall, to deliver oneself to it completely."[16] The Katkovian concept of national interest, Soloviev claimed with great prescience, would lead to the apotheosis of Ivan the Terrible.[17]

But the Russian intelligentsia—in too many ways the main culprit in the tragedy—has failed to understand national purposes outside the Muscovite framework. As a result, the Orwellian vision of Soloviev's antipode, Konstantin Leontiev, has come true that "no matter how the Socialists may feel towards the conservatives and towards the forms and means of conservatism, the essential aspects of conservative teachings will, nevertheless, be useful to them; they will need to make use of fear and discipline; they will need a tradition of submissiveness and a habit of obedience." That "a new kind of slavery will arise that will express itself in the most cruel form of individual submission to small and large institutions, which in turn will submit to the power of the state . . . ." That a "Slavic Orthodox Tsar will take into his hands the leadership of the Socialist movement . . . ."[18]

It would be, of course, absurd to ascribe Katkov any direct responsibility for what has happened to his country and the countries subjugated by it during the era of the "new obscurantists"; and it would be a gross oversimplification to assert that the latter had simply turned to the Muscovite ideology for guidance. Yet, however complex the process of their espousal of conservative teachings might be, it has to be stated nonetheless that covered by a slightly different phraseology, the method and the programme of "Katkovshchina" have materialized with an undreamed of consistency.

The ideal of a totalitarian dictatorship, where subjects have no political rights, only the obligation to serve the state, has been achieved. All the products of the "St. Petersburg cosmopolitanism" have been totally eradicated.

The concept of permanent vigilance, the constant campaigns against the hostile West and the traitors and deviationists inside the empire have been the backbone of what is called "ideological work."

Of all the major campaigns of the Strastnyi Boulevard, designed to inject strength into the state organism and safeguard the most cherished value, the unanimity of its subjects, only that of the "classicism" has never been resurrected.

In foreign policy, the Machiavellian-conceived state interest has been elevated into the highest, undisputed principle, too. The problem of Russian "security zones" and "safe borders" has been solved in the manner the Moscow publicist had advocated, notably in the writings on Bulgaria: the states and peoples in her steadily broadening spheres of influence "belong to Russia with no exception of race . . . form with her one system, one world," and the integrity of the whole system "is hardly less substantial and less dear to Russia than the integrity of her own territory." "Western plots" have been quelled, "liberated peoples" saved, Russian garrisons (re-) installed.

Most significantly, the Muscovy-Katkovite totalitarian model has been proclaimed the sole one in accordance with the "customs and tradition" not only of Russia but of all the territories under her tutelage, however substantially they may differ socially and culturally; and, worse still, this interpretation has been tacitly acknowledged in the "business as usual" political philosophy of the West, as the long beards of Moscow had always predicted it.

Thus, the heritage of the "Katkovshchina" is scarcely a lesser burden to bear now than was its authentic form in the "time of the Thunderer."

NOTES

Notes to the Introduction

1. A. J. P. Taylor, The Struggle for Mastery in Europe, 1848-1918, Oxford U. P. 1954, pp. 255-256.

2. Cf. P. A. Zaionchkovskii, Voennye reformy 1860-1870 godov v Rossii, Moskva 1952, p. 280.

3. Cf. Bernhard Fürst v. Bülow, Denkwürdigkeiten, vol. 4, Berlin 1931, p. 336.

4. W. L. Langer, European Alliances and Alignments 1871-1890, New York 1931, pp. 4-6.

5. N. V. Riasanovsky, Parting the Ways. Government and Educated Public in Russia, 1801-1955, Oxford 1976, p. VII.

6. G. F. Kennan, The Decline of Bismarck's European Order. Franco-Russian Relations, 1875-1890, Princeton U. P. 1979, p. 27. Cf. also D. Beyrau, Russische Orientpolitik und die Entstehung des Deutschen Kaiserreiches 1866-1870/71, Wiesbaden 1974, p. 16; I. Grüning, Die russische öffentliche Meinung und ihre Stellung zu den Grossmächten, 1878-1894, Berlin 1929, p. 17; R. Wittram, Die russisch-nationalen Tendenzen der achtziger Jahre im Spiegel der österreichisch-ungarischen diplomatischen Berichte aus St. Petersburg, in: W. Hubatsch, ed. Schicksalswege deutscher Vergangenheit, Düsseldorf 1950, pp. 323-324.

7. Dostoevskii put it as follows:
"The backward, wholly illiterate Russian people, i.e. the simplest village peasants . . . know nothing about the Slavs. . . . However, all our people, or their overwhelming majority, have heard and know that there are Orthodox Christians under Mohamedan yoke . . . ." And when Russia was at war with the Sultan this produced "a conscious national attitude of the people towards such a war. So that one shouldn't be surprised at the ardent sympathy of the people with such a war on the

mere grounds that they do not know history and geography. What they need–they know." (F. M. Dostoevsky, The Diary of a Writer, vol. 2, New York 1949, p. 804).

8. In sources and literature, the terms "elite," "society" (obshchestvo) and "public" are frequently in use. In this volume, the "elite" is mainly identified with higher officials and courtiers, while "society" is understood as the better educated, distinctly politcally minded and/or well-to-do portion of the "public."

9. B. H. Sumner, Russia and Panslavism in the Eighteen-seventies, TRHS, 4th ser., vol. 18, London 1935, p. 51. Sumner's classic, "Russia and the Balkans 1870-1880" (Oxford 1937), is still unparalleled in this field. For a recent well-balanced characteristics see also D. Geyer, Der russische Imperialismus, Göttingen 1977, pp. 27ff.

10. Grüning, p. 35. For similar opinions see Briefwechsel des Botschafters General v. Schweinitz, Berlin 1928, p. 30; A. Leroy-Beaulieu, L'Empire des Tsars, vol. 2, Paris 1882, p. 471, etc.

11. K. A. Skalkovskii, Nashi gosudarstvennye deiateli, St. Petersburg 1890, pp. 145-146.

12. Cf. A. N. Liubimov, Mikhail Nikiforovich Katkov i ego istoricheskaia zasluga, St. Petersburg 1889, p. 12; Vospominaniia E. M. Feoktistova, Za kulisami politiki i literatury 1848-1896, Leningrad 1929, p. 105; RA, *31:2*, 1893, pp. 427-430; Ju. B. Soloviev, Samoderzhavie i dvorianstvo v kontse XIX veka, Leningrad 1973, pp. 92ff.; Zapiski N. G. Zalesova, RS, *124*, 1905, pp. 21-22.

13. V. P. Meshcherskii, Vospominaniia o M. N. Katkove, RV, *250*, 1897, p. 49.

14. Pisma Pobedonostseva k Aleksandru III, vol. 2, Moskva-Leningrad 1925, p. 141.

15. Skalkovskii, p. 134.

16. V. A. Tvardovskaia, Ideologiia poreformennogo samoderzhaviia (M. N. Katkov i ego izdaniia), Moskva 1978, pp. 48-49).

17. MV, 1863, no. 81; 1865, no. 8.

18. Bismarck's attempts to buy Katkov off and the thick dossier—more than 250 pages covering only the year 1887 (Auswärtiges Amt. Akten: Russland 82, No. 4. Secr. Russ. Journalister [Katkov])—may serve as the best testimony.

Notes to Chapter 1

1.   Vozhd reaktsii 60-80kh godov (Pisma Katkova Aleksandru II i Aleksandru III), Byloe, 1917, no. 4 (26), p. 4.

2.   A. I. Gertsen, Polnoe sobranie sochinenii v 30-kh tomakh, vol. 14, Moskva 1958, p. 157.

3.   M. Katz, Mikhail N. Katkov, A Political Biography, The Hague 1966, pp. 17ff. Liubimov, pp. 16ff. S. S. Nevedenskii, Katkov i ego vremia, St. Petersburg 1888, pp. 2ff. RS, *119*, 1904, pp. 533ff.

4.   V. G. Belinskii, Polnoe sobranie sochinenii, vol. 12 (Pisma), Moskva 1956, pp. 10-12, 131, 140. Cf. also ibid., vol. 11, pp. 358-359, 372, 541-544, 557-558, 578; Katz, pp. 29ff.; Liubimov, pp. 19ff.; Nevedenskii, pp. 46ff.

5.   Feoktistov, pp. 84-88. Katz, pp. 23, 29-30, 36-39.

6.   A. Walicki, The Slavophile Controversy. History of a Conservative Utopia in Nineteenth-Century Russian Thought, Oxford 1975, p. 288.

7.   RA, *31:2*, 1893, p. 162.

8.   N. P. Barsukov, Zhizn i trudy N. P. Pogodina (St. Petersburg 1888-1910), vol. 11, pp. 253-254. Feoktistov, p. 88. Liubimov, pp. 42-45. Nevedenskii, pp. 97ff.

9.   RA, *25:2*, 1887, pp. 367-368. RS, *44*, 1884, pp. 67-68.

10.   His former student Chicherin wrote in the reminiscences on Moscow University that Katkov's lectures were unique in one aspect only—that nobody could comprehend them. "Who might have imagined that this unintelligible professor, this dim philosopher would later grow into a lively and talented journalist?" (Vospominaniia Borisa Nikolaevicha Chicherina. Moskva sorokovykh godov, Moskva 1929, pp. 59-60).

11.   Feoktistov, pp. 93-94. M. Lemke, Ocherki po istorii russkoi zhurnalistiki, St. Petersburg 1904, pp. 185ff.

12.   Katz, pp. 38ff. Liubimov, pp. 42ff. Nevedenskii, pp. 98ff. RS, *64*, 1889, p. 139; *116*, 1903, pp. 687-688.

13.   Barsukov, vol. 14, pp. 255ff. Feoktistov, pp. 93-94. Liubimov, pp. 46ff. RS, *33*, 1882, pp. 484ff.; *92*, 1897, pp. 355ff.

14.   V. P. Meshcherskii, Moi vospominaniia, vol. 1, St. Petersburg 1897, p. 62.

15.   Dnevnik D. A. Miliutina, vol. 1, Moskva 1947, p. 20.

16.   Meshcherskii, vol. 1, p. 151. See also A. A. Kornilov, Obshchestvennoe dvizhenie pri Aleksandre II (1855-1881), Moskva 1909, pp. 20-23, 28-34.

17.   During the first decade of Alexander II's reign, 66 newspapers and 156 journals were established. (E. Ambler, Russian Journalism and Politics 1861-1881, Detroit 1972, p. 41. For a general background cf. also Iu. I. Gerasimova, Iz istorii russkoi pechati v period revolutsionnoi situatsii kontsa 1850-kh—nachala 1860-kh godov, Moskva 1974, pp. 8ff.; Lemke, pp. 1ff., 311ff.

18.   A. V. Nikitenko, Dnevnik, vol. 2, Moskva 1955, p. 71. A. J. Rieber, The Politics of Autocracy, The Hague 1966, p. 45. RS, *40*, 1883, pp. 170ff.; *68*, 1890, pp. 155-157.

19.   R. F. Byrnes, Pobedonostsev, His Life and Thought, Indiana U. P. 1968, pp. 47ff.

20.   Kornilov, p. 86.

21.   RS, *34*, 1882, p. 122; *61*, 1889, pp. 191-193; *82*, 1897, pp. 31-32.

22.   Katz, pp. 44ff. Lemke, pp. 341ff.; Liubimov, pp. 100ff. Nevedenskii, pp. 107, 113ff.

23.   Kornilov, p. 75. Cf. also Barsukov, vol. 16, pp. 405-407; Chicherin, pp. 270-272.

24.   RV, *38*, 1862, pp. 452-453. E. Pyziur, Mikhail N. Katkov: Advocate of English Liberalism in Russia, 1856-1863, SEER, *45*, 1967, pp. 444-445.

25.   Katz, pp. 61ff. Nevedenskii, pp. 114ff. Pyziur, pp. 446-449.

26.   Cf. Liubimov, pp. 124ff.; V. N. Rozental, Obshchestvenno-politicheskaia programma russkogo liberalizma v seredine 50-kh godov XIX v., IZ, *70*, 1961, pp. 197ff.

27.   Gerasimova, p. 122. Lemke, p. 58. Liubimov, p. 127.

28.   Already in 1857, after publishing a highly critical article on the landowners' striving to prevent a satisfactory solution of the peasant question, the Third Section, responsible for internal security, requested its closure. The journal was allegedly saved by the liberal Minister for Public Instruction, Norov; but it was given a formal warning coupled with a ban on further comment on the highly explosive emancipation problem. Later came other warnings, mainly for "constitutional tendencies." (Feoktistov, pp. 94ff. Gerasimova, pp. 35, 66. G. K. Gradovskii, Iz minuvshego, RS, *133*, 1908, pp. 77ff. Kornilov, pp. 20-23, 86-88. Rieber, p. 45. RS, *92*, 1897, pp. 31-32.)

29.   Pyziur, p. 456.

30.   Meshcherskii, vol. 1, pp. 263-264.

31.   Pyziur, p. 456.

32.   Katz, p. 50. Cf. also N. A. Melgunov, Mezhdu Slavianofiliami i Zapadnikami, RS, *96*, 1898, pp. 551ff.

33.   Gertsen, vol. 11 (Byloe i dumy), p. 300. Katz, pp. 61-62.

34.   Pyziur, pp. 454-456.

35.   N. Berdyaev, The Origins of Russian Communism, London 1937, p. 50.

36.   Tvardovskaia, p. 20; quoting B. P. Kuzmin, Neskolko slov po povodu slova 'nigilizm,' in "Literatura i istoriia," Moskva 1969.

37.   Meshcherskii, vol. 1, p. 299. Miliutin, vol. 1, pp. 36-37.

38.   The most notable articles of Katkov on the subject were "K kakoi prinadlezhim my partii" (RV, *38*, 1862, pp. 382ff.) and "O nashem nigilizme po povodu romana Turgeneva" (RV, 41, 1862, pp. 402ff.). The then much discussed novel by Ivan Turgenev, "Ottsy i deti" (Fathers and Sons), carries the best testimony on the impact of the problem on Russian society.

39.   Katz, pp. 61ff. Kornilov, pp. 121ff. Liubimov, pp. 124ff., 144ff., 199ff. RS, *61*, 1889, pp. 126ff.; *108*, 1901, pp. 604ff.

40.   RV, 38, 1862, p. 383.

41.   Katz, pp. 74-75. Lemke, pp. 96ff. RV, *250*, 1897, pp. 3ff.

42.   Already in 1861, the editor had harvested first fruits: the *Russkii vestnik* was struck off from the Third Section's list of suspect periodicals and he was allowed to publish the *Sovremennaia letopis* as a separate weekly. (Gerasimova, pp. 140-141; cf. also pp. 130, 170, 182-184, 193.)

Notes to Chapter 2

1.   For the March memoranda see KA, *75*, 1936, pp. 45ff.; RA, *10*, 1872, pp. 337-340.

2.   Besides the loss of Southern Bessarabia, Russia was obliged to recognize in the treaty (a) the integrity of the Ottoman Empire; (b) the neutrality of the Black Sea, i.e renounce her rights to keep warships there and even fortify her coast; (c) the Sultan's suzerainty over Serbia and the Danubian Principalities of Moldavia and Wallachia; (d) a five-Power protectorate over the Ottoman Christians. In order to make sure that Tsardom would respect its commitments, England, France and Austria signed in April 1856 a special alliance agreement.

3.   RS, *40*, 1883, pp. 168ff.

4. "La Russie ne boude pas, la Russie se recueille." See Gorchakov's circular of September 1856 in S. S. Tatishchev, Imperator Alksandr II, vol. 1, St. Petersburg 1903, pp. 293-294.

5. On the main Gorchakov's programmatical analyses cf. L. I. Narochnitskaia, Rossiia i voiny Prussii v 60-e gody za obedinenie Germanii 'sverkhu,' Moskva 1960, pp. 78-79; S. A. Nikitin, Ocherki po istorii juzhnykh slavian i russko-balkanskikh sviazei v 50-70-e gody XIX v., Moskva 1970, pp. 149-151.

6. S. Goriainov, La question d'Orient à la veille du traité de Berlin (1870-1876) d'après des archives russes, Paris 1948, pp. 13-14.

7. S. A. Nikitin, Slavianskie komitety v Rossii v 1858-1876 godakh, Moskva 1960, pp. 14ff. M. B. Petrovich, The Emergence of Russian Panslavism, New York 1958, pp. 30-31.

8. Cf., for example, Petrovich, pp. 34ff., and Walicki, pp. 495ff.

9. Barsukov, vol. 9, p. 235. H. Kohn, Pan-Slavism, Univ. of Notre Dame 1953, pp. 130-131. Petrovich, pp. 25-26. Sumner, Russia and the Balkans, p. 60.

10. J. H. Billington, The Icon and the Axe, London 1966, pp. 318-320.

11. Ibid., p. 318.

12. U. Picht, M. P. Pogodin und die Slavische Frage, Stuttgart 1969, part. pp. 77-81. Petrovich, pp. 28-29. Istoriko-politicheskie pisma M. P. Pogodina, Moskva 1874, pp. 1ff.

13. Billington, pp. 342-343.

14. L. Pigarev, F. I. Tiutchev i problemy vneshnei politiki tsarskoi Rossii, Literaturnoe nasledstvo, 19-21, 1935, p. 193. Cf. also G. Florovsky, The Historical Premonitions of Tyutchev, SEER, 3, 1924-1925, pp. 337ff.; Meshcherskii, vol. 2, pp. 197ff.

15. Walicki, pp. 496-497.

16. Letters of Alexander II to Prince A. I. Bariatinskii, 1857-1864; in Rieber, pp. 120-121.

17. Nikitin, Slavianskie komitety, pp. 36ff.

Besides the members of the original initiating group including Aksakov, Pogodin and Katkov, the Committee was joined by prominent noblemen, high officials, officers and men of letters and learning. The nobility was its most numerous element, with some of the best families—Volkonskiis, Orlovs, Golitsyns, Obolenskiis—represented. Among the officers, those serving in the Caucasus were outstanding—General Prince Sviatopolk-Mirskii, General Kruzenshtern, Colonels Fadeev, Svistunov, Kishelski, Cossack atamans Ivanov and Kravtsov etc. Among the members belonging to officialdom were Minister for Public Instruction Kovalevskii, Senator Kruzenshtern, Governor of Vilna Zherebtsov. (Ibid., pp. 58ff.)

18.　Ju. Kartsov, Z kulisami diplomatii, RS, *133,* 1908, pp. 95-96.

19.　Ju. Kartsov, Sem let na Blizhnem Vostoke, St. Petersburg 1906, p. 252.

20.　Meshcherskii, vol. 1, pp. 335-336.

21.　RS, *133,* 1908, p. 96n.

22.　MV, 1865, no. 182. Nevedenskii, pp. 218-219.

23.　Aufzeichnungen und Erinnerungen aus dem Leben des Botschafters Joseph Maria v. Radowitz, vol. 1, Berlin 1925, p. 306. D. Mackenzie Wallace, Russia, vol. 2, London 1905, p. 40. Wittram, p. 329.

24.　I. Aksakov, Sochineniia, vol. 1, Moskva 1886, p. 9.

25.　RA, *11,* 1873, pp. 2489-2490. Walicki, pp. 471-472.

Notes to Chapter 3

1.　It will be shown later that the thesis "Russia must either extend her primacy to the Adriatic Sea or withdraw beyond the Dnieper" was to become a key extremist dogma, often repeated by Katkov.

2.　V. Cherkasskii, Dva slova po povodu Vostochnago voprosa, Russkaia beseda, 1858, no. 4, pp. 65ff.; extensively quoted in Petrovich, pp. 264-265.

3.　Aksakov, vol. 1, pp. 5-6, 9. Cf. also Nikitin, Slavianskie komitety, p. 29; Petrovich, pp. 35ff., 241ff.

4.　Phanar, the Greek quarter in Constantinople, was the center of their enormous influence within the Ottoman Empire.

5.　Nikitin, Ocherki, p. 186; Slavianskie komitety, p. 16.

6.　Nikitin, Slavianskie komitety, pp. 36-38.

7.　Ju. Bromley, ed., Slavianskie komitety i Rossia, Moskva 1972, pp. 126-127. D. Kosev, Russia, Frantsiia i balgarskoto osvoboditelno dvizhenie, 1860-1869, Sofia 1978, pp. 15-16. Nikitin, Ocherki, pp. 165-168.

8.　Aksakov, vol. 1, p. 43.

9.　RS, *13-15,* 1858. Liubimov, pp. 72ff.

10.　Barsukov, vol. 16, pp. 273-274. B. N. Bilunov, Iz istorii bolgarorusskikh zhurnalisticheskikh sviazei; in: Rossiia i vostochnyi krizis 70-kh godov XIX v., Moskva 1981, pp. 104-106. Nikitin, Ocherki, pp. 184ff. Zapiski Aleksandra Ivanovicha Kosheleva, Berlin 1884, p. 88.

11. This was the first occasion on which the Foreign Minister was directly attacked for the sin of passivity in the East and docility before Europe. "What is Russia itself doing in the arena of European politics? She keeps silent," wrote Pogodin. "For the sake of the balance of Europe, ten million Slavs must groan. . . ." (Barsukov, vol. 16, pp. 331-332, 450. S. Lukashevich, Ivan Aksakov 1823-1886, Harvard U. P. 1965, pp. 37-38, 120-121. Petrovich, pp. 115ff.

12. Nikitin, Slavianskie komitety, pp. 98ff. Petrovich, pp. 115ff., 132ff.

13. The annual report of the Singers' Bridge for 1856; quot. in N. S. Kiniapina, Vneshniaia politika Rossii vtoroi poloviny XIX v., Moskva 1975, p. 17.

14. Goriainov, La question, p. 13. Nikitin, Ocherki, pp. 162-164.

15. See Tatishchev, vol. 1, pp. 263-264.

16. Nikitin, Ocherki, p. 208.

17. "Poslanie k Serbam iz Moskvy," RA, 14, 1876, pp. 104ff. Aksakov, vol. 1, pp. 23ff. V. G. Karasev, ed., Zarubezhnye slaviane i Rossiia. Dokumenty arkhiva M. F. Raevskogo (40-80-e gody XIX v.), Moskva 1975, nos. 151, 185, 186. Nikitin, Ocherki, pp. 202ff.

18. D. MacKenzie, The Serbs and Russian Pan-Slavism, Cornell U. P. 1967, pp. 7-8.

19. Nikitin, Slavianskie komitety, pp. 91ff., 147ff.

20. Nikitin, Slavianskie komitety, p. 149. Zarubezhnye slaviane i Rossiia, nos. 152, 154.

21. The Diplomatic Reminiscences of Lord Augustus Loftus, vol. 2, London 1894, pp. 13ff.

22. Russian arms deliveries—allegedly 50,000 rifles and 30,000 pistols —came too late, in December 1862. (Cf. C. N. Velichi, La Roumanie et le mouvement révolutionaire bulgare de libération nationale, Bucureşti 1979, pp. 34-37.

23. Nikitin, Ocherki, pp. 163-164.

24. Aksakov, vol. 1, pp. 23-24. Nikitin, Ocherki, pp. 209-211.

25. Nikitin, Ocherki, pp. 207-209.

26. Wittram, pp. 336-337.

27. MV, 1877, no. 260; 1880, nos. 39, 94-A.

28. A. F. Koni, Na zhiznenom puti, vol. 2, St. Petersburg 1912, p. 91.

29. MV, 1868, no. 14; 1881, no. 141. S. Tatishchev, M. N. Katkov v inostrannoi politike, RV, *250*, 1897, pp. 120-122.

30. For the most important Katkov's comments on the subject see MV, 1864, nos. 117, 123; 1867, no. 285; 1873, no. 132-A; 1882, no. 91; 1883, no. 237; 1886, no. 197.

31. MV, 1880, no. 94-A.

32. Aksakov, vol. 1, pp. 29, 37. MV, 1881, no. 157.

33. N. Danilevskii, Rossiia i Evropa, St. Petersburg 1871, p. 488. Cf. also A. Florovsky, Dostoevsky and the Slavonic Question, SEER, *9*, 1931, p. 413; Pigarev, pp. 205-206.

Notes to Chapter 4

1. A. J. Rieber, The Politics of Autocracy, Paris-The Hague 1966, p. 23.

2. E. Crankshaw, The Shadow of the Winter Palace, London, 1976, p. 199.

3. S. J. Vite, Vospominaniia, vol. 1, Moskva 1955, p. 26.

4. A. L. Zisserman, Feldmarshal kniaz Aleksandr Ivanovich Bariatinskii, St. Petersburg 1890, vol. 2, p. 400.

5. Rieber, pp. 65ff. D. I. Romanovskii, General feldmarshal kn. A. I. Bariatinskii i kavkazskaia voina, RS, *130*, 1907, pp. 302ff. Zisserman, vol. 2, pp. 10ff., 94-95, 205-206; vol. 3, pp. 150ff. etc.

6. See the letters in Rieber, pp. 103-105.

7. Bariatinskii and his Chief of Staff, Miliutin, created five military districts and invested their commanders full powers including supervision of civil administration. This reorganization later served as a model for changes in the whole Russian army.

8. Zisserman, vol. 2, pp. 267-269.

9. Rieber, pp. 126-130. Zisserman, vol. 2, p. 268.

10. Tatishchev, vol. 1, pp. 284-285.

11. A. L. Zisserman, Kavkazskiia vospominaniia, RA, *23:1*, 1885, p. 615. Zisserman was a long-standing collaborator of the Katkovian press. When Katkov took over the *Moskovskiia vedomosti* in 1863, he became the main political commentator in the *Russkii vestnik*.

12. F. A. Miller, Dmitrii Miliutin and the Reform Era in Russia, Nashville, Ten. 1968, pp. 28-29. Rieber, pp. 88ff. Dnevnik P. A. Valueva, ministra vnutrennykh del, vol. 1, Moskva 1961, pp. 318-319. Vite, pp. 30-31. Zaionchkovskii, Voennye reformy, pp. 30-31, 47ff. Zisserman, vol. 3, pp. 400-401.

13. They were based on the assumption that troops would have to start their march in the Trans-Caucasia or Astrakhan and proceed along the route Astrabad-Meshed-Herat-Kandahar. (A. L. Popov, Iz istorii zavoevaniia Srednei Azii, IZ, 9, 1940, p. 220. E. L. Shteinberg, Angliiskaia versiia o "russkoi ugroze" Indii v XIX-XX vv., IZ, 33, 1950, pp. 53-55.

14. N. A. Khalfin, Politika Rossii v Srednei Azii, Moskva 1960, pp. 66ff.; Prisoedinenie Srednei Azii k Rossii, Moskva 1965, p. 88. Rieber, pp. 72-73. Zisserman, vol. 2, pp. 45-47, 120-122, 404ff.

15. Khalfin, Prisoedinenie, pp. 92ff.; Politika Rossii, pp. 67ff. RA, 20:3, 1882, pp. 42ff.; 27:2, 1889, pp. 299-300. Zisserman, vol. 3, pp. 172ff.

16. Rieber, p. 103.

17. Zisserman, vol. 2, p. 109.

18. Khalfin, Politika Rosii, pp. 120-123. N. S. Kiniapina, Sredniaia Aziia vo vneshnepoliticheskikh planakh tsarizma, VI, 1974, no. 2, pp. 39-43. Popov, pp. 202-203. Rieber, pp. 77-81. For the whole of Ignatiev's report see "Missiia v Khivu i Bukharu v 1858 godu Fligel-Adiutanta polkovnika N. Ignatieva," St. Petersburg 1897.

19. M. T. Florinsky, Russia, A History and an Interpretation, vol. 2, New York 1953, pp. 977-979.

20. Khalfin, Prisoedinenie, pp. 107ff.; Politika Rossii, pp. 119ff. M. A. Terentiev, Istoriia zavoevaniia Srednei Azii, vol. 1, St. Petersburg 1906, pp. 241ff. For the most interesting testimonies of Generals Duhamel and Zalesov see RA, 23:2, 1885, resp. RS, 114-115, 1903.

21. S. Becker, Russia's Protectorates in Central Asia: Bukhara nad Khiva, 1865-1924, Harvard U. P. 1968, p. 58.

22. Khalfin, Politika Rossii, p. 143; Prisoedinenie, pp. 128-129.

Notes to Chapter 5

1. Feoktistov, p. 155.

2. Cf. S. Lukashevich, Lonstantin Leontiev 1831-1891, New York 1967, p. 68.

3. Feoktistov, p. 345. Miller, p. 154. Nevedenskii, pp. 198-200. Tvardovskaia, pp. 24ff.

4. Katkov and his docile associate, Professor Pavel Leontiev, wished to manage a daily which was better suited for commenting on current affairs than the *Russkii vestnik* and *Sovremennaia letopis.* At first they were expected to take over the *St. Peterburgskiia vedomosti,* where powerful Count Bludov and his patriotic daughter supported their candidature. Then, Moscow University again offered them the *Moskovskiia vedomosti,* this time on a "free-hand" basis; and the Tsar approved the Katkov-Leontiev chocie among several contenders, "taking into account experience, knowledge and popularity of the new editors." (RS, *108,* 1901, pp. 521-523. RA, *31:2,* 1893, pp. 395ff. Tvardovskaia, p. 23.) Thus, at the beginning of 1863, the structure of the Katkovian press was firmly established. While the *Russkii vestnik* and *Sovremennaia letopis*—the latter was eventually closed down because of evident loss of purpose—were mainly devoted to current history and literature and run by his assistants, Katkov centered his work and direct supervision on the *Moskovskiia vedomosti.* For twenty-four years, he published, almost in every issue, up to three editorials, commenting on every important domestic and foreign policy problem.

5. Feoktistov, p. 345. Miller, pp. 153-154. For the concept and policies of the Miliutin group in the Polish question see D. Beyrau, Militär und Gesellschaft im vorrevolutionären Russland, Köln 1984, pp. 231ff.

6. MV, 1863, nos. 53, 55, 57, 68, 71, 75, 78, 96, 137, 168, 169, 180. RV, *44,* 1863, pp. 447ff., 933ff. Katz, pp. 118ff. Nevedenskii, pp. 170ff.

7. RS, *109,* 1902, pp. 270ff.; *128,* 1906, pp. 208. Tvardovskaia, p. 28.

8. Feoktistov, p. 137.

9. V. G. Revunenkov, Polskoe vosstanie 1863 i evropeiskaia diplomatiia, Leningrad 1957, p. 218.

10. Miller, pp. 146-147. Revunenkov, pp. 259ff., Valuev, vol. 1, pp. 225, 232.

11. W. E. Mosse, The European Powers and the German Question 1848-1871, Cambridge 1958, pp. 120-121.

12. MV, 1863, nos. 59, 68, 70, 83, 86, 96, 101, 104-106, 112, 114, 116, 128.

13. MV, 1863, nos. 125, 141, 144, 145, 195. About the actions directed by the Strastnyi Boulevard against the Grand Duke see RS, *120,* 1904, pp. 88-89.

14.   A. V. Nikitenko, Dnevnik v trekh tomakh, vol. 2 Moskva 1955, pp. 323-324. Cf. also Meshcherskii, vol. 1, p. 226; Tvardovskaia, pp. 27-32.

15.   Cf. the report of Ambassador Napier in Mosse, p. 121.

16.   R. F. Leslie, Reform and Insurrection in Russian Poland, 1856-1863, London 1963, pp. 186, 195. See also Mosse, European Powers, pp. 121ff.

17.   MV, 1863, nos. 161, 163.

18.   Cf. the Tsar's correspondence in "Posledniaia polskaia smuta," (RS, *36,* 1882, pp. 533ff.; *37,* 1883, pp. 323ff., 613ff.) and Shuvalov's testimony related by Baddeley (J. F. Baddeley, Russia in the "Eighties," London 1921, p. 377).

19.   Nevedenskii, p. 203. Pigarev, pp. 202-205. Valuev, vol. 1, p. 232.

20.   Baddeley, p. 376. Feoktistov, pp. 64-66.

21.   Liubimov, p. 236.

22.   V. Mustafin, ed., Mikhail Nikiforovich Katkov i graf Petr Aleksandrovich Valuev v ikh perepiske (1863-1879); RS, *161,* 1915, p. 279.

23.   Feoktistov, pp. 64-65. Meshcherskii, vol. 1, pp. 329ff.

24.   Tvardovskaia, pp. 51, 57-60.

25.   Crankshaw, The Shadow, p. 170.

26.   Western provinces, i.e. Lithuania, White Russia and western parts of the Ukraine, were claimed by the Poles in revolt as their own. Among about 15 million inhabitants they numbered just a million; they, however, formed an almost entire upper landowning stratum.

27.   Tatishchev, vol. 1, pp. 511-512. For Muraviev's own plea see RS, *37,* 1883, pp. 144ff.; *38,* 1883, pp. 207ff. For Katkov's proposals identical to those of the Hangman and his solidarity with him see MV, 1863, nos. 128, 139, 155, 161, 179, 184, 192, 193, 201, 221; 1864, nos. 6-A, 7-B, 8-B, 33, 48, 49, 54, 60, 75, 94, 99-B, 126, 157, 159, 167, 203; 1865, nos. 94, 102, 105, 252.

28.   Aksakov, vol. 3, pp. 118, 119, 272, 405, 409, 453. Barsukov, vol. 18, pp. 118ff. Lukashevich, Aksakov, p. 91. M. B. Petrovich, Russian Pan-Slavists and the Polish Uprising of 1863, Harvard Slavic Studies, *1,* 1953, pp. 238-239.

29.   Meshcherskii, vol. 1, p. 331, 433ff. RA, *32:1,* 1894, pp. 244. Tvardovskaia, pp. 32-34.

30.   Cf. particularly RA, *49:2,* 1911, p. 347; *49:3,* 1911, pp. 86-87.

31.   For Katkov's campaign against "cosmopolitanism" and "separatism" in general see MV, 1864, nos. 174, 246, 247, 252, 254; 1865, nos. 3,

137, 202, 211. For the campaign against "Polonism" and "Ukrainism" see MV, 1863, nos. 92, 117, 136, 169, 177, 191, 217, 252, 253, 283-A, B; 1864, nos. 30, 31, 134, 193. For the campaign against the Baltic Germans see MV, 1864, nos. 97, 109, 120, 125, 128-A, 208, 270; 1865, nos. 23, 103, 150, 151, 230-A, 234, 238, 284-A. Cf. also S. G. Isakov, Ostzeiskii vopros v russkoi pechati 1860-kh godov, Uchennye zapiski Tartuskogo gosudarstvennogo universiteta, *107*, 1961, pp. 28ff.

32. MV, 1867, no. 39; 1865, no. 131. Cf. also J. D. Morison, Katkov and Panslavism, SEER, *26*, 1968, pp. 423-424.

33. Wittram, p. 345.

34. MV, 1863, nos. 280, 283; 1864, no. 45. Tvardovskaia, pp. 38ff.

35. For the crucial Katkov's letter on the theme see RS, *163*, 1915, pp. 296-300.

36. Tvardovskaia, pp. 51ff.

37. Feoktistov, pp. 105, 131. Nevedenskii, pp. 219-220. For details about the atmosphere at Strastnyi Boulevard see Meshcherskii, vol. 2, pp. 83ff.

38. MV, 1865, no. 176. Nevedenskii, pp. 220-221, 264-265.

39. At the beginning of the Polish crisis, some adherents of the Panslav school (Aksakov, Pogodin, Samarin), embarrassed by possible effects of the confrontation on the Slavic world, professed their sympathies for appeasement; but when the Poles raised the issue of territorial historical rights, they quickly retreated back to the "patriotic" fold. On the attitude to Muraviev and to the Baltic question there was not even a shade of divergence between them and Katkov. (Lukashevich, Aksakov, pp. 76ff. Petrovich, Russian Panslavists and the Polish Uprising, pp. 219ff.)

40. Barsukov, vol. 19, pp. 31ff., 361-362. Nevedenskii, pp. 207ff. MV, 1863, nos. 187, 197; 1865, no. 54.

41. MV, 1863, nos. 139, 155; 1865, no. 102. Nevedenskii, pp. 258-260.

42. Nikitenko, vol. 2, pp. 73, 344, 353-355, 373-374.

43. RA, *49:2*, 1911, p. 359; *32:1*, 1894, p. 254.

44. Meshcherskii, vol. 1, pp. 265-266.

45. RA, *32:1*, 1894, pp. 235, 254, 432-433.

46. Tvardovskaia, p. 67.

47. Cf. particularly the letters in RS, *163*, 1915, pp. 206-213; *164*, 1915, pp. 92-94.

48. Liubimov, pp. 259ff. Nevedenskii, pp. 223-226. Valuev, vol. 1, pp. 251-252. Tvardovskaia, pp. 60ff.

49. Katz, p. 109.

50. Golovnin was the spiritus agens behind the conciliatory policies of Grand Duke Konstantin in Warsaw. Katkov also hated him for the inspiration he had given for the pamphlet of Schédo-Ferotti (Baron Firks), "Que fera-t-on de la Pologne" (Bruxelles 1864). The author, a correspondent of the *Independence Belge,* exposed in it the evil role of the Muscovite before the European public. (MV, 1864, nos. 195, 196, 212; 1865, no. 12. Nevedenskii, pp. 231ff. Tvardovskaia, pp. 68-69.)

51. MV, 1866, no. 81.

52. Valuev, vol. 1, pp. 307-308, 351. Feoktistov, pp. 130-131. Katz, pp. 101-102, 108-109, 126ff. RS, *163,* 1915, pp. 298ff.

53. MV, 1865, no. 12. Liubimov, pp. 280ff. Nevedenskii, pp. 238ff. Tvardovskaia, pp. 68-69. Valuev, vol. 1, pp. 307-308, 359. Soloviev, pp. 96ff.

54. Katz, p. 103n. Nevedenskii, pp. 222-223. RA, *32:1,* 1894, p. 262.

55. Nevedenskii, p. 240. Pigarev, p. 201. Valuev, vol. 2, pp. 37, 441.

56. MV, 1865, no. 210. Nevedenskii, p. 242.

57. Nikitenko, vol. 3, pp. 21-23.

58. Nikitenko, vol. 3, p. 23. Tvardovskaia, p. 70. RV, *250,* 1897, pp. 16-17.

59. MV, 1866, no. 61.

60. Katz, p. 138.

61. MV, 1866, no. 66. The editor, as it seems, made his formula deliberately unclear. But under the "supreme authority" he obviously understood autocracy which identified itself with the national interest, not simply the Tsar's personality.

62. Liubimov, pp. 316ff. Nevedenskii, pp. 242ff. Valuev, vol. 2, pp. 112, 463.

63. Cf. MV, 1866, nos. 69, 75, 81, 83, 85, 99.

64. Katz, pp. 139-141. Valuev, vol. 2, p. 131.

65. In June 1865, the Tsar received a Polish delegation and proclaimed that "he loved all his subjects equally—Russians, Poles, Finns, Livonians and others." In protest, Katkov stopped publishing his editorials for a week. (Cf. Nevedenskii, pp. 244-245.) Moreover, the editor was suspected of instigating the opposition of the Moscow nobility, expressed in the

"constitutionalist" address forwarded to the autocrat at the end of 1865. (Kornilov, pp. 171-174.)

66.　　Nikitenko, vol. 3, p. 35. Tvardovskaia, pp. 70-71. Valuev, vol. 2, p. 133.

67.　　Liubimov, pp. 316ff.; part. see pp. 341-343.

68.　　Cf. Vozhd reaktsii, pp. 21-22.

69.　　Nevedenskii, pp. 254-55. Valuev, vol. 2, pp. 131-134. RA, *32:1*, 1894, p. 428.

Notes to Chapter 6

1.　　The press regulations (1865) abolished preventive censorship for books over a certain number of pages, and for newspapers and magazines published in the two capitals. The main supervision was entrusted to the Interior Ministry and its censorship offices. If facts and problems were "improperly" presented, a punishment might ensue up to permanent closure of the periodical in question. Usually though, fines and warnings were applied; after three warnings a temporary suspension resulted. (For details see Ambler, pp. 23-25, Grüning, pp. 11ff.)

2.　　RA, *49:2*, 1911, p. 243.

3.　　MV, 1867, no. 51; SEER, *7*, 1928-1929, p. 43.

4.　　Barsukov, vol. 19, pp. 37ff. Katz, pp. 78ff. Nevedenskii, pp. 414ff., 464ff. Pyziur, p. 454. RA, *32:1*, 1894, pp. 432-433, 435; *49:2*, 1911, p. 243. Tvardovskaia, pp. 35-36.

5.　　Gertsen, vol. 11, p. 351.

6.　　SEER, *7*, 1928-1929, p. 43.

7.　　Nikitenko, vol. 2, pp. 546-547. Cf. also Valuev, vol. 2, pp. 74-75; RA, *49:1*, 1911, pp. 109, 116, 124, 125, 139.

8.　　H. Seton-Watson, The Imperial Russia 1801-1917, Oxford 1967, pp. 332-333.

9.　　Rieber, p. 21.

10.　　Gertsen, vol. 11, p. 312.

11.　　Meshcherskii, vol. 1, p. 413.

12.　　E. Crankshaw, Bismarck, London 1981, p. 353.

13.　　Miliutin, vol. 1, pp. 119-120; vol. 4, pp. 95-96, 99. Valuev, vol. 2, pp. 186, 203, 233.

14.　　Miller, pp. 142ff.

15.   For Katkov's veiled attacks on Shuvalov, particularly for his persecution of the "patriotic" press, see MV, 1867, nos. 151, 203; 1868, no. 48; 1869, nos. 18, 202, 250. For the essential editorials devoted to the danger of "cosmopolitanism" in general see MV, 1867, nos. 23, 89; 1869, no. 61; 1870, no. 186-A.

16.   Feoktistov, p. 240.

17.   In his revulsion against the city on the Neva, Katkov even backed the chimeric project to move the seat of the government from the "barrack-bureaucratic" stronghold to historical Kiev, put forward by Bariatinskii. (Cf. Zisserman, vol. 3, pp. 169-171.)

18.   Tvardovskaia, pp. 62-65.

19.   For general surveys see A. Henriksson, The Tsar's Loyal Germans, Columbia U. P. 1983, and R. Wittram, Baltische Geschichte, 1180-1918, München 1954.

20.   MV, 1867, nos. 46, 66, 78, 79, 97.

Already before 1867, Baltic Germans had identified the Strastnyi Boulevard as their sworn enemy. Their press organs stated that of 96 hostile articles published in the Russian press in 1865, almost half appeared in the Moskovskiia vedomosti. (MV, 1866, no. 81. Isakov, p. 158.)

21.   For Aksakov's writings on the Baltic question see his Sochineniia, vol. 3.

22.   Cf. Nikitenko, vol. 3, pp. 97ff.

23.   RV, 200, 1888, pp. 174-175.

24.   MV, 1867, nos. 170, 181, 201, 203, 265. Isakov, pp. 135ff.

25.   MV, 1867, no. 143-A. See also MV, 1867, nos. 39, 144, 145, 151, 170, 181, 222; 1868, nos. 149, 162, 169, 183-B, 230, 261, 266-B; 1869, nos. 12, 83, 87, 104-A, 107-A, etc. Isakov, pp. 147-148; Nevedenskii, pp. 301ff.

26.   Pogodin in his pamphlet on the "Ostsee question" (Ostzeiskii vopros, Moskva 1867) expressed the same thought flatly: "The Russification of the Ests, Letts and Kurlandians is a political necessity and one has to be blind not to see it." (Cf. Isakov, pp. 134ff.)

27.   E. C. Thaden, ed., Russification in the Baltic Provinces and Finland, 1855-1914, Princeton U. P. 1981, p. 216.

28.   APP, vol. 9, no. 441.

29.   For a brief analysis of Samarin's opus see Thaden, pp. 128-129.

30.   Cf. MV, 1868, nos. 191, 193, 194, 200; Isakov, pp. 150ff.

31. Isakov, pp. 154-157.

Samarin, too, in a letter to the Tsar declined to repent. His work, he argued similarly, had been "consecrated to the defense of Russian state interest against the immoderate and even increasing pretension of Baltic separatism." (Thaden, p. 134.)

32. APP, vol. 10, no. 265.

33. MV, 1868, nos. 153, 253, 266; 1869, nos. 23, 28, 31, 44, 48, 60, 86, etc. APP, vol. 10, no. 265. Nevedenskii, pp. 296ff.

34. Isakov, p. 162n.

Notes to Chapter 7

1. KA, *93,* 1939, p. 108. Narochnitskaia, p. 19.

2. S. A. Khrulev, Zapiska o pokhode v Indiiu, RA, *20:3,* 1882, pp. 42ff.

3. RS, *115,* 1903, pp. 322-324.

4. Khalfin, Prisoedinenie, pp. 148-150; Politika Rossii, pp. 171ff. D. MacKenzie, The Lion of Tashkent; the Career of General M. G. Cherniaev, Georgia U. P. 1974, pp. 30-31. Popov, pp. 210-211.

5. MacKenzie, p. 42.

6. Khalfin, Prisoedinenie, pp. 158ff.; Politika Rossii, pp. 168-169; MacKenzie, pp. 43-44.

7. Khalfin, Prisoedinenie, pp. 169-173; Politika Rossii, pp. 176-177.

8. A. H. Bilgrami, Afghanistan and British India 1793-1907, New Delhi 1972, p. 133.

9-10. For the text of the note see Tatishchev, vol. 2, pp. 107-108; Bilgrami, app. XVII, pp. 315ff.

11. Valuev, vol. 2, p. 60.

12. Khalfin, Politika Rossii, pp. 206ff.; Prisoedinenie, pp. 182ff. MacKenzie, The Lion, pp. 51ff. Popov, pp. 213-214. RS, *65,* 1890, pp. 661ff. Terentiev, vol. 1, pp. 326ff.

13. MV, 1866, no. 1.

14. Cf. Gorchakov's memorandum of November 1865, in KA, *93,* 1939, p. 108.

15. Mosse, European Powers, p. 220.

16. Ibid., p. 216.

17. W. E. Mosse, The Rise and Fall of the Crimean System, 1855-1871, London 1963, p. 129.

18.   MV, 1866, no. 256. The attitudes of the Russian and especially the Katkovian press have been analyzed in Nikitiin, Ocherki, pp. 193ff.

19.   MV, 1866, nos. 40-44, 52, 61, 72.

20.   Beyrau, Russische Orientpolitik, pp. 36ff. Mosse, European Powers, pp. 131ff.

21.   Zisserman, vol. 3, pp. 174-175.

22.   Aksakov, vol. 1, pp. 93, 206.

23.   MV, 1866, nos. 40-43, 61, 67, 138, 140, 152.

24.   MV, 1866, nos. 57, 61, 67, 92, 97.

25.   MV, 1866, nos. 138, 141, 145, 146, 160, 161, 222, 225, 246, 264; 1867, nos. 21, 41.

26.   Denkwürdigkeiten des Botschafters General v. Schweinitz, vol. 1, Berlin 1927, p. 194.

27.   For the most telling testimony see the memorandum circulated in September 1866 by Finance Minister Reutern, in W. Graf Reutern-Nolcken, Die finanzielle Sanierung Russlands nach der Katastroph des Krimkrieges 1862-1878 durch den Finanzminister Michael v. Reutern, Berlin 1914, pp. 16ff.

28.   Narochnitskaia, p. 78.

29.   Mosse, European Powers, pp. 256-257n. Zisserman, vol. 3, p. 175.

30.   Iu. A. Pisarev, Vosstanie v Bosnii i Gertsegovine i evropeiskie derzhavy (1875-1876), Novaia i noveishaia istoriia, 1876, no. 2, p. 55.

Notes to Chapter 8

1.   Kiniapina, Vneshniaia politika, p. 48.

2.   Nikitin, Ocherki, p. 147.

3.   L. M. Shneerson, Franko-prusskaia voina i Rossiia, Minsk 1976, p. 35.

4.   Quot. in Kiniapina, Vneshniaia politika, p. 15.

5.   The Polish question had left a strong imprint upon the Muscovite's feelikngs towards France and especially her Emperor. "The history of the First French Empire tells us convincingly that it is impossible to rely on a world-wide alliance with Napoleonic policy," he had contended. "Napoleonic France is precisely the Power with which Russia must on no occasion enter into an exclusive alliance." Before 1866, he repeatedly dismissed the belief in Russo-French cooperation in the East as Erroneous. (MV,

1863, nos. 215, 266; 1864, nos. 107, 111, 137, 141-B, 144, 146, 149, 156, 159, 241, 266, 260; 1865, no. 217 etc.) Already then, though, growing apprehension of Prussian ascendance had overshadowed anti-Napoleonic bitterness. The intimacy between the Romanovs and the Hohenzollerns made him unhappy from the outset; he had perceived it but as a deplorable remnant of the Holy Alliance tradition, untowardly enlivened by the Polish revolt. Similarly, although pronouncedly hostile to Austria and her Balkan aspirations, he had advised to support her in Germany to counterbalance Prussian "ambitious designs." (MV, 1863, no. 202; 1864, nos. 58, 111, 156, 228; 1865, no. 27. Nevedenskii, pp. 381ff.)

6.   MV, 1866, nos. 141, 157, 160, 170, 173; 1867, nos. 13, 50, 60, 185, 223, 250 etc. Beyrau, Russische Orientpolitik, pp. 54-55.

7.   N. P. Ignatiev, Zapiski 1875-1878, IsV, *135*, 1914, pp. 52, 161.

8.   IsV, *135*, 1914, p. 50.

9.   IsV, *135*, 1914, pp. 56-57.

10.   Cf. I. G. Senkevich, Rossiia i Kritskoe vosstanie, 1866-1869, Moskva 1970, pp. 39-43.

11.   IsV, *135*, 1914, p. 57.

12.   D. Dontas, Greece and the Great Powers, 1863-1875, Thessalonika 1966, pp. 66ff.; Senkevich, pp. 31ff.

13.   IsV, *135*, 1914, pp. 59ff.

14.   Cf. Beyrau, Russische Orientpolitik, p. 88.

15.   RA, *49:2*, 1911, pp. 466-467.

16.   Aksakov, vol. 1, pp. 107, 109-110, 130. Nikitin, Ocherki, p. 229.

17.   Cf. Senkevich, pp. 52-53.

18.   Mosse, European Powers, p. 257.

19.   Quot. in Nikitin, Ocherki, pp. 149-151; Shneerson, pp. 19-21.

20.   K. Bourne, Great Britain and the Cretan Revolt, SEER, *35*, 1854, pp. 81ff. Duke of Argyll, Our responsibilities for Turkey, London 1896, p. 44.

21.   Contrary to Aksakov and other Muscovites, Katkov distinctly approved Gorchakov's diplomatic effort; and, on the occasion of his fifty-year service in the Foreign Ministry and his promotion to the Chancellorship he again hailed him as the guardian of the "national interest" policy. His daily argued what was believed to be their common views: Russia had set herself free from the bondage of the Holy Alliance and instead of suffering a relapse, she should benefit from the regained liberty. If war were

to result from French-Prussian tensions, Russia should engage herself "neither for Prussia nor for France" as long as her interests were not at stake and the European balance did not shift to her disadvantage. If the French statesmen renounced their anti-Russian and pro-Polish proclivities beforehand, however, then it might be discovered that the goals of the Second Empire and Tsardom were identical. (MV, 1867, nos. 13, 29, 53, 55, 60, 65, 71, 105, 117, 147, 148, 164.)

22.   MV, 1867, nos. 245, 285; see also nos. 185, 223, 250.

23.   Aksakov, vol. 1, p. 117. Ignatiev, too, was hostile to Greek aggrandizement and allegedly even advised the Grand Vizier to resist pressures for the cession of Crete. (Dontas, p. 99.)

24.   The conflict was brought into open on Easter Sunday 1860 when Bulgarian Bishop Ilarion omitted the name of the Patriarch from the liturgy; instead, a special hymn of praise to the Sultan was sung. In response, the Greek hierarchy excommunicated and exiled Ilarion.

Ignatiev singularly failed in his subsequent conciliatory efforts. Although he managed on the one hand to direct a moderate, "Old" group among the Bulgarians to a gradualist approach, and on the other hand to win Patriarch Sophronius over into giving some concessions to them, the net result, though, was an uproar in the Greek community and a split in the Bulgarian ranks. While Sophronius was driven by his kinsmen to resignation (December 1866), the Bulgarian "maximalists" insisted on schism and turned against the Russian envoy.

25.   Nikitin, Ocherki, pp. 192-193.

26.   Cf. B. H. Sumner, Ignatiev at Constantinople, SEER, *11*, 1933, pp. 349ff.; A. Popov, Nastuplenie Tsarskoi Rossii na Balkhanakh, in "Avantiury russkogo tsarizma v Bolgarii," Moskva 1935, pp. 197ff.

27.   S. A. Nikitin, Diplomaticheskie otnosheniia Rossii s juzhnymi slavianami v 60-kh godakh XIX v., in: Slavianskii sbornik, Moskva 1947, p. 285; Ocherki, pp. 225, 229. Senkevich, pp. 53ff., 102ff., 128-130.

28.   Nikitin, Slavianskie komitety, pp. 152ff.

29.   Senkevich, pp. 65-66.

30.   APP, vol. 8, no. 311. Beyrau, Russische Orientpolitik, pp. 89ff. Nikitin, Diplomaticheskie otnosheniia, pp. 285-287; Slavianskie komitety, pp. 154ff.

31.   Popov, Nastuplenie, pp. 197-198.

32.   S. A. Nikitin, Slavianskie siezdy shestidesiatykh godov XIX v.; in: Slavianskii sbornik, Moskva 1948, p. 24.

33. MV, 1867, nos. 102-105, 110-113, 128, 247.

34. MV, 1867, no. 113.

35. Nikitin, Slavianskie komitety, pp. 222-225. MV, 1867, no. 128.

36. K. Kazbunda, Pout' Čechů do Moskvy 1867 a rakouská diplo-
macie, Praha 1924, p. 24.

37. Kohn, p. 142.

38. Nikitin, Slavianskie komitety, p. 250.

39. Ibid., p. 287.

40. APP, vol. 9, no. 115. Nikitin, Diplomatischeskie otnosheniia, p.
287.

41. Also the Russian military mission in Belgrade warned that "only
the most propitious moment circumstances, exhaustion and demoraliza-
tion of the Turks, considerable financial subsidies and influx of capable
Russian officers" could make the action possible. (Kosev, pp. 34ff. Nikitin,
Diplomaticheskie otnosheniia, pp. 286-287.)

42. Cf. Nikitin, Ocherki, pp. 171-172; Shneerson, p. 49. See also
Gorchakov's report of 4 January 1868, in Narochnitskaia, pp. 78-80.

43. APP, vol. 9, nos. 515, 559, 560; vol. 10, nos. 136, 225. Beyrau,
Russische Orientpolitik, p. 97. H. Müller-Link, Industrialisierung und
Aussenpolitik, Göttingen 1977, p. 55. Valuev, vol. 2, pp. 113ff.

44. Diplomatic documents of Western provenience also suggest that
on the Neva they still believed in the prospect which had roused them in
recent months. Neither the Tsar's conversations and Gorchakov's dispositions, nor the correspondence of key Russian diplomats, however, corroborate these allegations. Novikov clearly stated that "non-interference
will be damned in Greece as a withdrawal and diminish our prestige here."
Ignatiev wrote that the declaration would be a correct move only if
European Turkey were ready for revolt; yet this not being the case, it
would merely embolden the Turks and benefit Europe in binding Russian hands completely. (IMID, 1914, bd. 2, pp. 94-95. Mosse, European
Powers, pp. 280-281. Senkevich, pp. 141-143.

45. Cf. Beyrau, Russische Orientpolitik, pp. 84ff., 100ff. Tvardovskaia, pp. 75-76.

46. Aksakov, vol. 1, pp. 167-170, 182-183, 186. MV, 1867, no. 230.

47. APP, vol. 9, no. 366; cf. also no. 450.

48. Beyrau, Russische Orientpolitik, pp. 106ff. IMID, 1914, bk. 2,
p. 142. Shneerson, pp. 51, 248ff. Valuev, vol. 2, pp. 213ff.

49. APP, vol. 10, no. 293. IMID, 1914, bk. 2, pp. 72-73, 102.

50. Cf. APP, vol. 10, nos. 294, 470. IMID, 1914, bk. 2, pp. 102-105.

51. APP, vol. 10, nos. 470, 486. Bourne, p. 93.

52. Senkevich, p. 185.

53. Kiniapina, Vneshniaia politika, p. 71.

54. Ibid., p. 73.

55. MV, 1869, no. 138; cf. also nos. 188, 209, 227, 228, 238, 256, 268.

56. MV, 1868, no. 280; 1869, no. 39-B.

57. MV, 1867, nos. 276-A, 277, 278; 1868, no. 130-B; 1869, nos. 38-A, 55, 170; 1870, nos. 2-B, 45-B, 131, 184-B.

58. The group formed in the capital to organize the welcome for the guests of the Congress became the nucleus of the St. Petersburg section. Other sections were established at Kiev and Odessa. The Moscow Committee, however, overshadowed them by far in membership and importance; among its new recruits were many nobles and about 30 wealthy businessmen. Groups in Tiflis, Warsaw, Tver, Kharkov, Saratov, Kazan and other towns without local branches also adhered to the Moscow center. (Nikitin, Slavianskie komitety, pp. 45ff. Petrovich, Russian Panslavism, p. 139ff.)

59. For analyses see Kohn, pp. 147ff.; R. E. MacMaster, Danilevsky, A Russian Totalitarian Philosopher, Harvard U. P. 1967; E. C. Thaden, Conservative Nationalism in Nineteenth-Century Russia, Seattle U. P. 1964, pp. 102ff., 146ff.

60. Danilevskii, pp. 31-33.

61. R. Fadeev, Sobrannye sochineniia, vol. 2:1, St. Petersburg 1890, pp. 197-198.

62. Fadeev, vol. 2:1, pp. 35, 198, 204.

63. Ibid., p. 210.

64. Fadeev, vol. 1, pp. 54-55, vol. 2:2, pp. 296ff.

65. Ibid., vol. 2:2, pp. 253ff.

66. Ibid., pp. 297ff.

67. Ibid., pp. 300-301, 313.

68. Byrnes, pp. 117-118.

69. Danilevskii, pp. 5ff.

70. Ibid., p. 462.

71. Ibid., p. 384.

72. Danilevskii, pp. 384-385, 409-410, 451.
73. Ibid., pp. 416, 487-488, 497.

Notes to Chapter 9

1. Stremoukhov, the director of the Asiatic Department, was regarded as a "political friend of Katkov" and a "chauvinist in the Ministry (for Foreign Affairs) who hates everything opposing Russian policy in the East." Deeply distrustful of France, he differed from the publicist precisely in the belief that the pressing needs of Tsardom—the revision of the Paris Treaty, guarantees against Austrian action in Bosnia-Herce-govina—could be safeguarded only by an "intimate relationship with Prussia" (APP, vol 8, no 380; vol. 9, no. 11.). Ignatiev held the same view.

2. On the divisions see APP, vol. 8, no. 63; vol. 9, no. 146; Schweinitz, Briefwechsel, pp. 32-33.

3. APP, vol. 9, no. 559.

4. MV, 1867, nos. 207, 285.

5. MV, 1868, nos. 10, 13.

6. The Russian press, the Chancellor complained rather hypocritic-ally, was "unfortunately too independent" to be tamed; particularly the daily of Katkov, "regardless of all the signals he had given to it" had not been willing to behave reasonably. The Prussian Minister responded with similar lament: for a long time he had been observing that "the most influential paper with the acknowledged contacts with the cabinet" (i.e. with Gorchakov himself) was engaged in "mad incitements against his country, without any governmental organ opposing it even once." (APP, vol. 9, no 515.)

7. APP, vol. 9, no. 561.

8. APP, vol. 9, nos. 528, 539.

9. MV, 1868, no. 20.

10. If an armed conflict between France and Prussia would break out, Alexander suggested, Russia would hold Austria back by moving 100,000 troops up to the Galician border; Prussia was to send the same number of soldiers if Russia clashed with the Dual Monarchy. (APP, vol. 9, no. 644; see also nos. 559, 560, 562.) Like his Russian opponents, Bismarck was not anxious to bind his hands. Whatever importance he might have ascribed to Russian benevolent neutrality in the decisive

contest with Napoleon, he would not commit himself to a hostile stance towards Austria. So, recalling King William's "peaceful intentions and wishes to minimize the possibility of war," he put the proposal of the Tsar down; and instructed Reuss to ensure the Russian on every occasion of a friendly disposition but evade any debate on "special obligations." (APP, vol. 9, no. 662; cf. also no. 690.)

11.   Quot. in Shneerson, p. 74.

12.   MV, 1868, nos. 125, 132.

13.   MV, 1868, no. 184. Cf. also nos. 102, 107, 122, 125, 132, 257-260; APP, vol. 10, no. 353.

14.   APP, vol. 10, no. 353.

15.   Schweinitz, Briefwechsel, p. 30.

16.   APP, vol. 10, nos. 394, 445.

17.   APP, vol 10, no. 445. Foektistov, pp. 314-317, 324. MV, 1867, nos. 246, 263-B, 274, 282. Schweinitz, Briefwechsel, pp. 247, 263. Whether as a consequence of Katkov's threat or not, Schweinitz was soon transferred to Austria.

18.   MV, 1869, nos. 45, 49.

In a confidential communication, also Gorchakov took up the Paris episode to the same purpose: "In general," he stated, "the cooperation with Berlin in the East has been more in appearance than in reality"; "Prussia shows laxity or hesitation, whenever the talk starts on the proposition that she ought to join us . . . ." (Shneerson, p. 73.)

19.   Mosse, European Powers, pp. 293-295. Shneerson, pp. 74ff.

20.   MV, 1869, nos. 102, 252.

21.   Feoktistov, pp. 65ff.

22.   Mosse, European Powers, pp. 291-293, 398n.

23.   Beyrau, Russische Orientpolitik, pp. 148ff. Mosse, European Powers, pp. 291ff. Shneerson, pp. 74ff. H. Wereszcki, Soju trzech czesarzy, Warsawa 1965, pp. 141ff.

24.   Beyrau, Russische Orientpolitik, p. 148.

25.   Valuev, vol. 2, p. 504.

26.   Nikitenko, vol. 3, p. 161. Valuev, vol. 2, pp. 275, 504.

27.   MV, 1870, nos. 2, 3.

28.   Cf. Nikitenko, vol. 3, pp. 165-166. Both Katz and Tvardovskaia are silent on the episode.

29.   MV, 1870, no. 8.

30. For the uninterrupted anti-Prussian campaign see MV, 1870, nos. 23, 36-B, 43, 45-A, 50, 59, 74, 75, 136, 166-B, 176 etc.

31. The French statesmen did not even pretend to be interested in the Tsar's mediation; they badly handled the Spanish succession problem by resorting to war threats; furthermore, Prime Minister Ollivier announced highly inopportunely that the Paris Treaty constituted an "ummutable basis for the existing international order." In consequence, after a long time, the Russian press again severely criticized the Second Empire and Gorchakov with Miliutin branded its stance as "war provocation." (Shneerson, pp. 93ff.)

32. Beyrau, p. 187. Mosse, European Powers, p. 306.

33. MV, 1870, nos. 144, 148.

34. MV, 1870, nos. 174, 175.

35. The army was put on the alert, reequipment in the western military districts with modern rifles was speeded up. On 2 September, Miliutin submitted to Alexander his report based on the plans elaborated in 1867-1868: two armies—470,000 troops altogether—should be assembled with the task of keeping the Poles in check and invading Austria. (Shneerson, pp. 108-113.)

36. "We must stand closely side by side to prevent Prussia settling the matters alone and only to her advantage. I shall agree solely to such conditions as will safeguard a lasting peace; not to conditions unacceptable to France and harmful from the viewpoint of European equilibrium," the Tsar told Chotek.

It was precisely in the bid for Habsburg cooperation that Alexander diverted from his "inward stance" most. His promises were comprehensive: in the Balkans—to accept any arrangement save one-sided Austrian influence, and to stop the Panslav campaign; in Germany—to support Austrian preeminence south of the Main. If the understanding between Vienna and St. Petersburg was to be established, said the autocrat, "we can always find the means to force even victorious Prussia to listen to us." (Beyrau, Russische Orientpolitik, pp. 208. I Diószegi, Österreich-Ungarn und der französisch-preussische Krieg 1870-1871, Budapest 1974, pp. 163-166. Mosse, European Powers, pp. 308ff. Shneerson, pp. 107ff.)

37. MV, 1870, nos. 151, 168, 173-A, 176, 182, 192-B, 198, 200, 215, 248; 1871, no. 8.

38. Beyrau, p. 200.

39. For the Russian press reaction see Mosse, European Powers, app.C, pp. 389ff.

40. MV, 1870, no. 182.

41. Some of the dignitaries present must have felt highly uncomfortable. This applied above all to Gorchakov and Miliutin, the "anti-Prussians" who foresaw that the action would completely estrange London and Vienna, frustrate the effort to save the European balance, and, worse still, expose Russia to serious risks. The testimonies in Russian sources are contradictory. (Cf. Beyrau, Russische Orientpolitik, pp. 230ff.; Kiniapina, Vneshniaia politika, p. 91; Meshcherskii, vol. 2, pp. 135-136; Mosse, European Powers, pp. 342 ff.; Nikitin, Ocherki, pp. 264-265; Shneerson, pp. 193ff.; A. F. Tiutcheva, Pri dvore dvukh imperatorov, vol. 2, Leningrad 1929, p. 207.) Yet it appears that the War Minister alone voiced minor objections to the effect that only the restoration of Russian rights in the Black Sea ought to be demanded. With this alteration, Alexander got his initiative approved.

42. Feoktistiov, pp. 108-109. Cf. also Shneerson, pp. 210ff.

43. Pigarev, p. 253.

44. Tiutcheva, vol. 2, pp. 203-204.

45. MV, 1870, nos. 238-240, 243, 244, 251, 253, 259, 264, 274, 282; 1871, nos. 6-A, 22, 38. Cf. also RA, *32:2,* 1894, pp. 246ff.

46. Nikitenko, vol. 3, p. 188. Nikitin, Ocherki, pp. 266-268. RA, *32:2,* 1894, pp. 243-245.

47. Nikitin, Ocherki, pp. 267, 276. Pigarev, pp. 240-244. Tiutcheva, vol. 2, p. 213.

48. KA, *31,* 1928, pp. 144ff. Nikitin, Ocherki, pp. 268-270. RA, *32:2,* 1894, pp. 274ff.

49. A. Ramm, ed., The Diplomatic Correspondence of Mr. Gladstone and Lord Granville 1868-1876, vol. 1, London, 1952, nos. 364, 366, 374.

50. B. Jelavich, The Ottoman Empire, the Great Powers and the Straits Question 1870-1887, Indiana U.P. 1973, p. 38.

51. MV, 1871, no. 54. Cf. also Beyrau, Russische Orientpolitik, pp. 252ff.

53. Tiutcheva, vol. 2, pp. 218ff.

53. Nikitenko, vol. 3, pp. 224-225. RA, *32:2,* 1894, p. 52. Slavianskii sbornik, Moskva 1948, p. 146.

54. Nikitenko, vol. 3, p. 266.

Notes to Chapter 10

1. A. Toynbee, Experiences, Oxford U.P. 1969, p. 206.
2. W. N. Medlicott, Bismarck and Modern Germany, London 1965, p. 89.
3. R. Millman, Britain and the Eastern Question 1875-1878, Oxford 1979, p. 71.
4. W. N. Medlicott, Bismarck and the Three Emperors' Alliance, TRHS, 4th ser., *27*, 1945, p. 82.
5. Crankshaw, Bismarck, p. 311.
6. Radowitz, vol. 1, p. 263.
7. E. Eyck, Bismarck, Leben un Wek, vol. 3, Erlenbach-Zürich 1944, p. 244.
8. Ch. zu Hohenlohe-Schillingsfürst, Denkwürdigkeiten des Reich-skanzlerzeit, vol. 1, Berlin 1931, p. 201-202.
9. H. Wolter, Bismarcks Aussenpolitik 1871-1881, (East-) Berlin 1983, p. 197.
10. Goriaïnov, La question, p. 68.
11. Cf. G. Cecil, Life of Robert, Marquis of Salisbury, vol. 2, London 1921, pp. 103ff.; Lucius v. Ballhausen, Bismarck-Erinnerungen, Stuttgart 1921, p. 93; Schweinitz, Denkwürdigkeiten, vol. 1, pp. 355-356.
12. Hohenlohe, vol. 1, pp. 201-202.
13. Feoktistov, p. 111. Cf. also RA, *32:2*, 1894, pp. 243-245; *35:1*, 1897, pp. 106-107; Meshcherskii, vol. 2, p. 133; A. Z. Manfred, Vneshniaia politika Frantsii 1871-1891, Moskva 1952, pp. 79ff.; S. V. Obolenskaia, Franko-prusskaia voina i obshchestvennoe mnenie Germanii i Rossii, Moskva 1977; Shneerson, pp. 242ff.
14. The difference of outlook between the Tsar and his son, the heir, was perhaps best reflected in their reaction to the battle of Sedan. While the former was jubilant, the latter considered it "terrible news." (P.A. Zaionchkovskii, Rossiiskoe samoderzhavie v kontse XIX stoletiia, Moskva 1970, p. 38.)
15. MV, 1871, no. 150. For the analysis of the Russian press comments see Beyrau, Russische Orientpolitik, pp. 252ff.
16. MV, 1871, nos. 36-A, 106, 108, 123, 130, 167, 202, 273-A.

17. Kiniapina, Vneshniaia politika, pp. 123-125.

18. Tatishchev, vol. 2, p. 88.

19. MV, 1871, no. 274.

20. Müller-Link, p. 50.

21. Miliutin, vol. 1, p. 46.

22. A. Z. Manfred, Obrazovanie russko-francuzskogo soiuza, Moskva 1975, pp. 27-28.

23. Müller-Link, p. 48. Cf. also Obolenskaia, pp. 167ff.

24. Cf. A. Zaionchkovskii, Podgotovka Rossii k mirovoi voine; Plany voiny, Moskva-Leningrad 1926, pp. 31ff. The war plan of 1873, several times modified to give it increasingly offensive character, remained in force until 1909.

25. Meshcherskii, vol. 2, p. 184.

26. O. von Bismarck, Gedanke und Erinnerungen, München 1956, p. 355.

27. KA, 58, 1933, pp. 67-68.

28. Müller-Link, pp. 52-54.

29. E. Wertheimer, Graf Julius Andrássy, Sein Leben und seine Zeit, vol. 2, Stuttgart 1913, pp. 24-25.

30. H. Lutz, Politik und militärische Plannung in Österreich-Ungarn zu Beginn der Ära Andrássy, in: Geschichte und Gesellschaft, Wien 1974, pp. 23.

31. Gorianinov, La question, p. 36. A. Rupp, A Wavering Friendship, Harvard U.P. 1941, pp. 72-73.

32. Goriaïnov, La question, pp. 45-46.

33. Ibid., p. 41.

34. Rupp, p. 34n.

35. DDF-I, vol. 1, no 156; cf. also nos. 152, 153.

36. W. Taffs, Convesations between Lord Odo Russell and Andrassy, Bismarck and Gorchakov, SEER, 8, 1929-1930, p. 703ff.

37. Goriaïnov, La question, pp. 44-45. Kiniapina, Vneshniaia politika, p. 129. A. Meyendorff, Conversations of Gorchakov with Andrássy and Bismarck, SEER, 7, 1928, pp. 402ff. OBTI, vol. 1, no. 16.

38. Goriaïnov, La question, p. 49. KA, 1, 1922, pp. 10ff.

39. In the first article, the signatories of the convention promised each other to settle eventual disagreements in mutual goodwill and "to ensure that these disagreements do not prevail over considerations of

higher order"; further, "to prevent anyone from dividing them in respect to principles which they consider themselves solely able to safeguard, and, if necessary, to enforce the maintenance of European peace from any quarter whatever." In the second article, dealing with the "event of threat to peace arising from the aggression of a third Powers, they obliged themselves to "reach an understanding with each other first of all, and, without seeking or contracting new alliances, to agree on a line of action to be pursued in common." Only if "military action should become necessary" would the convention be according to its third article completed by a special convention. (GP, vol. 1, no. 128. KA, *1*, 1922, pp. 30-31.)

40.   Kiniapina, Vneshniaia politika, p. 135.

41.   Valuev, vol. 2, pp. 284-285. Cf. also Meshcherskii, vol. 2, pp. 143ff.

42.   Ramm, Correspondence, vol. 2, no. 810.

43.   Tvardovskaia, pp. 148ff.

44.   MV, 1867, no. 209. RV, *141*, 1879, p. 872.

45.   The most substantial editorials Katkov wrote on the subject (MV, 1864, nos. 172, 205, 233, 238, 286; 1865, nos. 273, 278; 1867, no 209; 1869, no. 188; 1871, nos. 99, 144, 156) were reprinted in RV, *141*, 1879 under the title "Nasha uchebnaia reforma." Cf. also Vozhd reaktsii, Byloe, 1917, no. 4 (26) pp. 66ff.

46.   There, "Bobby" Shuvalov matured into a fervent nationalist, opposing the "cosmopolitanism" of his powerful father; with him, a whole crop of young hawks, since the 1870s particularly prominent in diplomatic service, had grown in the lyceum.

47.   Feoktisov, pp. 162ff. Tvardovskaia, pp. 155-157. Cf. also P.D. Shestakov, Graf Dmitrii Andreevich Tolstoi RS, *69-70*, 1891; G.K. Gradovskii, Iz minuvshago, RS, *133*, 1908, pp. 82ff., *156*, 1913, pp. 142ff.

48.   MV, 1871, nos. 99, 156. RV, *141*, 1879, pp. 892, 918-920. Cf. also Florinsky, vol. 2, pp. 1035-1036; Valuev, vol. 2, p. 285.

49.   Tvardovskaia, p. 159.

50.   In consequence, two thirds of the curiculum was filled by the study of Latin, Greek and mathematics, while hours for Russian, rhetorics, history, geography, modern languages and even religion were reduced and natural sciences disappeared altogether. (Katz, pp. 142ff. A. Kornilov, Modern Russian History, London, 1917, pp. 165ff. MV, 1871, no. 91.

Nikitenko, vol. 3, pp. 203ff. A Sinel, The Classroom and the Chancellery: State Educational Reform in Russia under Count Dmitry Tolstoi, Harvard U.P. 1976, pp. 141ff. Tatishchev, vol. 2, pp. 266ff.)

51. The real gymnasia were abolished and in the real schools replacing them natural sciences were to be taught only "technologically." An enormous amount of mathematics and drawing filled the teaching hours.

52. For important comments on the tasks of the armed forces before the debate entered its decisive stage see MV, 1867, nos. 67, 72, 82; 1868, nos. 50, 62, 63-B, 236-A, 238, 248-B; 1870, nos. 31, 240-A; 1871, nos. 1, 18, 24, 28, 103-B, 110-B, 126, 140-B.

53. Cf. Beyrau, Militär, pp. 254ff.; Miller, pp. 26ff.; Zaionchkovskii, Voennye reformy, pp. 83ff.

54. Miller, pp. 192-93.

55. Schweinitz, Denkwürdigkeiten, vol. 2, p. 385.

56. The writings of Fadeev and the memoranda of Bariatinskii aimed primarily at the acceptance of the Prussian military-political system with the War Minister as a mere administrative figure and the Chief of the Imperial Headquarters as the supreme authority besides the Tsar. Otherwise, the recruitment praxis should remain unaltered, the traditional levies being, according to them, adequate. The Crimean episode taught, Fadeev affirmed, that a big standing army only exhausted Russian resources; and, moreover, if Miliutin's views were accepted, only chaos would ensue—the officer coprs would disintegrate under the influx of people not belonnging to the nobility, soldiers released after a seven-year service would become "displaced persons" endangering social balance. (For the main writings of Fadeev on the subject, "Vooruzhenye sily Rossii"/Armed forces of Russia/and "Nash voennyi vopros"/Our military question/ see his "Sochineniia"; the crucial memorandum of Bariatinskii was reprinted in Zisserman, vol. 3, pp. 209ff. Cf. also MacKenzie, The Lion, pp. 101ff.; Miller, pp. 202ff.; Zaionshkovskii, Voennye reformy, pp. 127ff. Beyrau, Militär, pp. 270ff.)

57. Cf. W. C. Askew, Russian Military Strength on the Eve of the Franco-Prussian War, SEER, *30*, 1951, pp. 185ff.; Miller, pp. 194-196; Valuev, vol. 2, pp. 284-286; Zaionshkovskii, Voennye reformy, pp. 259-261.

58. Beyrau, Militär, pp. 282ff. MacKenzie, The Lion, pp. 104-105. Miller, pp. 200ff. Zaionchkovskii, Voennye reformy, pp. 259ff.

59. Miliutin, vol. 1, p. 119.

60. Tvardovskaia, pp. 167-168.

61. Cf. MV, 1871, no. 250; 1872, nos. 217-A, 220-B, 223, 237-B, 266; 1873, no. 62.

62. Aside from the main theme—noble "purity" of the officer corps—Katkov canvassed for substantially shortened service (one year only) for the youth coming from the "improved" gymnasia and real schools and their equality with the graduates of the still "infected" universities. (MV, 1873, nos. 100-A, 106, 114, 187-A, 203, 216, 223, 301-B; 1874, no. 7.)

63. Miliutin, vol. 1, pp. 105ff.

64. Tvardovskaia, p. 169n.

65. All the male Russians were pronounced liable to military service. For illiterates, the period of service was to be six years, for those with primary and secondary education 2-4 years, and for university graduates six months. Military career was opened to all classes.

66. Cf. Müller-Link, pp. 48-49; Schweinitz, Briefwechsel, pp. 365-366.

Notes to Chapter 11

1. Cherniaev, the "Lion of Tashkent," who had performed the work of conquest in the initial stage, too often deliberately disregarded his superior's orders to be tolerated forever. "General Cherniaev merely communicates accomplished facts to me involving the necessity either to confirm measures wholly uncompatible with our general aims or revoke these measures and injure the prestige of our authority," the Governor General in Orenburg, Kryzhanovskii, complained to St. Petersburg. Jealous of his famous subordinate and anxious to be the great conqueror himself, Kryzhanovskii managed to persuade the Tsar and Miliutin that the unruly man must go before he would bring on Russia a big war. An abortive attempt to cross the Hungry Steppe and reach Bukhara (February 1866) provided a convenient pretext for the Lion's recall. (MacKenzie, The Lion, pp. 67ff. RS, 115, 1903, pp. 332-334. Valuev, vol. 2, pp. 100, 460. Terentiev, vol. 1, p. 322 ff.)

2. MacKenzie, The Lion, p. 89. Terentiev, vol. 1, p. 334.

3. General Terentiev, the historian of the Russian conquest, characterized the disposition to his colleague Romanovskii, appointed the Lion's successor in the New Kokand line, as an outstanding example of ambiguity in the official stance. (Op. cit., vol. 1, pp. 336-337.) The key sentence of the document elaborated by the ministries for foreign affairs and war and endorsed by the Tsar, namely read as follows: "While steadfastly striving not to extend our direct possessions in Central Asia, (you will) not reject, for the sake of this goal, such actions and orders which may be necessary, and in principle, (you will) above all keep in mind Russia's genuine interests."

But, the St. Petersburg position is shown in its true perspective if the instruction in compared with encouraging directive simultaneously dispatched by Miliutin to Kryzhanovskii–"His Majesty the Emperor hopes that Your Excellency will not fail to make every effort in virtue of safeguarding Russia's dignity and our influence"–and especially with the ensuing personal and political decisions taken in the capital. (Cf. Becker, pp. 28-31; Khalfin, Prisoedinenie, pp. 241ff.)

4. Terentiev, vol. 1, p. 336.

5. Becker, pp. 31ff.; Khalfin, Prisoedinenie, pp. 222ff.; MacKenzie, The Lion, pp. 95-96; Miliutin, vol. 4, p. 132; P. Morris, The Russians in Central Asia, SEER, 53, 1975, pp. 536-537.

6. It was precisely the dispute about the fate of Samarkand which demonstrated the rise of Kaufman's power. The action against Bukhara had been formally proclaimed a mere punitive expedition with no objectives of territorial aggrandizement. Even after the seizure of the city, special deliberations chaired by the Tsar had stressed an "unflinching allegiance to the adopted programme" and insisted that Samarkand must be returned to the Emir. Still, we are told, one audience granted to the Turkestan warlord by Alexander sufficed to bring about the change.

Allegedly, the standard reasoning–a better frontier must be created for eventual contest with the British–persuaded the Tsar. Also another argument was voiced, however: "Samarkand commands hydraulic installations for supplying water to all Bukharan possessions. Keeping Samarkand we shall always be able to deprive Bukhara of bread and water, condemn her to hunger and thirst and render it possible for us to regulate the passions of the fanatical population by the way of salutary diet." (Becker, pp. 36ff. Khalfin, Prisoedinenie, pp. 232ff., pp. 282ff. Terentiev, vol. 1, pp. 385ff. Popov, Iz istorii, pp. 218-219.)

7. Becker, p. 36. Cf. also D. MacKenzie, Kaufman of Turkestan, SR, *26*, 1967, pp. 265ff.

8. The main proponent of the doctrine, the Indian Governor General Sir John Lawrence, stated his position in a memoir of 3 October 1867. There, he aired the widespread spurious proposition that a rational approach dictated by economic requirements must eventually prevail in St. Petersburg:

"I do not pretend to know what is the policy of Russia in Central Asia, what may her views be hereafter in India. But it seems to me that common sense suggests that her primary interest is to consolidate her hold on these vast regions now in her possession . . . . Russia has indeed a task before her in which she may fail, and which must occupy her for generations. To attempt to advance until her power is firmly established, is to imperil all that she had hitherto accomplished."

Lawrence advised that Central Asia should be abandoned and "the Indus made the main line of a passive defence system." If Russia were even to continue her advance and dominate the states bordering India, she might "prove a safer ally—a better neighbour than the Mohamedan races of Central Asia and Kabul. She would introduce civilization; she would abate the fanaticism and ferocity of Mohamedanism, which still exercises so powerful an influence in India."

The protest against the "mastery inactivity" was most distinctly voiced by influential Sir Henry Rawlinson, who called precisely for the policy Gorchakov was afraid of: Russian control over Bujkhara ought to be responded by the annexation of Afghanistan and thus by moving the Indian defense perimeter on the Oxus (Amu-Daria) river. (For Lawrence's "minute" see G. Morgan, Anglo-Russian Rivalry in Central Asia, London 1981, pp. 266ff.; for the key memoir of Rawlinson his "England and Russia in the East," London 1875, pp. 272ff.)

9. Cf. AP, 1873, *75*, pp. 693ff.; Bilgrami, pp. 146ff.; FO 65-1150; G.A. Khidoiatov, Iz istorii anglo-russkikh otnoshenii v Srednei Azii v kontse XIX v. (60-70gg.), Tashkent 1969, pp. 67ff., 140ff.; A. Meyendorff, ed., Correspondence diplomatique de M. de Staal, vol. 1, Paris 1929, pp. 42ff. Tatishchev, vol. 2, pp. 114ff.

10. MV, 1872, no. 268.

11.   N. N. Knorring, General Mikhail Dmitrievich Skobelev, vol. 1, Paris, 1939, p. 26.

12.   Sumner, Russia and the Balkans, p. 50.

13.   Popov, Iz istorii, p. 236.

14.   Becker, pp. 71-72. Khalfin, Prisoedinenie, pp. 273ff. Khidoiatov, pp. 139ff. N. S. Kiniapina, Sredniaia Aziia, pp. 46-48. Loftus, vol. 1, pp. 105ff. Morris, pp. 524-525.

15.   Cf. Ch. Marvin, Reconnoitring Central Asia, London 1886, pp. 191ff.; E. Schuyler, Turkistan, vol. 2, New York 1876, pp. 347; Terentiev, vol. 2, pp. 147ff., 250ff.

16.   Schuyler, vol. 2, pp. 254ff. Terentiev, vol. 2, pp. 267ff. There is no point in repeating the description of the ghastly scenes. But it has to be pointed out that the Russians behaved worse than the Turks three years later, in the ill-famed Bulgarian massacres. In the Bulgarian case, irregulars and rabble turned wild; in the Yomuth case, it was a cool, premeditated mass murder engineered on orders from above.

17.   Backer, pp. 65ff., 77-78. Khalfin, Prisoedinenie, pp. 286ff., 306ff. Popov, Iz istorii, pp. 338-340. Tatishchev, vol. 2, pp. 124ff. Terentiev, vol. 2, pp. 124ff.

Notes to Chapter 12

1.   RS, *133,* 1908, p. 90.

2.   RS, *133,* 1908, pp. 90-91.

3.   The manner in which Ignatiev handled the Orthodox hierarchy and hand-picked its Patriarchs provides the most astounding example.

Looking for an entirely amenable Patriarch to help him to settle the Greco-Bulgarian Church dispute, he chose Gregorii VI, a senile octogenarian for decades retired, and induced the prelates to elect him in 1867. And he managed to repeat the performance in 1870, i.e. at the time when the Greeks intensely felt Russian betrayal in the Cretan affair, in the election of another ailing, deaf octogenarian—Anthim. (Cf. T. A. Meininger, Ignatiev and the Establishment of the Bulgarian Exarchate, 1864-1872, Madison 1970, pp. 79-80, 163-165.)

4.   IsV, 135, 1914, p. 72.

5.   Jelavich, The Ottoman Empire, pp. 81ff.

6.   According to the Ottoman tradition, after the demise of a Sultan the oldest member of the Osman House, not the oldest son of the ruler

received the throne. Abdülaziz (1861-1876) resolved to break the system and Ignatiev who backed the "reform" won his great confidence in the process.

7.   Sumner wrote a perfect brief character-study:

"Brilliantly aided by his seductive wife; himself combining great physical energy, unabashed self-confidence, ingratiating charm, jocular brusqueness, and unappeased talent for intrigue; supplied with a fantastic medley of agents and informers; Ignatiev with ten years' experience behind him and the closest relations with Abdülaziz could feel he was deservedly styled 'le vice-Sultan'". (Sumner, Russia in the Balkans, p. 32.)

8.   IMID, 1914, bk. 1, p. 53.

9.   Ramm, Correspondence, vol. 2, no. 936.

10.   Slavianskii sbornik. Slavianskii vopros i russkoe obshchestvo v 1867-1878 gg., Moskva 1948, p. 142.

11.   Feoktistov, pp. 61ff., 111-114.

12.   There were perhaps only two occasions when the editor put into his editorials more feelings. First, when during the visit of William I he stressed that "peace and order in Europe now safely rests in the hands of firm governments." (MV, 1873, nos. 93-A, 95-A, 100-B, 102-B, 111-A.) Second, when he attacked the concept of a strong France: the French debacle in 1870-1871, he now claimed, was a necessary result of moral decline of a country made rotten by revolutions. (MV, 1872, no. 190.)

In accordance with the Shuvalovian current, he advised that "pressing interests" turn Russia "inside her own borders" and that "by the logic of things" her foreign policy had to have a conservative character; he also praised Prussia as being "perhaps the most progressive country in Europe," because progress there "has been advancing patiently, without breaking the existing (order)." (MV, 1873, nos. 73, 190.) On the other hand, though, he evaded the Emperors' League theme and stated instead the improvement in "general confidence," the overall betterment in relations with "Turkey, England, Austria"; and, simultaneously, the continuing hostility of "some parties" in Austria-Hungary or "some politicians" in England. He put at the same level the friendship the Ottoman Empire— the accounts with which had "already been settled long ago"—and, "for example the friendship towards Germany, Sweden, or Austria" (MV, 1873, no 59-A; 1874, no. 234.)

Apart from occasionally favorably utterances on "sound and independent" Turkey, there is some indication of Katkov's sympathy for the

Ignatiev alternative in his recurrent attacks on the Austro-Hungarian press and the anti-Russian trend in Budapest. (MV, 1872, nos. 2, 26-A, 39, 42, 45, 49, 62, 63, 78, 82, 84, 106, 118, 125, etc.; 1873, nos. 51, 59-A, 183-A, 212, 218-A, 248.)

13. Crankshaw, Bismarck, p. 325.

14. Cf. V. Khvostov, ed., P. A. Shuvalov o Berlinskom Kongresse 1878 g., KA, *59*, 1933, pp. 106ff.; Rupp, pp. 52ff.

15. GP, vol. 1, nos. 114, 137, 147.

16. Miliutin, vol. 1, p. 153.

17. DDF-I, vol. 1, no 247; cf. also no. 371.

18. DDF-I, vol. 1, no 284. Wertheimer, vol. 2, pp. 106ff.

19. MV, 1874, nos. 35, 37-A.

20. W. Taffs, The War Scare, SEER, *9*, 1930-1931, pp. 336. Cf. also Wertheimer, vol. 2, pp.143ff.; Wolter, pp. 150-152, 160ff.

21. Manfred, Vneshniaia politika, pp. 148ff.; Tatishchev, vol. 2, p. 110. Radowitz in his memoirs maintains that he simply deputized for Reuss during his sick-leave and that the only task given to him was to "demonstrate warm friendship" and so to ease the relations strained by the French, "ultramontane" and Spanish issues. (Radowitz, vol 1, pp. 296ff.)

22. Soviet scholars consistently follow the lead of their Imperial predecessors in the claim that the German Chancellor wished to set out for a preventive war against France and do not question Gorchakov's allegations. Some of their Western colleagues like Hillgruber (Die Krieg-in-Sicht Krise 1875, in E. Schulin, ed., Gedenkschrift Martin Göhring, Wiesbaden 1968, pp. 238ff.) at least partly share this view, others, like Holborn (Bismarks europäische Politik zu Beginn der siebziger Jahre und die Mission Radowitz, Berlin 1925) or Kennan (op. cit., pp. 11ff.) deny it completely and consider Radowitz's and Bismarck's explanations correct. Recently, the East-German historian Wolter (op. cit., pp. 168ff.) backstepped somewhat from the customary "Soviet line."

23. Andrássy complained that Bismarck had "completely lost his common sense" and Queen Victoria, so far very pro-German, wrote to the same effect. The Conservative cabinet of Benjamin Disraeli, which had taken over in 1874, even tried to use the situation for splitting the Three Emperors' League. Ambassador Russell was instructed to assist Russian diplomatic initiative. (GP, vol. 1, no 176. S. Lee, King Edward

VII, vol. 1, London 1925, p. 351. Medlicott, Bismarck, pp. 117ff. Miliutin, vol. 1, pp. 196-197.

24.   DDF-I, vol. 1, 393. Miliutin, vol. 1, pp. 193-195. Cf. also KA, *91*, 1938, pp. 106ff.

25.   DDF-I, vol. 1, no. 442.

26.   The circular, orginally worded "The Russian Emperor is leaving Berlin entirely convinced of the conciliatory disposition which prevails there and which assures the maintenance of peace," was garbled to the effect that it read "which *now* assures the peace" instead of "assures the maintenance of peace." Worse still, the Tsar's telegram to the Queen of Württemberg—"I bring from Berlin formal assurances of peace" was wrongly read by a journalist as "the frenzied one in Berlin gives formal assurances of peace." (Cf. Kennan, pp. 20-21.)

Notes to Chapter 13

1.   S. Goriainow, Le Bosphore et les Dardanelles, Paris 1910, pp. 305ff. OBTI, vol. 1, no 16. Rupp, pp. 28, 42-43.

2.   IsV, *135*, 1914, pp. 72-75.

3.   MV, 1873, nos. 248, 258.

4.   MV, 1875, no. 17.

5.   Cf. F. R. Bridge, From Sadowa to Sarajevo, The Foreign Policy of Austria-Hungary, London 1972, pp. 45-46, 69-70; I. Diószegi, Andrássy und der Augstand von Herzegowina im Sommer des Jahres 1875, in "Medjunarodni naučni skup povodom 100-godišnijice ustanka u Bosni i Hercegovini, drugim balkanskim zemljama i istočnoj krizi 1875-1878 godine," vol. 1, Sarajevo 1977, pp. 367ff.; Rupp, pp. 34ff.; R. Seton-Watson, Les relations de l' Autriche-Hongrie et de Serbie entre 1868 et 1874, Le Monde Slave, 1926, no. 2, pp. 217ff., no. 5, pp. 186ff.

6.   Cf. H. Haselsteiner, Zur Haltung der Donaumonarchie in der Orientalischen Frage, in: R. Melville-H.-J. Schröder, ed., Der Berliner Kongress von 1878, Wiesbaden 1982, pp. 239-241.

7.   Rupp, pp. 38ff. Cf. also A. Suppan, Aussen- und militärpolitische Strategie Österreich-Ungarns vor Beginn des Bosnischen Augstandes 1875, Medjunarodni naučni skup, vol. 1, pp. 159ff.

8.   Bridge, pp. 72-74. Cf. also Diószegi, Andrássy, pp. 367ff.

9.　The first instructions of the Singers' Bridge after the outbreak in Hercegovina, written on 24 July by Gorchakov's deputy, Baron Jomini, were composed as if by Andrássy himself. No action should be taken which would incite Austrian distrust; and the unity of the Three Emperors' League should be "demonstrated in its role of peacemaker." Accordingly, the joint directives of the League ordered their diplomatic representatives to follow in mediating between the Porte and the insurgents the dispositions coming from the Ballplatz. (OBTI, vol. 1, no. 6. Cf. also Tatishchev, vol. 2, p. 293; Wertheimer, vol. 2, pp. 262-263.

10.　IsV, *135*, 1914, pp. 453ff., 805ff. Cf. also D. Harris, A Diplomatic History of the Balkan Crisis of 1875-1878, Stanford U. P. 1936, pp. 66f.; G. Hünigen, Nikolaj Pavlovič Ignat'ev und die russische Balkanpolitik, 1875-1878, Göttingen 1968, pp. 29ff.; Valuev, vol. 2, pp. 384-385.

11.　IsV, *135*, 1914, pp. 456-460, 463. Cf. also Sumner, Russia and the Balkans, pp. 144ff.; Tatishchev, vol. 2, pp. 296-297.

12.　IsV, *136*, 1914, p. 51.

13.　Kartsov, Sem let, p. 48; RS, *133*, 1908, p. 348.

14.　Millman, p. 80.

15.　Goriainov, La question, p. 61. IsV, *136*, 1914, p. 50.

16.　Wertheimer, vol. 2, pp. 271-272.

17.　OBTI, vol. 1, no. 15.

18.　MacKenzie, The Serbs, pp. 43ff. Millman, pp. 107-108, 504.

19.　Cf. MacKenzie, The Lion, pp. 117ff.; Nikitin, Slavianskie komitety, pp. 269ff.

20.　MV, 1875, nos. 204, 212, 236, 244.

21.　I. Kozmenko, ed., Slavianskii sbornik, Moskva 1948, p. 148.

22.　Cf. MacKenzie, The Serbs, pp. 57, 73-75.

23.　According to Aksakov, two-thirds of all donations came from this humble source. (Aksakov, vol. 1, p. 228. Cf. also Nikitin, Russkoe obshchestvo, p. 26; Slavianskie komitety, pp. 303ff.)

24.　Aksakov, vol. 1, p. 227. Nikitin, Slavianskie komitety, pp. 308ff.

25.　Nikitin, Russkoe obshchestvo, p. 11.

26.　MacKenzie, The Serbs, pp. 71ff. Nikitin, Slavianskie komitety, pp. 281ff. OBTI, vol. 1, nos. 63, 78, 79, 84, 86, 88. RS, *133*, 1908, pp. 348-349, 363-366.

27.　Schweinitz, Denkwürdigkeiten, vol. 1, pp. 317ff.

28.　MV, 1864, nos. 118-A, 168-A, 180; 1865, nos. 154, 194, 213, 221, 222, 250.

29.   MV, 1865, nos. 47, 60, 198, 246; 1866, no. 96; 1867, nos. 141, 146-B.

30.   RA, *49:2*, 1911, pp. 136-137.

31.   Aksakov, vol. 1, p. 425.

32.   MV, 1872, no. 303. Cf. also MV, 1868, nos. 115, 130-A, 159, 274; 1869, nos. 232, 238; 1870, nos. 97, 98; 1872, nos. 306, 310-A, 314-A.

33.   MV, 1872, no. 277-A; 1873, nost. 114-A, 116-A.

34.   MV, 1873, nos. 253, 270, 288-A, 294, 304, 306, 310.

35.   MV, 1873, nos. 176, 260, 271.

36.   MV, 1873, nos. 128, 186-A, 236-B; 1874, no. 223-A; 1876, nos. 63, 120-A.

37.   MV, 1873, nos. 152-A, 200, 231-A.

38.   Khidoiatov, p. 140.

39.   Cf. MV, 1874, nos. 1, 10, 58, 119, 133; 1875, nos. 56, 169, 170, 175, 193, 197.

40.   Under the impact of the Khiva campaign, the Afghan Emir Shere Ali thought about accepting British protection. The London Liberal cabinet, however, declined to exploit this unique opportunity; and, it intended to show to the Russians circumspection and even understanding when they—as Granville put it—"rightly or wrongly yield to the apparent necessity of protecting each new acquisition they make." (Ramm, Correspondence 1876-1886, vol. 2, no. 947.)

Not even the replacement of Gladstone by Disraeli (1874) brought about an immediate change. Foreign Secretary Lord Derby and Indian Secretary Lord Salisbury dwelled on a line evading "the risk of futile and costly war in Afghanistan." In his research on the Foreign Office files (FO 65-926, 65-927), Sumner discovered an astounding fact that the two cabinet members agreed in early 1875 to conceal secret reports coming from the St. Petersburg Embassy—obviously those containing "alarmist" analyses on Russian Asiatic policy—from their colleagues. (Sumner, Russia and the Balkans, p. 55n.)

Small wonder that Shere Ali, flattered by Kaufman, set out playing the Russian card, and that the Tsar found it safe and advantageous to let the military on the loose.

41.   Khalfin, Prisoedinenie, pp. 311ff. Khidoiatov, pp. 174ff. Knorring, vol. 1, pp. 53ff. Terentiev, vol. 2, pp. 327ff.

42.   Khalfin, Prisoedinenie, pp. 320-325, 335. Khidoiatov, pp. 178ff. Miliutin, vol. 1, p. 216; vol. 2, pp. 17-18. Morris, pp. 530-532.

43. IsV, *10*, 1882, pp. 110ff. Knorring, vol. 2, pp. 53ff.

44. Khalfin, Prisoedinenie, pp. 334ff. Sumner, Russia and the Balkans, pp. 54-55.

45. MV, 1875, no. 184; see also nos. 224, 239.

46. MV, 1876, no. 79; see also nos. 92, 101, 108.

47. Sumner, Russia and the Balkans, p. 155.

48. OBTI, vol. 1, no. 87; see also no. 92.

49. MV, 1875, nos. 269, 303, 305.

50. MV, 1876, no. 83; see also nos. 32, 38, 45, 51, 61, 65, 77.

51. MV, 1876, no. 71.

52. Miliutin, vol. 2, pp. 24-25. Valuev, vol. 2, pp. 302-304.

53. OBTI, vol. 1, no. 64; see also no. 81.

54. OBTI, vol. 1, no. 136. Cf. also nos. 29, 69, 74; MacKenzie, The Serbs, pp. 79-81.

55. Nikitin, Slavianskie komitety, pp. 278-279, 286-287, 291-293, 313.

56. Kartsov, Sem let, p. 51. MacKenzie, The Lion, pp. 119ff.; The Serbs, pp. 86-87. Miliutin, vol. 2, p. 53. OBTI, vol. 1, no. 113. RS, *113*, 1908, pp. 564ff.

57. In a memoir sent to the heir, Nelidov proposed to use the first opportunity and invade the Straits. Then, Constantinople should become a "free city under Russian protectorate" and the rest of the Ottoman Empire be divided. The English should be compensated in Egypt, the French in Syria, but Austria-Hungary, the bête-noire for the Ignatiev group, ought to be left empty-handed; the Balkan possessions of the Sultan were to be assigned to Serbia, Montenegro, Greece and the newly established principalities of Bulgaria and Macedonia. (A. Nelidov, Souvenirs d'avant et d'après la guerre de 1877-1878, Revue des deux mondes, *27*, 1915, no. 15, pp. 307ff. Valuev, vol. 2, p. 326.)

58. Cf. Miliutin, vol. 2, p. 61; Kartsov, pp. 171ff.; OBTI, vol. 1, no. 118n.

59. Miliutin, vol. 2, pp. 43, 46, 52-54, 57-58.

60. The repeated St. Petersburgs' claim that its only concern was with the "lot of the Christians" angered Bismarck. "Why that hypocrisy in confidential communications?", he noted on the margin of a Russian diplomatic dispatch. (GP, vol. 2, no. 308.)

61. Miliutin, vol. 2, p. 35.

62. Goriainov, Le Bosphore, pp. 314-315; La question, pp. 67-68.

63. MV, 1875, nos. 1, 17, 27, 36, 41, 45-A, 135, 148, 153, 204.

64. MV, 1876, no. 56.

65. KA, *58*, 1933, pp. 67-68.

66. Miliutin, vol. 2, p. 34.

67. MV, 1876, no. 105.

68. Harris, pp. 446ff.

69. Rupp, p. 74.

70. Cf. Bridge, pp. 394ff.; Goriainov, La question, pp. 67ff.; Harris, pp. 296-299; Rupp, pp. 96ff.

71. Cf. Gorchakov's memoir on the Berlin summit in Goriainov, La question, pp. 72-74.

Notes to Chapter 14

1. RS, *133*, 1908, pp. 72-74.

2. IsV, *135*, 1914, p. 72. Cf. also Hünigen, pp. 94ff.

3. Osobye pribavleniia k opisaniiu russko-turetskoi voiny 1877-1878gg. na Balkanskom poluostrove, vol. 1, St. Petersburg 1898, pp. 45ff.

4. The anti-Greek struggle for a national church had entirely dominated the Bulgarian scene until the early 1870s. The attempts to stir up the population to a rising against the Turks, initiated by exile groups from Russia, Rumania and Serbia, had enlisted little sympathy among their kin and ended accordingly: the guerrilla "chetas" sent across the border had been invariably chased, rounded up and annihilated by the enemy. Highly prosperous in comparison with other Balkan Slavs and held in check by numerous garrisons and Moslem enclaves, the Bulgarians felt no compulsion to emulate the Serbian and Montenegrin examples.

By achieving their first great aim—the independent Bulgarian Exarchate was established in 1872—however, their self-confidence rose appreciably and it seemed that also the deep-seated fear of repression withered away. About 200 secret committtees were set up and particularly the native intelligentsia (teachers, priests) exuded eagerness to start an armed struggle. New abortive action of an enthusiastic handful in 1875, although followed with mass arrests and deportations, appeared to have no adverse effects. Russian consuls reported that "all Bulgaria is only waiting for the opportune moment to rise en masse." (OBTI, vol. 1, no. 53; see also nos. 12, 18, 30, 41, 56, 60, 65.)

5. M. MacDermott, A History of Bulgaria, 1393-1885, London 1962, pp. 232-234. MacKenzie, The Serbs, pp. 96-97. Nikitin, Slavianskie komitety, pp. 288.

6. Millman, p. 153. Cf. also OBTI, vol. 1, nos. 82, 86, 91, 96.

7. Millman, pp. 148ff. R. W. Seton-Watson, Disraeli, Gladstone and the Eastern Question, London 1935, pp. 57-61.

8. IsV, 136, 1914, p. 56. OBTI, vol. 1, no. 118n. Nelidov, pp. 119, 334-336.

9. OBTI, vol. 1, no. 119.

10. RS, 134, 1908, pp. 70-71.

11. M. Gazenkampf, Moi dnevnik, St. Petersburg 1908, p. 470.

12. MacKenzie, The Lion, pp. 122ff.; The Serbs, p. 88. Nikitin, Slavianskie komitety, p. 301.

13. RS, 134, 1908, pp. 312-313.

14. In less vengeful terms, this was also the opinion initially prevalent in the Slavic committees and the press. An anonymous memoir originated in the Moscow committee envisaged that the organization would be able to muster up to 50,000 men and raise 4 million rubles to pay them; then, "if the matter will be pursued boldly," the sympathizers in the elite would arrange "big subsidies (directly) from the treasury." (Nikitin, Slavianskie komitety, p. 328.)

Katkov, too, at first conceived the triumph of the Serbs and Montenegrins, directed by Russian volunteers, the best outcome. (MV, 1876, nos. 141, 151, 154, 158, 165-A.)

15. Lukashevich, Aksakov, pp. 136-138. MacKenzie, The Lion, pp. 122ff. Nikitin, Russkoe obshchestvo, pp. 55, 62, 71-72; Slavianskie komitety, pp. 326-327.

16. Miliutin, vol. 2, p. 251.

17. MV, 1876, no. 110. The heavy doubts the editor raised about Austrian credibility now included Andrássy too. (MV, 1876, nos. 113, 115-B, 118, 123, 125, 134, 136, 140, 141, 168-A,B.)

18. Miliutin, vol. 2, pp. 64-65.

19. Goriainov, La question, pp. 80-81.

20. Goriainov, La question, pp. 91-94. Tatishchev, vol. 2, pp. 310-314.

21. If Ottoman rule were to collapse, the Vienna representatives approved of Russia getting Southern Bessarabia and Batumi, the Greeks

Thessaly and Epirus and Constantinople being proclaimed a free city. According to the Austrian version, however, they disagreed on Serbia and Montenegro obtaining large portions of Bosnia-Hercegovina and wrestled from their Russian counterparts an obligation that there would be no big compact Slavic state in the Balkans or independent states connected by a federal tie. (For the texts of the two versions see KA, *1,* 1922, pp. 36ff., or Sumner, Russia and the Balkans, pp. 583ff. For the analysis cf. Rupp, pp. 111ff.)

22.   Cf. Wertheimer, vol. 2, pp. 296ff.

23-24. W. F. Monypenny-G. E. Buckle, The Life of Benjamin Disraeli, vol. 6, London 1920, p. 54. For analyses see Millman, pp. 121ff.; Seton-Watson, pp. 73ff.; R. T. Shannon, Gladstone and the Bulgarian Agitation (1876), London 1963.

25.   This was mainly due to the impressive results achieved by Olga Novikova, a sister of the Kireev brothers and a correspondent of the *Moskovskiia vedomosti.* She had been friendly with Gladstone since 1873 and her salon at Claridge's Hotel attracted important personalities with pro-Russian affiliations—politicians, diplomats (Lord Napier, Sir Robert Morier), clerical figures, journalists and men of learning (Carlyle, Kinglake, Stead, etc.). Now these people formed the nucleus in the national-wide drive, willingly using in their propaganda materials delivered by Pobedonostsev and other Muscovites. The way Novikova managed to manipulate Gladstone and others who like him obsessively hated the "old corrupted Jew" Disraeli as well as persuade gullible clergymen that Tsardom was the true defender of Christianity, made her virtually an "M.P. for Russia." (See W. T. Steed, ed., The M. P. for Russia: Reminiscences of Madame Olga Novikoff, vol. 1, New York 1909; Kartsov, pp. 159ff.)

26.   MacKenzie, The Serbs, p. 109.

27.   KA, *1,* 1922, pp. 42-43. MV, 1876, nos. 168-B, 170, 173, 175-A, 190-A, 194-A, 196-B, 198-A, 199.

28.   MV, 1876, nos. 206, 207-B, 209-A, 212-A, 213-A.

29.   Cherniaev proclaimed in his war manifesto: "Behind us stands Russia. If fickle fortune should desert us, this holy ground will be drenched with the precious blood of our Russian brethren . . . . If we, wading in blood to our shoulders, are unable to open the doors to freedom and civilization, the iron hand of Russia will break them open. . . . " (MacKenzie, The Lion, p. 132.)

30.   OBTI, vol. 1, nos. 155, 156.

31.   RS, *134*, 1908, p. 308.

32.   Meshcherskii, vol. 2, pp. 282-283.

33.   Aksakov, vol. 1, pp. 224, 227, 233. MacKenzie, The Lion, pp. 139ff.; The Serbs, p. 122. Nikitin, Slavianskie komitety, pp. 313ff.

34.   The most important pamphlets on the issue were written by Meshcherskii (Pravda o Serbii, St. Petersburg 1877) and N. V. Maksimov (Dve voiny 1876-1878, St. Petersburg 1879).

35.   Meshcherskii, Moi vospominaniia, vol. 2, pp. 293, 297-298. K. A. Pushkarevich, Balkanskie slaviane i russkie "osvoboditeli," Trudy Instituta vostokovedenia AN SSSR, vol. 2, Leningrad 1934, pp. 211-213. RS, *134*, 1908, pp. 308ff.; *135*, 1909, pp. 81ff.

36.   Maksimov, p. 21. For well-balanced accounts see MacKenzie, The Serbs, pp. 120ff.; The Lion, pp. 139ff.

37.   Cf. MacKenzie, The Serbs, pp. 134-135.

38.   MV, 1876, no. 161.

39.   J. D. Morison, Katkov and Panslavism, SEER, *46*, 1968, p. 433.

40.   In another account, the Lion pictured his move as a blow "to the ministers (who) were disturbed by the fact that the power had passed out of their hands (into his own) and joined the general chorus for peace." (MacKenzie, The Serbs, p. 137. Nikitin, Russkoe obshchestvo, p. 1025.)

41.   MV, 1876, nos. 228, 234.

42.   Meshcherskii, vol. 2, p. 281. RNOBB, p. 11.

43.   OBTI, vol. 1, no. 200; cf. also no. 148.

44.   Nikitin, Slavianskie komitety, pp. 297-298.

45.   Miliutin, vol. 2, p. 70.

46.   Miliutin wrote in his diary: "War would inevitably be a misfortune for us, because its success depends . . . on diplomatic preparation and, on the other hand, on the competence of persons who actually lead the military operations. . . . But to my gnawing grief I must confess that in both matters we have only little hope. Our diplomacy is so directed that in case of war we would be necessarily alone, again without reliable allies and having almost the whole of Europe against us. At the same time, I do not see among the generals even one personality on whom one could place reliance on his strategic and tactical capabilities." (Miliutin, vol. 2, pp. 64-65.)

47.   Miliutin, vol. 2, p. 65.

48.   OBTI, vol. 1, no. 191; cf. also ibid., no. 206.

49.   Kartsov, Sem let, p. 45. Rupp, p. 153.

50.   On the Russian press campaign see RNOBB, pp. 11ff.

51.   MV, 1876, no. 213-B; see also nos. 212-A, 214-A, 217-A.

52.   MV, 1876, no. 225-B; see also nos. 232-A, 237, 238.

53.   The almost daily sessions of the Tsar's council were permanently or occasionally attended by Gorchakov, Miliutin, Adlerberg, Jomini, the heir, Ignatiev, Obruchev, Grand Duke Nikolai (Nikolaevich) and Reutern.

54.   Pisma Pobedonostseva k Aleksandru III, vol. 1, Moskva 1923, pp. 48-49. Cf. also Jomini's letters in Ch. and B. Jelavich, Russia in the East 1876-1880, Leiden 1959, pp. 20, 23ff.

55.   Porokhovshchikov described his Crimean mission in "Zapiski starozhila," IsV, 67, 1897, pp. 9ff.

56.   The Ignatiev memoir argued as follows: It would perhaps be more opportune to postpone the final solution of the Eastern Question, yet for many reasons further procrastination cannot be permitted. If the other Powers would deny her cooperation, Russia must proceed on her own way, taking advantage of the agitation in England and the military unpreparedness of Turkey; to wait until the next spring would only mean the loss of those advantages and additional financial and economic burdens. (IsV, 136, 1914, pp. 73ff. Cf. also Hünigen, pp. 132ff.)

57.   Pobedonostsev i ego korrespondenty, vol. 1, pp. 1016-1017.

58.   Dnevnik gosudarstvennogo sekretaria A. A. Polovtsova, Moskva 1966, vol. 2, pp. 186-187. Miliutin, vol. 2, p. 93. Reutern-Nolcken, pp. 119ff. RS, 143, 1910, p. 40.

59.   Goriainov, La question, pp. 145ff. IsV, 136, 1914, pp. 436-440. Miliutin, vol. 2, pp. 87ff.

60.   The bid for enlarging the diplomatic bridgehead gained by the Reichstadt understanding produced very little so far. The Tsar's proposals brought on 26 September to Vienna by his adjutant Sumarokov-Elston— that Russian troops should enter Bulgaria and Austrian troops Bosnia— was rejected. Only if the conference of the Powers failed, would such a move be legitimate, sounded the new Austrian position, wrestled by Andrássy from his Emperor and the military. (Cf. Goriainov, La question, pp. 122ff.; Rupp, pp. 152ff.)

61.   Miliutin, vol. 2, pp. 83-84. RS, 143, 1910, pp. 40, 46-48.

62.   MV, 1876, no. 247.

63.   MV, 1876, nos. 241, 242-B, 248, 250, 253, 256.

64.   MV, 1876, no. 258; see also nos. 242-A, 257.

65.   MV, 1876, no. 261; see also nos. 275, 302, 312, 317-A, 335-A.

66.   Goriainov, La question, pp. 158-162; Le Bosphore, pp. 326-327. Miliutin, vol. 2, pp. 102-103. RS, *40*, 1883, pp. 178-179. RNOBB, nos. 123, 124.

67.   Cf. IsV, *136*, 1914, pp. 448ff.

68.   In September, Marshal Manteuffel had brought to the Tsar a message repeating the assurances of German solidarity. As testified by Jomini's correspondence (Jelavich, Russia in the East, pp. 21-23), this time the reaction had been totally at variance with the cool dismissal of Bismarck's previous feelers. Questions were sent to Berlin on what would be the German stance if Russia were to clash with Austria-Hungary or went to war with Turkey alone. Now Schweinitz delivered the answer: there would be full diplomatic support, but no more: "We expected great things from you and you bring us nothing else but what we have already known for long. . . ." Gorchakov told the German Ambassador. His master must have been even more disappointed; although he had not shared Katkovian illusions about Bismarck's eagerness for the "big deal," he had evidently counted on a firm pledge ensuring Austrian restraint. (GP, vol. 2, nos. 251, 252. Schweinitz, Briefwechsel, pp. 115ff.; Denkwürdigkeiten, vol. 1, pp. 350ff. More about this fateful episode will be said in the next chapter.)

69.   Miliutin, vol. 2, p. 105.

70.   MV, 1876, no. 274; see also nos. 268, 269, 271, 273.

71.   Miliutin, vol. 2, pp. 104-105, 118, 120.

72.   Sumner, Russia and the Balkans, p. 227. Tatishchev, vol. 2, pp. 335-336.

73.   Aksakov, vol. 1, p. 238. MV, 1876, nos. 277-A, 281-A, 298-A, 299. Meshcherskii, vol. 2, pp. 305ff.

Notes to Chapter 15

1.   MV, 1876, nos. 264, 267, 270, 273, 282. RNOBB, no. 150.

2.   MacKenzie, The Serbs, pp. 146-147, 166.

3.   MacKenzie, The Serbs, pp. 144ff. Meshcherskii, vol. 2, pp. 293-295. Nikitin, Russkoe obshchestvo, p. 1035. Pushkarevich, p. 213.

4.   MacKenzie, The Serbs, pp. 146-147. Meshcherskii, vol. 2, pp.

313-317, 333. Schweinitz, Denkwürdigkeiten, vol. 1, pp. 336-337. G. Wittrock, Gorčakov, Ignatiev och Šuvalov, Stockholm 1931, p. 33.

5.   OBTI, vol. 1, nos. 320, 325, 329, 343, 350. RS, *143,* 1910, pp. 41-43. Rupp, pp. 259-261, 284.

6.   In the Guildhall speech of 9 November, Beaconsfield paraded his conviction that firmness towards Tsardom was the best way to prevent an assault on Turkey: "Though the policy of England is peace, there is no country as well prepared for war as our own. If she enters into a conflict in a righteous cause . . . her resources, I feel, are unexhaustible. She is not a country that, when she enters into a campaign, has to ask herself whether she can support a second or a third . . . . "

Yet he himself had to admit privately that "opinion in England as regards to Turkey changed." The campaign of the "Bulgarian horrors" had already been in eclipse, but it was powerful enough to put the hardliners under restraint. The national conference on the Eastern Question (on 8 December), attended by an impressive number of the aristocracy, clergy, businessmen, men of letters and learning, vocied views contradicting the tenets of the Palmerstonian school. So did Gladstone in his half honest, half demagogic way.

In the cabinet, Derby, Salisbury and Carnavon dwelled on the claim that "the Turk's teeth must be drawn, even if he be allowed to live." Neither should the English "be hanging on the coat-tails of Austria," Salisbury advised. Austrian existence "is no longer of the importance for us that it was in former times; he vocation is gone." Hence, the best chance for a "peaceful issue is . . . to come to an early understanding with Russia." (G. Cecil, The Life of Robert, Marquis of Salisbury, vol. 2, London 1922, pp. 84-86. Monypenny-Buckle, vol. 6, pp. 70-71. Millman, pp. 190ff. Seton-Watson, p. 102ff.)

It was Salisbury whom to Beaconsfield's considerable discomfort and Russian elation the cabinet selected to represent it at the Constantinople conference.

7.   OBTI, vol. 1, no. 352, see also no. 344.

8.   Millman, pp. 210-211, 533.

9.   For Serbia and Montenegro, it provided for the status quo with territorial improvements; for Bosnia-Hercegovina, for local autonomy based on Andrássy's and the insurgents' proposals. Bulgaria and Macedonia should be divided into two autonomous provinces under Christian governors, and protected by 6000 Belgian soldiers. (OBTI, vol. 1, no. 372.)

10.   Cecil, vol. 2, p. 112. Seton-Watson, p. 134.

11.   MV, 1876, no. 290; cf. also no. 284.

12.   MV, 1876, no. 285.

13.   MV, 1876, no. 304; 1877, no. 2. Cf. also MV, 1876, nos. 316, 333, 334; 1877, nos. 6, 8, 10, 17, 19, 22-A.

14.   MV, 1876, no. 306.

15.   RNOBB, p. 14.

16.   MV, 1877, nos. 26, 29, 30; see also nos. 6, 8, 13.

In the *Grazhdanin*, the Katkovian scheme was warmly sponsored by Dostoevskii. For the great novelist—and truly Russian reactionary and chauvinist—the German Chancellor was the only statesman properly perceiving the connection between French policy, "the universal Roman-Catholic conspiracy" and the "monster begotten by it—Socialism"; moreover, the man who fathomed that "Germany needs us, not for momentary political alliance, but forever": Germany's objective "is all Western mankind. She has selected for herself the European Western world where she seeks to inculcate her principles in lieu of the Roman and Romanic tenets, and henceforth to become its leader, leaving the East to Russia. Thus, two great peoples are destined to transform the face of this world." (Dostoevskii, vol. 2, pp. 908ff. For the writer's admiration of Katkov see ibid., vol. 1, p. 479, vol. 2, p. 821.)

17.   KA, *58,* 1933, pp. 67-68. Kartsov, Sem let, p. 138.

18.   Cf. F. Frahm, Bismarck vor der Option zwischen Russland und Österreich im Herbst 1876, Historische Zeitschrift, *149,* 1934, pp. 522ff.; Manfred, Vneshniaia politika, pp. 197ff.; Rupp, pp. 201ff.; S. D. Skazkin, Konets avstro-russko-germanskogo soiuza 1879-1884, Moskva 1928, pp. 46ff.; W. Schüssler, Bismarcks Bündnisangebot an Russland "Durch Dick und Dünn" im Herbst 1876, Historische Zeitschrift 1876, *147,* 1932, pp. 106ff.; Wolter, pp. 206ff. etc.

19.   Schweinitz, Briefwechsel, pp. 115ff.; Denkwürdigkeiten, vol. 1, pp. 350ff.

20.   Cf. Schweinitz, Denkwürdigkeiten, vol. 1, pp. 382ff.; Wolter, pp. 238ff. A memoir written by Moltke on 24 January 1877, suggests that the German military even feared that Tsardom might look for escape from its economic and political crisis in joining France instead of going to war with Turkey.

21.   KA, *1,* 1922, pp. 50ff. Cf. also Goriainov, La question, pp. 162ff.; Rupp, pp. 275ff.; Sumner, pp. 273ff.; Wertheimer, vol. 2, p. 384.

22. On the February councils see Miliutin, vol. 2, pp. 47-48, 139-141;
P. A. Valuev, Dnevnik 1877-1884, St. Petersburg 1919, pp. 5-7; RS, *143,*
1910, pp. 43-44. For Miliutin-Obruchev memoranda see Osobye pribavleniia, vol. 6, pp. 195-199; RNOBB, no. 164. For Reutern's memorandum
summing up the position of the peace party cf. Reutern-Nolcken, pp. 141-
146; for Ignatiev's statement IsV, *136,* 1914, pp. 841ff.

23. Cf., for example, Meshcherskii, vol. 2, p. 317; OBTI, vol. 1, no.
413.

24. The Rumanian convention was eventually signed in a different
situation, on 16 April 1877.

25. IsV, *136,* 1914, p. 465. Miliutin, vol. 2, pp. 130ff. OBTI, vol. 1,
nos. 390, 428.

26. Miliutin, vol. 2, p. 142.

27. On 5 February 1877, the short era of Turkish "constitutionalism"
ended. Abdülhamid ordered the deportation of Midhat and reestablished
the traditional system. To make it more easy to swallow for the British
public, however, a moderate (Edhem Pasha) was appointed the new Grand
Vizier and an Imperial decree promised improvements, partly corresponding with Andrássy's and the insurgents' demands—religious freedom, tax
reform, administrative reorganization and local autonomy.

28. MV, 1877, no. 42; see also nos. 34, 39, 40-A, B, 41.

29. MV, 1877, no. 51; see also nos. 43, 49, 50, 52, 53-B, 54, 56, 57,
61-B, 63-65, 67.

30. Bismarck again declared to Ignatiev that he could not give material help; nonetheless his pledges—to observe favorable neutrality and restrain Austria-Hungary—covered the most pressing Russian requirements.
In Vienna, the Emperor and the "Hofpartei" considered the Tsar's stance
beyond reproach and promised solidarity in the event of war. It did not
really matter that London rejected the St. Petersburg protocol, since
all the other Powers obliged themselves to support it, and since the
split among the English politicians was so profound that Ignatiev could
safely predict that the Turks would remain alone; that Beaconsfield and
Salisbury were willing to discuss with him the "peaceful liquidation" of
the Ottoman Empire, strengthened his conviction even more. (On the
Ignatiev mission see his "Poezdka grafa N. P. Ignatieva po evropeiskim
stolitsam pered voinoi 1877-1878 gg., RS, *157,* 1914, pp. 502ff.; *158,*
1914, pp. 447ff.; *159,* 1914, pp. 194ff., 402ff. Cf. also Hünigen, pp.
192ff.)

31.   Novikova, vol. 1, pp. 338-339.
32.   Miliutin, vol. 2, p. 147.
33.   MV, 1877, no. 73; cf. also nos. 69, 70, 72, 74.

Notes to Chapter 16

1.   For contemporary testimonies see Journal de Vicomte E. M. de Vogüé, Paris-St. Pétersbourg 1877-1883, Paris 1932, pp. 37-39; Koshelev, p. 228; Meshcherskii, vol. 2, p. 333; OBTI, vol. 2, no. 29.

2.   A. Florovsky, Dostoyevsky and the Slavonic Question, SEER, 9, 1930-1931, pp. 417-418.

3.   V. M. Khevrolina, Ob otnoshenii russkogo obshchestva k voine i osvobozhdeniiu Bolgarii ot turetskogo iga, Kratkie soobshcheniia IS AN SSSR, 40, 1964, pp. 45-46.

4.   Khevrolina, pp. 40ff. Miliutin, vol. 2, pp. 159, 164.

5.   Gazenkampf, p. 8.

6.   Gazenkampf, pp. 42-44, 60-61. Miliutin, vol. 2, p. 186. RA, 49:3, 1911, p. 585.

7.   Gazenkampf, app. 1.

8.   Osobye pribavleniia, vyp. 4, pp. 28ff. Gazenkampf, app. 4. Cf. also N. A. Beliaev, Russko-turetskaia voina 1877-1878, Moskva 1956, pp. 71-74.

9.   The Russians were rescued by Francis Joseph, who sent them maps used by the Austrian army, "incomparably more clear and suitable." "We wage wars with the Turks for 150 years, spend tens of millions on each one and have neither trustworthy spies, nor adequate maps, nor reliable statistical data," General Zotov complained. (RS, 49, 1886, p. 438. Cf. also Gazemkampf, pp. 10ff., 120-122; Skalon, vol. 1, pp. 47-48, 89.)

10.   Miliutin, vol. 2, p. 169.

11.   In the *Grazhdanin*, Meshcherskii denounced the advocates of the "little peace" (i.e. Gorchakov and Shuvalov above all) as "traitors and enemies" and Katkov attacked their initiative as a "real danger for Russia," worse than the British schemes. The latter contended to the following effect: The war resulted from a policy which had striven for peace at any price. Now the same people who had prosecuted this policy, would like to return to it under the pretext of grave external threat. In fact, in Europe

there are "no elements of a coalition hostile to us"; both England and Aus-tria-Hungary are impotent. However barren the course of concessions had been, it has brought beneficial results which must be exploited. "A clever policy of firmness would lead us to a peaceful outcome, but to insub-stantial and minor gains. The policy of retreat has led us to events of great significance." And the opportunity thus obtained must not be forfeited. (MV, 1877, nos. 79-A, 89, 115-A, 117-A. Cf. also MV, 1877, nos. 82, 87-A, 97-A, 123-A, 128, 130, 133, 139; Meshcherskii, vol. 2, pp. 335ff.; Skalon, vol. 1, pp. 119ff.)

12.   IsV, *137*, 1914, pp. 62ff. Miliutin, vol. 2, pp. 169ff. Skalon, vol. 1, pp. 111ff.

13.   Jelavich, Russia in the East, p. 61.

14.   Zaionchkovskii, Rossiiskoe samoderzhavie, p. 37.

15.   RS, *74*, 1892, p. 646.

16.   Miliutin, vol. 2, pp. 167-169. Skalon, vol. 1, p. 47. Valuev, Dne-vnik 1877-1884, p. 13.

17.   Meshcherskii, vol. 2, pp. 339ff. Cf. also Beyrau, Militär, pp. 396.

18.   RS, *49*, 1886, p. 253. Cf. also RNOBB, no. 209; Skalon, vol. 1, pp. 226ff.

19.   Miliutin, vol. 2, pp. 189ff., 204-205. Gazenkampf, p. 88. Skalon, vol. 1, p. 237.

20.   Tatishchev, vol. 2, p. 399.

21.   Beliaev, pp. 172-173.

22.   Miliutin, vol. 2, p. 201.

23.   When the Danube Army entered Rumania, Prince Charles expect-ed to be invited to join the war and given freedom of action on a part of the front assigned to him. The Grand Duke dismissed such an "intolerable proposition" and Alexander held the same view: "Rumanian cooperation is for us redundant." The Bucharest government was advised that its parti-cipation would be possible only if Rumanian forces unconditionally obey-ed the Russian Commander-in-Chief. (Gazenkampf, pp. 24-25. Osobye pribavleniia, vol. 6, pp. 32, 156. RS, *124*, 1905, pp. 607ff. Skalon, vol. 1, pp. 101-102. Tatishchev, vol. 2, p. 389.)

Prince Milan fared no better. Alexander, who would not embarrass the Austrians, warned him to keep quiet and wait until he was summoned. To appease Ignatiev and the Panslavs disliking this approach, he allowed the sending of Fadeev, Khitrovo and Prince Tseretelev to Athens and Belgrade to make arrangements for the hour of triumph. (Gazenkampf, pp. 37-38. IsV, *137*, 1914, pp. 65, 70ff. MacKenzie, The Serbs, pp. 171-174. Miliutin, vol. 2, pp. 161, 164, 177. Skalon, vol. 1, p. 129.)

Plevna created an entirely new situation. Now the Tsar implored an aide of the Serbian Prince: "Tell Milan that I love him like a son, that he may count on my protection under any circumstances . . . ; that if he enters the war within twelve days, he will be doing me a real service and I will take account of it. You have nothing to fear from Austria." (MacKenzie, The Serbs, pp. 220-221.)

Milan was evasive, pleading unpreparedness and financial distress; but Charles, mistakenly betting on Russian gratitude and subsequent territorial gains, entered the war and marched with his whole army to Plevna.

24.   Miliutin, vol. 2, pp. 215-216. RS, *129*, 1905, pp. 313-314. RNOBB, nos. 234, 235. Skalon, vol. 1, pp. 301ff.

25.   The opponents of the War Minister had always held him responsible for the war setbacks. They blamed him for everything—that the Guards were called too late, the campaign was started with insufficient forces, the arms were poor and soldiers without boots and proper clothing. (Cf. RA, *43:3*, 1911, pp. 592-593. Skalon, vol. 1, pp. 181, 223, 243-244.) Katkov shared this criticism. (MV, 1878, nos. 198-A, 208-A; 1879, no. 14.) Alexander, on the contrary, felt profound gratitude and unlimited confidence towards Miliutin from the September war council on, considering his firmness at that fateful moment decisive for Russian victory. When on 10 December 1877 Plevna finally capitulated, the ruler told his entourage: "Gentlemen, for that we are assembled here, we are obliged to Dmitrii Alekseevich Miliutin." (Tatishchev, vol. 2, pp. 249-250.)

26.   On the September war councils see Miliutin, vol. 2, pp. 214-216; RS, *129*, 1907, pp. 315-316; Skalon, vol. 1, pp. 308-310; Tatishchev, vol. 2, pp. 402-403.

27.   KA, *33*, 1933, p. 175. Sumner, Russia and the Balkans, pp. 336-337. Wittrock, p. 64.

28.   Pisma Pobedonostseva, vol. 1, pp. 67-68. For further revealing correspondence see ibid., pp. 68ff.

29.   MV, 1877, nos. 187-A, 188, 190-B, 195, 197, 198-A, 208-A, 211-A, 214-A, 228, 233-A.

30.   Cf. MV, 1877, nos. 186-A, 223, 235-B, 236, 249-A, 270, 271, 273, 274, 281.

31. Millman, pp. 277-278, 298-299, 326. Monypenny-Buckle, vol. 6, pp. 154ff. Seton-Watson, pp. 203ff.

32. Gazenkampf, p. 78. Rupp, pp. 367ff. Seton-Watson, pp. 145, 223. Skalon, vol. 1, p. 255. Wertheimer, vol. 3, pp. 38ff.

33. Monypenny-Buckle, vol. 6, p. 190.

34. Gazenkampf, p. 108. Forbes, the war correspondent of the *Daily News*, found the Tsar "gaunt, worn and haggard, his voice broken by nervousness and by the asthma that afflicted him, with an expression in his eyes as of a haunted deer." (Seton-Watson, p. 263.)

35. Pisma Pobedonostseva, vol. 1, p. 108; Skalon, vol. 1, p. 324. Cf. also Beyrau, Militär, pp. 402ff.; and for revealing illustrations S. P. Botkin, Pisma iz Bolgarii, St. Petersburg 1893, V. I. Nemirovich-Danchenko, God voiny, vols. 1-2, St. Petersburg 1879, and RNOBB, no. 255 [the diary of the Orlov Regiment].

36. Miliutin, vol. 2, pp. 222, 235. Cf. also Gazenkampf, pp. 136-137, 201-202. RS, *129*, 1907, p. 529. Skalon, vol. 1, 311-312, 326.

37. Cf. Rupp, pp. 410n., 420; Schweinitz, Denkwürdigkeiten, vol. 1, p. 438.

38. Gazenkampf, p. 94. Miliutin, vol. 2, pp. 226-229.

39. Gazenkampf, pp. 181-182. Goriainov, Le Bosphore, pp. 355ff. IsV, *137*, 1914, pp. 71ff. Jelavich, Russia in the East, pp. 64-65, 68-69. Miliutin, vol. 2, pp. 228ff. OBTI, vol. 2, no. 306. Tatishchev, vol. 2, pp. 425-426.

40. MV, 1877, no. 242-B.

41. MV, 1877, no. 262-V.

42. Gazenkampf, pp. 184-185.

43. Wittrock, pp. 61-65.

Notes to Chapter 17

1. IsV, *137*, 1914, pp. 74ff. Miliutin, pp. 252ff.

2. Skalon, vol. 2, pp. 41-42, 56-60.

3. Cecil, vol. 2, pp. 170-172. Millman, pp. 335ff. Monypenny-Buckle, vol. 6, pp. 193ff. OBTI, vol. 2, no. 311. Seton-Watson, pp. 233ff.

4. Rupp, pp. 427ff. Seton-Watson, pp. 249-250. Sumner, Russia and the Balkans, pp. 321-322.

5. Pisma Pobedonostseva, vol. 1, pp. 64-65.

6.   Goriainov, Le Bosphore, pp. 355-356. IsV, *137*, 1914, pp. 76-77. OBTI, vol. 2, nos. 342, 346. Rupp, p. 414.

7.   Gazenkampf, pp. 308, 323, 339. RS, *123*, 1905, p. 497. Skalon, vol. 2, p. 431. Tatishchev, vol. 2, pp. 430ff.

8.   Indeed, even the pampered Guards now had their feet mostly protected only by animal skins and reminded Skalon like all the other rather bands of medieval robbers. (Op. cit., vol. 2, p. 178.)

9.   Gazenkampf, pp. 339ff. OBTI, vol. 2, no. 377. Skalon, vol. 2, pp. 157ff. Tatischev, vol. 2, pp. 433ff.

10.   This violated the Reichstadt agreement obliging the Russians not to further the formation of a "big compact Slavic state." They argued that their obligation pertained only to a Greater Serbia, not a Greater Bulgaria. (OBTI, vol. 2, nos. 467, 469.)

11.   Rupp, pp. 439-441. Wertheimer, vol. 3, pp. 63-64.

12.   Gazenkampf, pp. 398ff. IsV, *137*, 1914, pp. 87-91; (N. P. Ignatiev, San Stefano), *139*, 1915, pp. 35ff.; (N. P. Ignatiev, Posle San Stefano), *143*, 1916, pp. 9-11; Miliutin, vol. 3, pp. 11-12. Skalon, vol. 2, pp. 189ff. Tatishchev, vol. 2, pp. 435-436.

13.   Cf. Gazenkampf, pp. 389ff.; Miliutin, vol. 3, pp. 14-15; OBTI, vol. 2, nos. 383, 391.

14.   Gazenkampf, pp. 391-392. RS, *123*, 1905, pp. 500, 505. Skalon, vol. 2, pp. 189ff. Sumner, Russia, pp. 340ff.

15.   Alarmed by Ambassador Layard that the Adrianople terms mean "the end of Turkish rule as well as the end of our influence in the East" and that "armistice does not stop Russian advance . . . the conduct of the Russian is inexplicable and treachery is suspected" (Sumner, p. 373), on 8 February the London cabinet motioned for the second time for sending warships. Again, however, the movements of the six ironclads led by Admiral Hornby indicated weak determination and provided an object for world-wide ironical comments.

The Sultan, in awe of Russian retaliation, refused Hornby the permission to pass through the Dardanelles; thus, the Admiral had to return to Besika Bay and ask for new orders. They instructed him to enter the Marmara Sea whatever the Turkish stance, but to stop at the Prince Islands and wait. Meanwhile, posters mocking London's diffidence appeared on the walls of the Turkish capital: "Lost! Between Besika Bay and the Sultan's Palace, a fleet of six fine ironclads, bearing the English flag. Anybody communicating to Lord Beaconsfield information as to their whereabouts will be suitably rewarded." (Millman, pp. 387ff. Seton-Watson, pp. 272ff.)

16. OBTI, vol. 2, no. 415.

17. MV, 1878, nos. 21-A, 25, 43-A. Cf. also nos. 18-B, 20, 22, 25, 30-A, B, 31, 33-A, 34-A, 36, 37, 40, 41-A, B, 43-B, 44-A.

18. Gazenkampf, pp. 428ff., 461ff. Miliutin, vol. 3, pp. 18-21. Tatishchev, vol. 2, pp. 441-442, 447-448. It may be presumed that the Tsar had been strongly emboldened by the telegrams sent from London by Shuvalov from 4 to 10 February. The Ambassador reported that "in the last week the hostility towards Russia developed to a degree of incomprehensible true madness," yet he judged British internal dissent profound enough to allow the seizure of Constantinople. Lord Derby, he wrote, had given him to understand that only the occupation of Gallipoli would mean war; otherwise, determination "will not provoke a breach, but prevent it (!). . . ." (KA, *59*, 1933, pp. 86, 90-91. Tatishchev, vol. 2, pp. 446-447.)

19. Miliutin, vol. 3, pp. 14-15. OBTI, vol. 2, nos. 391, 396.

20. Gazenkampf, pp. 389. IsV, *139*, 1915, pp. 376, 749ff.; *140*, 1915, pp. 36ff. 414-415. RS, *123*, 1905, pp. 511-512. Skalon, vol. 2, pp. 168, 189ff., 219ff., 254.

21. OBTI, vol. 2, no. 445.

22. IsV, *141*, 1915, pp. 369ff. OBTI, vol. 2, nos. 474, 478. RS, *75*, 1892, pp. 652-653; *123*, 1905, p. 516. Skalon, vol. 2, pp. 236ff.

23. Cf. OBTI, vol. 2, nos. 474, 493.

24. Meshcherskii, vol. 2, pp. 378-379.

25. Cf. OBTI, vol. 2, nos. 455-457.

26. For the text of the Treaty see Sumner, Russia, pp. 627ff.; for the best analysis ibid., pp. 399ff. For Katkov's comments MV, 1878, nos. 48-50, 53, 64, 71-A.

27. Skalon, vol. 2, p. 283. Tatishchev, vol. 2, pp. 466-467.

28. Rupp, p. 477.

29. Gazenkampf, pp. 541ff.; Miliutin, vol. 3, p. 24. RS, *123*, 1905, p. 524. Skalon, vol. 2, pp. 294ff. Tatishchev, vol. 2, pp. 476-477.

30. On 7 March, Andrássy dispatched a circulatory note formally inviting the Powers to Berlin to discuss the San Stefano terms. The Foreign Office reacted by a statement that Great Britain would take part in the diplomatic summit only if Russia assented to submit the San Stefano

treaty to revision in its entirety. (For the extraordinary councils see Miliutin, vol. 3, pp. 26ff.; OBTI, vol. 3, no. 15. For the diplomatic preparations for the Congress see GP, vol. 2, nos. 317-322, 334-338; OBTI, vol. 2, nos. 398, 400; Wertheimer, vol. 3, pp. 88-89.)

31.   MV, 1878, nos. 61-A, 64.

32.   MV, 1878, nos. 55, 62; see also nos. 50, 51, 55-59, 64, 66-A, B, 68, 69, 71-B, 76, 85-A, 103, 105, 106.

33.   On 21 March, the Austro-Hungarian delegations voted for a war credit of 60 million guldens. On 27 March, after the cabinet concurred with Beaconsfield's demand to call on the reserves and send an expeditionary force to the Mediterranean, Derby tendered his resignation and this was believed to be "the beginning of a British war declaration." (Millman, pp. 403ff. Seton-Watson, pp. 340ff.)

34.   MV, 1878, no. 46. Cf. also, 52, 54, 57, 61-A, B, 73, 75, 77, 92, 96.

35.   Morrison, p. 435.

36.   Byrnes, pp. 132ff. Miliutin, vol. 3, pp. 210, 236-237. Pisma Pobedonostseva, vol. 1, pp. 127, 253-254, 273-274, 417. De Vogüé, p. 83.

37.   OBTI, vol. 3, no. 9.

38.   Miliutin, vol. 3, pp. 26-27.

39.   Seton-Watson, pp. 343-344.

40.   On the Skobelev-Katkov correspondence see RS, 62, 1889, pp. 409-410.

41.   The relevant Skobelev papers were published in IsV, 10, 1882, pp. 110ff., 275ff.; 14, 1883, pp. 547ff.; and in "Voennaia entsyklopediia," vol. 10, St. Petersburg 1912, pp. 619ff. See also R. L. Greaves, Persia and the Defence of India 1884-1912, London 1959, p. 12; Knorring, vol. 1, pp. 62-65; Shteinberg, pp. 59-60.

42.   FO 181-539, nos. 27, 30, 35, 39; for further reports cf. FO 65-1029, 1030.

43.   Khidoiatov, pp. 259-260. Morris, pp. 526-527.

44.   Terentiev, vol. 2, pp. 431ff. Cf. also Ch Marvin, The Russian Advance towards India, London 1882, pp. 86ff.; Reconnoitring Central Asia, pp. 269-270.

45.   Terentiev, vol. 2, p. 435.

46.   Terentiev, vol. 2, pp. 428ff.; cf. also Khidoiatov, pp. 264-265.

47.   Nikitin, Slavianskie komitety, pp. 333ff. OBTI, vol. 1, no. 259. RA, 35:2, 1897, pp. 257ff.; 45:2, 1907, pp. 168-169.

48.   N. R. Ovsianyi, Blizhnii vostok i slavianstvo, St. Petersburg 1910, p. 10.

49.   RS, *84,* 1895, p. 78.

50.   Pisma Pobedonostseva, vol. 1, p. 78.

51.   One example would suffice to show how Cherkasskii understood his role.

Once he ordered that a magistrate should deliver a thousand loaves of bread for the Russian army; and if he failed to comply, he was to be beaten by a hazel-rod. When warned that this sort of punishment had not been in use even under the Turkish rule, he retorted: "This diplomacy is an utter nonsense. I don't need such considerations, I am here to work for Russia's sake." (RS, *66,* 1890, pp. 430-431.)

52.   E. I. Utin, Pisma iz Bolgarii, St. Petersburg 1879, p. 123. Cf. also ibid., pp. 115, 118; V. I. Nemirovich-Danchenko, Posle voiny, St. Petersburg 1880, pp. 93, 176 etc.

53.   Nemirovich-Danchenko, Posle voiny, p. 50.

54.   Nemirovich-Danchenko, Posle voiny, p. 82. OBTI, vol. 2, no. 233. RS, *58,* 1888, p. 485; *66,* 1890, pp. 434-435.

55.   OBTI, vol. 2, no. 352.

56.   MV, 1878, no. 301.

Katkov was equally disturbed by the anti-Bulgarian voices raised in Russia proper. Together with Meshcherskii, he sharply protested against a particularly provocative speech delivered by Novoselskii, the mayor of Odessa. (MV, 1877, no. 214-V.)

57.   Miliutin, vol. 2, p. 259. RS, *83,* 1895, pp. 18, 33.

58.   The Vienna Crown Councils in January-February and the ensuing intense debate remained inconclusive. The "Hofpartei" stayed unenthusiastic about the war prospects; and so did Francis Joseph, who "was enraged, no less than Andrássy, by Russian perfidy but feared war more." The anti-Russian option had not ceased to be suspected as purely emotional "Hungarian policy," a "revenge for Világos," harmful to the Habsburg Monarchy and devoid to any positive goal. "For what purpose is this war to be fought?" General Beck, the chief of the Imperial Military Chancery, asked the Emperor. "If Your Majesty demands half of Turkey as far as Salonika, then we know what we are fighting for; but merely to expel Russia (from the Balkans) is not worth the trouble." Scepticism about the English alliance even increased when London hesitated to

finance the mobilization. Andrássy appeared to dangle in political void and only Emperor's confidence allegedly saved him from forced resignation. (Rupp, pp. 427ff., 453-454. Wertheimer, vol. 3, pp. 76ff. Wittrock, p. 44.)

59.   Miliutin, vol. 3, pp. 32, 38-39. OBTI, vol. 3, nos. 9n., 34, 40, 44.

60.   Cf. IsV, *144*, 1916, pp. 32ff.

61.   On the shock of the Zasulich trial see MV, 1878, nos. 85, 87, 88-A, 89-B, 95-A, B, 106, 132-A; Meshcherskii, vol. 2, pp. 40ff., 397ff.; Miliutin, vol. 3, pp. 33, 41-42, 47-48.

62.   Cf. MV, 1878, nos. 90, 98, 101-B, 110-B, 118,-B, 130-B.

63.   Todleben made it clear that regardless of the enlivened zeal of his subordinates for the "second round," he would work only to remove deficiencies and take no chances. There were unconquered Turkish fortresses (Silistra, Ruse, Shumen and Varna) in the rear, he asserted, rising tension with Rumania as a result of the annexation of Southern Bessarabia, and, of course, the risk of British naval action and Austrian invasion in the valley of the Danube and Poland. All the Balkan Army could do under such circumstances, was to strengthen its defensive position in Bulgaria. (Sumner, Russia in the Balkans, p. 397. For Todleben's memoir see N. K. Shilder, Graf Eduard Ivanovich Totleben, ego zhizn i deiatelnost, vol. 2, St. Petersburg 1886, pp. 866ff.; Tatishchev, vol. 2, pp. 481-482.)

64.   Miliutin, vol. 3, pp. 32ff., 46, 48. OBTI, vol. 3, no. 47.

65.   Polovtsov, vol. 2, pp. 175-176.

66.   RS, *159*, 1914, p. 452.

67.   On Bariatinskii's campaign for the "second round" cf. KA, *33*, 1929, p. 195; Sumner, Russia, pp. 497-498; Zisserman, vol. 3, pp. 271-273.

68.   Miliutin, vol. 3, pp. 51-52. OBTI, vol. 3, no. 55.

69.   MV, 1878, no. 108; cf. also 111, 112.

70.   For the Shuvalov phase see KA, *59*, 1933, pp. 94-96; GP, vol. 2, nos. 388-392; IsV, *144*, 1916, pp. 36ff.; Rupp, pp. 508ff.

71.   Miliutin, vol. 3, p. 69, 73. OBTI, vol. 3, no. 67, encl. 1 and 2.

72.   Miliutin, vol. 3, pp. 59, 60, 63. Polovtsov, vol. 2, p. 185.

73.   Cf. KA, *59*, 1933, p. 96; Radowitz, vol. 2, pp. 24-25; N. Rich-H.M. Fisher, ed., The Holstein Papers, vol. 1, Cambridge 1955, pp. 119-122; RS, *149*, 1912, pp. 214-215; Tatishchev, vol. 2, pp. 486-487.

74.   RS, *150*, 1912, pp. 3-4.

75.   The Anglo-Austrian agreement of 6 June obliged the two Powers to urge together at congress /a/ "that the autonomous (Bulgarian) Principality shall not extend south or south-west of. . . the Balkans and west to the Morava river," /b/ "that Russian occupation south of the Danube shall be limited to six months." In addition, the English promised to "support any proposition with respect to Bosnia which Austria shall make." (Millman, pp. 439-440, 447-448.)

76.   As a sort of repayment for wrestling Cyprus from the Turks, London concluded on 4 June a secret defensive alliance with the Sultan securing his Asiatic possessions: if the Russians tried to take hold of territories beyond Batumi, Kars and Ardahan, Great Britain were to resist them by "force of arms." (Millman, pp. 443-445; Seton-Watson, pp. 421ff.)

77.   Seton-Watson, p. 451.

78.   Wertheimer, vol. 3, pp. 131ff.

79.   Gorchakov and Beaconsfield caused the greatest embarassment or merriment when they exchanged, by mistake, the most secret maps supplied to them by their respective general staffs.

80.   MV, 1878, 110-113, 115-A, 117-A, 119-121, 123-A, 139, 140.

81.   MV, 1878, nos. 144-146, 149-151.

82.   MV, 1878, nos. 152-154, 156, 159-B, 164-B.

83.   MV, 1878, no. 167.

84.   MV, 1878, nos. 169-171, 180. 181.

85.   MV, 1878, no. 185.

86.   MV, 1878, nos. 173-A, 177. See also MV, 1878, nos. 174-A, 176, 178, 179; RV, *136*, 1878, pp. 514ff.

87.   The text of the treaty see in Sumner, Russia, app. X, pp. 658ff.; for a still unsurpassed analysis of the congress see ibid., pp. 501ff. For contemporary testimonies see D. G. Anuchin, Kongres Berlina, RS, *149-152*, 1912, Carathéodory Pasha, Le rapport secret sur le Congrés de Berlin, Paris 1919; Radowitz, vol. 2, pp. 24ff. For the survey of sources and literature cf. I. Geiss, Der Berliner Kongress, eine historische Retrospektive; in "Der Berliner Kongress," pp. 31ff.

Notes to Chapter 18

1.   Miliutin put it most explicitly:
"On every occasion I have been trying to remind (them) that even

if the terms of the . . . Congress were to be extremely unfavorable to us, they would be incomparably less burdensome than those which we would have to expect in case of war, after inevitable defeat. Our military forces are so disorganized, so shattered, that it is impossible to speculate on any chance of success whatsoever." (Miliutin, vol. 3, pp. 68-69. For similar judgments see B. Nolde, L'alliance franco-russe. Les origines du système diplomatique d'avant guerre, Paris, 1936, pp. 207-209; Polovtsov, vol. 1, p. 119.

2.   FO 181-573, no. 572. For the press reaction see V. I. Ado, Berlinskii kongress 1878 i pomeshchichee-burzhuaznoe obshchestvennoe mnenie Rossii, IZ, 69, 1961, pp. 101ff; Grüning, pp. 56ff.)

3.   Aksakov, vol. 1, pp. 297ff. See also Koshelev, pp. 235ff., Nolde, pp. 200ff., Skazkin, pp. 87ff.

4.   Pisma Pobedonostseva, vol. 1, pp. 124-125.

5.   Ado, pp. 116ff. GP, vol. 2, nos. 440, 441. Miliutin, vol. 3, pp. 78ff. W. Windelband, Bismarck und die europäischen Grossmächte 1879-1885, Essen 1942, pp. 51ff. Wittrock, p. 5.

6.   Cf. Kennan, pp. 38-39.

7.   For prestige and financial reasons, Andrássy urged that the occupation should be performed with limited forces—the 40,000 strong corps of General Filipović. Lacking coordination in difficult terrain and surprised by stiff Moslem-Turkish resistance, the advancing units performed badly. Four additional corps had to be sent to complete the action. Besides the loss of face, Vienna had to cope with serious embarrassment—violent criticism from the Hungarians and Slavs, strained relations with Turkey, the Balkan neighbours and Italy.

8.   For Katkov's key comment see MV, 1878, no 202-B; cf. also nos. 184, 187-B, 191, 192-B, 195, 198, 199, 201-B, 206, 209, 216, 219-A, 230, 233.

9.   Kartsov, Sem let, pp. 41, 106. Miliutin, vol. 3, pp. 90, 93. RS, 75, 1892, pp. 678ff. Shilder, vol. 2, pp. 919ff., 932ff.

10.   D. Doinov, Kresnensko-razlozhkoto västanie 1878-1879, Sofia 1979, pp. 130ff. FO 181-573, nos. 887, 888, 924. OBTI, vol. 3, nos. 225, 323n. RS, 75, 1892, pp. 678-679.

11.   Cf. RS, 49, 1886, pp. 431-432; 61, 1889, pp. 587ff.; 62, 1889, pp. 389ff.

12.   Dnevnik E. A. Perettsa, 1880-1883, Moskva 1927, p. 140.

12.   Dnevnik E. A. Perettsa, 1880-1883, Moskva 1927, p. 140.

13.   Cf. HvB. no. 86.

14.   C. Jireček, Das Fürstenthum Bulgarien, Wien 1891, p. 371.

15.   Miliutin, vol. 3, pp. 93ff. OBTI, vol. 3, nos. 66, 75, 82, 109, 225, 341. N. R. Ovsianyi, ed., Sbornik materialov po grazhdanskomu upravleniiu i okkupatsii v Bolgarii v 1877-78-79 g.g. (St. Petersburg 1904-1905), vyp. 3, no 19; vyp. 5, nos. 140, 225. Shilder, vol. 2, pp. 348ff.

16.   Terentiev, vol. 2, p. 439.

17.   The Afghans begged Stoletov to stay away from their territories. He dismissed the plea as an "humiliation of Russia's name," resorted to threats and his intimidation tactics eventually proved effective. First the local officials and then Shere Ali Khan himself gave way. On 10 August the mission entered Kabul and without delay forwarded a proposal for a military alliance. The Khan, both afraid of Russian wrath—the General told him that he would soon be back with 30,000 troops—and tempted by the promise of rich spoils in India, assented to a treaty relationship establishing a de-facto Russian protectorate over his possessions. (Terentiev, vol. 2, p. 439. For a detailed account see I. L. Iavorskii, Puteshestvie russkogo posolstva po Afganistanu i Bukharskomu khanstvu 1878-1879, St. Petersburg 1880, 2 vols.)

18.   According to the Russian text (cf. Terentiev, vol. 2, pp. 451-454), Afghanistan was recognized as an independent country, but Tsardom obtained the right, in case of external threat or domestic crisis, "to intervene . . . by providing adequate help" (articles 1-2). In the further stipulations, mostly enlarging on this basic committment, Tsardom obliged itself explicitly to give military assistance against the British (article 5).

In the English version, the terms were supposed to contain the articles on the Russian march, on the establishment of a Russian garrison at Herat and the conquest of Punjab. (Bilgrami, pp. 188-189.)

19.   Terentiev, vol. 2, pp. 458ff.

20.   Bilgrami, p. 185. MV, 1878, no. 172. For Katkov's further campaign in this vein see MV, 1878, nos. 204, 226, 228, 232, 240, 243, 245, 251, 253, 261, 268, 273, 286, 291-A, 292, 316, 318, 332-A.

21.   The preparation for the Macedonian action was entrusted to the Sofia "Committee of unity," supervised by the members of Imperial Commissioner's council, Drinov and Alabin. Among financial contributors

were Russian Embassy at Constantinople, Slavonic committees and Bulgarian colonies in Russia. (Doinov, pp. 130ff. OBTI, vol. 3, nos. 119, 120, 123, 133, 152, 154, 163, 170, 203, 204, 212, 344.)

22.   OBTI, vol. 3, nos. 181, 212, 214, 221, 225. Cf. also B. Waller, Bismarck at the Crossroads, London 1974, pp. 43-44.

23.   Miliutin, vol. 3, p. 99. OBTI, vol. 3, no 171. N. R. Ovsianyi, Russkoe upravlenie v Bolgarii, vol. 2, St. Petersburg 1904, pp. 50-51.

24.   Khidoiatov, pp. 289-293. Miliutin, vol. 3, pp. 98-100. OBTI, vol. 3, no. 174.

25.   MV, 1878, nos. 295, 306; 1879, no. 31. In his comments, the editor also repeated other articles of the Muscovy faith: the "Crimean scare" was groundless, neither England nor Austria-Hungary were capable of waging a big war; the economic reasons were equally untenable, because the Russian situation in that respect had actually improved after the war. (MV, 1878, nos. 271, 275, 278, 282, 284, 295, 305, 311-B, 321.)

26.   MV, 1878, no. 285. See also nos. 260-B, 265, 267-A, 273, 287-A, 288-A, 289, 295, 300, 304, 310-A, 312, 313, 314-A.

27.   C. E. Black, The Establishment of Constitutional Government in Bulgaria, Princeton 1943, p. 77. Ovsianyi, Blizhnii vostok, pp. 53-55. Shilder, vol. 2, pp. 391ff.

28.   E. C. Corti, The Downfall of Three Dynasties, London 1934, p. 254. C. de Grunwald, Le tsar Alexandre II et son temps, Paris 1963, pp. 317-318.

29.   In Austria-Hungary, Shuvalov was confronted by the complaints about the conduct of Russian generals and by the insistence on a speedy withdrawal of the Balkan Army. Neither Andrássy nor Bismarck professed any interest in revitalizing the Emperors' League ties. On the other hand, from London the Ambassador reported "extreme moderation"; even there, however, Beaconsfield and Salisbury were unequivocal in the demand for the departure of Russian troops. (Cf. V. M. Khvostov, Problemy istorii vneshnei politiki Rossii i mezhdunarodnykh otnoshenii v kontse XIX i nachale XX veka, Moskva 1974, pp. 186ff.; Waller, pp. 46-49.)

30.   Khidoiatov, p. 296. Miliutin, vol. 3, pp. 107-108, 114ff. OBTI, vol. 3, nos. 280, 281, 285n. Schweinitz, Denkwürdigkeiten, vol. 2, p. 39. On Kaufman's unrelenting plea for the "second round" see Terentiev, vol. 2, pp. 458ff.

31. Cf. Dufferin's communications to Salisbury in FO 181-573 and 181-589; particularly see FO 181-573, no. 857; 181-589, nos. 8, 22, 23, 30, 41, 49.

32. On the negotiations see FO 181-589, nos. 32ff.; Miliutin, vol. 3, pp. 126ff.; OBTI, vol. 3, no. 333; Schweinitz, Denkwürdigkeiten, vol. 2, pp. 46, 57, 59.

33. P. A. Matveev, Bolgariia posle Berlinskogo kongressa, St. Petersburg 1887, pp. 239ff. OBTI, vol. 3, nos. 335, 341. Ovsianyi, Blizhnii vostok, pp. 60ff.; Russkoe upravlenie, vol. 3, pp. 277-278; Sbornik materialov, vol. 5, nos. 140, 225.

34. FO, 181-589, no. 139.

35. Miliutin, vol. 3, pp. 132. OBTI, vol. 3, no. 265. Ovsianyi, Sbornik materialov, vol. 6, no. 43.

36. For the continuing harangues of the Moscow editor in the already described vein see MV, 1879, nos. 7, 41, 56, 64, 65, 78-A, 93-A, 105, 107, 119, 129, 134, 145.

Notes to Chapter 19

1. Schweinitz, Denkwürdigkeiten, vol. 2, pp. 40ff; Briefwechsel, p. 358. For analysis see H. Heibronner, The Russian plague of 1878-1879, SR, *21*, 1962, pp. 89ff.

2. MV, 1879, nos. 16, 17, 19-22, 28-V, 29, 38, 40, 46, 47, 54, 106, 124, 214, 336. RV, *139*, 1879, pp. 950ff.; *140*, 1879, pp. 960ff. Cf. also Grüning, pp. 63ff.; Skazkin, pp. 65ff.

3. The study of Waller has been strongly tainted by this oversimplification. Cf. also Skazkin, pp. 69ff.; Sumner, Russian and the Balkans, p. 557.

4. GP, vol. 3, no. 447; cf. also nos. 451, 461, 482. Windelband, pp. 130-131.

5. Zaionchkovskii, Voennye reformy, pp. 272-273, 280ff.

6. For analyses see S. Kumpf-Korfes, Bismarck's "Draht nach Russland," (East-) Berlin 1968, pp. 5ff.; Müller-Link, pp. 58ff.

7. Grüning, pp. 66-68. Katz, pp. 110ff. L. Voronov, Finantsovo-ekonomicheskaia deiatelnost M. N. Katkova, RV, *250*, 1897, pp. 101 ff. Wolter, pp. 310ff.

8. The Moltke plan envisaged in the early stage defensive action in the west, against France, and a resolute advance in the east; only after

Russian forces were routed, would the mortal blow be delivered against the French. In 1880, the Austro-Hungarian army was included into operational calculations. (K. Canis, Bismarck und Waldersee, East-Berlin 1980, pp. 78-79. F.v. Schmerzfeld, ed., Moltke, Die deutschen Aufmarschpläne 1871-1890, Berlin, 1929, pp. 77ff.)

On general atmosphere see Müller-Link, p. 189; H. Rumboldt, Further Recollections of a Diplomatist, London 1903, p. 197; Schweinitz, Briefwechsel, p. 144, Denkwürdigkeiten, vol. 2, pp. 60, 80; Windelband, p. 59.

9.   GP, vol. 3, nos. 445, 446, 449, 455, 458, 461, 482. W. N. Medlicott, The Congress of Berlin and After, London 1938, pp. 370ff. Taylor, pp. 259ff. Wallter, pp. 177ff. Wolter, pp. 286ff.

10.   Cf. MV, 1879, no. 162; de Vogüé, pp. 150-153.

11.   GP, vol. 3, no 443. Miliutin, vol. 3, pp. 151, 153. R. Schaller, Der bulgarische Nationalismus und die Politik Bismarcks (Ph.D. dissertation), Frankfurt, a.M. 1975, pp. 22-23. Tatishchev, vol. 2, pp. 535-536.

12.   GP, vol. 3, no. 447. J. Y. Simpson, ed. The Saburov Memoirs, or Bismarck and Russia, Cambridge 1929, p. 63. Tatishchev, vol. 2, pp. 539-541. Nolde, pp. 216ff.

13.   MV, 1879, nos. 58-A, 233, 264, 270. Cf. also GP, vol. 3, no. 441; Skazkin, p. 70.

14.   KA, 1, 1922, pp. 78ff. Cf. also GP, vol. 3, no. 514; Radowitz, vol. 2, pp. 97ff.; Saburov, pp. 51ff.; Skazkin, pp. 105ff.; Schweinitz, Denkwürdigkeiten, vol. 2, p. 72.

15.   GP, vol. 3, nos. 457, 460, 465, 466. Miliutin, vol. 3, pp. 156ff. Radowitz, vol. 2, pp. 90-91.

16.   Miliutin, vol. 3, pp. 164-165. Saburov, pp. 60ff. Skazkin, pp. 110ff.

17.   Lucius v. Ballhausen, p. 177.

18.   Cf. GP, vol. 3, nos. 453-455, 458, 461, 469, 474, 475, 480, 482. Wolter, pp. 295ff.

19.   Hohenlohe, vol. 2, p. 274. See also Schweinitz, Denkwürdigkeiten, vol. 2, p. 80.

20.   GP, vol. 3, nos. 461, 482.

21.   Until the summer of 1879, Saburov had been just one of the second-raters. Although his connections at Court were excellent and his reports appreciated for stylistic brilliance, he had been taken for no more

more than a bleak copy of Ignatiev. The perfectly timed and worded memoir, though, catapulated him to the apex. Promoted in October to the very prestigious position of the Ambassador to Berlin and invited to take part in the deliberation in the Tsar's inner circle, he eagerly grasped his opportunity.

22.   GP, vol. 3, no. 514.

23.   Kumf-Korfes, pp. 28, 43. Skazkin, pp. 104ff.

24.   Miliutin, vol. 3, p. 148. Cf. also Tvardovskaia, pp. 183-184; Valuev, Dnevnik 1877-1884, pp. 47ff.; Zaionchkovskii, Krizis samoderzhaviia, pp. 124ff.

25.   SEER, 7, 1928-1929, pp. 44-45.

26.   MV, 1878, nos. 87-89, 106, 109; 1879, nos. 82, 83, 85, 97, 297; 1880, no. 36.

27.   Tvardovskaia, Ideologiia, pp. 173ff.; Ideolog samoderzhaviia v period krizisa "verkhov" na rubezhe 70-80 godov XIX v., IZ, 91, 1973, pp. 220ff.

28.   Indeed, Alexander's response to rampant terrorism was admirably mild. Tvardovskaia, of course, writes that "the country was covered by blood and gallows," meaning by it the sixteen revolutionaries executed in 1879 for the acts of political murder (Ideologiia, p. 185.); but could the learned Soviet lady and her peers made a comparison with, say, the number of executions after the Kirov assassination?

29.   The atmosphere is particularly well reflected in the diary of A. V. Bogdanovich (Tri poslednykh samoderzhtsa, Moskva 1924, pp. 11ff.). Cf. also Zaionchkovskii, Krizis samoderzhaviia, pp. 184ff.

30.   Miliutin, vol. 3, pp. 123ff. MV, 1879, nos. 183, 191, 196, 198, 204. Cf. also Dufferin's dispatches to Salisbury in FO 181-590, nos. 573ff.

31.   FO 181-590, nos. 510, 524, 527. MV, 1879, nos. 256, 259, 273. De Vogüé, p. 156. Waller, pp. 221-222.

32.   The expedition was initiated by the Tiflis military and the Russian minister to Teheran, Zinoviev, who supplied them with convenient reports. On 2 February 1879, an Extraordinary Council chaired by Grand Duke Mikhail tabled that the action must be undertaking to counterbalance the effect of the British success in Afghanistan on the neighbouring countries. On Miliutin's insistence, the objective was limited on the Akhal-Tekin oasis and the further advance on the oasis of Merv, situated

already within Afghan borders, was strictly prohibited; but according to the plan later elaborated by the General Staff and approved by the Tsar, the drive was conceived as the "decisive step to the final solution of the Merv question and to the closure of our frontiers." (Khalfin, Prisoedinenie, p. 344. Miliutin, vol. 3, p. 113. Terentiev, vol. 3, pp. 6-7. M. N. Tikhomirov, Prisoedinenie Merva k Rossii, Moskva 1960, p. 40.)

33. At first, following the conciliatory "Dufferin line," the London cabinet had tried to dampen aroused feelings. On Lytton's warnings that General Lomakin, the commander in the Trans-Caspian, had been operating deep in the Turkoman lands and that Merv might be his aim, the Indian Office responded in the style reminiscent of the "masterly inactivity" era: "Merv would bring Russia neither revenue nor subjects, nor security. Save as a basis for future advance towards India, the permanent occupation would be a needless and wanton waste of both money and military force." (Greaves, p. 30.)

When, however, the Singers' Bridge took back its promise that eventual military advance would be stopped 200 verstas from Merv and the press raised the demand to occupy the oasis "to bring the English to their senses," the Whitehall position stiffened accordingly. The Embassy on the Neva leaked a threat that "if Russia allowed her generals to interefere in the matters of Afghanistan there would be a war." (FO 181-539, no. 420; FO 181-509, nos. 319-321; FO 181-590, nos. 505, 506. RV, *142*, 1879, p. 913.)

34. The Turkoman nomadic tribes lived in a vast area including parts of Khiva, Persia and Afghanistan. The ordeal of the Yomuths of Khiva, who numbered 150,000, has already been described. Now came the turn of the Tekke Turcomans, whose lands lay south of the Yomuths, with Akhal-Tekin and Merv oases as centers. Still further south nomadized Sarakhs and other minor tribes.

35. MV, 1879, nos. 89, 165, 168, 272, 281-B, 282-B, 283, 299, 325-B.

36. See, Ch. Marvin, The eye-witnesses' account of the disastrous Russian campaign against Akhal Tekke Turcomans, London 1880, pp. 14ff.; on the criticism by the Russian press and particularly by the *Moskovskiia vedomosti* following the defeat ibid., pp. 313ff. Cf. also Khalfin, Prisoedinenie, pp. 347ff.; Knorring, vol. 2 pp. 158-159; Terentiev, vol. 3, 7ff.; Tikhomirov, pp. 38ff.

37. In early 1877, after the death of Yakub-beg, the Chinese re-established their control over Kashgaria; and soon they requested from St. Petersburg the return of the Ili region, which the Russian had occupied since 1871 under the pretext of protection of Chinese rights against a rebellion. Alexander himself recognized the hand-over as a "debt of honour," but Kaufman and his allies were obstinate. In order to find an escape from the dilemma, Miliutin and Giers lured the Chinese representative to sign the so called Livadi Treaty (October 1879), which postponed the withdrawal from Ili for an unspecified period and even enlarged Russian commercial privileges in the northwestern China. In Peking, the duplicity created uproar against the "northern barbarians" and forced the government to undertake war preparations.

38. MV, 1879, no 240. Cf. also nos. 243, 244.

39. Miliutin, vol. 3, pp. 167-169.

40. KA, *1*, 1922, pp. 64ff. Cf. also Kumpf-Korfes, pp. 21ff.; Nolde, pp. 241ff.; Skazkin, pp. 111ff.; Waller, pp. 183ff.; Wolter, pp 335ff.

41. Miliutin, vol. 3, pp. 167-169.

42. According to a memoir written by Jomini, the three preconditions were itemized at Livadia for a successful invasion of the Straits: "(1) the restoration of the financial balance . . . .(2) the creation of a fleet in the Black Sea, (3) an understanding with our neighbours to make sure of their neutrality." (S. Goriainov, The End of the Alliance of the Three Emperors, American Historical Review, *23*, 1918, no. 2, p. 326.)

43. Miliutin, vol. 3, pp. 173, 183, 186-188, 192. Skazkin, pp. 120ff.

44. GP, vol. 3, nos. 515-520. Nolde, pp. 246ff. Saburov, pp. 88ff., 110ff. Skazkin, pp. 122ff. Windelband, pp. 131ff.

45. For Katkov's participation see MV, 1879, nos. 240, 274, 281, 286, 288, 325-A; 1880, nos. 11, 15, 43, 53.

46. FO 181-603, no. 595. Miliutin, vol. 3, pp. 208, 225-227, 233-234. Saburov, pp. 97ff. Schweinitz, Briefwechsel, pp. 154-155; Denkwürdigkeiten, vol. 2, p. 84, 88, 92. Waller, pp. 224, 232ff.

Notes to Chapter 20

1. FO 181-539, no. 503; 181-601, nos. 42, 153, 167. Greaves, p. 59. Pisma Pobedonostseva, vol. 1, pp. 273-274.

2. FO 181-641, no. 29; see also no. 91.

3. Khalfin, Prisoedinenie, pp. 350ff. Khidoiatov, pp. 333ff. Miliutin, vol. 3, pp. 217-219, 223-224. Shteinberg, p. 59.

4. Byrnes, p. 132. Miliutin, vol. 3, pp. 210, 225, 236-237. Pisma Pobedonostseva, vol. 1, pp. 233ff.

5. On Gladstone's foreign-policy concept see W. N. Medlicott, Bismarck, Gladstone and the Concert of Europe, London 1956, pp. 17ff.

6. E. Fitzmaurice, The Life of Lord Granville, 1815-1891, London 1905, vol. 2, p. 204.

7. Medlicott, Bismarck, Gladstone, pp. 25ff. Windelband, pp. 155ff. Wolter, pp. 341ff.

8. Miliutin, vol. 3, p. 241. Cf. also FO 181-602, no. 229.

9. Medlicott, Bismarck, Gladstone, p. 57.

10. Cf. Ramm, Correspondence 1876-1886, no. 198.

11. Saburov, p. 130. See also Windelband, pp. 144-145.

12. Baddeley, p. 62. Cf. also Meshcherskii, vol. 2, pp. 441ff.

13. MV, 1880, nos. 37-A, 44, 47-A, 51. Zaionchkovskii, Krizis samoderzhaviia, pp. 149-150.

14. I.e. the editorial of 7/19.2.1880, no. 37-A.

15. Tvardovskaia, Ideologiia, pp. 189-191; Ideolog, pp. 235ff.

16. Tvardovskaia, Idelogiia, pp. 192-193; Ideolog, pp. 241ff.

17. On the Loris-Melikov episode see Koshelev, pp. 245ff.; Perets, pp. 1ff.; Valuev (1877-1884), pp. 59ff,; Tatishchev, vol. 2, pp. 625ff.; Zaionchkovskii, Krizis samoderzhaviia, pp. 148ff.

18. Tatishchev, vol. 2, pp. 625-626.

19. Bogdanovich, p. 34. Meshcherskii, vol. 2, pp. 466ff. Zaionchkovskii, Rossiiskoe samoderzhavie, pp. 213ff.

20. K. Pobedonostsev, L'autocratie russe, Paris 1927, p. 67. RS, 63, 1889, pp. 584-585. Tvardovskaia, Ideologiia, pp. 193-196; Ideolog, pp. 247-248.

21. FO 181-602; nos. 602, 603. Miliutin, vol. 3, pp. 244, 248, 260.

22. Miliutin, vol. 3, pp. 259-260; cf. also 243-244, 248, 255. For details see Medlicott, Bismarck, Gladstone, pp. 71ff.; Windelband, pp. 170ff.

23. MV, 1880, no. 64.

24. MV, 1880, nos. 81, 281, 289; see also nos. 131-A, 136, 140, 141, 145, 149, 156, 160, 172, 173, 188.

25.   Saburov, p. 165.

26.   Ibid., pp. 161-162. Windelband, pp. 199ff.

27.   W. N. Medlicott, Bismarck and the Three Emperors' Alliance 1881-1887; TRHS, 4th ser., *27*, 1945, pp. 46-47. Skazkin, pp. 135ff. Cf. also Miliutin, vol. 3, pp. 270-274, 278, 281.

28.   F. Martens, Rossia i Angliia v Srednei Azii, St. Petersburg 1880, pp. 4-5.

29.   MV, 1880, no. 350; cf. also MV, 1880, nos. 303, 338; 1881, nos. 3, 6, 16, 17, 28, 30, 42, 43, 50, 55, 57.

30.   FO 181-602, no. 361; 181-642, nos. 70, 71; 181-642, no. 44. Greaves, p. 59. Morris, 525-526.

31.   Miliutin, vol. 3, pp. 226, 274-275. Windelband, p. 168.

32.   GP, vol. 3, nos. 520-525. Medlicott, Bismarck, Gladstone, pp. 176ff. Saburov, pp. 142ff. Skazkin, pp. 139gg. Windelband, pp. 230ff. Wolter, pp. 344ff.

33.   Saburov, pp. 176-177.

34.   Cf. Müller-Link, pp. 192ff.

35.   Miliutin, vol. 4, pp. 20-25. Skazkin, pp. 143ff.

36.   Skazkin, pp. 147ff.

37.   The full text see in Skazkin, pp. 161-163.

38.   Knorring, vol. 2, pp. 156, 176.

39.   Terentiev, vol. 3, pp. 43-44.

40.   Ibid., p. 45.

41.   Cf. Tikhomirov, pp. 46-47.

42.   Ch. Marvin, The Russians at the gates of Herat, London 1886, pp. 5ff. Terentiev, vol. 3, pp. 200-201.

43.   Marvin, The Russian advance towards India, pp. 98-99.

44.   Baddeley, pp. 93-97. Schweinitz, Denkwürdigkeiten, vol. 2, pp. 142-143.

45.   Feoktistov, pp. 177ff. Koni, vol. 2, pp. 91-92. RS, *116*, 1903, pp. 635-637; *142*, 1910, p. 309. Tvardovskaia, Ideologiia, pp. 194ff.; Ideolog, pp. 247ff. Valuev, Dnevnik 1877-1884, pp. 142ff.

46.   KA, *31*, 1928, p. 121.

47.   For documents related to this so called "Loris-Melikov constitution" see Byloe, bk. 4-5, 1918, pp. 163ff.

48.   Peretts, pp. 35ff. RA, *45:2*, 1907, p. 93. Valuev, Dnevnik 1877-1884, pp. 142ff.

Notes to Chapter 21

1. Zaionchkovskii, Krizis samoderzhaviia, p. 382. For interesting details see KA, *14*, 1926, pp. 252ff.

2. Tvardovskaia, Ideolog, pp. 254ff.

3. Cf, KA, *14*, 1926, p. 254.

4. Zaionchkovskii, Krizis samoderzhaviia, p. 388. Cf. also I. M. Aronson, The attitudes of Russian Officials in the 1880s towards Jewish Assimilation, SR, *34*, 1975, pp. 1ff.; S. W. Baron, The Russian Jews under Tsars and Soviets, New York 1976, pp. 43ff.; Zaionchkovskii, Rossiiskoe samoderzhavie, pp. 131ff.

5. MV, 1881, nos. 66-A, 72-A, 74; see also nos. 63, 65-A, B, 72-B, 77, 78-B, 79-A, 91, 92, 96, 99-A, 104, 105, 112, 114, 119.

6. Tvardovskaia, Ideolog, pp. 262ff.; Ideologiia, pp. 200ff.

7. Byrnes, p. 153. Tvardovskaia, Ideologiia, pp. 208-209.

8. MV, 1881, no. 118. Tvardovskaia, Ideologiia, pp. 206-207.

9. It was believed that Katkov was also the co-author of the "restoration manifesto." Feoktistov, however, denied this proposition; according to him, the publicist privately disapproved the proclamation and opined that the Loris-Melikov episode should have been closed simply by the dismissal of the ministerial villains. (Cf. Feoktistov, p. 198: Meshcherskii, vol. 3, p. 23; Miliutin, vol. 4, p. 65; Skalkovskii, p. 141; Valuev, Dnevnik 1877-1884, p. 208; Tvardovskaia, Idelog, pp. 264-265.)

10. MV, 1881, no. 125. Pisma Pobedonostseva, vol. 1, p. 317.

11. GP, vol. 3, no. 526. Saburov, pp. 223-224. Schweinitz, Denkwürdigkeiten, vol. 2, p. 156.

12. Wittram, pp. 325-328.

13. Schweinitz, Briefwechsel, pp. 180-181. Valuev, Dnevnik 1877-1884, p. 169, 175. De Vogüé, p. 249. Thaden, Russification, p. 150. Windelband, pp. 270-271, 285.

14. Wittram, p. 329.

15. Schweinitz, Denkwürdigkeiten, vol. 2, p. 156. Cf. also Medlicott, Bismarck, Gladstone, pp. 282ff.,; Windelband, pp. 252ff.

16. Feoktistov, p. 379. Meshcherskii, vol. 2, p. 382.

17. Knorring, vol. 2, p. 189. De Vogüé, p. 187.

18. Bülow, vol. 4, p. 564.

19. Knorring, vol. 2, pp. 181ff. RS, *49*, 1886, pp. 431ff.

20.   K. P. Pobedonostsev, L'autocratie russe, pp. 200-203.

21.   MV, 1881, nos. 70, 91, 98.

22.   Skazkin, pp. 171-172.

23.   Ibid., pp. 184-186.

24.   Skazkin, p. 186.

25.   Medlicott, Bismarck and the Three Emperors Alliance, p. 78.

26.   Cf. Medlicott, Bismarck, Gladstone, pp. 241ff.; Nolde, pp. 248ff.; Skazkin, pp. 165ff.; Windelband, pp. 230ff.; Wolter, pp. 344ff.

27.   Taylor, pp. 270-271.

By the Three Emperors' Alliance treaty, the signatory Powers entered into following obligations:

(1) "In the event of one of the three Powers being at war with a fourth Great Power, the other two shall maintain a benevolent neutrality. . . . This stipulation shall apply likewise to a war between one of the three Powers and Turkey, but only in the case when a previous agreement has been reached . . . as to the results of the war . . . ." (2) ". . . The three Courts, desirous of avoiding all disagreements between them, undertake to respect their individual interests in the Balkan peninsula. They further promise one another that any new modification in the territorial status quo of Turkey can only be accomplished after a common agreement between them . . . ." (3) "The three Courts recognize the European and mutually obligatory character of the principle of the closure of the Straits . . . ."

In the enclosed protocol, Austria-Hungary was granted the right to annex Bosnia-Hercegovina formally; the return of Turkish troops to Eastern Rumelia was prohibited and on the other hand, the Bulgarian unification was to be accepted only "if it happens to arise by the force of circumstances," not by an invasion coming from the Principality. The representatives of the three Powers in the area were to be led to "smooth their differences by friendly dicussion." (The texts see in GP, vol. 3, no. 532.)

28.   Vite, vol. 1, p. 409.

29.   Feoktistov, p. 288. Pobedonostsev, L'autocratie russe, pp. 8-9.

30.   Chicherin, pp. 192-193. H. W. Whelan, Alexander III and the State Council, Ruthers, U.P. 1982, p. 68.

31.   Feoktistov, p. 225. Pobedonostsev, L'autocratie russe, pp. 233-234. Schweinitz, Denkwürdigkeiten, vol. 2, p. 217.

32. Cf. Florinsky, vol. 2, 1089-1090; GP, vol. 5, nos. 989, 990; HvB, no. 101; Miliutin, vol. 4, p. 106; Polovtsov, vol. 1, pp. 193, 461-462.

33. MV, 1881, no. 341.

34. A. Kizevetter, Na rubezhe dvukh stoletii, Praha 1929, p. 157.

35. RV, 250, 1897, pp. 6ff.

36. RS, 144, 1910, pp. 396-397.

37. Cf. Zaionchkovskii, Rossiiskoe samoderzhavie, pp. 53ff.

38. MV, 1880, no. 36; 1881, nos. 79, 99-A, 104, 105, 115-B, 116, 119, 126; RV, 159, 1882, p. 930; 250, 1897, pp. 27ff. See also Thaden, Conservative Nationalism, pp. 53ff.; Tvardovskaia, Ideologiia, pp. 201-202.

39. MV, 1881, no. 138.

40. Chicherin, p. 178.

41. Whelan, p. 20.

42. F. Toutain, Alexandre III et la République Française, Paris 1929, p. 53.

43. Cf. Meshcherskii, vol. 2, pp. 99-100.

44. MV, 1881, no. 99-A.

45. Skazkin, p. 183.

46. KA, 46, 1931, p. 180. Dnevnik V. N. Lamzdorfa 1891-1892, Moskva 1934, p. 269. Skazkin, p. 189.

47. Meshcherskii, vol. 3, pp. 138-139.

48. Vite, vol. 1, p. 411.

49. Cf. P. A. Zaionchkovskii, Samoderzhavie i russkaia armiia na rubezhe XIX-XX stoletii, Moskva 1973, p. 39.

50. Bülow, vol. 4, pp. 577-578. GP, vol. 5, nos. 979, 990. Holstein Papers, vol. 3, p. 170.

51. Miliutin, vol. 3, p. 251.

52. Bülow, vol. 4, p. 565.

53. Polovtsov, vol. 1, pp. 79, 102.

54. GP, vol. 3, no. 617. HvB, no. 280. Schweinitz, Briefwechsel, p. 197.

55. Windelband, p. 526.

56. In the literature on Pobedonostsev, opinions are at substantial variance. Byrnes pictures the Director General as a man of peace, while M. C. Wren ("Pobedonostsev and Russian influence in the Balkans, 1881-1887," Journal of Modern History, 19, 1947, pp. 130ff.) as an extremist.

In fact, his attitudes may be described as close to those of the Tsar. Like him, he underwent a profound change during the Turkish war and became at least partly "cured of his infatuation with the stormy and aggressive doctrine of Panslavism." (Byrnes, pp. 129-131, 134.) In crucial moments, when peace was at stake, he opposed risky solutions. On the other hand, he was heavily involved in the Volunteer Fleet scheme and during the whole reign of Alexander III stayed a source of inspiration for anti-Austrain policies. Considering the Dual Monarchy a "mortal enemy" and furthering Orthodox Church interests, he was also entangled in subversive activities, particularly in Galicia and Ruthenia. Moreover, he had always viewed "the situation abnormal that Russia does not rule the Straits." Since 1885, his assistance to Katkov in the reversal of Giers' policies was probably of paramount significance. (Cf. Pobedonostsev, L'autocratie russe, pp. 376-277; Pisma Pobedonostseva, vol. 1, pp. 64-65, 354-356; Pobedonostsev i ego korrespondenty, vol. 2, pp. 87-88; Dnevnik V. N. Lamzdorfa, 1886-1890, Moskva 1926, p. 36; Schweinitz, Denkwürdigkeiten, vol. 2, pp. 274-276, 301.)

Notes to Chapter 22

1. FO 181-647, nos. 462, 463, 466, 472, 487. Windelband, pp. 294ff., 325ff.

2. V. M. Khvostov, Problema zakhvata Bosfora v 90-kh godakh XIX veka, Istorik-marksist, *20,* 1930, p. 102.

3. MV, 1881, no. 265.

4. MV, 1881, nos. 219, 224-B, 233, 237, 249, 253.

5. MV, 1881, nos. 246, 257.

6. MV, 1881, no. 298-B.

7. MV, 1881, no. 298-B; 1882, nos. 14, 59, 79-B. Cf. also FO 65-1115, no. 547; Ch. Jelavich, Tsarist Russia and Balkan Nationalism, Univ. of California Press 1958, pp. 162ff.

8. FO 181-647, no. 642.

9. Pobedonostsev, L'autocratie russe, pp. 98-99. Jelavich, Tsarist Russia, pp. 178-179.

10. MV, 1881, nos. 301, 327; 1882, nos. 19, 31, 55, 64, 69, 72-A, 75-A, 102-A. Miliutin, vol. 4, p. 106. Windelband, p. 349.

11. Aksakov, vol. 1, p. 409. FO 78-3413, nos. 24, 34; FO 78-3414,

no. 50. Ch. Jelavich, The Revolt in Bosnia-Hercegovina, SEER, *31,* 1952, pp. 430ff. Skazkin, pp. 209-212.

12.   Jelavich, Revolt, p. 435. Peretts, p. 116. Skazkin, p. 209.

13.   Feoktistov, p. 379.

14.   From Serfdom to Bolshevism. The memoirs of Baron N. Wrangel, 1847-1920, London 1927, pp. 154-156.

15.   Cf. Knorring, vol. 2, p. 217.

16.   Knorring, vol. 2, p. 200. Valev, Dnevnik 1877-1884, p. 170.

17.   Baddeley, pp. 126-127. RA, *51:1,* 1913, p. 104.

18.   According to Tiutcheva, wife of Aksakov, her husband cautioned the General that "the government would have to denounce him in order to avoid open hostility with Germany"; that the country "was afraid of war, having not forgotten the terrible disappointment of the Berlin peace." She alleged that Skobelev had never "opened himself to my husband completely" and that the "pact" to bring about a "Russo-French anti-German coalition" had been struck only between him and Ignatiev, and even hinted that Katkov, who at the critical time visited St. Petersburg, might have been the partner in the "intrigue." (Tiutcheva, vol. 2, pp. 231-232.) But all the other testimonies differ from this explanation. They point, on the contrary, to a well-coordinated action of the triumvirate: while Skobelev and Aksakov made a public showing, Ignatiev remained true to his standard position of a back-stage schemer. (Cf. FO 181-651/1, no. 138. Knorring, vol. 2, pp. 224ff. Valuev, Dnevnik 1877-1884, pp. 183, 187.) This does not exclude a possibility of a particular Ignatiev-Skobelev "pact" but, on the other hand, Katkov is nowhere mentioned. Indeed, any participation of the Moscow editor appears highly improbable. Then, his interpretation of the Russian national interest was not at all identical with that in 1866-1871, and, as it will be shown, he was soon to attack fiercely the Interior Minister as well as the "intriguers" concept.

19.   O. M. (Olga Novikova), Skobelev and the Slavonic Cause, London 1883, pp. 253ff. Knorring, vol. 2, pp. 224-225.

20.   KA, *27,* 1928, pp. 219-220. Knorring, vol. 2, pp. 229ff. Novikova, Skobelev, pp. 283ff.

21.   Manfred, Vneshniaia politika, p. 305. Nolde, pp. 279ff. Tiutcheva, vol. 2, p. 232.

22.   DDF-I, vol. 4, nos. 260, 276. GP, vol. 3, nos. 548, 604. Schweinitz, Denkwürdigkeiten, vol. 2, pp. 183ff. Cf. also H. Herzfeld, Bismarck

und die Skobelew Episode, HZ, *142,* 1930, pp. 279ff.; E. R. von Rutkowski, General Skobelev, die Krise des Jahres 1882 und die Anfänge der militärischen Vereinbarungen zwischen Oesterreich-Ungarn und Deutschland, Ostdeutsche Wissenschaft, *10,* 1862, pp. 127ff.

23. Knorring, vol. 2, pp. 234ff. Peretts, p. 125. RS, *136,* 1908, p. 234.

24. FO 181-653/1, nos. 66, 84, 101, 138. Baddeley, pp. 131-132. IsV, *8,* 1882, pp. 157ff. Jelavich, Revolt, pp. 429-430. KA, *27,* 1928, p. 222. Schweinitz, Denkwürdigkeiten, vol. 2, pp. 182-185. De Vogüé, p. 294. Windelband, p. 359. Valuev, Dnevnik 1877-1884, pp. 186ff.

25. Pobedonostsev, L'autocratie russe, p. 91. Valuev, Dnevnik 1877-1884, pp. 183-184.

26. KA, *58,* 1933, p. 69. MV, 1882, nos. 47, 48, 51-B, 57-A, 76.

27. MV, 1882, (11./23.3.), no. 71. Cf. also Baddeley, p. 127.

28. MV, 1882, nos. 91, 95, 105-B, 108, 146-B, 155-B. Cf. also FO 181-656, no. 39.

29. Thornton to Granville, 24.4.1882; FO 181-653/1, no. 138. Cf. also Schweinitz, Denkwürdigkeiten, vol. 2, pp. 197-198.

30. Bogdanovich, p. 61. Feoktistov, pp. 200, 203. FO 181-653/1, nos. 124, 128. Meshcherskii, vol. 3, pp. 28ff. 88. Peretts, pp. 107, 125. Valuev, Dnevnik 1877-1884, pp. 174, 183-184, 186-187, 199. Zaionchkovskii, Krizis samoderzhaviia, pp. 379ff.

31. Pobedonostsev, L'autocratie russe, pp. 234-235.

32. Cf. RA, *51:1,* 1913, pp. 93ff.

33. Feoktistov, pp. 204ff. Pobedonostsev i ego korrespondenty, vol. 1, pp. 261-263. Dnevnik A. S. Suvorina, Moskva 1923. Zaionchkovskii, Krizis samoderzhaviia, pp. 439ff.

34. Pisma Pobedonostseva, vol. 1, pp. 379-381.

35. MV, 1882, no. 99.

36. MV, 1882, nos. 129, 130. See also MV, 1882, nos. 141-A, 147-B. Tvardovskaia, Ideologiia, pp. 214ff.; Valuev, Dnevnik 1877-1884, p. 438; Zaionchkovskii, Krizis samoderzhavia, pp. 451ff.

37. Feoktistov, pp. 209-210. Meshcherskii, vol. 3, pp. 93ff. Peretts, pp. 137-138.

38. MV, 1882, no. 152. The "A is equal to A" editorial created a sensation. The copy containing it was sold and resold for an exorbitant price, 2-3 rubles and more. (Tvardovskaia, Ideologiia, p. 222.)

39.   Feoktistov, pp. 211-213, 218. Tvardovskaia, Ideologiia, pp. 222-224. Vozhd reaktsii, p. 23.

40.   Knorring, vol. 2, p. 263. Cf. also RA, *51:1*, 1913, p. 188.

41.   Knorring, vol. 2, p. 275.

42.   Skobelev himself had already seen his chances only outside Russia. Another madcap plan, maturing in his venturesome mind, was centered in the Balkans. He decided to sell his vast landed property and with the money obtained—one million rubles, a very substantial sum in those days—to depart for Bulgaria. There, assisted by Prince Alexander, he wanted to initiate the final Slavic "liberation crusade," by a drive into Eastern Rumelia or Macedonia; in that way, a new Eastern crisis was to be reopened and St. Petersburg forced to abandon its "anti-national" course. (Knorring, vol. 2, p. 264. Cf. also Schweinitz, Denkwürdigkeiten, vol. 2, pp. 182-183.)

43.   Bülow, vol. 4, p. 564.

Notes to Chapter 23

1.   RA, *51:1*, 1913, p. 188.

2.   In describing the reaction prevalent under Alexander III, the literature has put a wrong emphasis on police repression instead of the overall mood dominating both the elite and the public. In fact, because of changed atmosphere and disarray in the revolutionary camp, there was much less punishment for acts connected with politics than in the previous period. The security apparatus remained—especially if compared with standards of our time—surprisingly miniscule. The entire gendarme corps counted in 1880 6800 men, in 1890 9400 men. In St. Petersburg, the ill-famed "Okhrana" had in 1883 only twelve regular, full-time employees, in Moscow six. The same may be said about the censorship, however heavy it might have appeared to contemporaries. In the 1880s, more than 95 million copies of books and journals were imported to Russia from the West; of them less than 10,000 were prohibited. (Cf. Zaionchkovskii, Rossiiskoe samoderzhavie, pp. 158ff., 301.)

3.   Byrnes, p. 358. Pisma Pobedonostseva, vol. 1, p. 150, 229; vol. 2, pp. 487, 493 etc.

4.   Schweinitz to Bismarck, 30.3.1887; AA, 1887, A 4189. Feoktistov, p. 252. Polovtsov, vol. 1, p. 461. Whelan, p. 71.

5. Feoktistov, pp. 211-213. Polovtsov, vol. 2, p. 6. Soloviev, pp. 107-108. Wittram, p. 335. Cf. also GP, vol. 5, no. 990.

6. Meshcherskii, vol. 3, pp. 232-235, 277-278. Soloviev, pp. 181ff. Zaionchkovskii, Rossiiskoe samoderzhavie, pp. 71-72, 368ff.

7. Chicherin, pp. 207ff. Meshcherskii, vol. 3, pp. 60ff. Miliutin, vol. 4, pp. 120, 137. Tvardovskaia, Ideologiia, pp. 256-257. Zaionchkovskii, Rossiiskoe samoderzhavie, pp. 70-71, 85, 309-311.

8. Polovtsov, vol. 1, p. 461.

9. MV, 1882, nos. 162, 174, 182, 220, 222. Tvardovskaia, Ideologiia, pp. 252ff.

10. Valuev, Dnevnik, 1877-1884, p. 479. Tvardovskaia, Ideologiia, pp. 256-257.

11. For the details of the whole dispute see Pobedonostsev, L'autocratie russe, pp. 283ff.; Polovtsov, vol. 1, p. 127ff., vol. 2, pp. 15ff.; G. I. Shchetinina, Universitety v Rossii i ustav 1884 goda, Moskva 1976; Sinel, pp. 112ff.; Zaionchkovskii, Krizis samoderzhaviia, pp. 276ff.; Rossiiskoe samoderzhavie, pp. 314ff.

12. Chicherin, p. 208.

13. "Zagrobnye zapiski," published by G. E. Snow as "The Years 1881-1884 in Russia: A Memorandum found in the papers of N. Kh. Bunge," Transactions of the American Philosophical Society, 71, pt. 6, Philadelphia 1981.

14. Ibid., p. 24.

15. Ibid., p. 37.

16. Ibid., p. 34.

17. Cf. Byrnes, pp. 75ff.; Thaden, Russification, pp. 56ff. Unfortunately, the Manasein report is available only in Latvian, in A. Dzirulis, Manaseina revizijä, Riga 1949.

18. Thaden, Russification, pp. 154-155.

19. Cf. Byrnes, pp. 303ff.; Polovtsov, vol. 1, pp. 353-354, vol. 2, pp. 60-61, 64, 473-474 etc.; Thaden, Russification, pp. 67ff., 161ff.

20. For the most important editorials on national economic policy themes in the 1880's see MV, 1880, nos. 175, 196, 296, 355, 356-A, 362; 1882, nos. 56, 63, 276; 1884, nos. 8-B, 77, 96, 100, 107, 110, 123, 124-B, 126, 135, 144, 148-A, 155, 157, 170, 185, 262; 1885, nos. 35, 52, 77, 98-A, 183; 1886, nos. 141, 183, 196; 1887, nos. 14, 16, 147.

21. MV, 1867, no. 24; 1869, nos. 260, 276; 1874, nos. 146, 147; 1875, nos. 61, 62. Cf. also Tvardovskaia, Ideologiia, pp. 74-81.

22. MV, 1884, no. 214. Cf. also 1882, nos. 92, 99; 1883, nos. 42, 188, 205, 251, 257.

23. Cf. MV, 1879, nos. 53, 90, 92, 97, 99; 1880, nos. 35, 46-B, 56, 71, 99-A, 113, 120, 129, 182; 1882, nos. 72-B, 90, 141, 161; 1883, nos. 51, 54, 88, 109, 174; 1884, nos. 93, 123, 126, 131, 213, 232, 271, 330, 341, 342, 346; 1885, nos. 146, 161, 243, 266; 1886, no. 73; 1887, nos. 41, 119.

24. Cf. Kennan, pp. 223ff.; Müller-Link, pp. 209ff., 268ff.; Pisma Pobedonostseva, vol. 2, p. 166; Polovtsov, vol. 1, pp. 352, 413, 424; *RS*, *86*, 1896, pp. 214-215; Soloviev, p. 179; V. Ia. Laverychev, Krupnaia burzhuaziia v poreformennoi Rossii (1861-1890), Moskva, 1974, pp. 169ff.

25. Zaionchkovskii, Rossiiskoe samoderzhavie, pp. 66ff.

26-27. Pobedonostsev, L'autocratie, pp. 306-307; cf. also Polovtsov, vol. 1, pp. 179-180, 197, 216, 218.

28. Whelan, p. 12. Cf. also ibid., pp. 38ff., 84-87, 107ff.

29. MV, 1882, nos. 30, 44, 116, 119; 1883, nos. 3, 44, 55, 99, 100; 1884, nos. 12, 26, 39, 112, 280, 353. Tvardovskaia, Ideologiia, pp. 243ff.

30. Polovtsov, vol. 1, p. 217.

31. Polovtsov, vol. 1, pp. 322-324. Whelan, pp. 159ff. Zaionchkovskii, Rossiiskoe samoderzhavie, pp. 243ff.

32. For Katkov's campaign see MV, 1885, nos. 46, 60, 110, 113, 164, 234, 254, 262; 1886, nos. 24, 174, 217; Tvardovskaia, Ideologiia, pp. 232ff.

33. Feoktistov, pp. 220-221. Pisma Pobedonostseva, vol. 2, pp. 105-106. Polovtsov, vol. 2, pp. 154ff. Soloviev, p. 165ff. Whelan, pp. 171ff. Zaionchkovskii, Rossiiskoe samoderzhavie, pp. 71-72, 92ff., 366ff.

34. Feoktistov, p. 222.

35. Polovtsov, vol. 1, p. 263.

36. Pobedonostsev, L'autocratie russe, pp. 233-234.

Notes to Chapter 24

1. FO 181-642, no. 199. GP, vol. 3, no. 527. Müller-Link, p. 210. Schweinitz, Denkwürdigkeiten, vol. 2, pp. 167-168.

2. Wittram, pp. 334, 337-338.

3. Cf. HvB, no. 283.

4. Polovtsov, vol. 1, pp. 52, 70, 72 etc.

5. FO 181-651/1, nos. 145, 154, 287. Polovtsov, vol. 1, pp. 29-30. Schweinitz, Briefwechsel, pp. 360ff.

6. Kartsov, Sem let, p. 103-104, 143-145. Schweinitz, Denkwürdig- keiten, vol. 2, pp. 297-298.

7. FO 181-653/1, nos. 153, 154.

8. Holstein Papers, vol. 2, pp. 15-16.

9. Cf. FO 181-653/1, nos. 157, 165, 218, 289.

10. Schweinitz, Denkwürdigkeiten, vol. 2, p. 436.

11. MV, 1882, no. 122; see also nos. 190-B, 193.

12. MV, 1882, nos. 204, 207, 215, 216-A, 218, 221, 227-B, etc.

13. MV, 1882, no. 178; see also RV, *160,* 1882, p. 434.

14. MV, 1882, no. 201-B; see also nos. 190-B, 195.

15. As long as Prince Lobanov had been in charge of the mission on the Golden Horn, its hawkish personnel had had not much chance to con- tinue the sort of activities they were accustomed to during the "vice-Sul- tanship" of Ignatiev. Lobanov called them with disrespect "those gentle- men who wish to be in charge of taking Constantinople," and they dubbed him en revanche "the pig with a scull-cap." With his successor Novikov, the well-known anti-Panslav, they fared not much better. The Ambassador used to shout at Turkish ministers as if they were his servants, but would not be a party to any intrigue. "In Constantinople there is no more a Rus- sian policy, there is only one, European policy," he blasphemed. Nelidov, a diplomat from the Ignatievian stable, with excellent position at Court and trusted by Alexander, however, brought the impatient warhorses fresh promises. His dispatches, wrote their leader Iurii Kartsov, a disciple of Kat- kov (not to be confused with his uncle, the former Consul General in Bel- grade), "perfectly corresponded with our views." (Kartsov, Sem let, pp. 4ff., 41, 72ff., 88ff.)

16. The text see in KA, *46,* 1931, pp. 179ff.

17. KA, *46,* 1931, p. 182.

18. Kartsov, Sem let, p. 166. Polovtsov, vol. 1, p. 31.

19. According to his memoir of 25 December 1881, two groups of states should be created: in the eastern Balkans, Rumania, Bulgaria and Serbia under Russian protectorate, with "Constantinople in our hands"; in the west, Montenegro, Albania, Macedonia and Greece under Austrian supremacy. (Skazkin, pp. 186-188.)

20. All the time, the publicist did not stop haranguing his readers against the Dual Monarchy, "a tottering state in its internal contradictions," hostile to Russia and the Slavs. (MV, 1882, no. 335-B; see also nos. 190-B, 200, 213, 228, 245, 251, 262, 267, 274, 277-A, 288-A, 297-B, 300, 305, 306.) Also his attitude to the Bismarckian system, after the Skobelev incident had ceased to be topical news, switched back to the usual tones. The November visit of Giers in Varzin and Berlin, designed to put the relations on better footing, prompted him to a warning against Austro-German intimity and to a repetition of the standard free-hand formula that "Russia has no reason to be the third in this alliance." (MV, 1882, no. 335-A; see also nos. 260, 266, 276, 291, 313, 347, 348, 353.)

21. MV, 1882, no. 362.

22. GP, vol. 3, no. 599; see also nos. 574, 605, 608, 609, 611.

23. Canis, pp. 114-115. GP, vol. 3, nos. 600-604. Müller-Link, pp. 239ff. Windelband, pp. 434ff., 447ff., 459-460.

24. Cf. Pobedonostsev, L'autocratie russe, pp. 254-258; Polovtsov, vol. 1, pp. 31, 52-53, 61, 177 etc.

25. Cf. Müller-Link, pp. 210ff. For Katkov's alarming comments see MV, 1883, nos. 47, 48, 63 etc.

26. Polovtsov, vol. 1, p. 21.

27. Kartsov, Sem let, pp. 136-138, 149-150, 163-165.

28. MV, 1883, nos. 111, 116, 117.

29. MV, 1883, nos. 71, 74, 245, 335-A. Alexander echoed Katkov, when the Prince of Montenegro visited St. Petersburg. "I drink to the only ally of Russia," he said in a toast. (Lukashevich, Aksakov, pp. 131-132.)

30. MV, 1883, nos. 1, 14, 27, 33, 36, 43, 61, 65-A, 69-B, 84-B, etc.

31. Skazkin, pp. 188-189.

32. Ibid., pp. 336-338.

33. Goriainov, The End of the Alliance, pp. 324-326. Kumpf-Korfes, pp. 45-47.

34. Kartsov, Sem let, pp. 164-165.

35. Ibid., p. 197.

Notes to Chapter 25

1. Jelavich, Tsarist Russia, p. 63. S. Radev, Stroitelite na savremenna Balgariia, Sofia 1911, vol. 1, p. 155.

2. Dostoevsky, vol. 2, pp. 897-901.

3. S. S. Tatischchev, Iz proshlago russkoi diplomatii, St. Petersburg 1890, p. 372. Cf. also Black, pp. 145ff.; R. J. Crampton, Bulgaria 1878-1918, Columbia U.P., 1983, pp. 27ff.

4. Corti, The Downfall, p. 258.

5. Saburov, p. 128. Cf. also FO 78-3117, no. 4; OBTI, vol. 3, no. 226; Jelavich, Tsarist Russia, pp. 52ff.

6. MV, 1880, nos. 1, 22.

7. Miliutin, vol. 3, p. 220.

8. Miliutin, vol. 3, pp. 205, 209-210, 213. Skazkin, pp. 230-232.

9. Black, pp. 156ff.; Crampton, pp. 35ff.; E. C. Corti, Alexander v. Battenberg, London 1954, pp. 81ff.; A. G. Drandar, Le Prince Alexandre de Battenberg en Bulgarie, Paris 1884, pp. 53ff.; Jelavich, Tsarist Russia, pp. 45ff.; A. Koch, Prince Alexander of Battenberg, London 1887, pp. 64-65; Matveev, pp. 121ff.; Miliutin, vol. 3, pp. 189ff., 209ff.; Radev, vol. 1, pp. 189ff.; Skazkin, pp. 228ff.

10. Corti, The Downfall, p. 270; Alexander, p. 65. See also Black, pp. 187ff.; FO 78-3308, nos. 11, 25-27, 40-42; Jelavich, Tsarist Russia, pp. 75ff.; Koch, pp. 87ff.; Radev, vol. 1, pp. 263ff.; RS, 52, 1886, pp. 475ff.; Skazkin, pp. 238ff.

11. MV, 1881, nos. 105, 116, 163-A, 168. Cf. also MV, 1881, nos. 133, 148, 195, 215; Aksakov, vol. 1, p. 324ff.; Jelavich, Tsarist Russia, pp. 84ff.; Koch, p. 79; Radev, vol. 1, p. 276.

12. Skazkin, pp. 248-249. Cf. also Black, pp. 198ff.; Corti, Alexander, pp. 66-67; Crampton, pp. 52ff.; FO 78-3007, nos. 39-43, FO 78-3008, no. 49, 78-3009, nos. 69, 70, 79, 82, 108-116; Matveev, pp. 148ff.; Radev, vol. 1, pp. 283ff., pp. 485ff.

13. Skazkin, pp. 251-252. Cf. also Kartsov, Sem let, pp. 138ff.

14. The Berlin Treaty stipulated that the Principality was to take over the railroad obligations of the Porte on its territory. These pertained above all to the Austrian interests related to the concession of Baron Hirsh, which entitled them to build a line connecting Constantinople with their railroad network. The claim presented an extremely serious problem of economic competition for Russia, because, as Jomini put it, she had "nothing to sell or buy in Bulgaria." The hawks demanded that not only should Vienna be prevented from enforcing its right, but a strategic railway be constructed instead, running from Ruse or Sistova to Tarnovo and Sofia, which could be used for transportation of troops in case another

drive to the Straits became acute. As representatives of the Russian financial group engaged in the scheme (Günzburg, resp. Günzburg-Poliakov group), General Struve emerged on the Bulgarian scene. (Jelavich, Tsarist Russia, pp. 66ff.; Skazkin, pp. 261ff.; E. Statelova, Diplomatiia na kniazhestvo Balgariia 1879-1886, Sofia 1978, pp. 43ff.)

15. Corti, Alexander, pp. 121-122; Jelavich, Tsarist Russia, pp. 95ff.; Kartsov, Sem let, pp. 140ff. Cf. also Black, pp. 210ff.; Crampton, pp. 59ff.; FO 78-3413, no. 8; Radev, vol. 1, pp. 311ff.; Skazkin, pp. 251ff.

16. FO 78-3413, nos. 24, 34; 78-3414, no. 50. D. Marinov, Stefan Stambolov i noveishata ni istoriia, Sofia 1909, pp. 181ff. Radev, vol. 1, pp. 339ff.

17. Aksakov, vol. 1, pp. 447-449. FO 78-3413, nos. 17, 40, 43, 47. A. F. Golowine, Fürst Alexander von Bulgarien, Wien 1896, pp. 192-193; MV, 1882, no. 126; Jelavich, Tsarist Russia, pp. 101-102; Skazkin, pp. 280-281.

18. Black, pp. 220-221; Radev, vol. 1, pp. 343ff.

19. Skazkin, p. 184n.

20. Sobolev himself estimated the construction costs for the Ruse-Sofia railway at 42 million francs, compared with 18 million for the Tsaribrod-Vakarel line. (L. N. Sobolev, K noveishei istorii Bolgarii, RS, 51, 1886, pp. 726-727.)

21. Jelavich, Tsarist Russia, pp. 106-108; Statelova, pp. 65-66. Skazkin, pp. 285ff. RS, 51, 1886, pp. 707ff.

22. Cf. Black, pp. 229ff.; Crampton, pp. 63ff.; Jelavich, Tsarist Russia, pp. 108ff.; Matveev, pp. 117ff.; Radev, vol. 1, pp. 365ff.; RS, 51, 1886, pp. 711ff.; A. N. Shcheglov, Russkoe ministerstvo v Bolgarii, IsV, 126, 1911, pp. 569ff.

23. FO 78-3414, nos. 72, 97; IsV, 126, 1911, pp. 587ff. Jelavich, Tsarist Russia, p. 116. Skazkin, p. 292.

24. Koch, pp. 135-137. See also IsV, 126, 1911, pp. 569-570; RS, 51, 1886, pp. 713ff.

25. K. Irechek, Balgarski devnik, vol. 2, Sofia 1934, p. 381. See also Black, p. 233; IsV, 126, 1911, p. 574; Radev, vol. 1, pp. 373-374.

26. RS, 52, 1886, pp. 724ff.

27. Corti, Alexander, pp. 79-80.

28. Corti, Alexander, pp. 83-84. Kartsov, Sem let, pp. 140ff. Schweinitz, Denkwürdigkeiten, vol. 2, pp. 235-236.

29.   MV, 1883, nos. 74, 151.

30.   Corti, Alexander, p. 87. Cf. also Corti, The Downfall, p. 288; Golowine, pp. 235-236.

31.   RS, *51*, 1886, pp. 733ff. Cf. also Black, pp. 236-237; IsV, *126*, 1911, p. 578; Tatishchev, Iz proshlago, pp. 328-329.

32.   The process of division in the Liberal ranks which had set out soon after the coup now entered an acute stage. Whereas the "radicals" inspired by Karavelov, still regarded the Prince and the Conservativess foes with whom a compromise was impossible, the "moderates" headed by Tsankov were willing for a deal with them rather than with the Russians, if the Tarnovo constitution were reintroduced. "He who knows what the Russian officers, officials and entrepreneurs have already indulged in in Bulgaria over the last four years, can understand the opposition of the Bulgarian population. Free my country from the Russians and the whole discord will quickly cease and order be introduced everywhere," Tsankov told an Austrian journalist. On 20 August, a first provisional Conservative-Liberal understanding was achieved. (Crampton, p. 66. FO 78-3413, nos. 3, 28, 32, 35, 39, 51. Golowine, p. 210. Radev, vol. 1, pp. 399ff.)

33.   By the Austro-Bulgarian convention (April 1883), Bulgaria undertook to build the Tsaribrod-Vakarel line and complete it by October 1886. Baron Hirsch renounced his rights.

34.   Corti, Alexander, p. 90.

35.   It has been alleged that the diplomat had cherished to sympathies for the too Asiatic-conditioned "gymnasist" Sobolev and had originally intended to handle the Bulgarian crisis softly. That may well be the truth. But being a Russian chinovnik who "had always been taking (in the end) the side of his superiors," he would unhesitantly adapt his conduct to the Tsar's mood and St. Petersburg's explicit disposition aiming at Battenberg's resignation. (Black, pp. 246-247; IsV, *126*, 1911, pp. 583-584; Jelavich, Tsarist Russia, pp. 124-125; Kartsov, pp. 146-149, 153, 163ff.; Schweinitz, Denkwürdigkeiten, vol. 2, pp. 239-242; Skazkin, pp. 294, 297-299.)

36.   Kartsov, Sem let, pp. 163-164.

37.   Corti, Alexander, pp. 91-92. Jelavich, Tsarist Russia, pp. 126-127. Koch, pp. 148-149. Skazkin, pp. 302-304.

38.   Jelavich, Tsarist Russia, p. 129. Koch, pp. 149-150. Skazkin, pp. 304-305.

39.   Golowine, p. 244. Jelavich, Tsarist Russia, pp. 130-131. Koch, pp. 150-151. Skazkin, p. 310n.

40. Lascelles to Granville, 1 and 2.9.1883; FO 78-3529, nos. 68, 69.
41. FO 78-3529, no. 72. Koch, p. 153. Radev, vol. 1, pp. 402ff.
42. FO 78-3529, nos. 70, 74, 77. Koch, pp. 153-154.
43. FO 78-3529, nos. 79-82, 85. Koch, pp. 154-155. Radev, vol. 1, pp. 409ff.
44. Kartsov, Sem let, pp. 153-154.

Notes to Chapter 26

1. A. Meyendorff, ed., Correspondance diplomatique de M. de Staal (1884-1900), vol. 1, Paris 1900, pp. 14ff.
2. GP, vol. 3, no. 605.
3. Crankshaw, Bismarck, p. 389.
4. Perhaps most succintly, Kálnoky postulated his tenets in a memoir written on 18 February 1881 to Haymerle:

"Your Excellency knows my conviction that our relationship with Russia which has so far been without any real basis, and neither good nor bad, cannot be maintained (in its present form) in the long run. We just cannot change the fact that we have this colossal empire on our frontiers, and we are faced with the alternative either to co-exist with Russia, or to hurl her back into Asia. The latter, every conscious statesmen must admit, is an impossibility for Austria-Hungary, either now or in the distant future. We must therefore, co-exist. And once that is admitted, then there can be no doubt that the most vital interests of the Monarchy demand a measure of stability in our relations with the great Slav empire, just because our interests clash in the Near East, (and) precisely because Russia's political, national and religious tentacles reach across our frontiers . . . . In any agreement with Russia the danger for us lies in the fact that in working it out we do not have such great and various means at our disposal, nor powerful weapons, as the Russians are wont to use. Because of this disparity an entente à deux between us and Russia is impossible. On the other hand, the situation is now unusually favorable for a sincere attempt at an agreement, because our close alliance with Germany gives us the necessary backing." (Cf. Bridge, pp. 398-399.)

5. Bridge, pp. 134-136. Canis, pp. 85ff. Rutkowski, pp. 104-142.
6. Müller-Link, p. 250. Windelband, pp. 432-433. GP, vol. 3, no. 611.
7. Müller-Link, pp. 251-252. H. O. Meissner, ed., Denkwürdigkeiten des General-Feldmarschalls Grafen von Waldersee, vol. 1, Stuttgart 1923, pp. 222-224. Windelband, pp. 437-439.

8. HvB, no. 89. Canis, pp. 114ff. Waldersee, vol. 1, pp. 326ff.

9. Following the French annexation of Tunisia, Germany, Austria-Hungary and Italy formed the Triple Alliance (May 1882), thereby substantially broadening the Bismarckian system in its anti-French dimension.

10. GP, vol. 3, nos. 583ff., 606, 608-611, 614, 615. Windelband, pp. 465ff.; 476ff., 493.

11. Medlicott, Bismarck and the Three Emperors' Alliance, p. 80.

12. Polovtsov, vol. 1, pp. 31, 34, 39, 72, 126.

13. MV, 1883, no. 106; cf. also nos. 86, 92, 99-A, 110, 111, 116, 117, 175.

14. MV, 1883, no. 233.

15. MV, 1883, no. 279.

16. Looking for ways to please the Germans, the Moscow editor even proposed them through his proxy Cyon that they could take over the *Golos,* just closed down by censorship, as their mouthpiece in Russia. (Cf. E. de Cyon, Histoire de l'Entente franco-russe 1886-1894, Paris 1895, pp. 125-127; Kennan, p. 96.)

17. GP, vol. 3, no. 607. Hohenlohe, vol. 2, pp. 343-344. Müller-Link, pp. 253-255. Polovtsov, vol. 1, pp. 126, 131. Schweinitz, Denkwürdigkeiten, vol. 2, pp. 248-249, 258-259. Valuev, Dnevnik, 1877-1884, p. 245.

18. GP, vol. 3, no. 607.

19. Taylor, p. 293.

20. In 1890, Herbert Bismarck summarized it in a letter to Schweinitz: "When we started colonial policy, we had to face a long reign by the Crown Prince, during which English influence would predominate. In order to forestall it, he (Bismarck the Elder) had to launch a colonial policy which was popular and could produce conflict with England at any moment." (Schweinitz, Briefwechsel, p. 193. Cf. also Holstein Papers, vol. 2, p. 161.)

21. Goriainov, The End, pp. 327-328. GP, vol. 5, nos. 622-628.

22. Adlerberg asserted that public opinion and the press were powerless to enforce the extremist course and that Obruchev was a mere "fantastico and theoretician." He advised Berlin to wait patiently until the Tsar acquired more independence from nationalist pressures and more determination. Shuvalov gave similar counsels. The complications were but the residues of the past Miliutin-Gorchakov era. The only problem with the present Tsar was that he had more confidence in "that beast Katkov"

than to any minister. By "showing his teech" the Chancellor helped Giers; now it remained only to get rid of Obruchev and the anti-German hatred would "fly away as a soap-bubble." (HvB, nos. 88-101.)

23. Polovtsov, vol. 1, p. 217. Nothing is known about their conversation. Cf. also GP, vol. 3, nos. 617, 618, 620, 621, 626.

24. Holstein Papers, vol. 3, pp. 101ff. HvB, nos. 90, 100. Polovtsov, vol. 1, p. 186. Valuev, Dnevnik, 1877-1884, p. 251.

25. GP, vol. 3, nos. 615, 617-621, 626. Holstein Papers, vol. 3, pp. 66-67. Kumpf-Korfes, p. 47. Nolde, pp. 284ff. Valuev, Dnevnik, 1877-1884, pp. 251-253.

26. While more circumspect and even cringing towards Germany, the Russian press had until late 1883 conducted its anti-Austrian campaign with unextinguished virulence and created an overall impression that the sole Tsardom's aim was to break the Austro-German alliance. Also the *Moskovskiia vedomosti* persevered in depicting the Dual Monarchy as an unnatural state organism at the verge of the breakdown and at the same time as a rabid anti-Russian plotter in the Balkans. (MV, 1883, nos. 164, 175, 181-B, 196, 203, 224, 227, 229, 234, 236, 242, 245, 258, 280, 286, 290, 291, 296, 303, 305, 308, 322, 328-B, 338, 354-A.) The Vienna government was so worried by this psychological warfare that it admonished its own press to avoid polemics. (Canis, pp. 119-120.)

27. MV, 1884, nos. 1, 4.

28. MV, 1884, nos. 55, 109-A, 149, 154, 243, 255.

29. MV, 1884, no. 260.

30. MV, 1884, nos. 52, 122-A, 214.

31. MV, 1884, nos. 156, 228, 264, 319, 326, 327, 333.

Notes to Chapter 27

1. Terentiev, vol. 3, pp. 206-207.

2. MV, 1881, no. 204.

3. L. N. Sobolev, Stranitsa iz istorii vostochnogo voprosa: anglo-afganskaia raspria.

4. Sobolev, Stranitsa, p. 46. Cf. also Ch. Marvin, The Russians at Merv and Herat, London 1883, p. 73.

5. Marvin, The Russians at Merv, p. 68. Sobolev, Stranitsa, pp. 226ff.

6. Khidoiatov, pp. 406ff., 420-421. Cf. also Marvin, The Russians at Merv, pp. 212ff.; Reconnoitring Central Asia, pp. 264ff., 384ff.

7. Tikhomirov, pp. 118-119. On the "Konshin caravan" see M. A. Alikhanov-Avarskii, Zakaspiiskie vospominaniia, Vestnik Evropy, 1904, no. 9 (several of Alikhanov's articles were published in June-July 1882 in the *Moskovskiia vedomosti*); Marvin, Reconnoitring Central Asia, pp. 361ff.; The Russians at the Gates of Herat, London 1886, pp. 15ff.; Tikhomirov, pp. 111ff.

8. Lessar reported that he had found Russian influence in Teheran predominant; that "the spell of the Russian standard is powerful far away to the east"; that there is no "natural barrier at all intervening between Herat and Merv" and a "vehicle could be driven without the slightest difficulty there."

9. Greaves, pp. 60-61, 64. Cf. also O. Hoetzsch. Russisch Turkestan und die Tendenzen der russischen Kolonialpolitik, in: Osteuropa und Deutscher Osten, Königsberg 1934, pp. 152ff.; Marvin, The Russians at the Gates, pp. 52ff.; Reconnoitring Central Asia, pp. 384ff.; The Russian Railway to Herat and India, London 1883.

10. Greaves, p. 64.

11. Khalfin, Prisoedinenie, p. 360.

12. Greaves, p. 82.

13. For Katkov's comments see MV, 1884, nos. 172, 180, 190, 194, 221, 232, 301, 352.

14. MV, 1884, no. 234. RV, *169*, 1884, pp. 892ff.; *171*, 1884, pp. 550ff.; *186*, 1886, pp. 935ff. Cf. also Kumpf-Korfes, pp. 62ff.; MV, 1883, nos. 4, 9, 12-B, 25-B, 28, 30, 40.

15. MV, 1882, nos. 222, 227.

16. MV, 1882, nos. 259, 299, 302, 306-A, 308-B, 312, 314, 323, 333, 344-B, 361-B; 1883, nos. 144, 146-B. In February 1883, against desperate opposition of the Finance Ministry, which saw in it a loss of considerable revenue, the Tsar ordered the closure of the transit. (Polovtsov, vol. 1, p. 36.)

17. Kumpf-Korfes, pp. 66-67.

18. Staal, vol. 1, pp. 17-18.

19. MV, 1883, no. 144. See also 1881, no. 184; 1882, nos. 119-B, 132-A.

20. RS, *141*, 1910, pp. 646-648.

21. Cherniaev had since the debate on the army reform hated Kaufman, the rival "merchant from the Miliutin shops." He attacked the

bureaucratic-colonial system introduced by him as a misplaced attempt to administer the Uzbeks "just like inhabitants of the Moscow region," by means of "violating the natural order of things to our detriment." When installed in Tashkent, already "in sere and yellow leaf," his rancor turned into senile urge to eradicate all that reminded of his predecessor. Among the acts of that "official vandalism," the liquidation of the Tashkent public library earned him the worst possible notoriety. (MacKenzie, The Lion, pp. 109-110, 211ff.; Terentiev, vol. 3, pp. 333ff. See also Marvin's interview with Cherniaev in "The Russian advance towards India," pp. 5ff., 128ff.

22. Khalfin, Prisoedinenie, pp. 408ff. MacKenzie, The Lion, pp. 223ff. Terentiev, vol. 3, p. 340. Tikhomirov, pp. 99-100.

23. Tikhomirov, p. 114. MacKenzie, The Lion, pp. 223ff.

24. For the final stage of the Merv affair see Tikhomirov, pp. 128ff.

25. Greaves, p. 65. HvB, no. 101.

26. MV, 1884, no. 36.

27. Bilgrami, p. 205. FO 181-656, nos. 155, 175, 208, 276, 287, 297. Greaves, p. 69. Cf. also Thornton's reports to Granville in FO 65-1171 and 65-1175.

28. Greaves, pp. 62-63, 65.

29. MV, 1884, no. 48.

30. Cf. Staal, vol. 1, pp. 80-81, 91-92.

31. Staal, vol. 1, pp. 26-27.

32. HvB, no. 101.

33. Terentiev, vol. 3, p. 248.

34. MV, 1884, no. 142. Cf. also nos. 129, 183; FO 65-1203, nos. 34, 37.

35. RS, *141*, 1910, p. 652.

36. Staal, vol. 1, p. 100.

37. Staal, vol. 1, p. 25ff. Cf. also Bilgrami, pp. 205-206; Terentiev, vol. 3, p. 248.

38. Staal, vol. 1, pp. 103-108, 115.

39. Lamzdorf, Dnevnik 1886-1890, pp. 44-45. Polovtsov, vol. 1, pp. 296, 302, 304. RS, *141*, 1910, pp. 653-654. Staal, vol. 1, p. 115.

40. RS, *141*, 1910, pp. 653-656. Staal, vol. 1, pp. 116-117, 136-137, 142-143.

41. RS, *141*, 1910, pp. 655-656.

42. For the St. Petersburg scene cf. Baddeley, pp. 207ff.; Novikova, vol. 2, pp. 212ff.; Staal, vol. 1, pp. 153ff.

43. Cf. Terentiev, vol. 3, pp. 249ff.

44. Baddeley, p. 219. Cf. also GP, vol. 4, nos. 773, 774, 778.

45. Staal, vol. 1, pp. 125-126, 160-163, 189-191.

46. Novikova, vol. 2, pp. 217-219.

47. Staal, vol. 1, pp. 199-200.

48. Polovtsov, vol. 1, pp. 304-306.

49. Polovtsov, vol. 1, p. 309.

50. MV, 1885, nos. 85, 100; cf. also nos. 56, 63, 64, 71, 79, 86, 87, 89-B, 91, 92-B, 96, 104, 105, 125.

51. The Council was chaired by the Tsar; present were Vannovskii, Shestakov, Bunge, Giers, Zinoviev and Grand Dukes Vladimir and Alexei.

52. Cf. Manfred, Obrazovanie, p. 189n.

53. While the moderates had requested a court-martial for Komarov, the Tsar had praised him. "Wire to him, that I appreciate fully his deeds and dispositions and approve them entirely," he had ordered. (RS, *142*, 1910, p. 42.)

54. Polovtsov, vol. 1, p. 315; vol. 2, pp. 111, 134-135.

55. HvB, no. 151.

56. Polovtsov, vol. 1, pp. 320-321, 325. Morris, pp. 528-529, 533-534, 537-538. Due to hawkish intransigency, the haggling on the frontier delimitation dragged for many months and the final protocol was signed under entirely different conditions, as late as July 1887. (Cf. Greaves, pp. 77ff.)

57. MV, 1885, nos. 128, 185, 206; see also nos. 137, 147, 148, 162, 199, 202.

58. Byrnes, pp. 231-234.

Notes to Chapter 28

1. HvB, no. 138.

2. Cf. MV, 1885, nos. 222, 226.

3. Cf. MV, 1885, no. 347.

4. Berlin wielded strong pressure on the Porte to prevent the opening of the Straits to the British navy. German officers, instructors in the Turkish army, supervised that the fortifications of the Dardenalles be

improved ready to repel any attempted break-through. (GP, vol. 4, nos. 762-772. Radowitz, vol. 2, p. 245.) Owing to the "Crimean complex," this was considered by the Russians as a huge service delivered.

5. MV, 1884, nos. 65-B, 66, 74, 76, 83, 103, 108-B, 150, 261, 352, 354, 357, 361 etc. See also RV, *173,* 1884, pp. 434ff.; *178,* 1885, pp. 427ff.; 1881, 1886, pp. 76ff.

6. "The whole psychological structure of her people" was carrying Abyssinia "to the Orthodox Church and consequently to Russia, to her Tsar as the great protector of Orthodoxy," wrote the publicist. (Cf. MV, 1884, no. 326, 336, 344; 1885, nos. 4-B, 12-A, 49.)

7. Polovtsov, vol. 1, pp. 309-310.

8. Cf. Giers' instructions to Orlov written before the signing of the renewed Treaty, in Goriainov, The End, pp. 327-328.

9. Cf. Kumpf-Korfes, p. 49.

10. MV, 1884, no. 260.

11. Aksakov, vol. 1, pp. 581-582, 586, 591. For similar Pobedonostev's views see Schweinitz, Denkwürdigkeiten, vol. 2, pp. 274-276, 290, 301.

12. GP, vol. 3, nos. 635-637, 639, 643-647. Schaller, pp. 85-87. Windelband, pp. 578-579, 609ff.

13. The Ballplatz had to face a criticism of listlessness and "postponement of the inevitable struggle," strongly reminiscent to that voiced by the Russian extremists against the Singers' Bridge. Crown Prince Rudolf was the most auspicious among the malcontents. "Our policy has a great goal it must follow—supremacy in the European (Near) East. To attain it, we need a successful war with Russia." His father's presence at Skiernewice was for him a "Canossa," "one of Kálnoky's biggest mistakes." (B. Hamman, ed., Kronprinz Rudolf, geheime und private Schriften, Wien 1979, pp. 134, 137-138, 158-159.) Andrássy and other Hungarian leaders agreed in essentials with him.

14. HvB, no. 166. See also GP, vol. 3, nos. 634, 638, 649.

15. Cf. MV, 1885, nos. 8-A, 13-A, 15, 27, 160, 188, 210.

16. Jelavich, Tsarist Russia, pp. 138ff.; Koch, pp. 156ff.

17. Skazkin, pp. 321ff.

18. MV, 1882, no. 126.

19. MV, 1883, no. 292.

20. MV, 1883, no. 299.

21. Holstein Papers, vol. 3, p. 89.

22.   "This action, consigning as it did to these two nongovernmental figures the virtual power of appointment to senior Russian positions in Bulgaria, stands as a revealing measure of the extent to which Russian policy in the Balkans was by this time removed from the effective control of the Foreign Ministry and shaped by people who had no place in the official governmental process," Kennan observed. (Kennan, p. 110.)

23.   Black, p. 148. Golowine, pp. 261ff. Kartsov, Sem let, p. 293. Jelavich, Tsarist Russia, pp. 148-151. Koch, pp. 174, 178-180.

24.   Skazkin, p. 329.

25.   Jelavich, Tsarist Russia, p. 115. Koch, pp. 195-196n. Kartsov (Sem let, pp. 213-214) gives us a different picture.

26.   Kartsov, Sem let, p. 217. Cf. also Golowine, p. 266; Kartsov, pp. 208ff., 228ff.; Koch, pp. 196-197.

27.   Crampton, pp. 73ff. Koch, pp. 164ff. Matveev, pp. 197ff. Radev, vol. 1, pp. 424ff. Statelova, pp. 196ff.

28.   GP, vol. 3, nos. 635, 636. Schaller, pp. 84ff. Windelband, pp. 571ff.

29.   Corti, Alexander, pp. 115ff. Holstein Papers, vol. 3, pp. 86-87. Lucius v. Ballhausen, p. 293.

30.   Windelband, pp. 520ff. Cf. also Schaller, p. 74.

31.   Corti, Alexander, pp. 102, 129; The Downfall, p. 299. Wilhelm II, Aus meinem Leben 1859-1888, Berlin 1928, p. 378.

32.   Corti, Alexander, p. 131; The Downfall, pp. 296, 300-302.

33.   Cf. ARTsB, no. 1.

34.   ARTsB, nos. 2, 3.

35.   Ibid., p. 9n.

36.   Ibid., no. 3.

37.   Hajek, p. 205. Cf. also Schaller, pp. 83ff.; Statelova, pp. 204ff.

38.   Irechek, vol. 2, p. 468. Matveev, pp. 278-279.

39.   Kartsov, Sem let, p. 232. Cf. also Koch, pp. 200ff.

Notes to Chapter 29

1.   MV, 1885, no. 212. DDF-I, vol. 6, no. 57.

2.   For the Prince's account of the Franzensbad parleys see Holstein Papers, vol. 3, pp. 149ff.

3.   Jones to Granville, 11.8.1881, FO 78-3311, no. 41. Kartsov, Sem let, pp. 107ff., 119ff. Matveev, pp. 254ff., 274ff. Crampton, pp. 85ff.

4. MV, 1882, no. 186-V.
5. Kartsov, Sem let, p. 225.
6. Radev, vol. 1, p. 406.
7. Hajek, pp. 209ff. Kartsov, pp. 220ff. Schaller, pp. 76ff.
8. Hajek, pp. 212ff. Radev, vol. 1, pp. 499ff. Statelova, pp. 158ff.
9. Golowine, pp. 272ff. Jelavich, pp. 214-215. Schaller, pp. 80-81.
10. Corti, Alexander, pp. 161-165. Jelavich, Tsarist Russia, pp. 215-217. Marinov, pp. 240ff. Radev, vol. 1, pp. 521ff. Schaller, pp. 95-97.
11. In both Bulgarias, Russian military and diplomatic personnel was initially mostly carried away by the general enthusiasm of the population or acted in the way they believed to be best. The men in charge in Plovdiv, Igelström and Chichagov, seem to have played a double game. They had allegedly taken part in the decisive meeting of the revolutionary committee and signed the resolution on the coup. When the Rumelians had risen, they made only irresolute moves "to stop them in the authority of the Russian name" and then joined them openly. In full-dress uniform they appeared at the town gate to welcome the Prince and Chichagov promised to accept the position of the new Chief-of-Staff in the united armed forces. Their colleagues in Sofia, Cantacuzène, became similarly involved by counter-signing the mobilization order issued by Battenberg. (FO 78-3770, nos. 67, 76. Corti, Alexander, pp. 165-166. Radev, vol. 1, pp. 533ff., 563ff. Statelova, pp. 152-153. Tatishchev, Iz proshlago, pp. 409ff.)
In Russia too, the first response at the Singers' Bridge and in the press was contradictory. Aksakov in the *Rus* rejoiced that the Berlin Treaty was destroyed and clamoured for further "active measures" including steps to solve the Bosphorus problem. (FO 181-665, nos. 314, 319, 322, 331, 335. For Aksakov's subsequent criticism of the Tsar's and Katkov's negative position see Kartsov, Sem let, pp. 253ff.)
12. MV, 1885, nos. 250, 251.
13. FO 65-1219, no. 400. Jelavich, Tsarist Russia, pp. 218-221. Radev, vol. 1, pp. 577ff.
14. AP, 75:1, 1886, nos. 54, 77. Kartsov, Sem let, p. 353. Radev, vol. 1, p. 587. Radowitz, vol. 2, p. 253.
15. Cecil, vol. 3, pp. 136, 231, 249. GP, vol. 4, no. 784. A. Ramm, Sir Robert Morier, Oxford 1973, p. 208.
16. Cecil, vol. 3, pp. 222ff., 257ff. GP, vol. 4, nos 779-784. Greaves, app. 2, pp. 237ff.

17. Cecil, vol. 3, p. 341. Letters of Victoria, ser. 2, vol. 3, pp. 690-695. W. N. Medlicott, The Powers and the Unification of the Two Bulgarias 1885, English Historical Review, *54*, 1939, pp. 73ff. C. L. Smith, The Embassy of Sir William White at Constantinople, 1886-1891, Oxford 1957, pp. 20-21.

18. Letters of Victoria, ser. 2, vol. 3, p. 397.

19. Radev, vol. 1, pp. 566-567. Tatishchev, Iz proshlago, pp. 422.

20. Cf. HvB, no. 195. Cecil, vol. 3, p. 231.

21. MV, 1885, nos. 258, 259, 262, 269.

22. KA, *46*, 1931, pp. 180ff. Cf. also ARTsB, pp. XV-XVI.

23. Polovtsov, vol. 2, pp. 135-136.

24. HvB, no. 195. Cf. also Cyon, p. 192.

25. "Je ne veux pas la guerre, je ne veux pas non plus qu'on se fiche de nous et je ne veux pas plus que cette canaille de Battenberg aide le dessus," the Tsar put it in a conversation with Grand Duke Vladimir in all clarity. (HvB, no. 185.)

26. Polovtsov, vol. 1, p. 348.

27. MV, 1885, no. 258. In the anti-Austrian vogue, too, the publicist was not in the forefront and even praised Francis Joseph, of whom the Tsar had taken a marked liking at Kremsier. (MV, 1885, no. 290.)

28. Kennan, pp. 141-142. For the documents and discussions of the conference see AP, 1886, *75:1*.

29. Medlicott, The Powers, pp. 263-264.

30. Cf. Staal, vol. 1, pp. 262-265.

31. FO 181-665, nos. 384, 385, 387.

32. FO 181-665, no. 380. HvB, no. 203. Kartsov, Sem let, pp. 262ff. Polovtsov, vol. 1, pp. 351, 374. (The Prince was promoted to a General of Russian army in 1879.)

33. MV, 1885, no. 300.

34. FO 78-3754, no. 443. Medlicott, The Powers, pp. 273ff. Smith, pp. 24, 31.

35. Cecil, vol. 3, pp. 245, 248. Canis, pp. 140-141. GP, vol. 5, nos. 959-961. Holstein Papers, vol. 2, pp. 255, 259, 263, 269, 276, 279-280, 287. Medlicott, Powers, pp. 68-69, 75-79, 266. Radowitz, vol. 2, pp. 252-253.

36. Holstein Papers, vol. 2, pp. 267ff. HvB, no. 207.

37. Understandably, the King appealed to his Austrian protectors for assistance. "The Danubian Empire should be grateful for my enterprising

spirit," he urged on Kálnoky; "every inch of conquered Bulgarian soil is a gain for the throne of Habsburg, which is the natural heir to Serbia." The chief of the Ballplatz, equally understandably, was far from tantalized by a prospect which threatened to precipitate a major Balkan conflagration, a situation he, Bismarck and Giers alike had striven to avoid. But he could not simply dismiss the possibility that Milan, with the army mobilized and the country in keen expectancy, might be overthown by his pro-Russian opponents, if he failed to grab some spoils. The critics of the "Skiernewice-Kremsier" course, led by Andrássy and the Crown Prince, were very emphatic on that point. It was presumably in their name that Count Khevenhüller-Meč, the Minister in Belgrade, told the King that the most secure way to reach traditional Serbian objects in Macedonia and Old Serbia went "through Sofia." Hence, Kálnoky had in the end to promise his benevolence to military action, once the Constantinople conference could not find means to restore the status quo or make arrangements for compensation.

Also Bismarck confidentially assented to the contingency provided that Austrian backing for the Serbian cause would not jeopardize the Russian entente. (Corti, Alexander, pp. 170ff. GP, vol. 5, nos. 956-959, 962. Medlicott, The Powers, pp. 76-78, 264-266, 282, 283. Jelavich, Tsarist Russia, pp. 228-230. Schaller, pp. 103ff.)

38.   Cecil, vol. 3, pp. 250-251. Medlicott, The Powers, pp. 282-283.

39.   MV, 1885, nos. 259, 307; see also nos. 265, 271, 273, 274, 276, 279, 281, 285, 286, 304, 309, 310, 311-B.

40.   MV, 1885, no. 307.

41.   Radev, vol. 1, p. 615.

42.   MV, 1885, no. 311-A.

43.   FO 78-3892, nos. 36, 167. Radev, vol. 1, p. 668.

44.   For a detailed analyses of the war from the military viewpoint see H. Klaeber, Fürst Alexander von Bulgarien, Dresden 1904, pp. 173ff.; Istoriia na särbsko-bälgarskata voina 1885, Sofia 1971.

45.   AP, 1886, 75:1, no. 560. Corti, Alexander, pp. 192-193. FO 78-3771, nos. 213, 214. GP, vol. 5, nos. 956-958, 966-968.

46.   GP, vol. 5, nos. 969-972. Kumpf-Korfes, pp. 79-80. Schaller, pp. 117-120. M. Ia. Zolotukhin, Bolgarskii krizis 1885-1886 gg. i. krakh avstro-russko-germanskogo soiuza, VI, 1984, no. 4, pp. 50-51.

47.   Nolde, p. 332.

48. Corti, Alexander, pp. 193-194. Jelavich, Tsarist Russia, p. 233.
GP, vol. 5, no. 967.

49. MV, 1885, nos. 317-A, 321-B, 322-B, 324-A, 327-A, 329, 332-A.

50. FO, 181-665, no. 419; HvB, no. 209. Cf. also FO, 181-665,
no. 423; GP, vol. 5, no. 967.

51. Appointed the member of the commission supervising the Serbo-
Bulgarian truce, Kaulbars advised the Prince to lay flattering unction
on the Tsar's and Katkov's souls and pronounce publicly gratitude to the
Russian officers who had trained his army; by giving them credit for the
victory achieved, he assured, good feelings would be restored. Though
with some apprehension—such a statement must have insulted his new
Bulgarian commanders, proud of their performance—Battenberg yielded
and issued an order of the day to that effect. Then, he asked his Romanov
relative for permission to come to St. Petersburg. (FO 78-3771, nos.
212-214, 181-665, no. 438. Corti, Alexander, p. 190. Jelavich, Tsarist
Russia, pp. 237-238. Radev, vol. 1, pp. 759-760.)

52. AP, 1886, *75:2,* no 12. FO 65-1219, nos. 405-A, 435, 436;
65-1256, nos. 4, 7; 181-665, nos. 440-441; 181-681/1, no. 10. GP, vol.
4, no. 788. Corti, Alexander, pp. 203-204. Kartsov, Sem let, pp. 273ff.
Polovtsov, vol. 1, pp. 366-367.

53. Polovtsov, vol. 1, p. 367. Cf. also FO 65-1256, no. 7; 78-3892,
no. 34.

54. Cf. HvB, nos. 209, 211.

55. MV, 1886, no. 4-A. Cf. also MV, 1885, nos. 315, 321-B, 324-B;
and FO 181-665, no. 447 for Katkov's opposition to any conciliatory
effort.

56. Corti, Alexander, pp. 200-201; FO 181-665, no. 435.

Notes to Chapter 30

1. ARTsB, nos. 4-6, 8. Cf. also Kartsov, Sem let, pp. 306-307.

2. Hajek, pp. 323-324. Miliukov, p. 82. Radev, vol. 1, pp. 790-
791. For the activities of the Russians and their clientele after the Serbo-
Bulgarian war see also FO 78-3770, nos. 114-116, 119, 121, 131.

3. MV, 1886, no. 155. Cf. also nos. 62-B, 87, 159, 168, 170-A, 223.

4. Cf. A. Huhn, Aus bulgarischen Sturmzeit, Leipzig 1886, p.
68.

5. Both parts of Bulgaria were to have a similar, but not common administration. The Prince was recognized the Governor General of Eastern Rumelia for life, provided that he would "faithfully execute his duties" to the Sultan; and he was to be reappointed after five years.

6. FO 78-3892, nos. 68, 75, 78, 82-84, 88. Radev, vol. 1, pp. 758ff. Schaller, pp. 134ff.

7. Cf. FO 181-681/1, nos. 17ff.; FO 65-1254, nos. 50ff.

8. Corti, Alexander, pp. 240ff. Hajek, pp. 324-325. Jelavich, Tsarist Russia, pp. 238-239, 249.

9. FO, 78-3893, nos. 82, 84, 88, 123, 128, 142.

10. FO 78-3893, nos. 135-138, 152, 154; 181-672, nos. 206, 219. Huhn, pp. 15ff. Golowine, pp. 399ff. Jelavich, Tsarist Russia, pp. 244-245.

11. Corti, Alexander, pp. 224-225. Golowine, pp. 405-406. Marinov, pp. 277-278. Radev, vol. 1, pp. 828-829. Cf. Huhn, pp. 23ff, 59ff., 203ff.

12. ARTsB, no. 10.

13. HvB, no. 215.

14. FO 65-1258, no. 179. For the analysis of Russian press comments see FO 181-681/1, no. 100.

15. Morier to Rosebery, 29.5.1886; FO 65-1258, no. 185.

16. Morier to Rosebery, 6.4.1886; FO 65-1258, no. 136.

17. Morier to Rosebery, 25.5.1886; FO 65-1258, no. 179.

18. FO 65-1258, no. 188.

19. Greaves, pp. 105-107.

20. FO 181-672, nos. 226-231, 244-246, 252-255. Kumpf-Korfes pp. 80-81. Ramm, Morier, pp. 223-225.

21. GP, vol. 5, no 978. HvB, no. 229.

22. GP, vol. 5, no. 979.

23. ARTsB, nos. 11, 12.

24. BgB, nos. 2, 3, 6. Corti, Alexander, pp. 225ff. FO 78-3894, nos. 216, 217, 219, 221. Hajek, pp. 329ff. Kartsov, Sem let, pp. 296ff. Koch, pp. 267ff. Radev, vol. 1, pp. 799ff. Huhn, pp. 32ff., 48ff.

25. J. V. Fuller, Bismarck's Diplomacy at its Zenith, Harvard U. P. 1922, pp. 64-65. Hajek, pp. 346ff. Holstein Papers, vol. 2, pp. 300, 304-305. Radev, vol. 2, pp. 199ff. Staal, vol. 1, pp. 304-306. Schaller, pp. 143ff.

26. MV, 1886, nos. 228, 235. For the analysis of Russian press comments see FO 65-1260, nos. 296, 298.

27. FO 78-3894, nos. 217, 218, 220. Hajek, pp. 350ff. Huhn, pp. 70ff. Radev, vol. 2, pp. 40ff.

28. Koch, p. 254.

29. Cf. ARTsB, nos. 11, 12; cf. also ARTsB, p. 19n.; Jelavich, Tsarist Russia, p. 249.

30. ARTsB, no. 14. Jelavich, Tsarist Russia, pp. 252-253. Radev, vol. 2, pp. 10-12, 17-18. S. Goriainov, Razryv Rossii s Bolgariei v 1886 godu, IsV, *147*, 1914, p. 187.

31. FO 78-3894, nos. 218, 221. Hajek, pp. 365ff. IsV, *147*, 1917, pp. 187-188. Radev, vol. 2, pp. 133ff.

32. IsV, *147*, 1917, pp. 188-189.

33. Corti, Alexander, pp. 194, 226ff. FO 65-1261, no. 314. IsV, *63*, 1896, pp. 933ff. Radev, vol. 2, pp. 177-178.

34. Corti, Alexander, pp. 235-236.

35. AA, 1887, A 2063. Kartsov, Sem let, pp. 259-260.

36. Corti, Alexander, pp. 237-239. FO 78-3894, nos. 223-225, 227, 229, 233-235, 237; 65-1261, nos. 306, 308-311, 329. Koch, p. 277. Radev, vol. 2, pp. 216-217.

37. Corti, Alexander, p. 240. Cyon, p. 158. IsV, *147*, 1917, p. 190. Kartsov, Sem let, p. 320. Polovtsov, vol. 1, p. 443.

38. MV, 1886, no. 235. For Russian press comments see FO 65-1261, nos. 322-323.

39. Corti, Alexander, pp. 241, 244. FO 78-3894, nos. 229, 230, 233, 237-239. IsV, 147, 1917, p. 193. Marinov, p. 309. Radev, vol. 2, pp. 227-228, 253.

40. Cf. IsV, *147*, 1917, pp. 192-193; Jelavich, Tsarist Russia, pp. 259-261; Radev, vol. 2, p. 255.

41. Radev, vol. 2, pp. 270-271.

42. Iddlesleigh to Morier, 20.9.1886; FO 65-1255, no. 219a. Kartsov has claimed in his memoirs that it was him who had persuaded Bogdanov to withhold the pledge. (Kartsov, Sem let, pp. 309ff.)

43. Cf. IsV, *147*, 1917, pp. 192-193.

44. Kartsov, Sem let, pp. 299ff.

45. Morier to Iddlesleigh, 15.9.1886; FO 65-1261, no. 331.

46. MV, 1886, nos. 23, 25, 43, 87; cf. also nos. 37-B, 40, 43, 45-B, 70, 72, 83-A.

47. MV, 1886, no. 3.

48.   MV, 1886, no. 181-A.

49.   MV, 1886, no. 223.

50.   This was also the reason for his somewhat ambiguous comments on Austrian policy: while peremptorily demeaning when dealing with its Balkan ramifications, he simultaneously suggested that if liberated from "alien" (i.e. German) mediation, it may attain an advantageous modus vivendi with Tsardom; no danger threatened the Dual Monarchy from the East, he assured, once she did not interefere in the Russian sphere. (MV, 1886, no. 205. On the "League of peace" theme see also nos. 208, 212-B, 214, 215, 243-B; FO 181-672, no. 274.)

51.   Cyon, pp. 129-130.

52.   Kennan, pp. 155ff. Manfred, Vneshniaia politika, pp. 370ff.; Obrazovanie, pp. 195-197. Toutain, pp. 24ff., 73ff.

53.   Cyon, pp. 141ff. Kennan, pp. 173-175.

54.   MV, 1886, no. 190. Canis, pp. 161-162. Kennan, pp. 171-172. Toutain, pp. 103ff.

55.   MV, 1886, no. 197. Cf. also Kennan, pp. 177ff.; Nolde, pp. 340ff.

56.   Holstein Papers, vol. 2, pp. 279-280.

57.   Ibid., p. 314.

58.   Cf. GP, vol. 5, nos. 977-980. Kumpf-Korfes, pp. 89ff. Nolde, pp. 345ff.

59.   AP, 1887, *91:1*, nos. 247, 257, Crampton, pp. 115ff. Corti, Alexander, p. 247. Radev, vol. 2, pp. 267ff. Schaller, pp. 147-149.

60.   Morier to Iddlesleigh, 11.9.1886; FO 65-1261, no. 234.

61.   FO 65-1260, nos. 302, 316. MV, 1886, nos. 242, 246, 250. Kartsov, Sem let, pp. 322ff. Radev, vol. 2, pp. 288, 317.

62.   AP, 1887, 91:1, no. 357. GP, vol. 5, nos. 987, 988, 995. Holstein Papers, vol. 3, p. 178. Kartsov, Sem let, pp. 292-293. DDF-I, vol. 6, no. 312. Tatishchev, Iz proshlago, p. 468.

63.   Kartsov, Sem let, p. 152. See also Jelavich, Tsarist Russia, pp. 263ff.; Kartsov, pp. 324ff.; Radev, vol. 2, pp. 333ff.; Schaller, pp. 149ff.

64.   Miliukov, pp. 92-93. The former Liberal-Conservative division lost all its importance. The majority of the radical Liberals (Stambolov, Radoslavov, Zakhari Stoianov), a group earlier wide open to Russian manipulations because of their anti-Prince predilections, now stood at the helm of the nationalist forces.

65. ARTsB, no. 16.

66. AP, 1887, *91:1*, no. 369. ARTsB, no. 20. FO 78-3894, nos. 266, 269, 270; 78-3895, nos. 273, 274.

67. Huhn, pp. 219ff. Radev, pp. 352-354. FO 78-3895, nos. 271, 275, 277.

69. FO 78-3895, nos. 282, 285, 290, 293, 297, 305, 314, 315. Kartsov, Sem let, pp. 330ff.

70. AP, 1887, 91:1, nos. 410, 540. ARTsB, nos. 21, 22. FO 78-3895, nos. 294-296, 299, 308, 334.

71. AP, 1887, *91:1*, no. 431. ARTsB, bos. 18, 20, 23. Radev, vol. 2, pp. 408-409. Tatishchev, Iz proshlago, p. 471.

72. ARTsB, no. 61.

73. MV, 1886, no. 254-A. Cf. also nos. 250, 256, 257.

74. MV, 1886, nos. 281, 285-B.

75. MV, 1886, nos. 259, 260, 263-A, 264-A, 265-A, 268-B, 270, 271-A, 273, 275-A, B, 280, 284, 289-A, 291, 292-B.

76. AP, 1887, *91:1*, no. 378. Jelavich, Tsarist Russia, pp. 264-265.

77. Morier to Iddlesleigh, 30.9.1886; FO 65-1261, no. 353. Cf. also FO 65-1261, no. 352, 356, 363; 65-1262, nos. 366, 378, 388a, 390; 65-1265, no. 433.

78. FO, 65-1262, no. 386a; 78-3895, nos. 323, 328, 330, 336, 341, 343, 348, 351; 78-3896, nos. 354, 355, 358, 359. Radev, vol. 2, pp. 437ff.

79. ARTsB, no. 27, 29.

80. Radev, vol. 2, pp. 440ff.

81. Staal, vol. 1, pp. 310-313. Cf. also FO 65-1255, nos. 288a, 234a, 253a, 259a, 273a; Schaller, pp. 153-155.

82. Canis, pp. 115-156, 159ff. GP, vol. 5, nos. 1009-112, 114-1127. HvB, no. 250, Lucius v. Ballhausen, p. 356. Schaller, pp. 155ff.

83. Fuller, pp. 86-87. For Katkov's reach MV, 1886, nos. 263-B, 268-A. For European reaction Huhn, pp. 285ff.

84. Canis, pp. 166-167. Holstein Papers, vol. 2, pp. 250ff., 307, 316. H. Krausnick, Holsteins Geheimpolitik in der Ära Bismarcks 1886-1890, Hamburg 1942, pp. 94ff.

85. GP, vol. 5, nos. 989, 990. Kennan, pp. 210-211. Holstein relates a very different version of the conversation. (Holstein Papers, vol. 3, pp. 193-194.)

86. GP, vol. 5, nos. 990, 992, 994-996.

87. ARTsB, no. 28. Canis, p. 165. Holstein Papers, vol. 3, pp. 192-193.

88. Morier to Iddlesleigh, 10.10.1886; FO 65-1261, no. 363; cf. also 65-1262, no. 376. Jomini's information presumably originated in the gathering of corps commanders summoned by Obruchev; its participants allegedly delivered a judgment that the Bulgarian invasion would be tantamount to a proclamation of European war and that the two divisions originally designated for the operation would be lost. (Kartsov, Sem let, pp. 363-364.)

89. ARTsB, no. 28.

90. Cf. FO 78-1261, nos. 354, 360, 375, 376, 381.

91. ARTsB, nos. 32-35. FO 78-3896, nos. 363, 366, 369, 373, 375, 376, 379; 78-3897, no. 425. Radev, vol. 2, pp. 476ff.

92. FO 78-3896, no. 380; see also nos. 382, 383, 394, 397.

93. Cecil, vol. 4, p. 5. Fuller, pp. 106-107. MV, 1886, no. 301. Staal, vol. 1, pp. 391-392.

94. BgB, no. 10. Fuller, pp. 104ff. Wertheimer, vol. 3, pp. 329ff. Cf. also GP, vol. 5, nos. 978, 988, 1008, 1010-1013.

95. Cf. GP, vol. 5, nos. 900-997, 1000, 1013.

96. MV, 1886, nos. 305-A, 306-A, see also nos. 294, 299-A, 303-B, 309-A, 319-B, 327-V.

97. MV, 1886, nos. 294, 296-A, 309-A, 313, 315.

98. Quoted from FO 78-1263, no. 430.

Notes to Chapter 31

1. Kennan, p. 200.

2. Staal, vol. 1, pp. 321-326. Cf. also FO 65-1262, no. 405, 406, 409, 411; GP, vol. 5, no. 993; Zolotukhin, p. 55.

3. MV, 1886, no. 309-A. Cf. also GP, vol. 5, no. 990; Schaller, pp. 162ff.

4. Polovtsov, vol. 1, p. 446. Cf. also FO 65-1263, no. 443.

5. Lamzdorf, Dnevnik 1886-1890, p. 10. Kartsov, pp. 336-337, 344.

6. ARTsB, no. 71.

7. A British Consul General reported from Sofia:
"There is no doubt a considerable amount of disorganization in the

military forces...and many of the officers are inclined to indulge in political intrigues...; nor would it be wise to ignore altogether the influence of the clergy who are for the most part partisans of Russia." But "the vast majority is made up of those who desire to prevent the country being a lucrative farm for Russian officers and capitalists." It was the return of Prince Alexander that people and the army were dreaming about—"time is clothing the episode of his reign in a popular legend"—and not rule by the Tsar's deputy.

Gadban Effendi, the Turkish plenipotentiary in Sofia considered a Russian tool, assessed that, at most, one fifth of the Assembly and the populace might support Karavelov's "realists" and the Tsankovites. (O' Connor to Iddlesleigh, 26.12.1886; FO 78-3897, no. 450.)

8. Kartsov, Sem let, pp. 353, 384. Tatishchev, Iz proshlago, pp. 418-419.

9. HvB, no. 259.

10. Kartsov, Sem let, p. 350.

11. FO 65-1255, no. 297a. Lamzdorf, Dnevnik 1886-1890, pp. 5-6, 13-14.

12. Iddlesleigh to Morier, 30.12.1886; FO 65-1255, no. 340.

13. FO 65-1295, nos. 11, 26; 78-3896, nos. 387, 388, 397, 410, 411, 413, 428, 437, 443. Kartsov, p. 329.

14. Cf. HvB, no. 270. Schaller, pp. 171ff.

15. Morier to Iddlesleigh, 15.10.1886; FO 65-1262, no. 370.

16. GP, vol. 5, no. 1000; cf. also nos. 1013, 1026.

17. GP, vol. 5, nos. 991, 992. HvB, nos. 259, 260.

18. Dnevnik akademika V. P. Bezobrazova, RS, *154*, 1913, pp. 530-531.

19. Polovtsov, vol. 1, p. 459; vol. 2, p. 15. Cf. also Manfred, Vneshniaia politika, pp. 374-375.

20. GP, vol. 5, no. 980; see also no. 986.

21. GP, vol. 5, no. 989.

22. GP, vol. 5, nos. 991, 992. Schweinitz, Briefwechsel, pp. 224-225, 228-230.

23. Schweinitz, Briefwechsel, pp. 224-225, 228-230. Cf. also Kumpf-Korfes, pp. 95ff.; Pobedonostsev i ego korrespondenty, vol. 2, pp. 727ff.; GP, vol. 5, no. 990.

24. MV, 1886, nos. 190, 200, 209, 214, 215, 217. Cf. also RV, *183*, 1886, pp. 913ff.; *184*, 1886, pp. 457ff.

25. GP, vol. 5, nos. 977, 980. Cf. also AA, 1886, A 9556.

26. GP, vol. 5, no. 977. Polovtsov, vol. 2, p. 54. Cf. also FO 65-1239, no. 145; Polovtsov, vol. 1, p. 450. On Katkov's connections see V. Ia. Laverychev, Russkie kapitalisty i periodicheskaia pechat vtoroi poloviny XIX v., Istoriia SSSR, 1972, no. 1, pp. 36ff.

27. After his death, Russian newspapers and foreign diplomats assessed Katkov's property at 2-3 million rubles. (Cf. Bülow to Bismarck, 4.11.1887; AA, 1887, A 13712.)

28. AA, 1886, A 9556.

29. Cf. Müller-Link, p. 272.

30. Russian foreign debts at that time amounted to about 2,000 million rubles and the German holdings are believed to have been worth about 1,200 million. (Kennan, p. 225.)

31. For general analyses see Canis, pp. 159ff.; Kennan, pp. 223ff.; Kumpf-Korfes, pp. 150ff.; Müller-Link, pp. 268ff.

32. FO 65-1261, no. 331. Schweinitz, Briefwechsel, pp. 224-225.

33. Kennan, pp. 203ff. Nolde, pp. 338ff. Toutain, pp. 130ff.

34. Cyon, pp. 163, 176ff. GP, vol. 6, nos. 1200-1205, 1212. Kennan, pp. 196-198. Manfred, Vneshniaia politika, p. 374. Nolde, p. 367.

35. GP, vol. 5, nos. 992, 994, 1009, 1014, 1015, 1017-1019, 1022-1024, 1027; vol. 6, no. 1207. Schaller, pp. 166ff. Schweinitz, Denkwürdigkeiten, vol. 2, p. 329.

36. Polovtsov, vol. 1, p. 459. Cf. also GP, vol. 5, no. 989.

37. MV, 1886, nos. 331, 333; cf. also nos. 334, 335, 342, 343, 347, 352, 355, 360.

38. Cf. BgB, no. 19.

39. The Ambassador to Berlin, Herbette, admonished the Paris government against "one sole word, one sole act" which would point to the intention of exploiting the growing chasm between Germany and Russia and this warning was strictly observed. The cool reaction on Kumani's feeler and the Strastnyi Boulevard campaign only confirmed that Paris was unwilling to play the Muscovite game. When Juliette Adam fully identified herself with the Thunderer and entrusted the editorship of La Nouvelle Revue to his lieutenant Cyon, her step was severely criticized. For republican organs, the Moscow editor was little more than a disgusting retrograde who should not be allowed to operate in their country. "In what sort of an epoch we live that a defamateur of the

Moskovskiia vedomosti should be directing one of the great French magazines?", the editor of the *Siècle* exclaimed in disgust. (DDF-I, vol. 6, no. 389. GP, vol. 6, nos. 1227, 1231, 1238. Kennan, pp. 215-216. Cyon, pp. 222ff.)

40.   Bülow, vol. 4, pp. 609-611. GP, vol. 6, nos. 1223-1225, 1228-1231, 1234. Lucius v. Ballhausen, pp. 355-358. Waldersee, vol. 1, pp. 301ff.

41.   Cf. GP, vol. 6, nos. 1186, 1205; Waldersee, vol. 1, pp. 316-317.

42.   DDF-I, vol. 6, no. 350. GP, vol. 5, nos. 989, 1006, 1007. HvB, nos. 263, 270. Lucius v. Ballhausen, p. 356.

43.   Lamzdorf, Dnevnik 1886-1890, p. 4. Cf. also GP, vol. 5, nos. 996-998.

44.   KA, *58,* 1933, p. 60n. Cf. also GP, vol. 5, no. 1000, 1003-1005.

45.   Lamzdorf, Dnevnik 1886-1890, pp. 22-24. Cf. also GP, vol. 5, nos. 1003-1005; Kennan, pp. 250ff.; Nolde, pp. 397ff., 447ff.

46.   Cf. GP, vol. 5, nos. 1032, 1033.

47.   GP, vol. 5, no. 1062.

48.   GP, vol. 5, no. 1062n.; vol. 6, nos. 1206, 1207. Cf. also vol. 5, nos. 1001, 1006.

49.   GP, vol. 5, no. 1063.

50.   DDF-I, vol. 6, no. 394. Cf. also Kennan, pp. 257-259; Nolde, pp. 404ff.

51.   DDF-I, vol. 6, nos. 415, 419, 427 etc; GP, vol. 6, nos. 1244-1247, 1250, 1253, 1256.

52.   DDF-I, vol. 6, nos. 397, 408, 415, 423, 426, 437. Morier, who travelled to St. Petersburg with Peter Shuvalov after the Berlin talks, reported: "How about the war I asked—war in the West and war in the East? There will be no war, he said . . . . Do you mean to tell me, said I, that the two Powers are to go on arming ad infinitum and never fly at each other's throats? I do not speak for the future, but for the present; and for the present, for this year, I am ready to bet you my entire fortune that there will be no war between France and Germany." (Ramm, Morier, p. 243.)

53.   GP, vol. 6, nos. 1236, 1237, 1239-1241, 1248, 1249, 1251, 1252, 1254. Lucius v. Ballhausen, pp. 366-367.

54.   V. M. Khvostov, Rossiia i germanskaia agressiia v dni evropeiskogo krizisa 1887 g., IZ, *18,* 1946, pp. 214-215.

55. Lamzdorf, Dnevnik 1886-1890, p. 28.

56. Staal, vol. 1, p. 336.

57. Holstein wrote in his diary on 7 and 11 January: "Herbert (Bismarck) had fallen completely under the spell of Peter Shuvalov's considerable charm of manner and would like to do everything he asks. . . . The wind has again shifted strongly against Austria here . . . Herbert controls his father completely . . . I cannot prevent his rapprochement with Russia: the magnetic force pulling Herbert and therefore his father to that direction is too strong." (Holstein Papers, vol. 2, pp. 331-332.)

58. Lamzdorf, Dnevnik 1886-1890, pp. 31-32. Polovtsov, vol. 2, p. 13. Schweinitz, Briefwechsel, p. 232; Denkwürdigkeiten, vol. 2, p. 322n.

59. AA, 1886, A 15368; AA, 1887, A 71, A 7510. Soloviev, pp. 84ff.

60. Schweinitz to Bismarck, 1.1.1887; AA, 1887, A 160. Schweinitz to Bismarck, 30.30.1887; AA, 1887, A 4189. Kartsov, Sem let, p. 144. Nolde, pp. 380ff. Polovtsov, vol. 2, pp. 9-10, 27, 468.

61. Polovtsov, vol. 2, p. 10.

62. KA, 58, 1933, pp. 74-75.

63. Kennan, p. 259.

64. KA, 58, 1933, pp. 61.

65. Ibid., pp. 62-64.

66. KA, 58, 1933, pp. 64-67.

67. Ibid., pp. 69-70.

68. Ibid., pp. 71-74.

69. KA, 58, 1933, pp. 77-79. Kumpf-Korfes, pp. 90ff.

70. MV, 1887, nos. 6, 7, 11.

71. BgB, no. 11. Manfred, Vneshniaia politika, pp. 394-395.

72. MV, 1887, no. 41; cf. also nos. 42, 56-B, 58-B, 66, 90, 92-B, 96, 99.

73. Feoktistov, p. 252.

74. Lamzdorf, Dnevnik 1886-1890, pp. 34-35.

75. Lamzdorf, p. 36. Cf. also GP, vol. 5, nos. 989, 900, 1000, 1005.

76. Polovtsov, vol. 2, pp. 9-10.

77. Lamzdorf, Dnevnik 1886-1890, p. 34.

78. Cf AA, 1887, A 2738.

79. HvB, nos. 279, 283.

80. Schweinitz, Briefwechsel, pp. 231, 234-237, 239.

81. HvB, no. 284.

82. Iddlesleigh wrote to Vienna: "We may not be primarily so much interested in the independence of Bulgaria and the smaller Balkan states as Austria-Hungary; but the growing power (?) of Russia in those states is of nearly as much consequences to us, and threatens us with almost as serious challenge as Austria-Hungary can herself comprehend." (B. Jelavich, Russia, Britain and the Bulgarian Question 1885-1888, Südostforschungen, 32, 1973, p. 174.)

83. GP, vol. 4, no. 861ff. Holstein Papers, vol. 3, pp. 206-207. Nolde, pp. 422ff. Schaller, pp. 173-175, 193ff.

84. Cecil, vol. 4, p. 71.

85. Ramm, Morier, pp. 235-238.

86. Ibid.

87. Bridge, pp. 164-167. Cecil, vol. 4, pp. 24-25.

88. Bismarck to Schweinitz, 28.2.1877; AA, 1887, A 2460. DDF-I, vol. 6, no. 470. GP, vol. 5, nos. 1007, 1034, 1068, 1070. Radowitz, vol. 2, pp. 266-267. Schweinitz, Denkwürdigkeiten, vol. 2, pp. 334-336.

89. Cecil, vol. 4, pp. 15ff. GP, vol. 4, nos. 883ff. Khvostov, Rossiia i germanskaia agressiia, pp. 228ff. Letters of Victoria, ser. 3, vol. 1, pp. 263ff. W. N. Medlicott, The Mediterranean Agreements of 1887, SEER, 5, 1926-1927.

90. Morier to Salisbury, 26.1.1887; FO 65-1295, no. 26.

91. Lamzdorf, p. 44.

92. Cyon, pp. 229ff. Feoktistov, pp. 259ff. Kennan, pp. 270ff. Kumpf-Korfes, pp. 102-103. Pobedonostsev i ego korrespondenty, vol. 1, p. 802. Toutain, pp. 162ff. Zaionchkovskii, Rossiiskoe samoderzhavie, p. 278.

93. Cyon, pp. 233ff. Kennan, pp. 289ff. Polovtsov, vol. 2, pp. 9-10.

Notes to Chapter 32

1. A rumor circulated about the way he handled the messy affair when his mentally unbalanced borther Methodius killed another "member of the family," Professor Leontiev. He allegedly promised Methodius to take care of his children if he would commit suicide to spare him the scandal of a public trial against "a Katkov"; and even smuggled into the prison the rope the man hanged himself with. (Kartsov, Sem let, p. 137n.)

2. Cyon, p. 244.

3. Cyon, pp. 272ff. Kartsov, Sem let, pp. 350ff., 376ff. Kumpf-Korfes, pp. 80n., 101n.

4. Pobedonostsev i ego korrespondenty, vol. 1, pp. 793-794. Polovtsov, vol. 1, pp. 216-217, 347, 372, 391, 395-396, 403, 418, 443-444, 460, 462-464; vol. 2, pp. 26-27.

5. Kennan, p. 295.

6. GP, vol. 5, no. 1013, Lamzdorf, Dnevnik 1886-1890, p. 41. Cf. also AA, 1887, A 160, A 1007; FO 65-1295, no. 21.

7. FO 65-1296, nos. 92, 96; HvB, no. 289.

8. Schweinitz to Bismarck, 1.1.1887; AA, 1887, A 160.

9. Staal, vol. 1, pp. 338-339. Cf. also DDF-I, vol. 6, no. 447; GP, vol. 5, no. 990; Khvostov, Rossiia i germanskaia agressiia, p. 236; Toutain, pp. 189ff. For a review of the Russian press comments on the subject see FO 65-1295,nos. 40, 49.

10. MV, 1887, nos. 27, 43, 59.

11. Pobedonostsev i ego korrespondenty, vol. 1, p. 608. Tatishchev, Iz proshlago, pp. 488-489. Lamzdorf, p. 35.

12. ARTsB, nos. 143-145. Radev, vol. 2, pp. 456ff. Tatishchev, Iz proshlago, p. 470. Cf. also the reports of O' Connor to Iddlesleigh in FO 78-4030, nos. 3, 6, 12, 13, 18-21, 23, 24, 29, 34; Schaller, pp. 177ff.

13. MV, 1887, nos. 21, 34-B, 47-A, 54, 56-B. Pobedonostsev i ego korrespondenty, vol. 1, p. 609.

14. Kartsov, Sem let, pp. 346ff., 365-366.

15. Lamzdorf, Dnevnik 1886-1890, p. 35.

16. ARTsB, nos. 41, 43.

17. MV, 1887, nos. 49-B, 53, 54.

18. ARTsB, nos. 47-62. FO 78-4030, nos. 72, 73, 76-80; 78-4031, nos. 88, 89, 91, 104, 105, 107-109, 112, 113, 115, 133, 137. Radev, vol. 2, pp. 661ff.

19. ARTsB, nos. 49, 53n. Cf. also FO 65-1297, nos. 202, 217, 234.

20. CF. FO 65-1295, nos. 60, 70, 72, 74.

21. ARTsB, nos. 71, 147.

22. GP, vol. 6, nos. 1029, 1210, 1211; Kennan, pp. 203ff.; Nolde, pp. 388ff.; Toutain, pp. 130ff., 177ff.

23. Reputedly promised cooperation by "very powerful French bankers," Poliakov proposed to buy up, under the guise of a Dutch company,

the shares in the companies hitherto controlled by the English and the Austrians. "To possess the railways in the East means virtually to possess the country, and so it would be for us a point of a great strength if the railways of Turkey, Bulgaria etc., were in Russian hands," the financier wrote to Pobedonostsev.

Katkov, Pobedonostsev and Vyshnegradskii were enthusiastic about the scheme which "with one coup, without the sacrifice of a ruble or a soldier, would turn Russian into a true master of the Balkans"; and from December 1886, they several times appealed to the Tsar to embark on it. However, they received only evasive answers. "Above all, no new complications. If we shall conquer the Balkans, the railways will fall ipso facto under our power; if not, whom will these railways serve?", Zinoviev transmitted the autocrat's opinion. (Cyon, pp. 338ff.; Kumpf-Korfes, pp. 73-74; Pobedonostsev i ego korrespondenty, vol. 1, pp. 554, 578-579, 653-654, 733ff.; Pisma Pobedonostseva, vol. 1, pp. 123-126.)

24. MV, 1887, no. 54; cf. also no. 59.

25. Morier to Salisbury, 26.3.1887; FO 65-1296, no. 101. Cf. also no. 103.

26. MV, 1886, no. 66. Cf. also Kennan, pp. 309ff.; Nolde, pp. 456ff.; Wittram, p. 340ff.

27. MV, 1886, no. 69.

28. Feoktistov, p. 253.

29. A careful analysis of Katkov's editorials reveals that he must have learned the essentials about the "treaty of Skiernewice" already sometime in 1884, probably from Zinoviev. Saburov was obviously correct in his subsequent defence that when he had passed his confidential papers to the editor (in 1887), the latter already was well apprised about the whole matter. (Cf. Kumpf-Korfes, p. 49; Kennan, pp. 434-435; Pobedonostsev i ego korrespondenty, vol. 1, p. 691.)

30. Bogdanovich, among other things, delivered a monetary reward to General Soussier for his pro-Russian toast at a gathering commemorating the battle of Sevastopol. More importantly, he was believed to be the author of the anonymous pamphlet "L'alliance franco-russe," in which Grand Duke Vladimir and other prominents of the German party had been fiercely assailed. (Cyon, pp. 318ff., 331; see also DDF-I, vol. 6, no. 529.)

31. Polovtsov, vol. 2, pp. 39-40. Cf. also Feoktistov, pp. 256-257.

32. Cf. AA, 1887, A 3299, A 4016, A 8187; FO 65-1296, no. 101.

33. Pisma Pobedonostseva, vol. 2, pp. 141-144.

34. Pobedonostsev i ego korrespondenty, vol. 1, pp. 644-645. Cf. also Feoktistov, pp. 254-255; Suvorin, p. 167; Polovtsov, vol. 2, pp. 45-46.

35. BgB, no. 22. Cyon, pp. 334-335. Feoktistov, pp. 255-256. Kumpf-Korfes, pp. 95ff.

36. Feoktistov, pp. 256-258. Kennan, p. 435n. Polovtsov, vol. 2, pp. 45-46. Cf. also AA, 1887, A 4043, A 4897; FO 65-1296, nos. 92, 96.

37. "C'est un fardeu que cet animal de Katkoff" was the style Alexander unburdened himself to his confidants. (Bülow to Bismarck, 20.4. 1887; AA, 1887, A 5613; cf. also A 5613.)

38. Morier to Salisbury, 6.4.1887; FO 65-1296, no. 119. Cf. also the reports of schweinitz to Bismarck in AA, 1887, A 2848, A 3992, A 4016.

39. Rechenberg to Bismarck, 26.2.1887; AA, 1887, A 4135. Cf. also, AA, 1887, A 4899; Pobedonostsev i ego korrespondenty, vol. 1, pp. 644-645.

40. AA, 1887, A 4492. Cyon, pp. 272-273. Feoktistov, pp. 258-259. Kartsov, Sem let, p. 385. FO 65-1296, no. 119. Kumpf-Korfes, p. 100. Nolde, pp. 458-460.

41. FO 65-1296, no. 119.

42. Feoktistov, pp. 258-259. FO 65-1296, no. 119.

43. Bülow to Bismarck, 9.4.1887; AA, 1887, A 4708. Cf. also A 4786 where Cherevin's explanation is corroborated by Giers.

44. FO 65-1296, no. 119.

45. DDF-I, vol. 6, no. 493. Kartsov, Sem let, pp. 383, 385.

46. KA, 58, 1933, pp. 79-85.

47. Lamsdorf, pp. 81-82.

48. The two men passed long excruciating hours on Easter eve in futile waiting for the messenger who should have brought the expected St. Vladimir order. Allegedly, the decoration with the appropriate rescript was prepared for the Tsar's signature, but the latter, warned by Pobedonostsev, did not dare to endorse it. (Kennan, p. 315-317. Lamzdorf, Dnevnik 1886-1890, pp. 81-83.)

49. AA, 1887, A 4665, A 5229. DDF-I, vol. 6, nos. 490, 503. FO 65-1296, nos. 125, 133, 134, 137, 144, 147, 148. BgB, nos. 23, 28.

50. AA, 1887, A 5376.

51.   Cf. AA, 1887, A 4646, A 4859.

52.   AA, 1887, A 4629.

53.   Cyon, p. 275. Cf. also Toutain, pp. 208ff.

54.   Cf. GP, vol. 5, nos. 992, 1034-1037, 1039-1041.

55.   Canis, pp. 202-203. GP, vol. 5, nos. 1071-1075, 1080. Lucius v. Ballhausen, pp. 376ff. Khvostov, Rossiia, pp. 345ff. Kumpf-Korfes, pp. 102-105. Polovtsov, vol. 2, p. 39.

56.   GP, vol. 5, nos. 1034-1036; cf. also nos. 1071-1075, 1080, 1083.

57.   Khvostov, Rossiia i germanskaia agressiia, p. 246n.

58.   Holstein Papers, vol. 2, p. 213. Cf. also GP, vol. 5, nos. 1040, 1042. Waldersee, vol. 2, pp. 320ff.

59.   Kennan, p. 320.

60.   GP, vol. 5, nos. 1040, 1042, 1073ff. KA, *1*, 1922, pp. 97ff. Nolde pp. 461ff. Schaller, pp. 197ff. For a detailed analysis see H. Hallman, ed., Zur Geschichte und Problematik des Deutsch-Russischen Rückversicherungsvertrages von 1887, Wege der Forschung, *13*, 1968 (Darmstadt).

61.   The treaty contained in its three articles (1) mututal guarantee of benevolent neutrality in the event of war with a third Power which, however, was not applicable in a conflict with France or Austria-Hungary; (2) German recognition of "historic rights appropriated by Russia in the Balkan peninsula and particularly the legitimacy of her preponderant and decisive influence in Bulgaria and Eastern Rumelia," and (3) recognition of the "European and mutually obligatory character of the principle of closure of the Straits."

In the "additional and top secret" protocol completing the stipulations of the second and third articles, Germany promised (a) her approval if Russia were to "establish in Bulgaria a regular and lawful government," and (b) "benevolent neutrality" and "moral support" to the measures which "His Majesty will judge necessary in order to take into his possession the key to his Empire." (For the texts see GP, vol. 5, no. 1092.)

62.   Canis, pp. 204-205. HvB, nos. 292, 303. GP, vol. 5, nos. 1093, 1094.

63.   GP, vol. 5, no. 1034n.

64.   Kennan, p. 320.

65.   Kennan, pp. 321-323. Toutain, pp. 173ff., 197ff.

66.   Feoktistov, pp. 260ff. Pobedonostsev i ego korrespondenty, vol. 1, pp. 644-645, 684ff., 711ff., 793ff. Cf. also AA, 1887, A 4499,

A 4686; DDF-I, vol. 6, no. 552, 553; KA, 72, 1935, pp. 72-73. Kennan, pp. 324-327; Kumpf-Korfes, p. 102; Nolde, pp. 466-467; Suvorin, p. 168.

67. Cf. reports, of 1, 8, 10.6.1887; AA, 1887, A 7072, A 7310, A 7352.

68. Cf. AA, 1887, A 8187, A 8662; GP, vol. 5, no. 1096.

69. Speaking to the British Ambassador about the reasons why the Russian government would not react on the election of Ferdinand by "active measures," Giers accentuated "the difference between 'now' and three years ago." Then, he said, "we were preponderant in Bulgaria. We had 300 Russian officers in the command of the Bulgarian army. We have no wish to have one there now. The dominant feeling, with the exception of the extreme Panslavs . . . is one of disgust at the ingratitude of the Bulgarian people and the folly which made Russia shed so much blood and wasted so much treasure on such people. . . ." (Morier to Salisbury, 26.7.1887; FO 65-1297, no. 260.)

Notes to the Conclusion

1. Staal, vol. 1, pp. 355-356.

2. For an analysis of Russian press comments see AA, 1887, A 9774.

3. The "Katkov file" in the Auswärtiges Amt provides us with extensive material on the matter: (AA, 1887), A 8820, A 9236, A 9469, A 9496, A 9692, A 9700, A 9774, A 10, 028, A 10 031, A 10 313, A 10 352, A 10 467, A 10 594, A 10 603, A 10 825, A 10 865, A 11 493.

4. Indeed, it would be of enormous value for the studies on Russian public opinion and Russian political culture, if an unbiased historian would analyze the publicist's correspondence from this "Katkov—the dark people" angle.

5. Staal, vol. 1, pp. 355-356.

6. Ibid.

7. AA, 1887, A 9529. Cyon, pp. 342ff. Kartsov, Sem let, pp. 388-390.

8. "With every true Russian," wrote the Tsar, "I share the profound grief at the loss you have suffered as I also suffer. The powerful words of your deceased husband, inspired by ardent love for the motherland, awakened the Russian spirit and strengthened sound judgment in moments of trouble. Russia will not forget his merits and everybody is joining you in prayer for the peace of his soul." (AA, 1887, A 10313.)

9. In his private diary, a Soviet historian tells us, the Tsar mentioned the death of Katkov in one "cool and indifferent" sentence; while, at the same time, he dedicated many lines to the fall of his favourite dog. (Manfred, Vneshniaia politika, p. 394n.)

10. AA, 1887, A 9469.

11. RV, 250, p. 131.

12. KA, 58, 1933, pp. 69-70. (Katkov's memoir of 7 January 1887.)

13. In the last edition of the "Great Soviet Encyclopedia," the entry on Katkov was reduced to six sentences. (Bolshaia sovetskaia entsyklopediia, vol. 20, Moskva 1953, p. 372.) The first Soviet monograph on him—burdened by all the usual dogmas and taboos and dealing with his role in internal policies only—was published as late as 1978. (Tvardovskaia).

14. In an astounding summarizing statement, Kennan declared Katkov "in the totality of his life's work a great man" and deplores that he was obliged in his volume "to occupy himself mainly with the abberations in matters of foreign policy that marred the final months of the activity of this formidable and talented personality and to leave aside the great services he rendered to Russia at another times and in other fields"(!). (Kennan, p. 327.)

15. Sobranie sochinenii Vladimira Sergeevicha Solovieva, vol. 5, St. Petersburg, s.d., pp. 206-207, 461.

16. Soloviev, vol. 5, pp. 196-199.

17. Ibid., pp. 199ff.

18. Lukashevich, Leontiev, pp. 130-131, 162.

SELECTED BIBLIOGRAPHY

Unpublished Sources

Germany. *Auswärtiges Amt. Akten: Russland* 82, no. 4. Secr. Russ. Journalister (Katkov).

Great Britain. Public Records Office. *The Records of the Foreign Office. Political Dispatches. General Correspondence.* Russia F.O. 65 (1878-1887).

General Correspondence. Turkey F.O. 78 (1878-1887).

Embassy and Consular Archives. Russia F.O. 181 (1878-1887).

Published Sources: Official Collections of Documents

Accounts and Papers. *Parliamentary Proceedings.* (Blue Books.) 1885-1888, London 1886-1890.

Brandenburg, E. et al., ed. *Die auswärtige Politik Preussens 1858-1871,* vols. 6-10. Berlin 1934-1939.

Documents diplomatiques français (1871-1914). 1ère série, vols. 2-6. Paris 1930-1938.

Lepsius, J. et al., ed. *Die grosse Politik der europäischen Kabinette 1871-1914,* vols. 1-6. Berlin 1922.

Narochnitskii, A. L., ed. *Rossiia i natsionalno-osvoboditelnaia borba na Balkanakh, 1875-1878.* Moskva 1978.

Nikitin, S. A., ed. *Osvobozhdenie Bolgarii ot turetskogo iga.* 3 vols. Moskva 1961-1967.

Osobye pribavleniia k opisaniiu russko-turetskoi voiny 1877-1878 gg. na Balkanskom poluostrove, vols. 1, 4, 6. S.-Peterburg 1898-1901.

Ovsianyi, N. R., ed. *Sbornik materialov po grazhdanskomu upravleniiu i okkupatskii v Bolgarii v 1877-1878 gg.* 6 vols.. S.-Peterburg 1904-1905.

Idem. *Russkoe upravlenie v Bolgarii v 1877-1879 gg.* 2 vols. S.-Peterburg 1906.

Pavlovich, P., ed. *Avantiury russkogo tsarizma v Bolgarii.* Moskva 1935.

Russko-germanskie otnosheniia (1873-1914). Sekretnye dokumenty. Krasnyi arkhiv, 1, 1922.

Schwertfeger, B., ed. *Zur europäischen Politik. Vol. 5. Revanche-Idee und Panslawismus.* Belgische Gesandtschaftsberichte. Berlin 1919.

Published Sources: Memoirs, Diaries, Private Correspondence and Collections, Memoranda

(Aksakov, I. S.) *Polnoe sobranie sochinenii I. S. Aksakova.* vol. 1 (Slavianskii vopros, 1860-1886). Moskva 1886.

Anuchin, D. G. *Kongress Berlina.* Russkaia starina, 149, 150, 152, 1912.

Baddeley, J. F. *Russia in the ‚'Eighties.'* London 1921.

Barsukov, N. P. *Zhizn i trudy M. P. Pogodina.* 22 vols. S.-Peterburg 1888-1910.

Belinskii, V. G. *Polnoe sobranie sochinenii.* Vols. 11, 12 (Pisma). Moskva 1956.

(Bezobrazov, V. P.) *Dnevnik Akademika V. P. Bezobrazova.* Russkaia starina, 154, 1913.

Bismarck, O. v. *Gedanken und Erinnerungen.* München 1956.

(Bogdanovich, A. V.) *Tri poslednykh samoderzhtsa. Dnevnik A. V. Bogdanovich.* Moskva-Leningrad 1924.

Buckle, G. E., ed. *The Letters of Queen Victoria.* 2nd ser., vols. 1-3; 3rd ser., vol. 1. London 1928-1930.

Bussman, W., ed. *Staatssekretär Graf Herbert v. Bismarck. Aus seiner politischer Privatkorrespondenz.* Göttingen 1964.

Bülow, B. v. *Denkwürdigkeiten.* Vol. 4. Berlin 1931.

Cecil, G. *The Life of Robert, Marquis of Salisbury.* 4 vols. London 1921-1931.

(Chicherin, B. N.) *Vospominaniia Borisa Nikolaevicha Chicherina.* Moskva sorokovykh godov. Moskva 1929.

Cyon, E. *Histoire de l'entente franco-russe, 1886-1894.* Paris 1895.

Dabizh, V. D. *San-Stefano i Konstantinopol v fevrale 1878g.* Russkaia starina, 57-58, 1888.

Ernrot, K. G.–Sobolev, L. N.) *K noveishei istorii Bolgarii.* Russkaia starina, 52, 1886.

Fadeev, R. *Sobrannye sochineniia.* 2 vols. S.-Peterburg 1890.

(Feoktistov, E. M.) *Vospominaniia E. M. Feoktistova. Za kulisami politiki i literatury, 1848-1896.* Leningrad 1929.

Grazenkampf, M. *Moi dnevnik, 1877-1878gg.* S. Peterburg 1908.

Gertsen [Herzen], A. *Polnoe sobranie sochinenii v 30-kh tomakh.* Vol. 11 (Byloe i dumy). Moskva 1955.

Golowine, A. F. *Fürst Alexander I. von Bulgarien, 1879-1886.* Wien 1896.

(Gorchakov, M. A.) *Kniaz Aleksandr Mikhailovich Gorchakov v ego rasskazakh iz proshlogo.* Russkaia starina, 40, 1883.

Hamman, B., ed. *Kronprinz Rudolf. Majestät, ich warne Sie... Geheime und private Schriften.* Wien-München 1979.

Holborn, H., ed. *Aufzeichnungen und Erinnerungen aus dem Leben des Botschafters Joseph Maria v Radowitz.* 2 vols. Berlin 1925.

Holstein, F.v. see Rich, N.

Ignatiev, N. P. *Zapiski grafa N. P. Ignatieva, 1864-1875.* Izvestiia ministerstva inostrannykh del, 1-6, 1914; 1-4, 1915.

idem. *Zpaiski (grafa N. P. Ignatieva).* Istoricheskii vestnik, 125-137, 1914.

idem. *Puteshestvie grafa N. P. Ignatieva iz Konstantinopolia v Peterburg posle konstantinopolskoi konferentsii.* Russkaia starina, 161, 1915.

idem. *Puteshestvie grafa N. P. Ignatieva po evropeiskim stolitsam pered voinoi 1877-1878 gg.* Russkaia starina, 157-159, 1914.

idem. *San Stefano.* Istoricheski vestnik, 139-142, 1915.

idem. *Pole San Stefano.* Istoricheskii vestnik, 143-144, 1916.

Irechek, K. *Balgarski dnevnik. 2 vols. Sofia 1930.*

Jelavich, Ch. and B. *Russia in the East 1876-1880. The Russo-Turkish War and the Kuldja crisis as seen through the letters of A. G. Jomini to N. K. Giers.* London 1959.

Karasev, V. G., ed. *Zarubezhnye slaviane i Rossiia. Dokumenty arkhiva M. F. Raevskogo (40-80e gody XIX v.).* Moskva 1975.

Kartsov, Iu. S. *Sem let na Blizhnem Vostoke, 1879-1886.* S.-Peterburg 1906.

idem. *za kulisami diplomatii,* Russkaia starina, 133-135, 1908.

(Katkov, M. N.) *Sobranie peredovykh statei "Moskovskikh vedomostei,"* *1863-1887.* 25 vols. Moskva 1897-1898.

idem. *Vozhd reaktsii 60-80-kh godov.* *Pisma Katkova Aleksandru II-omu i Aleksandru III-emu.* Byloe, 1917, no. 4 (26).

idem. *M. N. Katkov i Aleksandr III v 1886-1887 gg.* Krasnyi arkhiv, 58, 1933.

idem. see Mustafin, V.

(Khrulev, S. A.) *Zapiska o pokhode v Indiiu.* Russkii arkhiv, 20:2, 1882.

Kizevetter, A. *Na rubezhe stoletii.* Praha 1929.

Koch, A. *Prince Alexander of Battenberg: reminiscences of his reign in Bulgaria.* London 1887.

Koni, A. F. *Na zhiznenom puti.* 2 vols. S.-Peterburg 1912.

(Koshelev, A. I.) *Zapiski Aleksandra Ivanovicha Kosheleva (1812-1833 gody).* Berlin 1884.

(Lamzdorf, V. N.) *Dnevnik V. N. Lamzdorfs, 1886-1890.* Moskva-Leningrad 1926.

Léonoff, R., ed. *Documents secrets de la politique russe en Orient, 1881-1890.* Berlin 1893.

(Lebedev, K. N.) *Iz zapisok senatora K. N. Lebedeva,* Russkii arkhiv, 31:1, 1893.

(Loftus, A.) *The Diplomatic Reminiscences of Lord Augustus Loftus,* *1862-1879.* 2 vols. London 1894.

Lucius v. Ballhausen, R. *Bismarck-Erinnerungen.* Stuttgart-Berlin 1921.

Marvin, Ch. *The eye-witnesses' account of the disastrous Russian campaign against Akhal Tekke Turcomans.* London 1880.

Meissner, H. O., ed. *Denkwürdigkeiten des Generalfeldmarschalls Grafen von Waldersee,* 3 vols. Stuttgart 1923-1925.

Meshcherskii, V. P. *Moi vospominaniia.* 3 vols. S.-Peterburg 1897-1912.

idem. *Vospominaniia o M. N. Katkove.* Russkii vestnik, 250, 1987.

Meyendorff, A., ed. *Correspondence diplomatique de M. de Staal, 1884-1890.* Vol. 1. Paris 1929.

Miliutin, D. A. see Zaionchkovskii, P. A.

Monypenny, W. F.–Buckle, G. E. *The Life of Benjamin Disraeli.* Vols. 5-6. London 1920.

Mustafin, V., ed. *Mikhail Nikiforovich Katkov i graf Petr Aleksandrovich Valuev v ikh perepiske, 1863-1879.* Russkaia starina, 163-166, 1915-1916.

Nelidov, A. I. *Souvenirs d'avant et d'après la guerre de 1877-1878.* Revue des deux mondes, 27, 28, 30, 1930.

idem. *Zapiska A. I. Nelidova v 1882 g. o zaniatii prolivov.* Krasnyi arkhiv, 46, 1931.

Nemirovich-Danchenko, V. I. *God voiny.* 2 vols. S.-Peterburg 1879.

idem. *Posle voiny.* S.-Peterburg 1880.

(Nesselrode, K. V.) *Zapiska kantslera grafa K. V. Nesselroda o politicheskikh sootnosheniiakh Rossii.* Russkii arkhiv, 10:2, 1872.

Nikitenko, A. V. *Dnevnik v trekh tomakh.* 3 vols. Moskva 1955.

Novikova, O. see Stead, W. T.

Parensov, P. D. *Iz proshlago.* Vol. 3 (V Bolgarii). S.-Peterburg 1908.

(Peretts, E. A.) *Dnevnik E. A. Perettsa (1880-1883).* Moskva 1927.

(Pobedonostsev, K. P.) *K. P. Pobedonostsev i ego korrespondenty: pisma i zapiski.* Vol. 1. Moskva 1923.

idem. *Pisma Pobedonostseva k Aleksandru III.* 2 vols. Moskva 1926.

idem. *L'autocratie russe: mémoires politiques, 1881-1894.* Paris 1927.

(Polovtsov, A. A.) *Dnevnik gosudarstvennogo sekretaria A. A. Polovtsova.* 2 vols. Moskva 1966.

Porokhovshchikov, A. A. *Zapiski starozhila.* Istoricheskii vestnik, 67, 1897.

Posledniaia polskaia smuta. Russkaia starina, 36-37, 1882-1883.

Radowitz, J. M. v. see Holborn, H.

Ramm, A., ed. *The Political Correspondence of Mr. Gladstone and Lord Granville, 1868-1876.* 2 vols. London 1952.

idem. *The Political Correspondence of Mr. Gladstone and Lord Granville, 1876-1886.* Oxford 1962.

Reutern-Nolcken, W. v., ed. *Die finanzielle Sanierung Russlands nach der Katastrophe des Krimkrieges 1862-1878 durch den Finanzminister Michael von Reutern.* Berlin 1914.

Rich, N.-Fisher, H. M., ed. *The Holstein Papers.* 4 vols. Cambridge 1955.

Rieber, A. J., ed. *Letters of Alexander II to Prince A. I. Bariatinskii, 1857-1864.* In: A. J. Rieber, *The Politics of Autocracy,* Paris-The Hague 1966.

Saburov, P. see Simpson, J. Y.

Schuyler, E. *Turkistan: Notes of a Journey in Russian Turkestan, Khokand, Bukhara, and Kuldja.* 2 vols. New York 1876.

(Schweinitz, L. H. v.) *Denkwürdigkeiten des Botschafters General v. Schweinitz.* 2 vols. Berlin 1927.

idem. *Briefwechsel des Botschafters General v. Schweinitz.* Berlin 1928.

(Shuvalov, P. A.) *P. A. Shuvalov o Berlinskom kongresse.* Krasnyi arkhiv, 59, 1933.

Simpson, J. Y. *The Saburov Memoirs, or Bismarck and Russia.* Cambridge 1929.

Skalon, D. A. *Moi vospominaniia.* 2 vols. S.-Peterburg 1913.

(Skobelev, M. D.) *Posmertnye bumagi M. D. Skobeleva.* Istoricheskii vestnik, 10, 1882.

idem. *Proekt M. D. Skobeleva o pokhode v. Indiiu.* Istoricheskii vestnik, 14, 1883.

idem. *Rech generala Skobeleva v Parizhe v 1882g.* Krasnyi arkhiv, 28, 1928.

Snow, G. E., ed. *The Years 1881-1884 in Russia: A Memorandum found in the papers of N. Kh. Bunge.* Transactions of the American Philosophical Society, 71, pt 6. Philadelphia 1981.

Sobolev, L. N. *K noveishei istorii Bolgarii.* Russkaia starina, 51, 1886.

Stead, W. T., ed. *The M.P. for Russia: Reminiscences of M. Olga Novikoff.* 2 vols. New York 1909.

Staal, M. see Meyendorff, A.

(Sukhotin, S. M.) *Iz pamiatnykh tetradei S. M. Sukhotina.* Russkii arkhiv, 32:1, 32:2, 1894.

(Suvorin, A. S.) *Dnevnik A. S. Suvorina.* Moskva 1923.

(Terner, F. G.) *Vospominaniia zhizni F. G. Ternera.* Russkaia starina, 142-144, 1910.

Tiutcheva, A. F. *Pri dvore dvikh imperatorov.* Vol. 2 (Dnevnik 1855-1882). Leningrad 1929.

Toutain, E. *Alexandre III et la République française: souvenirs d'un témoin, 1885-1888.* Paris 1929.

Utin, E. I. *Pisma iz Bolgarii.* S.-Peterburg 1919.

Valuev, P. A. *Dnevnik, 1877-1884.* Petrograd 1919.

idem. *Dnevnik P. A. Valueva, ministra vnutrennykh del.* 2 vols. Moskva 1961.

Victoria, Queen see Buckle, G. E.

Vite, S. Iu. *Vospominaniia.* Vol. 1. Moskva 1960.

(Vogüé, E. M. de) *Journal du Vicomte E. M. de Vogüé: Paris-St. Pétersbourg, 1877-1883.* Paris 1932.

Waldersee, A. v. see Meissner, H. O.

Zaionchkovskii, P. A., ed. *Dnevnik D. A. Miliutina.* 4 vols. Moskva 1947-1950.

Zalesov, N. G. *Zapiski N. G. Zalesova*. Russkaia starina, 114-116, 123-124, 1903, 1905.

General Works

Ambler, E. *Russian Journalism and Politics, 1861-1881*. Detroit 1972.

Askew, W. C. *Russian Military Strength on the Eve of the Franco-Prussian War*. Slavonic and East European Review, 30, 1951-1952.

Becker, S. *Russia's Protectorate in Central Asia: Bukhara and Khiva, 1865-1924*. Cambridge, Mass. 1964.

Besançon, A. *Education et société en Russie dans le second tiers du XIX siècle*. Paris-The Hague 1974.

Beskrovnyi, L. G. *Russkaia armiia i flot v XIX veke*. Moskva 1973.

Beyrau, D. *Russische Orientpolitik und die Entstehung des Deutschen Kaiserreichs 1866-1870/1871*. Wiesbaden 1974.

idem. *Militär und Gesellschaft im vorrevolutionären Russland*. Köln-Wien 1984.

Bilgrami, A. H. *Afghanistan and British India 1793-1907*. New Delhi 1972.

Billington, J. H. *The Icon and the Axe. An interpretative history of Russian culture*. London 1966.

Black, C. E. *The Establishment of Constitutional Government in Bulgaria*. Princeton 1943.

Bridge, F. R. *From Sadowa to Sarajevo. The Foriegn Policy of Austria-Hungary*. London 1972.

Byrnes, R. F. *Pobedonostsev, His Life and Thought*. Indiana U. P. 1968.

Canis, K. *Bismarck und Waldersee. Die aussenpolitischen Krisenerscheinungen und das Verhalten des Generalstables (1882-1890)*. Berlin 1980.

Corti, E. C. *Alexander von Battenberg*. London 1954.

idem. *The Downfall of Three Dynasties*. London 1934.

Crampton, R. J. *Bulgaria 1878-1918. A History*. Boulder-Columbia, U.P. 1983.

Crankshaw, E. *The Shadow of the Winter Palace*. London 1976.

idem. *Bismarck*. London 1981.

Danilevskii, N. *Rossiia i Evropa*. S.-Peterburg 1871.

Druzhinin, N. M., ed. *Slavianskii sbornik. Slavianskii vopros i russkoe obshchestvo*. Moskva 1948.

Durman, K. *Lost illusions: Russian policies towards Bulgaria in 1877-1887*. Uppsala 1987.

Dzhanshiev, G. A. *Epokha velikikh reform.* S.-Peterburg 1900.

Erdman, A. v. *Nikolai Karlovič Giers, russischer Aussenminister 1882-1895.* Berlin 1936.

Eyck, E. *Bismarck: Leben und Werk.* 3 vols. Zürich 1941-1944.

Fischel, A. *Der Panslawismus bis zum Weltkrieg.* Stuttgart-Berlin 1919.

Florinsky, M. T. *Russia. A History and an Interpretation.* Vol. 2 New York 1955.

Fuller, J. V. *Bismarck's Diplomacy at its Zenith.* Cambridge, Mass. 1922.

Gerasimova. Iu. I. *Iz istorii russkoi pechativ v period revoliutsionnoi situatsii kontsa 1850-kh-nachala 1860-kh godov.* Moskva 1974.

Geyer, D., ed. *Der russischen Imperialismus.* Göttingen 1977.

Goriainow, S. *Le Bosphore et les Dardanelles.* Paris 1910.

idem. *Pazrvy Rossi s Bolgariei v 1886 godu.* Istoricheskii vestnik, 147, 1917.

idem. *The End of the Alliance of the Three Emperors.* American Historical Review, 13, 1918, no. 2.

idem. *La Question d'Orient à la veille du Traité de Berlin.* Paris 1948.

Greaves, R. L. *Persia and the Defense of India, 1884-1892.* London 1959.

Gringmut, V. A. *M. N. Katkov kak gosudarstvennyi deiatel.* Russkii vestnik, 250, 1897.

idem. *Zaslugi M. N. Katkova po prosveshcheniiu Rossii.* Russkii vestnik, 250, 1897.

Grüning, I. *Die russische öffentliche Meinung und ihre Stellung zu den Grossmächten, 1878-1894.* Berlin 1929.

Hajek, A. *Bulgariens Befreiung und staatliche Entwicklung unter seinem ersten Fürsten.* München 1939.

Henriksson, A. *The Tsar's Loyal Germans.* Boulder-Columbia U. P. 1983.

Hillgruber, A. *Bismarcks Aussenpolitik.* Freiburg 1972.

Hoetzsch, O. *Russland in Asien. Geschichte einer Expansion.* Stuttgart 1966.

Hünigen, G. *Nikolai Pavlovič Ignat'ev und die russische Balkanpolitik 1875-1878.* Göttingen 1968.

Isakov, S. G. *Ostzeiskii vopros v russkoi pechati 1860-kh godov.* Uchennye zapiski Tartuskogo gosudarstvennogo universiteta, 107, 1961.

Jelavich, B. *The Ottoman Empire, the Great Powers and the Straits Question, 1870-1887.* Indiana U. P. 1973.

idem. *Russia, Britain and the Bulgarian Question. 1885-1888.* Südost-Forschungen, 32, 1973.

Jelavich, Ch. *Tsarist Russia and Balkan Nationalism. Russian influence in the internal affairs of Bulgaria and Serbia, 1879-1886.* California U.P. 1958.

Katz, M. *Mikhail N. Katkov. A political biography 1818-1887.* The Hague 1966.

Kennan, G. F. *The Decline of Bismarck's European Order. Franco-Russian Relations 1875-1890.* Princeton U. P. 1978.

Khalfin, N. A. *Politika Rossii v Srednei Azii v 1857-1868 gg.* Moskva 1960.

idem. *Prisoedinenie Srednei Azii k Rossii (60-90-e gody XIX v.).* Moskva 1965.

Khidoiatov, G. A. *Iz istorii anglo-russkikh otnoshenii v Srednei Azii v kontse XIX v.* Tashkent 1969.

Khvostov, V. M. *Rossiia i germanskaia aggressiia v dni evropeiskogo krizisa 1887 g.* Istoricheskie zapiski, 18, 1946.

Kiniapina, N. S. *Vneshniaia politika Rossii vtoroi poloviny XIX v.* Moskva 1974.

Knorring, N. N. *General Mikhail Dmitrievich Skobelev.* 2 vols. Paris 1939-1940.

Kohn, H. *Panslavism. Its History and Ideology.* Univ. of Notre Dame Press 1953.

Kornilov, A. A. *Obshchestvennoe dvizhenie pri Aleksandre II (1855-1881).* Moskva 1909.

Kosev, D. *Rusiia, Frantsiia i balgarskoto osvoboditelno dvizhenie, 1860-1869.* Sofia 1978.

Kumpf-Korfes, S. *Bismarck's 'Dracht nach Russland.'* Berlin 1968.

Langer, W. L. *European Alliances and Alignments, 1871-1890.* New York 1931.

Lemke, M. *Ocherki po istorii russkoi zhurnalistiki i tsenzury XIX stoletiia.* S.-Peterburg 1904.

Leroy-Beaulieu, A. *L'Empire des Tsars et les Russes.* 3 vols. Paris 1898.

Liubimov, N. A. *Mikhail Nikiforovich Katkov i ego istoricheskaia zasluga.* S.-Peterburg 1888.

Livoff, G. *Michael Katkoff et son époque.* Paris 1897.

Lukashevich, S. *Konstantin Leontiev (1831-1891): A Study in Russian "Heroic Vitalism."* New York 1967.

idem. *Ivan Aksakov 1823-1886.* Cambridge, Mass. 1965.

MacKenzie, D. *The Serbs and Russian Panslavism, 1875-1878.* Cornell U.P. 1967.

idem. *The Lion of Tashkent. The Career of General M. G. Cherniaev.* Athens, Georgia U.P. 1974.

idem. *Kaufman of Turkestan: An Assessment of His Administration.* Slavonic and East European Review, 26, 1967.

MacMaster, R. E. *Danilevsky, A Russian Totalitarian Philosopher.* Harvard U.P. 1967.

Manfred, A. Z. *Vneshniaia politika Frantsii, 1871-1891.* Moskva 1952.

idem. *Obrazovanie russko-frantsuzskogo soiuza.* Moskva 1975.

Marinov, D. *Stefan Stambolov i noveishata ni istoriia.* Sofia 1909.

Marvin, Ch. *Reconnoitring Central Asia.* London 1886.

idem. *The Russian Advance toward India.* London 1882.

idem. *The Russians at the Gates of Herat.* London 1886.

idem. *The Russians at Merv and Herat.* London 1883.

Matveev, P. A. *Bolgariia posle Berlinskogo kongressa.* S.-Peterburg 1887.

Medlicott, W. N. *The Congress of Berlin and After.* London 1938.

idem. *The Powers and the Unification of the Two Bulgarias.* English Historical Review, 54, 1939.

idem. *Bismarck and the Three Emperors' Alliance 1881-1887.* Transactions of the Royal Historical Society, 4th ser., 27, 1945.

idem. *Bismarck, Gladstone and the Concert of Europe.* London 1956.

Meininger, T. A. *Ignatiev and the Establishment of the Bulgarian Exarchate, 1864-1872.* Madison 1970.

Miller, F. *Dmitrii Miliutin and the Reform Era in Russia.* Nashville 1968.

Millman, R. *Britain and the Eastern Question 1875-1878.* Oxford 1979.

Morgan, G. *Anglo-Russian Rivalry in Central Asia: 1810-1895.* London 1981.

Morison, J. D. *Katkov and Panslavism.* Slavonic and East European Review, 46, 1968.

Morris, P. *The Russians in Central Asia, 1870-1887.* Slavonic and East European Review, 53, 1975.

Mosse, W. E. *The European Powers and the German Question, 1848-1871.* Cambridge 1958.

idem. *The Rise and Fall of the Crimean System, 1855-1871.* London-New York 1963.

Müller-Link, H. *Industrialisierung und Aussenpolitik. Preussen-Deutschland und das Zarenreich von 1860 bis 1890.* Göttingen 1977.

Narochnitskaia, L. N. *Rossiia i voiny Prussii v 60-godakh XIX v. za obedinenie Germanii "sverkhu."* Moskva 1960.

Nevedenskii, S. S. *Katkov i ego vremia.* S.-Peterburg 1888.

Nikitenko, S. A. M. N. *Katkov sak redaktor 'Moskovskikh Vedomostei' i vozobnovitel 'Russkago Vestnika.'* Russkaia starina, 92, 1897.

Nikitin, S. A. *Diplomaticheskie otnosheniia Rossii s juzhnymi slavianami v 60-kh godakh XIX v.* In *Slavianskii sbornik,* Moskva 1947.

idem. *Slavianskie siezdy shestidesiatykh godov.* In: *Slavianskii sbornik,* Moskva 1948.

idem. *Slavianskie komitet v Rossii v 1858-1876 godakh.* Moskva 1960.

idem. *Ocherki po istorii juzhnykh slavian i russko-balkanskikh sviazei v 50-70-e gody XIX v.* Moskva 1970.

Nikitin, S. A.–Velev, L. B., ed. *Obshchestvenno-politischeskie i kulturnye sviazi narodov SSSR i Iugoslavii.* Moskva 1957.

Nolde, B. *L'alliance franco-russe. Les origines du système diplomatique d'avant-guerre.* Paris 1936.

Ovsianyi, N. R. *Blizhnii vostok i slavianstvo.* S.-Peterburg 1913.

Petrovich, M. B. *Russian Pan-Slavists and the Polish Uprising of 1863.* Harvard Slavic Studies, 1, 1953.

idem. *The Emergence of Russian Panslavism 1856-1870.* New York 1958.

Pigarev, K. F. I. *Tiutchev i problemy vneshnei politiki tsarskoi Rossii.* Literaturnoe nasledstvo, 19-21, 1935.

Picht, U. M. P. *Pogodin und die Slavische Frage.* Stuttgart 1969.

Pipes, R. *Russia under the Old Regime.* London 1974.

Pokrovskii, M. N. *Diplomatiia i voiny tsarskoi Rossii v XIX stoletii.* Moskva 1923.

Popov, A. L. *Ot Bosfora k Tikhomu Okeanu.* Istorik marksist, 34, 1934.

idem. *Nastuplenie tsarskoi Rossii na Balkanakh.* In: Pavlovich, P., ed., *Avantiury russkogo tsarisma v Bolgarii.* Moskva 1935.

idem. *Iz istorii zavoevaniia Srednei Azii.* Istoricheskie zapiski, 9, 1940.

Pushkarevich, K. A. *Balkanskie slaviane i russkie "osvoboditeli."* Trudy instituta vostokovedeniia Akademii Nauk SSSR, 2, Leningrad 1934.

Pypin, A. N. *Panslavism v proshlom i nastoiaschem.* S.-Peterburg 1913.

Pyziur, E. *Mikhail N. Katkov: Advocate of English Liberalism in Russia, 1856-1863.* Slavonic and East European Review, 45, 1967.

Radev, S. *Stroitelite na savremenna Bălgariia.* 2 vols. Sofia 1910-1911.

Raeff, M. *A Reactionary Liberal: M. N. Katkov.* Russian Review, 11, 1952.

Ramm, A. *Sir Robert Morier*. Oxford 1973.

Revunenkov, V. G. *Polskoe vosstanie 1863 g. i evropeiskaia diplomatiia*. Leningrad 1957.

Riasanovsky, N. *A Parting of Ways. Government and Educated Public in Russia, 1801-1855*. Oxford 1976.

Rieber, A. J. *The Politics of Autocracy*. Paris-The Hague 1966.

Rozental, V. N. *Obshchestvenno-politicheskaia programma russkogo liberalizma v seredine 50-kh godov XIX v*. Istoricheskie zapiski, 70, 1961.

Rupp, G. H. *A Wavering Friendship: Russia and Austria 1876-1878*. Harvard U.P. 1941.

Schaller, R. *Der bulgarische Nationalismus und die Politik Bismarcks*. (Diss.) Frankfurt a M. 1975.

Sementkovskii, P. I. *M. N. Katkov. Ego zhizn i literaturnaia deiatelnost*. S.-Peterburg 1892.

Senkevich, I. G. *Rossiia i kritskoe vosstanie 1866-1869*. Moskva 1970.

Seton-Watson, H. *The Russian Empire 1801-1917*. Oxford 1967.

Seton-Watson, R. W. *Disraeli, Gladstone and the Eastern Question*. London 1935.

Shcheglov, A. N. *Russkoe ministerstvo v Bolgarii. Vremia Aleksandra Battenbergskago*. Istoricheskii vestnik, 126, 1911.

Shilder, N. K. *Graf Eduard Ivanovich Totleben; ego zhizn i deiatelnost*. 2 vols. S.-Peterburg 1885-1886.

Shneerson, L. M. *Avstro-prusskaia voina 1866 g. i diplomatiia velkikh evropeiskikh derzhav*. Minsk 1962.

idem. *Franko-prusskaia voina i Rossiia*. Minsk 1976.

Shteinberg, E. L. *Angliiskaia versiia o russkoi ugroze Indii v XIX-XX vv*. Istoricheskie zapiski, 33, 1950.

Sinel, A. *The Classroom and Chancellery: State Educational Reform in Russia under Count Dmitry Tolstoi*. Harvard U.P. 1976.

Shalkovskii, K. A. *Nashi gosudarstvennye i obshchestvennye deiateli*. S.-Peterburg 1890.

Skazkin, S. D. *Konets avstro-russko-germanskogo soiuza, 1879-1884. Vol. 1. Moskva 1928*.

Soloviev, Iu. B. *Samoderzhavie i dvorianstvo v kontse XIX v*. Leningrad 1973.

Statelova, E. *Diplomatisiiata na kniazhestvo Balgariia*. Sofia 1979.

Stavrianos, L. S. *Balkan Federation: A History of the Movement towards Balkan Unity in Modern Times.* Northampton, Mass. 1943.

Strakhovsky, L. J. *General Count N. P. Ignatyev and the Pan-Slav Movement.* Journal of Central European Affairs, 17, 1957, no. 3.

Sumner, B. H. *Ignatyev at Constantinople, 1864-1874.* Slavonic and East European Review, 11, 1932-1933.

idem. *Russia and Pan-Slavism in the Eighteen-Seventies.* Transations of the Royal Historical Society, 4th ser., 18, 1935.

idem. *Russia and the Balkans 1870-1880.* Oxford 1937.

Tatishchev, S. S. *Iz proshlago russkoi diplomatii.* S.-Peterburg 1890.

idem. *M. N. Katkov v inostrannoi politike.* Russkii vestnik, 250, 1897.

idem. *Imperator Aleksandr II, ego zhizn i tsarstvovanie.* 2 vols. S.-Peterburg 1903.

Taylor, A. J. P. *The Struggle for Mastery in Europe, 1848-1918.* Oxford 1954.

Terentiev, M. A. *Istoriia zavoevaniia Srednei Azii.* 3 vols. S.-Peterburg 1906.

Thaden, E. C. *Conservative Nationalism in the 19th Century Russia.* Seattle 1964.

idem., ed. *Russification in the Baltic Provinces and Finland, 1855-1914.* Princeton U.P. 1981.

Tikhomirov, M. N. *Prisodinenie Merva k Rossii.* Moskva 1960.

Tvardovskaia, V. A. *Ideolog samoderzhaviia v period krizisa 'verkhov' na rubezhe 70-80-kh godov XIX v.* Istoricheskie zapiski, 91, 1973.

idem. *Ideologiia poreformennogo samoderzhaviia. (M. N. Katkov i ego izdaniia.)* Moskva 1978.

Voronov, L. N. *Finantsovo-ekonomicheskaia deiatelnost M. N. Katkova.* Russkii vestnik, 250, 1897.

Walicki, A. *The Slavophile Controversy. History of a Conservative Utopia in Nineteenth-Century Russian Thought.* Oxford 1975.

Waller, B. *Bismarck at the Crossroads.* London 1974.

Wehler, H.-U. *Bismarcks späte Russlandspolitik 1879-1890.* In: *Krisenherde des Kaiserreiches 1871-1918.* Göttingen 1970.

Wereszcki, H. *Sojusz trzech cesarzy. Geneza 1866-1872.* Warszawa 1965.

Wertheimer, E. v. *Graf Julius Andrassy. Sein Leben und seine Zeit.* 3 vols. Wien 1910-1913.

Whelan, H. W. *Alexander III and the State Council. Bureaucracy and Counter-Reform in Late Imperial Russia.* Rutgers U.P. 1982.

Windelband, W. *Bismarck und die europäischen Grossmächte 1879-1885.* Essen 1942.

Wittram, R. *Die russisch-nationalen Tendenzen der achtziger Jahre im Spiegel der österreichisch-ungarischen diplomatischen Berichte aus St. Petersburg.* In: W. Hubatsch, ed., *Schicksalswende deutscher Vergangenheit,* Düsseldorf 1950.

Wittrock, G. *Gorčakov, Ignatiev och Šuvalov.* Stockholm 1931.

Wolter, H. *Bismarcks Aussenpolitik 1871-1881.* Berlin 1983.

Wren, M. C. *Pobedonostsev and Russian Influence in the Balkans, 1881-1888.* Journal of Modern History, 19, 1947.

Zaionchkovskii, A. *Podgotovka Rossii k mirovoi voine. Plany voiny.* Moskva 1926.

Zaionchkovskii, P. A. *Voennye reformy 1860-1870-kh godov.* Moskva 1952.

idem. Krizis samoderzhaviia na rubezhe 1870-80-kh godov. Moskva 1964.

idem. *Rossiiskoe samoderzhavie v kontse XIX stoletiia.* Moskva 1970.

idem. *Samoderzhavie i russkaia armiia na rubezhe XIX-XX stoleii.* Moskva 1973.

idem. *Pravitelstvennyi apparat samoderzhavnoi Rossii v XIX v.* Moskva 1978.

Zisserman, A. L. *Kniaz general-feldmarshal A. I. Bariatinskii, 1815-1879.* 3 vols. S.-Peterburg 1890.

INDEX